DEBATES IN CONTEMPORARY POLITICAL PHILOSOPHY

Debates in Contemporary Political Philosophy is a comprehensive collection of influential essays that presents a balanced survey of the major ideas that have come out of this area of study in the past two decades. Each article has been carefully chosen to enable any student of political philosophy to grasp the main debates within the topic.

The book is divided into seven parts. Parts 1 to 3 deal with fundamental philosophical issues: the philosophy of social explanation, distributive justice and liberalism and communitarianism. Parts 4 to 7 contain seminal papers in more specific areas: citizenship and multiculturalism, nationalism, democracy and punishment.

Readings from the following thinkers are included:

Brian Barry	**Harry Frankfurt**	**Robert Nozick**	**Elliott Sober**
G.A. Cohen	**Amy Gutmann**	**Bhikhu Parekh**	**Charles Taylor**
Joshua Cohen	**Andrew Levine**	**Derek Parfit**	**Andrew von Hirsch**
Antony Duff	**Steven Lukes**	**John Rawls**	**Michael Walzer**
Jon Elster	**Alasdair MacIntyre**	**Michael Sandel**	**Erik Olin Wright**
Daniel Farrell	**David Miller**	**Roger Scruton**	**Iris Marion Young**

The readings represent a range of views and demonstrate the richness of the philosophical contribution to political thought. Each part has an introduction by the editors that situates the papers in the ongoing debate, and further reading sections feature at the end of each part.

Debates in Contemporary Political Philosophy will be an essential resource for any student studying a course in political philosophy.

Derek Matravers is Senior Lecturer at the Open University. He is the author of *Art and Emotions* (1998). **Jon Pike** is Lecturer and Staff Tutor at the Open University and is the author of *Aristotle to Marx* (1999). Together with Nigel Warburton they are joint editors of *Reading Political Philosophy* (Routledge, 2001).

DEBATES IN CONTEMPORARY POLITICAL PHILOSOPHY

An anthology

Edited by
Derek Matravers and
Jon Pike

Routledge
Taylor & Francis Group

LONDON AND NEW YORK

in association with

The Open
University

First published 2003
by Routledge in association with the Open University
11 New Fetter Lane, London EC4P 4EE

Simultaneously published in the USA and Canada
by Routledge
29 West 35th Street, New York, NY 10001

Routledge is an imprint of the Taylor & Francis Group

Typeset in Sabon and Frutiger by
Florence Production Ltd, Stoodleigh, Devon
Printed and bound in Great Britain by
TJ International Ltd, Padstow, Cornwall

British Library Cataloguing in Publication Data
A catalogue record for this book is available from the British Library

Library of Congress Cataloging in Publication Data
Debates in contemporary political philosophy : an anthology / edited by Derek
Matravers and Jonathan Pike.
p. cm.
Includes bibliographical references and index. 1. Political science – Philosophy.
I. Matravers, Derek. II. Pike, Jonathan E.
JA71 .D36 2003
320'.01–dc21   2002068245

ISBN 0–415–30210–2 (hbk)
ISBN 0–415–30211–0 (pbk)

This Reader is part of *Issues in Contemporary Social and
Political Philosophy* (A851) an Open University Masters course in Philosophy.
Details of this and other Open University courses can be obtained from the
Call Centre, PO Box 724, The Open University, Milton Keynes, MK7 6ZS,
United Kingdom; tel. +44 (0)1908 653231, email ces-gen@open.ac.uk. Alternatively,
you may visit the Open University web site at http://www.open.ac.uk
where you can learn more about the wide range of courses and
packs offered at all levels by the Open University

CONTENTS

Acknowledgements　　　　　　　　　　　　　　　　　　ix

1　Introduction　　　　　　　　　　　　　　　　　　　　1

Part 1
The philosophy of social explanation　　　　　　　　5

Introduction　　　　　　　　　　　　　　　　　　　　　7

2　Methodological individualism　　　　　　　　　　　12
　　STEVEN LUKES

3　Marxism, functionalism, and game theory: a case for methodological
　　individualism　　　　　　　　　　　　　　　　　　22
　　JON ELSTER

4　Reply to Elster on "Marxism, functionalism, and game theory"　　41
　　G.A. COHEN

5　Marxism and methodological individualism　　　　54
　　ERIK OLIN WRIGHT, ANDREW LEVINE AND ELLIOTT SOBER

Part 2
Distributive justice　　　　　　　　　　　　　　67

Introduction　　　　　　　　　　　　　　　　　　　69

6　Distributive justice　　　　　　　　　　　　　　73
　　ROBERT NOZICK

7　Equality as a moral ideal　　　　　　　　　　　82
　　HARRY FRANKFURT

8 Where the action is: on the site of distributive justice   100
G.A. COHEN

9 Equality and priority   115
DEREK PARFIT

Part 3
Liberalism and communitarianism   133

Introduction   135

10 Liberalism and the limits of justice   140
MICHAEL SANDEL

11 The domain of the political and overlapping consensus   160
JOHN RAWLS

12 Communitarian critics of liberalism   182
AMY GUTMANN

13 Cross-purposes: the liberal–communitarian debate   195
CHARLES TAYLOR

Part 4
Citizenship and multiculturalism   213

Introduction   215

14 Polity and group difference: a critique of the ideal of universal
citizenship   219
IRIS MARION YOUNG

15 Contemporary liberal responses to diversity   239
BHIKHU PAREKH

16 Theories of group rights   248
BRIAN BARRY

Part 5
Nationalism   265

Introduction   267

17 In defence of the nation   271
ROGER SCRUTON

18 Is patriotism a virtue?   286
ALASDAIR MACINTYRE

19 In defence of nationality   301
DAVID MILLER

Part 6
Democracy   319

Introduction   321

20 The market and the forum: three varieties of political theory   325
JON ELSTER

21 Deliberation and democratic legitimacy   342
JOSHUA COHEN

22 Philosophy and democracy   361
MICHAEL WALZER

Part 7
Punishment   381

Introduction   383

23 Punishment, communication and community   387
ANTONY DUFF

24 Punishment, penance and the state: a reply to Duff   408
ANDREW VON HIRSCH

Appendix: response to von Hirsch   423
ANTONY DUFF

25 The justification of general deterrence   428
DANIEL FARRELL

Index   448

ACKNOWLEDGEMENTS

Barry, B., 'Theories of Group Rights' from *Culture and Equality* (Polity Press, Cambridge, 2002).

Cohen, G.A., 'Reply to Elster on Marxism, Functionalism and Game Theory' *Theory and Society* 11, 1982, reprinted by permission of Kluwer Academic Publishers, Dordrecht.

Cohen, G.A., 'Where the Action Is' *Philosophy and Public Affairs* 25, no. 1, Winter, 1997. Copyright © 1997 PUP, reprinted by permission of Princeton University Press.

Cohen, Joshua, 'Deliberation and Democratic Legitimacy' from *The Good Polity* (eds Hamlin and Pettit) (Blackwell, Oxford, 1989).

Duff, R.A., 'Punishment, Communication and Community' from *Punishment and Political Theory* (ed. Matt Matravers) (Hart Publishing, Oxford, 1999).

Elster, J., 'Marxism, Functionalism and Game Theory' *Theory and Society* 11, 1982, reprinted by permission of Kluwer Academic Publishers, Dordrecht.

Elster, J., 'The Market and the Forum' from *Foundations of Social Choice Theory* (eds Elster and Hylland) (Cambridge University Press, Cambridge, 1986).

Farrell, Daniel M., 'The Justification of General Deterrence' *The Philosophical Review* XCIV, no. 3, July, 1985.

Frankfurt, H., 'Equality as a Moral Ideal' *Ethics* 98, 1987, The University of Chicago Press.

Gutmann, Amy, 'Communitarian Critics of Liberalism' *Philosophy and Public Affairs* 14, 1985. Copyright © 1985 PUP, reprinted by permission of Princeton University Press.

Lukes, S., *Individualism* pp. 110–24 (Oxford University Press, 1973. Copyright Blackwell Publishers).

MacIntyre, Alasdair, 'Is Patriotism a Virtue?' The Lindley Lecture, University of Kansas, reprinted in *Political Thought* (eds Rosen and Wolff) (OUP, Oxford, 1999).

Miller, David, 'In Defence of Nationality' *Journal of Applied Philosophy* 10, no. 1, 1993.

Nozick, R., *Anarchy, State and Utopia* pp. 160–4, 168–74 (Blackwell, Oxford, 1974).

Parekh, Bhikhu, 'Contemporary Liberal Responses to Diversity' from *Rethinking Multiculturalism* (Palgrave Macmillan, Basingstoke, 2000).

Parfit, D., 'Equality and priority' *Ratio* 10, no. 3, 1997, Blackwell Publishers, Oxford.

Rawls, J., 'The Domain of the Political and Overlapping Consensus' *The New York University Law Review* 64, 1989.

Sandel, M., *Liberalism and the Limits of Justice* pp. 82–95, 175–83 (Cambridge University Press, Cambridge, 1985).

Scruton, Roger, 'In Defence of the Nation' from *The Philosopher on Dover Beach* (Carcanet Press Ltd, Manchester, 1990).

Taylor, Charles, reprinted by permission of the publisher from 'Cross-purposes: The Liberal–Communitarian Debate' in *Liberalism and the Moral Life* (ed. Nancy Rosenblum), pp. 159–60, 163–8, 169–81 (Cambridge, MA: Harvard University Press. Copyright © 1989 by the President and Fellows of Harvard College).

von Hirsch, A., 'Punishment, Penance and the State: a Reply to Duff' from *Punishment and Political Theory* (ed. Matt Matravers) (Hart Publishing, Oxford, 1999).

Walzer, Michael, 'Philosophy and Democracy' *Political Theory* 9.3, 1981, Sage Publications Inc.

Wright, E.O., Sober, E. and Levine, A., 'Marxism and Methodological Individualism' *New Left Review* I/162, 1987.

Young, I.M., 'Polity and Group Difference: a Critique of the Ideal of Universal Citizenship' *Ethics* 99, 1989, The University of Chicago Press.

Every effort has been made to obtain permission to reproduce copyright material. If any proper acknowledgement has not been made, or permission not received, we invite copyright holders to inform us of the oversight.

1

INTRODUCTION

It is sensible to open an introduction to an anthology of papers and other readings by demarcating the field of contemporary political philosophy and by saying something about our selection criteria for this book. What, then, *is* contemporary political philosophy? First, all our selections were published after the publication of John Rawls' *A Theory of Justice* (1971) an event which substantially revived political philosophy. Second, the 'contemporary' in our title means we have chosen topics that are the ongoing foci of debate: the papers here are not museum pieces. Third, we have chosen pieces that are, in some sense, polemical, that take a position in the debates, rather than provide surveys of the field. The readings are all drawn from the anglophone, analytic tradition of philosophy. This is partly intellectual preference, and also a way of restricting the (still vast) literature available to us. However, the selection and organisation of the contributions has a wider justification.

We want to show that the discipline of political philosophy is flourishing. This is partly a result of drives internal to the arguments and debates, but also the result of the attempt to come to terms with political change and development in the world beyond the Academy. However, some might question this positive assessment. We would exaggerate if we characterised the terrain of contemporary political philosophy as footnotes to Rawls (just as Whitehead exaggerated when he characterised the whole of Western thought as footnotes to Plato), but there would nonetheless be some truth in the characterisation. Rawls' work is still extremely important, and, whatever might be said for the originality and analytical clarity of *A Theory of Justice*, Rawls works with the framework that dominates the actual political institutions of the Western world – liberalism. This may make it seem that the discipline is less flourishing than it actually is, because of relatively widespread agreement and the appearance that, on substantive matters, as well as approaches, we are all liberals now. This appearance is reinforced because of the decline of the major anti-liberal position: Marxism.

Up until the mid-1980s Marxism, in one form or another, held some significant moral and intellectual weight, not just in terms of the numbers of academics who would describe themselves as Marxists, but also because it offered an 'off the peg' critique of liberalism to social theorists and political philosophers. Whatever their relation to Marx's writings, the collapse of *soi-disant* regimes of 'actually existing socialism' after 1989 has changed this. In the assessment of liberalism, Marxism is simply not a major or straightforward influence any more. This has had many consequences. Contemporary political philosophy can be seen as a time when the critique of liberalism has been reinvented, rethought, or reconfigured by communitarians, egalitarians and feminists, amongst others. The critiques of liberalism now being offered up are 'bespoke' and consequently partial and contentious. This not to say, of course, that particular aspects of the critique derived from Marx – especially the critique of alienation – are not still significant. In addition, the critiques of liberalism that are on offer draw on some of the underpinnings of Marxist thought – such as in the rectification of injustice between groups over time. These controversies draw on the debate over methodological individualism in Marxism, and this is our opening section, on explanatory theory.

A second feature of the waning influence of Marxism has been that the terrain of political philosophy has in many respects become clearer. Whilst Marxism aimed to give a series of explanatory models for social theorists to apply in the explanation and analysis of events and processes, the liberal political philosophy articulated by Rawls had modest explanatory ambitions. It does, however, have grandiose normative ones. The political philosophy that has been written in the wake of *A Theory of Justice* has consolidated this turning away from grand explanatory frameworks, and from models for explaining events and processes. As the terrain of political philosophy has become more clearly and decidedly normative it has become closer to ethics. In fact, it is now much easier to see a distinction between political theory and political philosophy (the latter is normative, the former not), and much more difficult to see a clear distinction between political philosophy and ethics. This is not just a matter of the conceptual vagueness; it has institutional forms too. Some of the best articles published in journals such as *Ethics* are in political philosophy, and their equivalent in *Philosophy and Public Affairs* are in ethics. In many respects, political philosophy has moved closer to moral philosophy as it has moved away from any ambition to provide a quasi-sociological explanatory framework. Instead, applied ethics, including debates around abortion and bio-medical ethics, and the nest of issues around affirmative action, came to the foreground in American campuses, rocked by protests against US intervention in Vietnam in the late 1960s. Rawls' account of justice also emerged in this immensely fertile climate. Philosophers became increasingly willing to write articles and papers with direct implications for public policy. This phenomenon has reinforced and reinvigorated the discipline. So, the development of political philosophy in the decades since 1971 has seen a reconfiguration of the critique of liberalism, and, at the same time, a 'normative turn'. What are the results of these developments?

There are some welcome results: there is still considerable disagreement but this is not normally over the rules of argument, and there is a relative absence of accusations of bad faith. But the normative turn has had theoretical consequences. In particular, philosophers have asked themselves how, in the absence of commonly agreed moral foundations, is there to be reasonable argument about the grounding of norms?

Focusing on the grounds of normativity highlights the perspective that the moral agent is able to take on those norms: are our normative commitments something that we can stand outside of ourselves and assess, or are we – in some way – 'constituted' by our normative attachments? Whether we find the relatively abstract and quasi-Kantian approach of Rawls attractive (focusing on the *construction* of principles of justice), or whether we seek to root normativity in existing communities and traditions, we have to answer tough questions. The first approach just edges back the search for foundations for normativity one stage: the principles of justice are constructed, but from what materials? The second, so called 'communitarian', approach seems to leave us without the resources to defend our *found* normativity against the criticism that the result is unacceptably relativist.

The questions that underlie the debate on whether or not we can stand outside of ourselves and assess our normative commitments are important not least because our *actual* political locations, identities, and conceptions of the good are important. Who and what we think we are, what we can loosely call 'the politics of identity', has come to the forefront of political debate, and it is not surprising that political philosophy reflects this.

It would be wrong, however, to claim that political philosophy had become concerned solely with first order concerns about the grounds of normativity, or with the politics of identity. It is also the case that new work has been done on old topics. Distributive justice has been a concern of political philosophers since Aristotle, and there is widespread acceptance that some sort of equal respect for individual human beings needs to be reflected in the mechanisms for securing justice. Again, this debate stems from Rawls and in particular from his suggestion that, as people do not deserve their natural talents, they do not deserve the wealth that springs from them. However much there has been a shift of focus away from questions of resource inequality, and towards relations between dominant and subordinate groups delineated in quite different ways, the normative critique of inequality remains. Indeed it would be absurd to insist that justice required equality between groups unless we had answers to questions about what we meant by groups and what we meant by equality.

Our three opening sections, then, cover three key questions. To what extent does the individualism characteristic of liberalism provide a satisfactory explanatory strategy? In what ways is the notion of the unencumbered self central to liberal thought, and what are the consequences of its supposed centrality? What place is there for equality in our thinking about the just society?

Each of the next four sections covers topics on which there are direct implications for public policy, and where the philosophical debates arise from public concern themselves. They also represent areas where the liberal concern that, *ceteris paribus*, all are equally deserving, is under strain. Whilst Marxists took to task liberalism in many ways, they shared liberalism's universalist ambitions. The reconfigured critique does not. Ideas of national identity, and the conception of patriotism as a political virtue seem obviously to conflict with liberal universalism and with standard views about the constituency of the moral. They also stand opposed to the increasing geopolitical drive towards supranational identities and institutions that accompanies the trend towards an increasingly interconnected world.

Penal policy stands at the centre of a number of different issues. There are public policy debates, which deal with matters such as increasing prison populations and questions about the efficacy of punishment. These draw on philosophical debates about the nature of penal justice, whether punishment is compatible with the philosophical tradition underlying much contemporary liberal thought – the Kantian notion of respect for persons – and the extent to which any justification of punishment needs to be communitarian. Responses to this debate focus on the question of the grounding of norms referred to above.

Again, it used to be the case that a bespoke critique of liberal democracy was available: democracy was only formal and not real so long as it left deep structural economic inequalities untouched. The contemporary debate about democracy reconfigures this critique; it addresses questions such as – what sort of democratic accounting can prevent the dominance of self-interest and generate something closer to Rousseau's notion of the general will? And – given that in some respects they will conflict – what can be done to resolve the tensions between liberalism (particularly a commitment to rights which cannot be infringed by a powerful majority) and democracy (which vests political power and legitimacy in the hands of the majority)?

Last, the very basis of liberal universalism can be criticised. The shift of focus from the economic terrain to the terrain of identity and culture has been a reflection of the way in which such areas have become the prime sources of conflict in liberal democracies. Debates over multiculturalism, and the extent to which group rights, cultural differences and political representation of racial minorities should affect our notion of the just society, will be with us for many years to come. Close engagement with the texts we have selected will, we hope, enable readers to engage with those debates within a thriving discipline, and beyond.

Acknowledgements

We would like to thank Jackie Rossi, the course manager for 'Issues in Contemporary Political Philosophy', the Open University course for which this book is a Reader, Siobhan Pattinson at Routledge, and Professor Jo Wolff at University College London, as well as the anonymous publisher's readers who commented on our selections.

Part 1

THE PHILOSOPHY OF
SOCIAL EXPLANATION

Introduction

THE FIRST READING IN THIS PART is an excerpt from a book called *Individualism*, which was first published in 1973. In the book, Stephen Lukes traces the semantic history of individualism, before distinguishing some separate ways in which the term can be taken. It is worth bearing in mind the multiplicity of doctrines that fall under this general label, and Lukes distinguishes eleven distinct strands. They are: the dignity of man, autonomy, privacy, self-development, the abstract individual, political individualism, economic individualism, religious individualism, ethical individualism, epistemological individualism, and finally – our concern – methodological individualism.

Lukes identifies four types of predicates of individuals on a continuum from the least to the most social: 1) those that refer only to physical properties, 2) those that refer to mental states, and presuppose consciousness, 3) those that refer to minimally social and relational predicates and 4) those that refer to social institutions, or rely for their meaning on social institutions. He argues that to privilege the first set of predicates against the last is arbitrary. He outlines a series of views with which methodological individualism is sometimes conflated: truistic social atomism, a theory of meaning, a theory of ontology, a denial of the truth of sociological laws and a normative doctrine about individual ends.

Lukes' view is, that construed in one way, methodological individualism is false, because it arbitrarily rules out perfectly reasonable explanations of social phenomena that are not reducible to individual level explanation. Construed in another way, the notion is true, but trivially so. If Lukes is right, the task of the proponent of methodological individualism is either to accept this trivial status[1] or to outline a construal of methodological individualism that is both true and substantial.

The final part of the reading brings methodological individualism back into contact with some of the other strands of individualism. I have suggested above that it is important to recognise the distinctiveness of methodological individualism from normative claims about the individual, but, as Lukes indicates, the explanatory notion has 'affinities' with a series of other claims about the value of individuals. These can be depicted as below:

Table 1 Affinities between normative and methodological commitments

Normative commitment		Explanatory approach
Liberalism	⇒	Methodological individualism
Anti-liberalism (Marxism, conservatism)	⇒	Holism/functionalism

The arrows in Table 1 indicate the directions of affinity, which are suggested in the final paragraphs of Lukes' text. Note that the word 'affinity' means a connection that is quite weak – a much weaker connection than logical entailment. It conveys something like the idea of 'sitting well with' or 'having a family resemblance to'.

Since methodological individualism is normally thought to have an affinity with liberalism, linking it with explicitly Marxist modes of explanation is surprising. In Chapter 3, Jon Elster argues for methodological individualism, without which 'grand Marxist claims . . . remain at the level of speculation'. However, rather than presenting a straight case for methodological individualism, he argues that it is necessary to avoid the mistakes of functional explanation (and he cites a series of examples in which functional explanations go awry). A functional explanation is one in which the existence of an entity or process is explained by the functions that it carries out. In functional explanations, the why-question is answered by identifying a function.

Suppose that I wish to hang a picture in my living room. In order to do this, I need to put a screw in the wall, and in order to do that, I need to use a screwdriver. So, I get the screwdriver and bring it into the living room. Suppose I am asked – why is the screwdriver in the living room? It would be true, although more than a little odd, for me to answer that 'the screwdriver is in the living room because it is functional for the task of hanging pictures. Its being in the living room helps to satisfy the need for hanging pictures.' The *function* of the screwdriver – the fact that it is good at doing something that needs to be done, *explains* its spatio-temporal location. This is the general form of functional explanations: the function of an institution, activity, and so on, is what explains its existence.

What, though, was odd about the answer above? It was that the explanation made no reference to my deciding to hang a picture, and fetching the screwdriver. The functional benefits of the screwdriver are explanatory, but only indirectly – only through my desire to hang a picture and my belief that a screwdriver would be good for doing the job. I enter into the story as a purposive agent, and it is by acting on the screwdriver that I bring it about that the functional explanation is true. To say that 'the screwdriver is in the living room because it is functional for the task of hanging pictures' seems to suggest – contrary to the facts – that it got there on its own. But there was a very obvious mechanism by which the screwdriver came into the living room.

The first, negative, stage of Elster's article criticises functional explanations because they lack accounts of a mechanism. Functional explanations assume an intentional action by a system, without an account of the subject that could carry out the action. He characterises these as an objective teleology – a supposedly purposive explanation, but one that lacks an agent that can have purposes. The first crucial set of distinctions is between subjective teleology, objective teleology and teleonomy (see Table 2).

Elster's main task, then, is to replace the use of functional, structural and holist explanations with individual level explanations couched in terms of game theory. So he focuses particularly on problems of collective action, such as strikes. From one point of view it looks

Table 2 Types of explanation (drawn from Elster, Chapter 3)

Approach	Characterised as	Examples	Licit or illicit?
Objective teleology	Purposive processes without a purposive subject	Posner, Coser, Bordieu Marx, often (acc. Elster)	Illicit
Subjective teleology	Purposive processes with a purposive subject	Ordinary individual action, collective conspiracies	Licit

irrational for a worker to go on strike, even if the success of the strike would benefit him or her. This is because the contribution of one striker to a strike will not alter the chances of success of the strike. So each individual striker is faced with the following calculation: if the strike wins, I will gain whether or not I join it. If the strike loses, I will gain more if I do not join it than if I join it: so I should not join the strike. There is then a problem in showing how strikes can ever take place if individual strikers think rationally. But Elster is able to point to a plausible explanation of strike action getting off the ground when he considers 'assurance games' – these, he thinks, can explain why collective actions can take place. But the outcome of an assurance game is unstable: 'because there is no dominant strategy, the solution will be realised only if there is perfect information. Imperfect information leads to uncertainty, suspicion and play-safe behaviour.' However, if a consensus exists – if individual actors share the same preference rankings, and *know* that they share the same preference rankings – then a collective actor can emerge with particular, predictable modes of behaviour.

One way in which Elster's objection can be put is that, in functional explanations, the explanans (the thing that is explaining) comes after the explanandum (the thing to be explained). This flouts basic explanatory rules. However, in Chapter 4 Cohen argues that this objection can be rebutted. We can write generalisations of functional explanations in the form of 'consequence laws'. You should note Cohen's account of both a consequence law and functional explanation in the paper.

- A consequence law is a law justifying functional explanation, and
- A 'functional explanation is an explanation in which a dispositional fact explains the occurrence of the event-type mentioned in the antecedent of the hypothetical specifying the disposition'.

This second definition needs a little unpacking. A dispositional fact is just a fact about the disposition of an activity, or event. This may be a fact about its disposition to cause another activity or event. In the example Cohen gives:

$$(E \rightarrow F) \rightarrow E$$

Here, $(E \rightarrow F)$ is the dispositional fact, and E is the event-type mentioned in the antecedent of the hypothetical specifying the disposition (that is, the hypothetical $(E \rightarrow F)$). In rather simple terms, the fact that E would cause F is what explains E taking place.

Now, two things can be said about this account. First, Cohen has got functional explanations off one particular hook, because he has shown that they do not involve postulating an explanans that antedates an explanandum. The disposition of E to cause F exists before, not after, the occurrence of E.

But the second thing to be said is that he has done so without addressing the key concern of Elster in Chapter 3: *How* does the dispositional fact go to explain the occurrence of E? It is true that, in our earlier example, the disposition of the screwdriver explained the 'occurrence' of the screwdriver, but it did so through the mechanism of an intentional actor – me.

This concern refocuses the debate. We are no longer concerned with the question of whether any sort of functional explanations are legitimate: dispositions clearly can enter into explanations. The question is rather about the acceptability of functional explanations *in the absence of a mechanism*.

Wright, Levine and Sober, in Chapter 5, distinguish between type-reduction and token-reduction. You may be familiar with this distinction, but not with its being made in this context. There are tokens – particular instances of social phenomena and there are types of phenomena. Wright *et al.* endorse the notion of token–token reducibility, but argue that type–type reduction will prove 'a fruitless quest' if social phenomena can be multiply realised: that is, if there are lots of different configurations of individual intentional acts that can conceivably fill out an aggregate phenomenon. So if we want to explain an aggregate phenomenon (such as the tendency for capitalist societies to have strong economic growth) then we cannot do so by identifying particular mechanisms that operate at the micro level. This is because 'the social-level explanation of growth in terms of the macro processes of competitive market relations . . . can be realised by a vast array of possible micro-mechanisms'. The question of explanatory adequacy then, is just an empirical one. In some straightforward cases such as explaining the behaviour of water in terms of the atomic structure H_2O, reduction is justified. However, if social phenomena are multiply realised, then methodological individualism is a mistake.

How might a methodological individualist respond to this criticism? It is clear that the response by Wright *et al.* reduces the breadth of the issues at stake. They clearly accept that the actions that fill out aggregate social phenomena are the actions of flesh and blood individuals, not the actions of peculiar, invisible, supra-individual actors who select and dismiss social phenomena according to whether or not they are functional for the system. If this is the only claim the methodological individualist is pressing, that is, what Lukes calls truistic social atomism, then there is no dispute.

But the individualist might want to bite the bullet and insist on reductionism even in cases where it looked as if the same aggregate phenomenon was multiply realised.

A methodological individualist might argue as follows. 'In case A, we observe economic growth generated by one set of micro-level decisions taken by one set of individuals. In case B we observe economic growth generated by a different set of decisions taken by a different set of individuals. The anti-reductionist claims that multiple realisation of the same phenomenon rules out reductionist explanations. But this assumes that we are talking about the same phenomenon. Clearly (because each is differently filled out at the micro level) we are not talking about the same phenomenon. Economic growth in case A is, *ex hypothesi*, different from economic growth in case B and it should therefore be explained differently, by reference to the specific decisions taken by specific individuals.'

What should we make of this response? First, it does seem to show up an implicit assumption in the anti-reductionist approach taken by Wright *et al*. They assume that it is unproblematic to speak of types – 'strikes, class struggles, social conflicts, etc.' as if these are relatively stable entities that sit out in the social world waiting to be explained. But a persistent methodological individualist might insist that the existence of these social types, characterised in advance of their micro-level explanation, is just what is in question. Certain particular social phenomena share some characteristics, but to identify them as tokens of a particular type begs the question against methodological individualism.

NOTE

1   It may seem unlikely that an advocate of methodological individualism would take this option – accepting the triviality of methodological individualism – but Jon Elster did opt for it at a seminar I attended in 1986. The problem with accepting that methodological individualism is trivially true is that it is then not clear what opponents of the doctrine are up to. They are either deluded about the most obvious truths – that societies are made up of individuals – or they are attacking some other, more substantive doctrine, which is not trivial. If so, a bias towards the interesting would mean finding out what that second doctrine is, and addressing *it*, rather than a trivial methodological individualism.

2

METHODOLOGICAL INDIVIDUALISM

Steven Lukes

[. . .]

We must examine a doctrine which has had an important place in the history of individualism, but which needs to be very carefully analysed and distinguished from other doctrines which have often been held either to entail it, or to be entailed by it, or to be equivalent with it. Methodological individualism is a doctrine about explanation which asserts that all attempts to explain social (or individual) phenomena are to be rejected (or, according to a current, more sophisticated version, rejected as 'rock-bottom' explanations) unless they are couched wholly in terms of facts about individuals.

It was first clearly articulated by Hobbes, who held that 'it is necessary that we know the things that are to be compounded, before we can know the whole compound' for 'everything is best understood by its constitutive causes',[1] the causes of the social compound being Hobbesian men. It was taken up by the thinkers of the Enlightenment, among whom, with a few important exceptions (such as Vico and Montesquieu), an individualist mode of explanation became pre-eminent, though with wide divergences as to what was included, and in particular how much of a social nature was included, in the characterization of the explanatory elements. Man was seen by some as egoistic, by others as cooperative. Some presupposed the minimum about his social context in accounting for his nature; others (such as Diderot) employed a genuine social psychology. Those who did the former, reasoning as though the 'individuals' in question were prior to society and undetermined by their social environment, were putting to work the abstract conception of the individual [. . .]

Methodological individualism was confronted, from the early nineteenth century onwards, by a wide range of thinkers who brought to the understanding of social life a perspective according to which collective phenomena were given priority over individuals in explanation. In France, this tradition passed from the theocrats, Saint-Simon and Comte (who wrote that a society was 'no more decomposable into *individuals* than a geometric surface is into lines, or a line into points')[2] through Espinas to Durkheim, whose whole sociology was founded on the denial of methodological individualism. In Germany this was a pervasive trend, encompassing all the social studies, such as history, economics, law, psychology, and philology. Both Marxists and Hegelians have likewise been committed to such a denial, as in the mainstream of modern sociology.

On the other hand, Max Weber was inclined to uphold it: as he wrote in a letter shortly before he died, 'if I have become a sociologist . . . it is mainly in order to exorcize the spectre of collective conceptions which still lingers among us. In other words, sociology itself can only proceed from the actions of one or more separate individuals and must therefore adopt strictly individualistic methods'.[3] Again, the Utilitarians were at one with John Stuart Mill in maintaining that 'the laws of the phenomena of society are, and can be, nothing but the actions and passions of human beings', namely, 'the laws of individual human nature'.[4] Many social scientists have been tempted to adopt methodological individualism, most obviously all those who have appealed to fixed psychological elements as ultimately explanatory factors – such as Pareto ('residues'), McDougall ('instincts'), Sumner ('drives'), and Malinowski ('needs') – and, notably, the sociologist George Homans.[5]

The debate over methodological individualism has recurred in many different guises – in the dispute between the German 'historical' school in economics and the 'abstract' theory of classical and neo-classical economics (especially as expounded by Carl Menger and the Austrian school), in endless disputes among philosophers of history and between sociologists and psychologists, and in the celebrated controversy between Durkheim and Gabriel Tarde (in which most of the basic issues were most clearly brought out).[6] Among others, Georg Simmel[7] and Charles Horton Cooley[8] tried to resolve the dispute, as did Georges Gurvitch[9] and Morris Ginsberg,[10] but it constantly reappears, for example in the debate provoked by the polemical writings of Professors Hayek, Popper and Watkins in defence of methodological individualism, which we shall now briefly consider.[11]

Hayek, for example, writes that

> there is no other way toward an understanding of social phenomena but through our understanding of individual actions directed toward other people and guided by their expected behaviour.[12]

Similarly, according to Popper,

> all social phenomena, and especially the functioning of all social institutions, should always be understood as resulting from the decisions, actions, attitudes,

etc., of human individuals, and . . . we should never be satisfied by an explanation in terms of so-called 'collectives'.[13]

Finally we may quote Watkins's account of 'the principle of methodological individualism':

According to this principle, the ultimate constituents of the social world are individual people who act more or less appropriately in the light of their dispositions and understanding of their situation. Every complex social situation, institution or event is the result of a particular configuration of individuals, their dispositions, situations, beliefs, and physical resources and environment. There may be unfinished or half-way explanations of large-scale social phenomena (say, inflation) in terms of other large-scale phenomena (say full employment); but we shall not have arrived at rock-bottom explanations of such large-scale phenomena until we have deduced an account of them from statements about the dispositions, beliefs, resources and inter-relations of individuals. (The individuals may remain anonymous and only typical dispositions etc., may be attributed to them). And just as mechanism is contrasted with the organicist idea of physical fields, so methodological individualism is contrasted with sociological holism or organicism. On this latter view, social systems constitute 'wholes' at least in the sense that some of their large-scale behaviour is governed by macro-laws which are essentially *sociological* in the sense that they are *sui generis* and not to be explained as mere regularities or tendencies resulting from the behaviour of interacting individuals. On the contrary, the behaviour of individuals should (according to sociological holism) be explained at least partly in terms of such laws (perhaps in conjunction with an account, first of individuals' roles within institutions, and secondly of the functions of institutions within the whole social system). If methodological individualism means that human beings are supposed to be the only moving agents in history, and if sociological holism means that some super-human agents or factors are supposed to be at work in history, then these two alternatives are exhaustive.[14]

We can now turn to the task of distinguishing methodological individualism from a number of other, related theories, before analysing exactly what claims it advances. It has often, mistakenly, been taken to be the same as any or all of the following:

1. A set of such purely truistic assertions as that society consists of people, that groups consist of people, that institutions consist of people who follow rules and fill roles, that traditions, customs, ideologies, kinship systems and languages are ways that people act, think and talk. These are truistic propositions because they are analytically

true, in virtue of the meaning of words. Such a set of truisms has, of course, no implications as to the correct method of explaining social phenomena.

2. A theory of meaning to the effect that every statement about social phenomena is either a statement about individual human beings or else it is unintelligible and therefore not a statement at all. This theory entails that all predicates which range over social phenomena are definable in terms of predicates which range only over individual phenomena and that all statements about social phenomena are translatable without loss of meaning into statements that are wholly about individuals. As Jarvie has put it, ' "Army" is merely a plural of soldier and *all* statements about the Army can be reduced to statements about the particular soldiers comprising the Army'.[15]

It is worth noticing that this theory is only plausible on a crude verificationist theory of meaning (to the effect that the meaning of p is what confirms the truth of p). Otherwise, although statements about armies are true only in virtue of the fact that other statements about soldiers are true, the former are not equivalent in meaning to the latter, nor a fortiori are they 'about' the subject of the latter.

3. A theory of ontology to the effect that in the social world only individuals are real. This usually carries the correlative doctrine that social phenomena are constructions of the mind and 'do not exist in reality'. Thus Hayek writes, 'The social sciences ... do not deal with "given" wholes but their task is to constitute these wholes by constructing models from the familiar elements – models which reproduce the structure of relationships between some of the many phenomena which we always simultaneously observe in real life. This is no less true of the popular concepts of social wholes which are represented by the terms current in ordinary language; they too refer to mental models.'[16] Similarly, Popper holds that 'social entities such as institutions or associations' are 'abstract models constructed to interpret certain selected abstract relations between individuals'.[17]

If this theory means that in the social world only individuals are observable, it is evidently false. Some social phenomena simply can be observed (as both trees and forests can); and indeed, many features of social phenomena are observable (e.g. the procedure of a court) while many features of individuals are not (e.g. intentions). Both individual and social phenomena have observable and non-observable features. If it means that individual phenomena are easy to understand, while social phenomena are not (which is Hayek's view), this is highly implausible: compare the procedure of the court with the motives of the criminal. If the theory means that individuals exist independently of, e.g., groups and institutions, this is also false, since, just as facts about social phenomena are contingent upon facts about individuals, the reverse is also true. Thus, we can only speak of soldiers because we can speak of armies: only if certain statements are true of armies are others true of soldiers. If the theory means that all social phenomena are fictional and all individual phenomena are factual, that would entail that all assertions about social phenomena are false, or else neither true nor false, which is absurd. Finally, the theory may mean that only facts about individuals are explanatory, which alone would make this theory equivalent to methodological individualism.

4. A negative theory to the effect that sociological laws are impossible, or that law-like statements about social phenomena are always false. Hayek and Popper sometimes seem to believe this, but Watkins clearly repudiates it, asserting merely that such statements form part of 'half-way' as opposed to 'rock-bottom' explanations.

This theory, however, is clearly unacceptable – since not all law-like statements about social phenomena are false – as Popper himself recognizes.[18]

5. A doctrine which (ambiguously) asserts that society has as its end the good of individuals. When unpacked, this doctrine can be taken to mean any or all of the following: (a) that social institutions are to be explained as founded and maintained by individuals to fulfil their ends, framed independently of the institutions (as in, e.g., social contract theory); (b) that social institutions in fact satisfy individual ends; and (c) that social institutions ought to satisfy individual ends. (b) is typically held by economic individualists, such as Hayek, with respect to the market; (c) is typically held by political individualists who advocate a non-interventionist state on this ground, but neither (b) nor (c) either entails or is entailed by methodological individualism, whereas (a) is a version of it.

What, then, does methodological individualism claim? Briefly, we can say that it advances a range of different claims in accordance with how much of 'society' is built into the supposedly explanatory 'individuals'. Consider the following examples:

i   genetic make-up; brain-states; condition of central nervous system
ii   aggression; gratification; stimulus-response
iii co-operation; power; esteem
iv   cashing cheques; saluting; voting

What this exceedingly rudimentary list shows is at least this: that there is a continuum of what I shall henceforth call individual predicates from what one might call the most non-social to the most social. Propositions incorporating only predicates of type (i) are about human beings qua material objects and make no reference to and presuppose nothing about consciousness or any feature of any social group or institution. Propositions incorporating only individual predicates of type (ii) presuppose consciousness but still make no reference to and presuppose nothing about any feature of any social group or institution. Propositions incorporating only individual predicates of type (iii) do have a minimal social reference: they presuppose a social context in which certain actions, social relations and/or mental states are picked out and given a particular significance (which makes social relations of certain sorts count as 'cooperative', which makes certain social positions count as positions of 'power' and a certain set of attitudes count as 'esteem'). They still do not presuppose or entail any particular propositions about any particular form of group or institution. Finally, propositions incorporating only individual predicates of type (iv) are maximally social, in that they presuppose and sometimes directly entail propositions about particular types of group and institution. ('Voting Conservative' is at an even further point along the continuum.)

Methodological individualism can be seen to have confined its favoured explanations to any or all of these sorts of individual predicates. We may distinguish the following four possibilities:

(i) Attempts to explain in terms of type (i) predicates. The most celebrated eighteenth-century example of this kind of attempt is that made by the French materialist philosopher La Mettrie, author of *L'Homme machine*, who sought to demonstrate that the soul was physically or organically conditioned and that its faculties and activities were causally dependent on the central nervous system and the brain. The best contemporary example is the work of H. J. Eysenck. In his *The Psychology of Politics*, Eysenck writes that: 'Political actions are actions of human beings; the study of the direct cause of these actions is the field of the study of psychology. All other social sciences deal with variables which affect political action indirectly'.[19] (Compare this with Durkheim's famous statement that 'every time that a social phenomenon is directly explained by a psychological phenomenon, we may be sure that the explanation is false'.[20]) In this book, Eysenck sets out to classify attitudes along two dimensions – the Radical-Conservative and the Tough-minded-Tender-minded – on the basis of evidence elicited by questionnaires. Then, having classified the attitudes, his aim is to *explain* them by reference to antecedent conditions – in particular the modifications of the individual's central nervous system, in abstraction from the 'historical, economic, sociological, and perhaps even anthropological context'.[21]

(ii) Attempts to explain in terms of type (ii) predicates. Examples here are Hobbes's appeal to appetites and aversions, Pareto's 'residues' and those Freudian and other theories in which the sexual or aggressive instinct is seen as generating a type of undifferentiated activity that is (subsequently) channelled in particular social directions, or else repressed or sublimated.

(iii) Attempts to explain in terms of type (iii) predicates. Examples are those sociologists and social psychologists who favour explanations in terms of general and 'elementary' forms of social behaviour, which do invoke some minimal social reference, but are unspecific as to any particular form of group, institution, or society. It was in this way that Tarde sought to account for much of social life in terms of the process of 'imitation' and it is in this way too that George Homans attempts to use the principles of Skinnerian-type psychology and the terminology of 'costs' and 'rewards', arguing that 'within institutions', which differ greatly from society to society, 'in the face to face relations between individuals . . . characteristics of behaviour appear in which mankind gives away its lost unity'.[22]

(iv) Attempts to explain in terms of type (iv) predicates. Examples of these arc extremely widespread and comprise all those cases where features of concrete, un-abstracted, specifically-located individuals are invoked in explanations – as, for instance when an election result is explained in terms of voters' motivations. Here, the relevant features of the social context (e.g., the class structure and the party system) are, so to speak, incorporated into the characterization of the individuals (as, e.g., working-class deferential Conservatives). If one opens any empirical work of sociology, or of history, explanations of this sort leap to the eye.

This, then, is the range of types of explanation prescribed by methodological individualism. An attack on methodological individualism involves showing that these types of explanation are either implausible or unpromising or question-begging. I would certainly wish to claim that types (i) and (ii) are highly implausible and unpromising ways of approaching the explanation of social phenomena, that type (iii) is very partial and cannot account for the differences between institutions and societies, and that type (iv) is question-begging, because it builds crucial social factors or features of society into the allegedly explanatory individuals (that is, in order to explain working-class Conservatism, we need to look at the class structure and at the party system).[23] Thus the social phenomena have not really been eliminated; they have been swept under the carpet.

Methodological individualism is thus an exclusivist, prescriptive doctrine about what explanations are to look like. In the first three forms considered above, it excludes explanations which appeal to social forces, structural features of society, institutional factors, and so on, while in the fourth form, it only appears to exclude such an appeal.

Ideas have natural affinities for one another, though what seems natural varies from age to age. It has often been claimed that the ideas and doctrines distinguished above are naturally related, that to be committed to one is to be committed to some, most or all of the others [. . .]. Though many individual thinkers have upheld some of these ideas while rejecting others, it has long been supposed that there are connections that are more than merely historical and contingent between humanist and liberal values, a view of society as a combination of (abstract) individuals, political and economic liberalism, protestantism, an individualist view of morals, empiricism and methodological individualism.

This has been supposed both by those who adhere to these ideas and by those who oppose them. For example, among liberals, many, from Locke to Bertrand Russell, have believed that there was an inherent connection between liberalism in morals and politics and an empiricist theory of knowledge, while others such as Weber (but see note 3), Hayek and Popper, have seen it as a matter of moral and political importance to defend methodological individualism. The ideology of contemporary conservatism in America combines political, economic and religious individualism: 'Americanism', it has been said, 'means individualism, *laissez-faire* and Christianity, usually of the fundamentalist Protestant type'.[24] Likewise, anti-individualists have also seen these various ideas as inseparably related. As Lévi-Strauss has observed,

> The individualistic point of view of the eighteenth-century philosophers had been criticized by the theoreticians of reactionary thought, especially de Bonald, on the ground that social phenomena, having a reality *sui generis*, are not simply a combination of individual ones. There is a tradition linking individualism to humanism, while the assumption of the specificity of the collective in relation to the individual seems, also traditionally, to imply the higher value of the former over the latter.[25]

Culturally, it has been said, 'holism is intimately connected with hostility towards the liberal political individualism of the Western tradition'.[26] Conversely, anti-liberal thinkers on both left and right have been inclined to attack as 'individualism' an indistinct amalgam which comprises moral humanitarianism, an abstract view of 'the individual', the politics of liberal democracy and the economics of *laissez-faire* capitalism, protestantism and empiricism.

There are, clearly, interesting and complex relations of a logical or conceptual kind between some of these ideas and doctrines. [. . .]

NOTES

1 *English Works of Thomas Hobbes*, Vol. I, p. 67; Vol. II, p. xiv.
2 A. Comte, *Système de politique positive*, Paris, 1851, Vol. II, p. 181.
3 Quoted in W. Mommsen, 'Max Weber's Political Sociology and his Philosophy of World History', *International Social Science Journal*, XVII (1965), p. 25. Fortunately, Weber did not systematically follow this methodological principle in his substantive sociological work. Consider, for example, his theory of stratification, based on structural rather than subjective factors; his account of the decline of the Roman Empire in terms of structural changes in Roman agriculture; and his explanation of the rationalization of the modern world in terms of such structural factors as the separation of the household from the business enterprise. (*See* L. A. Coser, *Masters of Sociological Thought*, New York, 1971, p. 226).
4 J. S. Mill, *A System of Logic*, 9th ed., London, 1875, Vol. II, p. 469. Men are not, Mill continues, 'when brought together converted into another kind of substance, with different properties' (ibid.).
5 G. C. Homans, *The Nature of Social Science*, New York, 1968.

6 *See* S. Lukes, *Emile Durkheim*, London, 1973, Ch. 16, pp. 302–13.

7 *See The Sociology of Georg Simmel*, tr. and ed. with introduction by K. H. Wolff, Glencoe, Ill., 1950, esp. Chs. I, II and V. (e.g. 'Let us grant for the moment that only individuals "really" exist. Even then only a false conception of science could infer from this "fact" that any knowledge which somehow aims at synthesising these individuals deals with merely speculative abstractions and unrealities', pp. 4–5).

8 *See* C. H. Cooley, *Human Nature and the Social Order*, New York, 1912 For Cooley, society and the individual are merely 'the collective and distributive aspects of the same thing' (pp. 1–2).

9 *See* G. Gurvitch, 'Les Faux Problèmes de la sociologic au XIXe siècle' in *La Vocation actuelle de la sociologic*, Paris, 1950, esp. pp. 25–37.

10 *See* M. Ginsberg, 'The Individual and Society' in *On the Diversity of Morals*, London, 1956.

11 *See* the following discussions: F. A. Hayek, *The Counter-Revolution of Science*, Glencoe, Ill., 1952, Chs. 4, 6 and 8; K. R. Popper, *The Open Society and its Enemies*, London, 1945 (4th. revised edition, 1962) Ch. 14, and *The Poverty of Historicism*, London, 1957, Chs. 7, 23, 24 and 31; J. W. N. Watkins, 'Ideal Types and Historical Explanation', *Brit. J. Phil. Sci.*, Vol. III (1952) (reprinted in H. Feigl and M. Brodbeck, *Readings in the Philosophy of Science*, New York, 1953); 'The Principle of Methodological Individualism' (note) ibid., Vol. III (1952); 'Historical Explanation in the Social Sciences', ibid., Vol. VIII (1957); M. Mandelbaum, 'Societal Laws', ibid., Vol. VIII (1957); L. J. Goldstein, 'The Two Theses of Methodological Individualism' (note), ibid., Vol. IX (1958); Watkins, 'The Two Theses of Methodological Individualism' (note), ibid., Vol. IX (1959); Goldstein, 'Mr Watkins on the Two Theses' (note), ibid., Vol. X (1959); Watkins, 'Third Reply to Mr. Goldstein' (note), ibid., Vol. X (1959); K. J. Scott, 'Methodological and Epistemological Individualism' (note), ibid., Vol. XI (1961); Mandelbaum, 'Societal Facts', *Brit. J. Soc.*, Vol. VI (1955); E. Gellner, 'Explanations in History', *Proc. Aristotelian Soc.*, supplementary Vol. XXX (1956). (These last two articles together with Watkins's 1957 article above are reprinted in P. Gardiner (ed.), *Theories of History*, Glencoe, Ill., 1959, together with a reply to Watkins by Gellner. Gellner's paper is here retitled 'Holism and Individualism in History and Sociology'); M. Brodbeck, 'Philosophy of the Social Sciences', *Phil. Sci.*, Vol. XXI (1954); Watkins, 'Methodological Individualism: A Reply' (note), ibid., Vol. XXII (1955); Brodbeck, 'Methodological Individualisms: Definition and Reduction', ibid., Vol. XXV (1958); Goldstein, 'The Inadequacy of the Principle of Methodological Individualism', *J. Phil.*, Vol. LIII (1956); Watkins, 'The Alleged Inadequacy of Methodological Individualism' (note), ibid., Vol. LV (1958); C. Taylor, 'The Poverty of the Poverty of Historicism', *Universities and Left Review*, 1958 (Summer) followed by replies from I. Jarvie and Watkins, ibid., 1959 (Spring); J. Agassi, 'Methodological Individualism', *Brit. J. Soc.*, Vol. XI (1960); E. Nagel, *The Structure of Science*, 1961, pp. 535–46; A. C. Danto, *Analytical Philosophy of History*, Cambridge, 1965, Ch. XII; W. H. Dray, 'Holism and Individualism in History and Social Science' in P. Edwards (ed.), *The Encyclopedia of Philosophy*, New York, 1967; S. Lukes, 'Methodological Individualism Reconsidered' (containing much of the contents of this chapter), *Brit. J. Soc.*, XIX (1968), pp. 119–29; J. O. Wisdom, 'Situational Individualism and the Emergent Group Properties', in R. Borger and F. Cioffi (eds.), *Explanation in the Behavioural Sciences*, Cambridge, 1970. For a useful summary of some points in this debate, *see* I. C. Jarvie, *Concepts and Society*, London, 1972, Appendix: 'The Methodological Individualism Debate'.

12 Hayek, *Individualism and Economic Order*, p. 6.

13 Popper, *The Open Society*, Vol. II, p. 98.

14 Watkins, 'Historical Explanation in the Social Sciences', in P. Gardiner (ed.), *Theories of History* (see n. II, p. 113), p. 505. Cf: 'Large-scale *social* phenomena must be accounted for by the situations, dispositions and beliefs of individuals. This I call methodological individualism' (Watkins, 'Methodological Individualism: A Reply', *Phil. Sci.*, Vol. XXII (1955) (see n. II, p. 113), p. 58).

15 Jarvie, reply to Taylor (see n. II, p. 114), p. 57.

16 Hayek, *The Counter-Revolution of Science*, p. 56.

17 Popper, *The Poverty of Historicism* (paperback ed. 1961), p. 140.

18 *See* ibid., pp. 62–3.

19 H. J. Eysenck, *The Psychology of Politics*, London, 1954, p. 10.

20 É. Durkheim, *The Rules of Sociological Method*, New York, 1964, p. 104.

21 Eysenck, op. cit., p. 8.

22 G. C. Homans, *Social Behaviour: its Elementary Forms*, London, 1961, p. 6.

23 For a good example of just such a structural, sociological explanation, *see* F. Parkin, 'Working Class Conservatives', *Brit. J. Soc.*, XVIII (1967), pp. 278–90.

24 M. M. Goldsmith and Michael Hawkins, 'The New American Conservatism', *Political Studies*, XX (1972), p. 71.

25 C. Lévi-Strauss, 'French Sociology' in G. Gurvitch and W. E. Moore, (eds.), *Twentieth Century Sociology*, New York, 1945, p. 529.

26 M. Brodbeck, 'Methodological Individualisms: Definition and Reduction' (see n. II, p. 113), p. 3.

3

MARXISM, FUNCTIONALISM, AND GAME THEORY

The case for methodological individualism

Jon Elster

How should Marxist social analysis relate to bourgeois social science? The obvious answer is: retain and develop what is valuable, criticize and reject what is worthless. Marxist social science has followed the opposite course, however. By assimilating the principles of functionalist sociology, reinforced by the Hegelian tradition, Marxist social analysis has acquired an apparently powerful theory that in fact encourages lazy and frictionless thinking. By contrast, virtually all Marxists have rejected rational-choice theory in general and game theory in particular. Yet game theory is invaluable to any analysis of the historical process that centers on exploitation, struggle, alliances, and revolution.

This issue is related to the conflict over methodological individualism, rejected by many Marxists who wrongly link it with individualism in the ethical or political sense. By methodological individualism I mean the doctrine that all social phenomena (their structure and their change) are in principle explicable only in terms of individuals – their properties, goals, and beliefs. This doctrine is not incompatible with any of the following true statements. (a) Individuals often have goals that involve the welfare of other individuals. (b) They often have beliefs about supra-individual entities that are not reducible to beliefs about individuals. "The capitalists fear the working class" cannot be reduced to the feelings of capitalists concerning individual workers. By contrast, "The capitalists' profit is threatened by the working class" can be reduced to a complex statement about the consequences of the actions taken by individual workers.[1] (c) Many properties of individuals, such as "powerful," are irreducibly relational, so that accurate description of one individual may require reference to other individuals.[2]

The insistence on methodological individualism leads to a search for microfoundations of Marxist social theory. The need for such foundations is by now widely, but far from universally, appreciated by writers on Marxist economic theory.[3] The Marxist theory of the state or of ideologies is, by contrast, in a lamentable state. In particular, Marxists have not taken up the challenge of showing how ideological hegemony is created and entrenched at the level of the individual. What microeconomics is for Marxist economic theory, social psychology should be for the Marxist theory of ideology.[4] Without a firm knowledge about the mechanisms that operate at the individual level, the grand Marxist claims about macrostructures and long-term change are condemned to remain at the level of speculation.

THE POVERTY OF FUNCTIONALIST MARXISM

Functional analysis[5] in sociology has a long history. The origin of functionalist explanation is probably the Christian theodicies, which reach their summit in Leibniz: all is for the best in the best of all possible worlds; each apparent evil has good consequences in the larger view, and is to be explained by these consequences. The first secular proponent perhaps was Mandeville, whose slogan "Private Vices, Public Benefits" foreshadows Merton's concept of latent function. To Mandeville we owe the Weak Functional Paradigm: an institution or behavioral pattern often has consequences that are (a) beneficial for some dominant economic or political structure; (b) unintended by the actors; and (c) not recognized by the beneficiaries as owing to that behavior. This paradigm, which we may also call the invisible-hand paradigm, is ubiquitous in the social sciences. Observe that it provides no explanation of the institution or behavior that has these consequences. If we use "function" for consequences that satisfy condition (a) and "latent function" for consequences that satisfy all three conditions, we can go on to state the Main Functional Paradigm: the latent functions (if any) of an institution or behavior explain the presence of that institution or behavior. Finally, there is the Strong Functional Paradigm: all institutions or behavioral patterns have a function that explains their presence.

Leibniz invoked the Strong Paradigm on a cosmic scale; Hegel applied it to society and history, but without the theological underpinning that alone could justify it. Althusser sees merit in Hegel's recognition that history is a "process without a subject," though for Hegel the process still has a goal. Indeed, this is a characteristic feature of both the main and strong paradigms: *to postulate a purpose without a purposive actor* or, in grammatical terms, a predicate without a subject. (Functionalist thinkers characteristically use the passive voice.) I shall refer to such processes guided

23

by a purpose without an intentional subject *objective teleology*. They should be distinguished from both *subjective teleology* (intentional acts with an intentional subject) and *teleonomy* (adaptive behavior fashioned by natural selection). The main difference between subjective teleology and teleonomy is that the former, but not the latter, is capable of waiting and of using indirect strategies, of the form "one step backward, two steps forwards."[6] To the extent that the Main Functional Paradigm invokes teleonomy, as in the explanation of market behavior through a natural-selection model of competition between firms, there can be no objection to it. In the many more numerous cases where no analogy with natural selection obtains, latent functions cannot explain their causes.[7] In particular, long-term positive, unintended, and unrecognized consequences of a phenomenon cannot explain it when its short-term consequences are negative.[8]

Turning to examples of functional analysis in non-Marxist social science, consider this statement by Lewis Coser: "Conflict within and between bureaucratic structures provides the means for avoiding the ossification and ritualism which threatens their form of organization." If instead of "provides the means for avoiding," Coser had written "has the consequence of reducing," there could be no methodological quarrel with him. But his phrasing implies objective teleology, a simulation of human intentional adaptation without specification of a simulating mechanism. Alexander J. Field has observed that a similar functional explanation lies behind the Chicago school of "economic interpretation of the law."[10] For a somewhat grotesque example, consider a statement by Richard Posner:

> The economic case for forbidding marital dissolution out of concern for the children of the marriage is weakened if the parents love the child, for then the costs to the child of dissolution will be weighed by the parents in deciding whether to divorce, and they will divorce only if the gains to them from the divorce exceed the costs to the child, in which event the divorce will be welfare maximizing. If, as suggested earlier, love is a factor of growing importance in the production of children, this might help to *explain* why the law is moving toward easier standards for divorce.[11]

Posner and his school actually tend toward the Strong Functional Paradigm, which most sociologists have abandoned for the more subtle Main Paradigm. Merton, the leading exponent of the Main Paradigm, is also an acute critic of the Strong Paradigm.[12] In Radical and Marxist social science, however, both the crude Strong Paradigm and the less crude (but equally fallacious) Main Paradigm are flourishing. Although my main concern is with Marxism, a few comments on the closely related Radical approach may be in order. As exemplified in the work of Michel Foucault and Pierre Bourdieu, this tends to see every minute detail of social action as part of a vast design for oppression. For an example, we may take Bourdieu's assertion that when intellectuals play around with language and even deliberately violate the rules of grammar, this is a strategy designed to exclude the petty-bourgeois would-be intellectuals, who believe that culture can he assimilated by learning rules and who lose their footing when they see that it is rather a matter of knowing when to break them.[13] This sounds like a conspiratorial view, but actually is closer to functionalism, as can be seen from Bourdieu's incessant use of the phrase *"tout se passe comme si."*[4] If everything happens as if intellectuals thought of nothing but retaining their monopoly, then objectively this must be what explains their behavior. This argument is a theoretical analogue of envy – arising when "our factual inability to acquire a good is wrongly interpreted as a positive action against our desire."[15]

Marx recognized the Weak Functional Paradigm, but argued that what Sartre calls "counterfinality" – the systematic production of consequences that are harmful, unintended, and unrecognized – was equally important. In addition one can certainly trace to him the Main Functional Paradigm, and in at least one passage the Strong Paradigm as well. In the *Theories of Surplus-Value*, Marx reconstructs the rational core of an adversary's argument:

1   the various functions in bourgeois society mutually presuppose each other;
2   the contradictions in material production make necessary a superstructure of ideological strata, whose activity – whether good or bad – is good, because it is necessary;
3   all functions are in the service of the capitalist, and work out to his "benefit";
4   even the most sublime spiritual productions should merely be granted recognition, and *apologies* for them made to the bourgeoisie, that they are presented as, and falsely proved to be, direct producers of material wealth.[16]

Although the context is ambiguous and the text far from clear, a plausible reading suggests the Strong Paradigm. All activities benefit the capitalist class, and these benefits explain their presence. This conspiratorial world view, in which all apparently innocent activities, from Sunday picnics to health care for the elderly, are explained through their function for capitalism, is not, however, pervasive in Marx's work. Much more deeply entrenched, from the level of the philosophy of history to the details of the class struggle, is the Main Paradigm.

Marx had a theory of history, embedded in a philosophy of history: an empirical theory of the four modes of production based on class division, and a speculative notion that before and after the division there was, and will be, unity. In the latter idea, clearly, there is also present the Hegelian or Leibnizian[17] notion that the division is necessary to bring about the unity, and can be explained through this latent function. Marx's objective teleology is especially prominent in the 1862–63 notebooks, of which the middle third was published as the *Theories of Surplus-Value*, while the remaining parts are only now becoming available.[18] Consider in particular the argument that

> The original unity between the worker and the conditions of production ... has two main forms. ... Both are embryonic forms and both are equally unfitted to develop labour as *social* labour and the productive power of social labour. Hence the necessity for the separation, for the rupture, for the antithesis of labour and property ... The most extreme form of this rupture, and the one in which the productive forces of social labour are also most fully developed, is capital. The original unity can be reestablished only on the material foundations which capital creates and by means of the revolutions which, in the process of this creation, the working class and the whole society undergoes.[19]

Elsewhere Marx states that "insofar as it is the coercion of capital which forces the great mass of society to this [surplus labour] beyond its immediate needs, capital creates culture and exercises an historical and social function."[20] He also quotes one of his favorite verses from Goethe:

> Sollte diese Qual uns quälen,
> Da sie unsre Lust vermehrt,
> Hat nicht Myriaden Seelen
> Timur's Herrschaft aufgezehrt?[21]

It is difficult, although perhaps not impossible, to read these passages otherwise than as statements of an objective teleology. Marx, as all Hegelians, was obsessed with *meaning*. If class society and exploitation are necessary for the creation of communism, this lends them a significance that also has explanatory power. In direct continuation, Marx can also argue that various institutions of the capitalist era can be explained by their functions for capitalism, as in this analysis of social mobility:

> The circumstance that a man without fortune but possessing energy, solidity, ability and business acumen may become a capitalist in this manner [i.e., by receiving credit] – and the commercial value of each individual is pretty accurately estimated under the capitalist mode of production – is greatly admired by the apologists of the capitalist system. Although this circumstance continually brings an unwelcome number of new soldiers of fortune into the field and into competition with the already existing individual capitalists, it also reinforces the supremacy of capital itself, expands its base and enables it to recruit ever new forces for itself out of the substratum of society. In a similar way, the circumstance that the

Catholic Church in the Middle Ages formed its hierarchy out of the best brains in the land, regardless of their estate, birth or fortune, was one of the principal means of consolidating ecclesiastical rule and suppressing the laity. The more a ruling class is able to assimilate the foremost minds of a ruled class, the more stable and dangerous becomes its rule.[22]

By using the word "means" in the penultimate sentence, Marx suggests that the beneficial effects of mobility also explain it. In this case the explanatory assertion, although unsubstantiated, might be true, because the Catholic Church was in fact a corporate body, able to promote its interests by deliberate action. This cannot be true of social mobility under capitalism, however, because the capitalist class is not in this sense a corporate body, shaping and channeling everything for its own benefit. That mobility may have favorable consequences for "capital" is neither here nor there, as capital has no eyes that see or hands that move. Indeed, the German "capital logic" school represents a flagrant violation of the principle of methodological individualism, when it asserts or suggests that the needs of capital somehow bring about their own fulfillment.[23]

There is, however, one way in which the capitalist class may promote its collective interests: through the state. Here we confront the difficulty of specifying the capitalist character of the state in a capitalist society. Marx did not believe that the concrete states of the nineteenth century were a direct outgrowth and instrument of capitalist class rule. On the contrary, he argued that it was in the interest of the capitalist class to have a noncapitalist government – rule by the aristocracy in England, by the Emperor and his bureaucracy in France. It was useful for the English capitalists to let the aristocracy remain in power, so that the political struggle between rulers and ruled would blur the lines of economic struggle between exploiters and exploited.[24] Similarly, capitalism on the European continent could only survive with a state that apparently stood above the classes. In these analyses Marx asserts that the noncapitalist state was beneficial for capitalism. He never states or implies that this benefit was deliberately brought about by the capitalist class, and yet he strongly suggests that it explains the presence of the noncapitalist state:

The bourgeoisie confesses that its own interests dictate that it should be delivered from the danger of its *own rule*; that in order to restore the tranquillity in the country its bourgeois Parliament must, first of all, be given its quietus; that in order to preserve its social power intact its political power must be broken; that the individual bourgeois can continue to exploit the other classes and enjoy undisturbed property, family, religion and order only on condition that his class be condemned along with the other classes to like political nullity; that in order to save its purse it must forfeit the crown, and the sword that is to safeguard it must at the same time be hung over its own head as the sword of Damocles.[25]

I defy anyone to read this text without understanding it as an *explanation* of the Bonapartist regime. What else is it but a functional explanation? The anti-capitalist state is the indirect strategy whereby the capitalists retain their economic dominance; one step backward, two steps forward. But an explanation in terms of latent functions can never invoke strategic considerations of this kind. "Long-term functionalism" suffers from all the defects of ordinary functional explanations, notably the problem of a purpose in search of a purposive actor. Moreover, it is *arbitrary*, because the manipulation of the time dimension nearly always lets us find a way in which a given pattern is good for capitalism; *ambiguous* because the distinction between the short and long term may be read either as a distinction between transitional effects and steady-state effects, or as a distinction between two kinds of steady-state effects;[26] and *inconsistent*, because positive long-term effects could never dominate negative short-term effects in the absence of an intentional actor. It is not possible, then, to identify the state in a capitalist society as a capitalist state simply by virtue of its favorable consequences for bourgeois economic dominance.

From Marx I now turn to some recent Marxist writings. Consider first some writings by Marxist historians. In an otherwise important study, John Foster makes the following argument:

> The basic function of feudal social organization was, therefore, to maintain just that balance between population and land which (given technological conditions) would produce the biggest possible feudal surplus. . . . It was enough to ensure that [peasant] marriage and childrearing were strictly tied (by customary practice and religion) to the inheritance of land, and rely on peasant self-interest to do the rest.[27]

But what is the subject of the verbs "ensure" and "rely" in the last sentence? This is clearly a case of objective teleology, of an action in search of an actor.

E. P. Thompson writes that in pre-industrial England there were recurring revolts which, although usually unsuccessful in achieving their immediate objectives, had long-term success in making the propertied classes behave more moderately than they would have otherwise. He also seems to conclude that long-term success provides an (intentional or functional) explanation of the revolts. This, at any rate, is how I interpret his rhetorical question of whether the revolts "would have continued over so many scores, indeed hundreds of years, if they had consistently failed to achieve their objective."[28] If functional, the explanation fails for reasons by now familiar. If intentional, it fails for reasons related to a crucial difference between individual and collective action. If an individual acts in a way that he knows to be in his interest, we may conclude that he acted for the sake of that interest. But when a group of individuals act in a way that is to their collective benefit, we cannot conclude that they did so to bring about that benefit.[29]

The attempt to read meaning into behavior that benefits the actors can take one of three distinct forms. First, the functionalist, discussed above. Second, the consequences can be transformed into motives, as in the example from Thompson. This inference, although not always incorrect, is unwarranted in the cases where the benefits emerge only if the actions are performed by *all* the actors concerned, yet the *individual* has no incentive to perform them. For instance, it is beneficial for the capitalist class as a whole if all capitalists search for labor-saving inventions, for then the aggregate demand for labor and hence the wage rate will fall. And it may well be true that historically there has been a trend to labor-saving inventions. Yet the collective benefits cannot explain the trend, for they could never motivate the individual capitalist who, under conditions of perfect competition, is unable to influence the overall wage level. The trend, if there is one, must be explained by some other mechanism, of which the collective benefits are accidental byproducts. Third, one may invoke a conspiratorial design and seek one unifying but hidden intention behind the structure to be explained. Thus, if a pattern such as social mobility benefits the capitalist class as a whole, but not the "already existing individual capitalists," the conspiratorial explanation postulates a secret executive committee of the bourgeoisie. I do not deny that conspiracies occur, or that their existence may be asserted on indirect evidence. I simply argue the need for evidence – preferably direct or, if this is not available, as in the nature of the case it may not be, indirect – pointing to some hidden coordinating hand. Simply to invoke beneficial consequences supplies no such evidence.

Turning now from Marxist history to Marxist social science proper, we find that functionalism is rampant. Functional explanations pervade the theory of crime and punishment,[30] the analysis of education,[31] the study of racial discrimination,[32] and (most important) the analysis of the capitalist state, a Marxist growth industry during the last decade. Not all Marxist studies fall victim to the functionalist fallacies identified above, but most Marxist authors seem to believe that "everything that happens in a capitalist society necessarily corresponds to the needs of capital accumulation,"[33] so that the "correspondence between the actions (and structure) of the state and the requirements of capital accumulation [is] taken for granted."[34] Alternately, the "assumption is made that the capitalist state is universally functional for reproducing the dominance of the capitalist class."[35] These neo-Marxist works appear to be guided by the following principles. (i) All actions of the state serve the collective interest of the capitalist class. (ii) Any action that would serve the collective interest of the capitalist class is in fact undertaken by the state. (iii) Exceptions to the first principle are explained by "the relative autonomy of the state." (iv) Exceptions to the second principle are explained along the lines of Marx in the *Eighteenth Brumaire*: it is in the political interest of the bourgeoisie that the state should not always act in the economic interest of the bourgeoisie. Needless to say, the effect of the last two clauses is to render the first two virtually vacuous.

[...]

29

Obviously, an alternative approach is required. Having given my views elsewhere,[36] let me summarize them briefly. (1) There are three main types of scientific explanation: the *causal*, the *functional*, and the *intentional*. (2) All sciences use causal analysis. The physical sciences use causal analysis exclusively. (3) The biological sciences also use functional analysis, when explaining the structure or behavior of organisms through the benefits for reproduction. This procedure is justified by the theory of natural selection, according to which such beneficial effects tend to maintain their own causes. Intentional analysis, on the other hand, is not justified in biology – because natural selection is basically myopic, opportunistic, and impatient, as opposed to the capacity for strategic and patient action inherent in intentional actors. (4) The social sciences make extensive use of intentional analysis, at the level of individual actions. Functional analysis, however, has no place in the social sciences, because there is no sociological analogy to the theory of natural selection. (5) The proper paradigm for the social sciences is a mixed causal-intentional explanation – *intentional understanding* of the individual *actions*, and *causal explanation* of their *interaction*. (6) Individuals also interact intentionally. And here – in the study of the intentional interaction between intentional individuals – is where game theory comes in. The need for game theory arises as soon as individual actors cease to regard each other as given constraints on their actions, and instead regard each other as intentional beings. In parametric rationality each person looks at himself as a variable and at all others as constants, whereas in strategic rationality all look upon each other as variables. The essence of strategic thought is that no one can regard himself as privileged compared to the others: each has to decide on the assumption that the others are rational to the same extent as himself.

THE USES OF GAME THEORY IN MARXIST ANALYSIS

The basic premises of rational choice theory[37] are (1) that structural constraints do not completely determine the actions taken by individuals in a society, and (2) that within the feasible set of actions compatible with all the constraints, individuals choose those they believe will bring the best results. If the first premise is denied, we are left with some variety of structuralism – an element of which reasoning is present in Marx, and is most fully developed in French Structuralism. Although it may occasionally be true that the feasible set shrinks to a single point, a general theory to this effect cannot be defended – unless by the ptolemaic twist of counting preferences or ideologies among the constraints. True, the ruling class often manipulates the constraints facing the ruled class so as to leave it no choice, but this very manipulation itself presupposes some scope of choice for the rulers. If the second premise is denied, we are left with some variety of role theory, according to which individuals behave as they do because they have been socialized to, rather than because they try to realize some goal: causality vs. intentionality. Against this I would argue that what people acquire by socialization is not quasicompulsive tendencies to act in specific ways, but preference structures that – jointly with the feasible set – bring it about that some specific action is chosen. If the role theory was correct, it would be impossible to induce behavior modification by changing the feasible set (e.g., the reward structure), but clearly such manipulation is an omnipresent fact of social life.[38]

Game theory is a recent and increasingly important branch of rational choice theory, stressing the *interdependence of decisions*. If all violence were structural, class interests purely objective, and class conflict nothing but incompatible class interests, then game theory would have nothing to offer to Marxism. But because classes crystallize into collective actors that confront each other over the distribution of income and power, as well as over the nature of property relations, and as there are also strategic relations between members of a given class, game theory is needed to explain these complex interdependencies. In a "game" there are several players or actors. Each actor must adopt an action or a strategy. When all actors have chosen strategies, each obtains a reward that depends on the strategies chosen by him *and* by the others. *The reward of each depends on the choice of all*. The notion of a reward can be understood narrowly or broadly. In the narrow interpretation it signifies the material benefit received by each actor. In the broad interpretation, it covers everything in the situation of value to the actor, including (possibly) the rewards to other actors. *The reward of each depends on the reward of all*.[39] It is assumed that the actors strive to maximize their reward – to bring about a situation they prefer to other situations. When an actor chooses a strategy, he must take account of what the others will do. A strategy that is optimal against one set of strategies on the part of the others is not necessarily optimal against another set. To arrive at his decision, therefore, he has to *foresee their decisions*, knowing that they are trying to foresee his. *The choice of each depends on the choice of all*. The triumph of game theory is its ability to embrace simultaneously the three sets of interdependencies stated in the italicized sentences.[40] Nothing could be further from the truth, then, than the allegation that game theory portrays the individual as an isolated and egoistic atom.

An essential element of the situation is the *information* that the actors possess about each other. In games with perfect information, each individual has complete information about all relevant aspects of the situation. These include the capabilities of the other actors, their preferences, their information, and the payoff structure that maps sets of individual strategies into outcomes. The condition of perfect information is likely to be realized only in small and stable groups, or in groups with a coordinating instance. Also crucial is the notion of an *equilibrium point* – a set of strategies in which the strategy of each actor is optimal vis-à-vis those of the others. It is thanks to this notion that game theory can avoid the infinite regress of "I think that he thinks that

I think . . ." which plagued early attempts to understand the logic of interdependency. The notion of a *solution* can be defined through that of an equilibrium point. Informally, the solution to a game is the set of strategies toward which rational actors with perfect information will tacitly converge. If there is only one equilibrium point, it will automatically emerge as the solution – it is the only stable outcome, in the sense that no one gains from defection. If there are several such equilibria, the solution will be the one that is collectively optimal – the equilibrium point preferred by all to all the others. Not all games have solutions in this sense.

A brief typology of games may be useful. One basic distinction is between two-person and n-person games, both of which are important for Marxism. The struggle between capital and labor is a two-person game, the struggle between members of the capitalist class an n-person game. Often, however, complicated n-person games can be reduced without too much loss of generality to simpler two-person games – as games played between "me" and "everybody else."[41] The simplest two-person games are zero-sum games, in which the loss of one player exactly equals the gain of the other. This is the only category of games that always have a solution. The conceptual break-through that made proof of this proposition possible was the introduction of *mixed strategies*, i.e., the choice of a strategy according to some (optimal) probability distribution. In poker, for instance, a player may decide to bluff in one half of the cases, a policy implemented by tossing a coin in each case. Here the opponent may calculate how often the player will bluff, but not whether he will do so in any particular case. In variable-sum games not only the distribution of the rewards, but also the size of the total to be distributed, depends on the strategies chosen These games can be further divided into games of pure cooperation and games of mixed conflict and cooperation (whereas zero-sum games are games of pure conflict). Not all variable-sum games have a solution in the sense indicated above. They can, however, have a solution once we take the step from noncooperative to cooperative games. In cooperative games – which should not be confused with the (noncooperative) games of pure cooperation – there is joint rather than individual choice of strategies. The actors can coordinate their choices so as to avoid certain disastrous combinations of individual strategies. If there is a choice between left-hand and right-hand driving, the actors may agree to toss a coin between both driving on the right and both driving on the left – a *jointly-mixed strategy*. If they toss a coin individually, the chances are 50% that they will end up on a collision course.

The value of the cooperative approach to game theory is contested because it appears to beg the question by assuming that agreements to cooperate will be enforced. On general grounds of methodological individualism, noncooperative games are prior to cooperative games. Assuming that the actors will arrive at a cooperative solution is much like assuming that a functional need will create its own fulfillment. For this reason, and also because there are so many solution concepts for cooperative games, one will have to tread carefully when explaining the emergence of cooperative behavior in terms of cooperative games. Properly used, however, the method can yield important results, and in any case is fruitful for the purpose of normative analysis. For n-person games, the cooperative approach does not involve universal cooperation, but rather the cooperation of some actors against the others. The theory of coalitions in n-person game theory is an increasingly important branch of game theory for economic, political, and normative analysis.[42] The simplest solution concept for such games is that of the "core" – the set of all reward distributions in which no coalition of individuals can improve their lot by breaking out and acting on their own. Once again, the cooperative approach begs the question by assuming that coalitions can be formed and maintained whenever needed. And, once again, this is more an objection to the analytical-explanatory than to the normative use of the theory.

Turning now, from exposition to applications, I discuss in turn the logic of solidarity and cooperation within classes, the problem of worker-capitalist coalitions, and some static and dynamic aspects of the class struggle. These applications all presuppose that we have left behind us – if it ever existed – the capitalism of perfect competition, unorganized capital and unorganized labor. The income distribution that would emerge under perfect competition can serve as a baseline for comparison with the distributions that result when one or both of the main classes behave in an organized and strategic manner. Whether the classes will so behave is itself a question to be decided by game theoretic analysis. I define class consciousness as the capacity of a class to behave as a collective actor. Operationally, this means the capacity to overcome the free-rider problem. This problem arises within both the capitalist and the working classes. As well explained by Mancur Olson,[43] each worker is tempted by the prospect of a free ride, of benefiting from the strikes fought by the other workers without taking part in the action himself. Similarly, capitalists face the same difficulty with regard to cartelization, wage policy, etc. If, however, we want to penetrate past these generalities to the fine grain of the problem, some distinctions must be made. I assume that each actor within the class has a choice between a *solidary strategy* (S) and an *egoist strategy* (E). In the artificial two-person game between "me" and "everybody else," four possibilities can be distinguished:

A   Universal cooperation: everybody uses S
B   Universal egoism: everybody uses E
C   The free rider: "I" use E, "everybody else" uses S
D   The sucker: "I" use S, "everybody else" uses E.

Every individual in the society will rank these outcomes in a particular order, according to what he – in the role of "I" – would prefer. Excluding ties, there are twenty-four possible rankings of these four alternatives.[44] If we disregard all that rank

B before A, as we are permitted to do by the very nature of the problem under discussion, we are left with twelve cases. If we then exclude the "masochistic" cases that have D ranked above A, we are left with eight alternatives. I shall limit myself to four cases that have a central place in the literature on collective action. I shall also limit myself to the hypothesis that each "I" views the situation in the same way. Although mixed cases will be the rule in actual situations, the assumption of homogeneity makes for a more tractable analysis.[45]

The first case is the well-known Prisoners' Dilemma, defined by the ranking CABD and characterized by the following features. (1) Strategy E is dominant, i.e., for each actor it is the best choice regardless of what the others will do. Here, then, we need not impose any stringent information requirement for the solution to be realized. Also, it is not true here that "the choice of each depends on the choice of all." In a sense, therefore, it is a rather trivial game. (2) The solution to the game is universal egoism, which everybody ranks below universal cooperation. Individual rationality leads to collective disaster. (3) Universal cooperation is neither individually stable nor individually accessible: everybody will take the first step away from it, and no one the first step toward it We can apply this to the workers' predicament. For the individual there is no point in going on strike if his fellow workers do so, for by remaining at work he can derive the benefit from their action *and* be (highly) paid during the strike – and if they do not strike he has nothing to gain and much to lose by unilateral action.

Is there a "way out" of the Prisoners' Dilemma? Can individuals caught in this situation overcome the dilemma and behave cooperatively? No consensus has emerged from the extensive literature, but I believe that in the present context two approaches stand out as the most promising. In the case of working-class cooperation the most plausible explanation is by change of the preference structure. Through continued interaction the workers become both concerned and informed about each other. Concern for others changes the ranking of the alternatives, and information about others enables the actors to realize the solution of the ensuing game. This is the "Assurance Game," defined by the ranking ACBD and possessing the following features. (1) There is no dominant strategy in this game. Egoism is "my" best reply to egoism, solidarity the best reply to solidarity. (2) The optimum of universal cooperation is individually stable, but not individually accessible. (3) Universal egoism and universal solidarity are both, therefore, equilibrium points in the game. Because universal cooperation is preferred by all to universal egoism, the former emerges as the solution to the game. (4) Because there is no dominant strategy, the solution will be realized only if there is perfect information. Imperfect information – about preferences or information – easily leads to uncertainty, suspicion, and play-safe behavior. Amartya Sen has argued that Marx's *Critique of the Gotha Programme* can be interpreted in terms of the Assurance Game.[46] Solidarity can substitute for material incentives. I would tend to believe that quite generally working-class solidarity and collective action can he understood in these terms, although I shall later point to an alternative explanation.

Although the Prisoners' Dilemma and the Assurance Game differ profoundly in their structure, behavior – in cases of incomplete information – may occur *as if* the preferences were a Prisoner's Dilemma when in fact they form an Assurance Game. In tax evasion or suboptimal use of public transportation, for instance, the observed outcome may be the result of lack of information rather than of free-rider egoism. Likewise, the Assurance Game preferences should be distinguished from those of the Categorical Imperative, although behaviorally they may be indistinguishable. The Categorical Imperative is defined by the ranking ADBC, with solidarity as a dominant strategy. The history of the working class shows, in my opinion, that cooperative behavior typically is conditional rather than unconditional – motivated by the concern for doing one's share of a common task rather than by the spirit of sacrifice or disregard for actual consequences characteristic of the Categorical Imperative. Indeed, more harm than good sometimes ensues from heroic individual acts of revolt or disobedience, if the others are not willing to follow suit, because such acts may provide the authorities or the employers the excuse they need to crack down further on the workers. This, I believe, shows that Kant's individualistic ethic is not appropriate for collective action.[47]

The Assurance Game also provides an interpretation of Charles Taylor's notion of *common meaning*, designed to elucidate the meaning of consensus. In his polemic against methodological individualism Taylor asserts there are two forms of meaning that are irreducibly nonsubjective: the intersubjective meanings and the common meanings. Intersubjective meanings are, roughly, rules for social behavior whose negation cannot be generalized without contradiction. Thus promises should be kept because the notion of a society in which promises were never kept is logically contradictory. Common meanings illustrate the Assurance Game. Taylor distinguishes common meanings from shared subjective meanings by saying that "what is required for common meanings is that this shared value be part of the common world, that *this sharing itself be shared*."[48] The phrase I have italicized amounts to a condition of perfect information. For a consensus to be a living force, it must be known to exist. Everybody acts in a solidary manner because of knowing that the others are going to do so as well. This way of looking at consensus enables us to refute the following claim made by Taylor:

> Common meanings, as well as intersubjective meanings, fall through the net of mainstream social science. They can find no place in its categories. For they are not simply a converging set of subjective reactions, but part of the common world. What the ontology of mainstream social science lacks, is the notion of meaning as not simply for an individual subject; of a subject who can be a "we" as well as an "I".[49]

Game theory provides what Taylor claims is lacking – the notion of a subject that can be a "we" as well as an "I". Through the triple interdependence that game theory analyzes – between rewards, between choices, and between rewards and choices – the individual emerges as a microcosm epitomizing the whole network of social relations. A similar demystification makes good sense of Sartre's notion of the "group," even though he claims it cannot be rendered in the "neo-positivist" language of "analytical reason."[50]

[. . .]

The weakness of game theory, in its present state, is the lack of testable hypotheses. There are many experimental studies of gaming, within the noncooperative and the cooperative framework, but few applications to nonexperimental settings. The value of the theory, therefore, is mainly in illuminating the nature of social interaction and in creating more discriminating categories of sociological analysis. Yet I am confident that this is a transitory situation only, and that game theory will increasingly help us understand social and historical problems. My reasons for this belief are somewhat a priori. If one accepts that interaction is of the essence of social life, then I submit that the three, interlocking, sets of interdependencies set out above capture interaction better than does any alternative. Game theory provides solid microfoundations for any study of social structure and social change. Yet the problems of aggregation and statistical analysis still confound us when it comes to complex real life cases. This is not an argument for abandoning the search for microfoundations, but a compelling reason for forging better links between aggregate analysis and the study of individual behavior.

[. . .]

NOTES

1 The philosophical point invoked here is that in contexts of belief, desire, etc. it is not in general possible to substitute for each other expressions with the same reference, without change of truth value. We fear an object as described in a certain way, and we may not fear it under a different description.

2 For an analysis of this idea, see my *Logic and Society* (Chichester: Wiley, 1978), 20 ff.

3 A forceful statement of the need for microfoundations is in John Roemer, *Analytical Foundations of Marxian Economic Theory* (Cambridge University Press, 1981), Ch. 1 and *passim*.

4 I argue in more detail for this claim in Ch. V of my *Sour Grapes*, 1983b from Cambridge University Press.

5 For a fuller statement of my views on functional explanation, see Ch. 2 of my *Explaining Technical Change*, 1983a from Cambridge University Press; see also my exchange with G.A. Cohen in *Political Studies* XXVIII (1980), my exchange with Arthur Stinchcombe in *Inquiry*

23 (1980), and my review of P. van Parijs, *Evolutionary Explanation in the Social Sciences* (Totowa, NJ: Rowman and Littlefield, 1981), forthcoming in *Inquiry*.

6   For a fuller statement, see Ch. 1 of my *Ulysses and the Sirens* (Cambridge University Press, 1979).

7   Natural selection invokes competition between coexisting individuals. Arthur Stinchcombe (in his contribution to *The Idea of Social Structure: Papers in Honor of Robert K. Merton*, ed. Lewis A. Coser (Harcourt, Brace, Jovanovich, 1975)) points to an analogous model involving selection among successive social states. The model pictures social change as an absorbing Markov process – which for the present purposes may be summarized by saying that institutions undergo continuous change until they arrive in a state in which there is no pressure for further change (the "absorbing state"). This view could be used as a basis for functional explanation, with the modification that it would explain social states in terms of the absence of destabilizing consequences rather than through the presence of stabilizing ones. I would argue, however, that – unlike the biological case – there are no reasons for thinking that this adaptive process would ever catch up with the changing social environment.

8   A radically different account of functional explanation is offered by G.A. Cohen, *Karl Marx's Theory of History* (Oxford University Press, 1978). He argues that functional explanations can be sustained by *consequence laws*, of the form "Whenever x would have favourable consequences for y, then x appears." If a law of this form is established, we may affirm that x is explained by its favorable consequences for y, even if no mechanism is indicated (although Cohen asserts that some mechanism must indeed exist). To the (partially misguided) objections to this idea stated in my review of his book in *Political Studies* (note 5 above), I now would like to add the following. First, x and the y-enhancing effect of x might both be effects of some third factor z, and thus related by spurious correlation. Second, the definition of a consequence law is vitiated by the imprecise way in which the time dimension is brought in. The law could in fact be vacuously confirmed by suitably ignoring short-term in favor of long-term consequences.

9   "Social Conflict and the Theory of Social Change," in *Conflict Resolution: Contributions of the Behavioral Sciences*, ed. C.G. Smith (University of Notre Dame Press, 1971), 60.

10 "What's Wrong with the New Institutional Economics" (Mimeograph, Department of Economics, Stanford University, 1979).

11 *Economic Analysis of the Law* (Little, Brown, 1977), 106. Italics added, parentheses deleted.

12 R.K. Merton, *Social Theory and Social Structure*, rev. ed. (Free Press, 1957), 30 ff.

13 P. Bourdieu, *La Distinction* (Paris: Editions de Minuit, 1979), 285. For a critical discussion of this inverted sociodicy, which proceeds from the assumption that all is for the worst in the worst of all possible worlds, see my review in *London Review of Books*, 5–18 November 1981.

14 I counted 15 occurrences of this phrase in *La Distinction*.

15 M. Scheler, *Ressentiment* (Schocken, 1972), 52.

16 *Theories of Surplus-Value*, 3 vols. (Moscow: Progress, 1963–71), 1, 287.

17 "You know my admiration for Leibniz" (Marx to Engels, 10 May 1870). For the structure of Leibniz's philosophy of history, see Ch. VI of my *Leibniz et la Formation de l'Esprit Capitaliste* (Paris: Aubier-Montaigne, 1975).

18 The manuscript consists of 23 notebooks, of which books 6 to 15 were published by Kautsky as *Theories of Surplus-Value*. Books 1 to 5 and 16 to 18 have recently been published in the new *Marx-Engels Gesamt-Ausgabe*, and the remaining will soon be available

in the same edition. Just as Marx's *Grundrisse* testify to the influence of Hegel's *Logic*, these manuscripts bear witness to the influence of Hegel's philosophy of history.

19 *Theories of Surplus-Value*, 3, 422–3.

20 *Marx-Engels Gesamt-Ausgabe*, Zweite Abteilung, Band 3, Teil 1 (Berlin: Dietz, 1976), 173.

21 Ibid., 327. The verse is also quoted in Marx's article on "The British Rule in India" (*New York Daily Tribune*, 25 June 1853) and, in a more ironic vein, in *Neue Oder Zeitung*, 20 January 1855.

22 *Capital*, 3 vols. (International Publishers, 1967), 3, 600–1. For the distinction between short-term and long-term functionalism in Marxism, see also Roemer, *Analytical Foundations*, 9.

23 For surveys, see B. Jessop, "Recent Theories of the Capitalist State," *Cambridge Journal of Economics* 1 (1977), 353–74 and the Introduction to J. Holloway and S. Picciotta, eds., *State and Capital* (London: Edward Arnold, 1978). I should mention here that by "corporate body" I mean something different from what is later referred to as a "collective actor". The former refers to a juristic person, or more broadly to any kind of formal organization with a single decision-making center. The latter is defined below as any group of individuals who are able, by solidarity or enlightened self-interest, to overcome the free-rider problem. Another way of overcoming it is to create a corporate body with legal or effective power to keep individual members in line, but in the discussion below I mostly limit myself to cooperation emerging by tacit coordination.

24 *New York Daily Tribune*, 25 August 1852.

25 "The Eighteenth Brumaire of Louis Bonaparte," in Marx and Engels, *Collected Works* (Lawrence and Wishart, 1979), 143.

26 De Tocqueville, in *Democracy in America*, distinguishes both between the transitional effects of democratization and the steady-state effects of democracy: and between the inefficient use of resources and the efficient creation of resources that are both inherent in democracy as a going concern. For details, see Ch. 1 of my *Explaining Technical Change*.

27 *Class Struggle and the Industrial Revolution* (Methuen, 1974), 15. Thus Marxist functionalism explains the institutional arrangements of feudalism in terms of their favorable consequences for the surplus product, whereas non-Marxist functionalists such as D. North and R.P. Thomas (*The Rise of the Western World* (Cambridge University Press, 1973)) explain the same arrangements in terms of their favorable consequences for total product.

28 "The Moral Economy of the English Crowd in the Eighteenth Century," *Past and Present* 50 (1971), 120.

29 For an analysis of this fallacy, see my *Logic and Society*, 118 ff.

30 Stark examples include W.J. Chambliss, "The Political Economy of Crime: A Comparative Study of Nigeria and the USA," in *Critical Criminology*, ed. I. Taylor, *et al.* (Routledge and Kegan Paul, 1975), and W.J. Chambliss and T.E. Ryther, *Sociology: The Discipline and Its Direction* (McGraw-Hill, 1975), 348. The closely related Radical approach is exemplified by M. Foucault, *Surveiller et Punir* (Paris: Gallimard, 1915), 277 and *passim*.

31 S. Bowles and H. Gintis, *Schooling in Capitalist America* (Routledge and Kegan Paul, 1976), e.g., 103, 114, and 130 features many such examples. In the same vein is also M. Levitas, *Marxist Perspectives in the Sociology of Education* (Routledge and Kegan Paul, 1974). A Radical version is that of P. Bourdieu and J.-C. Passeron, *La Reproduction* (Paris: Editions de Minuit, 1910), e.g., 159.

32 H. Bowles and S. Gintis, "The Marxian Theory of Value and Heterogeneous Labour: a Critique and Reformulation," *Cambridge Journal of Economics* I (1977), 173–92;

J. Roemer, "Divide and Conquer: Microfoundations of a Marxian Theory of Wage Discrimination," *Bell Journal of Economics* 10 (1979), 695–705. The fallacy involved in both these articles is the belief that because internal cleavages in the working class benefit capitalist class domination, they are to be explained in terms of this benefit. This, however, is to confuse what Simmel (*Soziologic* (Berlin: Dunker und Humblot, 1908), 76 ff.) referred to as, respectively, *tertius gaudens* and *divide et impera*. Third parties may benefit from a struggle even when they have not been instrumental in setting it up.

33 As Jessop, "Recent Theories," 364, characterizes the "capital logic" school.

34 Introduction to Holloway and Picciotta, 12, characterizing Yaffe's work.

35 E.O. Wright, *Class, Crisis and the State* (New Left Books, 1978), 231.

36 Van Parijs, passim; also *Ulysses and the Sirens*, Ch. 1.

37 A standard treatment is R.D. Luce and H. Raiffa, *Games and Decisions* (Wiley, 1957). Some nonstandard problems are raised in *Ulysses and the Sirens*, especially Ch. 3.

38 For an elaboration of my critique of structuralism and role theory, see *Ulysses and the Sirens*, Ch. III.1 and III.6.

39 This could be part at what Marx meant by his statement in the *Communist Manifesto*: "In place of the old bourgeois society, with its classes and class antagonism, we shall have an association in which the free development for each is the condition for the free development of all." (Another possible reading is indicated in the next note.) If "each" and "all" are transposed in this passage, a more adequate expression occurs. Proper understanding of the philosophical anthropology behind this statement presupposes the idea that even for the single individual, the free development of all faculties is the condition for the free development of each faculty (*The German Ideology*, in Marx and Engels, *Collected Works* (Lawrence and Wishart, 1976), 5, 262). The freely-developed person is both a totality of freely-developed faculties and part of a totality of freely-developed persons. Hypertrophy is atrophy, in the individual and in society.

40 A fourth kind of independence falls outside game theory, however. It can be summed up by saying that the *preferences of each depend on the actions of all*, by socialization and more invidious mechanisms such as conformism, "sour grapes," etc. Game theory takes preferences as given, and has nothing to offer concerning preference formation. The transformation of a Prisoners' Dilemma into an Assurance Game (see below) must be explained by social psychology, not by game theory. We can explain behavior intentionally in terms of preferences, but the latter themselves are to be explained causally.

41 For n-person versions of some of the games discussed here, see A. Sen, "Isolation, Assurance and the Social Rate of Discount," *Quarterly Journal of Economics* 80 (1967) 112–24. For a treatment of heterogeneous preferences in n-person games, see the brilliant framework developed by T.S. Schelling, *Micromotives and Macrobehavior* (Norton, 1978).

42 The most general analysis, permitting overlapping coalitions, is J. Harsanyi, *Rational Behavior and Bargaining Equilibrium in Games and Social Situations* (Cambridge University Press, 1977). The economic theory of the core is made easily accessible by W. Hildebrand and A.P. Kirman, *Introduction to Equilibrium Theory* (Amsterdam: North-Holland, 1976). Applications to ethics include John Roemer, *A General Theory of Exploitation and Class* (Harvard University Press, 1990), and Roger Howe and John Roemer, "Rawlsian Justice as the Core of a Game," forthcoming in the *American Economic Review*.

43 *The Logic of Collective Action* (Harvard University Press, 1965), Ch. 4.

44 For a more fine-grained typology. see A. Rapoport, M.J. Guyer, and D.G. Gordon, *The 2×2 Game* (University of Michigan Press, 1976). For other discussions of the relation

among the preference structures analyzed here, see S.-C. Kolm, "Altruismes et Efficacités," *Social Science Information* 20 (1981), 293–344; and R. van der Veen, "Meta-Rankings and Collective Optimality," *Social Science Information* 20 (1981), 345–74.

45 For a brief discussion of some mixed cases, see my "Introduction" to the articles by Kuhn and van der Veen cited in the preceding note. See also Schelling.

46 A. Sen, *On Economic Inequality* (Oxford University Press, 1973), Ch. 4.

47 The point is that acting unilaterally on the Categorical Imperative may be downright unethical. A striking example could be unilateral disarmament, if the situation is such that other countries will rush in to fill the power vacuum. Instead of acting in a way that would lead to good results *if* everyone else did the same, one should act to promote the good on realistic assumptions about what others are likely to do. A little morality, like a little rationality, may be a dangerous thing. There is room and need for a "moral theory of the second best," corresponding to the economic theory of the second best which shows that if out of n conditions for an economic optimum, one is not fulfilled, the optimum may be more closely approached if additional conditions are violated. (R.G. Lipset and K. Lancaster, "The Economic Theory of Second Best," *Review of Economic Studies*, XXIV (1957–8), 133–62.)

48 C. Taylor, "Interpretation and the Sciences of Man," *Review of Metaphysics* 25 (1971), 31.

49 Ibid., 31–32.

50 J.-P. Sartre, *Critique de la Raison Dialectique* (Paris: Gallimard, 1960), 417, 404 ff.

4

REPLY TO ELSTER ON "MARXISM, FUNCTIONALISM, AND GAME THEORY"

G.A. Cohen

Jon Elster and I each worked sympathetically on Marxism for a long time, and each of us independently came to see that Marxism in its traditional form is associated with explanations of a special type, ones in which, to put it roughly, consequences are used to explain causes. In keeping with normal practice, Elster calls such explanations *functional* explanations, and I shall follow suit here.[1] He deplores the association between Marxism and functional explanation, because he thinks there is no scope for functional explanation in social science. It is, he believes, quite proper in biology, because unlike social phenomena, biological ones satisfy the presuppositions that justify its use. Elster therefore concludes that the Marxist theory of society and history should abandon functional explanation. He also thinks that it should, instead, draw for its explanations on the resources of game theory.

I do not think that course is open to historical materialism. I believe that historical materialism's central explanations are unrevisably functional in nature, so that if functional explanation is unacceptable in social theory then historical materialism cannot be reformed and must be rejected. But I do not think functional explanation is unacceptable in social theory. My judgment that historical materialism is indissolubly wedded to functional explanation naturally reflects my conception of the content of historical materialist theory. To display, then, the grounds of that judgment, I shall expound what I think historical materialism says. I shall provide a résumé of the theory that I attribute, on a textual basis, to Marx, and that I explicate and defend in my book *Karl Marx's Theory of History*.[2]

In my book I say, and Marx says, that history is, fundamentally, the growth of human productive power, and that forms of society rise and fall accordingly as they enable and promote, or prevent and discourage, that growth. The canonical text for this interpretation is the famous 1859 "Preface" to *A Contribution to the Critique of*

Political Economy, some sentences of which we shall look at shortly. I argue (in section 3 of Chapter VI) that the Preface makes explicit the standpoint on society and history to be found throughout Marx's mature writings, on any reasonable view of the date at which he attained theoretical maturity. In attending to the "Preface," we are not looking at just one text among many, but at that text which gives the clearest statement of the theory of historical materialism. The presentation of the theory in the "Preface" begins as follows:

> In the social production of their life men enter into definite relations that are indispensable and independent of their will, relations of production which *correspond* to a definite stage of development of their material productive forces. The sum total of these relations constitutes the economic structure of society, the real *basis*, *on which arises* a legal and political superstructure. (italics added)

These sentences mention three ensembles, the productive forces, the relations of production, and the superstructure, among which certain explanatory connections are asserted. Here I say what I think the ensembles are, and then I describe the explanatory connections among them. (All of what follows is argued for in *KMTH*, but not all of the argument is given in what follows, which may therefore wrongly impress the reader as dogmatic). The productive forces are those facilities and devices used in the process of production: means of production on the one hand, and labor power on the other. Means of production are physical productive resources; e.g., tools, machinery, raw materials, and premises. Labor power includes not only the strength of producers, but also their skills, and the technical knowledge (which they need not understand) they apply when laboring. Marx says, and I agree, that this subjective dimension of the productive forces is more important than the objective or means of production dimension; and within the more important dimension the part most capable of development is knowledge. In its higher stages, then, the development of the productive forces merges with the development of productively useful science.

Note that Marx takes for granted in the "Preface," what elsewhere he asserts outright, that "there is a continual movement of growth in productive forces."[3] I argue (in section 6 of Chapter 11 of *KMTH*) that the relevant standard for measuring that growth in power is how much (or, rather, how little) labor must be spent with given forces to produce what is required to satisfy the inescapable physical needs of the immediate producers.[4] This criterion of social productivity is less equivocal than others that may come to mind, but the decisive reason for choosing it is not any such "operational" advantage, but its theoretical appropriateness: if kinds of economic structure correspond, as the theory says they do, to levels of productive power, then this way of measuring productive power makes the theory's correspondence thesis more plausible.[5] (I do not say that the only explanatory feature of productive power is how much there is of it: qualitative features of productive forces also help to explain the character of economic structures. My claim is that insofar as quantity of productive power is what matters, the key quantity is how much time it takes to reproduce the producers.)

We turn to relations of production. They are relations of economic power, of the economic power[6] people enjoy or lack over labor power and means of production. In a capitalist society relations of production include the economic power capitalists have over means of production, the limited but substantial economic power workers (unlike slaves) have over their own labor power, and the lack of economic power workers have over means of production. The sum total of production relations in a given society is said to constitute the economic structure of that society, which is also called – in relation to the superstructure – the basis, or base, or foundation. The economic structure or base therefore consists of relations of production only: it does not include the productive forces. The "Preface" describes the superstructure as legal and political. So it at any rate *includes* the legal and state institutions of society. It is customary to locate other institutions within it too, and it is controversial what its correct demarcation is: my own view is that there are strong textual and systematic reasons for supposing that the superstructure is a lot smaller than many commentators think it is.[7] It is certainly false that every noneconomic social phenomenon is superstructural: artistic creation, for example, is demonstrably not, as such, superstructural for Marx. In these remarks I shall discuss the legal order only, which is uncontroversially a part of the superstructure.

So much for the identity of the three ensembles mentioned in the "Preface". Now relations of production are said to *correspond* to the level of development of the productive forces, and in turn to be a *foundation* on which a superstructure rises. I think these are ways of saying that the level of development of the productive forces explains the nature of the production relations, and that they in turn explain the character of the superstructure co-present with them. But what kind of explanation is ventured here? I argue that in each case what we have is a species of functional explanation.

What sort of explanation is that? It is, very roughly, an explanation in which an event, or whatever else, if there is anything else that can have an effect, is explained in terms of its effect. But now let us be less rough. Suppose we have a cause, e, and its effect, f. Then the form of the explanation is not: e occurred because f occurred – that would make functional explanation the mirror image of ordinary causal explanation, and then functional explanation would have the fatal defect that it represented a later occurrence as explaining an earlier one. Nor should we say that the form of the explanation is "e occurred because it caused f." Similar constraints on explanation and time order rule that candidate out: by the time e has caused f, e has occurred, so the fact that it caused f could not explain its occurrence. The only remaining candidate, which I therefore elect, is: *e* occurred because it *would* cause *f*, or, less tersely but more properly, *e* occurred because the situation was such that an event of type *E* would cause an event of type *F*.[8] So in my view a functional explanation is an explanation in which a dispositional fact explains the occurrence of the event-type mentioned in the antecedent of the hypothetical specifying the disposition. I called the laws justifying functional explanations *consequence laws*. They are of roughly this form: $(E \rightarrow F) \rightarrow E$ (a more precise specification of their form is given in section 4 of Chapter IX of *KMTH*). If this account of what functional explanations are is correct, then the main explanatory theses of historical materialism are functional explanations. For superstructures hold foundations together, and production relations control the development of productive forces: these are undeniable facts, of which Marx was aware. Yet he asserts that the character of the superstructure is explained by the nature of the base, and that the base is explained by the nature of the productive forces. If the intended explanations are functional ones, we have consistency between the effect of *A* on *B* and the explanation of *A* by *B*, *and I do not know any other way of rendering historical materialism consistent*.

I now expound in greater detail one of the two functional explanatory theses, that which concerns base and superstructure. The base, it will be recalled, is the sum total of production relations, these being relations of economic power over labor power and means of production. The capitalist's control of means of production is an illustration. And the superstructure, we saw, has more than one part, exactly what its parts are is somewhat uncertain, but certainly one *bona fide* part of it is the legal system, which will occupy us here. In a capitalist society capitalists have effective power over means of production. What confers that power on a given capitalist, say an owner of a factory? On what can he rely if others attempt to take control of the factory away from him? An important part of the answer is this: he can rely on the law of the land, which is enforced by the might of the state. It is his legal right that causes him to have his economic power. What he is effectively able to do depends on what he is legally entitled to do. And this is in general true in law-abiding society with respect to all economic powers and all economic agents. We can therefore say: in law-abiding society people have the economic powers they do because they have the legal rights they do.

That seems to refute the doctrine of base and superstructure, because here super-structural conditions – what legal rights people have – determine basic ones – what their economic powers are. But although it seems to refute the doctrine of base and superstructure, it cannot be denied. And it would not only seem to refute it, but actually would refute it, were it not possible, *and therefore mandatory* (for historical materialists), to present the doctrine of base and superstructure as an instance of functional explanation. For we can add, to the undeniable truth emphasized above, the thesis that the given capitalist enjoys the stated right because it belongs to a structure of rights, a structure that obtains because it sustains an analogous structure of economic power. The content of the legal system is explained by its function, which is to help sustain an economy of a particular kind. People do usually get their powers from their rights, but in a manner that is not only allowed but demanded by the way historical materialism explains superstructural rights by reference to basic powers. Hence the effect of the law of property on the economy is not, as is often supposed, an embarrassment to historical materialism. It is something that historical materialism is committed to emphasizing, because of the particular way it explains law in terms of economic conditions. Legal structures rise and fall accordingly as they sustain or frustrate forms of economy that, I now add, are favored by the productive forces. The addition implies an explanation why whatever economic structure obtains at a given time does obtain at that time. Once more the explanation is a functional one: the prevailing production relations prevail because they are relations that advance the development of the productive forces. The existing level of productive power determines what relations of production would raise its level, and relations of that type consequently obtain. In other words: if production relations of type R obtain at time t, then that is because R-type relations are suitable to the development of the forces at t, given the level of their development at t.[9]

Now to say that A explains B is not necessarily to indicate *how* A explains B. The child who knows that the match burst into flame because it was struck may not know how the latter event explains the former (because he is ignorant of the relationship between friction and heat, the contribution of oxygen to combustion, and so on).[10] In this sense of "how," we can ask: how does the fact that the economic structure promotes the development of the productive forces (or that the superstructure protects the base) explain the character of the economic structure (or the superstructure)? Consider an analogy: to say, correctly, that the species giraffe developed a long neck because of the utility of that feature in relation to the diet of giraffes (acacia tree leaves) is not to say how the utility of that feature accounted for its emergence or persistence. To that question Lamarck gave an unacceptable answer and Darwin an excellent one. To the corresponding questions within historical materialism no one has given excellent answers. I make some unexcellent attempts in Chapter X of my book. This seems to me an important area of future research for proponents of historical materialism, because the functional construal of the doctrine cannot be avoided.

Let me now summarize my argument for the thesis that the chief explanatory claims of historical materialism are functional in form. Historical materialism's central claims are that

1 The level of development of the productive forces in a society explains the nature of its economic structure, and
2 its economic structure explains the nature of its superstructure.

I take (1) and (2) to be functional explanations, because I cannot otherwise reconcile them with two further Marxian theses, namely that

3 the economic structure of a society promotes the development of its productive forces, and
4 the superstructure of a society stabilizes its economic structure.

(3) and (4) entail that the economic structure is functional for the development of the productive forces, and that the superstructure is functional for the stability of the economic structure. These claims do not by themselves entail that economic structures and superstructures are *explained* by the stated functions: *A* may be functional for *B* even when it is false that *A* exists, or has the character it does, *because* its existence or character is functional for *B*. But (3) and (4), *in conjunction with (1) and (2)*, do force us to treat historical materialist explanation as functional. No other treatment preserves consistency between the explanatory primacy of the productive forces over the economic structure and the massive control of the latter over the former, or between the explanatory primacy of the economic structure over the superstructure and the latter's regulation of the former. I did not come to associate historical materialism with functional explanation because I thought functional explanation a good thing and I therefore wanted Marxism to have it. I began with a commitment to Marxism, and my attachment to functional explanation arose out of a conceptual analysis of historical materialism. I do not see how historical materialism can avoid it, for better or for worse. Contrast Jon Elster's attitude to Marxism and game theory. He wants Marxism to liaise with game theory because he admires game theory and thinks Marxism can gain much from the match. He wants to put Marxism and game theory together. I would not say that I want to put together Marxism and functional explanation, because I think functional explanation is inherent in Marxism.

At the beginning of his article Elster complains that Marxist social analysis has been contaminated by the principles of functionalist sociology. I am sure that claim is both historically and conceptually incorrect. Marxists do not indulge in functional explanation because they are influenced by the bad bourgeois science of functionalist sociology, and it is not open to them to use the better bourgeois science of game theory instead. They indulge in functional explanation because they are committed to historical materialism. Because functional explanation cannot be removed from the center of historical materialism, game theory cannot be installed there in its stead. But it might be thought that game theory could also figure at the center of historical materialism, not as a replacement but as an addition. Yet that, too, I argue, is false. Game theory may be, as Elster says, "tailor-made for Marxist analysis,"[11] but it is irrelevant to historical materialism's central theses, which are propositions (1) and (2). Its relevance, as I now explain, is to theses immediately peripheral to (1) and (2).

Elster makes deft use of game theory in a discussion of the dialectics of class struggle that I greatly admire. And it is not surprising that game theory illuminates class behavior. But Marxism is *fundamentally* concerned not with behavior, but with the forces and relations constraining and directing it. When we turn from the immediacy of class conflict to its long-term outcome game theory provides no assistance, because that outcome, for historical materialism, is governed by a dialectic of forces and relations of production that is background to class behavior, and not explicable in terms of it. Game theory helps to explain the vicissitudes of the struggle, and the strategies pursued in it, but it cannot give a Marxist answer to the question why class wars (as opposed to battles) are settled one way rather than another. The Marxist answer is that the class that rules through a period, or emerges triumphant from epochal conflict, does so because it is the class best suited, most able and disposed, to preside over the development of the productive forces at the given time.[12] That answer may be untenable, but I cannot envisage a game-theoretical alternative to it that would qualify as historical materialist.

Elster says that "game theory is invaluable to any analysis of the historical process that centers on exploitation, struggle, alliances, and revolution." But for Marxian analysis those phenomena are not primary but, as it were, immediately secondary, on the periphery of the center: they are, in the words of the 1859 "Preface," the "forms in which men become conscious of the conflict [between forces and relations of production] and fight it out." To put the point differently, we may say that the items on Elster's list are the actions at the center of the historical process, but for Marxism there are also items more basic than actions at its center.[13] By "revolution" Elster must mean the political phenomenon of transfer of state power, as opposed to the transformation of economic structure political revolution initiates or reflects. Many facts about political revolutions are accessible to game-theoretical explanation, but not the world-historical facts that there was a bourgeois revolution and that there will be a proletarian one. Ester urges that game theory bears on strategic questions of great importance to Marxists. I accept that contention, which is amply supported by the excellent illustrations in his article. When faced with a strategic problem, such as how to transform society, we need strategic, not functionalist, thinking. But when Marx called on the workers to revolutionize society he was not asking them to bring about what would explain their doing so: the exhaustion of the progressive capacity of the capitalist order, and the availability of enough productive power to install a socialist one.

The concepts exercised in the previous sentence take us away from game theory to the fundamental context of historical materialism, that of forces and relations of production. There exists a splendid unpublished essay by Jon Elster entitled "Forces and Relations of Production." The essay makes no use of game theory. That is striking confirmation of my view that it is irrelevant to the foundational claims of Marxism:

it shows that Elster himself agrees, in practice, with that view. Having constructed a rigorous theory of contradiction between forces and relations of production, Elster says that "the great weakness of the theory is that it is very difficult to link it to action." Now despite my insistence on the centrality in historical materialism of things that are not actions, I do appreciate that actions are prominent proximate causes of social effects. If links with action cannot be forged, if the question *how* the functional explanations of historical materialism explain cannot even in principle be answered, then that would have lethal significance for historical materialism. And this brings me to Elster's critique of functional explanation.

I remarked earlier that even when A is functional for B, A's existence or character need not be *explained* by that fact. Thus to confer credibility on the claim that B functionally explains A one must supply evidence in excess of that needed to show that A is functional for B. Elster and I disagree about what sort of further evidence is necessary. He demands that the claim that B functionally explains A be supported by a plausible story that reveals *how* B functionally explains A, I think that is sufficient, but not necessary. For I think one can support the claim that B functionally explains A even when one cannot suggest what the mechanism is, if instead one can point to an appropriately varied range of instances in which, whenever A would be functional for B, A appears.[14] This is an application to functional explanatory claims of a general truth about explanatory claims. There are always two ways of backing them up. Suppose, for example, that Elster and I notice a dead body in the library of the country house the morning after the dinner party, and that we hypothesize that its owner died because of something he ate the night before. Further research can take either of two forms. We might open him up to see whether there are any poisons in him, which would be analogous to what Elster thinks we must do to back up functional explanations, or we might find out what he ate, what other guests ate, and which other guests took ill or died, and that would be analogous to the way I say we can proceed with functional explanations. In my procedure we look for appropriately consonant and discrepant parallel instances. In Elster's we rely on pre-existing knowledge about parallel instances at a more basic causal level and we look for a mechanism in the given case that is consonant with that knowledge.

I can illustrate what is at stake by reference to the case of Lamarck and Darwin. Darwin showed how functional facts about the equipment of organisms contribute to explaining why they have it: the answer lies in the mechanism of chance variation and natural selection. Now I claim, and Elster denies, that, before Darwin thereby advanced the science of natural history, the belief that the useful characters of organisms are there because they are useful was already justified, by the sheer volume of evidence of adaptation. The belief was certainly widely held, by people who had no idea how to elaborate it and by others, such as Lamarck, who had what proved to be an unsatisfactory idea of how to elaborate it. And I contend, and Elster denies, that it

48

was a justified belief. This debate is pursued elsewhere, and I shall not take it further here.[15]

Now because I concede that Marxists have not yet produced good elaborations of their functional explanatory theses, I concede that historical materialism is *at best* in a position like that occupied by natural history before Darwin transformed the subject. But I am not convinced that it has got even that far. For whereas Elster and I disagree strongly about what would confirm functional explanations, we disagree less about whether Marxists have actually produced well-confirmed functional explanations. The essays in Marxist functional explanation which he discusses are sadly representative, and I have no desire to defend them against his criticisms. Here we can make common cause. Many Marxist exercises in functional explanation fail to satisfy even the preliminary requirement of showing that *A is* functional for *B* (whether or not it is also *explained* by its function(s)).[16] Take, for example, the claim that the contemporary capitalist state functions to protect and sustain the capitalist system. Legislation and policy in the direct interest of the capitalist class can reasonably be regarded as confirming it. But what about putative counter-examples, such as social welfare provision and legal immunities enjoyed by trade unions? These too might be functional for capitalism in an indirect way, but that is something which needs to be argued with care, not just asserted. But those who propound the general claim about the state rarely trouble to say what sort of evidence would falsify or weaken it, and therefore every action of the state is treated as confirmatory, because there is always some way, legitimate or spurious, in which the action can be made to look functional. Methodological indiscipline is then compounded when, having established to his own satisfaction that state policy is functional, the theorist treats it, without further argument, as also functionally explained. He proceeds from "*A* is functional for *B*" to "*B* functionally explains *A*" without experiencing any need to justify the step, if, indeed, he notices that he has taken a step from one position to a distinct and stronger one.[17]

Most Marxists are methodologically unself-conscious. If they were more sophisticated, they might provide a better defense of the functional explanations they offer. And then, again, they might not. I do not know how to be confident about this, one way or the other. But I maintain my insistence, first, that historical materialism cannot shed its commitment to functional explanation, and, second, that there is nothing inherently suspect in it. Elster's philosophical criticisms of historical materialist functional explanation still strike me as without force, by contrast with his polemic against particular essays in functional explanation. Our philosophical disagreement is pursued in *Political Studies* and *Inquiry*. In note 8 of the previous chapter Elster offers two new objections to my own theory of functional explanation, both of which are misguided. His first objection is that even when it is true that whenever *A* would have favorable consequences for *B*, *A* appears, *A* might not be explained by its possession of such consequences, because a third factor, C, might both cause A to have favorable consequences for B, and cause A to appear, without causing the latter as a result of causing the former. That is so, but it is not an objection to my theory.[18] The form of an ordinary causal law is: whenever A occurs, B occurs. Once again, this might be caused by a third factor, C, so related to A and B that A does not qualify as causing B. But there are tests which, when appropriate results are forthcoming, render the hypothesis that there exists such a C implausible, and suitably analogous tests may be conducted in the case of consequence laws.[19] Elster's second fresh objection rests on the premise that I do not mention time in my characterization of consequence laws. It is true that I do not mention particular amounts of time when describing the form of such laws in general terms, just as one does not when one describes the form of ordinary causal laws as "whenever A occurs, B occurs." But causal laws are not therefore "vacuously confirmable," because particular causal laws include appropriate temporal specifications. All that need be said in general terms about consequence laws and time will be found on pp. 260–1 of *KMTH*.

I now take up two issues in the part of Elster's original article in which he successfully conjoins Marxism and game theory. In a highly original account of the ideology and practice of social democratic capitalism, Elster sets the stage by describing the dissolution of the marginalist illusion, and the action unfolds along lines scripted by Zeuthen and Nash on the one hand and Lancaster on the other. I have two criticisms of this treatment. The first is that Elster mis-identifies the illusion that survives after the marginalist one has been dissolved. He calls it "the presentist illusion" (472), and attributes it to "diachronic alienation" (474). Workers are alienated "from their own history, i.e., from past generations of workers who produced the means of production currently used," and they overcome that alienation "by taking possession of their history" (472). Elster would agree that unrevolutionary workers believe that the capitalist is entitled to a return because he is the morally legitimate owner of the means of production. He thinks the presentist illusion explains why they think the capitalist's ownership is legitimate. But in what does the illusion consist? In a false belief that the means of production were not produced by workers in the past? But workers know better than that. They know, if they reflect on the matter, that means of production were produced by earlier workers, but just as they believe that their own employer is entitled to a return, so, in parallel, they think the employer of earlier workers was; whence, in particular, employers of workers producing means of production came to possess them legitimately and passed them on, directly or indirectly, through market exchange and gift (especially inheritance), to the employers of today. If there exists any kind of presentist illusion, why should workers not project it backwards when they think about their predecessors?

My second criticism of the game theoretical part of Elster's original article concerns his remarks on the locus of exploitation. He writes that the exploitation of the working class ... does not consist *only* in the capitalists' appropriation of surplus-value, but also in the workers' exclusion from decisive investment choices that shape the future.

(476, my emphasis)

Much the same sentence occurs in an earlier version of Elster's article, except that the word "mainly" occurs where the word "only" appears in this final version. This reply was originally composed in response to that earlier version. Having read my response, Elster changed "mainly" to "only," thereby partly spoiling some criticisms I had made of the original version. I shall nevertheless enter the following paragraph of criticism of his original formulation (the one with "mainly") here, not only out of vanity but also because it still applies) if with reduced force, against his revised formulation, and most importantly because I think it is useful to try to identify rather precisely what exploitation consists in.

I do not doubt that workers are excluded from investment decisions, but I deny that they are thereby *exploited*. If someone robs me of the power to control my own life, he does not *ipso facto* use me unfairly to his own advantage, which is what, very roughly, exploitation is. Authoritarian parents do not, by virtue of being authoritarian, qualify as exploiters of their children, and authoritarian parenthood is a good analogue to the relationship Elster highlights here, which is one of subordination, not exploitation. That subordination is, moreover, a consequence of exploitation in the traditional sense, which is therefore not displaced by (what is anyway wrongly considered) a further form of exploitation. It is because capitalists appropriate surplus value that they are able to decide what to do with it, to consume and invest in whatever proportions they choose. And the exploitation of the worker lies in the appropriation, not in the subsequent disposal over what has been appropriated. Part of what moved Elster to make his (original) statement was the fact, which he emphasizes elsewhere, that only a small proportion of total social product remains for capitalist consumption after workers' income and capitalist investment have absorbed their shares.[20] But because there are relatively few capitalists, that small proportion enables them to enjoy a life of comfort and freedom inaccessible to workers. The difference in *per capita* personal income remains massive, and it matters a great deal to the self-perception and sense of dignity of working people. Working-class existence, even in America, is full of strain unknown to wealthy people. Elster's (original) formulation overlooks that sheer difference in standard of living between the classes remains a major part of the injustice of capitalism.

My present view about the matters in contention between Elster and myself is as follows: (1) Functional explanation lies at the heart of historical materialism. (2) Game theory therefore cannot replace functional explanation within Marxist social analysis. (3) Nor is there a place for game theory at the heart of historical materialism, alongside functional explanation. (4) But game theory is very helpful in relation to claims near, but not quite at, historical materialism's heart. (5) There is no methodological error in historical materialism's functional explanatory theses. (6) But Marxists have not done much to establish that they are true. If Marxian functional explanation remains as wanting in practice (as opposed to high theory) as it has been, the foundational claims of historical materialism might need to be severely modified. Positions of great traditional authority might have to be abandoned. One of Elster's achievements is that he has shown how fruitfully what would remain of the doctrine we have inherited can be enriched and extended.

NOTES

1 For reasons given in my "Functional Explanation, Consequence Explanation, and Marxism" (*Inquiry*, 1982) I am not certain that explanations of causes by consequences should be considered functional explanations, but that issue is irrelevant to Elster's article, so I shall here fall in with the standard practice of regarding what I would call *consequence* explanations as functional explanations. Much of this reply has already appeared in the *Inquiry* article mentioned above, and I am grateful to the editor of that journal for allowing it to be reproduced here.

2 G. A. Cohen, *Karl Marx's Theory of History* (Oxford and Princeton, 1978): henceforth referred to as *KMTH*.

3 *The Poverty of Philosophy*, in Marx and Engels, *Collected Works* (Lawrence and Wishart, 1976), Vol. 6, 166.

4 As opposed, for example, to their socially developed needs, reference to which would be inappropriate here (though not, of course, everywhere).

5 For a set of correspondences of relations to forces of production, see *KMTH*, 198.

6 I call such power "economic" in virtue of what it is power over, and irrespective of the means of gaining, sustaining or exercising the power, which need not be economic. See *KMTH*, 223–4.

7 The common practice of overpopulating the superstructure is criticized in my review of Melvin Rader's *Marx's Interpretation of History* (Oxford University Press, 1979) in *Clio*, X, 2 (1981), 229–33.

8 Small letters represent phrases denoting particular events, and capital letters represent phrases denoting types of event. Where the letters are the same, the particular event belongs to the type in virtue of the meanings of the phrases denoting them.

9 For a detailed account of the nature of the primacy of the forces, see section 5 of Chapter VI of *KMTH*, which also discusses the transitional case where relations of production fetter the development of the productive forces.

10 In a widely favored idiom, he may not know the *mechanism* linking cause and effect, or, as I prefer to say, he may be unable to *elaborate* the explanation. I use both forms of expression in the sequel.

11 Jon Elster, *Ulysses and the Sirens* (Cambridge University Press, 1979), 34.

12 See *KMTH*, 148–9.

13 Hence to say, as some Marxists do, that "class struggle is the motor of history," is to abandon historical materialism.

14 That is the simplest way of confirming a functional explanation without establishing a mechanism. For more complicated ways, see *KMTH*, Chapter IX, sections 5 and 7.

15 See the exchange between Elster and myself referred to in his fn. 5, especially 126, 133–4, and the *Inquiry* article mentioned in my fn. 1. One result reached in the latter article bears mention here. I show that if Elster is right about what functional explanation is (he says what it is in *Ulysses and the Sirens*), then he is wrong that natural selection is necessary to sustain functional explanations in biology. It follows that he is also wrong in the corresponding claims about sociological functional explanation at 455 and 463.

16 Elster does not always distinguish this criticism from the one I make in the next paragraph: see, for example, his comments (458) on the passage from the *Eighteenth Brumaire*. If he is right, both criticisms apply, but he does not properly separate them.

17 And sometimes it is unclear that a step has been taken from a statement of functionality to a functional explanation, and, therefore, it is correspondingly unclear that a fallacy has been committed. Thus, for example, I do not share Elster's confidence that Marx's use of the word "means" in the quotation from Volume III of *Capital* on p. 457 proves that Marx is offering a functional *explanation*, and I am sure that he is wrong when he claims (456) that Marx subscribed to "the main functional paradigm."

18 It is, indeed, a point I made myself: see *KMTH*, 267ff.

19 See, further, "Functional Explanation."

20 See "Exploring Exploitation," *Journal of Peace Research*, XV, (1978), 12, where he concludes that "in modern capitalist economies the notion of exploitation should be linked to the lack of power over investment decisions rather than to the fact (or to the possibility) of capitalists having a high level of consumption at the expense of workers."

5

MARXISM AND METHODOLOGICAL INDIVIDUALISM

Erik Olin Wright, Andrew Levine and Elliott Sober

It is often held that Marxism embodies distinctive methodological doctrines which distinguish it from 'bourgeois' social science.[1] The difference has been characterized in various ways: Marxism is scientific and materialist, bourgeois theory ideological and idealist; Marxism is holistic, bourgeois theory is individualistic; Marxism is dialectical and historical, bourgeois theory is linear and static; Marxism is anti-empiricist and anti-positivist, bourgeois theory empiricist and positivist. These claims have differed considerably in substance, but the near consensus view has been that an irreconcilable methodological fissure divides Marxism from its rivals.[2] Recently this unanimity has been broken by a current of Marxist theory, sometimes labeled 'analytical Marxism', which categorically rejects claims for Marxism's methodological distinctiveness.[3] In contrast to what has generally been maintained, authors such as Jon Elster, John Roemer, Adam Przeworski and G.A. Cohen have argued that what is distinctive in Marxism is its substantive claims about the world, not its methodology, and that the methodological principles widely held to distinguish Marxism from its rivals are indefensible, if not incoherent.

Perhaps the most striking example of the rejection of claims to Marxian methodological distinctiveness comes from those analytical Marxists who explicitly declare themselves proponents of 'methodological individualism', thereby endorsing a methodological position they attribute to sound social science, but one that virtually all Marxists have traditionally rejected.[4] As is well known, Marx inveighed against the 'individualism' of the classical economists and contractarian philosophers, heaping scorn on efforts to conceive individuals abstracted from social relations and on theories based upon the imputed choices of these 'abstracted individuals'. And nearly all

Marxists, whatever their differences, have accorded explanatory relevance to social 'totalities', in apparent opposition to the strictures of individualist forms of analysis. Furthermore, until quite recently, proponents of methodological individualism have been equally scornful of Marxism. Hayek and Popper, among others, have even promoted methodological individualism expressly as an alternative to Marxian explanatory practices. It is therefore ironic, to say the least, to maintain that what is worth taking seriously in Marx's thought can be reconstructed in methodological individualist fashion; and that only by recasting Marxian explanations in this way can we save the 'rational kernel' (as Marx might have put it) of Marx's thought from the indefensibility of so many of his own formulations and from the obscurantism that afflicts much of what has come to be identified as Marxism.

We are sympathetic to the idea that what is distinctive in Marxian theory is substantive, not methodological; and that as a science of society, the methodology adopted by Marxists ought to be just good scientific methodology. But methodological individualism is *not* good scientific methodology, even if, as we will show, some of the intuitions that motivate it are sound. The plausibility of Marxian methodological individualism depends, of course, on what methodological individualism is thought to be. Unfortunately, at the current stage of discussion, many of the obscurities that have always pervaded debates about methodological individualism are effectively reproduced in the Marxian context. One objective of this essay is to reduce this confusion by clarifying the stakes in claims for and against methodological individualism, both as these apply to the specific context of Marxian explanations and to social scientific explanations generally.

In the next section, we characterize methodological individualism by contrasting it with three other stances towards explanation in social science. This will be followed by a more intensive discussion of methodological individualism itself, suggesting that its reductionist ambitions cannot be fulfilled. Nevertheless we will argue, in the final section, that a practical implication of methodological individualism – that the microfoundations for macro-level theory should be elaborated – is timely and important, even if methodological individualism itself is not. Throughout this discussion, Jon Elster's book, *Making Sense of Marx*, will be a central point of reference.[5] Elster is among the most insightful of Marxian methodological individualists, and this book represents the most sustained attempt within the Marxian tradition to defend methodological individualism. It is therefore a useful point of departure for an examination of the doctrine's strengths, as well as its flaws.

I A TYPOLOGY OF METHODOLOGICAL POSITIONS ON EXPLANATION

Methodological individualism is a claim about *explanation*. It is the view that all social phenomena are best explained by the properties of the individuals who comprise the phenomena; or, equivalently, that any explanation involving macro-level, social concepts should in principle be reduced to micro-level explanations involving only individuals and their properties. In order to give methodological individualism a precise definition, it will be helpful to contrast it with three other possible views: *atomism, radical holism* and *anti-reductionism*. The first two of these positions, at least in their pure form, probably have no actual defenders, but they are implicit tendencies within social theory. Indeed, in debates over methodological individualism, disputants sometimes appear to confuse their opponents' views with one or the other of these positions. Thus defenders of methodological individualism depict anti-reductionists as radical holists, and defenders of anti-reductionist positions sometimes regard method-ological individualists as atomists. Therefore, in order to clarify the issues at stake, it will be useful to map out all four possibilities.

These methodological stances towards social scientific explanation differ in what they regard as explanatory. They can be distinguished on two dimensions: whether or not they regard the properties of and relations among aggregate social entities as *irre-ducibly* explanatory; and whether or not they regard relations among individuals as explanatory.[6] Aggregate social entities include such things as societies, groups, classes, organizations, nations, communities. Such entities have properties (e.g. inflation rates, institutional forms, distributions of income) and exist in a variety of relations to each other (e.g. relations between collectively organized classes). Individuals also have both properties (e.g. beliefs, abilities, resources) and exist in a variety of relations with other individuals (e.g. sibling relations, employer–employee relations, etc.). Taking these two dimensions together, we get the following typology of principles of explanation of social phenomena (see Figure 5.1).

Atomism

Atomism is a methodological stance which denies that relations – whether between individuals or between social entities – are ever genuinely explanatory. Consider any social phenomenon – for example, the transformation from feudalism to capitalism. An atomist would say that this transition can in principle be fully explained by causal processes strictly internal to individuals in the society in question. While *interactions* among these individuals matter for explaining the emergence of feudalism, the causal processes which govern the outcomes of such interactions are entirely intra-individual.[7]

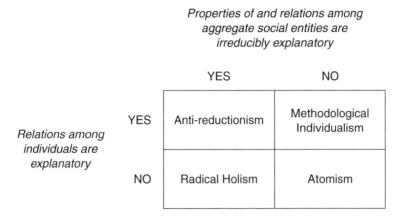

*Properties of and relations among
aggregate social entities are
irreducibly explanatory*

		YES	NO
Relations among individuals are explanatory	YES	Anti-reductionism	Methodological Individualism
	NO	Radical Holism	Atomism

Figure 1 What is explanatory of social phenomena?

The atomist would insist, in other words, that only entities which are fully constituted non-relationally are explanatory. On the face of it, atomism seems plainly unsustainable. In our everyday lives we exist within a network of relations to other people – as parents, siblings, employers, customers, and so on. These relations appear to be explanatory, and also, it would seem, irreducible: being a parent, for instance, necessarily involves another individual, the child. But atomism is not quite so implausible as may at first appear. The atomist might argue that everything that seems explanatory about irreducible relations between individuals actually is explanatory only because of the corresponding (non-relational) psychological states of these individuals; that what matters explanatorily in, say, power relations between individuals is not an irreducible relation between these individuals, but their beliefs and desires, considered atomistically. If I believe you will punish me if I do X and you believe that I have these beliefs, then we will each act in particular ways. The apparent power 'relation' between individuals, the argument would go, is really no more than a set of reciprocal beliefs, and it is these beliefs, rather than any 'objective relation', which explains actions.

Although we grant that beliefs and desires explain actions, it seems to us that the world outside the mind helps explain why agents think and want what they do. One plausible explanation for such things as beliefs about power is the objective power relations between people. Beliefs about power are formed, in part at least, by subjective effects of the *practices* of the powerful and the powerless. The enduring interconnection among these practices is precisely what is meant by the 'power relations' between the powerful and the powerless. If such relations help explain beliefs and beliefs help explain action then (assuming transitivity) such relational facts help explain agents' actions. Atomism *might* be right in claiming that relational facts affect actions only by virtue of their affecting (atomistic) mental states. But it is a *non sequitur* to conclude from this that irreducibly relational facts are explanatorily impotent. It is for this reason that theorists who insist on the reducibility of social explanations to individual explanations generally defend the explanatory importance of genuinely relational properties of individuals. This combination of methodological commitments – a belief in the reducibility of social explanations to individual explanations and a belief in the explanatory importance of relations among individuals – defines what is generally called methodological individualism.

Methodological individualism

Methodological individualism shares with atomism the view that social explanations are ultimately reducible to individual-level explanations. Elster states this claim explicitly at the beginning of *Making Sense of Marx*. He defines methodological individualism as 'the doctrine that all social phenomena – their structure and their change – are in principle explicable in ways that only involve individuals – their properties, their goals, their beliefs and their actions. To go from social institutions and aggregate patterns of behaviour to individuals is the same kind of operation as going from cells to molecules.'[8] Elster, however, is not an atomist because he does not proscribe irreducible relational properties of individuals from social scientific explanations. Indeed, Elster argues that the inventory of individual properties which are the basis for explaining social phenomena extends far beyond the beliefs, desires and other psychological properties of individuals. He concedes that 'many properties of individuals, such as "powerful", are inherently relational, so that an accurate description of one individual may involve reference to others.'[9] 'Relational properties' would also include being a sibling or a parent or an employer. Nowhere does Elster (or any other Marxist defender of methodological individualism) claim that these relational properties are reducible to atomistic properties.

It is sometimes thought that methodological individualism implies a rejection of the holistic claim that 'the whole is more than the sum of the parts'. While atomism unequivocally regards wholes as no more than collections of parts, the fact that methodological individualism accepts the explanatory relevance of relational properties implies that, unlike atomism, it can accept this central tenet of its putative rival. The issue hinges on what is meant by 'sum' and 'parts'. One way of reading the holistic claim is the following: the parts of society are individuals with *atomistic* properties, i.e., properties that can be defined for each individual independently of all other individuals. The whole, then, is 'greater' than the 'sum' of these parts in the sense that the properties of the whole come from the systematic relational patterns of *interaction* among these individuals – the relations that bind them together – and not simply from the aggregation of their atomistic (i.e. non-relational) properties. On the other hand, if *relational* properties are included in the descriptions of the parts themselves, then it is no longer true that the whole is more than the sum of its parts. Everything that was included in the word 'greater' in the holistic formulation has now been packed into the redescription of the 'parts'.[10]

[. . .]

Methodological individualism remains distinct from both radical holism and anti-reductionism in its insistence that only relations among individuals can be irreducibly explanatory. Methodological individualists deny that aggregate social categories are ever irreducibly explanatory. If a social property is explanatory, it is because it is reducible to relational properties of particular individuals. The property of a society 'being in a revolutionary situation', for example, is not irreducibly explanatory in the methodological individualist view. This property possesses whatever explanatory force it has in virtue of the properties of and relations among the individuals in the society. The aggregate social property 'revolutionary situation' is no more than an aggregation of all these particular individual properties and relations. It is only a *convenient* expression. Thus any explanation in which the expression 'revolutionary situation' appears can be reduced in principle to an explanation (no doubt of considerable complexity) involving only properties of and relations among individuals.

Radical holism

Radical holism stands in sharp contrast to methodological individualism. For radical holists, particular relations among individuals are essentially epiphenomenal with respect to social explanations. They are generated by the operation of the whole, and in their own right they explain nothing. It is not simply that 'the whole is more than the sum of its parts'. Rather, the whole is the sole genuine cause and the parts (even when constituted relationally) are mere artifacts. Macro-social categories – capitalism, the state, class relations – are not merely irreducible to micro-level processes. They are unaffected by these processes. It is difficult to find explicit defences of radical holism in its pure form, but there are certain explanatory tendencies in social science which reflect this kind of thinking. The Marxist tradition, because of its stress on the 'totality', has perhaps been particularly susceptible to such ideas. Three examples are worth mentioning: teleological reasoning in the theory of history, extreme formulations in arguments for structural causality, and what can be termed 'collectivist agency' arguments.

Holistic teleologies figure in accounts of history that see the trajectory of social change as objectively directed towards an ultimate goal which exists independently of the subjective goals of human actors. In these cases, explanatory force is ascribed to this 'end' of history. Individuals, then, are only agents of goal-achieving impersonal social forces; and what they do or choose is explained by – but does not explain – social phenomena. Their actions and choices are not mechanisms but consequences of the immanent principle whose career social science is supposed to trace. In putative explanations of this sort, social facts explain social facts directly without individual-level mechanisms playing any autonomous explanatory role.

A parallel tendency towards radical holism, of considerable importance in recent Western Marxism, is suggested by some of the more extravagant declarations of Louis Althusser and his followers.[11] Despite their express opposition to vestiges of Hegelian teleological thinking, Althusserians effectively reproduced some of its more dubious features. Thus Althusser proposed the obscure notion of 'structural causality', according to which structures cause structures and individuals are only 'supports' of social relations.[12] While such claims may simply reflect Althusser's rhetorical style, some Althusserian explanations appear to dispense with individual-level mechanisms in principle.

Collectivist-agency arguments are embodied in statements of the form: 'The bourgeoisie was unwilling to make compromises' or 'the proletariat took advantage of the crisis' or, to take a famous quote from Marx, 'mankind always sets itself only such tasks as it can solve'.[13] In most cases, such expressions are simply elliptical or at worst express a certain expository sloppiness rather than deep methodological error. The real referents in the statements could be, for example, organizations (parties, unions) which are viewed as representatives of the classes in question, or the statements could be claims about the distribution of beliefs in the relevant populations. There are times, however, when such expressions seem to imply a belief in collective consciousness and collective agency, where a class or even humanity as such thinks, chooses and acts. Generally, such non-elliptical treatments of collective subjects are linked to holistic teleologies of history: the objective purpose of history in the teleology is represented as the goal of a genuinely Collective Subject. But even when collective subjects are not linked to teleologies of history, positing such entities tends to marginalize the explanatory relevance of individual-level relations within a holistic argument.

Elster assails all these forms of radical holism – or what he calls 'methodological collectivism' – in Marx's work and the Marxist tradition. He has been particularly intent on attacking functional explanations within Marxism – explanations of the existence and persistence of particular social institutions because of their beneficial effects for ruling classes – on the grounds that they generally reflect teleological thinking about the nature of society and history and typically ignore the importance of specifying micro-level mechanisms. These errors, Elster argues, are derived from the methodological doctrines Marx inherited from Hegel. We believe instead that sloppiness and rhetorical excess is more nearly the culprit than considered, radical holist convictions. Few, if any, Marxists have ever imagined that functional relations could be established in the absence of micro-level mechanisms or that collective agents could ever be more than aggregations of individual actors. But Marxists (including Marx) have indeed failed rather frequently to trace out the implications of these (eminently sensible) beliefs. Elster has done well to identify instances, even if he has misrepresented their source and character. In any case, Elster is right insofar as he inveighs against radical holism. The plain fact that if there were no people there would be no societies underwrites the methodological assumption that causal mechanisms involving individuals must always be implicated in social explanations. The issue is not whether the individual level of analysis can be eliminated, but how it should be linked to macro-level social analysis. Methodological individualism maintains that macro-level phenomena can always be reduced to their micro-level realizations, at least in principle. Anti-reductionism rejects this thesis.

Anti-reductionism

Anti-reductionism acknowledges the importance of micro-level accounts in explaining social phenomena, while allowing for the irreducibility of macro-level accounts to these micro-level explanations. Methodological individualism insists that the ultimate goal of science is to reduce explanations to ever more micro-levels of analysis. For a methodological individualist, to explain a phenomenon is just to provide an account of the micro-mechanisms which produce it. Aggregate, supra-individual social categories are therefore admissible only *faute de mieux*, in consequence of our cognitive limitations or the inadequate state of our knowledge. In contrast, anti-reductionists do not prejudge in any given problem whether macro-level (social) explanations are finally reducible to micro-level (individualist) accounts. This may seem like a paradoxical stance: how can one be simultaneously committed to the irreducibility of social explanations to individual-level explanations and to the importance of elaborating micro-foundations? The resolution of this apparent paradox is discussed in the next section.

2 ANTI-REDUCTIONISM VERSUS METHODOLOGICAL INDIVIDUALISM

Methodological individualists insist that in principle it is desirable not simply to *add* an account of micro-causes to macro-explanations, but to *replace* macro-explanations with micro-explanations. Were we able, methodological individualists would have us ban aggregate social concepts or else tolerate them strictly as expository conveniences.[14]

The issue of reductionism of the macro to the micro in social explanations parallels issues familiar in the philosophy of mind.[15] Any particular distribution of properties

among individuals constitutes a particular social state. Similarly, any particular configuration of neurophysiological states of human brains constitutes a particular mental
state. It would therefore seem that a complete account of individual properties
(or neuro-physiological configurations) would constitute a full and adequate explanation of social phenomena (or mental states) and their effects. Thus it would seem
reasonable to conclude that we should be able, at least in principle, to reduce macro-
phenomena to micro-phenomena. To understand why this is not so, it will be helpful
to introduce the familiar distinction in the philosophy of science between *tokens* and
types.[16] 'Tokens' are particular instances: for example, a particular strike by a group
of workers in a particular factory or an idea in the head of a particular individual.
'Types' are characteristics that tokens may have in common. Thus a particular strike
– a token event – can be subsumed under a variety of possible 'types': *strikes, class
struggles, social conflicts*, etc. Similarly, being rich is a type of which Rockefeller is one
token. Types are general categories that subsume particular events or instances.

Reductionism raises different issues for tokens and types. Most Marxists, because
they are materialists, probably would endorse *token*-reductionism.[17] Thus, if current
views about the relation between human beings' minds and brains are correct, Marxists
(and most non-Marxists too) would concede that a particular mental state in a particular individual can be explained by describing the brain state of that individual at that
moment in time. Similarly, for social phenomena, particular instances can be explained
by appeal to the activities, properties and relations of the particular individuals
who collectively comprise the phenomenon. The real debate, then, concerns the
reducibility of macro-social types to micro-individual types. The distinction between
tokens and types can be applied both to social entities and to individuals. Thus, we can
define capitalism as a type of society and the United States in 1987 as a token instance
of that type. And we can define the capitalist–worker relation as a type of relation
among individuals, while the relation between the owner of a particular firm and the
employees of that firm would constitute a token instance of such a relation.[18] Both
methodological individualists and anti-reductionists admit the explanatory power of
type-concepts referring to individuals. Where they differ is in their view of the explanatory status of type-concepts referring to aggregate social entities: methodological
individualists insist that such type-concepts can be reduced to type-concepts referring
only to individuals; anti-reductionists argue that, in general, this is not possible.

The type/token distinction allows us to see that a science will have at least two sorts
of explanatory projects: it will seek to explain why *token* events occur and also to
explain the nature of the *types* that fall within its domain. Thus we would want
to explain why specific instances of capitalism emerged when and where they did but
also explain what capitalism is. The methodological individualist would be committed
to the micro-reducibility of both the token social event *and* the social type. Our quarrel
is not with the first of these claims, but with the second.

Our objection can be clarified by an example in which type-reductionism is justified. Consider 'water' (that is, a kind of substance, not a particular sample of water). When we say that water is reducible to H_2O, we mean that whatever effects water has can be reduced to effects of H_2O. In any explanation in which water plays an explanatory role, the effects of water come from the effects of aggregates of H_2O molecules. This reduction is possible for water because there is a single micro-property corresponding to the macro-property in question. Something is *water* if and only if it is an *ensemble of H_2O molecules*. However, in the case of social phenomena (and mental states), there is in fact no similarly unique correspondence between *types*. Consider mental states. For any kind of mental state – for example, the belief that snow is white, the intention to buy a chocolate bar, the feeling of pain – there are in principle many, perhaps infinitely many, physical states that could realize the mental state in question. This relationship is referred to as one of *supervenience*: mental states are *supervenient* on brain states. Similarly for social phenomena: many distributions of properties of individuals – their beliefs, desires, resources, interrelationships – can realize the same social type. In the case of supervenient properties and relations, type–type reductionism will not be possible.

The reason why reductionism is not possible in cases of supervenience is well illustrated by an example from evolutionary biology. The property of 'fitness' figures in many explanations in evolutionary theory. To every token instance of fitness (i.e. the fitness of a particular organism in a particular environment), there corresponds a particular configuration of physical facts about the organism in question. In each of these instances, we can say that the physical facts explain why this particular organism has the degree of fitness it does. There is no reason to believe, however, that any single physical property corresponds to the general category 'fitness', that the same mechanisms explain the fitness of, say, a frog and a giraffe. In all likelihood, fit organisms share no physical properties in virtue of which they are all fit. The *only* explanatorily relevant property they share is that they are instances of a single (supervenient) type. Thus, while a token reduction of individual instances of fitness to physical mechanisms is possible, a type reduction is not. Fitness is supervenient on its micro-realizations.[19]

Methodological individualists are type-reductionists with respect to social phenomena. But to insist on type-reductions as an a priori methodological requirement is plainly unwarranted. The feasibility of type-reduction is an empirical question. It *could* be the case that type-reductions actually are possible in this domain. But they almost certainly are not. Type-reductions would be possible if the relation between social phenomena and individual properties were like the relation between water and H_2O. But insofar as the relation of social facts to their micro-realizations is like the relation of mental states to brain states or like the relation of fitness to physical properties of morphology and physiology, type-reductionism will prove to be a fruitless quest.[20]

Consider the fact that capitalist societies have strong tendencies towards economic growth. This property is explicable, in part, as a consequence of the competitive character of capitalist markets, which generate innovations and continual investments that, cumulatively, produce growth. This process, in turn, is explained by the survival of those firms which most effectively make profits in the market. Survival and profit-making, in this explanation, are similar to 'fitness' in evolutionary biology. For each token instance of economic survival, we can identify a set of decisions made by individuals with particular beliefs, preferences, information and resources which explain why a particular firm survives. However, there need not be anything in common *at the micro-level* between the mechanisms which enable firm X to survive and the mechanisms which enable firm Y or Z to survive. X may survive because of the passivity of workers (enabling capitalists to introduce innovations without resistance); Y because of the ruthlessness of the owner; Z because of the scientific/technical rationality of the management team, and so on.[21] The social-level explanation of growth in terms of the macro-processes of competitive market relations, therefore, is supervenient on a vast array of possible micro-mechanisms. Accordingly, token-reductionism is possible in this case, but type-reductionism is not.

In short, the reductionist programme of methodological individualism fails because science has explanatory projects beyond the explanation of token events. Besides asking why this organism or that firm survived, we also want to explain what various objects and processes have in common. When the properties cited in answer to such questions supervene on properties at the micro-level, the explanations provided by the macro-theory will not, even in principle, be reducible to a micro-account. [. . .]

NOTES

1 'Methodology' here refers to views about theory construction and the conduct of research, including such things as the construction of explanations, the formation and transformation of concepts, and the gathering of data. We would like to thank Robert Brenner, Alan Carling, G. A. Cohen, Jon Elster, Robert Kahn, Margaret Levi, Joel Rogers, Phillipe Van Parijs and Beatrice Wright for comments on earlier drafts of this essay. Some of these individuals dissent strongly from the views advanced here.

2 Perhaps the most celebrated and extreme expression of this view is that of Lukács in his essay 'What Is Orthodox Marxism?' For Lukács, methodology alone differentiates Marxism from its rivals. All of the substantive claims of Marxian theory could be rejected, Lukács maintained, and yet Marxism would remain valid because of its distinctive method. Cf. Georg Lukács, *History and Class Consciousness: Studies in Marxist Dialectics*, London 1971, pp. 1–26.

3 For an anthology containing work of some of the prominent figures in the emerging analytical Marxist school, see John Roemer, ed., *Analytical Marxism*, Cambridge 1986.

4 Of course, not all Marxists working in an analytical style would follow Elster in this regard, but the position has been advanced by a number of influential figures. See, for instance,

Adam Przeworski, 'The Challenge of Methodological Individualism to Marxist Analysis', *Politics & Society* (forthcoming) and John Roemer, *A General Theory of Exploitation and Class*, Cambridge, Mass. 1982.

5 Cambridge University Press, 1985.

6 These dimensions are not strictly symmetrical since 'properties of individuals' is not included in the second dimension. The reason for this is that atomism accepts the explanatory relevance of properties of individuals but not relations among individuals.

7 If the concept of 'relation' is equated with 'interaction', then, plainly, no theorist could deny the explanatory relevance of relations. Even a radical atomist would acknowledge that the interactions of a parent with a child are consequential for the child. What is being claimed by atomists, therefore, is not that interactions have no consequences, but that interactions are governed entirely by mechanisms located within the atomistically constituted entities engaged in the interactions.

8 *Making Sense of Marx*, p. 5.

9 Ibid., p.6.

10 The familiar deflation of the holism/individualism debate is elaborated, for example, in Ernest Nagel, *The Structure of Science*, London 1961.

11 Cf. *For Marx*, NLB, London 1969, and *Reading Capital*, NLB, London 1970.

12 There are places in Althusser's work in which the treatment of individuals as 'bearers' and 'supports' of the structure can be interpreted as consistent with microfoundational reasoning. Thus, for example, in his analysis of ideology, Althusser discusses the process through which individuals are formed as subjects. This analysis of 'interpretation' could be considered an account of how social-structural causes shape micro-individual states which in turn have effects on the social structural relations themselves. See Louis Althusser, 'Ideology and Ideological Stare Apparatuses', in *Lenin and Philosophy*, NLB, London 1971. For a much more systematic development of these relatively primitive arguments of Althusser's which makes the micro-mechanisms of subject-formation much more explicit, see Göran Therborn, *The Power of Ideology and the Ideology of Power*, NLB/Verso, London 1982.

13 Karl Marx, 'Preface' to *A Contribution to the Critique of Political Economy* (1859).

14 A thorough methodological individualist reductionist would also argue that, in principle, individual-level explanations should be reduced to neuro-physiological explanations, and neuro-physiological explanations ultimately to explanations only involving atomic particles and their inter-relations. Like LaPlace's demon, the ultimate ambition of science is to reduce all phenomena to the operation of physical laws.

15 See, for example, the development of these ideas in Jerry Foder, *The Language of Thought*, New York 1975, Chapter 1, and Hilary Putnam, 'The Nature of Mental States', in Putnam, *Philosophical Papers*, vol. II, Cambridge 1975, pp. 429–40.

16 For a discussion of the type/token distinction as it figures in the problem of explanation, see Foder, op. cit., and Putnam, op. cit.

17 'Materialism', in this context, is the claim that tokens are 'modes' of matter. To oppose materialism would be to accord ontological status to (putatively) non-material entities (like disembodied minds or *élans vitaux*).

18 Discussions about 'social relations' often ignore the distinction between type concepts that are irreducibly social. For example, the 'capital–labour relation' is a type concept that identifies the theoretically salient properties that all of the particular instances of relations between capitalists and workers have in common. In this sense it is a micro-level type concept even if it is used to characterize an entire society. While this concept may be

irreducibly *relational* – that is, it cannot be represented in atomistic terms – it does not contravene the strictures of methodological individualism, since the relations it describes are among individuals. Ironically, perhaps, those 'fundamentalist Marxists' (as they are sometimes called) who emphasize the supreme explanatory importance of the capital–labour relation for understanding capitalism and who most categorically assert the methodological distinctiveness of Marxism may be closer to methodological individualism than those Marxists who emphasize the importance of various kinds of aggregate social entities such as class formations, state apparatuses, etc. Explanations based on the capital–labour relation may be very *abstract*, but they are still fundamentally rooted in a micro-logic. An abstract analysis of micro-type concepts is not equivalent to a macro-level analysis.

19 Cf. Sober, op. cit., Chapter One.

20 The argument that social type concepts cannot be reduced to individual-level type concepts is related to the frequent claim of holists in social science that macro-phenomena have 'emergent properties'. An emergent property is a property that can only be described at the macro-level. If, however, such properties were not supervenient, then any explanation in which they figured could be reduced to the corresponding micro-level explanation. The claim, therefore, that emergent properties are irreducibly *explanatory* depends upon the supervenience of the macro on the micro.

21 If a common property, specifiable at the micro-level, were discovered, a type-reduction of the macro- to the micro-level would be possible in this case. Our point is that this would be an *empirical discovery*, comparable to discovering in evolutionary biology, contrary to current theory, that all instances of fitness reflect a single micro-molecular mechanism.

FURTHER READING

Cohen, G.A. (1978). *Karl Marx's Theory of History: A Defence*. Princeton, Princeton University Press.

Elster, J. (1985). *Making Sense of Marx*. Cambridge, Cambridge University Press.

Elster, J. (1989). 'Marxism and Individualism.' *Knowledge and Politics*. M. Dascal. Boulder, Westview Press: 189–206.

Gould, C.C. (1997). 'Group Rights and Social Ontology.' *Philosophical Forum*: 28(1–2) 73–86.

Hollis, M. (1996). 'Philosophy of Social Science.' *The Blackwell Companion to Philosophy*. Bunnin, N.F. (ed.). Cambridge, Blackwell.

Ruben, D.H. (1982). 'The Existence of Social Entities.' *Philosophical Quarterly*: 32 295–310.

Ruben, D.H. (1985). *The Metaphysics of the Social World*. Routledge and Kegan Paul.

Ruben, D.H. (1998). 'The Philosophy of the Social Sciences.' *Philosophy 2: Further Through the Subject*. Grayling, A.C. (ed.). New York, Oxford University Press.

Part 2

DISTRIBUTIVE JUSTICE

Introduction

THE READING HERE FROM NOZICK'S *Anarchy, State and Utopia* (1974) outline his case against 'patterned' approaches to distributive justice. In Nozick's view, any stable pattern of holdings runs up against constraints put in place by individuals' property rights over themselves and over the products of their labour. In the much discussed Wilt Chamberlain example, he aims to show that free exchanges of resources will lead to instabilities in any pattern of resource distribution. Because the exchanges are uncoerced, there can be no complaint against them, and no injustice in a process that leads to inequality. By employing a modified version of Locke's account of appropriation, he aims to establish that widespread inequalities of holdings between individuals cannot justly be broken down by redistributive tax policies. This is because taxation is a form of forced labour, and so infringes the rights of individuals. The upshot of Nozick's argument is that intuitions about equality are trumped by intuitions about self-ownership and the property rights that these intuitions entail.

Nozick's approach has been widely influential and widely criticised. If the rights that self-owning individuals have over themselves and the products of their labour are absolute rights, that cannot be infringed without injustice, then his conclusion may follow. But it is not clear why the rights should be so construed, nor that all infringements of rights are violations (Thomson 1986; Kymlicka 1990). To suggest otherwise has been called 'rights fanaticism' (Otsuka 1998).

Like Nozick's work, Frankfurt's chapter is designed to get us to rethink any commitment to egalitarianism, but not because such a commitment leads us to infringe rights. Instead, Frankfurt suggests that egalitarians misidentify the morally relevant properties of distributive arrangements. We should not ask whether these arrangements manifest equality, but whether there are *sufficient* resources for individuals. He analyses the notion of sufficiency in some depth, making it clear, for example, that there may be arrangements of holdings where equality acts against the interests of everyone involved, condemning all to the equality of certain death. Equality is no good to us if we all have insufficient resources for life. Like Nozick, he directs some of his argument directly against Rawls, arguing that 'the only morally compelling reason for trying to make the worse off better off is, in my judgement, that their lives are in some degree bad lives' (note 17). But the worse off may not have bad lives. It may be that those who are worse off still have sufficient, in the sense that it may be reasonable for them to be content with having no more than they have.

It might be said that the simple existence of wide inequalities provides *prima facie* evidence for saying that those towards the bottom have worse lives than would be the case if shares were distributed more evenly. But the evidence is only *prima facie* – it is contingent upon the other possible arrangements that are available. Nonetheless, there is a marked contrast between the implications of Nozick's position and the implications of Frankfurt's argument for actually existing inequalities.

Where, then, does this leave our intuitions about equality? Parfit's paper is an invitation to get us to systematise any intuitions about equality, by proposing a number of thought experiments which isolate specific aspects of a commitment to equality. He distinguishes between telic and deontological egalitarians – for teleological (or telic) egalitarians, equality is an end which is valuable in itself, and inequality is bad, whereas, for deontological (or deontic) egalitarians, inequality is unjust, insofar as it is a sign of some wrongdoing. So the two sorts of egalitarians differ in their approaches to difference in natural talents. For telic egalitarians, this unevenness is a source of regret – it is in itself bad. For deontic egalitarians there is no question of wrongness or injustice involved in the natural lottery, and so nothing to regret. The difference is between a justice based commitment to equality, and a commitment to equality as a value in itself.

Each sort of egalitarianism can take pluralist or pure forms: equality can be viewed either as the sole value of schemes of distributive justice, or it can be one amongst a number of values. And egalitarianism needs to be carefully distinguished from views that look similar, such as various versions of the priority view. Priority views aim to demarcate a set of cases which count as priorities for assistance, or receipt of social spending, and they do so by identifying a common property of the set of individuals who deserve priority. One version of this is the Marxist commitment to distribution according to need. Another is the view that distributive arrangements ought to be constructed in order to improve the interests of the worse off. One difference between egalitarian views and priority views is that the latter are immune to the 'levelling down' objection. This is the objection that egalitarians are committed to levelling down in pursuit of equality, when the supposed improvement in the state of affairs is not an improvement for anyone. In at least some circumstances, priority views do not entail levelling down, since this does not favour those to whom priority should be given.

The objection to levelling down rests on some form of the 'person affecting' view of morality, according to which states of affairs are better or worse only in so far as they are worse for particular people. On this view, it is not possible for a state of affairs to be 'better' if it is better for no one, and this seems to apply to the levelling down of distributed bundles, when no particular person's bundle is increased.

As we have seen, in the 1980s G.A. Cohen set about reformulating classical Marxism in accordance with the constraints of analytical philosophy, and in the early 1990s, he took on Robert Nozick, particularly by pointing to the unattractiveness of the thesis of self-ownership which underpins the justification of inequality in *Anarchy, State and Utopia*. More recently he has engaged with Rawls. The Gifford lectures of 1996 (Cohen 2000) focus on *A Theory of Justice* and are situated on the terrain of normative political philosophy. In these lectures, and in the papers from which they came (Cohen 1992; Cohen 1995; Cohen 1997) Cohen argues that Rawls licenses far too much inequality, and that an adequate theory of justice would be much more egalitarian.

Cohen's critique, at least at first, is an internal one. He argues that Rawls endorses too much inequality. This is because Rawls restricts justice to 'the basic structure' – individual day to day choices are not covered by the same principles of justice that apply to the basic structure. There is no carrying over of – for example – the difference principle, from institutional structures such as a redistributive tax system to the everyday actions and life choices of individuals.

Rawls says that: 'The principles of justice for institutions must not be confused with the principles that apply to individuals and their actions in particular circumstances. These two kinds of principles apply to different subjects and must be discussed separately' (Rawls 1999: 47). However, while the principles of justice are limited to institutions, Rawls adds that people in a just society act *from* the principles of justice in their daily lives. Acting *from* the principles of justice, however, does not seem to exclude acting according to the economic disincentive of high levels of taxation. But a fairly obvious objection to Rawls is that individuals and their actions are clearly an input into institutions and help to determine what outputs those institutions produce. If the justice of institutions is to be judged by their output, then it is difficult to see how individuals and their decisions can be excluded.

Cohen builds his critique from one particular example of this objection: the actions of the talented who adapt their behaviour in pursuit of tax breaks, higher incomes or better conditions of employment. This has a practical political rendering: it is often said that tax rates must not be too high, managerial salaries must be sufficiently high, and post-tax income inequalities must be wide, otherwise there will be a disincentive effect on the talented. They, then, will decide not to work as hard, fail to innovate, opt to work in lower paid but less demanding occupations, or emigrate. The incentive argument for income inequality is familiar. And recall the argument for Rawls' famous difference principle that inequalities are only justifiable when they improve the position of the worst off. Then the incentive argument appears to justify widespread inequalities, since it is to the advantage of the worst off that talented people work hard, innovate, remain in demanding occupations and do not emigrate.

But those inequalities that are justified by the incentive argument only exist because the talented *choose* to behave in a certain way – such as refraining from exercising their talents in the absence of incentives. According to the argument Cohen is criticising, the decision whether or not to employ these talents is the preserve of the talented themselves, and is not open to criticism by means of comparison with those criteria of justice that apply to institutional arrangements. The propensity of the talented not to work in the absence of inegalitarian incentives is treated by Rawls as a given, and enters into the construction of justice at the beginning. But, argues Cohen, the decisions that give rise to that propensity, themselves generate inequality and they ought to be subject to scrutiny. Endorsing the feminist slogan that 'the personal is political' Cohen argues that the talented ought to act according to an 'egalitarian ethos' to put their abilities at the disposal of the less well off: 'A society that is just within the terms of the difference principle . . . requires not simply coercive *rules*, but also an *ethos* of justice that informs individual choices' (Cohen 2000: 128).

Within this egalitarian ethos, the activities of the talented would conform more closely to the principles of justice. The egalitarian intuitions that Rawls makes systematic in *A Theory of Justice* are, then, contentious in their scope. For theorists like Nozick, the intuitions are trumped by claims about self-ownership and property rights. For those such as Cohen, egalitarianism does not go far enough when it is applied only to the basic structure. Rather, the principles of justice to which these intuitions give rise apply to the actions of individuals themselves: the personal is also political.

REFERENCES

Cohen, G.A. (1992). 'Incentives, Inequality, and Community.' *The Tanner Lectures On Human Values*, *V13*, Grethe B. Petersen (ed.). Salt Lake City, University of Utah.

Cohen, G.A. (1995). 'The Pareto Argument for Inequality.' *Social Philosophy and Policy* 12: 160–85.

Cohen, G.A. (1997). 'Where the Action Is: On the Site of Distributive Justice.' *Philosophy and Public Affairs* 26(1): 3–30.

Cohen, G.A. (2000). *If You're an Egalitarian, How Come You're So Rich?* Harvard, Cambridge University Press.

Frankfurt, H. (1987). 'Equality as a Moral Ideal.' *Ethics* 98: 21–43.

Kymlicka, W. (1990). *Contemporary Political Philosophy*. Oxford, Oxford University Press.

Nozick, R. (1974). *Anarchy, State and Utopia*. New York, Basic Books.

Otsuka, M. (1998). 'Self-Ownership and Equality: A Lockean Reconciliation.' *Philosophy and Public Affairs* 27(1): 65–92.

Parfit, D. (1997). 'Equality and Priority.' *Ratio* 10(3) 202–21.

Rawls, J. (1999). *A Theory of Justice: Revised Edition*. Cambridge, Harvard University Press.

Thompson, J.J. and W. Parent (1986). *Rights, Restitution and Risk: Essays in Moral Theory*. Cambridge, Harvard University Press.

6

DISTRIBUTIVE JUSTICE

Robert Nozick

[...]

It is not clear how those holding alternative conceptions of distributive justice can reject the entitlement conception of justice in holdings. For suppose a distribution favored by one of these nonentitlement conceptions is realized. Let us suppose it is your favorite one and let us call this distribution D_1; perhaps everyone has an equal share, perhaps shares vary in accordance with some dimension you treasure. Now suppose that Wilt Chamberlain is greatly in demand by basketball teams, being a great gate attraction. (Also suppose contracts run only for a year, with players being free agents.) He signs the following sort of contract with a team: In each home game, twenty-five cents from the price of each ticket of admission goes to him. (We ignore the question of whether he is "gouging" the owners, letting them look out for themselves.) The season starts, and people cheerfully attend his team's games; they buy their tickets, each time dropping a separate twenty-five cents of their admission price into a special box with Chamberlain's name on it. They are excited about seeing him play; it is worth the total admission price to them. Let us suppose that in one season one million persons attend his home games, and Wilt Chamberlain winds up with $250,000, a much larger sum than the average income and larger even than anyone else has. Is he entitled to this income? Is this new distribution D_2, unjust? If so, why? There is *no* question about whether each of the people was entitled to the control over the resources they held in D_1; because that was the distribution (your favorite) that (for the purposes of argument) we assumed was acceptable. Each of these persons *chose* to give twenty-five cents of their money to Chamberlain. They could have spent it on going to the movies, or on candy bars, or on copies of *Dissent* magazine, or of *Monthly Review*. But they all, at least one million of them, converged on giving it to Wilt Chamberlain in exchange for watching him play basketball. If D_1 was

73

a just distribution, and people voluntarily moved from it to D_2, transferring parts of their shares they were given under D_1 (what was it for if not to do something with?), isn't D_2 also just? If the people were entitled to dispose of the resources to which they were entitled (under D_1), didn't this include their being entitled to give it to, or exchange it with, Wilt Chamberlain? Can anyone else complain on grounds of justice? Each other person already has his legitimate share under D_1. Under D_1, there is nothing that anyone has that anyone else has a claim of justice against. After someone transfers something to Wilt Chamberlain, third parties *still* have their legitimate shares; *their* shares are not changed. By what process could such a transfer among two persons give rise to a legitimate claim of distributive justice on a portion of what was transferred, by a third party who had no claim of justice on any holding of the others *before* the transfer?[1] To cut off objections irrelevant here, we might imagine the exchanges occurring in a socialist society, after hours. After playing whatever basketball he does in his daily work, or doing whatever other daily work he does, Wilt Chamberlain decides to put in *overtime* to earn additional money. (First his work quota is set; he works time over that.) Or imagine it is a skilled juggler people like to see, who puts on shows after hours.

Why might someone work overtime in a society in which it is assumed their needs are satisfied? Perhaps because they care about things other than needs. I like to write in books that I read, and to have easy access to books for browsing at odd hours. It would be very pleasant and convenient to have the resources of Widener Library in my back yard. No society, I assume, will provide such resources close to each person who would like them as part of his regular allotment (under D_1). Thus, persons either must do without some extra things that they want, or be allowed to do something extra to get some of these things. On what basis could the inequalities that would eventuate be forbidden? Notice also that small factories would spring up in a socialist society, unless forbidden. I melt down some of my personal possessions (under D_1) and build a machine out of the material. I offer you, and others, a philosophy lecture once a week in exchange for your cranking the handle on my machine, whose products I exchange for yet other things, and so on. (The raw materials used by the machine are given to me by others who possess them under D_1, in exchange for hearing lectures.) Each person might participate to gain things over and above their allotment under D_1. Some persons even might want to leave their job in socialist industry and work full time in this private sector. [. . .] Here I wish merely to note how private property even in means of production would occur in a socialist society that did not forbid people to use as they wished some of the resources they are given under the socialist distribution D_1.[2] The socialist society would have to forbid capitalist acts between consenting adults.

The general point illustrated by the Wilt Chamberlain example and the example of the entrepreneur in a socialist society is that no end-state principle or distributional patterned principle of justice can be continuously realized without continuous interference with people's lives. Any favored pattern would be transformed into one unfavored by the principle, by people choosing to act in various ways: for example, by people exchanging goods and services with other people, or giving things to other people, things the transferers are entitled to under the favored distributional pattern. To maintain a pattern one must either continually interfere to stop people from transferring resources as they wish to, or continually (or periodically) interfere to take from some persons resources that others for some reason chose to transfer to them. (But if some time limit is to be set on how long people may keep resources others voluntarily transfer to them, why let them keep these resources for any period of time? Why not have immediate confiscation?) It might be objected that all persons voluntarily will choose to refrain from actions which would upset the pattern. This presupposes unrealistically (1) that all will most want to maintain the pattern (are those who don't, to be "re-educated" or forced to undergo "self-criticism"?), (2) that each can gather enough information about his own actions and the ongoing activities of others to discover which of his actions will upset the pattern, and (3) that diverse and far-flung persons can coordinate their actions to dovetail into the pattern. Compare the manner in which the market is neutral among persons' desires, as it reflects and transmits widely scattered information via prices, and coordinates persons' activities.

It puts things perhaps a bit too strongly to say that every patterned (or end-state) principle is liable to be thwarted by the voluntary actions of the individual parties transferring some of their shares they receive under the principle. For perhaps some *very* weak patterns are not so thwarted.[3] Any distributional pattern with any egalitarian component is overturnable by the voluntary actions of individual persons over time; as is every patterned condition with sufficient content so as actually to have been proposed as presenting the central core of distributive justice. Still, given the possibility that some weak conditions or patterns may not be unstable in this way, it would be better to formulate an explicit description of the kind of interesting and contentful patterns under discussion, and to prove a theorem about their instability. Since the weaker the patterning, the more likely it is that the entitlement system itself satisfies it, a plausible conjecture is that any patterning either is unstable or is satisfied by the entitlement system.

[. . .]

Patterned principles of distributive justice necessitate *re*distributive activities. The likelihood is small that any actual freely-arrived-at set of holdings fits a given pattern; and the likelihood is nil that it will continue to fit the pattern as people exchange and give. From the point of view of an entitlement theory, redistribution is a serious matter indeed, involving, as it does, the violation of people's rights. (An exception is those takings that fall under the principle of the rectification of injustices.) From other points of view, also, it is serious.

Taxation of earnings from labor is on a par with forced labor.[4] Some persons find this claim obviously true: taking the earnings of a hours labor is like taking n hours from the person; it is like forcing the person to work n hours for another's purpose. Others find the claim absurd. But even these, *if* they object to forced labor, would oppose forcing unemployed hippies to work for the benefit of the needy.[5] And they would also object to forcing each person to work five extra hours each week for the benefit of the needy. But a system that takes five hours' wages in taxes does not seem to them like one that forces someone to work five hours, since it offers the person forced a wider range of choice in activities than does taxation in kind with the particular labor specified. (But we can imagine a gradation of systems of forced labor, from one that specifies a particular activity, to one that gives a choice among two activities, to . . .; and so on up.) Furthermore, people envisage a system with something like a proportional tax on everything above the amount necessary for basic needs. Some think this does not force someone to work extra hours, since there is no fixed number of extra hours he is forced to work, and since he can avoid the tax entirely by earning only enough to cover his basic needs. This is a very uncharacteristic view of forcing for those who *also* think people are forced to do something *whenever* the alternatives they face are considerably worse. However, *neither* view is correct. The fact that others intentionally intervene, in violation of a side constraint against aggression, to threaten force to limit the alternatives, in this case to paying taxes or (presumably the worse alternative) bare subsistence, makes the taxation system one of forced labor and distinguishes it from other cases of limited choices which are not forcings.[6]

The man who chooses to work longer to gain an income more than sufficient for his basic needs prefers some extra goods or services to the leisure and activities he could perform during the possible nonworking hours; whereas the man who chooses not to work the extra time prefers the leisure activities to the extra goods or services he could acquire by working more. Given this, if it would be illegitimate for a tax system to seize some of a man's leisure (forced labor) for the purpose of serving the needy, how can it be legitimate for a tax system to seize some of a man's goods for that purpose? Why should we treat the man whose happiness requires certain material goods or services differently from the man whose preferences and desires make such goods unnecessary for his happiness? Why should the man who prefers seeing a movie (and who has to earn money for a ticket) be open to the required call to aid the needy, while the person who prefers looking at a sunset (and hence need earn no extra money) is not? Indeed, isn't it surprising that redistributionists choose to ignore the man whose pleasures are so easily attainable without extra labor, while adding yet another burden to the poor unfortunate who must work for his pleasures? If anything, one would have expected the reverse. Why is the person with the non-material or nonconsumption desire allowed to proceed unimpeded to his most favored feasible alternative, whereas the man whose pleasures or desires involve material things and who must work for extra money (thereby serving whomever considers his activities valuable enough to pay him) is constrained in what he can realize? Perhaps there is no difference in principle. And perhaps some think the answer concerns merely administrative convenience. (These questions and issues will not disturb those who think that forced labor to serve the needy or to realize some favored end-state pattern is acceptable.) In a fuller discussion we would have (and want) to extend our argument to include interest, entrepreneurial profits, and so on. Those who doubt that this extension can be carried through, and who draw the line here at taxation of income from labor, will have to state rather complicated patterned *historical* principles of distributive justice, since end-state principles would not distinguish *sources* of income in any way. It is enough for now to get away from end-state principles and to make clear how various patterned principles are dependent upon particular views about the sources or the illegitimacy or the lesser legitimacy of profits, interest, and so on; which particular views may well be mistaken.

What sort of right over others does a legally institutionalized end-state pattern give one? The central core of the notion of a property right in X, relative to which other parts of the notion are to be explained, is the right to determine what shall be done with X; the right to choose which of the constrained set of options concerning X shall be realized or attempted.[7] The constraints are set by other principles or laws operating in the society; in our theory, by the Lockean rights people possess (under the minimal state). My property rights in my knife allow me to leave it where I will, but not in your chest. I may choose which of the acceptable options involving the knife is to be realized. This notion of property helps us to understand why earlier theorists spoke of people as having property in themselves and their labor. They viewed each person as having a right to decide what would become of himself and what he would do, and as having a right to reap the benefits of what he did.

This right of selecting the alternative to be realized from the constrained set of alternatives may be held by an *individual* or by a *group* with some procedure for reaching a joint decision; or the right may be passed back and forth, so that one year I decide what's to become of X, and the next year you do (with the alternative of destruction, perhaps, being excluded). Or, during the same time period, some types of decisions about X may be made by me, and others by you. And so on. We lack an adequate, fruitful, analytical apparatus for classifying the *types* of constraints on the set of options among which choices are to be made, and the *types* of ways decision powers can be held, divided, and amalgamated. A *theory* of property would, among other things, contain such a classification of constraints and decision modes, and from a small number of principles would follow a host of interesting statements about the *consequences* and effects of certain combinations of constraints and modes of decision.

When end-result principles of distributive justice are built into the legal structure of a society, they (as do most patterned principles) give each citizen an enforceable claim to some portion of the total social product; that is, to some portion of the sum total of the individually and jointly made products. This total product is produced by individuals laboring, using means of production others have saved to bring into existence, by people organizing production or creating means to produce new things or things in a new way. It is on this batch of individual activities that patterned distributional principles give each individual an enforceable claim. Each person has a claim to the activities and the products of other persons, independently of whether the other persons enter into particular relationships that give rise to these claims, and independently of whether they voluntarily take these claims upon themselves, in charity or in exchange for something.

Whether it is done through taxation on wages or on wages over a certain amount, or through seizure of profits, or through there being a big *social pot* so that it's not clear what's coming from where and what's going where, patterned principles of distributive justice involve appropriating the actions of other persons. Seizing the results of someone's labor is equivalent to seizing hours from him and directing him to carry on various activities. If people force you to do certain work, or unrewarded work, for a certain period of time, they decide what you are to do and what purposes your work is to serve apart from your decisions. This process whereby they take this decision from you makes them a *part-owner* of you; it gives them a property right in you. Just as having such partial control and power of decision, by right, over an animal or inanimate object would be to have a property right in it.

End-state and most patterned principles of distributive justice institute (partial) ownership by others of people and their actions and labor. These principles involve a shift from the classical liberals' notion of self-ownership to a notion of (partial) property rights in *other* people.

Considerations such as these confront end-state and other patterned conceptions of justice with the question of whether the actions necessary to achieve the selected pattern don't themselves violate moral side constraints. Any view holding that there are moral side constraints on actions, that not all moral considerations can be built into end-states that are to be achieved [. . .], must face the possibility that some of its goals are not achievable by any morally permissible available means. An entitlement theorist will face such conflicts in a society that deviates from the principles of justice for the generation of holdings, if and only if the only actions available to realize the principles themselves violate some moral constraints. Since deviation from the first two principles of justice (in acquisition and transfer) will involve other persons' direct and aggressive intervention to violate rights, and since moral constraints will not exclude defensive or retributive action in such cases, the entitlement theorist's problem rarely will be pressing. And whatever difficulties he has in applying the principle of rectification to persons who did not themselves violate the first two principles are difficulties in balancing the conflicting considerations so as correctly to formulate the complex principle of rectification itself; he will not violate moral side constraints by applying the principle. Proponents of patterned conceptions of justice, however, often will face head-on clashes (and poignant ones if they cherish each party to the clash) between moral side constraints on how individuals may be treated and their patterned conception of justice that presents an end-state or other pattern that *must* be realized.

May a person emigrate from a nation that has institutionalized some end-state or patterned distributional principle? For some principles (for example, Hayek's) emigration presents no theoretical problem. But for others it is a tricky matter. Consider a nation having a compulsory scheme of minimal social provision to aid the neediest (or one organized so as to maximize the position of the worst-off group); no one may opt out of participating in it. (None may say, "Don't compel me to contribute to others and don't provide for me via this compulsory mechanism if I am in need.") Everyone above a certain level is forced to contribute to aid the needy. But if emigration from the country were allowed, anyone could choose to move to another country that did not have compulsory social provision but otherwise was (as much as possible) identical. In such a case, the person's *only* motive for leaving would be to avoid participating in the compulsory scheme of social provision. And if he does leave, the needy in his initial country will receive no (compelled) help from him. What rationale yields the result that the person be permitted to emigrate, yet forbidden to stay and opt out of the compulsory scheme of social provision? If providing for the needy is of overriding importance, this does militate against allowing internal opting out; but it also speaks against allowing external emigration. (Would it also support, to some extent, the kidnapping of persons living in a place without compulsory social provision, who could be forced to make a contribution to the needy in your community?) Perhaps the crucial component of the position that allows emigration solely to avoid certain arrangements, while not allowing anyone internally to opt out of them, is a concern for fraternal feelings within the country. "We don't want anyone here who doesn't contribute, who doesn't care enough about the others to contribute." That concern, in this case, would have to be tied to the view that forced aiding tends to produce fraternal feelings between the aided and the aider (or perhaps merely to the view that the knowledge that someone or other voluntarily is not aiding produces unfraternal feelings).

[. . .]

NOTES

1 Might not a transfer have instrumental effects on a third party, changing his feasible options? (But what if the two parties to the transfer independently had used their holdings in this fashion?) I discuss this question below, but note here that this question concedes the point for distributions of ultimate intrinsic noninstrumental goods (pure utility experiences, so to speak) that are transferable. It also might be objected that the transfer might make a third party more envious because it worsens his position relative to someone else. I find it incomprehensible how this can be thought to involve a claim of justice.

Here and elsewhere in this chapter, a theory which incorporates elements of pure procedural justice might find what I say acceptable, *if* kept in its proper place; that is, if background institutions exist to ensure the satisfaction of certain conditions on distributive shares. But if these institutions are not themselves the sum or invisible-hand result of people's voluntary (nonaggressive) actions, the constraints they impose require justification. At no point does our argument assume any background institutions more extensive than those of the minimal night-watchman state, a state limited to protecting persons against murder, assault, theft, fraud, and so forth.

2 See the selection from John Henry MacKay's novel, *The Anarchists*, reprinted in Leonard Krimmerman and Lewis Perry, eds., *Patterns of Anarchy* (New York: Doubleday Anchor Books, 1966), in which an individualist anarchist presses upon a communist anarchist the following question: "Would you, in the system of society which you call 'free Communism' prevent individuals from exchanging their labor among themselves by means of their own medium of exchange? And further: Would you prevent them from occupying land for the purpose of personal use?" The novel continues: "[the] question was not to be escaped. If he answered 'Yes!' he admitted that society had the right of control over the individual and threw overboard the autonomy of the individual which he had always zealously defended; if on the other hand, he answered 'No!' he admitted the right of private property which he had just denied so emphatically.... Then he answered 'In Anarchy any number of men must have the right of forming a voluntary association, and so realizing their ideas in practice. Nor can I understand how any one could justly be driven from the land and house which he uses and occupies ... every serious man must declare himself: for Socialism, and thereby for force and against liberty, or for Anarchism, and thereby for liberty and against force.'" In contrast, we find Noam Chomsky writing, "Any consistent anarchist must oppose private ownership of the means of production," "the consistent anarchist then ... will be a socialist ... of a particular sort." Introduction to Daniel Guerin, *Anarchism: From Theory to Practice* (New York': Monthly Review Press, 1970), pages xiii, xv.

3 Is the patterned principle stable that requires merely that a distribution be Pareto-optimal? One person might give another a gift or bequest that the second could exchange with a third to their mutual benefit. Before the second makes this exchange, there is not Pareto co-optimality. Is a stable pattern presented by a principle choosing that among the Pareto-optimal positions that satisfies some further condition C? It may seem that there cannot be a counterexample, for won't any voluntary exchange made away from a situation show that the first situation wasn't Pareto-optimal? (Ignore the implausibility of this last claim for the case of bequests.) But principles are to be satisfied over time, during which new possibilities arise. A distribution that at one time satisfies the criterion of Pareto-optimality might not do so when some new possibilities arise (Wilt Chamberlain grows up and starts playing basketball); and though people's activities will tend to move then to a new Pareto-optimal position, *this* new one need not satisfy the contentful condition C. Continual

interference will be needed to insure the continual satisfaction of C. (The theoretical possibility of a pattern's being maintained by some invisible-hand process that brings it back to an equilibrium that fits the pattern when deviations occur should be investigated.)

4 I am unsure as to whether the arguments I present below show that such taxation merely *is* forced labor; so that "is on a par with" means "is one kind of." Or alternatively, whether the arguments emphasize the great similarities between such taxation and forced labor, to show it is plausible and illuminating to view such taxation in the light of forced labor. This latter approach would remind one of how John Wisdom conceives of the claims of metaphysicians.

5 Nothing hangs on the fact that here and elsewhere I speak loosely of *needs*, since I go on, each time, to reject the criterion of justice which includes it. If, however, something did depend upon the notion, one would want to examine it more carefully. For a skeptical view, see Kenneth Minogue, *The Liberal Mind* (New York: Random House, 1963), pp. 103–112.

6 Further details which this statement should include are contained in my essay "Coercion," in *Philosophy, Science, and Method*, ed. S. Morgenbesser, P. Suppes, and M. White (New York: St. Martin, 1969).

7 On the themes in this and the next paragraph, see the writings of Armen Alchian.

7

EQUALITY AS A MORAL IDEAL

Harry Frankfurt

First man: "How are your children?"
Second man: "Compared to what?"

I

Economic egalitarianism is, as I shall construe it, the doctrine that it is desirable for everyone to have the same amounts of income and of wealth (for short, "money").[1] Hardly anyone would deny that there are situations in which it makes sense to tolerate deviations from this standard. It goes without saying, after all, that preventing or correcting such deviations may involve costs which – whether measured in economic terms or in terms of noneconomic considerations – are by any reasonable measure unacceptable. Nonetheless, many people believe that economic equality has considerable moral value in itself. For this reason they often urge that efforts to approach the egalitarian ideal should be accorded – with all due consideration for the possible effects of such efforts in obstructing or in conducing to the achievement of other goods – a significant priority.[2]

In my opinion, this is a mistake. Economic equality is not, as such, of particular moral importance. With respect to the distribution of economic assets, what *is* important from the point of view of morality is not that everyone should have *the same* but that each should have *enough*. If everyone had enough, it would be of no moral consequence whether some had more than others. I shall refer to this alternative to egalitarianism – namely, that what is morally important with respect to money is for everyone to have enough – as "the doctrine of sufficiency."[3]

The fact that economic equality is not in its own right a morally compelling social ideal is in no way, of course, a reason for regarding it as undesirable. My claim that equality in itself lacks moral importance does not entail that equality is to be avoided. Indeed, there may well be good reasons for governments or for individuals to deal with problems of economic distribution in accordance with an egalitarian standard and to be concerned more with attempting to increase the extent to which people are economically equal than with efforts to regulate directly the extent to which the amounts of money people have are enough. Even if equality is not as such morally important, a commitment to an egalitarian social policy may be indispensable to promoting the enjoyment of significant goods besides equality or to avoiding their impairment. Moreover, it might turn out that the most feasible approach to the achievement of sufficiency would be the pursuit of equality.

But despite the fact that an egalitarian distribution would not necessarily be objectionable, the error of believing that there are powerful moral reasons for caring about equality is far from innocuous. In fact, this belief tends to do significant harm. It is often argued as an objection to egalitarianism that there is a dangerous conflict between equality and liberty: if people are left to themselves, inequalities of income and wealth inevitably arise, and therefore an egalitarian distribution of money can be achieved and maintained only at the cost of repression. Whatever may be the merit of this argument concerning the relationship between equality and liberty, economic egalitarianism engenders another conflict which is of even more fundamental moral significance.

To the extent that people are preoccupied with equality for its own sake, their readiness to be satisfied with any particular level of income or wealth is guided not by their own interests and needs but just by the magnitude of the economic benefits that are at the disposal of others. In this way egalitarianism distracts people from measuring the requirements to which their individual natures and their personal circumstances give rise. It encourages them instead to insist upon a level of economic support that is determined by a calculation in which the particular features of their own lives are irrelevant. How sizable the economic assets of others are has nothing much to do, after all, with what kind of person someone is. A concern for economic equality, construed as desirable in itself, tends to divert a person's attention away from endeavoring to discover – within his experience of himself and of his life – what he himself really cares about and what will actually satisfy him, although this is the most basic and the most decisive task upon which an intelligent selection of economic goals depends. Exaggerating the moral importance of economic equality is harmful, in other words, because it is alienating.[4]

To be sure, the circumstances of others may reveal interesting possibilities and provide data for useful judgments concerning what is normal or typical. Someone who is attempting to reach a confident and realistic appreciation of what to seek for himself may well find this helpful. It is not only in suggestive and preliminary ways like these, moreover, that the situations of other people may be pertinent to someone's efforts to decide what economic demands it is reasonable or important for him to make. The amount of money he needs may depend in a more direct way on the amounts others have. Money may bring power or prestige or other competitive advantages. A determination of how much money would be enough cannot intelligently be made by someone who is concerned with such things except on the basis of an estimate of the resources available to those with whose competition it may be necessary for him to contend. What is important from this point of view, however, is not the comparison of levels of affluence as such. The measurement of inequality is important only as it pertains contingently to other interests.

The mistaken belief that economic equality is important in itself leads people to detach the problem of formulating their economic ambitions from the problem of understanding what is most fundamentally significant to them. It influences them to take too seriously, as though it were a matter of great moral concern, a question that is inherently rather insignificant and not directly to the point, namely, how their economic status compares with the economic status of others. In this way the doctrine of equality contributes to the moral disorientation and shallowness of our time.

The prevalence of egalitarian thought is harmful in another respect as well. It not only tends to divert attention from considerations of greater moral importance than equality. It also diverts attention from the difficult but quite fundamental philosophical problems of understanding just what these considerations are and of elaborating, in appropriately comprehensive and perspicuous detail, a conceptual apparatus which would facilitate their exploration. Calculating the size of an equal share is plainly much easier than determining how much a person needs in order to have enough. In addition, the very concept of having an equal share is itself considerably more patent and accessible than the concept of having enough. It is far from self-evident, needless to say, precisely what the doctrine of sufficiency means and what applying it entails. But this is hardly a good reason for neglecting the doctrine or for adopting an incorrect doctrine in preference to it. Among my primary purposes in this chapter is to suggest the importance of systematic inquiry into the analytical and theoretical issues raised by the concept of having enough, the importance of which egalitarianism has masked.[5]

II

There are a number of ways of attempting to establish the thesis that economic equality is important. Sometimes it is urged that the prevalence of fraternal relationships among the members of a society is a desirable goal and that equality is indispensable to it.[6] Or it may be maintained that inequalities in the distribution of economic benefits are to be avoided because they lead invariably to undesirable discrepancies of other kinds – for example, in social status, in political influence, or in the abilities of people to make effective use of their various opportunities and entitlements. In both of these arguments, economic equality is endorsed because of its supposed importance in creating or preserving certain noneconomic conditions. Such considerations may well provide convincing reasons for recommending equality as a desirable social good or even for preferring egalitarianism as a policy over the alternatives to it. But both arguments construe equality as valuable derivatively, in virtue of its contingent connections to other things. In neither argument is there an attribution to equality of any unequivocally inherent moral value.

A rather different kind of argument for economic equality, which comes closer to construing the value of equality as independent of contingencies, is based upon the principle of diminishing marginal utility. According to this argument, equality is desirable because an egalitarian distribution of economic assets maximizes their aggregate utility.[7] The argument presupposes: (a) for each individual the utility of money invariably diminishes at the margin and (b) with respect to money, or with respect to the things money can buy, the utility functions of all individuals are the same.[8] In other words, the utility provided by or derivable from an nth dollar is the same for everyone, and it is less than the utility for anyone of dollar $(n - 1)$. Unless b were true, a rich man might obtain greater utility than a poor man from an extra dollar. In that case an egalitarian distribution of economic goods would not maximize aggregate utility even if a were true. But given both a and b, it follows that a marginal dollar always brings less utility to a rich person than to one who is less rich. And this entails that total utility must increase when inequality is reduced by giving a dollar to someone poorer than the person from whom it is taken.

In fact, however, both a and b are false. Suppose it is conceded, for the sake of the argument, that the maximization of aggregate utility is in its own right a morally important social goal. Even so, it cannot legitimately be inferred that an egalitarian distribution of money must therefore have similar moral importance. For in virtue of the falsity of a and b, the argument linking economic equality to the maximization of aggregate utility is unsound.

So far as concerns b, it is evident that the utility functions for money of different individuals are not even approximately alike. Some people suffer from physical, mental, or emotional weaknesses or incapacities that limit the satisfactions they are able to obtain. Moreover, even apart from the effects of specific disabilities, some people simply enjoy things more than other people do. Everyone knows that there are, at any given level of expenditure, large differences in the quantities of utility that different spenders derive.

So far as concerns a, there are good reasons against expecting any consistent diminution in the marginal utility of money. The fact that the marginal utilities of certain goods do indeed tend to diminish is not a principle of reason. It is a psychological generalization, which is accounted for by such considerations as that people often tend after a time to become satiated with what they have been consuming and that the senses characteristically lose their freshness after repetitive stimulation.[9] It is common knowledge that experiences of many kinds become increasingly routine and unrewarding as they are repeated.

It is questionable, however, whether this provides any reason at all for expecting a diminution in the marginal utility of *money* – that is, of anything that functions as a generic instrument of exchange. Even if the utility of everything money can buy were inevitably to diminish at the margin, the utility of money itself might nonetheless exhibit a different pattern. It is quite possible that money would be exempt from the phenomenon of unrelenting marginal decline because of its limitlessly protean versatility. As Blum and Kalven explain: "In . . . analysing the question whether money has a declining utility it is . . . important to put to one side all analogies to the observation that particular commodities have a declining utility to their users. There is no need here to enter into the debate whether it is useful or necessary, in economic theory, to assume that commodities have a declining utility. Money is infinitely versatile. And even if all the things money can buy are subject to a law of diminishing utility, it does not follow that money itself is."[10] From the supposition that a person tends to lose more and more interest in what he is consuming as his consumption of it increases, it plainly cannot be inferred that he must also tend to lose interest in consumption itself or in the money that makes consumption possible. For there may always remain for him, no matter how tired he has become of what he has been doing, untried goods to be bought and fresh new pleasures to be enjoyed.

There are in any event many things of which people do not, from the very outset, immediately begin to tire. From certain goods, they actually derive more utility after sustained consumption than they derive at first. This is the situation whenever appreciating or enjoying or otherwise benefiting from something depends upon repeated trials, which serve as a kind of "warming up" process: for instance, when relatively little significant gratification is obtained from the item or experience in question until the individual has acquired a special taste for it, has become addicted to it, or has begun in some other way to relate or respond to it profitably.

The capacity for obtaining gratification is then smaller at earlier points in the sequence of consumption than at later points. In such cases marginal utility does not decline; it increases. Perhaps it is true of everything, without exception, that a person will ultimately lose interest in it. But even if in every utility curve there is a point at which the curve begins a steady and irreversible decline, it cannot be assumed that every segment of the curve has a downward slope.[11]

III

When marginal utility diminishes, it does not do so on account of any deficiency in the marginal unit. It diminishes in virtue of the position of that unit as the latest in a sequence. The same is true when marginal utility increases: the marginal unit provides greater utility than its predecessors in virtue of the effect which the acquisition or consumption of those predecessors has brought about. Now when the sequence consists of units of money, what corresponds to the process of warming up – at least, in one pertinent and important feature – is *saving*. Accumulating money entails, as warming up does, generating a capacity to derive, at some subsequent point in a sequence, gratifications that cannot be derived earlier.

The fact that it may at times be especially worthwhile for a person to save money rather than to spend each dollar as it comes along is due in part to the incidence of what may be thought of as "utility thresholds." Consider an item with the following characteristics: it is nonfungible, it is the source of a fresh and otherwise unobtainable type of satisfaction, and it is too expensive to be acquired except by saving up for it. The utility of the dollar that finally completes a program of saving up for such an item may be greater than the utility of any dollar saved earlier in the program. That will be the case when the utility provided by the item is greater than the sum of the utilities that could be derived if the money saved were either spent as it came in or divided into parts and used to purchase other things. In a situation of this kind, the final dollar saved permits the crossing of a utility threshold.[12]

[. . .]

IV

It can easily be shown that, in virtue of the incidence of utility thresholds, there are conditions under which an egalitarian distribution actually minimizes aggregate utility.[13] Thus, suppose that there is enough of a certain resource (e.g., food or medicine) to enable some but not all members of a population to survive. Let us say that the size of the population is ten, that a person needs at least five units of the resource in question to live, and that forty units are available. If any members of this population are to survive, some must have more than others. An equal distribution, which gives each person four units, leads to the worst possible outcome, namely, everyone dies. Surely in this case it would be morally grotesque to insist upon equality! Nor would it be reasonable to maintain that, under the conditions specified, it is justifiable for some to be better off only when this is in the interests of the worst off. If the available resources are used to save eight people, the justification for doing this is manifestly not that it somehow benefits the two members of the population who are left to die.

An egalitarian distribution will almost certainly produce a net loss of aggregate utility whenever it entails that fewer individuals than otherwise will have, with respect to some necessity, enough to sustain life – in other words, whenever it requires a larger number of individuals to be below the threshold of survival. Of course, a loss of utility may also occur even when the circumstances involve a threshold that does not separate life and death. Allocating resources equally will reduce aggregate utility whenever it requires a number of individuals to be kept below *any* utility threshold without ensuring a compensating move above some threshold by a suitable number of others.

Under conditions of scarcity, then, an egalitarian distribution may be morally unacceptable. Another response to scarcity is to distribute the available resources in such a way that as many people as possible have enough or, in other words, to maximize the incidence of sufficiency. This alternative is especially compelling when the amount of a scarce resource that constitutes enough coincides with the amount that is indispensable for avoiding some catastrophic harm – as in the example just considered, where falling below the threshold of enough food or enough medicine means death. But now suppose that there are available, in this example, not just forty units of the vital resource but forty-one. Then maximizing the incidence of sufficiency by providing enough for each of eight people leaves one unit unallocated. What should be done with this extra unit?

It has been shown above that it is a mistake to maintain that *where some people have less than enough, no one should have more than anyone else.* When resources are scarce, so that it is impossible for everyone to have enough, an egalitarian distribution may lead to disaster. Now there is another claim that might be made here, which may appear to be quite plausible but which is also mistaken: *where some people have less than enough, no one should have more than enough.* If this claim were correct, then – in the example at hand – the extra unit should go to one of the two people who have nothing. But one additional unit of the resource in question will not improve the condition of a person who has none. By hypothesis, that person will die even with the additional unit. What he needs is not one unit but five.[14] It cannot be taken for granted that a person who has a certain amount of a vital resource is necessarily better off than a person who has a lesser amount, for the larger amount may still be too small to serve any useful purpose. Having the larger amount may even make a person worse off. Thus it is conceivable that while a dose of five units of some medication is therapeutic, a dose of one unit is not better than none but actually toxic. And while a person with one unit of food may live a bit longer than someone with no food whatever, perhaps it is worse to prolong the process of starvation for a short time than to terminate quickly the agony of starving to death.

The claim that no one should have more than enough while anyone has less than enough derives its plausibility, in part, from a presumption that is itself plausible but that is nonetheless false: to wit, giving resources to people who have less of them than enough necessarily means giving resources to people who need them and, therefore, making those people better off. It is indeed reasonable to assign a higher priority to improving the condition of those who are in need than to improving the condition of those who are not in need. But giving additional resources to people who have less than enough of those resources, and who are accordingly in need, may not actually improve the condition of these people at all. Those below a utility threshold are not necessarily benefited by additional resources that move them closer to the threshold. What is crucial for them is to attain the threshold. Merely moving closer to it either may fail to help them or may be disadvantageous.

By no means do I wish to suggest, of course, that it is never or only rarely beneficial for those below a utility threshold to move closer to it. Certainly it may be beneficial, either because it increases the likelihood that the threshold ultimately will be attained or because, quite apart from the significance of the threshold, additional resources provide important increments of utility. After all, a collector may enjoy expanding his collection even if he knows that he has no chance of ever completing it. My point is only that additional resources do not necessarily benefit those who have less than enough. The additions may be too little to make any difference. It may be morally quite acceptable, accordingly, for some to have more than enough of a certain resource even while others have less than enough of it.

V

Quite often, advocacy of egalitarianism is based less upon an argument than upon a purported moral intuition: economic inequality, considered as such, just seems wrong. It strikes many people as unmistakably apparent that, taken simply in itself, the enjoyment by some of greater economic benefits than are enjoyed by others is morally offensive. I suspect, however, that in many cases those who profess to have this intuition concerning manifestations of inequality are actually responding not to the inequality but to another feature of the situations they are confronting. What I believe they find intuitively to be morally objectionable, in the types of situations characteristically cited as instances of economic inequality, is not the fact that some of the individuals in those situations have *less* money than others but the fact that those with less have *too little*.

When we consider people who are substantially worse off than ourselves, we do very commonly find that we are morally disturbed by their circumstances. What directly touches us in cases of this kind, however, is not a quantitative discrepancy but a qualitative condition – not the fact that the economic resources of those who are worse off are *smaller in magnitude* than ours but the different fact that these people are so *poor*. Mere differences in the amounts of money people have are not in themselves distressing. We tend to be quite unmoved, after all, by inequalities between the well-to-do and the rich; our awareness that the former are substantially worse off than the latter does not disturb us morally at all. And if we believe of some person that his life is richly fulfilling, that he himself is genuinely content with his economic situation, and that he suffers no resentments or sorrows which more money could assuage, we are not ordinarily much interested – from a moral point of view – in the question of how the amount of money he has compares with the amounts possessed by others. Economic discrepancies in cases of these sorts do not impress us in the least as matters of significant moral concern. The fact that some people have much less than others is morally undisturbing when it is clear that they have plenty.

It seems clear that egalitarianism and the doctrine of sufficiency are logically independent: considerations that support the one cannot be presumed to provide support also for the other. Yet proponents of egalitarianism frequently suppose that they have offered grounds for their position when in fact what they have offered is pertinent as support only for the doctrine of sufficiency. Thus they often, in attempting to gain acceptance for egalitarianism, call attention to disparities between the conditions of life characteristic of the rich and those characteristic of the poor. Now it is undeniable that contemplating such disparities does often elicit a conviction that it would be morally desirable to redistribute the available resources so as to improve the circumstances of the poor. And, of course, that would bring about a greater degree of economic equality. But the indisputability of the moral appeal of improving the condition of the poor by allocating to them resources taken from those who are well off does not even tend to show that egalitarianism is, as a moral ideal, similarly indisputable. To show of poverty that it is compellingly undesirable does nothing whatsoever to show the same of inequality. For what makes someone poor in the morally relevant sense – in which poverty is understood as a condition from which we naturally recoil – is not that his economic assets are simply of lesser magnitude than those of others.

[. . .]

My suggestion that situations involving inequality are morally disturbing only to the extent that they violate the ideal of sufficiency is confirmed, it seems to me, by familiar discrepancies between the principles egalitarians profess and the way in which they commonly conduct their own lives. My point here is not that some egalitarians hypocritically accept high incomes and special opportunities for which, according to the moral theories they profess, there is no justification. It is that many egalitarians (including many academic proponents of the doctrine) are not truly concerned whether they are as well off economically as other people are. They believe that they themselves have roughly enough money for what is important to them, and they are therefore not terribly preoccupied with the fact that some people are considerably richer than they. Indeed, many egalitarians would consider it rather shabby or even reprehensible to care, with respect to their own lives, about economic comparisons of that sort. And, notwithstanding the implications of the doctrines to which they urge adherence, they would be appalled if their children grew up with such preoccupations.

VI

The fundamental error of egalitarianism lies in supposing that it is morally important whether one person has less than another regardless of how much either of them has. This error is due in part to the false assumption that someone who is economically worse off has more important unsatisfied needs than someone who is better off. In fact the morally significant needs of both individuals may be fully satisfied or equally unsatisfied. Whether one person has more money than another is a wholly extrinsic matter. It has to do with a relationship between the respective economic assets of the two people, which is not only independent of the amounts of their assets and of the amounts of satisfaction they can derive from them but also independent of the attitudes of these people toward those levels of assets and of satisfaction. The economic comparison implies nothing concerning whether either of the people compared has any morally important unsatisfied needs at all nor concerning whether either is content with what he has.

This defect in egalitarianism appears plainly in Thomas Nagel's development of the doctrine. According to Nagel: "The essential feature of an egalitarian priority system is that it counts improvements to the welfare of the worse off as more urgent than improvements to the welfare of the better off. . . . What makes a system egalitarian is the priority it gives to the claims of those . . . at the bottom. . . . Each individual with a more urgent claim has priority . . . over each individual with a less urgent claim."[15] And in discussing Rawls's Difference Principle, which he endorses, Nagel says: the Difference Principle "establishes an order of priority among needs and gives preference to the most urgent."[16] But the preference actually assigned by the Difference Principle is not in favor of those whose needs are most urgent; it is in favor of those who are identified as worst off. It is a mere assumption, which Nagel makes without providing any grounds for it whatever, that the worst off individuals have urgent needs. In most societies the people who are economically at the bottom are indeed extremely poor, and they do, as a matter of fact, have urgent needs. But this relationship between low economic status and urgent need is wholly contingent. It can be established only on the basis of empirical data. There is no necessary conceptual connection between a person's relative economic position and whether he has needs of any degree of urgency.[17]

It is possible for those who are worse off not to have more urgent needs or claims than those who are better off because it is possible for them to have no urgent needs or claims at all. The notion of "urgency" has to do with what is *important*. Trivial needs or interests, which have no significant bearing upon the quality of a person's life or upon his readiness to be content with it, cannot properly be construed as being urgent to any degree whatever or as supporting the sort of morally demanding claims to which genuine urgency gives rise. From the fact that a person is at the bottom of some economic order, moreover, it cannot even be inferred that he has *any* unsatisfied needs or claims. After all, it is possible for conditions at the bottom to be quite good; the fact that they are the worst does not in itself entail that they are bad or that they are in any way incompatible with richly fulfilling and enjoyable lives.

Nagel maintains that what underlies the appeal of equality is an "ideal of acceptability to each individual."[18] On his account, this ideal entails that a reasonable person should consider deviations from equality to be acceptable only if they are in his interest in the sense that he would be worse off without them. But a reasonable person might well regard an unequal distribution as entirely acceptable even though he did not presume that any other distribution would benefit him less. For he might believe that the unequal distribution provided him with quite enough, and he might reasonably be unequivocally content with that, with no concern for the possibility that some other arrangement would provide him with more. It is gratuitous to assume that every reasonable person must be seeking to maximize the benefits he can obtain, in a sense requiring that he be endlessly interested in or open to improving his life. A certain deviation from equality might not be *in* someone's interest because it might be that he would in fact be better off without it. But as long as it does not *conflict* with his interest, by obstructing his opportunity to lead the sort of life that it is important for him to lead, the deviation from equality may be quite acceptable. To be wholly satisfied with a certain state of affairs, a reasonable person need not suppose that there is no other available state of affairs in which he would be better off.[19]

Nagel illustrates his thesis concerning the moral appeal of equality by considering a family with two children, one of whom is "normal and quite happy" while the other "suffers from a painful handicap."[20] If this family were to move to the city the handicapped child would benefit from medical and educational opportunities that are unavailable in the suburbs, but the healthy child would have less fun. If the family were to move to the suburbs, on the other hand, the handicapped child would be deprived but the healthy child would enjoy himself more. Nagel stipulates that the gain to the healthy child in moving to the suburbs would be greater than the gain to the handicapped child in moving to the city: in the city the healthy child would find life positively disagreeable, while the handicapped child would not become happy "but only less miserable."

Given these conditions, the egalitarian decision is to move to the city; for "it is more urgent to benefit the [handicapped] child even though the benefit we can give him is less than the benefit we can give the [healthy] child." Nagel explains that this judgment concerning the greater urgency of benefiting the handicapped child "depends on the worse off position of the [handicapped] child. An improvement in his situation is more important than an equal or somewhat greater improvement in the situation of the [normal] child." But it seems to me that Nagel's analysis of this matter is flawed [. . .]. The fact that it is preferable to help the handicapped child is not due, as Nagel asserts, to the fact that this child is worse off than the other. It is due to the fact that this child, and not the other, suffers from a painful handicap. The handicapped child's claim is important because his condition is *bad* – significantly undesirable – and not merely because he is *less well off* than his sibling.

This does not imply, of course, that Nagel's evaluation of what the family should do is wrong. Rejecting egalitarianism certainly does not mean maintaining that it is always mandatory simply to maximize benefits and that therefore the family should move to the suburbs because the normal child would gain more from that than the handicapped child would gain from a move to the city. However, the most cogent basis for Nagel's judgment in favor of the handicapped child has nothing to do with the alleged urgency of providing people with as much as others. It pertains rather to the urgency of the needs of people who do not have enough.[21]

VII

What does it mean, in the present context, for a person to have enough? One thing it might mean is that any more would be too much: a larger amount would make the person's life unpleasant, or it would be harmful or in some other way unwelcome. This is often what people have in mind when they say such things as "I've had enough!" or "Enough of that!" The idea conveyed by statements like these is that *a limit has been reached*, beyond which it is not desirable to proceed. On the other hand, the assertion that a person has enough may entail only that *a certain requirement or standard has been met*, with no implication that a larger quantity would be bad. This is often what a person intends when he says something like "That should be enough." Statements such as this one characterize the indicated amount as sufficient while leaving open the possibility that a larger amount might also be acceptable.

In the doctrine of sufficiency the use of the notion of "enough" pertains to *meeting a standard* rather than to *reaching a limit*. To say that a person has enough money means that he is content, or that it is reasonable for him to be content, with having no more money than he has. And to say this is, in turn, to say something like the following: the person does not (or cannot reasonably) regard whatever (if anything) is unsatisfying or distressing about his life as due to his having too little money. In other words, if a person is (or ought reasonably to be) content with the amount of money he has, then insofar as he is or has reason to be unhappy with the way his life is going, he does not (or cannot reasonably) suppose that money would – either as a sufficient or as a necessary condition – enable him to become (or to have reason to be) significantly less unhappy with it.[22]

It is essential to understand that having enough money differs from merely having enough to get along or enough to make life marginally tolerable. People are not generally content with living on the brink. The point of the doctrine of sufficiency is not that the only morally important distributional consideration with respect to money is whether people have enough to avoid economic misery. A person who might naturally and appropriately be said to have just barely enough does not, by the standard invoked in the doctrine of sufficiency, have enough at all.

There are two distinct kinds of circumstances in which the amount of money a person has is enough – that is, in which more money will not enable him to become significantly less unhappy. On the one hand, it may be that the person is suffering no substantial distress or dissatisfaction with his life. On the other hand, it may be that although the person is unhappy about how his life is going, the difficulties that account for his unhappiness would not be alleviated by more money. Circumstances of this second kind obtain when what is wrong with the person's life has to do with non-economic goods such as love, a sense that life is meaningful, satisfaction with one's own character, and so on. These are goods that money cannot buy; moreover, they are goods for which none of the things money can buy are even approximately adequate substitutes. Sometimes, to be sure, noneconomic goods are obtainable or enjoyable only (or more easily) by someone who has a certain amount of money. But the person who is distressed with his life while content with his economic situation may already have that much money.

It is possible that someone who is content with the amount of money he has might also be content with an even larger amount of money. Since having enough money does not mean being at a limit beyond which more money would necessarily be undesirable, it would be a mistake to assume that for a person who already has enough the marginal utility of money must be either negative or zero. Although this person is by hypothesis not distressed about his life in virtue of any lack of things which more money would enable him to obtain, nonetheless it remains possible that he would enjoy having some of those things. They would not make him less unhappy, nor would they in any way alter his attitude toward his life or the degree of his contentment with it, but they might bring him pleasure. If that is so, then his life would in this respect be better with more money than without it. The marginal utility for him of money would accordingly remain positive.

To say that a person is content with the amount of money he has does not entail, then, that there would be no point whatever in his having more. Thus someone with enough money might be quite *willing* to accept incremental economic benefits. He might in fact be *pleased* to receive them. Indeed, from the supposition that a person is content with the amount of money he has it cannot even be inferred that he would not *prefer* to have more. And it is even possible that he would actually be prepared to *sacrifice* certain things that he values (e.g., a certain amount of leisure) for the sake of more money.

But how can all this be compatible with saying that the person is content with what he has? What *does* contentment with a given amount of money preclude, if it does not preclude being willing or being pleased or preferring to have more money or even being ready to make sacrifices for more? It precludes his having an *active interest* in getting more. A contented person regards having more money as *inessential* to his being satisfied with his life. The fact that he is content is quite consistent with his recognizing that his economic circumstances could be improved and that his life might as a consequence become better than it is. But this possibility is not important to him. He is simply not much interested in being better off, so far as money goes, than he is. His attention and interest are not vividly engaged by the benefits which would be available to him if he had more money. He is just not very responsive to their appeal. They do not arouse in him any particularly eager or restless concern, although he acknowledges that he would enjoy additional benefits if they were provided to him.

In any event, let us suppose that the level of satisfaction that his present economic circumstances enable him to attain is high enough to meet his expectations of life. This is not fundamentally a matter of how much utility or satisfaction his various activities and experiences provide. Rather, it is most decisively a matter of his attitude toward being provided with that much. The satisfying experiences a person has are one thing. Whether he is satisfied that his life includes just those satisfactions is another. Although it is possible that other feasible circumstances would provide him with greater amounts of satisfaction, it may be that he is wholly satisfied with the amounts of satisfaction that he now enjoys. Even if he knows that he could obtain a greater quantity of satisfaction overall, he does not experience the uneasiness or the ambition that would incline him to seek it. Some people feel that their lives are good enough, and it is not important to them whether their lives are as good as possible.

[. . .]

It may seem that there can be no reasonable basis for accepting less satisfaction when one could have more, that therefore rationality itself entails maximizing, and, hence, that a person who refuses to maximize the quantity of satisfaction in his life is not being rational. Such a person cannot, of course, offer it as his reason for declining to pursue greater satisfaction that the costs of this pursuit are too high; for if that were his reason then, clearly, he would be attempting to maximize satisfaction after all. But what other good reason could he possibly have for passing up an opportunity for more satisfaction? In fact, he may have a very good reason for this: namely, *that he is satisfied with the amount of satisfaction he already has.* Being satisfied with the way things are is unmistakably an excellent reason for having no great interest in changing them. A person who is indeed satisfied with his life as it is can hardly be criticized, accordingly, on the grounds that he has no good reason for declining to make it better.

He might still be open to criticism on the grounds that he *should not* be satisfied – that it is somehow unreasonable, or unseemly, or in some other mode wrong for him to be satisfied with less satisfaction than he could have. On what basis, however, could *this* criticism be justified? Is there some decisive reason for insisting that a person ought to be so hard to satisfy? Suppose that a man deeply and happily loves a woman who is altogether worthy. We do not ordinarily criticize the man in such a case just because we think he might have done even better. Moreover, our sense that it would be inappropriate to criticize him for that reason need not be due simply to a belief that holding out for a more desirable or worthier woman might end up costing him more than it would be worth. Rather, it may reflect our recognition that the desire to be happy or content or satisfied with life is a desire for a satisfactory amount of satisfaction and is not inherently tantamount to a desire that the quantity of satisfaction be maximized.

Being satisfied with a certain state of affairs is not equivalent to preferring it to all others. If a person is faced with a choice between less and more of something desirable, then no doubt it would be irrational for him to prefer less to more. But a person may be satisfied without having made any such comparisons at all. Nor is it necessarily irrational or unreasonable for a person to omit or to decline to make comparisons between his own state of affairs and possible alternatives. This is not only because making comparisons may be too costly. It is also because if someone is satisfied with the way things are, he may have no motive to consider how else they might be.[23]

Contentment may be a function of excessive dullness or diffidence. The fact that a person is free both of resentment and of ambition may be due to his having a slavish character or to his vitality being muffled by a kind of negligent lassitude. It is possible for someone to be content merely, as it were, by default. But a person who is content with resources providing less utility than he could have may not be irresponsible or indolent or deficient in imagination. On the contrary, his decision to be content with those resources – in other words, to adopt an attitude of willing acceptance toward the fact that he has just that much – may be based upon a conscientiously intelligent and penetrating evaluation of the circumstances of his life.

It is not essential for such an evaluation to include an *extrinsic* comparison of the person's circumstances with alternatives to which he might plausibly aspire, as it would have to do if contentment were reasonable only when based upon a judgment that the enjoyment of possible benefits has been maximized. If someone is less interested in whether his circumstances enable him to live as well as possible than in whether they enable him to live satisfyingly, he may appropriately devote his evaluation entirely to an *intrinsic* appraisal of his life. Then he may recognize that his circumstances do not lead him to be resentful or regretful or drawn to change and that, on the basis of his understanding of himself and of what is important to him, he accedes approvingly to his actual readiness to be content with the way things are. The situation in that case is not so much that he rejects the possibility of improving his circumstances because he thinks there is nothing genuinely to be gained by attempting to improve them. It is rather that this possibility, however feasible it may be, falls as a matter of fact to excite his active attention or to command from him any lively interest.[24]

[. . .]

NOTES

1 This version of economic egalitarianism (for short, simply "egalitarianism") might also be formulated as the doctrine that there should be no inequalities in the *distribution* of money. The two formulations are not unambiguously equivalent because the term "distribution" is equivocal. It may refer either to a pattern of possession or to an activity of allocation, and there are significant differences in the criteria for evaluating distributions in the two senses. Thus it is quite possible to maintain consistently both that it is acceptable for people to have unequal amounts of money and that it is objectionable to allocate money unequally.

2 Thus, Thomas Nagel writes: "The defense of economic equality on the ground that it is needed to protect political, legal and social equality . . . [is not] a defense of equality *per se* – equality in the possession of benefits in general. Yet the latter is a further moral idea of great importance. Its validity would provide an independent reason to favor economic equality as a good in its own right" ("Equality," in his *Mortal Questions* [Cambridge: Cambridge University Press, 1979], p. 107).

3 I focus attention here on the standard of equality in the distribution of money chiefly in order to facilitate my discussion of the standard of sufficiency. Many egalitarians, of course, consider economic equality to be morally less important than equality in certain other matters: e.g., welfare, opportunity, respect, satisfaction of needs. In fact, some of what I have to say about economic egalitarianism and sufficiency applies as well to these other benefits. But I shall not attempt in this essay to define the scope of its applicability, nor shall I attempt to relate my views to other recent criticism of egalitarianism (e.g., Larry S. Temkin, "Inequality," *Philosophy and Public Affairs* 15 [1986]: 99–121; Robert E. Goodin, "Epiphenomenal Egalitarianism," *Social Research* 52 [1985]: 99–117).

4 It might be argued (as some of the editors of *Ethics* have suggested to me) that pursuing equality as an important social ideal would not be so alienating as pursuing it as a personal goal. It is indeed possible that individuals devoted to the former pursuit would be less immediately or less intensely preoccupied with their own economic circumstances than those devoted to the latter. But they would hardly regard the achievement of economic equality as important for the society unless they had the false and alienating conviction that it was important for individuals to enjoy economic equality.

5   I shall address some of these issues in Sec. VII below.

6   In the Sterling Memorial Library at Yale University (which houses 8.5 million volumes), there are 1,159 entries in the card catalog under the subject heading "liberty" and 326 under "equality." Under "fraternity," there are none. This is because the catalog refers to the social ideal in question as "brotherliness." Under that heading there are *four* entries! Why does fraternity (or brotherliness) have so much less salience than liberty and equality? Perhaps the explanation is that, in virtue of our fundamental commitment to individualism, the political ideals to which we are most deeply and actively attracted have to do with what we suppose to be the rights of individuals, and no one claims a right to fraternity. It is also possible that liberty and equality get more attention in certain quarters because, unlike fraternity, they are considered to be susceptible to more or less formal treatment. In any event, the fact is that there has been very little serious investigation into just what fraternity is, what it entails, or why it should be regarded as especially desirable.

7   Nagel endorses this argument as establishing the moral importance of economic equality. Other formulations and discussions of the argument may be found in: Kenneth Arrow, "A Utilitarian Approach to the Concept of Equality in Public Expenditures," *Quarterly Journal of Economics* 85 (1971): 409–10; Walter Blum and Harry Kalven, *The Uneasy Case for Progressive Taxation* (Chicago: University of Chicago Press, 1966); Abba Lerner, *The Economics of Control* (New York: Macmillan Publishing Co., 1944); Paul Samuelson, *Economics* (New York: McGraw-Hill Book Co., 1973), and "A. P. Lerner at Sixty," in *Collected Scientific Papers of Paul A. Samuelson*, ed. Robert C. Merton, 3 vols. (Cambridge, Mass.: MIT Press, 1972), vol. 3, pp. 643–52.

8   Thus, Arrow says: "In the utilitarian discussion of income distribution, equality of income is derived from the maximization conditions if it is further assumed that individuals have the same utility functions, each with diminishing marginal utility" (p. 409). And Samuelson offers the following formulation: "If each extra dollar brings less and less satisfaction to a man, and if the rich and poor are alike in their capacity to enjoy satisfaction, a dollar taxed away from a millionaire and given to a median-income person is supposed to add more to total utility than it subtracts" (*Economics*, p. 164, n. 1).

9   "With successive new units of [a] good, your total utility will grow at a slower and slower rate because of a fundamental tendency for your psychological ability to appreciate more of the good to become less keen. This fact, that the increments in total utility fall off, economists describe as follows: as the amount consumed of a good increases, the *marginal utility* of the good (or the extra utility added by its last unit) tends to decrease" (Samuelson, *Economics*, p. 431).

10 Blum and Kalven, pp. 57–58.

11 People tend to think that it is generally more important to avoid a certain degree of harm than to acquire a benefit of comparable magnitude. It may be that this is in part because they assume that utility diminishes at the margin, for in that case the additional benefit would have less utility than the corresponding loss. However, it should be noted that the tendency to place a lower value on acquiring benefits than on avoiding harms is sometimes reversed: when people are so miserable that they regard themselves as "having nothing to lose," they may well place a higher value on improving things than on preventing them from becoming (to a comparable extent) even worse. In that case, what is diminishing at the margin is not the utility of benefits but the disutility of harms.

12 In virtue of these thresholds, a marginal or incremental dollar may have conspicuously greater utility than dollars that do not enable a threshold to be crossed. Thus, a person who uses his spare money during a certain period for some inconsequential improvement in his

routine pattern of consumption – perhaps a slightly better quality of meat for dinner every night – may derive much less additional utility in this way than by saving up the extra money for a few weeks and going to see some marvelous play or opera. The threshold effect is particularly integral to the experience of collectors, who characteristically derive greater satisfaction from obtaining the item that finally completes a collection – whichever item it happens to be – than from obtaining any of the other items in the collection. Obtaining the final item entails crossing a utility threshold: a complete collection of twenty different items, each of which when considered individually has the same utility, is likely to have greater utility for a collector than an incomplete collection that is of the same size but that includes duplicates. The completeness of the collection itself possesses utility, in addition to the utility provided individually by the items of which the collection is constituted.

13 Conditions of these kinds are discussed in Nicholas Rescher, *Distributive Justice* (Indianapolis: Bobbs-Merrill Co., 1966), pp. 28–30.

14 It might be correct to say that he does need one unit if there is a chance that he will get four more, since in that case the one unit can be regarded as potentially an integral constituent of the total of five that puts him across the threshold of survival. But if there is no possibility that he will acquire five, then acquiring the one does not contribute to the satisfaction of any need.

15 Nagel, p. 118.

16 Ibid., p. 117.

17 What I oppose is the claim that when it comes to justifying attempts to improve the circumstances of those who are economically worst off, a good reason for making the attempt is that it is morally important for people to be as equal as possible with respect to money. The only morally compelling reason for trying to make the worse off better off is, in my judgment, that their lives are in some degree bad lives. The fact that some people have more than enough money suggests a way in which it might be arranged for those who have less than enough to get more, but it is not in itself a good reason for redistribution.

18 Nagel, p. 123.

19 For further discussion, see Sec. VII below.

20 Quotations from his discussion of this illustration are from Nagel, pp. 123–24.

21 The issue of equality or sufficiency that Nagel's illustration raises does not, of course, concern the distribution of money.

22 Within the limits of my discussion it makes no difference which view is taken concerning the very important question of whether what counts is *the attitude a person actually has* or *the attitude it would be reasonable for him to have*. For the sake of brevity, I shall henceforth omit referring to the latter alternative.

23 Compare the sensible adage: "If it's not broken, don't fix it."

24 People often adjust their desires to their circumstances. There is a danger that sheer discouragement, or an interest in avoiding frustration and conflict, may lead them to settle for too little. It surely cannot be presumed that someone's life is genuinely fulfilling, or that it is reasonable for the person to be satisfied with it, simply because he does not complain. On the other hand, it also cannot be presumed that when a person has accommodated his desires to his circumstances, this is itself evidence that something has gone wrong.

8

WHERE THE ACTION IS

On the site of distributive justice

G.A. Cohen

Only when the actual, individual man has taken back into himself the abstract citizen and in his everyday life, his individual work, and his individual relationships has become a *species-being*, only when he has recognized and organized his own powers as *social* powers so that social power is no longer separated from him as *political* power, only then is human emancipation complete.

Karl Marx, "On the Jewish Question"

1

I now present a preliminary reply to the basic-structure objection. It is preliminary in that it precedes my interrogation, in section 2, of what the phrase "basic structure" denotes, and also in that, by contrast with the fundamental reply that will follow that interrogation, there is a certain way out for Rawls, in face of the preliminary reply. That way out is not costless for him, but it does exist.

Although Rawls says often enough that the two principles of justice govern only justice in basic structure, he also says three things which tell against that restriction. This means that, in each case, he must either uphold the restriction and repudiate the comment in question, or maintain the comment, and drop the restriction.[1]

First, Rawls says that, when the difference principle is satisfied, society displays *fraternity*, in a particularly strong sense: its citizens do not want "to have greater advantages unless this is to the benefit of others who are less well off. . . . Members of a family commonly do not wish to gain unless they can do so in ways that further the interests of the rest. Now, wanting to act on the difference principle has precisely this consequence."[2] But fraternity of that strong kind is not realized when all the justice delivered by the difference principle comes from the basic structure, and, therefore, whatever people's motivations in economic interaction may be. Wanting not "to gain unless they can do so in ways that further the interests of the rest" is incompatible with the self-interested motivation of market maximizers, which the difference principle, in its purely structural interpretation, does not condemn.[3]

Second, Rawls says that the worst off in a society governed by the difference principle can bear their inferior position with dignity, since they know that no improvement of it is possible, that they would lose under any less unequal dispensation. Yet that is false, if justice relates to structure alone, since it might then be necessary for the worst off to occupy their relatively low place only because the choices of the better off tend strongly against equality. Why should the fact that no purely structurally induced improvement in their position is possible suffice to guarantee the dignity of the worst off, when their position might be very inferior indeed, because of unlimited self-seekingness in the economic choices of well-placed people?[4] Suppose, for example, that (as politicians now routinely claim) raising rates of income taxation with a view to enhancing benefits for the badly off would be counterproductive, since the higher rates would induce severe disincentive effects on the productivity of the better off. Would awareness of that truth contribute to a sense of dignity on the part of the badly off?

Third, Rawls says that people in a just society act with a sense justice *from* the principles of justice in their daily lives; they strive to apply those principles in their own choices. And they do so because they "have a desire to express their nature as free and equal moral persons, and this they do most adequately by acting *from* the principles that they would acknowledge in the original position. When all strive to comply with these principles and each succeeds, then individually and collectively their nature as moral persons is most fully realized, and with it their individual and collective good."[5] But why do they have to act *from* the principles of justice, and "apply" them "as their circumstances require,"[6] if it suffices for justice that they choose as they please within a structure designed to effect an implementation of those principles? And how can they, without a redolence of hypocrisy, celebrate full realization of their natures as moral persons, when they know that they are out for the most that they can get in the market?

Now, as I said, these inconsistencies are not decisive against Rawls. For, in each case, he could stand pat on his restriction of justice to basic structure, and give up, or weaken, the remark that produces the inconsistency. And that is indeed what he is disposed to do, at least with respect to the third inconsistency that I have noted. He said[7] that *A Theory of Justice* erred by in some respects treating the two principles as defining a *comprehensive* conception of justice;[8] he would, accordingly, now drop the high-pitched homily which constitutes the text to note 5 above. But this accommodation carries a cost: it means that the ideals of dignity, fraternity, and full realization of people's moral natures can no longer be said to be delivered by Rawlsian justice.[9]

2

I now provide a more fundamental reply to the basic-structure objection. It is more fundamental in that it shows, decisively, that justice requires an ethos governing daily choice which goes beyond one of obedience to just rules,[10] on grounds which do not, as the preliminary reply did, exploit things that Rawls says in apparent contradiction of his stipulation that justice applies to the basic structure of society alone. The fundamental reply interrogates, and refutes, that stipulation itself.

A major fault line in the Rawlsian architectonic not only wrecks the basic-structure objection but also produces a dilemma for Rawls's view of the subject[11] of justice – a dilemma from which I can imagine no way out. The fault line exposes itself when we ask the apparently simple question: What (exactly) is the basic structure? For there is a fatal ambiguity in Rawls's specification of the basic structure, and an associated discrepancy between his criterion for what justice judges and his desire to exclude the effects of structure-consistent personal choice from the purview of its judgment.

The basic structure, the primary subject of justice, is always said by Rawls to be a set of institutions, and, so he infers, the principles of justice do not judge the actions of people within (just) institutions whose rules they observe. But it is seriously unclear *which* institutions are supposed to qualify as part of the basic structure. Sometimes it appears that coercive (in the legal sense) institutions exhaust it, or, better, that institutions belong to it only insofar as they are (legally) coercive.[12] In this widespread interpretation of what Rawls intends by the "basic structure" of a society that structure is legible in the provisions of its constitution, in such specific legislation as may be required to implement those provisions, and in further legislation and policy which are of central importance but which resist formulation in the constitution itself.[13] The basic structure, in this first understanding of it, is, so one might say, the *broad coercive outline* of society, which determines in a relatively fixed and general way what people may and must do, in advance of legislation that is optional, relative to the principles of justice, and irrespective of the constraints and opportunities created and destroyed by the choices that people make within the given basic structure, so understood.

Yet it is quite unclear that the basic structure is *always* to be so understood, in exclusively coercive terms, within the Rawlsian texts. For Rawls often says that the basic structure consists of the *major* social institutions, and he does not put a particular accent on coercion when he announces *that* specification of the basic structure.[14] In this second reading of what it is, institutions belong to the basic structure whose structuring can depend far less on law than on convention, usage, and expectation; a signal example is the family, which Rawls sometimes includes in the basic structure and sometimes does not.[15] But once the line is crossed, from coercive ordering to the noncoercive ordering of society by rules and conventions of accepted practice, then the ambit of justice can no longer exclude chosen behavior, since, at least in certain cases, the prescriptions that constitute informal structure (think, again, of the family) are bound up with the choices that people customarily make.

"Bound up with" is vague, so let me explain how I mean it here. One can certainly speak of the structure of the family, and it is not identical with the choices that people customarily make within it; but it is nevertheless impossible to claim that the principles of justice which apply to family structure do not apply to day-to-day choices within it. For consider the following contrast. The *coercive* structure, let us provisionally accept,[16] arises independently of people's quotidian choices: it is formed by those specialized choices which legislate the law of the land. But the noncoercive structure of the family has the character it does only because of the choices that its members routinely make. The constraints and pressures that sustain the noncoercive structure reside in the dispositions of agents which are actualized as and when those agents choose to act in a constraining or pressuring way. With respect to coercive structure, one may, perhaps, fairly readily distinguish the choices which institute and sustain a structure from the choices that occur within it.[17] But with respect to informal structure, that distinction, though conceptually intelligible, is compromised extensionally. When A chooses to conform to the prevailing usages, the pressure on B to do so is reinforced; and no such pressure exists, the very usages themselves do not exist, in the absence of conformity to them. Structure and choice remains distinguishable, but not from the point of view of the applicability to them of principles of justice.

Now, since that is so, since appropriately conforming behavior is (at least partly) *constitutive* of *non*coercive structure, it follows that the only way of sustaining the basic-structure objection against my claim that the difference principle condemns maximizing economic behavior (and, more generally, of sustaining the restriction of justice to the basic structure against the insistence that the personal, too, is political) is by holding fast to a purely coercive specification of the basic structure. But that way out is not open to Rawls, because of a further characterization that he offers of the basic structure: this is where the discrepancy adverted to in the second paragraph of this section appears. For Rawls says that "the basic structure is the primary subject of justice because its effects are so profound and present from the start."[18] Nor is this further characterization of the basic structure optional: it is needed to explain why it *is* primary, as far as justice is concerned. Yet it is false that only the *coercive* structure causes profound effects, as the example of the family once again reminds us:[19] if the "values [that] govern the basic [political] framework of social life" thereby govern "the very groundwork of our existence,"[20] so too do the values that govern our nurture and conduct in the family. Accordingly, if Rawls retreats to coercive structure, he contradicts his own criterion for what justice judges, and he lands himself with an arbitrarily narrow definition of his subject matter. So he must let other structure in, and that means, as we have seen, letting chosen behavior in. What is more, even if behavior did not, as I claim it does, partly constitute the noncoercive structure, it will come in by direct appeal to the profundity-of-effect criterion for what justice governs. So, for example, we need not decide whether or not a regular practice of favoring sons over daughters in the matter of providing higher education forms part of the *structure* of the family to condemn it as unjust, under that criterion.[21]

Given, then, his stated rationale[22] for exclusive focus on the basic structure – and what *other* rationale could there be for calling it the *primary* subject of justice? – Rawls is in a dilemma. For he must either admit application of the principles of justice to (legally optional) social practices, and, indeed, to patterns of personal choice that are not legally prescribed, *both* because they are the substance of those practices, *and* because they are similarly profound in effect, in which case the restriction of justice to structure, in any sense, collapses; or, if he restricts his concern to the coercive structure only, then he saddles himself with a purely arbitrary delineation of his subject matter. I now illustrate this dilemma by reference to [. . .] the family and the market economy.

Family structure is fateful for the benefits and burdens that redound to different people, and, in particular, to people of different sexes, where "family structure" includes the socially constructed expectations which lie on husband and wife. And such expectations are sexist and unjust if, for example, they direct the woman in a family where both spouses work outside the home to carry a greater burden of domestic tasks. Yet such expectations need not be supported by the law for them to possess informal coercive force: sexist family structure is consistent with sex-neutral family law. Here, then, is a circumstance, outside the basic structure, as that would be coercively defined, which profoundly affects people's life-chances, *through the choices people make in response to the stated expectations, which are, in turn, sustained by those choices.*[23] Yet Rawls must say, on pain of giving up the basic-structure objection that (legally uncoerced) family structure and behavior have no implications for justice in the sense of "justice" in which the basic structure has implications for justice, since they are not a consequence of the formal coercive order. But that implication of the stated position is perfectly incredible: no such differentiating sense is available.

John Stuart Mill taught us to recognize that informal social pressure can restrict liberty as much as formal coercive law does. And the family example shows that informal pressure is as relevant to distributive justice as it is to liberty. One reason why the rules of the basic structure, when it is coercively defined, do not by themselves determine the justice of the distributive upshot is that, by virtue of circumstances that are relevantly independent of coercive rules, some people have much more power than others to determine what happens *within* those rules.

The second illustration of discrepancy between what coercive structure commands and what profoundly affects the distribution of benefits and burdens is my own point about incentives. Maximizing legislation,[24] and, hence, a coercive basic structure that satisfies the difference principle, are consistent with a maximizing ethos across society which, under many conditions, will produce severe inequalities and a meager level of provision for the worst off; yet both have to be declared just by Rawls, if he stays with a coercive conception of what justice judges. And that implication is, surely, perfectly incredible.

Rawls cannot deny the difference between the coercively defined basic structure and that which produces major distributive consequences: the coercively defined basic structure is only an instance of the latter. Yet he must, to retain his position on justice and personal choice, restrict the ambit of justice to what a coercive basic structure produces. But, so I have (by implication) asked: Why should we *care* so dispropor-tionately, about the coercive basic structure, when the major reason for caring about it, its impact on people's lives, is *also* a reason for caring about informal structure and patterns of personal choice? To the extent that we care about coercive structure because it is fateful with regard to benefits and burdens, we must care equally about the ethic that sustains gender inequality, and inegalitarian incentives. And the simi-larity of our reasons for caring about these matters will make it lame to say: Ah, but only the caring about coercive structure is a caring about *justice*, in a certain distin-guishable sense. That thought is, I submit, incapable of coherent elaboration.[25]

My response to the basic-structure objection is now fully laid out; but before we proceed, in the sections that follow, to matters arising, it will be useful to rehearse, in compressed form, the arguments that were presented in [. . .] this book [. . .].

My original criticism of the incentives argument ran, in brief, as follows:

(1) Citizens in a just society adhere to its principles of justice.

But

(2) They do not adhere to the difference principle if they are acquisitive maxi-mizers in daily life.

Therefore

(3) In a society that is governed by the difference principle, citizens lack the acquisitiveness that the incentives argument attributes to them.

The basic-structure objection to that criticism is of this form:

(4) The principles of justice govern only the basic structure of a just society.

Therefore,

(5) Citizens in a just society may adhere to the difference principle whatever their choices may be within the structure it determines, and, in particular, even if their economic choices are entirely acquisitive.

Therefore,

(6) Proposition (2) lacks justification.

My preliminary reply to the basic-structure objection says:

(7) Proposition (5) is inconsistent with many Rawlsian statements about the relationship between citizens and principles of justice in a just society.

And my fundamental reply to the basic-structure objection says:

(8) Proposition (4) is unsustainable.

Let me emphasize that my rebuttal of the basic-structure objection does not *itself* establish that the difference principle properly evaluates not only state policy but everyday economic choice. [. . .] I do not say that *because* everyday choice cannot be, as the basic-structure objection says it is, beyond the reach of justice, simply because it is everyday choice, it then follows that everyday economic choice is indeed within its reach; that would be a non sequitur. I say, rather, that it is no objection to my argument for the claim that justice evaluates everyday economic choice that everyday choice is (in general) beyond the reach of justice, since it is not.

This point about the structure of my argument is easily missed, so let me explain it in a different way. I have not tried to show that a robust structure/choice distinction cannot be sustained in the case of the economy – that claim is false. What I argued is that choices within the economic structure cannot be placed outside the primary purview of justice *on the ground* that the only thing (quite generally) which is within its primary purview is structure. The family case refutes that *argument*. That refutation doesn't, I would agree, exclude treating economic choices like the choices of a game player who obeys the rules (and therefore plays not unjustly), while trying to score as many points as he can.[26]

3

So the personal is indeed political: personal choices to which the writ of the law is indifferent are fateful for social justice.

But that raises a huge question, with respect to *blame*. The injustice in distribution which reflects personal choices within a just coercive structure can plainly not be blamed on that structure itself, nor, therefore, on whoever legislated that structure. Must it, then, be blamed, in our two examples, on men[27] and on acquisitive people, respectively?

I shall presently address, and answer, that question about blame; but before I do so, I wish to explain why I could remain silent in the face of it – why, that is, my argument in criticism of Rawls's restricted application of the principles of justice requires no judgment about blaming individual choosers. The conclusion of my argument is that the principles of justice apply not only to coercive rules but also to the pattern in people's (legally) uncoerced choices. Now, if we judge a certain set of rules to be just or unjust, we need not add, as pendant to that judgment, that those who legislated the rules in question should be praised or blamed for what they did.[28] And something analogous applies when we come to see that the ambit of justice covers the pattern of choices in a society. We can believe whatever we are inclined to do about how responsible and/or culpable people are for their choices, and that includes believing that they are not responsible and/or culpable for them at all, while affirming the view on which I insist: that the pattern in such choices is relevant to how just or unjust a society is.

That said, let me now face the question of how blameable individuals are. It would be inappropriate to answer it here by first declaring my position, if indeed I have one, on the philosophical problem of the freedom of the will. Instead, I shall answer the question about blame on the pre-philosophical assumptions which inform our ordinary judgments about when, and how much, blame is appropriate. On such assumptions, we should avoid two opposite mistakes about how culpable chauvinistic men and self-seeking high fliers are. One is the mistake of saying: there is no ground for blaming these people *as individuals*, for they simply participate in an accepted social practice, however tawdry or awful that practice may be. That is a mistake, since people do have choices: it is, indeed, *only* their choices that reproduce social practices; and some, moreover, choose *against* the grain of nurture, habit, and self-interest. But one also must not say: look how each of these people shamefully decides to behave so badly. That, too, is unbalanced, since, although there exists personal choice, there is heavy social conditioning behind it and it can cost individuals a lot to depart from the prescribed and/or permitted ways. If we care about social justice, we have to look at four things: the coercive structure, other structures, the social ethos, and the choices of individuals: and judgment on the last of those must be informed by awareness of the power of the others. So, for example, a properly sensitive appreciation of these matters allows one to hold that an acquisitive ethos is profoundly unjust in its effects, without holding that those who are gripped by it are commensurately unjust. It is essential to apply principles of justice to dominant patterns in social behavior – that, as it were, is where the action is – but it doesn't follow that we should have a persecuting attitude to the people who display that behavior. We might have good reason to exonerate the perpetrators of injustice, but we should not deny, or apologize for, the injustice itself.[29]

On an extreme view, which I do not accept but need not reject, a typical husband in a thoroughly sexist society – one, that is, in which families in their overwhelming majority display an unjust division of domestic labor – is literally incapable of revising his behavior, or capable of revising it only at the cost of cracking up, to nobody's benefit. But even if that is true of typical husbands, we know it to be false of husbands in general. It is a plain empirical fact that some husbands are capable of revising their behavior, since some husbands have done so, in response to feminist criticism. These husbands, we could say, were moral pioneers. They made a path which becomes easier and easier to follow as more and more people follow it, until social pressures are so altered that it becomes harder to stick to sexist ways than to abandon them. That is a central way in which a social ethos changes. Or, for another example, consider the recent rise in environmental awareness. At first, only a few people bother to save and recycle their paper, plastic, and so forth, and they seem freaky because they do so. Then, more people start doing that, and, finally, it becomes not only difficult not to do it but easy to do it. It is pretty easy to discharge burdens that have become part of the normal round of everybody's life. Expectations determine behavior, behavior determines expectations, which determine behavior, and so on.

Are there circumstances in which a similar incremental process could occur with respect to economic behavior? I do not know. But I do know that universal maximizing is by no means a necessary feature of a market economy. For all that much of its industry was state-owned, the United Kingdom from 1945 to 1951 had a market economy. But salary differentials were nothing like as great as they were to become, or as they were then, in the United States. Yet, so I hazard, when British executives making five times what their workers did met American counterparts making fifteen times what their (anyhow better paid) workers did, many of the British executives would *not* have felt: *we* should press for more. For there was a social ethos of reconstruction after war, an ethos of common project, that moderated desire for personal gain. It is not for a philosopher to delimit the conditions under which such – and even more egalitarian – ethi can prevail. But a philosopher can say that a maximizing ethos is not a necessary feature of society, or even of a market society, and that, to the extent that such an ethos prevails, satisfaction of the difference principle is prejudiced.

In 1988, the ratio of top-executive salaries to production-worker wages was 6.5 to 1 in West Germany and 17.5 to 1 in the United States.[30] Since it is not plausible to think that Germany's lesser inequality was a disincentive to productivity, since it *is* plausible to think that an ethos which was relatively friendly to equality[31] protected German productivity in the face of relatively modest material incentives, we can conclude that the said ethos caused the worst paid to be better paid than they would have been under a different culture of reward. It follows, on my view of the matter, that the difference principle was better realized in Germany in 1988 than it would have been if its culture of reward had been more similar to that of the United States.[32] But Rawls cannot say that, since the smaller inequality that benefited the less well off in Germany was a matter not of law but of ethos. I think that Rawls's inability to regard

Germany as having done comparatively well with respect to the difference principle is a grave defect in his conception of the site of distributive justice.

4

I should like, now, to modify the distinction drawn in section 2 above between coercive and other social structure. The modification will strengthen my argument against the basic-structure objection.

The legally coercive structure of society functions in two ways. It *prevents* people from doing things by erecting insurmountable barriers (fences, police lines, prison walls, and so forth), and it *deters* people from doing things by ensuring that certain forms of unprevented behavior carry an (appreciable risk of) penalty.[33] The second (deterrent) aspect of coercive structure may be described counterfactually, in terms of what would or might happen to someone who elects the forbidden behavior: knowledge of the relevant counterfactual truths motivates the complying citizen's choices.

Not much pure prevention goes on within the informal structure of society: not none, but not much. Locking errant teenagers in their rooms would represent an instance of pure prevention, which, if predictable for determinate behavior, would count as part of a society's informal structure: it would be a rule in accordance with which that society operates. That being set aside, informal structure manifests itself in predictable sanctions such as criticism, disapproval, anger, refusal of future cooperation, ostracism, beating (of, for example, spouses who refuse sexual service), and so on.

Finally, to complete this conceptual review, the ethos of a society is the set of sentiments and attitudes in virtue of which its normal practices, and informal pressures, are what they are.

Now, the pressures that sustain the informal structure lack force save insofar as there is a normal practice of compliance with the rules they enforce. That is especially true of that great majority of pressures (beating does not belong to that majority) which have a moral coloring: criticism and disapproval are ineffective when they come from the mouths of those who ask others not to do what they do themselves. To be sure, that is not a conceptual truth, but a social-psychological one. Even so, it enables us to say that what people ordinarily do supports and partly constitutes (again, not conceptually, but in effect) the informal structure of society, in such a way that it makes no sense to pass judgments of justice on that structure while withholding such judgment from the behavior that supports and constitutes it; that point is crucial to the anti-Rawlsian inference presented in section 2 above.[34] Informal structure is not a behavioral pattern but a set of rules, yet the two are so closely related that, so one might say, they are *merely* categorically different. Accordingly, so I argued, to include (as one must) informal structure within the basic structure is to countenance behavior, too, as a primary object of judgments of justice.

Now, two truths about legally coercive structure might be thought to cast doubt on the contrast that I allowed between it and informal structure in section 2 above. First, although the legally coercive structure of society is indeed discernible in the ordinances of society's political constitution and law, those ordinances count as delineating it only on condition that they enjoy a broad measure of compliance.[35] And, second, legally coercive structure achieves its intended social effect only in and through the actions which constitute compliance with its rules.

In light of those truths, it might be thought that the dilemma I posed for Rawls (see section 2 above), and by means of which I sought to defeat his claim that justice judges structure *as opposed to* the actions of agents, was misframed. For I said, against that claim, that the required opposition between structure and actions works for coercive structure only, with respect to which a relevantly strong distinction can be drawn between structure-sustaining and structure-conforming action, but that coercive structure could not reasonably be thought to exhaust the structure falling within the purview of justice. Accordingly, so I concluded, justice must also judge (at least some) everyday actions.

The truths rehearsed two paragraphs back challenge that articulation of the distinction between coercive structure and action within it. They thereby also challenge the contrast drawn in section 2 between two relationships: that between coercive structure and action, and that between informal structure and action. And to the extent that the first relationship is more like the second, the first horn of the dilemma I posed for Rawls becomes sharper than it was. It is sharp not only for the reason I gave, namely, the consideration about "profound effect," but also for the same reason that the second horn is sharp, namely, that everyday behavior is too germane to the very existence of (even) coercive structure to be immune to the principles of justice that apply to the coercive structure.

The distinction, vis-à-vis action, between coercive and informal structure, so I judge, is more blurred than section 2 allowed – not, of course, because informal structure is more separable from action than I originally claimed, but because coercive structure is less separable from it than I originally allowed. Accordingly, even if the dilemma constructed in section 2 was for the stated reasons misframed, the upshot would hardly be congenial to Rawls's position – that justice judges structure rather than actions – it would, rather, be congenial to my own rejection of it. But I wish to emphasize that this putative strengthening of my argument is not essential. In my opinion, the argument was strong enough already.[35]

NOTES

1 Because of these tensions in Rawls, people have resisted my incentives critique of him in two opposite ways. Those convinced that his primary concern is the basic structure object [. . .]. But others do not realize how important that concern is to him: they accept my (as I see it, anti-Rawlsian) view that the difference principle should condemn incentives, but they believe that Rawls would also accept it, since they think his commitment to the principle is relevantly uncompromising. They therefore do not regard what I say about incentives as *a criticism* of Rawls.

   Those who respond in that second fashion seem not to realize that Rawls's liberalism is jeopardized if he takes the route that they think open to him. He then becomes a radical egalitarian socialist, whose outlook is very different from that of a liberal who holds that "deep inequalities" are "inevitable in the basic structure of any society" (*A Theory of Justice*, p. 7).

2 Rawls, *A Theory of Justice*, p. 105.

3 See, further, Cohen, "Incentives, Inequality, and Community," pp. 321–322; and idem, "The Pareto Argument for Inequality," pp. 178–179. Note that I do not here deny that there is *more* fraternity when high earners willingly submit to taxation shaped by the difference principle than when they insist on laissez-faire.

4 See, further, Cohen, "Incentives," pp. 320–321.

5 Rawls, *A Theory of Justice*, p. 528, my emphasis. See, further, [. . .] and Cohen, "Incentives," pp. 316–320.

6 Rawls, "Justice as Fairness: A Briefer Restatement," p. 154.

7 Rawls made this point in reply to a lecture that I gave at Harvard in March 1993.

8 That is, as (part of) a complete moral theory, as opposed to a purely political one. See, for explication of that distinction, Rawls, *Political Liberalism*, passim, in particular pp. xv–xvii, xliii–xlvii.

9 See Cohen, "Incentives," p. 322.

10 Though not necessarily an ethos embodying the very principles that the rules formulate; [. . .] Justice will be shown to require an ethos, and the basic structure objection will thereby be refuted, but it will be a contingent question whether the ethos required by justice can be discerned in the content of the just principles themselves. Still, as I suggested [. . .], the answer to this question is almost certainly yes.

11 That is, the subject matter that principles of justice judge. I follow Rawls's usage here – e.g., in the title of Lecture 7 of *Political Liberalism* ("The Basic Structure as Subject"). [. . .]

12 Throughout the rest of this lecture, I shall use "coercive," coercion," etc. to mean "legally coercive," "legal coercion," etc.

13 Thus, the difference principle, though pursued through (coercively sustained) state policy, cannot, so Rawls thinks, be aptly inscribed in a society's constitution. See Rawls, *Political Liberalism*, pp. 227–230.

14 Consider, for example, the passage from *A Theory of Justice* (pp. 7–8) in which the concept of the basic structure is introduced:

   "Our topic . . . is that of social justice. For us the primary subject of justice is the basic structure of society, or more exactly, the way in which the major social institutions distribute fundamental rights and duties and determine the division of advantages from social cooperation. By major institutions I understand the political constitution and the principal economic and social arrangements. Thus the legal protection of freedom of thought and liberty of conscience, competitive markets, private property in the means of production, and the monogamous family are examples of major social institutions. . . . I shall not consider the justice of institutions and social practices generally. . . . [The two principles of justice] may not work for the rules and practices of private associations or for those of less comprehensive social groups. They may be irrelevant for the various informal conventions and customs of everyday life; they may not elucidate the justice or, perhaps better, the fairness of voluntary cooperative arrangements or procedures for making contractual agreements."

I cannot tell from those statements what is to be included in, and what excluded from, the basic structure, nor, more particularly, whether coercion is the touchstone of inclusion. Take, for example, the case of the monogamous family. Is it simply its "legal protection" that is a major social institution, in line with a coercive definition of the basic structure (if not, perhaps, with the syntax of the relevant sentence)? Or is the monogamous family itself part of that structure? And, in that case, are its typical usages part of it? They certainly constitute a "principal social arrangement," yet they may also count as "practices of private associations or . . . of less comprehensive social groups," and they are heavily informed by the "conventions and customs of everyday life." (Section 5 of Rawls's essay "The Idea of Public Reason Revisited" offers an exceedingly interesting account of the family as a component of the basic structure. It does not, however, expressly address the question whether it is only in virtue of the coercive rules that govern it that the family belongs to that structure. But I think it tends, on the whole, to answer that question in the negative.)

Puzzlement with respect to the bounds of the basic structure is not relieved by examination of the relevant pages of *Political Liberalism* – to wit, 11, 68, 201–202, 229, 258, 268, 271–272, 282–283, and 301. Some formulations on those pages lean toward a coercive specification of the basic structure. Others do not.

15 [. . .]

16 I severely qualify this acceptance in section 4 below, and I thereby strengthen the present reply to the basic-structure objection.

17 In section 4 below, I entertain a doubt about the strength of the distinction drawn here, but, as I indicate, if that doubt is sound, then my case against Rawls is strengthened.

18 Rawls, *A Theory of Justice*, p. 7. "Present from the start" means, here, "present from birth"; see ibid., p. 96. But what matters, surely, is the asserted profundity of effect, whether or not it is "present from birth."

19 Or consider access to that primary good which Rawls calls "the social basis of self-respect." While the law may play a large role in securing that good to people vulnerable to racism, legally unregulable racist attitudes also have an enormous negative impact on how much of that primary good they get.

20 Rawls, *Political Liberalism*, p. 139.

21 Note that one can condemn the said practice without condemning those who engage in it. For there might be a collective action problem here, which weighs heavily on poor families in particular. If, in addition to discrimination in education, there is discrimination in employment, then a poor family might sacrifice a great deal through choosing evenhandedly across the sexes with whatever resources it can devote to its children's education. This illustrates the important distinction between condemning injustice and condemning the people whose actions perpetuate it. See further, section 3 below.

22 See the text to note 18 above.

23 Hugo Adam Bedau noticed that the family falls outside the basic structure, under the coercive specification of it often favored by Rawls, but he did not notice the connection between noncoercive structure and choice that I emphasize in the above sentence. See Bedau, "Social Justice and Social Institutions," p. 171.

24 That is, legislation which maximizes the size of the primary-goods bundle held by the worst off people, given whatever is correctly expected to be the pattern in the choices made by economic agents.

25 As Liam Murphy points out, Rawls's focus on just institutional structure is utterly implausible for the case where institutions are unjust. On Rawls's intrinsically institutional approach, the only duty of justice that then falls on individuals is to *promote* just institutions (rather than to *comply* with them, since they do not obtain). But the worst off might be better served in an unjust society through direct assistance, rather than through a possibly fruitless, or less productive, attempt to improve the justice of institutions. (Private communication, 19 January 1997. And see Murphy, "Institutions and the Demands of Justice.")

26 [...]

27 We can here set aside the fact that women often subscribe to, and inculcate, male-dominative practices.

28 We can distinguish between how unjust past practices (e.g., slavery) were and how unjust those who protected and benefited from those unjust practices were. Most of us (rightly) do not condemn Lincoln for his (conditional) willingness to tolerate slavery as strongly as we would a statesman who did the same in 1999, but the slavery institution itself was as unjust in Lincoln's time as it would be today.

What made slavery unjust in, say, Greece, is exactly what would make slavery (with, of course, the very same rules of subordination) unjust today – to wit, the content of its rules. But sound judgments about the justice and injustice of people are much more contextual; they must take into account the institutions under which people live, the prevailing level of intellectual and moral development, collective action problems such as the one delineated in note 21 above, and so forth. The morally best slave-holder might deserve admiration. The morally best form of slavery would not. (Of some relevance here is the brilliant discussion of "how far our rejection of [ancient slavery] . . . depends on modern conceptions that were not available in the ancient world" (p. 106) in Bernard Williams, *Shame and Necessity*, Chapter 5.)

29 See note 28.

30 See Mishel and Frankel, *The State of Working America*, p. 122.

31 That ethos need not have been a (relatively) egalitarian one. For present purposes, it could have been an ethos which disendorsed acquisitiveness as such (see note 10 above [. . .]), other than on *behalf* of the worst off. (I have here supposed that the stated difference in salary ratios was not due, or not wholly due, to social legislation that raised the wages of German workers, and/or other features of Germany's basic structure. If that supposition is false, the example can be treated as invented. It would still make the required point.)

32 And note how implausible it would be to say that Germany's (relatively speaking) equality-friendly ethos reduced the *liberty* of the German better off. I make this point in anticipation of the objection that my extension of the difference principle to everyday life violates the first principle of Rawlsian justice.

33 The distinction given above corresponds to that between the difficulty and the cost of actions [. . .]

34 See the last sentence of the fourth paragraph of section 2.

35 It does not follow that they are not *laws* unless they enjoy such compliance. Perhaps they are nevertheless laws, if they "satisfy a test set out in a Hartian rule of recognition, even if they are themselves neither complied with nor accepted" (Joshua Cohen, in comment on a draft of this lecture). But such laws (or "laws") are not plausibly represented as part of the basic structure of society, so the statement in the text can stand as it is.

36 My 1997 article "Where the Action Is" [. . .] has attracted a number of published and as yet unpublished responses. Among those that have been published of which I am aware, I should like to mention two very considerable ones.

The first is David Estlund's "Liberalism, Equality and Fraternity in Cohen's Critique of Rawls." Estlund exploits (in the best sense of the word) my friendliness to a Scheffler-like personal prerogative [. . .] to argue, very powerfully, that "inequality-producing incentives will still be required by many conscientious citizens exercising" not only that prerogative but three other "prerogatives that Cohen must allow" (p. 101). I believe that I would accede to some, but not all, of Estlund's criticism. I have to express myself in that guarded way because I have not had the time fully to take the measure of Estlund's critique. I am, however, fairly confident that the interesting position he develops is not, as he thinks it is, entirely consistent with Rawls's view, but a substantial revision of it, a kind of halfway house between Rawls's view and my own.

The other very considerable critique of "Where the Action Is" that I must mention is Andrew Williams' "Incentives, Inequality, and Publicity." In the course of a beautifully organized argument, Williams claims that my view that the difference principle must apply to economic choice fails the publicity requirement that Rawls says principles must satisfy to qualify as principles of justice, a requirement that Williams defends. I believe, however, that publicity, as Williams (following Rawls) explicates that notion, is demonstrably not a requirement of justice, and that the difference-principle-sensitive ethos that I require for justice meets every *defensible* publicity requirement on justice. These claims need, of course, to be argued, but I cannot provide the arguments for them here.

9

EQUALITY AND PRIORITY[1]

Derek Parfit

In his article 'Equality', Nagel imagines that he has two children, one healthy and happy, the other suffering from some painful handicap. Nagel's family could either move to a city where the second child could receive special treatment, or move to a suburb where the first child would flourish. Nagel writes:

> This is a difficult choice on any view. To make it a test for the value of equality, I want to suppose that the case has the following feature: the gain to the first child of moving to the suburb is substantially greater than the gain to the second child of moving to the city.

He then comments:

> If one chose to move to the city, it would be an egalitarian decision. It is more urgent to benefit the second child, even though the benefit we can give him is less than the benefit we can give to the first child.[2]

My aim, in this chapter, is to discuss this kind of reasoning.

1

Nagel's decision turns on the relative importance of two facts: he could give one child a greater benefit, but the other child is worse off. There are countless cases of this kind. In these cases, when we are choosing between two acts or policies, one relevant fact is how great the resulting benefits would be. For Utilitarians, that is all that matters. On their view, we should always aim for the greatest sum of benefits. But,

115

for egalitarians, it also matters how well off the beneficiaries would be. We should sometimes choose a smaller sum of benefits, for the sake of a better distribution.

Should we aim for a better distribution? If so, when and how? These are difficult questions, but their subject matter is, in a way, simple. It is enough to consider different possible states of affairs, or outcomes, each involving the same set of people. We imagine knowing how well off, in these outcomes, these people would be. We then ask whether either outcome would be better, or would be the outcome that we ought to bring about.

Some writers reject these questions. Nozick objects, for example, that these questions wrongly assume that there is something to be distributed. Most goods, he argues, are not up for distribution, or redistribution.[3] They are goods to which particular people already have entitlements, or special claims. Others make similar claims about desert.

These objections we can set aside. We can assume that, in the cases we are considering, no one deserves to be better off than anyone else; nor does anyone have special claims to whatever we are distributing. Since there are *some* cases of this kind, we have a subject. If we can reach conclusions, we can then consider how widely these apply. Like Rawls and others, I believe that, at the fundamental level, most cases are of this kind.

To ask my questions, we need only two assumptions. First, some people can be worse off than others, in ways that are morally relevant. Second, these differences can be matters of degree. To describe my imagined cases, I shall use figures. Nagel's choice, for example, can be shown as follows:

	The first child	The second child
Move to the city:	20	10
Move to the suburb:	25	9

Such figures misleadingly suggest precision. Even in principle, I believe, there could not be precise differences between how well off different people are. I intend these figures to show only that the choice between these outcomes makes much more difference to Nagel's first child, but that, in both outcomes, the second child would be much worse off.

One point about my figures is important. Each unit is a roughly equal benefit, however well off the person is who receives it. If someone rises from 99 to 100, this person benefits as much as someone else who rises from 9 to 10. Without this assumption we cannot ask some of our questions. Thus we cannot ask whether some benefit would matter more if it came to someone who was worse off.

Since each extra unit is an equal benefit, however well off the recipient is, these units should not be thought of as equal quantities of resources. The same increase in resources usually brings greater benefits to those who are worse off. But these benefits need not be thought of in Utilitarian terms, as involving greater happiness, or desire-fulfilment. They might be improvements in health, or length of life, or education, or range of opportunities, or involve any other goods that we take to be morally important.[4]

2

Most of us believe in some kind of equality. We believe in political equality, or equality before the law, or we believe that everyone has equal rights, or that everyone's interests should be given equal weight. Though these kinds of equality are of great importance, they are not my subject here. I am concerned with people's being *equally well off*. To be egalitarians, in my sense, this is the kind of equality in which we must believe.

Some egalitarians believe that, if people were equally well off, that would be a better state of affairs. If we hold this view, we can be called *Teleological* – or, for short, *Telic* – Egalitarians. We accept

> *The Principle of Equality*: It is in itself bad if some people are worse off than others.[5]

Suppose that the people in some community could all be either equally well off, or equally badly off. The Principle of Equality does not tell us that the second would be worse. To explain that obvious truth, we might appeal to

> *The Principle of Utility*: It is in itself better if people are better off.

When people would be on average better off, or would receive a greater sum of benefits, we can say, for brevity, that there would be more *utility*.

If we cared only about equality, we would be *Pure* Egalitarians. If we cared only about utility, we would be Utilitarians. Most of us accept a *pluralist* view: one that appeals to more than one principle or value. According to *Pluralist Egalitarians*, it would be better both if there was more equality, and if there was more utility. In deciding which of two outcomes would be better, we give weight to both these values.

These values may conflict. One of two outcomes may be in one way worse, because there would be more inequality, but in another way better, because there would be more utility. We must then decide which of these two facts would be more important. Consider, for example, the following possibilities:

117

(1) Everyone at 150
(2) Half at 199   Half at 200
(3) Half at 101   Half at 200

For Pure Egalitarians, (1) is the best outcome, since it contains the least inequality. For Utilitarians, (1) is the worst outcome, since it contains the least utility. For most Pluralist Egalitarians, (1) would be neither the best nor the worst of these outcomes. (1) would be, on balance, worse than (2), since it would be *much* worse in terms of utility, and only *slightly* better in terms of equality. Similarly, (1) would be better than (3), since it would be much better in terms of equality, and only slightly worse in terms of utility.

In many cases the Pluralist View is harder to apply. Compare

(1) Everyone at 150

with

(4) Half at N Half at 200.

If we are Pluralist Egalitarians, for which values of N would we believe (1) to be worse than (4)? For some range of values – such as 120 to 150 – we may find this question hard to answer. And it may not have an answer. The relative importance of equality and utility may be, even in principle, imprecise.

We should next distinguish two kinds of value. If we claim that equality is good, we may mean only that it has good effects. If people are unequal, for example, that can produce conflict, or damage the self-respect of those who are worst off, or put some people in the power of others. If we care about equality because we are concerned with such effects, we believe that equality has *instrumental* value, or is good as a means. But I am concerned with a different idea. For true Egalitarians, equality has *intrinsic* value, or is in itself good.

This distinction is important. If we believe that, besides having bad effects, inequality is in itself bad, we shall think it to be worse. And we shall think it bad even when it has no bad effects.

To illustrate this second point, consider what I shall call *the Divided World*. The two halves of the world's population are, we can suppose, unaware of each other's existence. Perhaps the Atlantic has not yet been crossed. Consider next two possible states of affairs:

(1) Half at 100   Half at 200
(2) Everyone at 145

Of these two states, (1) is in one way better than (2), since people are on average better off. But we may believe that, all things considered, (1) is worse than (2). How could we explain this view?

If we are Telic Egalitarians, our explanation would be this. While it is good that, in (1), people are on average better off, it is bad that some people are worse off than others. The badness of this inequality morally outweighs the extra benefits.

In making such a claim, we could not appeal to inequality's bad effects. Since the two halves of the world's population are quite unconnected, this inequality has no effects. If we are to claim that (1) is worse because of its inequality, we must claim that this inequality is in itself bad.[6]

3

We can now turn to a different kind of egalitarian view. According to *Deontic Egalitarians,* though we should sometimes aim for equality, that is *not* because we would thereby make the outcome better. On this view, it is not in itself bad if some people are worse off than others. When we ought to aim for equality, that is always for some other moral reason.

Such a view typically appeals to claims about *comparative* justice. Whether people are unjustly treated, in this comparative sense, depends on whether they are treated *differently* from other people. Thus it may be unfair if, in a distribution of resources, some people are denied their share. Fairness may require that, if certain goods are given to some, they should be given to all.

Another kind of justice is *non-comparative*. Whether people are unjustly treated, in this other sense, depends only on facts about them. It is irrelevant whether others are treated differently. Thus, if we treated no one as they deserved, this treatment would be unjust in the non-comparative sense. But, if we treated everyone equally unjustly, there would be no comparative injustice.[7]

It can be hard to distinguish these two kinds of justice, and there are difficult questions about the relation between them.[8] One point should be mentioned here. Non-comparative justice may require us to produce equality. Perhaps, if everyone were equally deserving, we should make everyone equally well off. But such equality would be merely the effect of giving people what they deserved. Only comparative justice makes equality our aim.

When I said that, in my examples, no one deserves to be better off than others, I did not mean that everyone is equally deserving. I meant that, in these cases, questions of desert do not arise. It is only comparative justice with which we are here concerned.

There is another relevant distinction. In some cases, justice is *purely procedural*. It requires only that we act in a certain way. For example, when some good cannot be divided, we may be required to conduct a lottery, which gives everyone an equal chance to receive this good. In other cases, justice is in part *substantive*. Here too, justice may require a certain kind of procedure; but there is a separate criterion of what the outcome ought to be. One example would be the claim that people should be given equal shares.[9]

We can now redescribe our two kinds of Egalitarianism. On the Telic View, inequality is bad; on the Deontic View, it is unjust.

It may be objected that, when inequality is unjust, it is, for that reason, bad. But this does not undermine this way of drawing our distinction. On the Deontic View, injustice is a special kind of badness, one that necessarily involves wrong-doing. What is unjust, and therefore bad, is not strictly the state of affairs, but the way in which it was produced.

There is one kind of case which most clearly separates these two views: those in which some inequality cannot be avoided. For Deontic Egalitarians, if nothing can be done, there can be no injustice. In Rawls's words, if some situation 'is unalterable . . . the question of justice does not arise.'[10]

Consider, for example, the inequality in our natural endowments. Some of us are born more talented or healthier than others, or are more fortunate in other ways. If we are Deontic Egalitarians, we shall not believe that such inequality is in itself bad. We might agree that, if we *could* distribute talents, it would be unjust or unfair to distribute them unequally. But, except when there are bad effects, we shall see nothing to regret in the inequalities produced by the random shuffling of our genes. Many Telic Egalitarians take a different view. They believe that, even when such inequality is unavoidable, it is in itself bad.[11]

These views differ in several other ways. The Telic View, for example, is likely to have wider scope. If we believe that inequality is in itself bad, we may think it bad whoever the people are between whom it holds. It may seem to make no difference whether these people are in the same or different communities. We may also think it irrelevant what the respects are in which some people are worse off than others: whether they have less income, or worse health, or are less fortunate in other ways. *Any* inequality, if undeserved and unchosen, we may think bad. Nor, third, will it seem to make a difference how such inequality arose. That is implied by the very notion of intrinsic badness. When we ask whether some state is in itself bad, it is irrelevant how it came about.

If we are Deontic Egalitarians, our view may have none of these features. Though there are many versions of the Deontic View, one large group are broadly contractarian. Such views often appeal to the idea of reciprocity, or mutual benefit. On some views of this kind, when goods are co-operatively produced, and no one has special claims, all the contributors should get equal shares. There are here two restrictions. First, what is shared are only the fruits of co-operation. Nothing is said about other goods, such as those that come from nature. Second, the distribution covers only those who produce these goods. Those who cannot contribute, such as the handicapped, or children, or future generations, have no claims.[12]

Other views of this kind are less restrictive. They may cover all the members of the same community, and all kinds of good. But they still exclude outsiders. It is irrelevant that, in other communities, there are people who are much worse off. On such views, if there is inequality between people in different communities, this need not be anyone's concern. Since the greatest inequalities are on this global scale, this restriction has immense importance.

Consider next the question of causation. The Telic View naturally applies to all cases. On this view, we always have a reason to prevent or reduce inequality, if we can. If we are Deontic Egalitarians, we might think the same; but that is less likely. Since our view is not about the goodness of outcomes, it may cover only inequalities that result from acts, or only those that are intentionally produced. And it may tell us to be concerned only with the inequalities that we ourselves produce. On such a view, when we are responsible for some distribution, we ought to distribute equally. But, when no one is responsible, inequality is not unjust. In such cases, there is nothing morally amiss. We have no reason to remove such inequality, by redistribution. Here again, since this view has narrower scope, this can make a great practical difference.

4

Let us now consider two objections to the Telic View.

On the widest version of this view, *any* inequality is bad. It is bad, for example, that some people are sighted and others are blind. We would therefore have a moral reason to take single eyes from the sighted and give them to the blind. That conclusion may seem horrific.

Such a reaction is, I believe, mistaken. To set aside some irrelevant complications, we can imagine a simplified example. Suppose that, after some genetic change, children are henceforth born as twins, one of whom is always blind. And suppose that, as a universal policy, operations are performed after every birth, in which one eye from the sighted twin is transplanted into its blind sibling. That would be non-voluntary redistribution, since new-born babies cannot give consent. But I am inclined to believe that such a policy would be justified.

Some people would reject this policy, believing that it violates the rights of the sighted twins. But that belief provides no ground for rejecting the Telic View. As pluralists, Telic Egalitarians could agree that the State should not redistribute organs. Since they do not believe equality to be the only value, they could agree that, in this example, some other principle has greater weight, or is overriding. Their belief is only that, if we all had one eye, this would be *in one way* better than if half of us had two eyes and the other half had none. Far from being horrific, that belief is clearly true. If we all had one eye, that would be much better for all of the people who would otherwise be blind.[13]

121

A second objection is more serious. If inequality is bad, its disappearance must be in one way a change for the better, however this change occurs. Suppose that, in some natural disaster, those who are better off lose all their extra resources, and become as badly off as everyone else. Since this change would remove the inequality, it must be in one way welcome, on the Telic View. Though this disaster would be worse for some people, and better for no one, it must be, in one way, a change for the better. Similarly, it would be in one way an improvement if we destroyed the eyes of the sighted, not to benefit the blind, but only to make the sighted blind. These implications can be more plausibly regarded as monstrous, or absurd. The appeal to such examples we can call *the Levelling Down Objection*.[14]

It is worth repeating that, to criticize Egalitarians by appealing to this objection, it is not enough to claim that it would be *wrong* to produce equality by levelling down. Since they are pluralists, who do not care only about equality, Egalitarians could accept that claim. Our objection must be that, if we achieve equality by levelling down, there is *nothing* good about what we have done. Similarly, if some natural disaster makes everyone equally badly off, that is not in any way good news. These claims do contradict the Telic Egalitarian View.

I shall return to the Levelling Down Objection. The point to notice now is that, on a Deontic view, we avoid this objection. If we are Deontic Egalitarians, we do not believe that inequality is bad, so we are not forced to admit that, on our view, it would be in one way better if inequality were removed by levelling down. We may believe that we have a reason to remove inequality only *when*, and only *because*, our way of doing so benefits the people who are worse off. Or we may believe that, when some people are worse off than others, through no fault or choice of theirs, they have a special claim to be raised up to the level of the others, but they have no claim that others be brought down to their level.

Given these differences between the Telic and Deontic Views, it is important to decide which view, if either, we should accept. If we are impressed by the Levelling Down Objection, we may be tempted by the Deontic View. But, if we give up the Telic View, we may find it harder to justify some of our beliefs. If inequality is not in itself bad, we may find it harder to defend our view that we should often redistribute resources. And some of our beliefs might have to go. Reconsider the Divided World, in which the two possible states are these:

(1) Half at 100   Half at 200
(2) Everyone at 145

In outcome (1) there is inequality. But, since the two groups are unaware of each other's existence, this inequality was not deliberately produced, or maintained. Since this inequality does not involve wrong-doing, there is no injustice. On the Deontic View, there is nothing more to say. If we believe that (1) is worse, and because of the inequality we must accept the Telic form of the Egalitarian View. We must claim that the inequality in (1) is in itself bad.

We might, however, give a different explanation. Rather than believing in equality, we might be especially concerned about those people who are worse off. That could be our reason for preferring (2).

Let us now consider this alternative.

5

In discussing his imagined case, Nagel writes:

> If one chose to move to the city, it would be an egalitarian decision. It is more urgent to benefit the second child . . . This urgency is not necessarily decisive. It may be outweighed by other considerations, for equality is not the only value. But it is a factor, and it depends on the worse off position of the second child. An improvement in his situation is more important than an equal or somewhat greater improvement in the situation of the first child.[15]

This passage contains the idea that equality has value. But it gives more prominence to another idea. It is more important, Nagel claims, to benefit the child who is worse off. That idea can lead us to a quite different view.

Consider first those people who are badly off: those who are suffering, or those whose basic needs have not been met. It is widely believed that we should give priority to helping such people. This would be claimed even by Utilitarians, since, if people are badly off, they are likely to be easier to help.

Nagel, and others, make a stronger claim. On their view, it is more urgent to help these people even if they are *harder* to help. While Utilitarians claim that we should give these people priority when, and because, we can help them *more*, this view claims that we should give them priority, even when we can help them *less*.

Some people apply this view only to the two groups of the well off and the badly off.[16] But I shall consider a broader view, which applies to everyone. On what I shall call

The Priority View: Benefiting people matters more the worse off these people are.

For Utilitarians, the moral importance of each benefit depends only on how great this benefit would be. For *Prioritarians*, it also depends on how well off the person is to whom this benefit comes. We should not give equal weight to equal benefits, whoever receives them. Benefits to the worse off should be given more weight.[17] This priority is not, however, absolute. On this view, benefits to the worse off could be morally outweighed by sufficiently great benefits to the better off. If we ask what would be sufficient, there may not always be a precise answer. But there would be many cases in which the answer would be clear.[18]

On the Priority View, I have said, it is more important to benefit those who are worse off. But this claim does not, by itself, amount to a different view, since it would be made by all Egalitarians. If we believe that we should aim for equality, we shall think it more important to benefit those who are worse off, since such benefits reduce inequality. If *this* is why we give such benefits priority, we do not hold the Priority View. On this view, as I define it here, we do *not* believe in equality. We do not think it in itself bad, or unjust, that some people are worse off than others. That is what makes this a distinctive view.

The Priority View can be easily misunderstood. On this view, if I am worse off than you, benefits to me matter more. Is this *because* I am worse off than you? In one sense, yes. But this has nothing to do with my relation to you.

It may help to use this analogy. People at higher altitudes find it harder to breathe. Is this because they are higher up than other people? In one sense, yes. But they would find it just as hard to breathe even if there were no other people who were lower down. In the same way, on the Priority View, benefits to the worse off matter more, but that is only because these people are at a lower *absolute* level. It is irrelevant that these people are worse off *than others*. Benefits to them would matter just as much even if there *were* no others who were better off.

The chief difference is, then, this. Egalitarians are concerned with *relativities*: with how each person's level compares with the level of other people. On the Priority View, we are concerned only with people's absolute levels. This is a fundamental structural difference. Because of this difference, there are several ways in which these views have different implications.

One example concerns scope. Telic Egalitarians may, I have said, give their view wide scope. They may believe that inequality is bad even when it holds between people who have no connections with each other. This may seem dubious. Why would it matter if, in some far off land, and quite unknown to me, there are other people who are better off than me?

On the Priority View, there is no ground for such doubts. This view naturally has universal scope. If it is more important to benefit one of two people, because this person is worse off, it is irrelevant whether these people are in the same community, or are aware of each other's existence. The greater urgency of benefiting this person does not depend on her relation to the other person, but only on her lower absolute level.

These views differ in other ways, which I have no space to discuss here. But I have described the kind of case in which these views most deeply disagree. These are the cases which raise the Levelling Down Objection. Egalitarians face this objection because they believe that inequality is in itself bad. If we accept the Priority View, we avoid this objection. On this view, except when it is bad for people, inequality does not matter.

6

Though equality and priority are different ideas, this distinction has been often over-looked.

One reason is that, especially in earlier centuries, Egalitarians have often fought battles in which this distinction did not arise. They were demanding legal or political equality, or attacking arbitrary privileges, or differences in status. These are not the kinds of good to which our distinction applies. And it is here that the demand for equality is most plausible.

Second, when Egalitarians considered other kinds of good, they often assumed that, if equality were achieved, this would either increase the sum of these goods, or would at least not reduce this sum. In either of these cases, equality and priority cannot conflict.

Third, even when a move to equality would reduce the total sum of benefits, Egalitarians often assumed that such a move would at least bring *some* benefits to the people who were worse off. In such cases, equality and priority could not deeply conflict. Egalitarians ignored the cases in which equality could not be achieved except by levelling down.

Since this distinction has been overlooked, some writers have made claims that are not really about equality, and would be better stated as claims about priority. For example, Nagel writes:

> To defend equality as a good in itself, one would have to argue that improvements in the lot of people lower on the scale of well-being took priority over greater improvements to those higher on the scale.[19]

In the example with which we began, Nagel similarly claims that it would be 'more urgent' to benefit the handicapped child. He then writes:

> This urgency is not necessarily decisive. It may be outweighed by other considerations, for equality is not the only value.[20]

These remarks suggest that, to the question 'Why is it more urgent to benefit this child?', Nagel would answer, 'Because this would reduce the inequality between these two children'. But I doubt that this is really Nagel's view. Would it be just as urgent to benefit the handicapped child, even if he had no sibling who was better off? I suspect that, on Nagel's view, it would. Nagel would then, though using the language of equality, really be appealing to the Priority View.[21]

Consider next the idea of distribution according to need. Several writers argue that, when we are moved by this idea, our aim is to achieve equality. Thus Raphael writes:

125

If the man with greater needs is given more than the man with lesser needs, the intended result is that each of them should have (or at least approach) the same level of satisfaction; the inequality of nature is corrected.[22]

When discussing the giving of extra resources to meet the needs of the ill, or handicapped, Norman similarly writes:

the underlying idea is one of equality. The aim is that everybody should, as far as possible, have an equally worthwhile life.[23]

As before, if that were the aim, it could be as well achieved by levelling down. This cannot be what Norman means. He could avoid this implication by omitting the word 'equally', so that his claim became: 'the aim is that everybody should, as far as possible, have a worthwhile life.' With this revision, Norman could not claim that equality is the underlying idea. But that, I believe, would strengthen his position. Distribution according to need is better regarded as a form of the Priority View.[24]

What these writers claim about need, some have claimed about all kinds of distributive principle. For example, Ake writes:

Justice in a society as a whole ought to be understood as a complete equality of the overall level of benefits and burdens of each member of that society.

The various principles of distributive justice, Ake claims, can all be interpreted as having as their aim 'to restore a situation of complete equality to the greatest degree possible'.[25] Some writers even make such claims about retributive justice. They argue that, by committing crimes, criminals make themselves better off than those who keep the law. The aim of punishment is to restore them to their previous level.

These writers, I believe, claim too much for equality. But there are some plausible views which are rightly expressed in egalitarian terms. For example, Cohen suggests that 'the right reading of egalitarianism' is that 'its purpose is to eliminate involuntary disadvantage'.[26] He means by this *comparative* disadvantage: being worse off than others. This is an essentially relational idea. Only equality could eliminate such disadvantage. Cohen's view could not be re-expressed in the language of priority. Similar assumptions underlie Rawls's view, whose complexity leads me to ignore it here.

Some Egalitarians are not moved by the Levelling Down Objection. For example, Ake writes

What about the case of someone who suddenly comes into good fortune, perhaps entirely by his or her own efforts? Should additional burdens . . . be imposed on that person in order to restore equality and safeguard justice? . . . Why wouldn't it be just to impose any kind of additional burden whatsoever on him in order to restore the equality? The answer is that, strictly speaking, it would be.[27]

Ake admits that, on his view, it *would* be just to level down, by imposing burdens on this person. What he concedes is only that the claim of justice would here be over-ridden. Levelling down would be in one way good, or be something that we would have a moral reason to do. Similarly, Temkin writes:

> I, for one, believe that inequality is bad. But do I *really* think that there is some respect in which a world where only some are blind is worse than one where all are? Yes. Does this mean I think it would be better if we blinded everybody? No. Equality is not all that matters.[28]

Several other writers make such claims.[29]

7

Since some writers are unmoved by the Levelling Down Objection, let us now recon-sider that objection. Consider these alternatives:

(1) Everyone at some level
(2) Some at this level   Others better off

In outcome (1) everyone is equally well off. In outcome (2), some people are better off, but in a way that is worse for no one. For Telic Egalitarians, the inequality in (2) is in itself bad. Could this make (2), all things considered, a worse outcome than (1)?

Some Egalitarians answer Yes. These people do not believe that the avoidance of inequality always matters most. But they regard inequality as a great evil. On their view, a move to inequality can make an outcome worse, even when this outcome would be better for everyone. Those who hold this view we can call *Strong Egalitarians*.

Others hold a different view. Since they believe that inequality is bad, they agree that outcome (2) is *in one way* worse than outcome (1). But they do not believe that (2) is worse all things considered. In a move from (1) to (2), some people would become better off. According to these Egalitarians, the loss of equality would be morally outweighed by the benefits to these people. (2) would be, on balance, better than (1). Those who hold this view we can call *Moderates*.

This version of Egalitarianism is often overlooked, or dismissed. People assume that, if we are Egalitarians, we must be against a move to inequality, even when this move would be bad for no one. If we regard such inequality as outweighed by the extra benefits, our view must, they assume, be trivial.[30]

That assumption is mistaken. If some change would increase inequality, but in a way that is worse for no one, the inequality must come from benefits to certain people. And there cannot be a *great* loss of equality unless these benefits are also great. Since these gains and losses would roughly march in step, there is room for Moderates to hold a significant position. They believe that, in all such cases, the gain in utility would outweigh the loss in equality.

That is consistent with the claim that, in many other cases, that would not be so. Moderates can claim that *some* gains in utility, even if *great*, would *not* outweigh some losses in equality. Consider, for example, these alternatives:

(1) All at 100
(4) Half at 100   Half at 200
(5) Half at 70   Half at 200.

Moderates believe that, compared with (1), (4) is better. But they might claim that (5) is worse. Since (5) would involve a much greater sum of benefits, that is not a trivial claim.

Return now to the Levelling Down Objection. Strong Egalitarians believe that, in some cases, a move towards inequality, even though it would be worse for no one, would make the outcome worse.[31] This view may seem incredible. One of two outcomes *cannot* be worse, we may claim, if it would be worse for no one. To challenge Strong Egalitarians, it would be enough to defend this claim. To challenge Moderates, we must defend the stronger claim that, when inequality is worse for no one, it is not in any way bad.

Many of us would make this stronger claim. It is widely assumed that nothing can be bad if it is bad for no one. This we can call the *Person-affecting View*.

This view might be defended by an appeal to some account of the nature of morality, or moral reasoning. According to some writers, for example, to explain the impersonal sense in which one of two outcomes can be worse – or worse, period – we must appeal to claims about what would be worse *for* particular people. The Person-affecting View can also be supported by various kinds of contractualism.[32]

Egalitarians might reply by defending a different meta-ethical view. Or they might argue that, when the Person-affecting View is applied to certain other questions, it has unacceptable implications, since it conflicts too sharply with some of our beliefs.[33] Since I have no space to discuss these questions here, I shall merely express an opinion. The Person-affecting View has, I believe, less plausibility than, and cannot be used to strengthen, the Levelling Down Objection.

8

I shall now summarise what I have claimed. According to Telic Egalitarians, it is in itself bad, or unfair, if some people are worse off than others through no fault or choice of theirs. Though this view is widely held, and can seem very plausible, it faces the Levelling Down Objection. This objection seems to me to have great force, but is not, I think, decisive.

Suppose that we began by being Telic Egalitarians, but we are convinced by this objection. We cannot believe that, if the removal of inequality would be bad for some people, and better for no one, this change would be in any way good. If we are to salvage something of our view, we then have two alternatives.

We might become Deontic Egalitarians. We might come to believe that, though we should sometimes aim for equality, that is not because we would thereby make the outcome better. We must then explain and defend our beliefs in some other way. And the resulting view may have narrower scope. For example, it may apply only to goods of certain kinds, such as those that are co-operatively produced, and it may apply only to inequality between members of the same community.

We may also have to abandon some of our beliefs. Reconsider the Divided World:

(1) Half at 100   Half at 200
(2) Everyone at 145

On the Deontic View, we cannot claim that it would be better if the situation changed from (1) to (2). This view is only about what people ought to do, and makes no comparisons between states of affairs.

Our alternative is to move to the Priority View. We could then keep our belief about the Divided World. It is true that, in a change from (1) to (2), the better off would lose more than the worse off would gain. That is why, in utilitarian terms, (2) is worse than (1). But, on the Priority View, though the better off would lose more, the gains to the worse off count for more. Benefits to the worse off do more to make the outcome better. That could be why (1) is worse than (2).

The views that I have been discussing often coincide. But, as I have tried to show, they are quite different. They can support different beliefs, and policies, and they can be challenged and defended in different ways. Taxonomy, though unexciting, needs to be done. Until we have a clearer view of the alternatives, we cannot hope to decide which view is true, or is the best view.

NOTES

1   This paper is a greatly shortened version of my Lindley Lecture 'Equality or Priority?' (42 pp.), published by the University of Kansas in 1995. That lecture owes much to the ideas of, or comments from, Brian Barry, David Brink, John Broome, Jerry Cohen, Robert Goodin, James Griffin, Shelley Kagan, Dennis McKerlie, David Miller, Thomas Nagel, Robert Nozick, Richard Norman, Ingmar Persson, Janet Radcliffe Richards, Joseph Raz, Thomas Scanlon, and Larry Temkin.

2   Thomas Nagel, *Mortal Question* (Cambridge: Cambridge University Press, 1979), pages 123–4. See also Nagel's *Equality and Partiality* (New York: Oxford University Press, 1991).

3   Robert Nozick, *Anarchy, State, and Utopia* (New York: Basic Books, 1974), pages 149–50.

4   For two such broader accounts of well-being, see Amartya Sen, 'Capability and Well-Being', in *The Quality of Life*, edited by Martha Nussbaum and Amartya Sen (Oxford: Oxford University Press, 1993), Amartya Sen, *Inequality Reexamined* (Oxford: Oxford University Press, 1992), Chapter 3; and Thomas Scanlon, 'Value, Desire, and the Quality of Life', in Nussbaum and Sen, op. cit.

5   We might add, 'through no fault or choice of theirs'. In a fuller statement of this principle, we would need to assess the relative badness of different patterns of inequality. But we can here ignore these complications. They are well discussed in Larry Temkin's *Inequality* (New York: Oxford University Press, 1993).

6   In his paper [. . .], which I cannot properly discuss here, Richard Norman writes: [Parfit] asks us whether (1) is worse that (2). I have to confess that I do not know how to answer that question, and I do not think that this is simply a personal confession on my part. . . . I want to say of Parfit's Divided world example that when you abstract the question from the social context in which we make judgements about equality and inequality, it is no longer clear how to answer it' [. . .]. It is, I agree, not obvious whether the inequality in (1) is bad. But that it is not because we cannot make value judgments about such examples. It is clear that (1) would be better than

(3) Half at 100, Half at 50,

but worse than

(4) Everyone at 200.

7   Cf. Joel Feinberg, 'Noncomparative Justice', *Philosophical Review*, 83 (1974).

8   Cf. Philip Montague, Comparative and Non-comparative Justice', *Philosophical Quarterly*, 30 (1980).

9   There is an intermediate case. Justice may require a certain outcome, but only because this avoids a procedural flaw. One such flaw is partiality. Suppose that we have to distribute certain publicly owned goods. If we could easily divide these goods, others might be rightly suspicious if we gave to different people unequal shares. That might involve favouritism, or wrongful discrimination. We may thus believe that, to avoid these flaws, we should distribute these goods equally.

How does this view differ from a view that requires equality for substantive reasons? One difference is this. Suppose that we have manifestly tried to distribute equally, but our procedure has innocently failed. If we aimed for equality only to avoid the taint of partiality or discrimination, there would be no case for correcting the result. (For discussions of these points, see Robert Goodin, 'Egalitarianism, Fetishistic and Otherwise', *Ethics*, 98 (1987); and Lawrence Sager and Lewis Kornhauser, 'Just Lotteries', *Social Science Information* (Sage, London, Newbury Park and New Delhi, Vol 27, 1988).)

10 John Rawls, *A Theory of Justice* (Cambridge: Harvard University Press, 1971), page 291.

11 There is now a complication. Those who hold this second view do not merely think that such inequality is bad. They often speak of natural injustice. On their view, it is unjust or unfair that some people are born less able, or less healthy, than others. Similarly, it is unfair if nature bestows on some richer resources. Talk of unfairness here is sometimes claimed to make no sense. I believe that it does make sense. But, even on this view, our distinction stands. According to Telic Egalitarians, it is the state of affairs which is bad, or unjust; but Deontic Egalitarians are concerned only with what we ought to do.

12 See, for example, David Gauthier, *Morals by Agreement* (Oxford: Oxford University Press, 1980), pages 18 and 268.

13 Cf. Nozick, op. cit., page 206 (though Nozick's target here is not the Principle of Equality but Rawls's Difference Principle).

14 Such an objection is suggested, for example, in Joseph Raz, *The Morality of Freedom* (Oxford: Oxford University Press, 1986), Chapter 9, and Larry Temkin, op. cit., pages 247–8.

15 Nagel, op. cit., page 124.

16 Cf. H. Frankfurt, *The Importance of What We Care About* (Cambridge: Cambridge University Press, 1988), Chapter 11, and Joseph Raz, op. cit., Chapter 9.

17 Several other writers have suggested such a view. See, for example, Thomas Scanlon, 'Nozick on Rights, Liberty, and Property', *Philosophy & Public Affairs*, 6 (1976), pages 6 to 10, Joseph Raz, op. cit., Harry Frankfurt, 'Equality as a Moral Ideal', in *The Importance of What We Care About* (Cambridge: Cambridge University Press, 1988), David Wiggins, 'Claims of Need', in his *Needs, Values, Truth* (Oxford: Blackwell, 1987), Dennis McKerlie, 'Egalitarianism', *Dialogue*, 23 (1984), and 'Equality and Priority', *Utilitas*, 6 (1994).

18 Like the belief in equality, the Priority View can take either Telic or Deontic forms. It can be a view about which outcomes would be better, or a view that is only about what we ought to do. But, for our purposes here, this difference does not matter.

19 *Reading Nozick*, edited by Jeffrey Paul (Oxford: Blackwell, 1981), page 203.

20 Op. cit., p. 124.

21 Similar remarks apply to section 117 of my *Reasons and Persons* (Oxford: Oxford University Press, 1984). For a later discussion of the choice between these views, see Nagel's *Equality and Partiality*, op. cit., Chapters 7 and 8.

22 D.D. Raphael, *Justice and Liberty* (London: Athlone Press, 1980), page 10. Cf. page 49.

23 Richard Norman, *Free and Equal* (Oxford: Oxford University Press, 1987), page 80.

24 See, however, the excellent discussion in David Miller, 'Social Justice and the Principle of Need', in *The Frontiers of Political Theory*, ed. Michael Freeman and David Robertson (Brighton: Harvester Press, 1980).

25 Christopher Ake, 'Justice as Equality', *Philosophy & Public Affairs*, 5 (1975), pages 71 and 77.

26 G.A. Cohen, 'On the Currency of Egalitarian Justice', *Ethics*, 99 (1989).

27 Op cit., page 73.

28 *Inequality*, page 282.

29 See, for example, Amartya Sen, *Inequality Reexamined* (Oxford: Oxford University Press, 1992), pages 92–3.

30 See, for example, Antony Flew, *The Politics of Procrustes* (Buffalo, New York: Prometheus, 1981), page 26. McKerlie, 'Egalitarianism', op. cit., p. 232. See also Nozick, op. cit., p. 211.

31 I am assuming here that inequality is not in itself bad for people. It is not bad for me if, unknown to me and without affecting me, there exist some other people who are better off

than me. That assumption is implied, not only by hedonistic theories about well-being, but also by plausible versions both of desire-fulfilment theories, and of theories that appeal to what Scanlon calls *substantive goods*. For a contrary view, however, which would need a further discussion, see John Broome, *Weighing Goods* (Oxford: Blackwell, 1991), Chapter 9.

32 Such as the view advanced in Thomas Scanlon's 'Contractualism and Utilitarianism', in ed. Amartya Sen and Bernard Williams, *Utilitarianism and Beyond* (Cambridge: Cambridge University Press, 1982).

33 See Temkin, op. cit., Chapter 9. Another objection to the Person-affecting View comes from what I have called the *Non-Identity Problem* (in my *Reasons and Persons*), Chapter 16).

FURTHER READING

Anderson, E.S. (1999). 'What Is the Point of Equality?' *Ethics* 109(2): 287–337.

Arneson, R.J. (1989). 'Equality and Equal Opportunity for Welfare.' *Philosophical Studies* 55: 77–93.

Cohen, G.A. (1989). 'On the currency of egalitarian justice,' *Ethics* 99: 906–44.

Dworkin, R.M. (2000). *Sovereign Virtue*, Harvard University Press.

Nagel, T. (1991). *Equality and Partiality*. New York, Oxford University Press.

Scheffler, S. (1992). 'Responsibility, Reactive Attitudes and Liberalism in Philosophy and Politics.' *Philosophy and Public Affairs* 21(4): 10 pages.

Sen, A. (1982). 'Rights and Agency.' *Philosophy and Public Affairs* 11: 3–39.

Temkin, L.S. (1993). *Inequality*. OUP.

Wolff, J. (1998). 'Fairness, Respect, and the Egalitarian Ethos.' *Philosophy and Public Affairs* 27(2): 97–122.

Part 3

LIBERALISM AND COMMUNITARIANISM

Introduction

LIBERAL POLITICAL PHILOSOPHY RECEIVED an enormous boost in 1971 with the publication of *A Theory of Justice* by John Rawls. The book appeared to provide (and arguably did provide) a reasoned and convincing defence of a liberal conception of justice. As with any book of comparable stature, it provoked much response from a wide range of opponents. Objections from within moral philosophy included scepticism about Rawls' methodology, and the rejection of consequentialism as a principle of distributive justice. From political philosophy there were Marxist-inspired criticisms that saw in Rawls a regrettable return to liberal individualism. Over the next thirty years, the latter became distanced from their Marxist roots, and evolved into what came to be called 'communitarian' objections to liberalism. You will need to judge for yourselves the extent to which the various criticisms referred to thus deserve a common label.

The first reading in this section is an excerpt from Michael Sandel's influential book, *Liberalism and the Limits of Justice* (Cambridge: Cambridge University Press, 1982). One theme of that book is that justice should not dominate our lives; it should not, for example, govern relations between friends. That theme is not, however, the focus of this excerpt. Instead we focus on two further themes: the 'unencumbered self' and the role of desert.

The first theme is an examination of the theoretical foundations of what Sandel calls 'deontological liberalism'. The core thesis of this is that society, which is composed of a plurality of persons each with their own conception of the good life, should organise itself in a way that favours none of these conceptions. This is sometimes put by saying that 'the right' (that is, the right way to run politics) is prior to that of 'the good' (that is, individual ideals of a good life) (Rawls 1999: 27–28). Sandel examines the notion of the self this presupposes. He rejects what he calls 'the sociological objection' to deontological liberalism: namely, the claim that it is undermined by the fact that our individual values are shaped by social conditions. Instead, he argues that deontological liberalism supposes that when we are arguing about what is right for society, we can extract ourselves from our conceptions of the good (as the right is neutral with respect to the good). Hence, we can in theory distance ourselves from our ideal of a good life and remain ourselves. Against this Sandel argues that 'my enduring attachments and commitments . . . partly define the person I am'. Hence, the attenuated self supposed by deontological liberalism is going to ignore or distort fundamental issues. It is worth reading what Sandel says carefully; his objection is not that liberalism implies that we are 'beings without purpose or incapable of moral ties'. The point is narrower; it is that we cannot stand back and regard our conceptions of the good as a matter of choice. The second theme examines Rawls' attitude to desert. As indicated in the

Introduction to this Reader, Rawls' view is that our considered opinion on justice is that people do not deserve their natural assets, any more than they deserve anything else they have as a matter of brute contingency (Rawls 1999: 13–14). Sandel considers a reply to this by Robert Nozick: that desert rests on attributes that we just have – 'It needn't be that the foundations underlying desert are themselves deserved, *all the way down*' (Nozick 1974: 225). However, the conception of the self discussed above can rescue Rawls here. Nozick's view depends on there being a self with a certain attribute (say, strength) and it not making sense to ask whether or not the person deserves that attribute. It is part of what the person is that they are strong. However, Rawls' conception is of a self we can think of independently of its attributes. If this is the case, we can ask whether those attributes *are* deserved. There is an additional discussion here concerning Rawls' views on the punishment of offenders. It seems to be part of Rawls' view of the justification of punishment that it is bound up with desert. This is doubtfully consistent with his overall position, but, as Sandel says, this inconsistency 'need not do serious damage to the theory as a whole'.

There are a number of questions you should ask yourself in reading this extract. Is our conception of the good so bound up with identity that we *cannot* stand back from it and regard it as a matter of choice? Do we *deserve* the consequences of our natural endowments? If the answer to either of these questions is 'yes', then Sandel's attack on deontological liberalism has struck home.

A Theory of Justice appeared in a revised second edition in 1999. Rawls also continued to develop his thought in a number of papers, and a major restatement of his views appeared in *Political Liberalism* in 1993. Our second paper is from this period (published in 1989). Although the focus has changed, Rawls' views have not, I think, altered radically. I shall outline the main thread of 'The Domain of the Political and Overlapping Consensus' before commenting on the differences between the views expressed here and the views expressed in *A Theory of Justice*.

First, let us clarify the problem Rawls is trying to solve. There are, he says, some general facts about sociology and psychology, some of which (at least) are not 'mere historical conditions that soon pass away' but 'a permanent feature of the public culture of democracy'. In summary, these describe a society with many different 'comprehensive doctrines'. A doctrine is comprehensive 'when it includes conceptions of what is of value in human life, ideals of personal virtue and character, and the like, that inform much of our nonpolitical conduct'. The imposition of any particular comprehensive doctrine in the political sphere would require the oppressive use of state power. Hence, we need a 'public basis for justification . . . that widely different and even irreconcilable comprehensive doctrines can endorse'. The problem is to formulate this 'domain of the political'.

Rawls' account comes in two stages. For the first he appeals to 'certain fundamental intuitive ideas' to come up with 'free standing political conception' of justice as fairness. Briefly stated, it requires that the domain of the political uses justifications that do not favour any particular comprehensive conception. In other words, political discourse must appeal to the reason of everyone affected by the decision, regardless of his or her comprehensive conception of the good. It is only when the conception of justice has been formulated that 'overlapping consensus' is introduced at the second stage. A society governed by the principle of justice so formulated will aim to acquire allegiance from everyone, regardless of their conception of the good, to make those institutions stable. There will not be a strict divide between conceptions of the good and the domain of the political; rather, as justice is recognised to be valuable, the domain of the political will be a part of each of the conceptions of the good that flourish in that society. This in turn will make it possible to appeal, from the domain of the political, to each person in that society in their own terms.

What is the contrast with the earlier work? Rawls explicitly warns us against taking his view to be that our conception of justice is simply grounded in contingent political realities. Rather, as he says himself, it is that the notion of the political conception is broader than justice as fairness (and has it as a part). In addition, justice as fairness in now explicitly characterised as a free-standing political conception and not a comprehensive doctrine. This allows Rawls to pay much greater attention to the pluralism to which his earlier views in fact lead. One issue you might like to think about when reading this paper is the extent to which justice as fairness is universal. Philosophers schooled in ethical theory tend to focus on the question as to whether or not ethical claims are necessary. If they are necessary, then it follows that they apply universally (even if the claims are not recognised locally). From Rawls' gnomic comments on this question, I think we will get further if we recognise more than a simple 'yes' or 'no' to answer the question of universality. It is clear that Rawls does not think his account applies, as a matter of fact, to all societies. However, some such account is a necessary part of democratic institutions (because pluralism is inevitable in a constitutional democracy). Second, the requirements of 'a just international society' will inevitably put pressure on states to become constitutional democracies, and hence fall within the range of Rawls' account.

Finally, you might like to consider the question of whether the domain of the political is, as claimed, not a comprehensive conception of the good. You might think there is a circularity here. Rawls claims that the institutions are made stable by being grounded in an overlapping consensus of reasonable conceptions of the good. However, a conception of the good is only reasonable if it is willing to participate in public reason (and so be part of that overlapping consensus). Is liberalism committed to coercing those it does not see as reasonable? Is it, then, as neutral as it claims?

Amy Gutmann's contribution came out, as you will see from her footnotes, after some important re-statements by Rawls, but before both *Political Liberalism* and the previous chapter in this Reader. In it she replies to two 'communitarian' critics of liberalism. In doing so, she also states clearly that to which she thinks the liberal is committed. Communitarianism is not so much a clearly defined position as a tendency of thought, characterised by the view that liberalism, for various reasons, overestimates the individual as the bearer of value at the expense of goods inherent in community.

The first of the two critics Gutmann responds to is Michael Sandel. She argues that Sandel is wrong in thinking that liberalism presupposes some doubtful metaphysics, arguing instead that it is a response to certain facts about contemporary pluralistic society. Two points in this counter argument deserve particular attention. Gutmann points out an embarrassment for the communitarian. If our identities are taken partly from the values of our community, then our identities will include a commitment to liberal justice (as liberal justice is a feature of modern constitutional democracies). Hence, there is a pragmatic inconsistency in communitarian opposition to liberalism (cf. Waldron 1989). Second, Gutmann admits that liberalism is committed to rejecting something Sandel affirms: namely, that our identities can be so determined by community given ends that we cannot stand back from our conceptions of what is good so as to appreciate the value of justice. Here we seem to have a straightforward clash of views.

The second critic to whom Gutmann responds is Alasdair MacIntyre. MacIntyre, according to Gutmann, argues that our ethical beliefs once made sense; when they were grounded in a different type of society. In our society such beliefs, especially beliefs in rights, are not so grounded. Gutmann's response is to argue that, unlike ancient societies, constitutional democracies throw up exactly the question to which liberal justice is the answer (as she rather nicely puts it, 'the unencumbered self is . . . the encumbrance of our modern social condition'). It is, as Gutmann admits and as MacIntyre would certainly want to press, an open question as to whether this is or is not a good thing (MacIntyre 1985: 244–56).

In the final section of her chapter Gutmann presciently suggests an accommodation between the two views: that communitarianism can supplement rather than supplant liberal values. The suggested result would be a liberalism that gave up some of its impartiality, and favoured some conceptions of the good over others. In particular, Gutmann suggests it should be explicitly concerned with preventing the disruption of local communities. How much a conception of justice can borrow from particular conceptions of the good and remain liberal is a question you might want to think about (cf. Raz 1986).

In our final chapter, Charles Taylor takes a side-long look at the debate between the (so-called) communitarians and liberals. It is important, he argues, to distinguish what he calls questions of ontology from questions of advocacy. Ontology, a branch of metaphysics, concerns 'what you recognize as the factors you will invoke to account for your social life'. In short, can social life be accounted for in terms of the psychology of individuals (what Taylor calls 'atomism') or does it need to invoke the social context (what Taylor calls 'holism')? Advocacy concerns 'the moral stand or policy one adopts'. The question here is whether to be an individualist or collectivist. Presumably, these terms refer to either end of a spectrum, which moves from the unfettered free market to a social arrangement such as communism. Taylor argues that these questions can be answered separately. Furthermore, getting the answer to the ontological question right can 'structure the field of possibilities in a more perspicuous way', making it easier to answer questions of advocacy.

Taylor's main concern in this paper is with what he calls 'the viability question'. Every political society 'requires some sacrifices and demands some disciplines from its members'.

If liberals are concerned with individuals pursuing their own conception of the good, will such sacrifices and disciplines be forthcoming? That is, if the liberal attitude to society is instrumental to individual well-being, will there be sufficient identification with the common good?

Taylor argues for a holist answer to the ontology question. The argument in this paper is sketchy, but has been given more fully by Taylor elsewhere (Taylor 1985). Armed with this holism, Taylor sketches various non-liberal answers to the viability question: specifically patriotism and republicanism (by which is meant the view that citizens can and should find their dignity in political participation). Such replies might well provide an answer, but they are not ones that sit well with the prevailing liberal sentiment. Hence, Taylor considers possible replies the liberal could make. It is important to realise that, although the liberal maintains that each individual should pursue their own commitment their own ideal of a good life, liberals are also committed to an impartial justice between all these individuals. Hence, the viability of a society might be sustained by a liberal commitment to justice. Taylor's principal thesis is that, because of a mistaken confusion between the ontological and advocacy questions, liberals tend to think they are committed to atomism. Hence, they tend to think they are forced to rest their commitment to justice on such matters as enlightened self-interest.

Taylor argues, by invoking a series of events from recent American political history, that enlightened self-interest simply does not explain the commitment citizens have to the common good. However, as the ontological and advocacy questions are separate, liberals can be holists, and, if they are, further possibilities open up: specifically, a greater citizen involvement in politics. Taylor presents us with two models of citizenship. The first is likely to be favoured by liberal atomists, the second by those who think of freedom as, in part, a matter of participation in politics. His point is not so much to provide a definite answer to the advocacy question, as to argue that there is a whole range of questions about the viability of society in practice. How liberal and atomistic can we be before we have no answer to the viability question? How republican can we become without compromising our liberal freedoms?

REFERENCES

MacIntyre, A. (1985). *After Virtue*. London, Duckworth.

Nozick, R. (1974). *Anarchy, State and Utopia*. Oxford, Blackwell.

Rawls, J. (1999). *A Theory of Justice*. Oxford, Oxford University Press.

Raz, J. (1986). *The Morality of Freedom*. Oxford, Oxford University Press.

Taylor, C. (1985). 'Atomism.' *Philosophy and the Human Sciences. Philosophical Papers, Vol. 2* Cambridge, Cambridge University Press: 187–210.

Waldron, J. (1989). 'Particular Values and Critical Morality.' *California Law Review* 77: 561–89.

10

LIBERALISM AND THE LIMITS OF JUSTICE

Michael Sandel

The notion of possession leads naturally to claims of desert and entitlement. The argument over what people possess, and on what terms, has a direct bearing on the question of what people deserve or are entitled to as a matter of justice. It is to the issues of desert and entitlement that we now turn, to consider the second strand of Nozick's critique of justice as fairness. Rawls rejects the principles of natural liberty and liberal equality on the grounds that they reward assets and attributes which, being arbitrary from a moral point of view, people cannot properly be said to deserve, and adopts the difference principle on the grounds that it nullifies this arbitrariness. Nozick attacks this line of reasoning by arguing first that arbitrariness does not undermine desert, and second that, even if it did, a version of natural liberty and not the difference principle would emerge as the preferred result

Stated in terms of possession, Rawls' objection to natural liberty and liberal equality is that under these principles, persons are allowed unfairly to benefit (or suffer) from natural and social endowments that do not properly *belong* to them, at least not in the strong, constitutive sense of belonging. To be sure, the various natural assets with which I am born may be said to 'belong' to me in the weak, contingent sense that they reside accidentally within me, but this sense of ownership or possession cannot establish that I have any special rights with respect to these assets or any privileged claim to the fruits of their exercise. In this attenuated sense of possession, I am not really the owner but merely the guardian or repository of the assorted assets and attributes located 'here'. By failing to acknowledge the arbitrariness of fortune, the principles of natural liberty and liberal equality go wrong in assuming that 'my' assets belong to me in the strong, constitutive sense, and so allowing distributive shares to depend on them.

Expressed in terms of desert, Rawls' objection to the principles of natural liberty and liberal equality is that they reward assets and attributes that people cannot properly be said to deserve. Though some may think the fortunate deserve the things that lead to their greater advantage, 'this view is surely incorrect'.

> It seems to be one of the fixed points of our considered judgments that no one deserves his place in the distribution of native endowments, any more than one deserves one's initial starting place in society. The assertion that a man deserves the superior character that enables him to make the effort to cultivate his abilities is equally problematic; for his character depends in large part upon fortunate family and social circumstances for which he can claim no credit. The notion of desert seems not to apply to these cases. (104)

Because no one deserves his good luck in the genetic lottery, or his favored starting place in society, or for that matter the superior character that motivates him to cultivate his abilities conscientiously, no one can be said to deserve the benefits these assets produce. It is this deduction that Nozick disputes. 'It is not true,' he argues, 'that a person earns Y (a right to keep a painting he's made, praise for writing *A Theory of Justice*, and so on) only if he's earned (or otherwise *deserves*) whatever he used (including natural assets) in the process of earning Y. Some of the things he uses he just may *have*, not illegitimately. It needn't be that the foundations underlying desert are themselves deserved, *all the way down*' (1974: 225).

Now what are we to make of this claim? If I do not necessarily have to *deserve* everything I use in producing a thing in order to deserve the thing, what *does* my desert depend on? Nozick says that some of the things I use I 'just may *have*, not illegitimately' (and, presumably, possibly arbitrarily). Once again, the notion of possession enters the scene. To see whether my having a thing, not illegitimately, can enable me to deserve what it helps me produce, we must explore in greater detail the relation between possession and desert, and sort out once more the sense of possession being appealed to.

For this purpose, it may be helpful to consider a discussion of justice and personal desert by Joel Feinberg, who analyzes the bases of desert with an admirable clarity in terms suggestive for the arguments before us (1970). Feinberg begins with the observation that no one can deserve anything unless there is some basis for the desert. 'Desert without a basis is simply not desert'. But the question immediately arises what *kind* of basis is necessary. As Feinberg writes, 'Not any old basis will do'. Once again, the notion of possession provides the key. 'If a person is deserving of some sort of treatment, he must, necessarily, be so in virtue of some *possessed characteristic* or prior activity' [emphasis added] (1970: 48).

A characteristic of mine cannot be a basis for a desert of yours unless it somehow reveals or reflects some characteristic of yours. In general, the facts which constitute the basis of a subject's desert must be facts about that subject. If a student deserves a high grade in a course, for example, his desert must be in virtue of some fact about *him* – his earlier performances, say, or his present abilities. . . . It is necessary that a person's desert have a basis and that the basis consist in some fact about himself.

(1970: 58–9, 61)

Feinberg's analysis, tying a person's desert to some fact about the person, would appear to support Nozick's claim that 'the foundations underlying desert needn't themselves be deserved, *all the way down*'. In fact, the reliance of desert on some possessed characteristic of the person suggests a thesis even stronger than Nozick's: that the foundations underlying desert *cannot* themselves be deserved, *all the way down*, any more than the foundations underlying possession can themselves be possessed, *all the way down*. We have already seen how the notion of possession requires that somewhere, 'down there', there must be a subject of possession that is not *itself* possessed (for this would deny its agency), a subject 'doing the possessing', so to speak. The analogy for desert must be a *basis* of desert ultimately prior to desert. For consider: if desert presupposes some possessed characteristic, and if possessed characteristics presuppose some subject of possession which is not itself possessed, then desert must presuppose some subject of possession which is not itself possessed, and therefore some basis of desert which is not itself deserved. Just as there must be some subject of possession prior to possession, so there must be some basis of desert prior to desert. This is why the question whether someone deserves (to have) his sterling character, for example, is notoriously difficult (for it is unclear who or what is left to judge once his character has been removed), and why, beyond a certain point, asking just wholesale whether someone deserves to be the (kind of) person he is becomes incoherent altogether. Somewhere, 'down there', there must be a basis of desert that is not itself deserved. The foundations underlying desert cannot themselves be deserved, all the way down.

This result would seem amply to confirm Nozick's claim against Rawls that I do not necessarily have to *deserve* everything I use in producing a thing in order to deserve the thing, that some of what I use I 'just may *have*, not illegitimately'. And if this claim can be established, then it would appear that Rawls' argument from arbitrariness fails to undermine desert after all. To say, as Rawls does, that I do not deserve the superior character that led me to realize my abilities is no longer enough. To deny my desert, he must show that I do not *have* the requisite character, or alternatively, that I *have* it, but not in the requisite sense.

But this is precisely the argument Rawls' theory of the person allows him to make. For given his sharp distinction between the self, taken as the pure subject of possession, and the aims and attributes it possesses, the self is left bare of any substantive feature or characteristic that could qualify as a desert base. Given the distancing aspect of possession, the self *itself* is dispossessed. On Rawls' theory of the person, the self, strictly speaking, *has nothing*, nothing at least in the strong, constitutive sense necessary to desert. In a move similar to the one invoked to show that the difference principle does not use a *person* as a means, only a person's *attributes*, Rawls can accept that some undeserved desert base is necessary to desert, only to claim that, on an adequate understanding of the person, this condition could never in principle be met! On Rawls' conception, the characteristics I possess do not *attach* to the self but are only *related* to the self, standing always at a certain distance. This is what makes them attributes rather than constituents of my person; they are *mine* rather than *me*, things I *have* rather than *am*.

We can see in this light how Rawls' argument from arbitrariness undermines desert not directly, by claiming I cannot *deserve* what is arbitrarily given, but indirectly, by showing I cannot *possess* what is arbitrarily given, that is, that 'I', qua subject of possession, cannot possess it in the undistanced, constitutive sense necessary to provide a desert base. An arbitrarily-given asset cannot be an essential constituent but only an accidental attribute of my person, for otherwise my identity would hang on a mere contingency, its continuity constantly vulnerable to transformation by experience, my status as a sovereign agent dependent on the conditions of my existence rather than epistemologically guaranteed. On Rawls' conception, no one can properly be said to deserve anything because no one can properly be said to possess anything, at least not in the strong, constitutive sense of possession necessary to the notion of desert.

A theory of justice without desert would seem a dramatic departure from traditional conceptions, but Rawls is at pains to show that it is not. In his opening pages, Rawls acknowledges that his approach 'may not seem to tally with tradition', but seeks to reassure that in fact it does.

> The more specific sense that Aristotle gives to justice, and from which the most familiar formulations derive, is that of refraining from *pleonexia*, that is, from gaining some advantage for oneself by seizing *what belong to another*, his property, his reward, his office, and the like, or by denying a person that which is due to him. . . . *Aristotle's definition clearly presupposes, however, an account of what properly belongs to a person, and of what is due to him. Now such entitlements are, I believe, very often derived from social institutions and the legitimate expectations to which they give rise.* There is no reason to think that Aristotle would disagree with this, and certainly he has a conception of social justice to account for these claims. . . . There is no conflict with the traditional notion.
>
> [emphasis added] (10–11)*

---

* All references to Rawls in this chapter not specifically cited are to Rawls 1971.

In comparing justice as fairness with traditional conceptions, Rawls confirms its novelty rather than denies it. What he presents as an incidental qualification to justice as classically conceived turns out on inspection to signal a striking departure. As Rawls suggests, traditional notions freely refer to 'what properly belongs to a person', institutions, presumably, aside; they presuppose thickly-constituted persons with a fixity of character, certain features of which are taken to be essential, 'all the way down'. On Rawls' conception, however, none of these concepts is available. In so far as a theory of justice 'presupposes an account of what properly belongs to a person' (in the strong sense of 'belongs'), Rawls effectively acknowledges that he has none. Nor, he seems to imply, given the precedence of plurality, the priority of right, and the theory of the person they require, is it reasonable to think that such a theory of justice could be true. We are not essentially thick enough selves to bear rights and deserts antecedent to the institutions that define them. Given these constraints, the only alternative is to opt for a theory of justice based on entitlements to legitimate expectations, ruling out desert altogether. Rawls hedges this claim at first, saying only that 'such entitlements are, I believe, *very often* derived from social institutions and the legitimate expectations to which they give rise' [emphasis added] (10). But as the full consequences of Rawls' view emerge, 'very often' becomes 'always', for it becomes clear that 'such entitlements' can arise in no other way. While Aristotle might not disagree that entitlements can arise in this way, it seems far from his view that they can arise in no other way. In denying that justice has to do with giving people what they deserve, justice as fairness departs decisively from the traditional notion after all.

Rawls' apparent view that no one can properly be said to deserve anything, and the connection of this view with the notion of the self as 'essentially unencumbered', emerges more fully in his discussion of legitimate expectations and moral desert. He begins by acknowledging that justice as fairness, in rejecting desert, runs counter to common sense.

> There is a tendency for common sense to suppose that income and wealth, and the good things in life generally, should be distributed according to moral desert. Justice is happiness according to virtue. While it is recognized that this ideal can never be fully carried out, it is the appropriate conception of distributive justice, at least as a prima facie principle, and society should try to realize it as circumstances permit. Now justice as fairness rejects this conception. Such a principle would not be chosen in the original position. There seems to be no way of defining the requisite criterion in that situation. (310–11)

There seems to be no way of defining the requisite criterion of a person's virtue or moral worth in the original position because no substantive theory of the person antecedent to social institutions exists. For moral desert to provide an independent criterion of justice, there must be some substantive theory of the person, or of the worth of persons, to get it going. But for Rawls, the worth of persons is subsequent to institutions, not independent of them. And so a person's moral claims must await their arrival.

This leads to the distinction between moral desert and legitimate expectations. Once a person does the various things established institutions encourage him to do, he acquires certain rights, but not before. He is entitled that institutions honor the claims they announce they will reward, but he is not entitled that they undertake to reward any particular kind of claim in the first place.

> A just scheme, then, answers to what men are entitled to; it satisfies their legitimate expectations as founded upon social institutions. But what they are entitled to is not proportional to nor dependent upon their intrinsic worth. The principles of justice that regulate the basic structure and specify the duties and obligations of individuals do not mention moral desert, and there is no tendency for distributive shares to correspond to it. (311)

The principles of justice do not mention moral desert because, strictly speaking, no one can be said to deserve anything. Similarly, the reason people's entitlements are not proportional to nor dependent upon their intrinsic worth is that, on Rawls' view, *people have no intrinsic worth*, no worth that is intrinsic in the sense that it is theirs prior to or independent of or apart from what just institutions attribute to them.

> The essential point is that the concept of moral worth does not provide a first principle of distributive justice. This is because it cannot be introduced until after the principles of justice and of natural duty and obligation have been acknowledged. ... [T]he concept of moral worth is secondary to those of right and justice, and it plays no role in the substantive definition of distributive shares. (312–13)

Rawls could agree with Feinberg that 'desert is a *moral* concept in the sense that it is logically prior to and independent of public institutions and their rules', but would deny that there is any 'antecedent standard for its definition', and so disagree with Feinberg that 'one of the aims of [a system of public bestowals] is to give people what they deserve' (1970: 86). For Rawls, the principles of justice aim neither at rewarding virtue nor at giving people what they deserve, but instead at calling forth the resources and talents necessary to serve the common interest.

> None of the precepts of justice aims at rewarding virtue. The premiums earned by scarce natural talents, for example, are to cover the costs of training and to

encourage the efforts of learning, as well as to direct ability to where it best furthers the common interest. The distributive shares that result do not correlate with moral worth. (311)

To illustrate the priority of just institutions with respect to virtue and moral worth, Rawls suggests an analogy to the relation between the rules of property and the law of robbery and theft.

> These offenses and the demerits they entail presuppose the institution of property which is established for prior and independent social ends. For a society to organize itself with the aim of rewarding moral desert as a first principle would be like having the institution of property in order to punish thieves. The criterion to each according to his virtue would not, then, be chosen in the original position. (313)

The analogy is intriguing, but one wonders whether it works entirely to Rawls' advantage. While it is apparent that the institution of property has a *certain* priority with respect to its correlative offenses, it is less clear why the dependence must run only in one direction, especially given Rawls' own commitment to the method of reflective equilibrium. For example, is our belief in the validity of the institution of property in no way enhanced by a conviction that robbery and theft are wrong? Would our confidence in the institution of property in no way be diminished if it turned out that those it defined as robbers and thieves were invariably good and virtuous men? And what of more extreme cases? While the norms and rules protecting human life can no doubt be defended on a variety of grounds, such as keeping people alive, avoiding suffering, and so on, is it logically mistaken to think that one justification of prohibitions against murder could be to punish murderers?

Rawls' position here appears especially perplexing in the light of a contrast he draws between distributive justice and retributive justice, suggesting that in the second case, some notion of moral desert may he appropriate after all. The view that distributive shares should match moral worth to the extent possible, writes Rawls, 'may arise from thinking of distributive justice as somehow the opposite of retributive justice'. But the analogy is mistaken. In a reasonably well-ordered society, 'Those who are punished for violating just laws have normally done something wrong. This is because the purpose of the criminal law is to uphold basic natural duties ... and punishments are to serve this end'.

> They are not simply a scheme of taxes and burdens designed to put a price on certain forms of conduct and in this way to guide men's conduct for mutual advantage. It would be far better if the acts prescribed by penal statutes were never done.

Thus a propensity to commit such acts is a mark of bad character, and in a just society legal punishments will only fall upon those who display these faults.

It is clear that the distribution of economic and social advantages is entirely different. These arrangements are not the converse, so to speak, of the criminal law so that just as the one punishes certain offenses, the other rewards moral worth. The function of unequal distributive shares is to cover the costs of training and education, to attract individuals to places and associations where they are most needed from a social point of view, and so on. . . . *To think of distributive and retributive justice as converses of one another is completely misleading and suggests a moral basis of distributive shares where none exists.*

[emphasis added] (314–15)

Unlike the benefits that flow from distributive arrangements, the punishments and prohibitions associated with the criminal law are not simply a non-moral system of incentives and deterrents designed to encourage some forms of behavior and discourage others. For Rawls, the pre-institutional moral notions excluded in distributive justice somehow find meaning for retributive purposes, and there is a tendency for punishment to correspond to them.

The immediate puzzle is how this account can possibly fit with the analogy of property and theft. If retributive justice differs from distributive justice precisely in virtue of its prior moral basis, it is difficult to see how the example of property and theft could demonstrate the priority of social institutions with respect to virtue and moral worth, if this priority holds for distributive justice alone. This relatively minor confusion aside, the more basic question is how Rawls can admit desert in retributive justice without contradicting the theory of the self and related assumptions that ruled it out for purposes of distributive justice. If such notions as pre-institutional moral claims and intrinsic moral worth are excluded from a theory of distributive justice in virtue of an essentially unencumbered self too slender to support them, it is difficult to see how retributive justice could differ in any relevant way.[1]

Do not the same arguments from abitrariness exclude desert as a basis for punishment as for distributive shares? Is the propensity to commit crimes, any less than the propensity to do good, the result of factors arbitrary from a moral point of view? And if not, why would the parties to the original position not agree to share one another's fate for the purpose of criminal liability as well as distributive arrangements? Since under the veil of ignorance, none can know whether he shall have the misfortune to be born into the unfavorable social and family circumstances that lead to a life of crime, why would the parties not adopt a kind of difference principle for punishments as well as distributive shares, and agree, in effect, to regard the distribution of natural and social liabilities as a common burden?

Rawls holds that 'those who are punished for violating just laws have normally done something wrong', and so deserve their punishment (314). But suppose, by an act of vandalism, I deprive the community of a certain measure of well-being, say by throwing a brick through a window. Is there any reason why I deserve to bear the full costs of my destructiveness any more than the person who produced the window *deserves* to enjoy the full benefits of his productiveness? Rawls may reply that my 'propensity to commit such acts is a mark of bad character'. But if the worker's industriousness in making the window is not a mark of good character (in the moral, pre-institutional sense), why is my maliciousness in breaking the window a mark of bad character (in the moral pre-institutional sense)? To be sure (following Rawls, p. 103), given a just system of criminal law, those who have done what the system announces it will punish are properly dealt with accordingly and in his sense are 'deserving' of their penalty. 'But this sense of desert presupposes the existence of the [retributive] scheme; it is irrelevant to the question whether in the first place the scheme is to be designed in accordance with the difference principle or some other criterion' (103).

Some may think that the criminal deserves his punishment in the strong moral sense because he deserves the low character his criminality reflects. Perhaps this is what Rawls has in mind when he writes that 'propensity to commit such acts is a mark of bad character', and punishments properly fall on those who display these faults. Because the transgressor is less worthy in this sense, he deserves the misfortune that befalls him. But again (following Rawls, p. 104), this view is surely incorrect. It seems to be one of the fixed points of our considered judgments that no one deserves his place in the distribution of native endowments or liabilities, any more than one deserves one's initial starting place in society. The assertion that a man deserves the inferior character that prevents him from overcoming his liabilities is equally problematic; for his character depends in large part upon unfortunate family and social circumstances for which he cannot be blamed. The notion of desert seems not to apply to these cases. None of which is to say that, generally speaking, a non-moral theory of distributive justice is incompatible with a moral, or desert-based theory of punishment, only that given Rawls' reasons for rejecting desert-based distributive arrangements, he seems clearly committed to rejecting desert-based retributive ones as well.

The apparent inconsistency between Rawls' retributive and distributive theories need not do serious damage to the theory as a whole. Given the method of reflective equilibrium, 'justification is a matter of the mutual support of many considerations, of everything fitting together into one coherent view' (21). From the standpoint of the overall theory, little hangs on Rawls' retributive theory, apart from the measure of plausibility it lends justice as fairness for those committed to a strong, desert-based notion of punishment. If Rawls distinction succeeds, they need not choose between their retributive intuitions and the difference principle; if it does not, one or the other of those convictions must give way. If, on reflection, a non-moral theory of punishment appears unacceptable, even in the light of the arbitrariness of criminal characteristics and dispositions, then the difference principle – rejecting as it does the notion of desert – would be called into serious question. If, on the other hand, our intuition that criminals deserve punishment proves no more indispensable than our intuition that virtue deserves reward (an intuition of common sense Rawls explicitly rejects), then we may adjust our intuitions in a direction that affirms the difference principle rather than opposes it. Desert would be rejected as the basis for both distributive and retributive arrangements, and so the inconsistency resolved.

But such a resolution returns us to the larger difficulties of a theory of justice without desert and a notion of the self as essentially dispossessed, or barren of constituent traits. Nozick argues against Rawls that the foundations underlying desert need not themselves be deserved, all the way down. But as we have seen, Rawls' denial of desert does not depend on the thesis Nozick refutes, but instead on the notion of the self as a pure, unadulterated, 'essentially unencumbered' subject of possession. Rawls is not committed to the view that a person can only deserve a thing he produces if he deserves everything he used in producing it, but rather to the view that no one possesses anything in the strong, constitutive sense necessary to a desert base. No one can be said to deserve anything (in the strong, pre-institutional sense), because no one can be said to possess anything (in the strong, constitutive sense). This is the philosophical force of the argument from arbitrariness.

That the argument from arbitrariness works in this way can be seen by viewing the moves from natural liberty to fair opportunity to the democratic conception, as traced by Rawls, as stages in the dispossession of the person. With each transition, a substantive self, thick with particular traits, is progressively shorn of characteristics once taken to be essential to its identity; as more of its features are seen to be arbitrarily given, they are relegated from presumed constituents to mere attributes of the self. More becomes *mine*, and less remains *me*, to recall our earlier formulation, until ultimately the self is purged of empirical constituents altogether, and transformed into a condition of agency standing beyond the objects of its possession. The logic of Rawls' argument might be reconstructed as follows:

At the far end of the spectrum, even before natural liberty appears, are aristocratic and caste societies; in such societies, a person's life prospects are tied to a hierarchy into which he is born and from which his person is inseparable. Here, the self is most fully ascribed, merged almost indistinguishably with its condition, embedded in its situation. The system of natural liberty removes fixed status of birth as an assumed constituent of the person, and regards each as free, given his capacities and resources, to compete in the marketplace as best he can, and to reap his reward. By shifting the basis of expectations from status to contract, the system of natural liberty repairs the arbitrariness of hierarchical societies by taking the person more narrowly, so to speak, as distinct and separable from his surroundings. Still, some arbitrariness remains, most notably in the form of social and cultural contingencies. In the regime of natural liberty, a person's life prospects are governed by factors no more ascribable to the person (in the strong, constitutive sense) than his inherited status. Having relieved the person of his hierarchical baggage, the principle of natural liberty still conceives a thickly-constituted self, burdened by the accidents of social and cultural contingency. And so the move to fair opportunity, which strips the self of social and cultural accidents as well as inherited status. In a 'fair meritocracy', the effects of class status and cultural disadvantage are understood to reflect more on the society and less on the person. Those with comparable talents and 'the same willingness to use them, should have the same prospects of success regardless of their initial place in the social system, that is, irrespective of the income class into which they are born' (73). In this way, the meritocratic conception extends the logical of natural liberty by ascribing less to the self and more to its situation.

But even the principle of fair opportunity, in rewarding individual effort, conceives the province of the self too expansively. For even 'the effort a person is willing to make is influenced by his natural abilities and skills and the alternatives open to him. The better endowed are more likely, other things equal, to strive conscientiously, and there seems to be no way to discount for their greater good fortune' (312). The self is still over-ascribed. Given its arbitrariness, even the character that determines a person's motivation cannot properly be regarded as an essential constituent of his identity. And so finally the move to the democratic conception, in which the self, shorn of all contingently-given attributes, assumes a kind of supra-empirical status, essentially unencumbered, bounded in advance and given prior to its ends, a pure subject of agency and possession, ultimately thin. Not only my character but even my values and deepest convictions are relegated to the contingent, as features of my condition rather than as constituents of my person. 'That we have one conception of the good rather than another is not relevant from a moral standpoint. In acquiring it we are influenced by the same sort of contingencies that lead us to rule out a knowledge of out sex and class' (Rawls 1975: 537). Only in this way is it possible to install the self as invulnerable, to assure its sovereignty once and for all in a world threatening always to engulf it. Only if the fate of the self is thus detached from the fate of its attributes and aims, subject as they are to the vagaries of circumstances, can its priority be preserved and its agency guaranteed.

This is the vision of the person that Nozick and Bell, as defenders of natural liberty and meritocracy, respectively, emphatically reject, even if they do not spell out in any detail the conception of the self they rely on instead. Both object that the argument from arbitrariness, consistently applied, leads ineluctably to the dissolution of the person, and the abnegation of individual responsibility and moral choice. 'This line of argument can succeed in blocking the introduction of a person's autonomous choices and activities (and their results) only by attributing *everything* noteworthy about the person completely to certain sorts of "external" factors', writes Nozick. Echoing his argument against the notion of common assets, Nozick questions whether, on Rawls' account, any coherent conception of the person remains, and if so, whether it is any longer the kind of person worth the moral fuss deontological liberalism makes on its behalf.

> So denigrating a person's autonomy and prime responsibility for his actions is a risky line to take for a theory that otherwise wishes to buttress the dignity and self-respect of autonomous beings; especially for a theory that founds so much (including a theory of the good) upon a person's choices. One doubts that the unexalted picture of human beings Rawls' theory presupposes and rests upon can be made to fit together with the view of human dignity it is designed to lead to and embody.
>
> (1974: 214)

Bell summarizes the objection in an epigram: 'The person has disappeared. Only attributes remain' (1973: 419). Where Rawls seeks to assure the autonomy of the self by disengaging it from the world, his critics say he ends by dissolving the self in order to preserve it.

To recapitulate our reconstructed version of the argument between Rawls and Nozick on the issue of desert: Nozick first argues that the arbitrariness of assets does not undermine desert, because desert may depend not only on things I deserve, but also on things I just *have*, not illegitimately. Rawls' response is to invoke the distinction between the self and its possessions in the strongest version of that distinction, and so to claim that, strictly speaking, there *is* nothing that 'I', qua pure subject of possession, *have* – nothing that is attached, rather than related, to *me* – nothing at least in the strong, constitutive sense of possession necessary to a desert base. Nozick's rejoinder is that this defense cannot succeed for long, for it has the consequence of leaving us with a subject *so* shorn of empirically identifiable characteristics as to resemble once more the Kantian transcendent or disembodied subject Rawls resolved to avoid. It makes the individual inviolable only by making him invisible, and calls into question the dignity and autonomy this liberalism seeks above all to secure.

[. . .]

CONCLUSION

For justice to be the first virtue, certain things must be true of us. We must be creatures of a certain kind, related to human circumstance in a certain way. We must stand at a certain distance from our circumstance, whether as transcendental subject in the case of Kant, or as essentially unencumbered subject of possession in the case of Rawls. Either way, we must regard ourselves as independent: independent from the interests and attachments we may have at any moment, never identified by our aims but always capable of standing back to survey and assess and possibly to revise them (Rawls 1979: 7; 1980: 544–5).

Deontology's liberating project

Bound up with the notion of an independent self is a vision of the moral universe this self must inhabit. Unlike classical Greek and medieval Christian conceptions, the universe of the deontological ethic is a place devoid of inherent meaning, a world 'disenchanted' in Max Weber's phrase, a world without an objective moral order. Only in a universe empty of *telos*, such as seventeenth-century science and philosophy affirmed,[2] is it possible to conceive a subject apart from and prior to its purposes and ends. Only a world ungoverned by a purposive order leaves principles of justice open to human construction and conceptions of the good to individual choice. In this the depth of opposition between deontological liberalism and teleological world views most fully appears.

Where neither nature nor cosmos supplies a meaningful order to be grasped or apprehended, it falls to human subjects to constitute meaning on their own. This would explain the prominence of contract theory from Hobbes onward, and the corresponding emphasis on voluntarist as against cognitive ethics culminating in Kant. What can no longer be found remains somehow to be created.[3] Rawls describes his own view in this connection as a version of Kantian 'constructivism'.

> The parties to the original position do not agree on what the moral facts are, as if there were already such facts. It is not that, being situated impartially, they have a clear and undistorted view of a prior and independent moral order. Rather (for constructivism), *there is no such order*, and therefore no such facts apart from the procedure as a whole.
>
> [emphasis added] (1980: 568)

Similarly for Kant, the moral law is not a discovery of theoretical reason but a deliverance of practical reason, the product of pure will. 'The elementary practical concepts have as their foundation the form of a pure will given in reason', and what makes this will authoritative is that it legislates in a world where meaning has yet to arrive. Practical reason finds its advantage over theoretical reason precisely in this voluntarist faculty, in its capacity to generate practical precepts directly, without recourse to cognition. 'Since in all precepts of the pure will it is only a question of the determination of will,' there is no need for these precepts 'to wait upon intuitions in order to acquire a meaning. This occurs for the noteworthy reason that *they themselves produce the reality of that to which they refer*' [emphasis added] (1788: 67–8).

It is important to recall that, on the deontological view, the notion of a self barren of essential aims and attachments does not imply that we are beings wholly without purpose or incapable of moral ties, but rather that the values and relations we have are the products of choice, the possessions of a self given prior to its ends. It is similar with deontology's universe. Though it rejects the possibility of an objective moral order, this liberalism does not hold that just anything goes. It affirms justice, not nihilism. The notion of a universe empty of intrinsic meaning does not, on the deontological view, imply a world wholly ungoverned by regulative principles, but rather a moral universe inhabited by subjects capable of constituting meaning on their own – as agents of *construction* in case of the right, as agents of *choice* in the case of the good. Qua noumenal selves, or parties to the original position, we arrive at principles of justice; qua actual, individual selves, we arrive at conceptions of the good. And the principles we construct as noumenal selves constrain (but do not determine) the purposes we choose as individual selves. This reflects the priority of the right over the good.

The deontological universe and the independent self that moves within it, taken together, hold out a liberating vision. Freed from the dictates of nature and the sanction of social roles, the deontological subject is installed as sovereign, cast as the author of the only moral meanings there are. As inhabitants of a world without *telos*, we are free to construct principles of justice unconstrained by an order of value antecedently given. Although the principles of justice are not strictly speaking a matter of choice, the society they define 'comes as close as a society can to being a voluntary scheme' (13), for they arise from a pure will or act of construction not answerable to a prior moral order. And as independent selves, we are free to choose our purposes and ends unconstrained by such an order, or by custom or tradition or inherited status. So long as they are not unjust, our conceptions of the good carry weight, whatever they are, simply in virtue of our having chosen them. We are 'self-originating sources of valid claims' (Rawls 1980: 543).

Now justice is the virtue that embodies deontology's liberating vision and allows it to unfold. It embodies this vision by describing those principles the sovereign subject is said to construct while situated prior to the constitution of all value. It allows the vision to unfold in that, equipped with these principles, the just society regulates each person's choice of ends in a way compatible with a similar liberty for all. Citizens governed by justice are thus enabled to realize deontology's liberating project – to exercise their capacity as 'self-originating sources of valid claims' – as fully as circumstances permit. So the primacy of justice at once expresses and advances the liberating aspirations of the deontological world view and conception of the self.

But the deontological vision is flawed, both within its own terms and more generally as an account of our moral experience. Within its own terms, the deontological self, stripped of all possible constitutive attachments, is less liberated than disempowered. As we have seen, neither the right nor the good admits of the voluntarist derivation deontology requires. As agents of construction we do not really construct, and as agents of choice we do not really choose. What goes on behind the veil of ignorance is not a contract or an agreement but if anything a kind of discovery; and what goes on in 'purely preferential choice' is less a choosing of ends than a matching of pre-existing desires, undifferentiated as to worth, with the best available means of satisfying them. For the parties to the original position, as for the parties to ordinary deliberative rationality, the liberating moment fades before it arrives; the sovereign subject is left at sea in the circumstances it was thought to command.

The moral frailty of the deontological self also appears at the level of first-order principles. Here we found that the independent self, being essentially dispossessed, was too thin to be capable of desert in the ordinary sense. For claims of desert presuppose thickly-constituted selves, beings capable of possession in the constitutive sense, but the deontological self is wholly without possessions of this kind. Acknowledging this lack, Rawls would found entitlements on legitimate expectations instead. If we are incapable of desert, at least we are entitled that institutions honor the expectations to which they give rise.

But the difference principle requires more. It begins with the thought, congenial to the deontological view, that the assets I have are only accidentally mine. But it ends by assuming that these assets are therefore common assets and that society has a prior claim on the fruits of their exercise. This either disempowers the deontological self or denies its independence. Either my prospects are left at the mercy of institutions established for 'prior and independent social ends' (313), ends which may or may not coincide with my own, or I must count myself a member of a community defined in part by those ends, in which case I cease to he unencumbered by constitutive attachments. Either way, the difference principle contradicts the liberating aspiration of the deontological project. We cannot be persons for whom justice is primary and also be persons for whom the difference principle is a principle of justice.

Character, self-knowledge, and friendship

If the deontological ethic fails to redeem its own liberating promise, it also fails plausibly to account for certain indispensable aspects of our moral experience. For deontology insists that we view ourselves as independent selves, independent in the sense that our identity is never tied to our aims and attachments. Given our 'moral power to form, to revise, and rationally to pursue a conception of the good' (Rawls

1980: 544), the continuity of our identity is unproblematically assured. No transformation of my aims and attachments could call into question the person I am, for no such allegiances, however deeply held, could possibly engage my identity to begin with.

But we cannot regard ourselves as independent in this way without great cost to those loyalties and convictions whose moral force consists partly in the fact that living by them is inseparable from understanding ourselves as the particular persons we are – as members of this family or community or nation or people, as bearers of this history, as sons and daughters of that revolution, as citizens of this republic. Allegiances such as these are more than values I happen to have or aims I 'espouse at any given time'. They go beyond the obligations I voluntarily incur and the 'natural duties' I owe to human beings as such. They allow that to some I owe more than justice requires or even permits, not by reason of agreements I have made but instead in virtue of those more or less enduring attachments and commitments which taken together partly define the person I am.

To imagine a person incapable of constitutive attachments such as these is not to conceive an ideally free and rational agent, but to imagine a person wholly without character, without moral depth. For to have character is to know that I move in a history I neither summon nor command, which carries consequences none the less for my choices and conduct. It draws me closer to some and more distant from others; it makes some aims more appropriate, others less so. As a self-interpreting being, I am able to reflect on my history and in this sense to distance myself from it, but the distance is always precarious and provisional, the point of reflection never finally secured outside the history itself. A person with character thus knows that he is implicated in various ways even as he reflects, and feels the moral weight of what he knows.

This makes a difference for agency and self-knowledge. For, as we have seen, the deontological self, being wholly without character, is incapable of self-knowledge in any morally serious sense. Where the self is unencumbered and essentially dispossessed, no person is left for *self*-reflection to reflect upon. This is why, on the deontological view, deliberation about ends can only be an exercise in arbitrariness. In the absence of constitutive attachments, deliberation issues in 'purely preferential choice', which means the ends we seek, being mired in contingency, 'are not relevant from a moral standpoint' (Rawls 1975: 537).

When I act out of more or less enduring qualities of character, by contrast, my choice of ends is not arbitrary in the same way. In consulting my preferences, I have not only to weigh their intensity but also to assess their suitability to the person I (already) am. I ask, as I deliberate, not only what I really want but who I really am, and this last question takes me beyond an attention to my desires alone to reflect on my identity itself. While the contours of my identity will in some ways be open and subject to revision, they are not wholly without shape. And the fact that they are not enables me to discriminate among my more immediate wants and desires; some now appear essential, others merely incidental to my defining projects and commitments. Although there may be a certain ultimate contingency in my having wound up the person I am – only theology can say for sure – it makes a moral difference none the less that, being the person I am, I affirm these ends rather than those, turn this way rather than that. While the notion of constitutive attachments may at first seem an obstacle to agency – the self, now encumbered, is no longer strictly prior – some relative fixity of character appears essential to prevent the lapse into arbitrariness which the deontological self is unable to avoid.

The possibility of character in the constitutive sense is also indispensable to a certain kind of friendship, a friendship marked by mutual insight as well as sentiment. By any account, friendship is bound up with certain feelings. We like our friends; we have affection for them, and wish them well. We hope that their desires find satisfaction, that their plans meet with success, and we commit ourselves in various ways to advancing their ends.

But for persons presumed incapable of constitutive attachments, acts of friendship such as these face a powerful constraint. However much I might hope for the good of a friend and stand ready to advance it, only the friend himself can know what that good is. This restricted access to the good of others follows from the limited scope for self-reflection, which betrays in turn the thinness of the deontological self to begin with. Where deliberating about my good means no more than attending to wants and desires given directly to my awareness, I must do it on my own; it neither requires nor admits the participation of others. Every act of friendship thus becomes parasitic on a good identifiable in advance. 'Benevolence and love are second-order notions: they seek to further the good of beloved individuals that is already given' (191). Even the friendliest sentiments must await a moment of introspection itself inaccessible to friendship. To expect more of any friend, or to offer more, can only be a presumption against the ultimate privacy of self-knowledge.

For persons encumbered in part by a history they share with others, by contrast, knowing oneself is a more complicated thing. It is also a less strictly private thing. Where seeking my good is bound up with exploring my identity and interpreting my life history, the knowledge I seek is less transparent to me and less opaque to others. Friendship becomes a way of knowing as well as liking. Uncertain which path to take, I consult a friend who knows me well, and together we deliberate, offering and assessing by turns competing descriptions of the person I am, and of the alternatives I face as they bear on my identity. To take seriously such deliberation is to allow that my friend may grasp something I have missed, may offer a more adequate account of the way my identity is engaged in the alternatives before me. To adopt this new description is to see myself in a new way; my old self-image now seems partial or occluded, and I may say in retrospect that my friend knew me better than I knew myself. To deliberate with friends is to admit this possibility, which presupposes in turn a more richly-constituted self than deontology allows. While there will of course remain times when friendship requires deference to the self-image of a friend, however flawed, this too requires insight; here the need to defer implies the ability to know.

So to see ourselves as deontology would see us is to deprive us of those qualities of character, reflectiveness and friendship that depend on the possibility of constitutive projects and attachments. And to see ourselves as given to commitments such as these is to admit a deeper commonality than benevolence describes, a commonality of shared self-understanding as well as 'enlarged affections'. As the independent self finds its limits in those aims and attachments from which it cannot stand apart, so justice finds its limits in those forms of community that engage the identity as well as the interests of the participants.

To all of this, deontology might finally reply, with a concession and a distinction: it is one thing to allow that 'citizens in their personal affairs . . . have attachments and loves that they believe they would not, or could not, stand apart from', that they 'regard it as unthinkable . . . to view themselves without certain religious and philo-sophical convictions and commitments' (Rawls 1980: 545). But with public life it is different. There, no loyalty or allegiance could be similarly essential to our sense of who we are. Unlike our ties to family and friends, no devotion to city or nation, to party or cause, could possibly run deep enough to be defining. By contrast with our private identity, our 'public identity' as moral persons 'is not affected by changes over time' in our conceptions of the good (Rawls 1980: 544–5). While we may be thickly-constituted selves in private, we must be wholly unencumbered selves in public, and it is there that the primacy of justice prevails.

But once we recall the special status of the deontological claim, it is unclear what the grounds for this distinction could be. It might seem at first glance a psychological distinction; detachment comes more easily in public life, where the ties we have are typically less compelling; I can more easily step back from, say, my partisan allegiances than certain personal loyalties and affections. But as we have seen from the start, deon-tology's claim for the independence of the self must be more than a claim of psychology or sociology. Otherwise, the primacy of justice would hang on the degree of benevo-lence and fellow-feeling any particular society managed to inspire. The independence of the self does not mean that I can, as a psychological matter, summon in this or that circumstance the detachment required to stand outside my values and ends, rather that I must regard myself as the bearer of a self distinct from my values and ends, what-ever they may be. It is above all an epistemological claim, and has little to do with the relative intensity of feeling associated with public or private relations.

Understood as an epistemological claim, however, the deontological conception of the self cannot admit the distinction required. Allowing constitutive possibilities where 'private' ends are at stake would seem unavoidably to allow at least the possibility that 'public' ends could be constitutive as well. Once the bounds of the self are no longer

fixed, individuated in advance and given prior to experience, there is no saying in principle what sorts of experiences could shape or reshape them, no guarantee that only
'private' and never 'public' events could conceivably be decisive.

Not egoists but strangers, sometimes benevolent, make for citizens of the deontological republic; justice finds its occasion because we cannot know each other, or our
ends, well enough to govern by the common good alone. This condition is not likely
to fade altogether, and so long as it does not, justice will be necessary. But neither is
it guaranteed always to predominate, and in so far as it does not, community will be
possible, and an unsettling presence for justice.

Liberalism teaches respect for the distance of self and ends, and when this distance
is lost, we are submerged in a circumstance that ceases to be ours. But by seeking to
secure this distance too completely, liberalism undermines its own insight. By putting
the self beyond the reach of politics, it makes human agency an article of faith rather
than an object of continuing attention and concern, a premise of politics rather than
its precarious achievement. This misses the pathos of politics and also its most inspir-
ing possibilities. It overlooks the danger that when politics goes badly, not only disap-
pointments but also dislocations are likely to result. And it forgets the possibility that
when politics goes well, we can know a good in common that we cannot know alone.

NOTES

1   In a footnote (315), Rawls cites Feinberg in apparent support of this claim, but Feinberg
    allows a role for desert in both distributive and retributive justice. Feinberg's point is that
    retributive justice involves what he calls polar desert (where one either deserves good or
    deserves ill), whereas distributive justice involves nonpolar desert (where, as a prize, some
    deserve and others do not). But both cases involve desert in the moral, pre-institutional
    sense (Feinberg 1970: 62).
2   For discussion of the moral, political, and epistemological consequences of the seventeenth-
    century scientific revolution and world-view, see Strauss 1953; Arendt 1958: 248–325;
    Wolin 1960: 239–85; and Taylor 1975: 3–50.
3   As one liberal writer boldly asserts, 'The hard truth is this: There is no moral meaning
    hidden in the bowels of the universe. . . . Yet there is no need to be overwhelmed by the
    void. We may create our own meanings, you and I' (Ackerman 1980: 368). Oddly enough,
    he insists nonetheless that liberalism is committed to no particular metaphysic or episte-
    mology, nor any 'Big Questions of a highly controversial character' (356–7, 361).

REFERENCES

Ackerman, B.A. (1980). *Social Justice in the Liberal State*. Yale University Press, New Haven.
Arendt, H. (1958). *The Human Condition*. University of Chicago Press, Chicago.

Bell, D. (1973). *The Coming of Post-industrial Society*. Penguin, Harmondsworth.

Feinberg, J. (1970). *Doing and Deserving*. Princeton University Press, Princeton.

Kant, I. (1788). *Critique of Pure Reason*. Hackett, Indianapolis.

Nozick, R. (1974). *Anarchy, State and Utopia*. Basic Books, New York.

Rawls, J. (1971). *A Theory of Justice*. Oxford University Press, Oxford.

Rawls, J. (1975). 'Fairness to Goodness.' *Philosophical Review*, 84, 536–54.

Rawls, J. (1979). 'A Well-ordered Society.' In P. Laslett and J. Fishkin (eds) *Philosophy, Politics and Society*, 5th Series. pp. 6–20. Oxford University Press, Oxford.

Rawls, J. (1980). 'Kantian Constructivism in Moral Theory.' *Journal of Philosophy* 77, 515–72.

Strauss, L. (1953). *Natural Right and History*. Chicago University Press, Chicago.

Taylor, C. (1975). *Hegel*. Cambridge University Press, Cambridge.

Wolin, S. (1960). *Politics and Vision*. Little, Brown, Boston, MA.

11

THE DOMAIN OF THE POLITICAL AND OVERLAPPING CONSENSUS

John Rawls

In this paper I shall examine the idea of an overlapping consensus[1] and its role in a political conception of justice for a constitutional regime. A political conception, I shall suppose, views the political as a special domain with distinctive features that call for the articulation within the conception of the characteristic values that apply to that domain. Justice as fairness, the conception presented in my book *A Theory of Justice*,[2] is an example of a political conception and I refer to it to fix ideas. By going over these matters I hope to allay misgivings about the idea of an overlapping consensus, especially the misgiving that it makes political philosophy political in the wrong way.[3] That is, this idea may suggest to some the view that consensus politics is to be taken as regulative and that the content of first principles of justice should be adjusted to the claims of the dominant political and social interests.

This misgiving may have resulted from my having used the idea of an overlapping consensus without distinguishing between two stages in the exposition of justice as fairness and without stressing that the idea of an overlapping consensus is used only in the second. To explain: in the first stage justice as fairness should be presented as a free-standing political conception that articulates the very great values applicable to the special domain of the political, as marked out by the basic structure of society. The second stage consists of an account of the stability of justice as fairness, that is, its capacity to generate its own support,[4] in view of the content of its principles and ideals as formulated in the first stage. In this second stage the idea of an overlapping consensus is introduced to explain how, given the plurality of conflicting comprehensive religious, philosophical, and moral doctrines always found in a democratic society – the kind of society that justice as fairness itself enjoins – free institutions may gain the allegiance needed to endure over time.

I FOUR GENERAL FACTS

I begin with some background. Any political conception of justice presupposes a view of the political and social world, and recognizes certain general facts of political sociology and human psychology. Four general facts are especially important.

The first fact is that the diversity of comprehensive religious, philosophical, and moral doctrines found in modern democratic societies is not a mere historical condition that may soon pass away; it is a permanent feature of the public culture of democracy. Under the political and social conditions that the basic rights and liberties of free institutions secure, a diversity of conflicting and irreconcilable comprehensive doctrines will emerge, if such diversity does not already exist. Moreover, it will persist and may increase. The fact about free institutions is the fact of pluralism.

A second and related general fact is that only the oppressive use of state power can maintain a continuing common affirmation of one comprehensive religious, philosophical, or moral doctrine. If we think of political society as a community when it is united in affirming one and the same comprehensive doctrine, then the oppressive use of state power is necessary to maintain a political community. In the society of the Middle Ages, more or less united in affirming the Catholic faith, the Inquisition was not an accident; preservation of a shared religious belief demanded the suppression of heresy. The same holds, I believe, for any comprehensive philosophical and moral doctrine, even for secular ones. A society united on a form of utilitarianism, or on the liberalism of Kant or Mill, would likewise require the sanctions of state power to remain so.

A third general fact is that an enduring and secure democratic regime, one not divided into contending doctrinal confessions and hostile social classes, must be willingly and freely supported by at least a substantial majority of its politically active citizens. Together with the first general fact, this means that for a conception of justice to serve as the public basis of justification for a constitutional regime, it must be one that widely different and even irreconcilable comprehensive doctrines can endorse. Otherwise the regime will not be enduring and secure. As we shall see later, this suggests the need for what I have referred to as a political conception of justice.[5]

A fourth fact is that the political culture of a reasonably stable democratic society normally contains, at least implicitly, certain fundamental intuitive ideas from which it is possible to work up a political conception of justice suitable for a constitutional regime. This fact is important when we come to specify the general features of a political conception of justice and to elaborate justice as fairness as such a view.

II THE BURDENS OF REASON

These facts, especially the first two – namely, the fact that a diversity of comprehensive doctrines is a permanent feature of a society with free institutions, and that this diversity can be overcome only by the oppressive use of state power – call for explanation. For why should free institutions with their basic rights and liberties lead to diversity, and why should state power be required to suppress it? Why does our sincere and conscientious attempt to reason with one another fail to lead us to agreement? It seems to lead to agreement in science, or if disagreement in social theory and economics often seems intractable, at least – in the long run – in natural science.

There are, of course, several possible explanations. We might suppose that most people hold views that advance their own more narrow interests; and since their interests are different, so are their views. Or perhaps people are often irrational and not very bright, and this mixed with logical errors leads to conflicting opinions.

But such explanations are too easy, and not the kind we want. We want to know how reasonable disagreement is possible, for we always work at first within ideal theory. Thus we ask: how might reasonable disagreement come about?

One explanation is this. We say that reasonable disagreement is disagreement between reasonable persons, that is, between persons who have realized their two moral powers[6] to a degree sufficient to be free and equal citizens in a democratic regime, and who have an enduring desire to be fully cooperating members of society over a complete life. We assume such persons share a common human reason, similar powers of thought and judgment, a capacity to draw inferences and to weigh evidence and to balance competing considerations, and the like.

Now the idea of reasonable disagreement involves an account of the sources, or causes, of disagreement between reasonable persons. These sources I shall refer to as the "burdens of reason." The account of these burdens must be such that it is fully compatible with, and so does not impugn, the reasonableness of those who disagree among themselves.

What, then, goes wrong? If we say it is the presence of prejudice and bias, of self- and group-interest, of blindness and willfulness – not to mention irrationality and stupidity (often main causes of the decline and fall of nations) – we impugn the reasonableness of at least some of those who disagree. We must discover another explanation.

An explanation of the right kind is that the burdens of reason, the sources of reasonable disagreement among reasonable persons, are the many hazards involved in the correct (and conscientious) exercise of our powers of reason and judgment in the ordinary course of political life. Except for the last two sources below, the ones I mention now are not peculiar to reasoning about values; nor is the list I give complete. It covers only the more obvious sources of reasonable disagreement:

a   The evidence – empirical and scientific – bearing on the case may be conflicting and complex, and hence hard to assess and evaluate.

b   Even where we agree fully about the kinds of considerations that are relevant, we may disagree about their weight, and so arrive at different judgments.

c   To some extent all of our concepts, not only our moral and political concepts, are vague and subject to hard cases; this indeterminacy means that we must rely on judgment and interpretation (and on judgments about interpretations) within some range (not itself sharply specifiable) wherein reasonable persons may differ.

d   To some unknown extent, our total experience, our whole course of life up to now, shapes the way we assess evidence and weigh moral and political values, and our total experiences surely differ. Thus, in a modern society with its numerous offices and positions, its various divisions of labor, its many social groups and often their ethnic variety, the total experiences of citizens are disparate enough for their judgments to diverge, at least to some degree, on many if not most cases of any significant complexity.

e   Often there are different kinds of normative considerations of different force on both sides of a question, and it is difficult to make an overall assessment.[7]

f   Finally, since any system of social institutions can admit only a limited range of values, some selection must be made from the full range of moral and political values that might be realized. This is because any system of institutions has, as it were, but a limited social space. In being forced to select among cherished values, we face great difficulties in setting priorities, and other hard decisions that may seem to have no clear answer.[8]

These are some sources of the difficulties in arriving at agreement in judgment, sources that are compatible with the full reasonableness of those judging. In noting these sources – these burdens of reason – we do not, of course, deny that prejudice and bias, self- and group-interest, blindness and willfulness, play an all-too-familiar part in political life. But these sources of unreasonable disagreement stand in marked contrast to sources of disagreement compatible with everyone's being fully reasonable.

I conclude by stating a fifth general fact: we make many of our most important judgments subject to conditions which render it extremely unlikely that conscientious and fully reasonable persons, even after free discussion, can exercise their powers of reason so that all arrive at the same conclusion.

III PRECEPTS OF REASONABLE DISCUSSION

Next I consider how, if we are reasonable, we should conduct ourselves in view of the plain facts about the burdens of reason. I suppose that, as reasonable persons, we are

163

fully aware of these burdens, and try to take them into account. On this basis we recognize certain precepts to govern deliberation and discussion. A few of these follow.

First, the political discussion aims to reach reasonable agreement, and hence so far as possible it should be conducted to serve that aim. We should not readily accuse one another of self- or group-interest, prejudice or bias, and of such deeply entrenched errors as ideological blindness and delusion. Such accusations arouse resentment and hostility, and block the way to reasonable agreement. The disposition to make such accusations without compelling grounds is plainly unreasonable, and often a declaration of intellectual war.

Second, when we are reasonable we are prepared to find substantive and even intractable disagreements on basic questions. The first general fact means that the basic institutions and public culture of a democratic society specify a social world within which opposing general beliefs and conflicting comprehensive doctrines are likely to flourish and may increase in number. It is unreasonable, then, not to recognize the likelihood – indeed the practical certainty – of irreconcilable reasonable disagreements on matters of the first significance. Even when it seems that agreement should in principle be possible, it may be unattainable in the present case, at least in the foreseeable future.[9]

Third, when we are reasonable, we are ready to enter discussion crediting others with a certain good faith. We expect deep differences of opinion, and accept this diversity as the normal state of the public culture of a democratic society. To hate that fact is to hate human nature, for it is to hate the many not unreasonable expressions of human nature that develop under free institutions.[10]

I have suggested that the burdens of reason sufficiently explain the first two general facts – the facts of pluralism, given free institutions, and the necessity of the oppressive use of state power to maintain a political community (a political society united on a comprehensive doctrine) – whatever further causes those facts might have. Those facts are not, then, mere historical contingencies. Rather, they are rooted in the difficulties of exercising our reason under the normal conditions of human life.

IV FEATURES OF A POLITICAL CONCEPTION OF JUSTICE

Recall that the third general fact was that an enduring and stable democratic regime is one that at least a substantial majority of its politically active citizens freely support. Given this fact, what are the more general features of a political doctrine underlying a regime able to gain such allegiance? Plainly, it must be a doctrine that a diversity of comprehensive religious, philosophical, and moral doctrines can endorse, each from its own point of view.[11] This follows not only from the third general fact but also from the first, the fact of pluralism: for a democratic regime will eventually, if not from the outset, lead to a pluralism of comprehensive doctrines.

Let us say that a political conception of justice (in contrast to a political regime) is stable if it meets the following condition: those who grow up in a society well-ordered by it – a society whose institutions are publicly recognized to be just, as specified by that conception itself – develop a sufficient allegiance to those institutions, that is, a sufficiently strong sense of justice guided by appropriate principles and ideals, so that they normally act as justice requires, provided they are assured that others will act likewise.[12]

Now what more general features of a political conception of justice does this definition of stability suggest? The idea of a political conception of justice includes three such features:[13]

First, while a political conception of justice is, of course, a moral conception, it is worked out for a specific subject, namely, the basic structure of a constitutional democratic regime. This structure consists in society's main political, social, and economic institutions, and how they fit together into one unified system of social cooperation.

Second, accepting a political conception of justice does not presuppose accepting any particular comprehensive doctrine. The conception presents itself as a reasonable conception for the basic structure alone.[14]

Third, a political conception of justice is formulated so far as possible solely in terms of certain fundamental intuitive ideas viewed as implicit in the public political culture of a democratic society. Two examples are the idea of society as a fair system of social cooperation over time from one generation to the next, and the idea of citizens as free and equal persons fully capable of engaging in social cooperation over a complete life. (That there are such ideas is the fourth general fact.) Such ideas of society and citizen are normative and political ideas; they belong to a normative political conception, and not to metaphysics or psychology.[15]

Thus the distinction between political conceptions of justice and other moral conceptions is a matter of scope, that is, of the range of subjects to which a conception applies, and of the wider content which a wider range requires. A conception is said to be general when it applies to a wide range of subjects (in the limit to all subjects); it is comprehensive when it includes conceptions of what is of value in human life, ideals of personal virtue and character, and the like, that inform much of our nonpolitical conduct (in the limit, our life as a whole).

Religious and philosophical conceptions tend to be general and fully comprehensive; indeed, their being so is sometimes regarded as a philosophical ideal to be attained. A doctrine is fully comprehensive when it covers all recognized values and virtues within one rather precisely articulated scheme of thought; whereas a doctrine is partially comprehensive when it comprises certain, but not all, nonpolitical values and virtues and is rather loosely articulated. By definition, then, for a conception to be even partially comprehensive it must extend beyond the political and include nonpolitical values and virtues.

Keeping these points in mind, political liberalism tries to articulate a workable political conception of justice. The conception consists in a view of politics and of the kind of political institutions which would be most just and appropriate when we take into account the five general facts. From these facts rises the need to found social unity on a political conception that can gain the support of a diversity of comprehensive doctrines. Political liberalism is not, then, a view of the whole of life: it is not a (fully or partially) comprehensive doctrine.

Of course, as a liberalism, it has the kind of content we historically associate with liberalism. It affirms certain basic political and civil rights and liberties, assigns them a certain priority, and so on. Justice as fairness begins with the fundamental intuitive idea of a well-ordered society as a fair system of cooperation between citizens regarded as free and equal. This idea together with the five general facts shows the need for a political conception of justice, and such a conception in turn leads to the idea of "constitutional essentials," as we may refer to them.

A specification of the basic rights and liberties of citizens – rights and liberties they are to have in their status as free and equal – falls under those essentials. For such rights and liberties concern the fundamental principles that determine the structure of the political process – the powers of the legislative, executive, and the judiciary, the limits and scope of majority rule, as well as the basic political and civil rights and liberties legislative majorities must respect, such as the right to vote and to participate in politics, freedom of thought and liberty of conscience, and also the protections of the rule of law.

These matters are a long story; I merely mention them here. The point is that a political understanding of the constitutional essentials is of utmost urgency in securing a workable basis of fair political and social cooperation between citizens viewed as free and equal. If a political conception of justice provides a reasonable framework of principles and values for resolving questions concerning these essentials – and this must be its minimum objective – then a diversity of comprehensive doctrines may endorse it. In this case a political conception of justice is already of great significance, even though it may have little specific to say about innumerable economic and social issues that legislative bodies must regularly consider.

V THE SPECIAL DOMAIN OF THE POLITICAL

The three features of a political conception[16] make clear that justice as fairness is not applied moral philosophy. That is, its content – its principles, standards, and values – is not presented as an application of an already elaborated moral doctrine, comprehensive in scope and general in range. Rather, it is a formulation of a family of highly significant (moral) values that properly apply to basic political institutions; it gives a specification of those values which takes account of certain special features of the political relationship, as distinct from other relationships.

The political relationship has at least two significant features:

First, it is a relationship of persons within the basic structure of society, a structure of basic institutions we enter only by birth and exit only by death (or so we may appropriately assume).[17] Political society is closed, as it were; and we do not, and indeed cannot, enter or leave it voluntarily.

Second, the political power exercised within the political relationship is always coercive power backed by the state's machinery for enforcing its laws. In a constitutional regime political power is also the power of equal citizens as a collective body. It is regularly imposed on citizens as individuals, some of whom may not accept the reasons widely thought to justify the general structure of political authority (the constitution), some of whom accept that structure but do not regard as well grounded many of the statutes and other laws to which they are subject.

Political liberalism holds, then, that there is a special domain of the political identified by at least these features. So understood, the political is distinct from the associational, which is voluntary in ways that the political is not; it is also distinct from the personal and the familial, which are affectional domains, again in ways the political is not.[18]

Taking the political as a special domain, let us say that a political conception formulating its basic values is a "free-standing" view. It is a view for the basic structure that formulates its values independent of nonpolitical values and of any specific relationship to them. Thus a political conception does not deny that there are other values that apply to the associational, the personal, and the familial; nor does it say that the political is entirely separate from those values. But our aim is to specify the special domain of the political in such a way that its main institutions can gain the support of an overlapping consensus.

As a form of political liberalism, then, justice as fairness holds that, with regard to the constitutional essentials, and given the existence of a reasonably well-ordered constitutional regime, the family of very great political values expressed by its principles and ideals normally will have sufficient weight to override all other values that may come into conflict with them. Justice as fairness also holds, again with respect to constitutional essentials, that so far as possible, questions about those essentials should be settled by appeal to those political values alone. For it is on those questions that agreement among citizens who affirm opposing comprehensive doctrines is most urgent.

Now, in holding these convictions we clearly imply some relation between political and nonpolitical values. Thus, if it is said that outside the church there is no salvation,[19] and that hence a constitutional regime, with its guarantees of freedom of religion, cannot be accepted unless it is unavoidable, we must make some reply. From the point of view of political liberalism, the appropriate reply is to say that the conclusion is unreasonable:[20] it proposes to use the public's political power – a power in which citizens have an equal share – to enforce a view affecting constitutional essentials about which citizens as reasonable persons, given the burdens of reason, are bound to differ uncompromisingly in judgment.

It is important to stress that this reply does not say that a doctrine *Extra ecclesiam nulla salus* is not true. Rather, it says that it is unreasonable to use the public's political power to enforce it. A reply from within an alternative comprehensive view – the kind of reply we should like to avoid in political discussion – would say that the doctrine in question is incorrect and rests on a misapprehension of the divine nature. If we do reject the enforcement by the state of a doctrine as unreasonable we may of course also regard that doctrine itself as untrue. And there may be no way entirely to avoid implying its lack of truth, even when considering constitutional essentials.[21]

Note, however, that in saying it is unreasonable to enforce a doctrine, we do not necessarily reject it as incorrect, though we may do so. Indeed, it is vital to the idea of political liberalism that we may with perfect consistency hold that it would be unreasonable to use political power to enforce our own comprehensive religious, philosophical, or moral views – views which must, of course, affirm as true or reasonable (or at least as not unreasonable).

VI HOW IS POLITICAL LIBERALISM POSSIBLE?

The question now arises: how, as I have characterized it, is political liberalism possible? That is, how can the values of the special domain of the political – the values of a sub-domain of the realm of all values – normally outweigh any values that may conflict with them? Or put another way: how can we affirm our comprehensive doctrines as true or reasonable and yet hold that it would not be reasonable to use the state's power to gain the allegiance of others to them?[22]

The answer to this question has two complementary parts. The first part says that values of the political are very great values indeed and hence not easily overridden. These values govern the basic framework of social life, "the very groundwork of our existence,"[23] and specify the fundamental terms of political and social cooperation. In justice as fairness some of these great values are expressed by the principles of justice for the basic structure: the values of equal political and civil liberty, of fair equality of opportunity, of economic reciprocity, the social bases of mutual respect among citizens, and so on.

Other great values fall under the idea of free public reason, and are expressed in the guidelines for public inquiry and in the steps taken to secure that such inquiry is free and public, as well as informed and reasonable. These values include not only the appropriate use of the fundamental concepts of judgment, inference, and evidence, but also the virtues of reasonableness and fair-mindedness as shown in the adherence to the criteria and procedures of common-sense knowledge, and to the methods and conclusion of science when not controversial, as well as respect for the precepts governing reasonable political discussion.[24]

Together these values give expression to the liberal political ideal that since political power is the coercive power of free and equal citizens as a corporate body, this power should be exercised, when constitutional essentials are at stake, only in ways that all citizens can reasonably be expected to endorse publicly in the light of their own common, human reason.[25]

So far as possible, political liberalism tries to present a free-standing account of these values as those of a special domain – the political. It is left to citizens individually, as part of their liberty of conscience, to settle how they think the great values of the political domain relate to other values within their comprehensive doctrine. We hope that by doing this we can, in working political practice, firmly ground the constitutional essentials in those political values alone, and that these values will provide a satisfactory shared basis of public justification.

The second part of the answer as to how political liberalism is possible complements the first. This part says that the history of religion and philosophy shows that there are many reasonable ways in which the wider realm of values can be understood so as to be either congruent with, or supportive of, or else not in conflict with, the values appropriate to the special domain of the political as specified by a political conception of justice for a democratic regime. History tells of a plurality of not unreasonable comprehensive doctrines. That these comprehensive doctrines are divergent makes an overlapping consensus necessary. That they are not unreasonable makes it possible. A model case of an overlapping consensus of the kind I have considered elsewhere shows how this is so.[26] Many other such cases could make the same point.

VII THE QUESTION OF STABILITY

Justice as fairness, as I have said, is best presented in two stages.[27] In the first stage it is worked out as a free-standing political (but of course moral) conception for the basic structure of society. Only when this is done and its content – its principles of justice and ideals – is provisionally on hand do we take up, in the second stage, the problem of stability and introduce the idea of an overlapping consensus: a consensus in which a diversity of conflicting comprehensive doctrines endorse the same political conception, in this case, justice as fairness.

In describing the second stage, let us agree that a political conception must be practicable, that is, must fall under the art of the possible. This contrasts with a moral

169

conception that is not political; a moral conception may condemn the world and human nature as too corrupt to be moved by its precepts and ideals.

There are, however, two ways in which a political conception may be concerned with stability.[28] In one way, we suppose that stability is a purely practical matter: if a conception fails to be stable, it is futile to try to base a political structure upon it. Perhaps we think there are two separate tasks: one is to work out a political conception that seems sound, or reasonable, at least to us; the other is to find ways to bring others who reject the conception to share it in due course, or failing that, to act in accordance with it, prompted if need be by penalties enforced by state power. As long as the means of persuasion or enforcement can be found, the conception is viewed as stable; it is not utopian in the pejorative sense.

But as a liberal conception, justice as fairness is concerned with stability in a second, very different way. Finding a stable conception is not simply a matter of avoiding futility. Rather, what counts is the kind of stability and the nature of the forces that secure it. The idea is that, given certain assumptions specifying a reasonable human psychology[29] and the normal conditions of human life, those who grow up under basic institutions that are just – institutions that justice as fairness itself enjoins – acquire a reasoned and informed allegiance to those institutions sufficient to render the institutions stable. Put another way, the sense of justice of citizens, in view of their traits of character and interests as formed by living under a just basic structure, is strong enough to resist the normal tendencies to injustice. Citizens act willingly so as to give one another justice over time. Stability is secured by sufficient motivation of the appropriate kind acquired under just institutions.[30]

The kind of stability required of justice as fairness is based, then, on its being a liberal political view, one that aims at being acceptable to citizens as reasonable and rational, as well as free and equal, and so addressed to their free public reason. Earlier we saw how this feature of liberalism connects with the feature of political power in a constitutional regime, namely, that it is the power of equal citizens as a collective body. It follows that if justice as fairness were not expressly designed to gain the reasoned support of citizens who affirm reasonable although conflicting comprehensive doctrines – the existence of such conflicting doctrines being a feature of the kind of public culture which that conception itself encourages – it would not be liberal.[31]

The point, then, is that, as a liberal conception, justice as fairness must not merely avoid futility; the explanation of why it is practicable must be of a special kind. The problem of stability is not the problem of bringing others who reject a conception to share it, or to act in accordance with it by workable sanctions if necessary – as if the task were to find ways to impose that conception on others once we are ourselves convinced it is sound. Rather, as a liberal political conception, justice as fairness relies for its reasonableness in the first place upon generating its own support in a suitable way by addressing each citizen's reason, as explained within its own framework.[32]

170

Only in this manner is justice as fairness an account of political legitimacy. Only so does it escape being a mere account of how those who hold political power can satisfy themselves, in the light of their own convictions, whether political or fully comprehensive, that they are acting properly – satisfy themselves, that is, and not citizens generally.[33] A conception of political legitimacy aims for a public basis of justification and appeals to free public reason, and hence to all citizens viewed as reasonable and rational.

VIII COMPARISON WITH *A THEORY OF JUSTICE*

It may seem that the idea of an overlapping consensus and related topics are a significant departure from *Theory*. They are some departure certainly; but how much? *Theory* never discusses whether justice as fairness is meant as a comprehensive moral doctrine or as a political conception of justice. In one place it says that if justice as fairness succeeds reasonably well, a next step would be to study the more general view suggested by the name "rightness as fairness."[34]

But *Theory* holds that even this view would not be fully comprehensive: it would not cover, for example, our relations to other living things and to the natural order itself.[35] *Theory* emphasizes the limited scope of justice as fairness, and the limited scope of the kind of view it exemplifies; the book leaves open the question of how far its conclusions might need revision once these other matters are taken into account. There is, however, no mention of the distinction between a political conception of justice and a comprehensive doctrine. The reader might reasonably conclude, then, that justice as fairness is set out as part of a comprehensive view that may be developed later were success to invite it.

This conclusion is supported by the discussion of the well-ordered society of justice as fairness in Part III of *Theory*.[36] There it is assumed that the members of any well-ordered society, whether it be a society of justice as fairness or of some other view, accept the same conception of justice and also, it seems, the same comprehensive doctrine of which that conception is a part, or from which it can be derived. Thus, for example, all the members of a well-ordered society associated with utilitarianism (classical or average) are assumed to affirm the utilitarian view, which is by its nature (unless expressly restricted) a comprehensive doctrine.

Although the term was introduced in another context,[37] the idea of an overlapping consensus was first introduced to think of the well-ordered society of justice as fairness in a different and more realistic way.[38] Given the free institutions which that conception itself enjoins, we can no longer assume that citizens generally, even if they accept justice as fairness, also accept the particular comprehensive view in which it might seem to be embedded in *Theory*. We now assume citizens hold two distinct views; or perhaps better, we assume their overall view has two parts. One part can be seen to be, or to coincide with, a political conception of justice; the other part is a (fully or partially) comprehensive doctrine to which the political conception is in some manner related.[39]

The political conception may be simply a part of, or an adjunct to, a partially comprehensive view; or it may be endorsed because it can be derived within a fully articulated comprehensive doctrine. It is left to citizens individually to decide for themselves in what way their shared political conception is related to their wider and more comprehensive views. A society is well-ordered by justice as fairness so long as, first, citizens who affirm reasonable comprehensive doctrines generally endorse justice as fairness as giving the content of their political judgments; and second, unreasonable comprehensive doctrines do not gain enough currency to compromise the essential justice of basic institutions.

This is a better and no longer utopian way of thinking of the well-ordered society of justice as fairness. It corrects the view in *Theory*, which fails to take into account the condition of pluralism to which its own principles lead.

Moreover, because justice as fairness is now seen as a free-standing political conception that articulates fundamental political and constitutional values, endorsing it involves far less than is contained in a comprehensive doctrine. Taking such a well-ordered society as the aim of reform and change does not seem altogether impracticable; under the reasonably favorable conditions that make a constitutional regime possible, that aim is a reasonable guide and may be in good part realized. By contrast, a free democratic society well-ordered by any comprehensive doctrine, religious or secular, is surely utopian in a pejorative sense. Achieving it would, in any case, require the oppressive use of state power. This is as true of the liberalism of rightness as fairness, as it is of the Christianity of Aquinas or Luther.

IX IN WHAT SENSE POLITICAL?

To trace our steps, I put before the reader this brief summary.[40] I have suggested that once we recognize the five general facts[41] and the inevitable burdens of reason even under favorable conditions,[42] and once we reject the oppressive use of state power to impose a single comprehensive doctrine as the way to achieve social unity, then we are led to democratic principles and must accept the fact of pluralism as a permanent feature of political life. Hence, to achieve social unity for a well-ordered democratic regime, what I have called political liberalism introduces the idea of an overlapping consensus and along with it the further idea of the political as a special domain. Political liberalism does this not only because its content includes the basic rights and liberties the securing of which leads to pluralism, but also because of the liberal ideal

172

of political legitimacy, namely, that social cooperation, at least as it concerns the constitutional essentials, is to be conducted so far as possible on terms both intelligible and acceptable to all citizens as reasonable and rational. Those terms are best stated by reference to the fundamental political and constitutional values (expressed by a political conception of justice) that, given the diversity of comprehensive doctrines, all citizens may still be reasonably expected to endorse.

We must, however, be careful that a political conception is not political in the wrong way. It should aim to formulate a coherent view of the very great (moral) values applying to the political relationship and to set out a public basis of justification for free institutions in a manner accessible to free public reason. It must not be political in the sense of merely specifying a workable compromise between known and existing interests, nor political in looking to the particular comprehensive doctrines known to exist in society and in then being tailored to gain their allegiance.

In this connection let us ensure that the assumptions about pluralism do not make justice as fairness political in the wrong way. Consider first the five general facts reviewed in Parts I and II. These we suppose are accepted from the point of view of you and me as we try to develop justice as fairness. When the original position is viewed as a device of representation, these facts are made available to the parties in that position as they decide which principles of justice to select. So if principles that require free democratic institutions are accepted in the first stage, then the account of the stability in the second stage must show how justice as fairness can be endorsed by an overlapping consensus. As we have seen, this follows because free institutions themselves lead to pluralism.

The crucial question, then, is whether the five general facts, along with other premises allowed by the constraints of the original position in the first stage, suffice to lead the parties to select the two principles of justice;[43] or whether certain further assumptions related to pluralism are also needed, assumptions that make justice as fairness political in the wrong way. I cannot settle this matter here; it would require a survey of the argument from the original position.

I believe we need only suppose in the first stage that the parties assume the fact of pluralism to obtain, that is, that a plurality of comprehensive doctrines exists in society.[44] The parties must then protect against the possibility that the person each party represents may be a member of a religious, ethnic, or other minority. This suffices for the argument for the equal basic liberties to get going. In the second stage, when stability is considered, the parties again assume that pluralism obtains. They confirm principles leading to a social world that allows free play to human nature and thus, we hope, encourages a diversity of reasonable rather than unreasonable comprehensive doctrines, given the burdens of reason.[45] This makes stability possible.

Now it is often said that the politician looks to the next election, the statesman to the next generation. To this we add that the student of philosophy looks to the standing conditions of human life, and how these affect the burdens of reason. Political philosophy must take into account the five general facts we noted, among them the fact that free institutions encourage a diversity of comprehensive doctrines. But in doing this we abstract from the particular content of these doctrines, whatever it may be, and from the many contingencies under which the doctrines exist. A political conception so arrived at is not political in the wrong way but suitably adapted to the public political culture that its own principles shape and sustain. And although such a conception may not apply to all societies at all times and places, this does not make it historicist, or relativist; rather, it is universal in virtue of its extending appropriately to specify a reasonable conception of justice among all nations.[46]

X CONCLUDING REMARKS

The foregoing shows, I think, that the freedoms discussed have a dual role. On the one hand, they are the result of the working out, at the most basic level (in what I called the first stage of justice as fairness), of the fundamental ideas of a democratic society as a fair system of cooperation between citizens as free and equal. On the other hand, in the second stage, we know on the basis of general facts and the historical condition of the age that a conception of political justice leading to free institutions must be acceptable to a plurality of opposing comprehensive doctrines. That conception must, therefore, present itself as independent of any particular comprehensive view and must firmly guarantee for all citizens the basic rights and liberties as a condition of their sense of security and their peaceful, mutual recognition.

As the first role is perhaps clearer than the second, I comment on the latter. We know from the burdens of reason that even in a well-ordered society, where the basic freedoms are secure, sharp political disagreement will persist on their more particular interpretation. For instance, where exactly should the line be drawn between church and state? Or, granting there is no such crime as seditious libel, who precisely belongs to the class of public persons in regard to whom the law of libel is relaxed? Or, what are the limits of protected speech? So the question arises: if disagreements on such constitutional essentials always remain, what is gained by a publicly recognized political conception? Isn't the aim – to underwrite the basic rights and liberties of citizens by achieving an overlapping consensus, thereby giving everyone the sense that their rights are indeed secure – still unresolved?

There are two replies to this. First, by securing the basic rights and liberties, and assigning them a due priority, the most divisive questions are taken off the political agenda. This means that they are publicly recognized as politically settled, once and for all, and so contrary views on those questions are emphatically rejected by all political parties.[47] Though disagreements remain, as they must, they occur in areas of less central significance, where reasonable citizens equally attached to the political conception may reasonably be expected to differ. If liberty of conscience is guaranteed and separation of church and state is enjoined, we still expect there to be differences about what more exactly these provisions mean. Differences in judgment on the details in matters of any complexity even among reasonable persons are a condition of human file. But with the most divisive questions off the political agenda, it should be possible to reach a peaceful settlement within the framework of democratic institutions.

A second reply, complementing the first, is that the political conception, when properly formulated, should guide reflective judgment both to an agreed enumeration of the basic rights and liberties and to an agreement about their central range of significance. This it can do by its fundamental intuitive idea of society as a fair system of cooperation between citizens as free and equal persons, and by its idea of such persons as having the two moral powers, one a capacity for a sense of justice and the other a capacity for a conception of the good, that is, a conception of what is worthy of their devoted pursuit over a complete life.[48] Basic rights and liberties secure the conditions for the adequate development and exercise of those powers by citizens viewed as fully cooperating members of society. Citizens are thought to have and to want to exercise these powers whatever their more comprehensive religious, philosophical, or moral doctrine may be. Thus, the equal political liberties and freedom of speech and thought enable us to develop and exercise these powers by participating in society's political life and by assessing the justice and effectiveness of its laws and social policies; and liberty of conscience and freedom of association enable us to develop and exercise our moral powers in forming, revising, and rationally pursuing our conceptions of the good that belong to our comprehensive doctrines and affirming them as such.[49]

But in view of the truism that no conception, whether in law, morals, or science, interprets and applies itself, we should expect various interpretations of even the constitutional essentials to gain currency. Does this jeopardize the rule of law? Not necessarily. The idea of the rule of law has numerous elements and it can be specified in a variety of ways. But however this is done, it cannot depend on the idea of a clear, unambiguous directive that informs citizens, or legislators, or judges what the constitution enjoins in all cases. There can be no such thing. The rule of law is not put in jeopardy by the circumstance that citizens, and even legislators and judges, may often hold conflicting views on questions of interpretation.

Rather, the rule of law means the regulative role of certain institutions and their associated legal and judicial practices. It may mean, among other things, that all officers of the government, including the executive, are under the law and that their acts are subject to judicial scrutiny, that the judiciary is suitably independent, and that civilian authority is supreme over the military. Moreover, it may mean that judges' decisions rest on interpreting existing law and relevant precedents, that judges must justify their verdicts by reference thereto and adhere to a consistent reading from case to case, or else find a reasonable basis for distinguishing them, and so on. Similar constraints do not bind legislators; while they may not defy basic law and can try politically to change it only in ways the constitution permits, they need not explain or justify their vote, though their constituents may call them to account. The rule of law exists so long as such legal institutions and their associated practices (variously specified) are conducted in a reasonable way in accordance with the political values that apply to them: impartiality and consistency, adherence to law and respect for precedent, all in the light of a coherent understanding of recognized constitutional norms viewed as controlling the conduct of all government officers.[50]

Two conditions underwrite the rule of law so understood: first, the recognition by politically engaged citizens of the dual role of the basic rights and liberties; and second, its being the case that the main interpretations of those constitutional essentials take the most divisive matters off the political agenda and specify the central range of significance of the basic liberties in roughly the same way. The ideas of the domain of the political and of an overlapping consensus indicate how these conditions strengthen the stability of a political conception.

It is important for the viability of a just democratic regime over time for politically active citizens to understand those ideas. For in the long run, the leading interpretations of constitutional essentials are settled politically. A persistent majority, or an enduring alliance of strong enough interests, can make of the Constitution what it wants.[51] This fact is simply a corollary to the third general fact – that an enduring democratic regime must be freely supported by a substantial majority of its politically active citizens. As a fact, we must live with it and see it as specifying further one of the conditions of achieving a well-ordered constitutional state.

NOTES

1   An overlapping consensus exists in a society when the political conception of justice that regulates its basic institutions is endorsed by each of the main religious, philosophical, and moral doctrines likely to endure in that society, from one generation to the next. [. . .] The idea is introduced in *A Theory of Justice* (Cambridge, Mass.: Harvard University Press, 1971), pp. 387–388.
2   Hereafter referred to as *Theory of Justice*.
3   For an awareness of these misgivings I am indebted to the comments of G. A. Cohen and Paul Seabright (soon after the lecture "Overlapping Consensus" was given at Oxford in May 1986), and to discussions with Jürgen Habermas (at Harvard the following October). For a better understanding of and suggestions for how to deal with the misgivings, I am greatly indebted to Ronald Dworkin, Thomas Nagel, and T. M. Scanlon. I also have gained much from Wilfried Hinsch, to whom I owe the important idea of a reasonable comprehensive doctrine, which I have simply elaborated a bit. This idea, when joined with suitable companion ideas such as the burdens of reason (see Section II) and the precepts of

reasonable discussion (see Section III), imposes an appropriate limit on the comprehensive doctrines we may reasonably expect to be included in an overlapping consensus.

4   See Section VIII.

5   See Section VII.

6   These powers are those of a capacity for a sense of justice and a capacity for a conception of the good. See *Theory of Justice*, p. 505; Chapter 28, sec. III.

7   This source of disagreement I have expressed in a somewhat flat way. It could be put more strongly by saying, as Thomas Nagel does, that there are basic conflicts of value in which there seem to be decisive and sufficient (normative) reasons for two or more incompatible courses of action; and yet some decision must be made. See T. Nagel, "The Fragmentation of Value," in *Mortal Questions* (Cambridge: Cambridge University Press, 1979), pp. 128–141. Moreover, these normative reasons are not evenly balanced, and so it matters greatly what decision is made. The lack of even balance holds because in such cases the values are incomparable. They are each specified by one of the several irreducibly different perspectives within which values arise, in particular, the perspectives that specify obligations, rights, utility, perfectionist ends, and personal commitments. Put another way, these values have different bases which their different formal features reflect. These basic conflicts reveal what Nagel thinks of as the fragmentation of value (ibid.). I find much in Nagel's discussion very plausible, and I might endorse it were I stating my own (partially) comprehensive moral doctrine; since I am not doing that, but rather trying so far as possible to avoid controversial philosophical theses and to give an account of the difficulties of reason that rest on the plain facts open to all, I refrain from any statement stronger than (e).

8   This point has often been stressed by Sir Isaiah Berlin, most recently in his article "On the Pursuit of the Ideal," *New York Review of Books*, March 17, 1988, p. 11.

9   For instance, consider the questions of the causes of unemployment and the more effective ways to reduce it.

10 I have adopted this idea from Pliny the Younger's remarks, "He who hates vice, hates mankind," quoted in Judith Shklar, *Ordinary Vices* (Cambridge, Mass.: Harvard University Press, 1984), p. 192.

11 Here I assume that any substantial majority will include citizens who hold conflicting comprehensive doctrines.

12 Note that this is a definition of stability for political conception of justice. It is not to be mistaken for a definition of stability, or of what I call the security, of a political regime (as a system of institutions).

13 The features of a political conception of justice are discussed in more detail in John Rawls, "Justice as Fairness; Political not Metaphysical," *Philosophy and Public Affairs*, 14 (1985), secs. I–III.

14 A political conception for the basic structure must also generalize to, or else fit in with, a political conception for an international society of constitutionally democratic states; but here I put this important matter aside. See note 46 below.

15 See Rawls, "Justice as Fairness", sec. V, and n. 22 (discussing a "political conception of the person").

16 See Section IV.

17 The appropriateness of this assumption rests in part on a point I shall only mention here, namely, that the right of emigration does not make the acceptance of political authority voluntary in the way than freedom of thought and liberty of conscience make the acceptance of ecclesiastical authority voluntary. This brings out a further feature of the domain of the political, one that distinguishes it from the associational.

18 The associational, the personal, and the familial are only three examples of the nonpolitical; there are others.

19 The common medieval maxim *Extra ecclesiam nulla salus* ("Outside the church there is no salvation") was used, for example, in the famous bull "Unam sanctam" of November 18, 1302, by Pope Boniface VIII; reprinted in *Enchiridion symbolorum definitionum et delcarationum de rebus fidei et morum*, 870, p. 279 (33d ed., H. Denzinger and A. Schoenmetzer, eds., 1965).

20 For clarity on this point I owe thanks to Wilfried Hinsch and Peter de Marneffe.

21 See John Rawls, "The Idea of an Overlapping Consensus", *Oxford Journal of Legal Studies*, (1987), sec. IV.

22 Recall here the formulation of political liberalism a few lines back, namely, given the existence of a well-ordered institutional democratic regime, the family of great values expressed by its principles and ideals, and realized in its basic institutions, normally has sufficient weight to override whatever other values may come into conflict with them. See Section IV above.

23 J. S. Mill, *Utilitarianism* (3rd ed., 1867), ch. 5, par. 25.

24 See Section III.

25 On this point see the instructive discussion by Jeremy Waldron, "Theoretical Foundations of Liberalism", *Philosophical Quarterly*, 37 (1987): 127.

26 See Rawls, "Justice as Fairness", sec. VI. The model case of an overlapping consensus is one in which the political conception is endorsed by three comprehensive doctrines: the first endorses justice as fairness, say, because its religious beliefs and understanding of faith lead to the principle of toleration and support the basic equal liberties; the second doctrine affirms justice as fairness as a consequence of a comprehensive liberal conception such as that of Kant or Mill; while the third affirms justice as fairness as a political conception, that is, not as a consequence of a wider doctrine but as in itself sufficient to express very great values that normally outweigh whatever other values might oppose them, at least under reasonably favorable conditions. Ibid. See also Rawls, "The Idea of an Overlapping Consensus", sec. III (more fully discussing this model case).

27 These two stages correspond to the two parts of the argument from the original position for the two principles of justice contained in *Theory of Justice*. In the first part the parties select principles without taking the effects of the special psychologies into account (ibid., pp. 118–193). In the second part they ask whether a society well-ordered by the principles selected in the first part would be stable, that is, would generate in its members a sufficiently strong sense of justice to counteract tendencies to injustice (ibid., pp. 395–587). The argument for the principles of justice is not complete until the principles selected in the first part are shown in the second part to be sufficiently stable. So in *Theory of Justice* the argument is not complete until the next to last section, sec. 86 (ibid., pp. 567–577). For these two parts, see ibid., pp. 144, 530–531.

28 In this and the next several paragraphs I am indebted to a very helpful discussion with T. M. Scanlon.

29 The assumptions of such a psychology are noted briefly in Rawls, "The Idea of an Overlapping Consensus", sec. VII. In section VI of the same essay I also consider the way in which a political conception can gain an allegiance to itself that may to some degree shape comprehensive doctrines to conform to its requirements. This is plainly an important aspect of stability and strengthens the second part of the answer as to how political liberalism is possible. See Section VI.

I wish to thank Francis Kamm or pointing out to me several significant complications in the relation between a political conception and the comprehensive doctrines it shapes to accord with it, and how far as a result the viability of political liberalism depends on the support of such doctrines. It seems best not to pursue these matters here but to postpone them until a more complete account of stability can be given.

30 As stated in *Theory of Justice*, the question is whether the just and the good are congruent (see ibid., pp. 395, 567–577). In section 86 of *Theory of Justice*, it is argued that a person who grows up in a society well-ordered by justice as fairness, and who has a rational plan of life, and who also knows, or reasonably believes, that everyone else has an effective sense of justice, has sufficient reason, founded on that person's good (and not on justice), to comply with first institutions (ibid., pp. 567–577). These institutions are stable because the just and the good are congruent. That is, no reasonable and rational person in the well-ordered society of justice as fairness is moved by rational considerations of the good not to honor what justice requires.

31 Recall that reasonable comprehensive doctrines are ones that recognize the burdens of reason and accept the fact of pluralism as a condition of human life under free democratic institutions, and hence accept freedom of thought and liberty of conscience. See Sections II and III.

32 The force of the phrase "within its own framework" as used in the text emerges in the two parts of the argument from the original position in *Theory of Justice*. Both parts are carried out within the same framework and subject to the same conditions embedded in the original position as a device of representation.

33 For this distinction, see Thomas Nagel, "What Makes Political Theory Utopian?" p. 5 (unpublished paper, April 1988, on file at New York University Law Review).

34 *Theory of Justice*, p. 17.

35 Ibid., p. 512.

36 Ibid., pp. 453–462.

37 Ibid., pp. 387–388.

38 See Rawls, "Justice as Fairness", sec. VI.

39 For example, in the well-ordered society of justice as fairness, some may hold a form of utilitarianism as their comprehensive doctrine, provided they understand that doctrine, as I believe J. S. Mill did, so as to coincide in its requirements with justice as fairness, at least for the most part. See Mill, *Utilitarianism*, ch. 3, par. 10.

40 I am grateful to Erin Kelley for valuable discussion about how to put this summary.

41 See Sections I and II.

42 See Section II.

43 These two principles are: (1) each person has an equal right to a fully adequate scheme of equal basic rights and liberties, which scheme is compatible with a similar scheme for all; (2) social and economic inequalities are to satisfy two conditions: first they must be attached to offices and positions open to all under conditions of fair equality of opportunity; and second, they must be to the greatest benefit of the least advantaged members of society. See Rawls, "Justice as Fairness", sec. II.

44 I should like to thank David Chow for very helpful comments on this point.

45 The reasons for thinking reasonable rather than unreasonable doctrines are encouraged are sketched briefly in Rawls, "The Idea of an Overlapping Consensus", secs. VI–VII.

46 Perhaps I should explain briefly that the political conception so arrived at may not apply to some societies because the general facts we have assumed may not appropriately obtain in their case. Nevertheless, those facts do obtain widely in the modern world, and hence

the political conception implies. Its not applying in some cases, however, does not make that conception relativist or historicist so long as it provides grounds for judging the basic institutions of different societies and their social policies. Thus the appropriate test of a conception's universality is whether it can be extended to, or developed into, a reasonable political conception of justice for an international society of nation-states. In *Theory of Justice*, pp. 377–379, I noted briefly how, after the principles of justice have been adopted for the basic structure of society (viewed as a closed scheme of cooperation), the idea of the original position can be used once more at the higher level. The parties are now seen as representatives of states. We start with (closed) societies and build up to the international society of states. Doing this locates us where we are and follows the historical tendencies of democratic societies. Others may want to begin with an original position in which the parties are seen as representatives of citizens of the world society. I supposed that in any case the outcome would be sometimes like the familiar principles of international justice governing a society of states rather than a world state, for example, a principle of equality among peoples as organized into states, though states who recognize certain duties toward other states. For I think that Kant is right that a world state would likely be either highly oppressive if not autocratic, or else torn by civil strife as separate peoples and cultures tried to win their autonomy. See Immanuel Kant, "Perpetual Peace: A Philosophical Sketch" (1795), trans. Lewis White Beck (1949). If so, the principles of international justice will also include a principle of equality among peoples as organized into states, and there will also be, I think, principles for forming and regulating loose confederations of states, and standards of fairness for various cooperative arrangements between them, and so on. In such a confederation or arrangement, one role the state, however arbitrary its boundaries may appear from a historical point of view, is to be the representative of a people as they take responsibility for their territory and the numbers they put on it, and especially for maintaining its environmental integrity and its capacity to sustain them in perpetuity.

Theory of Justice does not pursue these larger matters but only mentions the extension to the international system as background for discussing conscientious refusal in section 58, pp. 377–382. But given this extension, as briefly indicated, we can see that justice as fairness as a political conception is universal in at least two ways. First, its principles extend to the international society and bind all its members, the nation-states; and second, insofar as certain of a society's domestic institutions and policies are likely to lead to war or to expansionist aims, or to render a people unreliable and untrustworthy as partners in a confederation of states or in a cooperative arrangement, those institutions and policies are open to censure and sanctions of varying degrees of severity by the principles of international justice. Here violations of what are recognized as human rights may be particularly serious. Thus, the requirements of a just international society may reflect back and impose constraints downward on the domestic institutions of states generally. But these constraints will already be met, I assume, by a just constitutional regime.

I cannot pursue these matters further here, and have appended this note only to indicate why I think the political conception of justice as fairness is in a suitable way universal, and not relativist or historicist, even though it may not apply to all societies at all times and places. See John Rawls, "The Law of Peoples", *Collected Papers* (ed.) Samuel Freeman (Cambridge, Mass., Harvard University Press, 1993), pp. 529–564. Thomas Pogge's work *Realizing Rawls* (Ithaca: Cornell University Press, 1989) includes an account of international justice from within a conception much like justice as fairness, but very importantly revised and extended in a different way to the global sphere. His much fuller discussion will sustain, I believe, the same general point about the universality of such a conception, although his approach to international justice is very different.

47 For example, it is not on the political agenda whether certain groups are to have the vote, or whether certain religious or philosophical views have the protections of liberty of conscience and freedom of thought.

48 This conception of the person, which characterizes citizens, is also a political conception. See Rawls, "Justice as Fairness", sec. V. I added that persons understand their own conceptions of the good against the background of their own comprehensive doctrines.

49 For further discussion of the basic rights and liberties, see my book *Political Liberalism* (New York: Columbia University Press, 1993), ch. 8.

50 I owe thanks to T. M. Scanlon for helpful discussion of the rule of law as summarized in the last two paragraphs.

51 On this point, see Alexander Bickel, *The Least Dangerous Branch* (Indianapolis: Bobbs-Merrill, 1962), pp. 244–272, discussing the politics of *Dred Scott v. Sanford*, 60 U.S. (19 Haw.) 393 (1857), and the school segregation cases, notably *Brown v. Board of Education*, 347 U.S. 483 (1954).

12

COMMUNITARIAN CRITICS OF LIBERALISM*

Amy Gutmann

We are witnessing a revival of communitarian criticisms of liberal political theory. Like the critics of the 1960s, those of the 1980s fault liberalism for being mistakenly and irreparably individualistic. But the new wave of criticism is not a mere repetition of the old. Whereas the earlier critics were inspired by Marx, the recent critics are inspired by Aristotle and Hegel. The Aristotelian idea that justice is rooted in "a community whose primary bond is a shared understanding both of the good for man and the good of that community" explicitly informs Alasdair MacIntyre in his criticism of John Rawls and Robert Nozick for their neglect of desert;[1] and Charles Taylor in his attack on "atomistic" liberals who "try to defend . . . the priority of the individual and his rights over society."[2] The Hegelian conception of man as a historically conditioned being implicitly informs both Roberto Unger's and Michael Sandel's rejection of the liberal view of man as a free and rational being.[3]

The political implications of the new communitarian criticisms are correspondingly more conservative. Whereas the good society of the old critics was one of collective property ownership and equal political power, the good society of the new critics is one of settled traditions and established identities. For many of the old critics, the role of women within the family was symptomatic of their social and economic oppression; for Sandel, the family serves as a model of community and evidence of a good greater than justice.[4] For the old critics, patriotism was an irrational sentiment that stood in the way of world peace; for MacIntyre, the particularistic demands of patriotism are no less rational than the universalistic demands of justice.[5] The old critics were inclined to defend deviations from majoritarian morality in the name of nonrepression; the new critics are inclined to defend the efforts of local majorities to ban offensive activities in the name of preserving their community's "way of life and the values that sustain it."[6]

The subject of the new and the old criticism also differs. The new critics recognize that Rawls's work has altered the premises and principles of contemporary liberal theory. Contemporary liberals do not assume that people are possessive individualists; the source of their individualism lies at a deeper, more metaphysical level. According to Sandel, the problem is that liberalism has faulty foundations: in order to achieve absolute priority for principles of justice, liberals must hold a set of implausible metaphysical views about the self. They cannot admit, for example, that our personal identities are partly defined by our communal attachments.[7] According to MacIntyre, the problem is that liberalism lacks any foundations at all. It cannot be rooted in the only kind of social life that provides a basis for moral judgments, one which "views man as having an essence which defines his true end".[8] Liberals are therefore bound either to claim a false certainty for their principles or to admit that morality is merely a matter of individual opinion, that is, is no morality at all.

The critics claim that many serious problems originate in the foundational faults of liberalism. Perhaps the most troubling for liberals is their alleged inability to defend the basic principle that "individual rights cannot be sacrificed for the sake of the general good."[9] Because Sandel and MacIntyre make the most detailed and, if true, devastating cases against believing in a liberal politics of rights, I shall focus for the rest of this review on their arguments.

The central argument of Sandel's book is that liberalism rests on a series of mistaken metaphysical and metaethical views: for example, that the claims of justice are absolute and universal; that we cannot know each other well enough to share common ends; and that we can define our personal identity independently of socially given ends. Because its foundations are necessarily flawed, Sandel suggests in a subsequent article that we should give up the "politics of rights" for a "politics of the common good."[10]

MacIntyre begins his book with an even more "disquieting suggestion": that our entire moral vocabulary, of rights and the common good, is in such "grave disorder" that "we have – very largely, if not entirely – lost our comprehension, both theoretical and practical, of morality."[11] To account for how "we" have unknowingly arrived at this unenviable social condition, MacIntyre takes us on an intriguing tour of moral history, from Homeric Greece to the present. By the end of the tour, we learn that the internal incoherence of liberalism forces us to choose "Nietzsche or Aristotle," a politics of the will to power or one of communally defined virtue.[12]

THE LIMITS OF COMMUNITARIAN CRITICISM

Do the critiques succeed in undermining liberal politics? If the only foundations available to liberal politics are faulty, then perhaps one need not establish a positive case for communitarian politics to establish the claim that liberal politics is philosophically indefensible.[13] Although this is the logic of Sandel's claim concerning the limits of liberal justice, he gives no general argument to support his conclusion that liberal rights are indefensible.[14] He reaches this conclusion instead on the basis of an interpretation and criticism of Rawls's theory, which he reasonably assumes to be the best theory liberalism has yet to offer.

Sandel argues that despite Rawls's efforts to distance himself from Kantian metaphysics, he fails. Sandel attributes Rawls's failure to his acceptance of the "central claim" of deontology, "the *core conviction* Rawls seeks *above all* to defend. It is the claim that 'justice is the first virtue of social institutions.'"[15] As Rawls presents it, the "primacy of justice" describes a moral requirement applicable to institutions. Sandel interprets Rawls as also making a metaethical claim: that the foundations of justice must be independent of all social and historical contingencies without being transcendental.[16]

Why saddle Rawls's moral argument for the primacy of justice with this meaning? To be sure, Rawls himself argues that "embedded in the principles of justice . . . is an ideal of the person that provides an Archimedean point for judging the basic structure of society."[17] But to translate this passage into a claim that the grounds of justice can be noncontingent ignores most of what Rawls says to explain his Archimedean point, the nature of justification, and Kantian constructivism.[18] "Justice as fairness is not at the mercy, so to speak, of existing wants and interests. It sets up an Archimedean point . . . *without invoking a priori considerations*."[19] By requiring us to abstract from our particular but not our shared interests, the original position with its "veil of ignorance" and "thin theory of the good" avoids reliance on both existing preferences and a priori considerations in reasoning about justice. The resulting principles of justice, then, clearly rely on certain contingent facts: that we share some interests (in primary goods such as income and self-respect), but not others (in a particular religion or form of family life); that we value the freedom to choose a good life or at least the freedom from having one imposed upon us by political authority. If we do not, then we will not accept the constraints of the original position.

Rawls's remarks on justification and Kantian constructivism make explicit the contingency of his principles of justice. The design of the original position must be revised if the resulting principles do not "accommodate our firmest convictions."[20] Justification is not a matter of deduction from certain premises, but rather "a matter of the mutual support of many considerations, of everything fitting together into one coherent view."[21] Since Rawls accords the view "that justice is the first virtue of social institutions" the status of a "common sense conviction,"[22] this view is part of what his theory must coherently combine. Rawls therefore does not, nor need he, claim more for justice as fairness than that "given our history and the traditions embedded in our public life, it is the most reasonable doctrine for us. We can find no better charter for our social world."[23]

Rawls could be wrong about our firmest convictions or what is most reasonable for us. But instead of trying to demonstrate this, Sandel argues that Rawls must show that the content and claims of justice are independent of all historical and social particularities.[24] If this is what constitutes deontological metaphysics, then it is a metaphysics that Rawls explicitly and consistently denies.

What metaphysics must Rawlsian liberalism then embrace? Several commentators, along with Rawls himself, have argued that liberalism does not presuppose metaphysics.[25] The major aim of liberal justice is to find principles appropriate for a society in which people disagree fundamentally over many questions, including such metaphysical questions as the nature of personal identity. Liberal justice therefore does not provide us with a comprehensive morality; it regulates our social institutions, not our entire lives. It makes claims on us "not because it expresses our deepest self-understandings," but because it represents the fairest possible *modus vivendi* for a pluralistic society.[26]

The characterization of liberalism as nonmetaphysical can be misleading however. Although Rawlsian justice does not presuppose only *one* metaphysical view, it is not compatible with *all* such views. Sandel is correct in claiming that the Kantian conception of people as free and equal is incompatible with the metaphysical conception of the self as "radically situated" such that "the good of community . . . [is] so thoroughgoing as to reach beyond the motivations to the subject of motivations."[27] Sandel seems to mean that communally given ends can so totally constitute people's identities that they cannot appreciate the value of justice. Such an understanding of human identity would (according to constructivist standards of verification) undermine the two principles.[28] To be justified as the *political* ideals most consistent with the "public culture of a democratic society,"[29] Rawlsian principles therefore have to express some (though not all) of our deepest self-understandings. Rawls must admit this much metaphysics – that we are not radically situated selves – if justification is to depend not on "being true to an order antecedent to and given to us, but . . . [on] congruence with our deeper understanding of ourselves and our aspirations."[30]

If this, rather than Kantian dualism, is the metaphysics that liberal justice must admit, Sandel's critique collapses. Rawls need not (and he does not) claim that "justice is the first virtue of social institutions" in *all* societies to show that the priority of justice obtains *absolutely* in those societies in which people disagree about the good life and consider their freedom to choose a good life an important good.[31] Nor need Rawls assume that human identity is *ever* totally independent of ends and relations to others to conclude that justice must *always* command our moral allegiance unless love and benevolence make it unnecessary.[32] Deontological justice thus can recognize the conditional priority of justice without embracing "deontological metaethics" or collapsing into teleology. Sandel has failed therefore to show that the foundations of rights are mistaken.

MISSING FOUNDATIONS?

MacIntyre argues that the foundations are missing:

> The best reason for asserting so bluntly that there are no such rights is indeed of precisely the same type as the best reason which we possess for asserting that there are no witches . . .: every attempt to give good reasons for believing there *are* such rights has failed.[33]

The analogy, properly drawn, does not support MacIntyre's position. The best reason that people can give for believing in witches is that the existence of witches explains (supposedly) observed physical phenomena. Belief in witches therefore directly competes with belief in physics, and loses out in the competition. The best reason for taking rights seriously is of a different order: believing in rights is one way of regulating and constraining our behavior toward one another in a desirable manner. This reason does not compete with physics; it does not require us to believe that rights "exist" in any sense that is incompatible with the "laws of nature" as established by modern science.[34]

MacIntyre offers another, more historical argument for giving up our belief in rights. "Why," he asks, "should we think about our modern uses of *good*, *right*, and *obligatory* in any different way from that in which we think about late eighteenth-century Polynesian uses of taboo?"[35] Like the Polynesians who used *taboo* without any understanding of what it meant beyond "prohibited," we use *human right* without understanding its meaning beyond "moral trump." If the analogy holds, we cannot use the idea correctly because we have irretrievably lost the social context in which its proper use is possible.

But on a contextualist view, it is reasonable for *us* to believe in human rights: many of the most widely accepted practices of our society – equality of educational opportunity, careers open to talent, punishment conditional on intent – treat people as relatively autonomous moral agents. Insofar as we are committed to maintaining these practices, we are also committed to defending human rights.[36] This argument parallels MacIntyre's contextualist defense of Aristotelian virtue: that the established practices of heroic societies supported the Aristotelian idea that every human life has a socially determined *telos*. Each person had a "given role and status within a well-defined and highly determinate system of roles and statuses," which fully defined his identity: "a man who tried to withdraw himself from his given position . . . would be engaged in the enterprise of trying to make himself disappear."[37]

If moral beliefs depend upon supporting social practices for their validity, then we have more reason to believe in a liberal politics of rights than in an Aristotelian politics of the common good. In *our* society, it does not logically follow that: "I am someone's son or daughter, someone else's cousin or uncle; I am a citizen of this or that city, a member of this or that guild or profession; I belong to this clan, that tribe, this nation[,] *hence* what is good for me *has* to be THE good for one who inhabits these roles."[38] One reason it does not follow is that none of these roles carries with it only one socially given good. What follows from "what is good for me has to be the good for someone who was born female, into a first-generation American, working-class Italian, Catholic family"? Had Geraldine Ferraro asked, following Sandel, "Who am I?" instead of "What ends should I choose?" an answer would not have been any easier to come by.[39] The Aristotelian method of discovering the good by inquiring into the social meaning of roles is of little help in a society in which most roles are not attached to a single good. Even if there is a single good attached to some social roles (as caring for the sick is to the role of a nurse, or searching for political wisdom to the function of political philosophers, let us suppose), we cannot accurately say that our roles determine our good without adding that we often choose our roles because of the good that is attached to them. The unencumbered self is, in this sense, the encumbrance of our modern social condition.

But the existence of supporting social practices is certainly not a sufficient condition, arguably not even a necessary one, for believing in liberal rights rather than Aristotelian virtue. The practices that support liberal rights may be unacceptable to us for reasons that carry more moral weight than the practices themselves; we may discover moral reasons (even within our current social understandings) for establishing new practices that support a politics of the common good. My point here is not that a politics of rights is the only, or the best, possible politics for our society, but that neither MacIntyre's nor Sandel's critique succeeds in undermining liberal rights because neither gives an accurate account of their foundations. MacIntyre mistakenly denies liberalism the possibility of foundations; Sandel ascribes to liberalism foundations it need not have.

THE TYRANNY OF DUALISM

The critics' interpretive method is also mistaken. It invites us to see the moral universe in dualistic terms: either our identities are independent of our ends, leaving us totally free to choose our life plans, or they are constituted by community, leaving us totally encumbered by socially given ends; either justice takes absolute priority over the good or the good takes the place of justice; either justice must be independent of all historical and social particularities or virtue must depend completely on the particular social practices of each society; and so on. The critics thereby do a disservice to not only liberal but communitarian values, since the same method that reduces liberalism to an extreme metaphysical vision also renders communitarian theories unacceptable.

By interpreting Rawls's conception of community as describing "just a feeling," for example, Sandel invites us to interpret Aristotle's as describing a fully constituted identity. The same mode of interpretation that permits Sandel to criticize Rawls for betraying "incompatible commitments" by uneasily combining into one theory "intersubjective and individualistic images" would permit us to criticize Sandel for suggesting that community is "a mode of self-understanding *partly* constitutive" of our identity.[40] Neither Sandel's interpretation nor his critique is accurate.

MacIntyre's mode of interpreting modern philosophy similarly divides the moral world into a series of dualisms. The doomed project of modern philosophy, according to MacIntyre, has been to convert naturally egoistical men into altruists. "On the traditional Aristotelian view such problems do not arise. For what education in the virtues teaches me is that my good as a man is one and the same as the good of those others with whom I am bound up in human community."[41] But the real, and recognized, dilemma of modern liberalism, as we have seen, is not that people are naturally egoistical, but that they disagree about the nature of the good life. And such problems also arise on any (sophisticated) Aristotelian view, as MacIntyre himself recognizes in the context of distinguishing Aristotelianism from Burkean conservatism: "when a tradition is in good order it is always partially constituted by an argument about the goods the pursuit of which gives to that tradition its particular point and purpose."[42]

The dualistic vision thus tyrannizes over our common sense, which rightly rejects all "easy combinations" – the individualism MacIntyre attributes to Sartre and Goffman "according to which the self is detachable from its social and historical roles and statuses" such that it "can have no history,"[43] as well as the communitarian vision MacIntyre occasionally seems to share with Roberto Unger according to which the "conflict between the demands of individuality and sociability would disappear."[44] Because the critics misinterpret the metaphysics of liberalism, they also miss the appeal of liberal politics for reconciling rather than repressing most competing conceptions of the good life.

BEYOND METAPHYSICS: COMMUNITARIAN POLITICS

Even if liberalism has adequate metaphysical foundations and considerable moral appeal, communitarian politics might be morally better. But MacIntyre and Sandel say almost nothing in their books to defend communitarian politics directly. Sandel makes a brief positive case for its comparative advantage over liberalism in a subsequent article. "Where libertarian liberals defend the private economy and egalitarian liberals defend the welfare state," Sandel comments, "communitarians worry about the concentration of power in both the corporate economy and the bureaucratic state, and the erosion of those intermediate forms of community that have at times sustained a more vital public life." But these worries surely do not distinguish communitarians from most contemporary liberals, unless (as Sandel implies) communitarians therefore oppose, or refuse to defend, the market or the welfare state.[45] Sandel makes explicit only one policy difference: "communitarians would be more likely than liberals to allow a town to ban pornographic bookstores, on the grounds that pornography offends its way of life and the values that sustain it." His answer to the obvious liberal worry that such a policy opens the door to intolerance in the name of communal standards is that "intolerance flourishes most where forms of life are dislocated, roots unsettled, traditions undone." He urges us therefore "to revitalize those civic republican possibilities implicit in out tradition but fading in our time."[46]

What exactly does Sandel mean to imply by the sort of civic republicanism "implicit within our tradition"? Surely not the mainstream of our tradition that excluded women and minorities, and repressed most significant deviations from white, Protestant morality in the name of the common good. We have little reason to doubt that a liberal politics of rights is morally better than that kind of republicanism. But if Sandel is arguing that when members of a society have settled roots and established traditions, they will tolerate the speech, religion, sexual, and associational preferences of minorities, then history simply does not support his optimism. A great deal of intolerance has come from societies of selves so "confidently situated" that they were sure repression would serve a higher cause.[47] The common good of the Puritans of seventeenth-century Salem commanded them to hunt witches; the common good of the Moral Majority of the twentieth century commands them not to tolerate homosexuals. The enforcement of liberal rights, not the absence of settled community, stands between the Moral Majority and the contemporary equivalent of witch hunting.

The communitarian critics want us to live in Salem, but not to believe in witches. Or human rights. Perhaps the Moral Majority would cease to be a threat were the United States a communitarian society; benevolence and fraternity might take the place of justice. Almost anything is possible, but it does not make moral sense to leave liberal politics behind on the strengths of such speculations.[48]

Nor does it make theoretical sense to assume away the conflicts among competing ends – such as the conflict between communal standards of sexual morality and individual sexual preference – that give rise to the characteristic liberal concern for rights. In so doing, the critics avoid discussing how morally to resolve our conflicts and therefore fail to provide us with a political theory relevant to our world. They also may overlook the extent to which some of their own moral commitments presuppose the defense of liberal rights.

CONSTRUCTIVE POTENTIAL

Even if the communitarian critics have not given good reasons for abandoning liberalism, they have challenged its defenders. One should welcome their work if for no other reason than this. But there is another reason. Communitarianism has the potential for helping us discover a politics that combines community with a commitment to basic liberal values.

The critics' failure to undermine liberalism suggests not that there are no communitarian values but that they are properly viewed as supplementing rather than supplanting basic liberal values. We can see the extent to which our moral vision already relies on communitarian values by imagining a society in which no one does more or less than respect everyone else's liberal rights. People do not form ties of love and friendship (or they do so only insofar as necessary to developing the kind of character that respects liberal rights). They do not join neighborhood associations, political parties, trade unions, civic groups, synagogues, or churches. This might be a perfectly liberal, arguably even a just society, but it is certainly not the best society to which we can aspire. The potential of communitarianism lies, I think, in indicating the ways in which we can strive to realize not only justice but community through the many social unions of which the liberal state is the super social union.

What might some of those ways be? Sandel suggests one possibility: states might "enact laws regulating plant closings, to protect their communities from the disruptive effects of capital mobility and sudden industrial change."[49] This policy is compatible with the priority Rawls gives to liberty and may even be dictated by the best interpretation of the difference principle. But the explicit concern for preventing the disruption of local communities is an important contribution of communitarianism to liberalism. We should also, as Sandel suggests, be "troubled by the tendency of liberal programs to displace politics from smaller forms of association to more comprehensive ones." But we should not therefore oppose all programs that limit – or support all those that expand – the jurisdiction of local governments. We may be able to discover ways in which local communities *and* democracy can be vitalized without violating individual rights. We can respect the right of free speech by opposing local efforts to ban pornographic bookstores, for example, but still respect the values of community and democratic participation by supporting local (democratic) efforts to regulate the location and manner in which pornographic bookstores display their wares. Attuned to the dangers of dualism, we can appreciate the way such a stand combines – uneasily – liberal and communitarian commitments.

Some ways of fostering communal values – I suspect some of the best ways – entail creating new political institutions rather than increasing the power of existing institutions or reviving old ones. By restoring "those intermediate forms of community that have at times sustained a more vital public life," we are unlikely to control "the concentration of power in both the corporate economy and the bureaucratic state" that rightly worries both communitarians and liberals.[50] If large corporations and bureaucracies are here to stay, we need to create new institutions to prevent them from imposing (in the name of either efficiency or expertise) their values on those of potentially more democratic communities. Realizing the relatively old idea of workplace democracy would require the creation of radically new economic institutions.[51] Recently mandated citizen review boards in areas such as health care, education, and community development have increased interest in democratic participation. Wholehearted political support of such reforms and others yet untried is probably necessary before we can effectively control bureaucratic power.[52] Although the political implications of the communitarian criticisms of liberalism are conservative, the constructive potential of communitarian values is not.

Had they developed the constructive potential of communitarian values, the critics might have moved further toward discovering both the limits of Rawlsian liberalism and a better charter for our social world. Instead, MacIntyre concludes that we should be "waiting not for a Godot, but for another – doubtless very different – St. Benedict."[53] The critics tend to look toward the future with nostalgia. We would be better off, by both Aristotelian and liberal democratic standards, if we tried to shape it according to our present moral understandings. At the end of his book, Sandel urges us to remember "the possibility that when politics goes well, we can know a good in common that we cannot know alone." But he has neglected the possibility that the only common good worth striving for is one that is not "an unsettling presence for justice."[54] Justice need not be the only virtue of social institutions for it to be better than anything we are capable of putting in its place. The worthy challenge posed by the communitarian critics therefore is not to replace liberal justice, but to improve it.

NOTES

* This review essay concentrates on the arguments presented in Michael Sandel, *Liberalism and the Limits of Justice* (New York: Cambridge University Press, 1982); Sandel, "Morality and the Liberal Ideal," *The New Republic*, May 7, 1984. pp. 15–17; Alasdair MacIntyre, *After Virtue* (Notre Dame: Notre Dame University Press, 1981); and MacIntyre, "Is Patriotism a Virtue?" *The Lindley Lecture* (University of Kansas: Department of Philosophy, March 26, 1984). Other works to which I refer are Benjamin Barber, *Strong Democracy: Participatory Politics for a New Age* (Berkeley: University of California Press, 1984); Charles Taylor, "Atomism", in Alkis Kontos, ed., *Powers, Possessions and Freedom: Essays in Honor of C. B. Macpherson* (Toronto: University of Toronto Press, 1979), pp. 39–61, and "The Diversity of Goods," in *Utilitarianism and Beyond*, ed. Amartya Sen and Bernard Williams (New York: Cambridge University Press, 1982), pp. 129–44; Roberto Mangabeira Unger, *Knowledge and Politics* (New York: Free Press, 1975); and Michael Walzer, *Spheres of Justice* (New York: Basic Books, 1983)

1 MacIntyre, *After Virtue*, pp. 232–33.

2 "Atomism," p. 39.

3 *Knowledge and Politics*, pp. 85, 191–231; *Limits*, pp. 179–80.

4 Sandel, *Limits*, pp. 30–31, 33–34, 169.

5 "Is Patriotism a Virtue?" pp. 15–18 and passim.

6 Sandel, "Morality and the Liberal Ideal," p. 17.

7 *Limits*, pp. 64–65, 168–73.

8 *After Virtue*, p. 52.

9 Sandel, "Morality and the Liberal Ideal," p. 16.

10 Ibid., p. 17.

11 *After Virtue*, pp. 1–5.

12 *Ibid.*, pp. 49, 103–13, 238–45.

13 I say "perhaps" because if defensibility is relative to our alternatives, then Sandel still would have to establish the positive case for communitarian politics before claiming that the faulty foundations of liberal politics render it indefensible.

14 The general argument that can he constructed from Sandel's work (using his conceptual framework) is, I think, the following: (1) To accept a politics based on rights entails believing that justice should have absolute priority over all our particular ends (our conception of the good): (2) To accept the priority of justice over our conception of the good entails believing that our identities can be established prior to the good (otherwise our conception of the good will enter into our conception of justice); (3) Since our identities are constituted by our conception of the good, justice cannot be prior. Therefore we cannot consistently believe in the politics of rights. But each of the steps in this argument are suspect: (1) We may accept the politics of rights not because justice is prior to the good, but because our search for the good requires society to protect our right to certain basic freedoms and welfare goods; (2) Justice may be prior to the good not because we are "antecedently individuated," but because giving priority to justice may be the fairest way of sharing the goods of citizenship with people who do not accept our conception of the good; (2) Our identities are probably not constituted, at least not exclusively, by our conception of the good. If they were, one could not intelligibly ask: "What kind of person do I want to become?" Yet the question reflects an important part (although not necessarily the whole) of our search for identity. If, however, we assume by definition that our identities are constituted by our good, then we must consider our sense of justice to be part of our identities. My commitment to treating other people as equals, and therefore to respecting their freedom of religion, is just as elemental a part of my identity (on this understanding) as my being Jewish, and therefore celebrating Passover with my family and friends.

15 *Limits*, p. 15. Emphasis added. See *Theory of Justice* (Cambridge, MA: Harvard University Press, 1971), pp. 3–4, 36.

16 *Limits*, pp. 16–17. Rawls must, in Sandel's words, "find a standpoint neither compromised by its implication in the world nor dissociated and so disqualified by detachment."

17 Rawls, *A Theory of Justice*, p. 584: see also pp. 260–62.

18 In interpreting Rawls, I rely (as does Sandel) on passages from both *Theory of Justice* and "Kantian Constructivism in Moral Theory: the Dewey Lectures 1980," *The Journal of Philosophy* 77, no. 9 (September 1980), pp. 515–72. Someone might reasonably argue that not until "The Dewey Lectures" does Rawls consistently and clearly defend the position on justification that I attribute to him. Had Sandel directed his criticism only against *A Theory*

of Justice, his interpretation would have been more credible. But he still could not have sustained his central claim that Rawls's principles and liberalism more generally *must* rest on implausible metaethical grounds.

19 *A Theory of Justice*, p. 261. Emphasis added. See also "The Dewey Lectures," esp. pp. 564–67.

20 *A Theory of Justice*, p. 20. The reasoning is circular, but not viciously so, since we must also be prepared to revise our weaker judgments when principles match our considered convictions, until we reach "reflective equilibrium."

21 Ibid., pp. 21, 579.

22 Ibid., p. 586.

23 "The Dewey Lectures," p. 519. Cf. Sandel, *Limits*, p. 30.

24 *Limits*, p. 30. Sometimes Sandel comes close to making a more limited but potentially more plausible argument – that Rawls derives his principles of justice from the wrong set of historical and social particularities: from (for example) our identification with all free and rational beings rather than with particular communities. Such an argument, if successful, would establish different limits, and limits of only Rawlsian liberalism.

25 See Rawls, "The Independence of Moral Theory," *Proceedings and Addresses of the American Philosophical Association* 48 (1975), pp. 5–22.

26 Charles Larmore, "Review of *Liberalism and the Limits of Justice*," *The Journal of Philosophy* 81, no. 6 (June 1984): 338. See also Rawls, "The Dewey Lectures," p. 542.

27 Sandel, *Limits*, pp, 20–21, 149.

28 Rawls, "The Dewey Lectures," pp. 534–35, 564–67. See also *A Theory in Justice*, p. 260: "The theory of justice does, indeed, presuppose a theory of the good, but *within wide limits* this does not prejudge the choice of the sort of persons that men want to be." (Emphasis added.)

29 Rawls, "The Dewey Lectures," p. 518.

30 Ibid., p. 519.

31 Ibid., pp. 516–24. Cf. Sandel, *Limits*, pp. 28–40.

32 Rawls, *A Theory of Justice*, pp. 560–77. Cf. Sandel, *Limits*, pp. 47–65.

33 *After Virtue*, p. 67.

34 I am grateful to Thomas Scanlon for suggesting this reply.

35 *After Virtue*, p. 107.

36 We need not be committed to a thoroughly deontological moral apparatus. Sophisticated consequentialist theories justify these same practices and are consistent with believing in rights.

37 *After Virtue*, pp. 117, 119.

38 Ibid., pp. 204–5 (emphases added). Sandel makes a very similar point in *Limits*, p. 179.

39 *Limits*, pp. 58–59.

40 Ibid., p. 150. When Sandel characterizes his own preferred "strong" view of community, it is one in which people conceive their identity "as defined to *some extent* by the community of which they are a part." (Emphases added.)

41 *After Virtue*, pp. 212–13.

42 Ibid., p. 206.

43 Ibid., p. 205. See also Sandel, *Limits*, pp. 40, 150. Cf. p. 180.

44 *Knowledge and Politics*, p. 220.

45 "Morality and the Liberal Ideal," p. 17.

46 Ibid.

47 Sandel may be correct in claiming that *more* intolerance has come – in the form of fascism – from societies of "atomized, dislocated, frustrated selves." But the truth of this claim does not establish the case for communitarian over liberal politics unless our only choice is to support a society of totally "atomized" or one of totally "settled" selves. This dualistic interpretation of our alternatives seems to lead Sandel to overlook the moral value of establishing some balance between individualism and community, and to underestimate the theoretical difficulty of determining where the proper balance lies.

48 Sandel might want to argue that societies like Salem were not "settled." Perfectly settled communities would not be repressive because every individual's identity would be fully constituted by the community or completely compatible with the community's understanding of the common good. This argument, however, is a truism: a perfectly settled society would not be repressive, because perfect settlement would leave no dissent to repress.

49 "Morality and the Liberal Ideal," p. 17.

50 Ibid.

51 For a communitarian defense of economic democracy that is not based on a rejection of liberal values, see Michael Walzer, *Spheres of Justice*, pp. 161 and 291–303.

52 For a suggestive agenda of democratic reforms, see Benjamin Barber, *Strong Democracy*, pp. 261–307. Although Barber attacks liberal theory as fundamentally flawed in the first nine chapters, the aim of his agenda for reform in the last chapter is "to reorient liberal democracy toward civic engagement and political community, not to raze it" (p. 308).

53 Ibid., p. 245. Roberto Unger similarly concludes *Knowledge and Politics* waiting for God to speak (p. 235).

54 Cf. Sandel, *Limits*, p 183.

I am grateful to Robert Amdur, Michael Doyle, Steven Lukes, Susan Moller Okin, Judith Shklar, Dennis Thompson, Michael Walzer, Susan Wolf, and the Editors of *Philosophy & Public Affairs* for their helpful suggestions.

13

CROSS-PURPOSES: THE LIBERAL–COMMUNITARIAN DEBATE

Charles Taylor

We often hear talk of the difference between "communitarians" and "liberals" in social theory, and in particular in the theory of justice.[1] Certainly a debate seems to have been engaged between two "teams," with people like Rawls, Dworkin, Nagel, and Scanlon on one side (team L), and Sandel, MacIntyre, and Walzer on the other (team C). There are genuine differences, but I think there are also a lot of cross-purposes, and just plain confusion in this debate. That is because two quite different issues tend to get run together in it. We can call these, respectively, ontological issues and advocacy issues.

The ontological questions concern what you recognize as the factors you will invoke to account for social life. Or, put in the "formal mode," they concern the terms you accept as ultimate in the order of explanation. The big debate in this area, which has been raging now for more than three centuries, divides atomists from holists, as I propose to call them.[2] The former are often referred to as methodological individualists. They believe that in (a), the order of explanation, you can and ought to account for social actions, structures, and conditions, in terms of properties of the constituent individuals; and in (b), the order of deliberation, you can and ought to account for social goods in terms of concatenations of individual goods. In recent decades, Popper has declared himself a militant advocate of (a), while (b) is a key component of what Amartya Sen has defined as "welfarism," a central if often inarticulate belief of most writers in the field of welfare economics.[3]

Advocacy issues concern the moral stand or policy one adopts. Here there is a gamut of positions, which at one end give primacy to individual rights and freedom, and at the other give higher priority to community life or the good of collectivities. We could describe the positions on this scale as more or less individualist and collectivist. At one extreme we would find people like Nozick and Friedman and other libertarians; at the other, Enver Hodja's Albania, or the Red Guards of the cultural revolution define the ultimate benchmarks. Of course most sane people, when not in the grip of some relentless ideology, find themselves much closer to the middle; but there are still significant differences between, say, liberals à la Dworkin who believe that the state should be neutral between the different conceptions of the good life espoused by individuals, on one hand,[4] and those who believe that a democratic society needs some commonly recognized definition of the good life, on the other – a view which later I will defend.

The relation between these two congeries of issues is complex. On the one hand, they are distinct, in the sense that taking a position on one does not force your hand on the other. On the other hand, they are not completely independent, in that the stand one takes on the ontological level can be part of the essential background of the view one advocates. Both these relations, the distinctness and the connection, are inadequately appreciated, and this confuses the debate.

[. . .]

My belief is that the misconstruals occur because there has been widespread insensitivity to the difference between the two kinds of issue. The portmanteau terms "liberal" and "communitarian" will probably have to be scrapped before we can get over this, because they carry the implication that there is only one issue here, or that someone's position on one determines what he holds on the other. But a cursory look at the gamut of actual philosophical positions shows exactly the contrary. Either stand on the atomism–holism debate can be combined with either stand on the individualist–collectivist question. There are not only atomist individualists (Nozick) and holist collectivists (Marx), but also holist individualists, like Humboldt – and even atomist collectivists, as in the nightmare, programmed utopia of B. F. Skinner, "beyond freedom and dignity."[5] This last category may be of interest only for the student of the bizarre or the monstrous, but I would argue that Humboldt and his ilk occupy an extremely important place in the development of modern liberalism. They represent a trend of thought that is fully aware of the (ontological) social embedding of human agents, but at the same time prizes liberty and individual differences very highly. Humboldt was one of the important sources for Mill's doctrine of liberty. In the face of this, it is astonishing that anyone should read a defense of holism as entailing an advocacy of collectivism. But the rich tradition that Humboldt represents seems to have been forgotten by Mill's heirs in the English-speaking world.

Recovering the distinction I am making here is therefore worth the trouble, if it can allow this tradition to return to its rightful place in the debate. This is a big part of my (not so hidden) agenda, because it is the line of thought that I identify with.

But I also believe that the confusion of issues has contributed to a kind of eclipse of ontological thinking in social theory. Since this is the level at which we face important questions about the real choices open to us, the eclipse is a real misfortune. Sandel's first book was very important because he put on the agenda some issues that a properly aware liberalism ought to face. The reaction of the "liberal" consensus (to use one of the portmanteau terms I have just impugned) was that to obtrude issues about identity and community into the debate on justice was an irrelevancy. My thesis is that, quite the contrary, these matters are highly relevant, and the only alternative to discussing them is relying on an implicit and unexamined view of them. Moreover, in that the unexamined views on these matters in Anglo-Saxon philosophical culture tend to be heavily infected with atomist prejudices, the implicit understanding tends to be – according to my, holistic outlook – wrong. The result is that an ontologically disinterested liberalism tends to be blind to certain important questions. I would like in the remainder of this chapter to try to sketch why I think this is so.

There is a family of theories of liberalism that is now very popular, not to say dominant, in the English-speaking world, which I want to call "procedural." It sees society as an association of individuals, each of whom has his or her conception of a good or worthwhile life, and correspondingly, his or her life plan. The function of society ought to be to facilitate these life plans, as much as possible, and following some principle of equality. That is, the facilitation ought not to be discriminatory, although there is obviously some room for serious question as to exactly what this means: whether the facilitation ought to aim at equality of results, or of resources, or of opportunities, or of capacities, or whatever.[6] But many writers seem to agree on the proposition that the principle of equality or nondiscrimination would be breached if society itself espoused one or other conception of the good life. This would amount to discrimination, because we assume that in a modern pluralist society, there is a wide gamut of views about what makes a good life. Any view endorsed by society as a whole would be that of some citizens and not others. These latter, in seeing their views denied official favor, would not in effect be treated with equal respect in relation to their compatriots espousing the established view.

Thus, it is argued, a liberal society should not be founded on any particular notion of the good life. The ethic central to a liberal society is an ethic of the right, rather than the good. That is, its basic principles concern how society should respond to and arbitrate the competing demands of individuals. These principles would obviously include the respect of individual rights and freedoms, but central to any set that could be called liberal would be the principle of maximal and equal facilitation. This does not in the first instance define what goods the society will further, but rather how it will determine the goods to be advanced, given the aspirations and demands of its component individuals. What is crucial here are the procedures of decision, which is why I want to call this brand of liberal theory "procedural."[7]

There are grave problems with this model of liberalism, which only can be properly articulated when one opens up the ontological issues of identity and community I have been referring to. There are questions about the viability of a society which would really meet these specifications, and an issue about the applicability of this formula in societies other than the United States (and perhaps also Britain), where it has been mainly developed, which also have a prima facie right to be called liberal. In other words, the theory can be taxed with being unrealistic and ethnocentric. Both of these objections are directed against procedural liberalism's exclusion of a socially endorsed conception of the good.

The viability issue has been raised by thinkers in the civic humanist tradition. One of the central themes of this line of thought concerns the conditions for a free society. "Free" is understood here not in the modern sense of negative liberty, but more as the antonym to "despotic." Ancient writers, followed by such moderns as Machiavelli, Montesquieu, and Tocqueville, have all tried to define the conditions in terms of political culture in which a participatory regime can flourish. The underlying reasoning, in its different forms, has been of the following sort: every political society requires some sacrifices and demands some disciplines from its members: they have to pay taxes, or serve in the armed forces, and in general observe certain restraints. In a despotism, a regime where the mass of citizens are subject to the rule of a single master, or a clique, the requisite disciplines are maintained by coercion. In order to have a free society, one has to replace this coercion with something else. This can only be a willing identification with the polis on the part of the citizens, a sense that the political institutions in which they live are an expression of themselves. The "laws" have to be seen as reflecting and entrenching their dignity as citizens, and hence to be in a sense extensions of themselves. This understanding that the political institutions are a common bulwark of citizen dignity is the basis of what Montesquieu called "vertu," the patriotism which is "une préférence continuelle de l'intérêt public au sien propre,"[8] an impulse which cannot be placed neatly in the (very modern) classification egoistic-altruistic. It transcends egoism in the sense that people are really attached to the *common* good, to *general* liberty. But it is quite unlike the apolitical attachment to universal principle that the Stoics advocated, or that is central to modern ethics of the right.

The difference is that patriotism is based on an identification with others in a particular common enterprise. I am not dedicated to defending the liberty of just anyone, but I feel the bond of solidarity with my compatriots in our common enterprise, the common expression of our respective dignity. Patriotism is somewhere between friendship, or family feeling, on one side, and altruistic dedication on the other. The latter has no concern for the particular: I am inclined to act for the good of anyone anywhere. The former attach me to particular people. My patriotic allegiance does not bind me to individual people in this familial way; I may not know most of my compatriots, and may not particularly want them as friends when I do meet them. But particularity enters in because my bond to these people passes through our participation in a common political entity. Functioning republics are like families in this crucial respect, that part of what binds people together is their common history. Family ties or old friendships are deep because of what we have lived through together, and republics are bonded by time and climactic transitions.

Here is where we find ourselves pushed back into the ontological issues of community and identity I have been discussing. Of course there was a (premodern) time in the history of our civilization when patriotism was intellectually unproblematic. But the last three centuries have seen the growing power of atomist modes of thought, particularly in the English-speaking world, and more, these have fostered the constitution of an unreflecting common sense which is shot through with atomist prejudices. According to this outlook, there are individuals, who have inclinations and goals and life plans. These inclinations include affection for others, which may be mutual and hence bring about bonding. Families and friendships thus find a place. But beyond these, common institutional structures have to be understood as in the nature of collective instruments. Political societies in the understanding of Hobbes, Locke, Bentham, or the twentieth-century common sense that they have helped shape are established by collections of individuals to obtain benefits through common action that they could not secure individually. The action is collective, but the point of it remains individual. The common good is constituted out of individual goods, without remainder. This construal of society incorporates the atomist component of Sen's "welfarism" that I have already mentioned.

This implicit ontology has no place for functioning republics, societies bonded by patriotism in the above sense. For these are grounded on a common good of a stronger kind than atomism allows. To see this we have to dive deeper into the ontological level. I want to take a plunge now for a few paragraphs and raise an issue wider than the political, before returning to this question of the nature of republics.

There is a distinction largely ignored, or mischaracterized, in post-Cartesian thought: that between matters which are for me and for you, on one hand, and those which are for us, on the other. This distinction, plays a tremendously important and pervasive role in human affairs, in ways both banal and fateful. In a banal context, we transfer matters from one category to the other when we open an ordinary conversation over the back fence. "Fine weather we're having," I say to my neighbor. Prior to this, he was aware of the weather, may have been attending to it; obviously I was as well. It was a matter for him, and also for me. What the conversation-opener does is make it now a matter for *us*: we are attending to it now together. It is important to see that this attending-together is not reducible to an aggregation of attendings-separately. Obviously it involves something more than each of us enjoying the weather on our own. But our atomist prejudices may tempt us to try to account for this more in terms of aggregations of monological mind-states: for example, now I know that you are attending, and you know that I am attending, and you know that I know that you know, and so on.[9] But just adding these monological states does not get us the dialogic condition where things are for us. In certain circumstances, I can know just by seeing you that you are enjoying the weather, and you know the same of me, and since we're both in plain view of each other, each will know that the other knows, and so on. Nevertheless, it is very different when we actually start conversing.

A conversation is not the coordination of actions of different individuals, but a common action in this strong, irreducible sense; it is *our* action. It is of a kind with – to take a more obvious example – the dance of a group or a couple, or the action of two men sawing a log. Opening a conversation is inaugurating a common action. This common action is sustained by little rituals which we barely notice, like the interjections of accord ('unhunh") with which the presently nonspeaking partner punctuates the discourse of the speaker, and with rituals which surround and mediate the switch of the "semantic turn" from one to the other.[10]

This threshold, which conversation takes us over, is one which matters in all sorts of ways and on all sorts of levels in human life. In human terms, we stand on a different footing when we start talking about the weather. That is the main point of conversation, where frequently the actual new information imparted may be sparse or nonexistent. Certainly I do not tell you anything new with my opener. On a deeper level, those whom I talk to about the things that matter to me are my intimates. Intimacy is an essentially dialogic phenomenon: it is a matter of what we share, of what's for us. One could never describe what it is to be on an intimate footing with someone in terms of monological states. On a transpersonal, institutional level, the same difference can play an important role. The steamy personal life of a political candidate may be for long an open secret, known to all insiders, journalists, politicians, even cab drivers in the capital. But a significant line is crossed when it breaks into the media and becomes "public knowledge." This has to do with the number and kind of people (unsophisticated country folks, for example), who know about it of course, but not only. It is also a matter of the way in which even those who "always" knew, now know: it is now for us, out there in public space. Analogous thresholds exist in the diplomatic world between states. Some things unsaid, or kept discreet, can be tolerated, which you have to react to once they are public. The move from the for-me-for-you to the for-us, the move into public space, is one of the most important things we bring about in language, and any theory of language has to take account of this.[11]

[. . .]

What has all this to do with republics? That it is essential to them, as I have characterized them, that they are animated by a sense of a shared immediate common good.

To that degree, the bond resembles that of friendship, as Aristotle saw.[12] The citizen is attached to the laws as the repository of his and others' citizen dignity. That might sound like the way I'm indebted to the Montreal Urban Community for its police service. But the crucial difference is that the latter relationship secures what we all understand as a merely convergent good, whereas the identification of the citizen with the republic as a common enterprise is essentially the recognition of a common good. My attachment to the MUC for its police service is based on enlightened self-interest. My (frequently inoperative) moral commitment to the welfare of all humans is altruistic. But the bond of solidarity with my compatriots in a functioning republic is based on a sense of shared fate, where the sharing itself is of value. This is what gives this bond its special importance, what makes my ties with these people and to this enterprise peculiarly binding, what animates my "virtu," or patriotism.

In other words, the very definition of a republican regime as classically understood requires an ontology different from atomism, and which falls outside atomism-infected common sense. It requires that we probe the relations of identity and community, and distinguish the different possibilities, in particular, the possible place of we-identities as against merely convergent I-identities, and the consequent role of common as against convergent goods. If we abstract from all this, then we are in danger of losing the distinction between collective instrumentality and common action, of misconstruing the republic as a hyped-up version of the Montreal Urban Community, delivering a product of much greater importance, and about which the beneficiaries feel (on grounds which are hard to fathom, but which have possibly irrational roots) particularly strongly.[13]

Perhaps this does not matter too much practically, if this kind of regime has no relevance to the modern world. And such is the view of many students of modern politics. But if we are going even to consider the basic thesis of the civic humanist tradition, we cannot simply just assume this from the outset. This thesis, to repeat, is that the essential condition of a free (nondespotic) regime is that the citizens have this kind of patriotic identification. This may have seemed self-evident to them because of their concept of freedom. This was not defined mainly in terms of what we would call negative liberty. Freedom was thought of as citizen liberty, that of the active participant in public affairs. This citizen was "free" in the sense as having a say in the decisions in the political domain, which would shape his and others' lives. Since participatory self-government is itself usually carried out in common actions, it is perhaps normal to see it as properly animated by common identifications. Since one exercises freedom in common actions, it may seem natural that one value it as a common good.

The underlying reasoning of the thesis, as I have said, is that the disciplines that would be externally imposed by fear under a despotism have to be self-imposed in its absence, and only patriotic identification can provide the motivation. But the case could also be argued in slightly different terms. We could say that a free, that is, participatory regime calls on the citizens to provide themselves for things which a despotism may provide for them. The foremost example of this was national defense. A despotic regime may raise money and hire mercenaries to fight for it; a republican regime will generally call on its citizens to fight for their own freedom. The causal links run in both directions. Citizen armies guarantee freedom because they are an obstacle to despotic takeover, just as large armies at the disposal of powerful generals invite a coup, as the agony of the Roman Republic illustrates. But at the same time, only people who live in and cherish a free regime will be motivated to fight for themselves. This relation between citizen armies and freedom was one of the main themes of Machiavelli's work.

So we could say that republican solidarity underpins freedom, because it provides the motivation for self-imposed discipline; or else that it is essential for a free regime, because this calls on its members to do things that mere subjects can avoid. In one case, we think of the demands on members as the same, and the difference concerns the motivation to meet them: fear of punishment versus inwardly generated sense of honor and obligation. In the other, the demands of freedom are defined as more onerous, and the issue concerns what can motivate this extra effort.

The second formulation very much depends on seeing freedom in participatory terms. Free regimes are more onerous, because they require service in public life, both military and political, that the unfree do not. The importance of this latter formulation in the civic humanist tradition shows the degree to which freedom was understood in terms of participation. But one can extract a thesis from this tradition about the essential bases of nondespotic society which is broader than this. The thesis would define nondespotism not just in terms of participation, but by a broader gamut of freedoms, including negative ones. It would draw on the first formulation to argue a link between the solidarity of patriotism and free institutions, on the grounds that a free society needs this kind of motivation to provide what despotisms get through fear; to engender the disciplines, the sacrifices, the essential contributions it needs to keep going, as well as to mobilize support in its defense when threatened.

If we call this basic proposition connecting patriotism and freedom the "republican thesis," then we can speak of narrower and broader forms of this, with the former focused purely on participatory freedom, and the latter taking in the broader gamut of liberties. With all these preliminaries behind us, we can finally address the first criticism of procedural liberalism, that it offers a nonviable formula for a free regime.

We can see right off how this kind of liberalism *seems* to run athwart the republican thesis. It conceives of society as made up of individuals with life plans, based on their conceptions of the good, but without a commonly held conception espoused by the society itself. But that seems to be the formula for an instrumental society, designed to seek merely convergent goods; it seems to exclude the republican form altogether.

This is the usual reaction of people steeped in the civic humanist tradition when they first confront the definitions of procedural liberalism. I confess that I find myself reacting this way. But this criticism as it stands is not quite right. There are confusions here, but what is interesting is that they are not all on one side, not only in the mind of the critic.

What is wrong with the criticism? The liberal can respond to the republican that he is not at all committed to a merely instrumental society. His formula does indeed exclude there being a societally endorsed common *good*, but not at all that there be a common understanding of the *right*; actually, it calls for this. The misunderstanding turns on two senses of "good." In the broad sense, it means anything valuable which we seek; in the narrower sense, it refers to life plans or ways of living which are so valued. Procedural liberalism cannot have a common good in the narrow sense, because society must be neutral on the question of the good life. But in the broader sense, where a rule of right can also count as "good," there can be an extremely important shared good.

So procedural liberalism can parry the objection of nonviability. This objection, to recall, came out of the republican thesis, and reading this type of liberal society as necessarily instrumental, saw it as essentially lacking citizen identification with a common good. But since this is a condition of a nondespotic regime, it judged this form of liberalism to be by its very nature self-undermining. A free society, which thus needs to call on a strong spontaneous allegiance from its members, is eschewing the indispensable basis of this: strong citizen identification around a sense of common good – what I have been calling "patriotism."

One reply to this attack would remain entirely within the assumptions of modern atomism. It would simply reject the republican thesis, and suppose that viable liberal societies can rely on quite different bases; either the eighteenth-century view that the citizens' allegiance could be grounded on enlightened self-interest; or the idea that modern civilization has educated people to higher moral standards, so that citizens are sufficiently imbued with the liberal ethos to support and defend their society; or else the idea current in modern "revisionist" democratic theory, that in fact a mature liberal society does not demand very much of its members, as long as it delivers the goods and makes their lives prosperous and secure. As a matter of fact, on this view it is better if the citizens do not try to participate too actively, but rather elect governments every few years and then let them get on with it.[14]

But procedural liberalism need not reply in this way. It can accept the republican thesis, and plead that it *does* have a place for a common good, and hence patriotism, hence that it can be viable as a free society.

Which reply ought liberalism to make? Those of an atomist outlook will opt for the first. They will think that the republican thesis, whatever its validity in ancient times, is irrelevant in modern mass bureaucratic society. People in the modern age have become individualist, and societies can only be held together in one or other of the ways I have just described. To hanker after the unity of earlier republics is to indulge in bootless nostalgia. If this is right, then all the ontological discussion of the previous pages, designed to make sense of republican societies, is of purely antiquarian interest, and the civic humanist critique of liberalism can be shrugged off.

But plausible as this atomist view might seem to us today, it is wide of the mark. We can see this if we look at the recent history of the United States, which is after all the main society of reference for procedural liberals. Think of the reaction to Watergate and, to a lesser degree, to the Iran-Contra misdemeanors. In the first case, citizen outrage actually drove a president from power. Now I want to make two, admittedly contestable, points about these reactions, which together amount to an important confirmation of the continuing relevance of the republican thesis.

The first is that the capacity of the citizenry to respond with outrage to this kind of abuse is an important bulwark of freedom in modern society. It is true that Americans are perhaps especially sensitive to acts of executive abuse, in comparison to other contemporary democracies – think, for instance, of the (absence of) French reaction to the *Rainbow Warrior* incident. But the general point would be that, although the targets might vary from society to society, most democratic electorates are disposed to react to violations of the norms of liberal self-rule, and this is a crucial supporting factor to the stability of these regimes. Where this disposition has been relatively lacking – as, for example, in a number of Latin American countries, where a large number of people are ready to tolerate "disappearances" perpetrated by semi-clandestine arms of the military, or to welcome army putsches – then one is in danger of ending up with an Argentine Junta or a murderous Pinochet regime.

The second point is that this capacity for outrage is not fueled from any of the sources already enumerated that are recognized by atomism. People do not respond this way because they calculate that it is in their long-term interest. Or rather, we should admit that some do, but they are comparatively few. Nor do most people respond just because of their general commitment to the principles of liberal democracy. This too plays a role, but by itself it would not lead to, say, an American reacting more vigorously to Nixon's violations than to Pinochet's or Enver Hodja's. Now there are certainly some people who feel very strongly about the fate of democracy everywhere, but they too are, alas, a relatively small minority of most modern electorates. Thirdly, people would barely respond at all if they thought of their society purely instrumentally, as the dispenser of security and prosperity.

What generates the outrage is something in none of the above categories, neither egoism nor altruism, but a species of patriotic identification. In the case of the United States, there is a widespread identification with "the American way of life," a sense of Americans sharing a common identity and history, defined by a commitment to certain ideals, articulated famously in the Declaration of Independence, Lincoln's Gettysburg address, and such documents, which in turn derive their importance from their connection to certain climactic transitions of this shared history. It is this sense of identity, and the pride and attachment which accompanies it, that is outraged by the shady doings of a Watergate, and this is what provokes the irresistible reaction.

In other terms, my second point is that republican patriotism remains a force in modern society, one that was very palpably operative during the days of Watergate. It goes unnoticed, partly because of the hold of atomist prejudices on modern theoretical thinking, and partly because its forms and locus are somewhat different from those of classical times. But it is still very much with us and plays an essential role in maintaining our contemporary liberal democratic regimes. Of course patriotism is also responsible for a lot of evil, today as at any time. It can also take the form of virulent nationalism, and in its darker forms encourages an Oliver North to violate the norms of a free society, even as it is generating a healthy defense against the danger he creates. But whatever menace the malign effects have spawned, the benign ones have been essential to the maintenance of liberal democracy.[15]

This is my second point. It is of course controversial. It involves a certain reading of recent history, and of its causes, which is far from being universally agreed. But I should like to make the point even stronger. Not only has patriotism been an important bulwark of freedom in the past, but it will remain unsubstitutably so for the future. The various atomist sources of allegiance have not only been insufficient to generate the vigorous defensive reaction à la Watergate; they will never be able to do so, in the nature of things. Pure enlightened self-interest will never move enough people strongly enough to constitute a real threat to potential despots and putschists. Nor will there, alas, be enough people who are moved by universal principle, unalloyed with particular identifications, moral citizens of cosmopolis, Stoic or Kantian, to stop these miscreants in their tracks. As for those who support a society because of the prosperity and security it generates, they are only fair-weather friends and are bound to let you down when you really need them. In other words, I want to claim that the republican thesis is as relevant and true today, in its peculiar contemporary application, as it was in ancient or early modern times, when the paradigm statements of civic humanism were articulated.

If I am right about this, then liberalism cannot answer the charge of nonviability just by assuming atomism and dismissing the republican thesis. To do so would be to be blind to the crucial dynamics of modern society. But that leaves the other answer: that a procedural liberal society can be a republican one in a crucial respect. And indeed, that is one way of reading the Watergate reaction. What the outraged citizens saw as violated was precisely a rule of right, a liberal conception of rule by law. That is what they identified with, and that is what they rose to defend as their common good. We no longer need to argue that, in theory, procedural liberalism allows for patriotism; we have a living case, or at least a close approximation, of such a patriotism of the right. The confusion in the mind of the critic would be to have thought that procedural liberalism entails an atomist ontology, on the grounds that it speaks of individual life plans, and that hence it can only draw allegiance from the atomist sources, which are manifestly inadequate to sustain it. But in fact a procedural liberal can be a holist; what is more, holism captures much better the actual practice of societies that approximate to this model. Thus runs a convincing answer to the critic – which incidentally illustrates again how essential it is not to confuse the ontological issue of atomism–holism with questions of advocacy opposing individualism and collectivism.

Now here it is the critics who seem to have fallen prey to this confusion. But they may not be the only victims. For once we understand procedural liberalism holistically, certain questions arise which its protagonists rarely raise.

(i) We can question whether a patriotic liberal regime really meets the full proceduralist demands. The common good is, indeed, a rule of right. But we have to remember that patriotism involves more than converging moral principles; it is a common allegiance to a particular historical community. Cherishing and sustaining this has to be a common goal, and this is more than just consensus on the rule of right. Put differently, patriotism involves beyond convergent values a love of the particular. Sustaining this specific historical set of institutions and forms is and must be a socially endorsed common end.

In other words, while the procedural liberal state can indeed be neutral between (a) believers and unbelievers in God, or (b) people with homo- and heterosexual orientations, it cannot be between (c) patriots and antipatriots. We can imagine its courts hearing and giving satisfaction to those who, under (a), object to school prayers, or those who, under (b), petition to ban a manual of sex education that treats homosexuality as a perversion. But supposing someone, under (c), objected to the pious tone with which American history and its major figures are presented to the young. The parents might declare themselves ready to abide by the rules of the procedural republic and to educate their children to do so, but this they will do for their own hyper-Augustinian reasons, that in this fallen world of depraved wills, such a modus vivendi is the least dangerous arrangement. But they'll be damned (no mere figure of speech, this!) if they'll let their children be brainwashed into taking as their heroes the infidel Jefferson, and the crypto-freethinker Washington, and indoctrinated into their shallow and impious cant about human perfectibility. Or else we might imagine a less ideological objection, where parents who espouse an apolitical life-style object to the implicit endorsement of active citizenship that flows from the patriots' view of American history.

These examples sound fanciful, and they are, indeed, very unlikely to happen. But why? Is it not because, while fighting about religion in schools has become a very

American thing to do and the battle continues well beyond the point where another less litigious people might have settled on a workable compromise, just because Americans on both sides feel that what they advocate is dictated by the constitution, so a questioning of the value of patriotism is profoundly un-American, and is close to unthinkable as a public act?[16] But logically such a challenge is possible, and it would be no more illegitimate on the terms of procedural liberalism than those under (a) and (b). But any court which gave satisfaction to such a suit would be undermining the very regime it was established to interpret. A line has to be drawn here before the demands of proceduralism.

This may not be a major problem. No political theory can be implemented in all the purity of its original model. There have to be some compromises with reality, and a viable procedural republic would have to be non-neutral about its own regime patriotism. But another issue, touched on earlier, must be explored.

(ii) This patriotic liberal regime differs from the traditional republican model. We have imagined that the values enshrined in the historically endorsed institutions are purely those of the rule of right, incorporating something like: the rule of law, individual rights, and some principles of fairness and equal treatment. What this leaves out is the central good of the civic humanist tradition: participatory self-rule. In fact, one could say that the center of gravity of the classical theory was at the opposite end of the spectrum: ancient theories were not concerned with individual rights, and they allowed some pretty hairy procedures judged by our modern standards of personal immunity – such as ostracism. Moreover, their notions of equal treatment applied very selectively from our point of view. But they did think citizen rule was of the very essence of the republic.

Now the question arises of what we make of this good in our modern liberal society. Procedural liberals tend to neglect it, treating self-rule as purely instrumental to the rule of law and equality. And indeed, to treat it as the republican tradition does, which sees self-rule as essential to a life of dignity, as the highest political good in itself, would take us beyond the bounds of procedural liberalism. Because a society organized around this proposition would share and endorse qua society at least this proposition about the good life. This is a clear, unconfused point of conflict between procedural liberals and republicans. Thinkers like Hannah Arendt and Robert Bellah clearly have an incompatible political ideal, which this liberalism cannot incorporate.[17] Well, so what? Why is that a problem for procedural liberalism?

Perhaps it is not, but important questions arise before we can be sure. The issue is, can our patriotism survive the marginalization of participatory self-rule? As we have seen, a patriotism is a common identification with an historical community founded on certain values. These can vary widely, and there can of course be patriotisms of unfree societies, for example, founded on race or blood ties, and finding expression in despotic forms, as in Fascism; or the patriotism of Russians, under tsars and Bolsheviks, which was/is linked to authoritarian forms of rule. A free society requires a patriotism, according to the republican thesis. But it must be one whose core values incorporate freedom. Historically republican patriotism has incorporated self-rule in its definition of freedom. Indeed, as we have seen, this has been at the core of this definition.

Does this have to be so? The point is, that the patriotism of a free society has to celebrate its institutions as realizing a meaningful freedom, one which safeguards the dignity of citizens. Can we define a meaningful freedom in this sense, which can capture people's allegiance, which does not include self-rule as a central element?

We could argue this point in general terms: What will moderns recognize as genuine citizen dignity? This has to be defined not only in terms of what is to be *secured* for a citizen; the modern notion of the dignity of the person is essentially that of an agent, who can affect his or her own condition. Citizen dignity involves a notion of citizen capacity. Two major models are implicit in much of my discussion.

A. One focuses mainly on individual rights and equal treatment, as well as a government performance which takes account of the citizen's preferences. This is what has to be secured. Citizen capacity consists mainly in the power to retrieve these rights and ensure equal treatment, as well as to influence the effective decisionmakers. This retrieval may take place largely through the courts, in systems with a body of entrenched rights, such as we find in the United States (and recently also in Canada). But it will also be effected through representative institutions. Only in the spirit of this model, these institutions have an entirely instrumental significance. They tend to be viewed as they were on the "revisionist" model mentioned earlier. That means that no value is put on participation in rule for its own sake. The ideal is not "ruling and being ruled in turn,"[18] but having clout. This is compatible with not engaging in the participatory system at all, provided one can wield a credible threat to those who are so engaged, so that they will take notice; or with engaging in it in an adversarial way, in which the actual governors are defined as "them" to our "us," and pressured through single-issue campaigns, or petitions or lobbies, to take us into account.

B. The other model, by contrast, defines participation in self-rule as of the essence of freedom, as part of what must be secured. This is thus also seen as an essential component of citizen capacity. In consequence, a society in which the citizen's relation to government is normally adversarial, even where he or she manages to bend it to his or her purposes, has not secured citizen dignity and allows only a low degree of citizen capacity. Full participation in self-rule is seen as being able, at least part of the time, to have some part in the forming of a ruling consensus, with which one can identify along with others. To rule and be ruled in turn means that at least some of the time the governors can be "us," not always "them." The sense of citizen capacity is seen as incompatible with our being part of an alien political universe, which one can perhaps manipulate but never identify with.

These two kinds of capacity are incommensurable. We cannot say simpliciter which is greater. For people of an atomist bent, there is no doubt that A will seem preferable, and for republicans B will seem the only genuine one. But ranking them in the abstract is not the issue. The point is to see which can figure in the definition of citizen dignity in a viable patriotism. This requires us to share an allegiance to and cherish in common a historical set of institutions as the common bulwark of our freedom and citizen dignity. Can definition A be the locus of some such common sentiment?

The reasons for being skeptical are that this model of citizen capacity is so adversarial that it would seem impossible to combine it with the sense that our institutions are a shared bulwark of dignity. If I win my way by manipulating the common institutions, how can I see them as reflecting a purpose common to me and those who participate in these institutions? But there are also reasons to be skeptical of a too simple logic. Once again the reality of United States experience gives us pause. One could argue that America has moved in the last century more and more toward a definition of its public life based on A. It has become a less participatory and more "procedural" republic.[19] Judicial retrieval has become more important; at the same time, participation in elections seems to be declining. Meanwhile, political action committees (PACs) threaten to increase the leverage of single-issue politics.

These are exactly the developments that republicans deplore, seeing in them a decline in civic spirit, and ultimately a danger for free society. But liberals could counterargue that the continuing vigor of American political life shows that a patriotism of model A is viable; that underlying the adversarial relation to the representative institutions is a continuing sense that the political structure of which they are a part remains a common bulwark of freedom. The law invites us to litigate as adversaries to get our way; but it entrenches and enshrines for both sides their freedom and capacity as citizens. After all, they may add, the agon of citizens struggling for office and honor was central to the classical polis. That regime too united adversaries in solidarity.

I do not know who will turn out to be right on this. Republicans argue that the continued growth of bureaucratic, centralized society and the consequent exacerbation of participant alienation cannot but undermine patriotism in the long run. Liberals will reply that the resources of rights retrieval will increase to empower people *pari passu* with the spread of bureaucratic power. Such measures as the freedom of information acts already show that countervailing power can be brought to bear.

But the question cannot be settled in purely general terms. It is not just a matter of whether in the abstract people can accommodate to one or other model of citizen dignity. The question must be particularized to each society's tradition and culture.

Procedural liberals seem to assume that something like model *A* is consonant with the American tradition, but this is vigorously contested by others, who argue that participation was an important part of early American patriotism and remains integral to the ideal by which American citizens will ultimately judge their republic.[20]

My aim cannot be to settle this issue. I raise it only to show how placing procedural liberalism against the background of a holist ontology, while answering the oversimple charge of nonviability in principle, opens a whole range of concrete questions about its viability in practice. These questions can be properly addressed only after we have settled issues on the ontological level, in fact in favor of holism. Both my main theses about the relation of the two levels are illustrated here: Once you have opted for holism, extremely important questions remain open on the level of advocacy; but at the same time, one's ontology structures the debate between the alternatives, and forces you to face certain questions. Clarifying the ontological question restructures the debate about advocacy.

When I said that procedural liberals might be confused about these levels, and not only those who proffer the simple republican criticism, I was referring to this. Certainly this liberalism has an answer to the in principle nonviability objection, and perhaps it will prove viable in practice. But procedural liberals seem quite unaware that this issue has to be addressed. Could it be that they are still too much in the thrall of common-sense atomist-infected notions, of the instrumental model of society, or of the various atomist sources of allegiance to see that there are questions here? That they are too insensitive to the ontological issues to see the point of the republican critique? I suspect that this is so. And thus they fail to articulate the distinction between ontological and advocacy questions, and take their communitarian critics to be simply advancing a different *policy*, which they vaguely apprehend as more collectivist; instead of seeing how the challenge is based on a redrawn map of political possibilities.

[. . .]

NOTES

1   This chapter applies a distinction which has been defined and explored in depth by Mimi Bick in her dissertation for Oxford, "The Liberal-Communitarian Debate: A Defense of Holistic Individualism" (unpub. diss., Trinity, 1987). My discussion owes a great deal to her work.

2   I am here following Mimi Bick's terminology; "Liberal-Communitarian Debate," chap. 1.

3   Sen's definition, which appears in Amartya Sen, "Utilitarianism and Welfarism," *The Journal of Philosophy* 76 (1979): 463–489, runs: "Welfarism: The judgement of the relative goodness of states of affairs must be based exclusively on, and taken as an increasing function of, the respective collections of individual utilities in these states." I have discussed the atomist component of welfarism so defined in "Irreducibly Social Goods" (forthcoming).

4   See Ronald Dworkin, "Liberalism," in Stuart Hampshire, ed., *Public and Private Morality* (Cambridge: Cambridge University Press, 1978); and "What Liberalism Isn't," *The New York Review of Books* 20 (January 1983): 47–50.

5   Mimi Bick, "Liberal-Communitarian Debate,' pp. 164–168, cites the case of Morelly as another example in this category.

6   See the debate between Amartya Sen, "Equality of What?" in *Choice, Welfare and Measurement* (Oxford: Blackwell, 1982), and "Capability and Well-Being," in Nussbaum, Martha C. and Sen, A. (eds.), *The Quality of Life* (New York: Oxford University Press, 1993), pp. 30–53; G. A. Cohen, "Equality of What? On Welfare, Resources and Capabilities," in Nussbaum, Martha C. and Sen, A. (eds.), *The Quality of Life* (New York: Oxford University Press, 1993), pp. 9–29.

7   I have tried to sketch the common features that unite the theories of Dworkin, "Liberalism," "What Liberalism Isn't," and "What is Equality?"; Rawls, *Theory of Justice*; Nagel, "Moral Conflict and Political Legitimacy," *Philosophy and Public Affairs* 16 (Summer 1987): 215–240; and T. M. Scanlon, "Contractualism and Utilitarianism," in Sen, Amartya and Williams, Bernard (eds.), *Utilitarianism and Beyond* (Cambridge: Cambridge University Press, 1982).

8   Montesquieu, *Esprit des Lois*, bk. IV, chap. 5.

9   See Stephen Schiffer's account of "mutual knowledge" in *Meaning* (Oxford: Oxford University Press, 1972), pp. 30ff.

10 See Greg Urban, "Ceremonial Dialogues in South America," *American Anthropologist* 88 (1986): 371–386.

11 I have tried to argue this in Charles Taylor, "Theories of Meaning," *Human Agency and Language* (Cambridge: Cambridge University Press, 1985).

12 *Nicomachean Ethics*, 1167b3.

13 There is another version of the civic humanist tradition, and of what I later refer to as its republican thesis, which has been articulated by Quentin Skinner and attributed by him to Machiavelli. See Quentin Skinner, "The Idea of Negative Liberty: Philosophical and Historical Perspectives," in Richard Rorty, J. B. Schneewind, and Quentin Skinner (eds.), *Philosophy in History* (Cambridge: Cambridge University Press, 1984). According to this, the appeal of the theory is purely to instrumental considerations. The only way to defend any of my freedoms is to sustain a regime of activity participation, because otherwise I shall be at the mercy of others who are far from having my interest at heart. On this version, we do without common goods altogether, and freedom is redefined as a convergent value. Skinner may be right about Machiavelli, though I am unconvinced. But this interpretation could not capture, for example, Montesquieu, Rousseau, Tocqueville, Mill (in *On Representative Government*), or Hannah Arendt. (Skinner does not claim that it does.) In that sense, the description that I am offering remains historically very relevant. The issue concerns which of these variants is relevant to today's politics. I am convinced that mine is.

14 For this revisionist, or elite, theory of democracy, see Joseph Schumpeter, *Capitalism, Socialism and Democracy*, 3rd ed. (New York: Harper, 1950).

15 The United States is peculiarly fortunate in that, from the very beginning, its patriotism welded together the sense of nationality with a liberal representative regime. For other Western nations these have been distinct, and even in tension. Think of France, where until recent decades a strong sense of national identity went along with a deep rift in the society, where an important segment rejected liberal democracy, even saw the greatness of France as entailing its rejection. The stability of contemporary Western democracies results from a fusion between national identity and free regimes finally having been achieved, so that

now Atlantic countries are proud to share a democratic civilization. But what happened at the beginning in the United States was achieved late and sometimes painfully in some other countries, for example, Germany or Spain – and perhaps now in Argentina? I have discussed this issue in "Alternative Futures," in Alan Cairns and Cynthia Williams (eds.), *Constitutionalism, Citizenship and Society in Canada* (Toronto: University of Toronto Press, 1985).

16 Of course there *have* been challenges to the requirement to take the pledge of allegiance, and the issue of whether it should be imposed was the occasion of some fairly base demagoguery in the 1988 presidential election. But this punctual challenge to a particular ritual on, say, religious grounds, although it poses a dilemma for a republican regime, does not frontally attack the central beliefs and attitudes that patriotism lives by, as my constructed examples were meant to do.

17 See Hannah Arendt, *The Human Condition* (Chicago: University of Chicago Press, 1958), Robert Bellah *et al.*, *Habits of the Heart* (Berkeley: University of California Press, 1985), and William Sullivan, *Reconstructing Public Philosophy* (Berkeley: University of California Press, 1982).

18 Aristotle, *Politics*, 1259b5.

19 See Michael Sandel, "The Procedural Republic and the Unencumbered Self," *Political Theory* 12 (February 1984): 81–96.

20 John Rawls seems to define the American liberal tradition pretty well exclusively in terms of the procedural ideal. See "Justice as Fairness: Political not Metaphysical," *Philosophy and Public Affairs* 14 (Summer 1985): 223–251. Michael Sandel takes issue with this view of American history, arguing for the recent hegemony of the procedural republic. See Sandel, "Procedural Republic," and also his forthcoming book. The issue is also hotly debated among American historians.

FURTHER READING

Caney, S. (1992). "Liberalism and Communitarianism: a Misconceived Debate." *Political Studies* 40: 273–89.

Mendus, S. (ed.) (1988). *Justifying Toleration: Conceptual and Historical Perspectives.* Cambridge, Cambridge University Press.

Mill, J. S. (1974). *On Liberty.* London, Penguin.

Miller, R. (1974). "Rawls and Marxism." *Philosophy and Public Affairs* 3(2): 167–91.

Nussbaum, M. C. (1993). *The Quality of Life.* New York, Oxford University Press.

Rawls, J. (1985). "Justice as Fairness: Political not Metaphysical." *Philosophy and Public Affairs* 14(3): 223–51.

Rawls, J. (1993). *Political Liberalism.* New York, Columbia University Press.

Rawls, J. (1999). *A Theory of Justice: Revised Edition.* Oxford, Oxford University Press.

Sayre-McCord, G. (2000). "Contractarianism." *The Blackwell Guide to Ethical Theory.* H. LaFollette (ed.). Oxford, Blackwell: 347–67.

Taylor, C. (1985). "Atomism." *Philosophy and the Human Sciences. Philosophical Papers,* Vol. 2. Cambridge, Cambridge University Press: 187–210.

Walzer, M. (1990). "The Communitarian Critique of Liberalism." *Political Theory* 18(1): 6–23.

Part 4

CITIZENSHIP AND MULTICULTURALISM

Introduction

IN THE TIME SINCE THE PUBLICATION of *A Theory of Justice*, liberals have had to come to terms with a changing world. They have been confronted by a world in which societies are divided on the ground of race and ethnicity, religious, national and regional antagonisms, and which are marked by a plurality of cultural identities within a single political structure. These realities seem to confront the universalism implicit in the liberal tradition. Can a liberal conception of citizenship cope with these sorts of strain? Can liberals be multiculturalists?

This chapter includes papers on this theme. Iris Marion Young's seminal and controversial article 'Polity and Group Difference' was published in 1989, and is one of the key papers in the emergence of a philosophically grounded critique of liberalism. In this paper and in her books such as *Justice and the Politics of Difference* (1990) Young makes the case for 'differentiated citizenship' – that is, a conception of citizenship in which rights, for example, for political representation, are not uniform but vary between groups and are distributed on a special, group basis. She asks why, historically, the extension of equal citizenship has not led to social justice and equality. Her prescription of special group rights and a heterogeneous public arises from her diagnosis of this gap between equal citizenship and social justice.

Addressing this disparity, Young points to a tension between three conceptions of citizenship – universality as inclusion, universality as generality and universality as equal treatment. For Young, the first is in tension with the second and third conceptions, and the tension ought to be resolved, to favour universal participation, by radical alterations to the second and third conceptions. The idea of citizenship expressing a general will implicitly supports exclusions and homogeneity, whilst differences between groups require 'the articulation of special rights that attend to group differences in order to undermine oppression and disadvantage'. The different conceptions of citizenship are shown below in Table 3.

Her radical conclusion is that a democratic polity should provide special mechanisms for the effective representation of those of its constituent groups that are oppressed or disadvantaged within it. This extends up to (for example) a veto on changes of the law on reproductive rights, for women as a self-organised group. The concrete proposals are for a 'constitutional convention' which would determine which groups deserve special representation, and then for those groups to organise themselves – with group assemblies which would delegate group representatives.

The public acknowledgement of group particularities with different and special rights in this way, is thought to be a problem for liberals. Young attempts to defuse these concerns by suggesting that they rest on a false, essentialist account of universal capacities, needs, culture, and so on: 'acknowledging group differences in capacities, needs, culture, and cognitive styles poses a problem for those seeking to eliminate oppression only if difference

Table 3 Different conceptions of citizenship

Liberal citizenship	Differentiated citizenship
Citizenship as the inclusion and participation of everyone	Universal inclusion and participation are endorsed but in tension with general will and equal treatment
Activities of citizenship express or create a general will	Unity suppresses and excludes perspectives – heterogeneous public
Citizenship as equal treatment	Equal, on what norm? Group representation and special rights

Source: Drawn from Young: *Polity and Group Difference*

is understood as deviance or deficiency'. But group differences should not be seen in this way – in fact, rectification of injustice ought to take account of those differences, and adapt the world external to the different in such a way as to make it more habitable. 'Difference-blind' liberalism ignores much of what is important and valuable to individuals, and it wrongly assumes an essentialist account of what it is to be fully human, organising the principles of justice on that false basis. Universal laws depend on norms that are neutral, but, argues Young, these norms simply do not exist. 'Equal treatment requires everyone to be measured according to the same norms, but in fact there are no neutral norms of behaviour and performance'.

In many cases of difference, this is a plausible account. The shift from seeking medical treatment for people with disabilities, to seeking to alter the spatial environment within which we live in order to make it more hospitable to those with disabilities, signifies a move away from an essentialist account that generates norms of behaviour and performance. But this new model for the rectification of injustice is perhaps not universally applicable. First, the question of whether, and to what extent, cultural attributes are the stuff of justice is likely to remain contentious. Liberals often privatise such concerns, away from the public sphere. Barry takes this point up in the excerpt below. Second, it could be objected that there are some norms of behaviour and performance – such as literacy – which do, *pace* Young, provide a basis for judgements of deficiency, and therefore the basis for a more essentialist approach to justice (Wolff 2002).

In the excerpt from his book, *Rethinking Multiculturalism*, Bhikhu Parekh (who formerly chaired Britain's Commission for Racial Equality) takes on three liberal thinkers – John Rawls, Jo Raz, and Will Kymlicka. All three have tried to reconcile liberal account of justice and rights with cultural diversity. In particular, liberals have highlighted the value of group membership, and hence the importance of groups in securing the conditions for the full exercise of individual autonomy. However, Parekh signals three problems with liberal accounts – first, that the ghost of a 'transcultural and culturally untainted power of autonomy' figures in their work. It is clear that there are affinities between this approach and the criticism of liberalism offered by communitarian thinkers such as Sandel. Second, Parekh alleges that liberals are guilty of 'absolutising' liberalism. This involves the granting to liberalism of a privileged status, and of enshrining its key value – autonomy – as a sort of 'metavalue' coming before all others. Third, Parekh argues that, for liberals, tolerance of non-liberal cultures is dependent on the acceptance of 'thinned down' liberal principles. This then raises a critical issue concerning the status of these principles. Can this acceptance be demanded of others without infringing their moral autonomy? If not, then the negotiations with non-liberals begin to look morally coercive. What, asks Parekh, is the genuinely universal basis on which liberalism rests?

Controversially, Parekh also argues that sensitivity to cultural difference requires a rethinking of the liberal commitment to equality of opportunity. He argues that 'opportunity is a subject dependent concept' and for a sensitivity to the way in which the absence of social and cultural resources make 'mute' some apparent opportunities. This notion of opportunity as subject-dependent has some affinities to the Marxist distinction between formal and real freedom. Just as Marxists argue that 'formal' equality before the law still left inequalities of resources and advantage untouched, Parekh looks to spread a similar argument to the cultural sphere.

Brian Barry's *Culture and Equality*, published in 2001, is the most recent major work of liberal individualism to be openly sceptical of the claims of multiculturalism. Barry endorses the traditional liberal approach to religious beliefs of constraining them to the private sphere – a strategy of 'privatisation'. He is, therefore, critical of the call in Parekh and others for special arrangements to accommodate religious and cultural beliefs, and particularly critical of the claim that these are demanded by justice. He concedes that they may sometimes be sensible for reasons of political prudence.

His first move is to consider whether the inequality of impact of laws between groups with different religious beliefs provides a basis for considering those laws to be unjust. He argues that inequality of impact means nothing, in and of itself, and to think that it does 'is simply a mistake'. This is because all laws impact differently on different individuals and groups, depending on how they behave. But does this change when the inequality of impact is determined by different sets of religious beliefs? To suggest that this is not the case, Barry appeals to an argument that comes from discussions of distributive justice. If we were concerned to secure equality of enjoyment, then we would skew distribution to those for whom enjoyment was only achieved expensively. If I have expensive tastes – for fine claret – then it will be expensive to satisfy those tastes.

But, Barry says, it is false that expensive preferences should skew distribution of goods towards their possessors in order to equalise satisfaction. This is because distributive justice is a matter of the distribution of rights, resources and opportunities. It is not relevant, from the standpoint of distributive justice, how much enjoyment is gained from these resources.

So my possession of expensive tastes is likely to mean that I derive less satisfaction from a just distribution of resources. Is this analogous to saying that if I have a particular set of beliefs, I will get less satisfaction from a series of just laws – but that impact on me does not thereby make them any less just? Whether it is analogous or not depends on the analogy between tastes and beliefs. It might be said that we can change our tastes but not our beliefs. Because we can change our preferences, but not our beliefs, justice ought to adapt to different beliefs in a way that it ought not to adapt to different preferences. However, Barry argues that this is not so. He endorses preference involuntarism and belief involuntarism – whilst we can try to strengthen both beliefs and preferences, at bottom, neither are matters of choice. It is, then, a mistake to skew institutions of justice and representation towards those who have 'expensive' cultural attributes.

Barry is critical of the view that liberalism is founded on the promotion of diversity. Liberalism offers limited cultural or group rights, but it can't accommodate 'deep diversity' – since liberals, in so far as they are liberals, need to insist on certain norms – such as respect for individual autonomy. This claim does perhaps seem open to the charge of Parekh that liberals 'absolutise' liberalism. He also endorses the Millian argument that a liberal values diversity not in itself, but because it promotes individuality, and Barry argues that the liberals' concern is not with diversity as such but with ensuring that behaviour is compatible with the existence of liberal institutions.

The debate between different versions of liberalism, and the plural cultural attachments that characterise the contemporary world, is by no means complete. Individual communities continue to try to reach a *modus vivendi* with the liberal order. Global institutions confront the problems raised by notions of cosmopolitan citizenship in a world marked by pluralism. In practice, as well as in theory, this is one of the most testing arenas for liberalism.

REFERENCES

Barry, B. (2001). *Culture and Equality*. Cambridge, Polity.

Kymlicka, W. (1995). *Multi-cultural Citizenship*. Oxford, Oxford University Press.

Kymlicka, W. (2001). *Politics in the Vernacular: Nationalism, Multiculturalism and Citizenship*. Oxford, Oxford University Press.

Raz, J. (1986). *The Morality of Freedom*. Oxford, Oxford University Press.

Wolff, J. (2002). 'Addressing Disadvantage and the Human Good.' *Journal of Applied Philosophy* 19, 3.

Young, I.M. (1989). 'Polity and Group Difference: A Critique of the Ideal of Universal Citizenship.' *Ethics* 99: 250–74.

Young, I.M. (1990). *Justice and the Politics of Difference*. Princeton, Princeton University Press.

14

POLITY AND GROUP DIFFERENCE

A critique of the ideal of universal citizenship

Iris Marion Young

An ideal of universal citizenship has driven the emancipatory momentum of modern political life. Ever since the bourgeoisie challenged aristocratic privileges by claiming equal political rights for citizens as such, women, workers, Jews, blacks, and others have pressed for inclusion in that citizenship status. Modern political theory asserted the equal moral worth of all persons, and social movements of the oppressed took this seriously as implying the inclusion of all persons in full citizenship status under the equal protection of the law.

Citizenship for everyone, and everyone the same qua citizen. Modern political thought generally assumed that the universality of citizenship in the sense of citizenship for all implies a universality of citizenship in the sense that citizenship status transcends particularity and difference. Whatever the social or group differences among citizens, whatever their inequalities of wealth, status, and power in the everyday activities of civil society, citizenship gives everyone the same status as peers in the political public. With equality conceived as sameness, the ideal of universal citizenship carries at least two meanings in addition to the extension of citizenship to everyone: (a) universality defined as general in opposition to particular; what citizens have in common as opposed to how they differ, and (b) universality in the sense of laws and rules that say the same for all and apply to all in the same way; laws and rules that are blind to individual and group differences.

During this angry, sometimes bloody, political struggle in the nineteenth and twentieth centuries, many among the excluded and disadvantaged thought that winning full citizenship status, that is, equal political and civil rights, would lead to their freedom and equality. Now in the early twenty-first century, however, when citizenship rights have been formally extended to all groups in liberal capitalist societies, some groups still find themselves treated as second-class citizens. Social movements of oppressed and excluded groups have recently asked why extension of equal citizenship rights has not led to social justice and equality. Part of the answer is straightforwardly Marxist: those social activities that most determine the status of individuals and groups are anarchic and oligarchic; economic life is not sufficiently under the control of citizens to affect the unequal status and treatment of groups. I think this is an important and correct diagnosis of why equal citizenship has not eliminated oppression, but in this article I reflect on another reason more intrinsic to the meaning of politics and citizenship as expressed in much modern thought.

The assumed link between citizenship for everyone, on the one hand, and the two other senses of citizenship – having a common life with and being treated in the same way as the other citizens – on the other, is itself a problem. Contemporary social movements of the oppressed have weakened the link. They assert a positivity and pride in group specificity against ideals of assimilation. They have also questioned whether justice always means that law and policy should enforce equal treatment for all groups. Embryonic in these challenges lies a concept of *differentiated* citizenship as the best way to realize the inclusion and participation of everyone in full citizenship.

In this article I argue that far from implying one another, the universality of citizenship, in the sense of the inclusion and participation of everyone, stands in tension with the other two meanings of universality embedded in modern political ideas: universality as generality, and universality as equal treatment. First, the ideal that the activities of citizenship express or create a general will that transcends the particular differences of group affiliation, situation, and interest has in practice excluded groups judged not capable of adopting that general point of view; the idea of citizenship as expressing a general will has tended to enforce a homogeneity of citizens. To the degree that contemporary proponents of revitalized citizenship retain that idea of a general will and common life, they implicitly support the same exclusions and homogeneity. Thus I argue that the inclusion and participation of everyone in public discussion and decision making requires mechanisms for group representation. Second, where differences in capacities, culture, values, and behavioral styles exist among groups, but some of these groups are privileged, strict adherence to a principle of equal treatment tends to perpetuate oppression or disadvantage. The inclusion and participation of everyone in social and political institutions therefore sometimes requires the articulation of special rights that attend to group differences in order to undermine oppression and disadvantage.

I CITIZENSHIP AS GENERALITY

Many contemporary political theorists regard capitalist welfare society as depoliticized. Its interest group pluralism privatizes policy-making, consigning it to back-room deals and autonomous regulatory agencies and groups. Interest group pluralism fragments both policy and the interests of the individual, making it difficult to assess issues in relation to one another and set priorities. The fragmented and privatized nature of the political process, moreover, facilitates the dominance of the more powerful interests.[1]

In response to this privatization of the political process, many writers call for a renewed public life and a renewed commitment to the virtues of citizenship. Democracy requires that citizens of welfare corporate society awake from their privatized consumerist slumbers, challenge the experts who claim the sole right to rule, and collectively take control of their lives and institutions through processes of active discussion that aim at reaching collective decisions.[2] In participatory democratic institutions citizens develop and exercise capacities of reasoning, discussion, and socializing that otherwise lie dormant, and they move out of their private existence to address others and face them with respect and concern for justice. Many who invoke the virtues of citizenship in opposition to the privatization of politics in welfare capitalist society assume as models for contemporary public life the civic humanism of thinkers such as Machiavelli or, more often, Rousseau.[3]

With these social critics I agree that interest group pluralism, because it is privatized and fragmented, facilitates the domination of corporate, military, and other powerful interests. With them I think democratic processes require the institutionalization of genuinely public discussion. There are serious problems, however, with uncritically assuming as a model the ideals of the civic public that come to us from the tradition of modern political thought.[4] The ideal of the public realm of citizenship as expressing a general will, a point of view and interest that citizens have in common which transcends their differences, has operated in fact as a demand for homogeneity among citizens. The exclusion of groups defined as different was explicitly acknowledged before [the twentieth] century. In our time, the excluding consequences of the universalist ideal of a public that embodies a common will are more subtle, but they still obtain.

The tradition of civic republicanism stands in critical tension with the individualist contract theory of Hobbes or Locke. Where liberal individualism regards the state as a necessary instrument to mediate conflict and regulate action so that individuals can have the freedom to pursue their private ends, the republican tradition locates freedom and autonomy in the actual public activities of citizenship. By participating in public discussion and collective decision making, citizens transcend their particular self-interested lives and the pursuit of private interests to adopt a general point of view from which they agree on the common good. Citizenship is an expression of the universality of human life; it is a realm of rationality and freedom as opposed to the heteronomous realm of particular need, interest, and desire.

Nothing in this understanding of citizenship as universal as opposed to particular, common as opposed to differentiated, implies extending full citizenship status to all groups. Indeed, at least some modern republicans thought just the contrary. While they extolled the virtues of citizenship as expressing the universality of humanity, they consciously excluded some people from citizenship on the grounds that they could not adopt the general point of view, or that their inclusion would disperse and divide the public. The ideal of a common good, a general will, a shared public life leads to pressures for a homogeneous citizenry.

Feminists in particular have analyzed how the discourse that links the civic public with fraternity is not merely metaphorical. Founded by men, the modern state and its public realm of citizenship paraded as universal values and norms which were derived from specifically masculine experience: militarist norms of honor and homoerotic camaraderie; respectful competition and bargaining among independent agents; discourse framed in unemotional tones of dispassionate reason.

Several commentators have argued that in extolling the virtues of citizenship as participation in a universal public realm, modern men expressed a flight from sexual difference, from having to recognize another kind of existence that they could not entirely understand, and from the embodiment, dependency on nature, and morality that women represent.[5] Thus the opposition between the universality of the public realm of citizenship and the particularity of private interest became conflated with oppositions between reason and passion, masculine and feminine.

The bourgeois world instituted a moral division of labor between reason and sentiment, identifying masculinity with reason and femininity with sentiment, desire, and the needs of the body. Extolling a public realm of manly virtue and citizenship as independence, generality, and dispassionate reason entailed creating the private sphere of the family as the place to which emotion, sentiment, and bodily needs must be confined.[6] The generality of the public thus depends on excluding women, who are responsible for tending to that private realm, and who lack the dispassionate rationality and independence required of good citizens.

In his social scheme, for example, Rousseau excluded women from the public realm of citizenship because they are the caretakers of affectivity, desire, and the body. If we allowed appeals to desires and bodily needs to move public debates, we would undermine public deliberation by fragmenting its unity. Even within the domestic realm, moreover, women must be dominated. Their dangerous, heterogeneous sexuality must be kept chaste and confined to marriage. Enforcing chastity on women will keep each family a separated unity, preventing the chaos and blood mingling that would be produced by illegitimate children. Chaste, enclosed women in turn oversee men's desire by tempering its potentially disruptive impulses through moral education. Men's desire for women itself threatens to shatter and disperse the universal, rational realm of the public, as well as to disrupt the neat distinction between the public and private. As guardians of the private realm of need, desire, and affectivity, women must ensure that men's impulses do not subvert the universality of reason. The moral neatness of the female-tended hearth, moreover, will temper the possessively individualistic impulses of the particularistic realm of business and commerce, since competition, like sexuality, constantly threatens to explode the unity of the polity.[7]

It is important to recall that universality of citizenship conceived as generality operated to exclude not only women, but other groups as well. European and American republicans found little contradiction in promoting a universality of citizenship that excluded some groups, because the idea that citizenship is the same for all translated in practice to the requirement that all citizens be the same. The white male bourgeoisie conceived republican virtue as rational, restrained, and chaste, not yielding to passion or desire for luxury, and thus able to rise above desire and need to a concern for the common good. This implied excluding poor people and wage workers from citizenship on the grounds that they were too motivated by need to adopt a general perspective. The designers of the American constitution were no more egalitarian than their European brethren in this respect; they specifically intended to restrict the access of the laboring class to the public, because they feared disruption of commitment to the general interests.

[. . .]

Contemporary critics of interest group liberalism who call for a renewed public life certainly do not intend to exclude any adult persons or groups from citizenship. They are democrats, convinced that only the inclusion and participation of all citizens in political life will make for wise and fair decisions and a polity that enhances rather than inhibits the capacities of its citizens and their relations with one another. The emphasis by such participatory democrats on generality and commonness, however, still threatens to suppress differences among citizens.

[. . .]

A repoliticization of public life should not require the creation of a unified public realm in which citizens leave behind their particular group affiliations, histories, and needs to discuss a general interest or common good. Such a desire for unity suppresses but does not eliminate differences and tends to exclude some perspectives from the public.[8] Instead of a universal citizenship in the sense of this generality, we need a group differentiated citizenship and a heterogeneous public. In a heterogeneous public, differences are publicly recognized and acknowledged as irreducible, by which I mean that persons from one perspective or history can never completely understand and adopt the point of view of those with other group-based perspectives and histories. Yet commitment to the need and desire to decide together the society's policies fosters communication across those differences.

II DIFFERENTIATED CITIZENSHIP AS GROUP REPRESENTATION

In her study of the functioning of a New England Town Meeting government, Jane Mansbridge discusses how women, blacks, working-class people, and poor people tend to participate less and have their interests represented less than whites, middle-class professionals, and men. Even though all citizens have the right to participate in the decision-making process, the experience and perspectives of some groups tend to be silenced for many reasons. White middle-class men assume authority more than others and they are more practiced at speaking persuasively; mothers and old people often find it more difficult than others to get to meetings.[9] Amy Gutmann also discusses how participatory democratic structures tend to silence disadvantaged groups. She offers the example of community control of schools, where increased democracy led to increased segregation in many cities because the more privileged and articulate whites were able to promote their perceived interests against blacks' just demand for equal treatment in an integrated system.[10] Such cases indicate that when participatory democratic structures define citizenship in universalistic and unified terms, they tend to reproduce existing group oppression.

Gutmann argues that such oppressive consequences of democratization imply that social and economic equality must be achieved before political equality can be instituted. I cannot quarrel with the value of social and economic equality, but I think its achievement depends on increasing political equality as much as the achievement of political equality depends on increasing social and economic equality. If we are not to be forced to trace a utopian circle, we need to solve now the "paradox of democracy" by which social power makes some citizens more equal than others, and equality of citizenship makes some people more powerful citizens. That solution lies at least in part in providing institutionalized means for the explicit recognition and representation of oppressed groups. Before discussing principles and practices involved in such a solution, however, it is necessary to say something about what a group is and when a group is oppressed.

The concept of a social group has become politically important because recent emancipatory and leftist social movements have mobilized around group identity rather than exclusively class or economic interests. In many cases such mobilization has consisted in embracing and positively defining a despised or devalued ethnic or racial identity. In the women's movement, gay rights movement, or elders' movements, differential social status based on age, sexuality, physical capacity, or the division of labor has been taken up as a positive group identity for political mobilization.

I shall not attempt to define a social group here, but I shall point to several marks which distinguish a social group from other collectivities of people. A social group involves first of all an affinity with other persons by which they identify with one another, and by which other people identify them. A person's particular sense of history, understanding of social relations and personal possibilities, her or his mode of reasoning, values, and expressive styles are constituted at least partly by her or his group identity. Many group definitions come from the outside, from other groups that label and stereotype certain people. In such circumstances the despised group members often find their affinity in their oppression. The concept of social group must be distinguished from two concepts with which it might be confused: aggregate and association.

An aggregate is any classification of persons according to some attribute. Persons can be aggregated according to any number of attributes, all of them equally arbitrary – eye color, the make of car we drive, the street we live on. At times the groups that have emotional and social salience in our society are interpreted as aggregates, as arbitrary classifications of persons according to attributes of skin color, genitals, or years lived. A social group, however, is not defined primarily by a set of shared attributes, but by the sense of identity that people have. What defines black Americans as a social group is not primarily their skin color; this is exemplified by the fact that some persons whose skin color is fairly light, for example, identify as black. Though sometimes objective attributes are a necessary condition for classifying oneself or others as a member of a certain social group, it is the identification of certain persons with a social status, a common history that social status produces, and a self-identification that defines the group as a group.

Political and social theorists tend more often to elide social groups with associations rather than aggregates. By an association I mean a collectivity of persons who come together voluntarily – such as a club, corporation, political party, church, college, union, lobbying organization, or interest group. An individualist contract model of society applies to associations but not to groups. Individuals constitute associations; they come together as already formed persons and set them up, establishing rules, positions, and offices.

Since one joins an association, even if membership in it fundamentally affects one's life, one does not take that association membership to define one's very identity in the way, for example, being Navajo might. Group affinity, on the other hand, has the character of what Heidegger calls "thrownness": one finds oneself as a member of a group, whose existence and relations one experiences as always already having been. For a person's identity is defined in relation to how others identify him or her, and others do so in terms of groups which always already have specific attributes, stereotypes, and norms associated with them, in reference to which a person's identity will be formed. From the thrownness of group affinity it does not follow that one cannot leave groups and enter new ones. Many women become lesbian after identifying as heterosexual, and anyone who lives long enough becomes old. These cases illustrate thrownness precisely in that such changes in group affinity are experienced as a transformation in one's identity.

A social group should not be understood as an essence or nature with a specific set of common attributes. Instead, group identity should be understood in relational terms. Social processes generate groups by creating relational differentiations, situations of clustering and affective bonding in which people feel affinity for other people. Sometimes groups define themselves by despising or excluding others whom they define as other, and whom they dominate and oppress. Although social processes of affinity and separation define groups, they do not give groups a substantive identity. There is no common nature that members of a group have.

As products of social relations, groups are fluid; they come into being and may fade away. Homosexual practices have existed in many societies and historical periods, for example, but gay male group identification exists only in the West in the twentieth century. Group identity may become salient only under specific circumstances, when in interaction with other groups. Most people in modern societies have multiple group identifications, moreover, and therefore groups themselves are not discrete unities. Every group has group differences cutting across it.

I think that group differentiation is an inevitable and desirable process in modern societies. We need not settle that question, however. I merely assume that ours is now a group differentiated society, and that it will continue to be so for some time to come. Our political problem is that some of our groups are privileged and others are oppressed.

But what is oppression? In another place I give a fuller account of the concept of oppression.[11] Briefly, a group is oppressed when one or more of the following conditions occurs to all or a large portion of its members: (1) the benefits of their work or energy go to others without those others reciprocally benefiting them (exploitation); (2) they are excluded from participation in major social activities, which in our society means primarily a workplace (marginalization); (3) they live and work under the authority of others, and have little work autonomy and authority over others themselves (powerlessness); (4) as a group they are stereotyped at the same time that their experience and situation is invisible in the society in general, and they have little opportunity and little audience for the expression of their experience and perspective on social events (cultural imperialism); (5) group members suffer random violence and harassment motivated by group hatred or fear. In the United States today at least the following groups are oppressed in one or more of these ways: women, blacks, Native Americans, Chicanos, Puerto Ricans and other Spanish-speaking Americans, Asian

Americans, gay men, lesbians, working-class people, poor people, old people, and mentally and physically disabled people.

Perhaps in some utopian future there will be a society without group oppression and disadvantage. We cannot develop political principles by starting with the assumption of a completely just society, however, but must begin from within the general historical and social conditions in which we exist. This means that we must develop participatory democratic theory not on the assumption of an undifferentiated humanity, but rather on the assumption that there are group differences and that some groups are actually or potentially oppressed or disadvantaged.

I assert, then, the following principle: a democratic public, however that is constituted, should provide mechanisms for the effective representation and recognition of the distinct voices and perspectives of those of its constituent groups that are oppressed or disadvantaged within it. Such group representation implies institutional mechanisms and public resources supporting three activities: (1) self-organization of group members so that they gain a sense of collective empowerment and a reflective understanding of their collective experience and interests in the context of the society; (2) voicing a group's analysis of how social policy proposals affect them, and generating policy proposals themselves, in institutionalized contexts where decision makers are obliged to show that they have taken these perspectives into consideration; (3) having veto power regarding specific policies that affect a group directly, for example, reproductive rights for women, or use of reservation lands for Native Americans.

The principles call for specific representation only for oppressed or disadvantaged groups, because privileged groups already are represented. Thus the principle would not apply in a society entirely without oppression. I do not regard the principle as merely provisional, or instrumental, however, because I believe that group difference in modern complex societies is both inevitable and desirable, and that wherever there is group difference, disadvantage or oppression always looms as a possibility. Thus a society should always be committed to representation for oppressed or disadvantaged groups and ready to implement such representation when it appears. These considerations are rather academic in our own context, however, since we live in a society with deep group oppressions the complete elimination of which is only a remote possibility.

Social and economic privilege means, among other things, that the groups which have it behave as though they have a right to speak and be heard, that others treat them as though they have that right, and that they have the material, personal, and organizational resources that enable them to speak and be heard in public. The privileged are usually not inclined to protect and further the interests of the oppressed partly because their social position prevents them from understanding those interests, and partly because to some degree their privilege depends on the continued oppression of others. So a major reason for explicit representation of oppressed groups in discussion and decision making is to undermine oppression. Such group representation also exposes in public the specificity of the assumptions and experience of the privileged. For unless confronted with different perspectives on social relations and events, different values and language, most people tend to assert their own perspective as universal.

Theorists and politicians extol the virtues of citizenship because through public participation persons are called on to transcend merely self-centered motivation and acknowledge their dependence on and responsibility to others. The responsible citizen is concerned not merely with interests but with justice, with acknowledging that each other person's interest and point of view is as good as his or her own, and that the needs and interests of everyone must be voiced and be heard by the others, who must acknowledge, respect, and address those needs and interests. The problem of universality has occurred when this responsibility has been interpreted as transcendence into a general perspective.

I have argued that defining citizenship as generality avoids and obscures this requirement that all experiences, needs, and perspectives on social events have a voice and are respected. A general perspective does not exist which all persons can adopt and from which all experiences and perspectives can be understood and taken into account. The existence of social groups implies different, though not necessarily exclusive, histories, experiences, and perspectives on social life that people have, and it implies that they do not entirely understand the experience of other groups. No one can claim to speak in the general interest, because no one of the groups can speak for another, and certainly no one can speak for them all. Thus the only way to have all group experience and social perspectives voiced, heard, and taken account of is to have them specifically represented in the public.

Group representation is the best means to promote just outcomes to democratic decision-making processes. The argument for this claim relies on Habermas's conception of communicative ethics. In the absence of a Philosopher King who reads transcendent normative verities, the only ground for a claim that a policy or decision is just is that it has been arrived at by a public which has truly promoted free expression of all needs and points of view. In his formulation of a communicative ethic, Habermas retains inappropriately an appeal to a universal or impartial point of view from which claims in a public should be addressed. A communicative ethic that does not merely articulate a hypothetical public that would justify decisions, but proposes actual conditions tending to promote just outcomes of decision-making processes, should promote conditions for the expression of the concrete needs of all individuals in their particularity.[12] The concreteness of individual lives, their needs and interests, and their perception of the needs and interests of others, I have argued, are structured partly through group-based experience and identity. Thus full and free expression of concrete needs and interests under social circumstances where some groups are silenced or marginalized requires that they have a specific voice in deliberation and decision making.

The introduction of such differentiation and particularity into democratic proce-dures does not encourage the expression of narrow self-interest; indeed, group repre-sentation is the best antidote to self-deceiving self-interest masked as an impartial or general interest. In a democratically structured public where social inequality is miti-gated through group representation, individuals or groups cannot simply assert that they want something; they must say that justice requires or allows that they have it. Group representation provides the opportunity for some to express their needs or inter-ests who would not likely be heard without that representation. At the same time, the test of whether a claim on the public is just, or a mere expression of self-interest, is best made when persons making it must confront the opinion of others who have explicitly different, though not necessarily conflicting, experiences, priorities, and needs. As a person of social privilege, I am not likely to go outside of myself and have a regard for social justice unless I am forced to listen to the voice of those my privilege tends to silence.

Group representation best institutionalizes fairness under circumstances of social oppression and domination. But group representation also maximizes knowledge expressed in discussion, and thus promotes practical wisdom. Group differences not only involve different needs, interests, and goals, but probably more important different social locations and experiences from which social facts and policies are understood. Members of different social groups are likely to know different things about the structure of social relations and the potential and actual effects of social policies. Because of their history, their group-specific values or modes of expression, their relationship to other groups, the kind of work they do, and so on, different groups have different ways of understanding the meaning of social events, which can contribute to the others' understanding if expressed and heard.

Emancipatory social movements in recent years have developed some political prac-tices committed to the idea of a heterogeneous public, and they have at least partly or temporarily instituted such publics. Some political organizations, unions, and feminist groups have formal caucuses for groups (such as blacks, Latinos, women, gay men and lesbians, and disabled or old people) whose perspectives might be silenced without them. Frequently these organizations have procedures for caucus voice in organization discussion and caucus representation in decision making, and some organizations also require representation of members of specific groups in leadership bodies. Under the influence of these social movements asserting group difference, during some years even the Democratic party, at both national and state levels, has instituted delegate rules that include provisions for group representation.

Though its realization is far from assured, the ideal of a "rainbow coalition" expresses such a heterogeneous public with forms of group representation. The tradi-tional form of coalition corresponds to the idea of a unified public that transcends particular differences of experience and concern. In traditional coalitions, diverse groups work together for ends which they agree interest or affect them all in a similar way, and they generally agree that the differences of perspective, interests, or opinion among them will not surface in the public statements and actions of the coalition. In a rainbow coalition, by contrast, each of the constituent groups affirms the presence of the others and affirms the specificity of its experience and perspective on social issues.[13] In the rainbow public, blacks do not simply tolerate the participation of gays, labor activists do not grudgingly work alongside peace movement veterans, and none of these paternalistically allow feminist participation. Ideally, a rainbow coalition affirms the presence and supports the claims of each of the oppressed groups or political movements constituting it, and it arrives at a political program not by voicing some "principles of unity" that hide differences but rather by allowing each constituency to analyze economic and social issues from the perspective of its experience. This implies that each group maintains autonomy in relating to its constituency, and that decision-making bodies and procedures provide for group representation.

To the degree that there are heterogeneous publics operating according to the principles of group representation in contemporary politics, they exist only in organizations and movements resisting the majority politics. Nevertheless, in principle participatory democracy entails commitment to institutions of a heterogeneous public in all spheres of democratic decision making. Until and unless group oppression or disadvantages are eliminated, political publics, including democratized workplaces and government decision-making bodies, should include the specific representation of those oppressed groups, through which those groups express their specific understanding of the issues before the public and register a group-based vote. Such structures of group representation should not replace structures of regional or party representation but should exist alongside them.

Implementing principles of group representation in national politics in the United States, or in restructured democratic publics within particular institutions such as factories, offices, universities, churches, and social service agencies, would require creative thinking and flexibility. There are no models to follow. European models of consociational democratic institutions, for example, cannot be taken outside of the contexts in which they have evolved, and even within them they do not operate in a very democratic fashion. Reports of experiments with publicly institutionalized self-organization among women, indigenous peoples, workers, peasants, and students in contemporary Nicaragua offer an example closer to the conception I am advocating.[14]

The principle of group representation calls for such structures of representation for oppressed or disadvantaged groups. But what groups deserve representation? Clear candidates for group representation in policy making in the United States are women, blacks, Native Americans, old people, poor people, disabled people, gay men and lesbians, Spanish-speaking Americans, young people, and nonprofessional workers. But it may not be necessary to ensure specific representation of all these groups in all public contexts and in all policy discussions. Representation should be designated whenever the group's history and social situation provide a particular perspective on the issues, when the interests of its members are specifically affected, and when its perceptions and interests are not likely to receive expression without that representation.

An origin problem emerges in proposing a principle such as this, which no philosophical argument can solve. To implement this principle a public must be constituted to decide which groups deserve specific representation in decision-making procedures. What are the principles guiding the composition of such a "constitutional convention"? Who should decide what groups should receive representation, and by what procedures should this decision take place? No program or set of principles can found a politics, because politics is always a process in which we are already engaged; principles can be appealed to in the course of political discussion, they can be accepted by a public as guiding their action. I propose a principle of group representation as a part of such potential discussion, but it cannot replace that discussion or determine its outcome.

What should be the mechanisms of group representation? Earlier I stated that the self-organization of the group is one of the aspects of a principle of group representation. Members of the group must meet together in democratic forums to discuss issues and formulate group positions and proposals. This principle of group representation should be understood as part of a larger program for democratized decision-making processes. Public life and decision-making processes should be transformed so that all citizens have significantly greater opportunities for participation in discussion and decision making. All citizens should have access to neighborhood or district assemblies where they participate in discussion and decision making. In such a more participatory democratic scheme, members of oppressed groups would also have group assemblies, which would delegate group representatives.

[. . .]

III UNIVERSAL RIGHTS AND SPECIAL RIGHTS

A second aspect of the universality of citizenship is today in tension with the goal of full inclusion and participation of all groups in political and social institutions: universality in the formulation of law and policies. Modern and contemporary liberalism hold as basic the principle that the rules and policies of the state, and in contemporary liberalism also the rules of private institutions, ought to be blind to race, gender, and other group differences. The public realm of the state and law properly should express its rules in general terms that abstract from the particularities of individual and group histories, needs, and situations to recognize all persons equally and treat all citizens in the same way.

231

As long as political ideology and practice persisted in defining some groups as unworthy of equal citizenship status because of supposedly natural differences from white male citizens, it was important for emancipatory movements to insist that all people are the same in respect of their moral worth and deserve equal citizenship. In this context, demands for equal rights that are blind to group differences were the only sensible way to combat exclusion and degradation.

Today, however, the social consensus is that all persons are of equal moral worth and deserve equal citizenship. With the near achievement of equal rights for all groups, with the important exception of gay men and lesbians, group inequalities nevertheless remain. Under these circumstances many feminists, black liberation activists, and others struggling for the full inclusion and participation of all groups in this society's institutions and positions of power, reward, and satisfaction, argue that rights and rules that are universally formulated and thus blind to differences of race, culture, gender, age, or disability, perpetuate rather than undermine oppression.

Contemporary social movements seeking full inclusion and participation of oppressed and disadvantaged groups now find themselves faced with a dilemma of difference.[15] On the one hand, they must continue to deny that there are any essential differences between men and women, whites and blacks, able-bodied and disabled people, which justify denying women, blacks, or disabled people the opportunity to do anything that others are free to do or to be included in any institution or position. On the other hand, they have found it necessary to affirm that there are often group-based differences between men and women, whites and blacks, able-bodied and disabled people that make application of a strict principle of equal treatment, especially in competition for positions, unfair because these differences put those groups at a disadvantage. For example, white middle-class men as a group are socialized into the behavioral styles of a particular kind of articulateness, coolness, and competent authoritativeness that are most rewarded in professional and managerial life. To the degree that there are group differences that disadvantage, fairness seems to call for acknowledging rather than being blind to them.

Though in many respects the law is now blind to group differences, the society is not, and some groups continue to be marked as deviant and as the other. In everyday interactions, images, and decision making, assumptions continue to be made about women, blacks, Latinos, gay men, lesbians, old people, and other marked groups, which continue to justify exclusions, avoidances, paternalism, and authoritarian treatment. Continued racist, sexist, homophobic, ageist, and ableist behaviors and institutions create particular circumstances for these groups, usually disadvantaging them in their opportunity to develop their capacities and giving them particular experiences and knowledge. Finally, in part because they have been segregated and excluded from one another, and in part because they have particular histories and traditions, there are cultural differences among social groups – differences in language, style of living, body comportment and gesture, values, and perspectives on society.

Acknowledging group difference in capacities, needs, culture, and cognitive styles poses a problem for those seeking to eliminate oppression only if difference is understood as deviance or deficiency. Such understanding presumes that some capacities, needs, culture, or cognitive styles are normal. I suggested earlier that their privilege allows dominant groups to assert their experience of and perspective on social events as impartial and objective. In a similar fashion, their privilege allows some groups to project their group-based capacities, values, and cognitive and behavioral styles as the norm to which all persons should be expected to conform. Feminists in particular have argued that most contemporary workplaces, especially the most desirable, presume a life rhythm and behavioral style typical of men, and that women are expected to accommodate to the workplace expectations that assume those norms.

Where group differences in capacities, values, and behavioral or cognitive styles exist, equal treatment in the allocation of reward according to rules of merit composition will reinforce and perpetuate disadvantage. Equal treatment requires everyone to be measured according to the same norms, but in fact there are no "neutral" norms of behavior and performance. Where some groups are privileged and others oppressed, the formulation of law, policy, and the rules of private institutions tend to be biased in favor of the privileged groups, because their particular experience implicitly sets the norm. Thus where there are group differences in capacities, socialization, values, and cognitive and cultural styles, only attending to such differences can enable the inclusion and participation of all groups in political and economic institutions. This implies that instead of always formulating rights and rules in universal terms that are blind to difference, some groups sometimes deserve special rights.[16] In what follows, I shall review several contexts of contemporary policy debate where I argue such special rights for oppressed or disadvantaged groups are appropriate.

The issue of a right to pregnancy and maternity leave, and the right to special treatment for nursing mothers, is highly controversial among feminists today. I do not intend here to wind through the intricacies of what has become a conceptually challenging and interesting debate in legal theory. As Linda Krieger argues, the issue of rights for pregnant and birthing mothers in relation to the workplace has created a paradigm crisis for our understanding of sexual equality, because the application of a principle of equal treatment on this issue has yielded results whose effects on women are at best ambiguous and at worst detrimental.[17]

In my view an equal treatment approach on this issue is inadequate because it either implies that women do not receive any right to leave and job security when having babies, or it assimilates such guarantees under a supposedly gender neutral category of "disability." Such assimilation is unacceptable because pregnancy and childbirth are normal conditions of normal women, they themselves count as socially necessary work, and they have unique and variable characteristics and needs.[18] Assimilating pregnancy into disability gives a negative meaning to these processes as "unhealthy." It suggests, moreover, that the primary or only reason that a woman has a right to leave and job security is that she is physically unable to work at her job, or that doing so would be more difficult than when she is not pregnant and recovering from childbirth. While these are important reasons, depending on the individual woman, another reason is that she ought to have the time to establish breastfeeding and develop a relationship and routine with her child, if she chooses.

The pregnancy leave debate has been heated and extensive because both feminists and nonfeminists tend to think of biological sex difference as the most fundamental and irradicable difference. When difference slides into deviance, stigma, and disadvantage, this impression can engender the fear that sexual equality is not attainable. I think it is important to emphasize that reproduction is by no means the only context in which issues of same versus different treatment arise. It is not even the only context where it arises for issues involving bodily difference. The last twenty years have seen significant success in winning special rights for persons with physical and mental disabilities. Here is a clear case where promoting equality in participation and inclusion requires attending to the particular needs of different groups.

Another bodily difference which has not been as widely discussed in law and policy literature, but should be, is age. With increasing numbers of willing and able old people marginalized in our society, the issue of mandatory retirement has been increasingly discussed. This discussion has been muted because serious consideration of working rights for all people able and willing to work implies major restructuring of the allocation of labor in an economy with already socially volatile levels of unemployment. Forcing people out of their workplaces solely on account of their age is arbitrary and unjust. Yet I think it is also unjust to require old people to work on the same terms as younger people. Old people should have different working rights. When they reach a certain age they should be allowed to retire and receive income benefits. If they wish to continue working, they should be allowed more flexible and part-time schedules than most workers currently have.

Each of these cases of special rights in the workplace – pregnancy and birthing, physical disability, and being old – has its own purposes and structures. They all challenge, however, the same paradigm of the "normal, healthy" worker and "typical work situation." In each case the circumstance that calls for different treatment should not be understood as lodged in the differently treated workers, per se, but in their interaction with the structure and norms of the workplace. Even in cases such as these, that is, difference does not have its source in natural, unalterable, biological attributes, but in the relationship of bodies to conventional rules and practices. In each case the political claim for special rights emerges not from a need to compensate for an inferiority, as some would interpret it, but from a positive assertion of specificity in different forms of life.[19]

Issues of difference arise for law and policy not only regarding bodily being, but just as importantly for cultural integrity and invisibility. By culture I mean group-specific phenomena of behavior, temperament, or meaning. Cultural differences include phenomena of language, speaking style or dialectic, body comportment, gesture, social practices, values, group-specific socialization, and so on. To the degree that groups are culturally different, however, equal treatment in many issues of social policy is unjust because it denies these cultural differences or makes them a liability.

[...]

The universalist finds a contradiction in asserting both that formerly segregated groups have a right to inclusion and that these groups have a right to different treatment. There is no contradiction here, however, if attending to difference is necessary in order to make participation and inclusion possible. Groups with different circumstances or forms of life should be able to participate together in public institutions without shedding their distinct identities or suffering disadvantage because of them. The goal is not to give special compensation to the deviant until they achieve normality, but rather to denormalize the way institutions formulate their rules by revealing the plural circumstances and needs that exist, or ought to exist, within them.

Many opponents of oppression and privilege are wary of claims for special rights because they fear a restoration of special classifications that can justify exclusion and stigmatization of the specially marked groups. Such fear has been particularly pronounced among feminists who oppose affirming sexual and gender difference in law and policy. It would be foolish for me to deny that this fear has some significant basis.

Such fear is founded, however, on accession to traditional identification of group difference with deviance, stigma, and inequality. Contemporary movements of oppressed groups, however, assert a positive meaning to group difference, by which a group claims its identity as a group and rejects the stereotypes and labeling by which others mark it as inferior or inhuman. These social movements engage the meaning of difference itself as a terrain of political struggle, rather than leave difference to be used to justify exclusion and subordination. Supporting policies and rules that attend to group difference in order to undermine oppression and disadvantage is, in my opinion, a part of that struggle.

Fear of claims to special rights points to a connection of the principle of group representation with the principle of attending to difference in policy. The primary means of defense from the use of special rights to oppress or exclude groups is the self-organization and representation of those groups. If oppressed and disadvantaged groups are able to discuss among themselves what procedures and policies they judge will best further their social and political equality, and have access to mechanisms to make their judgments known to the larger public, then policies that attend to difference are less likely to be used against them than for them. If they have the institutionalized right to veto policy proposals that directly affect them, and them primarily, moreover, such danger is further reduced.

In this article I have distinguished three meanings of universality that have usually been collapsed in discussions of the universality of citizenship and the public realm. Modern politics properly promotes the universality of citizenship in the sense of the inclusion and participation of everyone in public life and democratic processes. The realization of genuinely universal citizenship in this sense today is impeded rather than furthered by the commonly held conviction that when they exercise their citizenship, persons should adopt a universal point of view and leave behind the perceptions they derive from their particular experience and social position. The full inclusion and participation of all in law and public life is also sometimes impeded by formulating laws and rules in universal terms that apply to all citizens in the same way.

In response to these arguments, some people have suggested to me that such challenges to the ideal of universal citizenship threaten to leave no basis for rational normative appeals. Normative reason, it is suggested, entails universality in a Kantian sense: when a person claims that something is good or right he or she is claiming that everyone in principle could consistently make that claim, and that everyone should accept it. This refers to a fourth meaning of universality, more epistemological than political. There may indeed be grounds for questioning a Kantian-based theory of the universality of normative reason, but this is a different issue from the substantive political issues I have addressed here, and the arguments in this paper neither imply nor exclude such a possibility. In any case, I do not believe that challenging the ideal of a unified public or the claim that rules should always be formally universal subverts the possibility of making rational normative claims.

NOTES

1 Theodore Lowi's classic analysis of the privatized operations of interest group liberalism remains descriptive of American politics; see *The End of Liberalism* (New York: Norton, 1969). For more recent analyses, see Jürgen Habermas, *Legtimation Crisis* (Boston: Beacon, 1973); Claus Offe, *Contradictions of the Welfare State* (Cambridge, Mass.: MIT Press, 1984); John Keane, *Public Life in Late Capitalism* (Cambridge, Mass.: MIT Press, 1984); Benjamin Barber, *Strong Democracy* (Berkeley: University of California Press, 1984).

2 For an outstanding account of the virtues of and conditions for such democracy, see Philip Green, *Retrieving Democracy* (Totowa, N.J.: Rowman & Allanheld, 1985).

3 Barber and Keane both appeal to Rousseau's understanding of civic activity as a model for contemporary participatory democracy, as does Carole Pateman in her classic work, *Participation and Democratic Theory* (Cambridge: Cambridge University Press, 1970). (Pateman's position has, of course, changed.) See also James Miller, *Rousseau: Dreamer of Democracy* (New Haven, Conn.: Yale University Press, 1984).

4 Many who extol the virtues of the civic public, of course, appeal also to a model of the ancient polis. For a recent example, see Murray Bookchin, *The Rise of Urbanization and*

the Decline of Citizenship (San Francisco: Sierra Club Books, 1987). In this article, however, I choose to restrict my claims to modern political thought. The idea of the ancient Greek polis often functions in both modern and contemporary discussion as a myth of lost origins, the paradise from which we have fallen and to which we desire to return; in this way, appeals to the ancient Greek polis are often contained within appeals to modern ideas of civic humanism.

5   Hannah Pitkin performs a most detailed and sophisticated analysis of the virtues of the civic public as a flight from sexual difference through a reading of the texts of Machiavelli; see *Fortune Is a Woman* (Berkeley: University of California Press, 1984). Carole Pateman's writing also focuses on such analysis. See, e.g., Carole Pateman, *The Social Contract* (Stanford, Calif.: Stanford University Press, 1988). See also Nancy Hartsock, *Money, Sex and Power* (New York: Longman, 1983), chaps. 7 and 8.

6   See Susan Okin, "Women and the Making of the Sentimental Family," *Philosophy and Public Affairs* 11 (1982): 65–88; see also Linda Nicholson, *Gender and History: The Limits of Social Theory in the Age of the Family* (New York: Columbia University Press, 1986).

7   For analyses of Rousseau's treatment of women, see Susan Okin, *Women in Western Political Thought* (Princeton, N.J.: Princeton University Press, 1978); Lynda Lange, "Rousseau: Women and the General Will," in *The Sexism of Social and Political Theory,* ed. Lorenne M., G. Clark and Lynda Lange (Toronto: University of Toronto Press, 1979); Jean Bethke Elshtain, *Public Man, Private Woman* (Princeton, N.J.: Princeton University Press, 1981), chap. 4. Mary Dietz develops an astute critique of Elshtain's "maternalist" perspective on political theory; in so doing, however, she also seems to appeal to a universalist ideal of the civic public in which women will transcend their particular concerns and become general; see "Citizenship with a Feminist Face: The Problem with Maternal Thinking," *Political Theory* 13 (1985): 19–37. On Rousseau on women, see also Joel Schwartz, *The Sexual Politics of Jean-Jacques Rousseau* (Chicago: University of Chicago Press, 1984).

8   On feminism and participatory democracy, see Pateman.

9   Jane Mansbridge, *Beyond Adversarial Democracy* (New York: Basic Books, 1980).

10 Amy Gutmann, *Liberal Equality* (Cambridge: Cambridge University Press, 1980), pp. 191–202.

11 See Iris Marion Young, "Five Faces of Oppression," *Philosophical Forum* (1988).

12 Jürgen Habermas, *Reason and the Rationalization of Society* (Boston: Beacon, 1983), pt. 3. For criticism of Habermas as retaining too universalist a conception of communicative action, see Seyla Benhabib, *Critique, Norm and Utopia* (New York: Columbia University Press, 1986); and Young, "Impartiality and the Civic Public: Some Implications of Feminist Critiques of Moral and Political Theory," in *Feminism as Critique,* ed. S. Benhabib and D. Cornell (Oxford: Polity Press, 1987), pp. 56–76.

13 The Mel King for mayor campaign organization exhibited the promise of such group representation in practice, which was only partially and haltingly realized; see special double issue of *Radical America* 17, no. 6, and 18, no. 1 (1984). Sheila Collins discusses how the idea of a rainbow coalition challenges traditional American political assumptions of a "melting pot," and she shows how lack of coordination between the national level rainbow departments and the grassroots campaign committees prevented the 1984 Jackson campaign from realizing the promise of group representation; see *The Rainbow Challenge: The Jackson Campaign and the Future of U.S. Politics* (New York: Monthly Review Press, 1986).

14 See Gary Ruchwarger, *People in Power: Forging a Grassroots Democracy in Nicaragua* (Hadley, Mass.: Bergin & Garvey, 1985).

15 Martha Minow, "Learning to Live with the Dilemma of Difference: Bilingual and Special Education," *Law and Contemporary Problems*, no. 48 (1985), pp. 157–211.

16 I use the term "special rights" in much the same way as Elizabeth Wolgast, in *Equality and the Rights of Women* (Ithaca, N.Y.: Cornell University Press, 1980). Like Wolgast, I wish to distinguish a class of rights that all persons should have, general rights, and a class of rights that categories of persons should have by virtue of particular circumstances. That is, the distinction should refer only to different levels of generality, where "special" means only "specific." Unfortunately, "special rights" tends to carry a connotation of *exceptional*, that is, specially marked and deviating from the norm. As I assert below, however, the goal is not to compensate for deficiencies in order to help people be "normal," but to denormalize, so that in certain contexts and at certain levels of abstraction everyone has "special" rights.

17 Linda J. Krieger, "Through a Glass Darkly: Paradigms of Equality and the Search for a Women's Jurisprudence," *Hypatia: A Journal of Feminist Philosophy* 2 (1987): 45–62. Deborah Rhode provides an excellent synopsis of the dilemmas involved in this pregnancy debate in feminist legal theory in "Justice and Gender" (typescript), chap. 9.

18 See Ann Scales, "Towards a Feminist Jurisprudence," *Indiana Law Journal* 56 (1980): 375–444. Christine Littleton provides a very good analysis of the feminist debate about equal vs. different treatment regarding pregnancy and childbirth, among other legal issues for women, in "Reconstructing Sexual Equality," *California Law Review* 25 (1987): 1279–1337. Littleton suggests, as I have stated above, that only the dominant male conception of work keeps pregnancy and birthing from being conceived of as work.

19 Littleton suggests that difference should be understood not as a characteristic of particular sorts of people, but of the interaction of particular sorts of people with specific institutional structures. Minow expresses a similar point by saying that difference should be understood as a function of the relationship among groups, rather than located in attributes of a particular group.

15

CONTEMPORARY LIBERAL RESPONSES TO DIVERSITY

Bhikhu Parekh

GENERAL COMMENTS

Three contemporary thinkers (Raz, Kymlicka and Rawls) have perceptively reinterpreted, refined or even redefined liberalism to make it more hospitable to cultural and moral plurality. I have argued that although their thought marks a considerable advance over that of their classical predecessors and opens up new lines of inquiry, it remains inadequate. In each case the nature of, and the reasons for, their inadequacy have been indicated. It would be useful to highlight several common tendencies in their and other liberal writings which prevent liberals from developing a coherent and persuasive response to cultural and moral diversity.

• First, although liberals have begun to appreciate the cultural embeddedness of human beings, they still have considerable difficulty overcoming the traditional transcultural view of them. For Hobbes, Locke, Bentham, even J. S. Mill and others, human beings are naturally endowed with certain wants, needs and capacities, and social life either merely realizes these or at best adds new ones to them. Although Raz, Kymlicka and even Rawls rightly challenge this view and appreciate the profound ways in which culture shapes, structures, reconstitutes and channels human wants and capacities, they still remain too deeply committed to it to exploit their insights fully. Take their account of autonomy. As they understand it, culture helps individuals develop their capacity for autonomy, which then transcends it and views it and the wider world untainted by its provenance. This is a misleading account of the relation between the two. Although human beings are not determined by their culture in the sense of being unable to take a critical view of it and appreciate and learn from others, they are not transcendental beings contingently and externally related to it either. Their culture shapes them in countless ways, forms them into certain kinds of persons, and culti-vates certain attachments, affections, moral and psychological dispositions, taboos and modes of reasoning. Far from being purely formal and culturally neutral, their capacity for autonomy is structured in a particular way, functions within flexible but determi-nate limits, and defines and assesses options in certain ways. Although Raz appreciates this more than most other liberals, the ghost of a transcultural and culturally untainted power of autonomy continues to shadow even his thought. Liberals cannot take a transcultural view of human powers and expect culture to play an obligingly passive role in developing them.

• Second, directly or indirectly and subtly or crudely, liberals continue to absolutize liberalism. Hence their persistent tendency to make it their central frame of reference, divide all ways of life into liberal and nonliberal, equate the latter with illiberal, and to talk of tolerating and rarely of respecting or cherishing them. The crudity of this dis-tinction would become clear if someone were to divide all religions into Christianity and non-Christianity and equate the latter with anti-Christianity. If liberals are to do justice to alternative ways of life and thought, they need to break away from this crude binary distinction. They cannot do so unless they stop absolutizing the liberal way of life and making it their central point of comparison. And that in turn requires them to accept the full force of moral and cultural pluralism and acknowledge that the good life can be lived in several different ways, some better than others in certain respects but none is the best. Once they do so, their perspective undergoes a profound change. They would deabsolutize though not relativize liberal ways of life and thought, see these as both valuable and limited, and take a critical view of them. The spirit of crit-ical self-understanding opens up a vitally necessary theoretical and moral space for a critical but sympathetic dialogue with other ways of life, now seen not as objects of willing or grudging tolerance but as conversational partners in a common search for a deeper understanding of the nature, potentialities and grandeur of human life.

• Third, in their discussions of how to treat the so-called nonliberal ways of life, liberal writers adopt one of two strategies. Some, mostly of teleological persuasion, confront nonliberals with a full-blooded liberal vision and attack them for failing to measure up to it (Barry, 1991, pp. 23–39).[1] Others, many but not all of whom are deontological liberals, thin down liberal principles to what they take to be their minimum content, and make tolerance of nonliberal cultures conditional upon their acceptance of it. As seen earlier the first strategy is incoherent, rests on circular reasoning, and has been a source of much violence and moral arrogance. Although the second is better, it too is flawed. If the minimum that the liberal insists upon is essen-tially liberal in nature and cannot be shown to be morally binding on all, it cannot be demanded of nonliberals without violating their moral autonomy. If, on the other hand, it is universally binding, then there is nothing particularly liberal about it except the contingent historical fact that liberals happened to appreciate its importance more than others. In other words liberals need to rise to a higher level of abstraction than they have done so far, and distinguish between a universal and a liberal moral minimum, insisting on the former in all circumstances and on the latter when it does not violate the universal minimum and can be shown to be central to a liberal society's historically inherited cultural character.

Liberals often argue that since the modern western society is liberal, it is entitled to ask its members to live by basic liberal values. Even if we accepted this premise, deep disagreements would remain concerning what these values are, and we would get caught up in an interminable and unnecessary quasi-theological controversy concerning what a 'truly' liberal society stands for, what its 'real' identity consists in, what principles it 'cannot' betray, and so on. There is no obvious reason, however, why we should accept the liberal premise in the first instance. Modern western society includes nonliberal groups such as conservatives, socialists, communists, Marxists, religious communities, indigenous peoples, long-established ethnic communities and newly-arrived immigrants who cannot be excluded from its self-definition by an ideologically biased act of linguistic appropriation. Although all its institutions are touched by the liberal spirit, some are not and cannot be fully liberal; for example religion, the family, and perhaps schools. The fact that its political and economic institutions and some of its social practices are liberal does not make its entire way of life liberal any more than the fact that the state is largely secular entitles us to call the whole society secular. Again, liberals are not and perhaps cannot be liberal in all areas of life, and entertain and live by nonliberal ideas, a mixture of liberal and nonliberal ideas, or even by instincts, faith and habits in matters relating to intimate interpersonal relations, moral values, ethnic, political or national loyalties, and religious beliefs. In short as is only to be expected in a society with a long and rich history, contemporary western society is characterized by an interplay of several mutually regulating and historically sedimented impulses, some liberal, some nonliberal, some others a mixture of both, yet others too complex to fall into either category. Its members harbour and sometimes feel attached to all of these, and attempts to simplify their identity by purging it of all but the liberal impulses deprive them of their history, do injustice to their complex self-understanding, arouse avoidable hostility against liberalism, and rarely succeed.[2]

To call contemporary western society liberal is not only to homogenize and over-simplify it but also to give liberals a moral and cultural monopoly of it and treat the rest as illegitimate and troublesome intruders. When one then goes on to say that *because* the society is liberal, it should or should not allow certain practices or be guided by certain principles, one is guilty of bad logic and even bad faith. One abstracts a particular, albeit an extremely important aspect of modern society, turns it into its sole defining feature, and uses it to delegitimize other moral sensibilities and reshape the entire society in its image. One also gives the liberal the double advantage of setting nonliberals the challenging task of defending their principles to his satisfaction while more or less exempting himself from it. Earlier writers called contemporary western society open, free, public, civil or humane rather than liberal. These terms are ideologically less narrow and biased, and socially more inclusive. They too, however, are not free of difficulties, and that only goes to show both the danger and the futility of bringing the entire society under a single description. Paradoxical as it may seem, it is the glory of liberal (that is, tolerant, open and free) society that it is not, and does not need or even seek to become, exclusively or entirely liberal (that is, committed to a strong sense of autonomy, individualism, self-creation, and so on). Liberal writers misunderstand its inner logic and strength when they seek to turn it into one.

[. . .]

EQUALITY IN A MULTICULTURAL SOCIETY

Much of the traditional discussion of equality suffers from a weakness derived from the mistaken theory of human nature in which it is grounded. As we saw earlier, many philosophers understand human beings in terms of a substantive theory of human nature and treat culture as of no or only marginal importance. Broadly speaking they maintain that human beings are characterized by two sets of features, some common to them all such as that they are made in the image of God, have souls, are noumenal beings, have common capacities and needs or a similar natural constitution; and others varying from culture to culture and individual to individual. The former are taken to constitute their humanity and are ontologically privileged. Human beings are deemed to be equal because of their shared features or similarity, and equality is taken to consist in treating them in more or less the same way and giving them more or less the same body of rights.

I have argued that this view of human beings is deeply mistaken. Human beings are at once both natural and cultural beings, sharing a common human identity but in a culturally mediated manner. They are similar and different, their similarities and differences do not passively coexist but interpenetrate, and neither is ontologically prior or morally more important. We cannot ground equality in human uniformity because the latter is inseparable from and ontologically no more important than human differences. Grounding equality in uniformity also has unfortunate consequences. It requires us to treat human beings equally in those respects in which they are similar and not those in which they are different. While granting them equality at the level of their shared human nature, we deny it at the equally important cultural level. In our discussions of the Greek, Christian and liberal philosophers we have seen that it is also easy to move from uniformity to monism. Since human beings are supposed to be basically the same, only a particular way of life is deemed to be worthy of them, and those failing to live up to it either do not merit equality or do so only after they are suitably civilized. The idea of equality thus becomes an ideological device to mould humankind in a certain direction. A theory of equality grounded in human uniformity is both philosophically incoherent and morally problematic.

Human beings do share several capacities and needs in common, but different cultures define and structure these differently and develop new ones of their own. Since human beings are at once both similar and different, they should be treated equally because of both. Such a view, which grounds equality not in human uniformity but in the interplay of uniformity and difference, builds difference into the very concept of equality, breaks the traditional equation of equality with similarity, and is immune to monist distortion. Once the basis of equality changes so does its content. Equality involves equal freedom or opportunity to be different, and treating human beings equally requires us to take into account both their similarities and differences. When the latter are not relevant, equality entails uniform or identical treatment; when they are, it requires differential treatment. Equal rights do not mean identical rights, for individuals with different cultural backgrounds and needs might require different rights to enjoy equality in respect of whatever happens to be the content of their rights. Equality involves not just rejection of irrelevant differences as is commonly argued, but also full recognition of legitimate and relevant ones.

Equality is articulated at several interrelated levels. At the most basic level it involves equality of respect and rights, at a slightly higher level that of opportunity, self-esteem, self-worth and so on, and at a yet higher level, equality of power, well-being and the basic capacities required for human flourishing. Sensitivity to differences is relevant at each of these levels. We can hardly be said to respect a person if we treat with contempt or abstract away all that gives meaning to his life and makes him the kind of person he is. Respect for a person therefore involves locating him against his cultural background, sympathetically entering into his world of thought, and interpreting his conduct in terms of its system of meaning. A simple example illustrates the point. It was recently discovered that Asian candidates for jobs in Britain were systematically underscored because their habit of showing respect for their interviewers by not looking them in the eye led the latter to conclude that they were shifty and devious and likely to prove unreliable. By failing to appreciate the candidates' system of meaning and cultural practices, interviewers ended up treating them unequally with their white counterparts. Understandably but wrongly, they assumed that all human beings shared and even perhaps ought to share an identical system of meaning which predictably turned out to be their own. This relatively trivial example illustrates the havoc we can easily cause when we uncritically universalize the categories and norms of our culture.

Like the concept of equal respect, that of equal opportunity, too, needs to be interpreted in a culturally sensitive manner. Opportunity is a subject-dependent concept in the sense that a facility, a resource, or a course of action is only a mute and passive possibility and not an opportunity for an individual if she lacks the capacity, the cultural disposition or the necessary cultural knowledge to take advantage of it. A Sikh is in principle free to send his son to a school that bans turbans, but for all practical purposes it is closed to him. The same is true when an orthodox Jew is required to give up his yarmulke, or the Muslim woman to wear a skirt, or a vegetarian Hindu to eat beef as a precondition for certain kinds of jobs. Although the inability involved is cultural not physical in nature and hence subject to human control, the degree of control varies greatly. In some cases a cultural inability can be overcome with relative ease by suitably reinterpreting the relevant cultural norm or practice; in others it is constitutive of the individual's sense of identity and even self-respect and cannot be overcome without a deep sense of moral loss. Other things being equal, when a culturally derived incapacity is of the former kind, the individuals involved may rightly be asked to overcome it or at least bear the financial cost of accommodating it. When it is of the latter kind and comes closer to a natural inability, society should bear at least most of the cost of accommodating it. Which cultural incapacity falls within which category is often a matter of dispute and can only be resolved by a dialogue between the parties involved.

Equality before the law and equal protection of the law, too, need to be defined in a culturally sensitive manner. Formally a law banning the use of drugs treats all equally, but in fact it discriminates against those for whom some drugs are religious or cultural requirements as is the case with Peyote and Marijuana respectively for the American Indians and Rastafarians. This does not mean that we might not ban their use, but rather that we need to appreciate the unequal impact of the ban and should have strong additional reasons for denying exemption to these two groups. The United States government showed the requisite cultural sensitivity when it exempted the ceremonial use of wine by Jews and Catholics during Prohibition.

Equal protection of the law, too, may require different treatment. Given the horrible reality of the Holocaust and the persistent streak of anti-semitism in German cultural life, it makes good sense for that country to single out physical attacks on Jews for harsher punishment or ban utterances denying the Holocaust. In other societies, other groups such as blacks, Muslims and gypsies might have long been demonized and subjected to hostility and hatred, and then they too might need to be treated differently. Although the differential treatment of these groups might seem to violate the principle of equality, in fact it only equalizes them with the rest of their fellow-citizens.

In a culturally homogeneous society, individuals share broadly similar needs, norms, motivations, social customs and patterns of behaviour. Equal rights here mean more or less the same rights, and equal treatment involves more or less identical treatment. The principle of equality is therefore relatively easy to define and apply, and discriminatory deviations from it can be identified without much disagreement. This is not the case in a culturally diverse society. Broadly speaking equality consists in equal treatment of those judged to be equal in relevant respects. In a culturally diverse society citizens are likely to disagree on what respects are relevant in a given context, what response is appropriate to them, and what counts as their equal treatment. Furthermore, once we take cultural differences into account, equal treatment would mean not identical but differential treatment, raising the question as to how we can ensure that it is really equal across cultures and does not serve as a cloak for discrimination or privilege.

IMPLICATIONS

When we take legitimate cultural differences into account, as we should, equal treatment is likely to involve different or differential treatment, raising the question as to how we can ensure that the latter does not amount to discrimination or privilege. There is no easy answer to this. As a general rule it would seem that different treatments of individuals or groups are equal if they represent different ways of realizing the same right, opportunity or in whatever other respect they are intended to be treated equally, and if as a result none of the parties involved is better-off or worse-off. The Sikh who is allowed to carry a *kirpan* and a Christian who is not are treated differently but equally because they are both exercising the same right in different ways and because the former does not secure an advantage over or at the expense of the latter. And an Asian girl whose marriage is declared void when contracted under threat of parental ostracism, and a white girl whose marriage under similar circumstances is not, are both treated equally though differently because they are subject to the same general rule that duress voids a marriage. In all such cases we need to consider the nature and the purpose of the right or the rule involved, and show that the differential treatment is justified in terms of it. Disagreements are bound to arise at both levels, especially the former. Since there is no way to resolve them conclusively, cross-cultural application of equality will always remain vulnerable to the opposite charges of privileging or discriminating against a particular group.

In a multicultural society one might sometimes need to go further and grant not only different but also additional rights to some groups or individuals. This may be necessary either to equalize them with the rest or to achieve such worthwhile collective goals as political integration, social harmony and encouragement of cultural diversity. If some groups have long been marginalized or suppressed, lack the confidence and the opportunity to participate as equals in mainstream society, or are subjected to vigorous assimilation, we might need to give them rights not available to others, such as special or disproportionate representation in parliament, the cabinet and other government bodies and the right to consultation and even perhaps a veto over laws relating to them. The purpose of such additional rights is to draw the groups involved into the mainstream of society and give substance to the principle of equal citizenship.

There may also be groups in society who have been traumatized by their recent history, or feel culturally insecure, or are under particular threat. We may then need to give them rights not available to the majority in order to reassure them, promote social harmony, give them a stake in the country's political stability and foster a common sense of belonging. Born in the trauma of the partition of the country and the enormous intercommunal violence that accompanied it, the Constitution of India wisely decided to grant its minorities several additional rights. In Canada and the USA, indigenous peoples enjoy negative and positive rights required to protect their ways of life that are not available to others. Some countries such as Australia, Canada and India place a high value on cultural diversity and give extra resources and rights to their cultural minorities to help them flourish and contribute towards the creation of a rich and plural society. In these and other cases minorities are clearly favoured and in some respects even privileged, but that is justified if it is in the larger interest of society. Such additional rights and resources can easily arouse a sense of injustice and resentment among the majority, and even become a cloak to buy minority electoral support. They must therefore be granted only when justified, and their purpose should be clearly stated and explained.

Liberals, who insist that all citizens should enjoy equal rights, feel troubled by such additional rights to minorities, and either disapprove of them or justify them on the ground that they are intended to equalize these groups with the rest of their fellow-citizens. Their first response represents the triumph of dogma over prudence and is sometimes a recipe for disharmony and disorder in a multicultural society. Their second response makes moral and political sense but misrepresents the basis of the rights. While some additional rights of minorities are meant to equalize them with the rest, others are designed to promote such worthwhile collective goals as social harmony, cultural diversity and a common sense of belonging. Like equality, they too are important values and we need to balance their competing demands.

Although society has a duty to treat all its citizens equally, its ability to do so is necessarily limited. It has a dominant language, and no language is culturally neutral. While it should cherish its minority languages and help their speakers acquire competence in the dominant language, it cannot always give these an equal public status. Every society also has a historically inherited cultural structure which informs its conduct of public life. While it has a duty to modify it to accommodate the legitimate demands of its minorities, it cannot do so beyond a certain point without losing its coherence and causing widespread disorientation, anxiety and even resistance. This is likely to lead to unequal treatment of its cultural minorities in certain areas, about which in spite of all its good intentions it might be able to do little. In all western societies Sunday is a day of rest for obvious cultural and religious reasons. This puts Muslims at a disadvantage who, unlike Christians, cannot join communal prayer on Friday, their holy day. Although provisions should be made to accommodate Muslim employees and reduce the inequality, it is difficult to see how it can be eliminated altogether without unscrambling the prevailing cultural structure and incurring an enormous social and financial cost. Such inescapable inequalities occur in even more acute forms in other areas of life as well. Which inequalities are eliminable, at what cost, and who should bear it are bound to be a matter of dispute. Since often there is no one just or rational way to resolve the disputes, they are best settled by discussion, negotiation and compromise.

NOTES

1 Barry, B. (1991) *Liberty and Justice: Essays in Political Theory* 2 (Oxford, Clarendon Press).
2 For a perceptive critique of liberalism from a pluralist perspective and suggestions as to how it can come to terms with pluralism, see Kekes, J. (1993) *The Morality of Pluralism* (Princeton, Princeton University Press).

16

THEORIES OF GROUP RIGHTS

Brian Barry

EQUAL TREATMENT

[. . .]

The strategy of privatization entails a rather robust attitude towards cultural diversity. It says, in effect, 'Here are the rules which tell people what they are allowed to do. What they choose to do within those rules is up to them. But it has nothing to do with public policy.' A simple model of rational decision making, but one adequate for the present purpose, would present the position as follows: the rules define a choice set, which is the same for everybody: within that choice set people pick a particular course of action by deciding what is best calculated to satisfy their underlying preferences for outcomes, given their beliefs about the way in which actions are connected to outcomes. From an egalitarian liberal standpoint, what matters are equal opportunities. If uniform rules create identical choice sets, then opportunities are equal. We may expect that people will make different choices from these identical choice sets, depending on their preferences for outcomes and their beliefs about the relation of actions to the satisfaction of their preferences. Some of these preferences and beliefs will be derived from aspects of a culture shared with others; some will be idiosyncratic. But this has no significance: either way it is irrelevant to any claims based on justice. since justice is guaranteed by equal opportunities.

None of this means, of course, that people will not in fact feel hard done by and complain that the system of uniform laws treats them unfairly. Many such complaints are, indeed, made. The question that has to be asked is what merit there is in these complaints. That will be the subject of the rest of the chapter. The main conclusion for which I shall argue is that a popular political response – and one that multiculturalists would like to see made more common – is actually very hard to justify in any particular case, even though it cannot be ruled out a priori. This is the approach that keeps the rule objected to for most of the population but allows members of cultural or religious minorities to opt out of the obligation to obey it. More precisely, I shall concede that this approach, which I shall call the rule-and-exemption approach, may sometimes be defensible on the basis of political prudence or an estimate of the balance of advantages. But I shall reject the characteristic case made by the supporters of multiculturalism, that a correct analysis would show exemptions for cultural minorities to be required in a great many cases by egalitarian liberal justice.

An example of the rule-and-exemption approach is the exemption from humane slaughter regulations that many countries have enacted to accommodate the beliefs of Jews and Muslims. Another is a family of exemptions from laws designed to reduce head injuries which have the effect of permitting turban-wearing Sikhs to ride motorcycles, work in the construction industry, and so on. I shall discuss both of these in the next section. Most, though not all, of these exemptions are claimed on the basis of religious belief. Indeed, Peter Jones has gone so far as to suggest that, if we leave aside the 'religious components of culture', there should be 'few, if any problems of mutual accommodation' arising from cultural diversity.[1] We shall see in the course of this book how often demands for special treatment – by individuals and by organizations – are based on religious belief. This is, perhaps, to be expected if we recognize the tendency for religious precepts to be experienced as more peremptory than norms that are supported only by custom.

We should at the same time, however, appreciate that claims based on religion are more likely to be sympathetically received by outsiders than claims based on custom, especially in largely Protestant (or ex-Protestant) countries, in which there is a traditional reluctance to 'force tender consciences'. This tendency is reinforced in the United States by the constitutional guarantee of 'freedom of religion', which encourages the packaging of custom as religion. The result is, for example, that wearing a *yarmulke* (skull cap) is presented as a religious obligation rather than as the traditional practice that it is for some Orthodox Jews. Even without this incentive, however, it is perceived as advantageous to press claims on the basis of religion wherever possible. Thus, it is questionable that the wearing of a turban is a religious obligation for Sikhs, as against a customary practice among some.[2] In the parliamentary debate on the proposal to exempt turban-wearing Sikhs from the requirement that all motorcyclists must wear a crash helmet, those who favoured the exemption thought it important to insist on the religious standing of the turban, while those who were opposed to it argued for its customary status.[3] There is, however, a countervailing force in Britain, as we shall see below: outside Northern Ireland, discrimination on the basis of religion is not illegal, but discrimination on the basis of race or ethnicity is. This means that there is an incentive to code what may plausibly be a religious obligation (e.g. the wearing of some kind of head-covering by Muslim women) as an ethnic cultural practice, so as to bring it within the scope of the Race Relations Act.

The strong claim made by many theorists of multiculturalism is that special arrangements to accommodate religious beliefs and cultural practices are demanded by justice. The argument is that failure to offer special treatment is in some circumstances itself a kind of unequal treatment. For, it is said, the same law may have a different impact on different people as a result of their religious beliefs or cultural practices. Thus, the liberal claim that equal treatment is generated by a system of uniform laws is invalid. What can be said of this argument? There can be no question that any given general law will have a different impact on different people. But is there anything inherently unfair about this? The essence of law is the protection of some interests at the expense of others when they come into conflict. Thus, the interests of women who do not want to be raped are given priority over the interests of potential rapists in the form of the law that prohibits rape. Similarly, the interests of children in not being interfered with sexually are given priority over the interests of potential paedophiles in the form of the law that prohibits their acting on their proclivities. These laws clearly have a much more severe impact on those who are strongly attracted to rape and paedophilia than on those who would not wish to engage in them even if there were no law against them. But it is absurd to suggest that this makes the laws prohibiting them unfair: they make a fair allocation of rights between the would-be rapist or paedophile and the potential victim.

The point is a completely general one. If we consider virtually any law, we shall find that it is much more burdensome to some people than to others. Speed limits inhibit only those who like to drive fast. Laws prohibiting drunk driving have no impact on teetotallers. Only smokers are stopped by prohibitions on smoking in public places. Only those who want to own a handgun are affected by a ban on them, and so on *ad infinitum*. This is simply how things are. The notion that inequality of impact is a sign of unfairness is not an insight derived from a more sophisticated conception of justice than that previously found in political philosophy. It is merely a mistake. This is not, of course, to deny that the unequal impact of a law may in some cases be an indication of its unfairness. It is simply to say that the charge will have to be substantiated in each case by showing exactly how the law is unfair. It is never enough to show no more than that it has a different impact on different people.

All of this bears on a line of thought in recent political philosophy according to which a legitimate claim for additional income can, in principle at least, be made by those with expensive tastes – people who have to eat plovers eggs and drink vintage claret (to take a famous example) if they are to achieve the same level of satisfaction as others can achieve with sausages and beer. The usual reaction to the idea that those with expensive tastes should get extra resources is that it is absurd, and such a reaction is perfectly sound. This is not simply because the proposal is unworkable: those who put forward the idea are usually quite willing to concede that. The error lies in thinking that, even as a matter of principle, fair treatment requires compensation for expensive tastes. To explain what is wrong with the idea, we have to invoke the fundamental premise that the subject of fairness is the distribution of rights, resources and opportunities. Thus, a fair share of income is a fair share of income: income is the stuff whose distribution is the subject of attributions of fairness. Suppose that you and I have an equal claim on society's resources, for whatever reason. Then it is simply not relevant that you will gain more satisfaction from using those resources than I will. What is fair is that our equal claim translates into equal purchasing power: what we do with it is our own business.

If we rule out the claim that equal treatment entails equal impact, there may still be other arguments for special arrangements to accommodate cultural practices or religious beliefs. But what are they? One natural recourse is to suggest that what I have said so far may be all very well for costs arising from preferences, but that costs arising from beliefs are a different kettle of fish. It is very hard to see why this proposition should be accepted, however confidently it is often advanced. Consider, for example, the way in which people's beliefs may make some job opportunities unattractive to them. Pacifists will presumably regard a career in the military as closed to them. Committed vegetarians are likely to feel the same about jobs in slaughterhouses or butchers' shops. Similarly, if legislation requires that animals should he stunned before being killed, those who cannot as a result of their religious beliefs eat such meat will have to give up eating meat altogether.

Faced with a meatless future, some Jews and Muslims may well decide that their faith needs to be reinterpreted so as to permit the consumption of humanely slaughtered animals. And indeed this has already happened. According to Peter Singer, 'in Sweden, Norway and Switzerland, for example, the rabbis have accepted legislation requiring the stunning [of animals prior to killing] with no exceptions for ritual slaughter'.[4] The case for saying that humane slaughter regulations are not unfair does not, however, depend upon the claim that beliefs are a matter of choice, so that it is somehow people's own fault if they are incommoded by their beliefs. (That is not the point about expensive tastes either.) If we want to say, as Yael Tamir does, that people should be 'free to adhere to cultures and religions of their choice', that should be taken to mean only that they should not be penalized for changing their minds about the value of their current religious or cultural commitments.[5] It should not be interpreted to mean that these commitments are the product of choice. It makes no sense to say that we can decide what to believe. Similarly, we can say if we like that people are responsible for their own beliefs, but that should be understood simply as a way of saying that they own them: their beliefs are not to be conceived of as some sort of alien affliction. (The same may, again, be said in general about preferences.) Talking, as Michael Sandel does, about people being 'encumbered' by their beliefs feeds this sense of alienation.[6]

The position regarding preferences and beliefs is similar. We can try to cultivate certain tastes (by, for example, developing a familiarity or skill), and we can try to strengthen certain beliefs (by, for example, deliberately exposing ourselves to messages tending to confirm them), but in neither case is there any guarantee of success. Moreover, the decision to make the attempt must come from somewhere: we must already have a higher-order preference for developing the taste or a higher-order belief that it would be a good thing to strengthen the belief. Choice cannot, in either case, go all the way down. I suspect that one source of the idea that many preferences are easily changeable is a result of a tendency to muddle together preferences and choices. Suppose, for example, that I have a preference for vanilla over strawberry ice cream, other things being equal. That entails that, if other things are actually equal, I will choose vanilla. But this preference may be a weak one, which means that things do not have to be very unequal before my choice switches to strawberry. The weakness of my preference would be revealed by my willingness to pay only a little more for vanilla and my lack of reluctance to let somebody else have the last vanilla ice cream. Even so, the preference itself, even if weak, may be solidly based in physiology and almost impossible to change. The upshot is, then, that beliefs and preferences are in the same boat: we cannot change our beliefs by an act of will but the same can be said equally well of our preferences. It is false that the changeability of preferences is what makes it not unfair for them to give rise to unequal impact. It is therefore not true that the unchangeability of beliefs makes it unfair for them to give rise to unequal impacts.

Beliefs are not an encumbrance in anything like the way in which a physical disability is an encumbrance. Yet precisely this claim is sometimes made. Thus, Bhikhu Parekh argues that giving people special treatment on the basis of their beliefs 'is like two individuals who both enjoy the right to equal medical attention but who receive different treatments depending on the nature of their illness'.[7] A disability – for example, a lack of physical mobility due to injury or disease – supports a strong prima facie claim to compensation because it limits the opportunity to engage in activities that others are able to engage in. In contrast, the effect of some distinctive belief or preference is to bring about a certain pattern of choices from among the set of opportunities that are available to all who are similarly placed physically or financially. The position of somebody who is unable to drive a car as a result of some physical disability is totally different from that of somebody who is unable to drive a car because doing so would be contrary to the tenets of his or her religion. To suggest that they are similarly situated is in fact offensive to both parties. Someone who needs a wheelchair to get around will be quite right to resent the suggestion that this need should be assimilated to an expensive taste. And somebody who freely embraces a religious belief that prohibits certain activities will rightly deny the imputation that this is to be seen as analogous to the unwelcome burden of a physical disability.

The critical distinction is between limits on the range of opportunities open to people and limits on the choices that they make from within a certain range of opportunities. Parekh deliberately blurs this distinction by writing that 'opportunity is a subject-dependent concept', so that 'a facility, a resource, or a course of action' does not constitute an opportunity for you, even if it is actually open to you, unless you have 'the cultural disposition … to take advantage of it'.[8] This proposal actually destroys the meaning of the word opportunity, which originally related to Portunus, who was (and for anything I know to the contrary still is) the god who looks after harbours.[9] When the wind and the tide were propitious, sailors had the opportunity to leave or enter the harbour. They did not have to do so if they did not want to, of course, but that did not mean (as Parekh's proposal would imply) that the opportunity then somehow disappeared. The existence of the opportunity was an objective state of affairs. That is not to say that opportunity could not be individualized: whether a certain conjunction of wind and tide created an opportunity for a particular ship might depend on its build and its rigging. But it did not depend on the 'cultural disposition' of the crew 'to take advantage of it'. They might, perhaps, have chosen not to sail because setting out on a voyage was contraindicated by a religious omen, but that simply meant that they had passed up the opportunity.

Lily Bart, the heroine of *The House of Mirth* (in the sense in which Becky Sharp is the heroine of Thackeray's *Vanity Fair*), spends a lot of time in the novel bemoaning the way in which the wealth of her relatives and friends provides them with opportunities – a word she uses several times in this context – that they do not take up because their horizons are limited by the stifling culture of upper-crust New York, and she reflects on the advantage she would be able to take of the same opportunities. If Parekh were right, we would have to convict Miss Bart and her creator, Edith Wharton, of commiting a conceptual mistake. On Parekh's analysis, Lily Bart would have had to think that, if she had the wealth of her relatives and friends, she would have had a lot of opportunities that they did not have. But this would be, I submit, to lose the point of her complaint, which was precisely that they had the opportunities yet did not use them. Similarly, the opportunity to read a wide range of books is ensured by literacy plus access to a public library or (provided you have the money) a bookshop. If you belong to some Christian sect that teaches the sinfulness of reading any book except the Bible, you will choose not to avail yourself of this opportunity. But you still have exactly the same opportunity to read books as somebody who is similarly placed in all respects except for not having this particular belief.

The peculiar implications of Parekh's analysis are well illustrated by his treatment of one example of 'giving people special treatment on the basis of their beliefs'. At issue here is the exemption that Sikhs enjoy from the 'provisions designed to penalize those who carry knives and other sharply pointed objects' contained in the Criminal Justice Act of 1988, which 'specifically states that it is a defence for an accused to prove that he had the article with him in a public place "for religious reasons"', a provision that was 'introduced . . . to permit Sikhs to carry their *kirpans* (swords or daggers) in public places without fear of prosecution'.[10] Parekh asks if non-Sikhs can 'legitimately complain of discrimination or unequal treatment' and replies that 'there is no discrimination involved both because their [i.e. non-Sikhs'] religious requirements are not ignored, and because they [i.e. non-Sikhs] do not suffer adversely as a result of the law respecting those [religious requirements] of the Sikhs'.[11] However, the rationale of a law against the carrying of knives in public must be that unarmed citizens (pleonastically) 'suffer adversely' if some other people are going around carrying weapons. Unless a knife confers an advantage on its possessor, there is no point in having a law restricting the carrying of knives at all. Assuming that the law's rationale is sound, it is absurd to deny that granting an exemption to it for members of one group inevitably reduces the personal security of all the rest of the population.

Parekh also argues that 'as for the complaint of inequality, there is a prima facie inequality of rights in the sense that Sikhs can do what others cannot. However the alleged inequality grows out of the requirements of the principle of equal respect for all, and it is not so much inequality as an appropriate translation of that principle in a different religious context.[12] But the inequality of rights is not prima facie – it is real. The right to carry knives amidst a population none of whom can legally do the same is an inequality of rights, however we look at it. Whether or not it is a justifiable inequality is another matter. But it is playing with words to suggest that it is really a superior form of equality to the liberal one that says we have equal rights when we have the same ones.

I have argued so far that the differential impact of a general law cannot in itself found a claim that the law is unjust. But justice is not the only basis on which the argument for an exemption from the law might be made. If it is true that a law bears particularly harshly on some people, that is at the very least a reason for examining it to see if it might be modified so as to accommodate those who are affected by it in some special way. Prudence or generosity might support such a move. From a utilitarian point of view, we could pose the question by asking if it is worth giving up some of the benefits of the law in order to reduce the costs of complying with it. It does not follow, though, that the best approach is to keep the general rule unchanged and simply add an exemption for the members of some specific group. The alternative is to work out some less restrictive alternative form of the law that would adequately meet the objectives of the original one while offering the members of the religious or cultural minority whatever is most important to them. This avoids the invidiousness of having different rules for different people in the same society. In practice, however, it is the rule-and-exemption approach that is usually followed. [. . .]

Once we accept, however, that the case for exemptions must be based on the alleviation of hardship rather than the demands of justice, it seems to me much more problematic to make it out than is widely assumed. I do not wish to rule out the possibility that there will be cases in which both the general law and the exemption are defensible. Usually, though, either the case for the law (or some version of it) is strong enough to rule out exemptions, or the case that can be made for exemptions is strong enough to suggest that there should be no law anyway. Consider, for example, the claim that 'the core of Rastafarian religiosity resides in the revelatory dimensions induced by the sacramental use of *ganja* [cannabis], in which a new level of consciousness is attained. Adherents to the movement are enabled more easily to perceive Haile Selassie as the redeemer and to appreciate their own identities.'[13] It might perhaps be said of many other religious truths that they too would be more easy to believe in under the influence of mind-altering substances.[14] However, there would obviously be insuperable practical problems in legalizing the use of cannabis for Rastafarians only, such as the difficulty of restricting its use to Rastafarian religious ceremonies, the absurdity of trying to distinguish 'genuine' from 'opportunistic' Rastafarians, and the virtual impossibility of preventing Rastafarian cannabis from 'leaking' into the general population.[15] For the same reasons, claims for religiously based exemptions to laws prohibiting use of marijuana in the United States have been ruled out even by those Supreme Court judges sympathetic to such exemptions in general: 'the Ethiopian Zionist Coptic Church . . . teaches that marijuana is properly smoked "continually all day"', and even if its use were officially prescribed only within the context of a religious ceremony, 'it would be difficult to grant a religious exemption without seriously compromising law enforcement efforts'.[16] The best case for making cannabis legal for Rastafarians or members of the Ethiopian Zionist Coptic Church would be to argue that it is far less harmful than either alcohol or tobacco, both of which are legal.[17] But this is an argument whose scope is not confined to Rastafarians. Rather, if it is valid, it constitutes a case for legalizing the consumption of cannabis by anybody.

[. . .]

LIBERALISM AND DIVERSITY

The partisans of diversity or tolerance are absolutely right to insist on the importance of freedom of association. They are in error, however, in suggesting that liberals are somehow inhibited by their principles from recognizing its value. It is true that liberal individualism has the implication that a group has no value over and above its value to its members (and to other people outside it), but this is quite compatible with a full recognition of the role played in our well-being by the communities and associations to which we belong.

It should be borne in mind that liberalism is, in the first instance, a doctrine about the way in which states should treat people. Over time, it has gradually come to be accepted that, in addition, states must impose certain standards on non-state organizations. It would, for example, make a mockery of the principle that equally qualified candidates should have equal access to jobs if firms in the private sector could flout it with impunity. Similarly, it would be absurd to hold that non-discrimination among passengers should be required only of municipally run bus companies, with the implication that privately owned companies would be perfectly free to order blacks to sit at the back of the bus. Interventions of this kind are essential to ensure that the principle of equal treatment is not rendered nugatory in central areas of people's lives such as employment, housing and travel. But that is far from entailing that every community and every association must operate within the constraints that it is appropriate to impose on a polity. There is no liberal principle to the effect that family decisions have to be taken by majority vote or that parents cannot censor their children's television viewing. Again, there is nothing to stop people from belonging to a church that vests ultimate authority in a Pope or Patriarch or is run autocratically by a charismatic preacher. Nor is there any liberal principle that forbids a church to instruct its members not to read certain books or watch certain films. The whole point of liberal institutions is to leave people with a great deal of discretion in their conduct, and one of the ways in which they can exercise that discretion is voluntarily to follow the orders issued by bodies whose authority they acknowledge.

It may be wondered what, in that case, all the fuss is about. What do the partisans of diversity or tolerance want that liberal principles are incapable of delivering? We can approach an answer to this question by observing that liberal principles limit the power of groups over their members. Thus, the condition on which churches can legitimately tell their members what to do is that those members are free to disobey without being liable to any penalty (in this world, anyway) except expulsion. In contrast, a church that could call on the Secular Arm (as the Inquisition called it) to punish heresy, apostasy or disobedience would clearly be out of bounds. Equally unacceptable, on liberal principles, would be a church whose members could without fear of legal sanctions inflict physical injuries on those who left it or disobeyed its rulings.

Similarly, while a liberal state can allow a good deal of discretion to parents in bringing up their children, that power must again be limited. Children need to be protected against parents who would inflict physical harm on them, even if this is prescribed by the parents' beliefs or customs. A familiar example is that of parents whose religious beliefs would lead them to withhold life-saving medical treatment from their children. Another well-publicized example is the practice, or more precisely set of practices, often referred to under the names of female circumcision or clitoridectomy but more comprehensively and accurately described as female genital mutilation. There is nothing specifically liberal about the view that the state should override the wishes of the parents in such cases. Any doctrine that gives the state the duty to prevent physical injury and death from being inflicted on its inhabitants will have the implication that the state should intervene. All that has to be said is that a liberal state is such a state.

If this is the liberal position, what do the critics think is wrong with it? I quoted [...] from an essay by Bhikhu Parekh on 'the narrowness of liberalism from Mill to Rawls'. How, we may ask, does this narrowness manifest itself? 'The liberal', says Parekh, '"privatises" non-liberal ways of life and denies them public recognition, status and support.'[18] Now to say that liberalism 'privatizes' non-liberal ways of life is simply to say that members of illiberal groups enjoy exactly the same rights as anybody else. It they so choose, they are perfectly free to participate with others in, say, the observance of a religious faith that is autocratic, misogynistic and bigoted. But the terms on which they can do so are just the same as those open to all their fellow citizens. The state does not lend any special weight to the norms of illiberal – or liberal – groups. This is, indeed, the essence of what it means to say that a society is a liberal society.

What of Parekh's alternative? If 'public recognition, status and support' are to amount to more than verbal gestures by politicians, they must consist of measures granting special legal immunities and powers to the leaders of illiberal groups that will enable them to control their members in ways that would otherwise violate the law. It requires little imagination to see how liberal rights for individuals are liable to be undermined by concessions whose intention and effect is to strengthen groups against their members. We may be reminded of Charles Taylor's complaint [...] that 'difference-blind' liberalism is inhospitable to diversity because its principles cannot make room for policies aimed at thwarting 'those who might want to cut loose in the name of some individual goal of self-development'.[19] We may also, indeed, recall Parekh's own depiction of free speech as a benefit to writers and a cost to everybody else, and his proposed remedy, the suppression of non-respectful writings about religion.

I asked earlier if a theory that made it the primary task of the state to promote autonomy could properly be described as a liberal theory at all. Without great conviction, I suggested that it just might scrape in as one. When it comes to the alleged version of liberalism that makes diversity or tolerance central to it, however, the case seems to me completely clear. In the current context, 'diversity' and 'autonomy' refer to policies that would systematically enfeeble precisely those rights of individuals to protection against groups that liberal states ought to make it their business to guarantee. How can a theory that would gut liberal principles be a form of liberalism?

[...]

Suppose we were to imagine the principles laid down in the Peace of Augsburg applied not between states but within states. We would then indeed get an approximation to a policy of promoting group diversity by state action. To the principle that 'Where there is one ruler, there should be only one religion' would correspond the maxim 'Where there is one group, there should be only one set of beliefs and norms.'[10] And the provision of a 'right to emigration . . . for subjects unwilling to accept their prince's religion' would be endorsed for groups by most contemporary partisans of diversity and tolerance, who often emphasize the importance of a right of exit. They tend not to insist that people must really be able to exercise this right, however, and here too there is an analogy, since 'emigration required paying off one's debts to the prince, which could be economically impossible'.[21]

The point of all this is not simply that 'Reformation liberalism' is an oxymoron. The deeper point is that the policies advocated in its name are not liberal. If this is so, it is natural to ask why it should be thought by anybody that policies aimed at promoting diversity or tolerance (as they are defined by contemporary political philosophers) have any claim to count as implications of liberalism. The most important reason is that liberalism has in recent years been equated by many people with cultural relativism. I shall show [. . .] how surprisingly pervasive this strange idea has become. In the remainder of the present section, I shall examine briefly three other lines of thought that crop up again and again among those who seek to argue that there is an authentic strain of liberalism devoted to the pursuit of diversity or tolerance.

The first argument runs as follows: 'The liberal is in theory committed to equal respect for persons. Since human beings are culturally embedded, respect for them entails respect for their cultures and ways of life.'[22] This particular formulation comes from Bhikhu Parekh, but the idea is common enough: it animates much of the rhetoric in James Tully's *Strange Multiplicity* [. . .].[23] The obvious problem with this argument is that illiberal cultures typically – I am tempted to say necessarily – are committed to violating the canons of equal respect. Equal respect for people cannot therefore entail respect for their cultures when these cultures systematically give priority to, say, the interests of men over the interests of women.

It does not follow, however, that groups whose norms contravene the canons of equal respect can legitimately be repressed by a liberal state. Freedom of association is, to repeat, a core liberal value, and it protects the freedom of groups whose norms mandate, among other things, the unequal treatment of men and women. The only condition on a group's being able to impose norms on its members is that the sanctions backing these norms must be restricted to ones that are consistent with liberal principles. What this means is primarily that, while membership of the group can be made contingent upon submission to these unequal norms, those who leave or are expelled may not be subjected to gratuitous losses. [. . .] What I want to emphasize here is that the value underwriting the freedom of groups to operate in illiberal ways is not respect for their culture but rather an acknowledgement of the significance in people's lives of free association.

An example [. . .] is [. . .] Jewish and Muslim divorce law. Although this treats men and women unequally, it is beyond the scope of a liberal state to rewrite it, as long as the only reason for anybody's adhering to it is the wish to remain a member in good standing of a certain religious community. What a liberal state cannot do, however, is give the force of law to religious rules that contravene liberal principles of equal treatment. If we define 'group rights' so that they are 'self-government rights and means [for communities] to protect their religious and cultural practices', then we have to say, with Yael Tamir, that such rights are

> either dangerous or of little importance. They are dangerous if they can be turned inwards to restrict the rights and freedom of members; they are of little importance if they can only be bestowed upon groups which treat their members with equal concern and respect. Very few of the groups that demand group rights, if any, accord with this description.[24]

Indeed, Chandran Kukathas has made it clear that the usual reason for demanding group rights is precisely so as to violate the demands of equal concern and respect among the members of the group. 'If liberalism describes a nation-state governed by the principles of liberal justice, then the liberal state cannot condone deep cultural diversity. For many, the cultural rights it can offer are not worth having.'[25] Maybe this is so, but it does not follow that there is an alternative understanding of liberalism that would accommodate 'deep cultural diversity' by withdrawing standard liberal protections for individuals or putting the force of the state behind practices that violate basic liberal tenets of freedom and equality. The conclusion I would wish to draw is, rather, that liberalism cannot accommodate 'deep diversity' and that it is right not to do so.

A second argument purporting to establish a connection between liberalism and the promotion of diversity by the state may also be discussed in the form in which it is presented by Parekh. According to this, 'the liberal . . . argues [that] cultural diversity increases the range of available options'.[26] Any liberal who did so argue would be mistaken. Parekh himself says a little later in the same article that 'cultures are not options', from which it obviously follows that the existence of a variety of different cultures does not 'increase our range of "options"'.[27] In fact, multiculturalism tends to restrict the range of options open to any given individual. 'Although seeking to "legitimize heterogeneity in British national culture"... multicultural policies have paradoxically "created a space for separatist and fundamentalist movements which seek to impose uniformity and homogeneity on all their adherents."'[28] My only quarrel with that way of putting it is that I can see nothing paradoxical about the combination of heterogeneity between groups and homogeneity within them. If the state is going to lend its coercive powers to attempts to maintain the cultural distinctiveness of groups, it is hard to imagine how this can be done in any way that does not strengthen the hands of those within each group who wish to impose on its members uniform beliefs and standards of conduct.

A variant of Parekh's move that is sometimes made is to point to John Stuart Mill's enthusiasm for diversity in *On Liberty* and then draw the conclusion that, since Mill is an archetypal liberal, diversity must be a liberal value. Now it is quite true that, towards the end of Chapter 3 of *On Liberty*, Mill argues that it is the 'remarkable diversity of character and culture' that 'has made the European family of nations an improving, instead of a stationary portion of mankind'.[29] Nevertheless, it has to be recalled that the title of this chapter is 'Of individuality, as one of the elements of well-being', not 'Of diversity . . .'. Diversity is indeed valuable for Mill. But only in as far as it is an expression of individuality. As Mill puts it, in a passage of rather embarrassing floweriness:

> It is not by wearing down into uniformity all that is individual in themselves, but by cultivating it and calling it forth, within the limits imposed by the rights and interests of others, that human beings become a noble and beautiful object of contemplation: and as the works partake the character of those who do them, by the same process human life also becomes rich, diversified, and animating.[30]

It is surely apparent that Mill's praise for diversity cannot without grotesque distortion be brought to bear in support of, for example, Charles Taylor's so-called difference-friendly liberalism: the kind that is not 'neutral between those who value remaining true to the culture of our ancestors and those who might want to cut loose in the name of some individual goal of self-development'.[31] Throwing the force of the state behind the ancestral values may promote diversity between groups by preventing voluntary assimilation to some other set of values. But it can do so only by trampling on the individuality that was prized by Mill. 'As one would expect,' writes Parekh, 'Millian liberalism cherishes not diversity *per se* but *liberal* diversity.'[32] So indeed, one *should* expect, provided that 'liberal diversity' is understood to mean simply whatever diversity is compatible with liberal institutions.

Parekh himself does not, it need hardly be said, understand 'liberal diversity' in this way: he follows Galston and Kymlicka in supposing that the only diversity permitted by Millian liberalism is that which is 'confined within the narrow limits of the individualist model of human excellence', which he equates with autonomy.[33] If 'the liberal way of life' and 'the autonomous way of life' are treated as synonymous, in the way that they are by Parekh, it is clear that we are once again being offered the false choice between autonomy and diversity.[34] Liberal ways of life should be defined simply as those ways of life, whatever they may be, that are not incompatible with the existence of liberal institutions. We can then point out – what Parekh's conceptual sleight of hand conceals – that liberal ways of life so understood do not have to value autonomy.

The third and last argument that I shall look at here invokes the public–private distinction. It has become virtually an orthodoxy, in particular among feminist critics of liberalism, that it is a doctrine uniquely attached to the protection of a 'private sphere'. This is then taken to mean that liberals are committed to withdrawing from public scrutiny and intervention what goes on within families. This claim is historically inaccurate to the point of perversity. It would be more correct to say that the condition of most societies that have existed in the world has been one in which the public sphere has concerned relations between households: in effect, the polity has been a league of households, represented by their heads. Within the household, its (male) head has had a more or less free hand over his wife (or wives), children, servants and, where they have existed, slaves. Thus, John Stuart Mill observed in *The Subjection of Women* that 'the man had anciently (but this was anterior to Christianity) the power of life and death over his wife. She could invoke no law against him: he was her sole tribunal and law.'[35] In ancient Rome, the father also had the power of life and death over his children. Now this is the separation of the public and private spheres with a vengeance. But it would be a travesty to suggest that it is a characteristically liberal idea. Quite the reverse: it is liberals who have been in the forefront of efforts to remove the legal disabilities of women, to make marital rape a punishable offence, to press for more active involvement by the police in incidents of domestic violence and for the prosecution of child-abusers, and to insist that parents should be legally obliged to provide for the education of their children.

Mill is exemplary here. So far from endorsing the notion that families belong to the 'private sphere', he argued that they constitute 'a case where ... [the sentiment of liberty] is altogether misplaced. A person should be free to do as he likes in his own concerns; but he ought not to be free to do as he likes in acting for another, under the pretext that the affairs of the other are his own affairs.'[36] Mill's strictures continue to have force. There is still an insidious tendency to assume that the interests of children are somehow subsumed under those of their parents. It is, however, conservatives touting so-called 'family values' who are typically guilty of this error – just as in Mill's day. Liberals are more typically concerned to protect children against parents by pressing for the prohibition of abuses such as corporal punishment, the genital mutilation of girls and parental coercion to marry. In this, liberals run up against objections from the more consistent enthusiasts for cultural diversity.

NOTES

1 Jones, P. 'Rushdie, Race and Religion', *Political Studies* 38 (1990), p. 694.
2 'The Sikh's turban no longer remains a cultural symbol, which is what it largely is, and becomes a religious requirement.' Bhikhu Parekh, 'Cultural Diversity and Liberal Democracy', pp. 202–27 in Gurpreet Mahajan, ed., *Democracy, Difference and Social Justice* (Delhi: Oxford University Press, 1998), p. 208.
3 Sebastian Poulter, *Ethnicity, Law and Human Rights: The English Experience* (Oxford: Clarendon Press, 1988), pp. 294–5.

4   Peter Singer, *Animal Liberation* (London: HarperCollins, 2nd edn, 1991), p. 154.

5   Yael Tamir, *Liberal Nationalism* (Princeton, NJ: Princeton University Press, 1993), p. 39.

6   See especially Michael Sandel, *Democracy's Discontent* (Cambridge, Mass.: Harvard University Press. 1996).

7   Bhikhu Parekh, 'Equality in a Multiracial Society', pp. 123–55 in Jane Franklin, ed., *Equality* (London: Institute for Public Policy Research, 1997), p. 135.

8   Ibid., pp. 150–1.

9   See *The Oxford English Dictionary* under 'Opportune' and, for more information about Portunus, Manfred Lurker, *Dictionary of Gods and Goddesses, Devils and Demons* (London and New York: Routledge and Kegan Paul, 1987), p. 286.

10 Sebastian Poulter, *Ethnicity, Law and Human Rights: The English Experience* (Oxford: Clarendon Press, 1988), p. 322, n. 271. See also p. 48.

11 Parekh, 'Equality in a Multiracial Society', p. 135.

12 Ibid.

13 Poulter, *Ethnicity, Law and Human Rights*, p. 356.

14 This thought was anticipated by A. E. Housman when he wrote in the penultimate poem in *A Shropshire Lad* (62) that 'malt does more than Milton can / To justify God's ways to man.'

15 Poulter, *Ethnicity, Law and Human Rights*, pp. 372–3.

16 Dissent by Justices Blackmun, Brennan and Marshall in *Employment Division, Department of Human Resources of Oregon et al.* v. *Alfred L. Smith et al.*, 494 US 872 (1990), p. 918.

17 Poulter, *Ethnicity, Law and Human Rights*, pp. 366–9.

18 Bhikhu Parekh, 'Superior People: The Narrowness of Liberalism from Mill to *Rawls*', *Times Literary Supplement*, 25 February 1994, pp. 11–13, p. 13.

19 Charles Taylor, 'The Politics of Recognition', pp. 25–73 in Amy Gutmann, ed., *Multiculturalism: Examining the Politics of Difference* (Princeton, NJ: Princeton University Press, 1994), p. 58.

20 Carter Lindberg, *The European Reformations* (Oxford: Blackwell, 1996), p. 247.

21 Ibid.

22 Parekh, 'Superior People', p. 13. The same claim is made (in the same words) in Bhikhu Parekh, 'Cultural Diversity and Liberal Democracy', pp. 202–27 in Gurpreet Mahajan, ed., *Democracy, Difference and Social Justice* (Delhi: Oxford University Press, 1998), p. 206.

23 James Tully, *Strange Multiplicity: Constitutionalism in an Age of Diversity* (Cambridge: Cambridge University Press, 1995), esp. pp. 1–17 and pp. 188–91.

24 Yael Tamir, 'Who Do You Trust?', *Boston Review* 22 (October/November 1997), 32–3, p. 33.

25 Chandran Kukathas, 'Multiculturalism as Fairness: Will Kymlicka's *Multicultural Citizenship*', *Journal of Political Philosophy* 5 (1997), 406–27, p. 426.

26 Parekh, 'Cultural Diversity and Liberal Democracy', p. 207.

27 Ibid., p. 212.

28 R. D. Grillo, *Pluralism and the Politics of Difference: State, Culture and Ethnicity in Comparative Perspective* (Oxford: Clarendon Press, 1998), p. 212; internal quotation from N. Yuval-Davis, 'Fundamentalism, Multiculturalism and Women in Britain', pp. 278–91 in J. Donald and A. Rattansi, eds, *'Race', Culture and Difference* (London: Sage, 1992), p. 283.

29 Mill, *On Liberty*, p. 72.

30 Ibid., p. 63.

31 Taylor, 'The Politics of Recognition', p. 58.

32 Parekh, 'Superior People', p. 12, emphasis in original.
33 Ibid.
34 Parekh, 'Cultural Diversity and Liberal Democracy', p. 207.
35 John Stuart Mill, *The Subjection of Women*, in Collini, ed., *On Liberty and Other Writings*, pp. 146–7.
36 Mill, *On Liberty*, pp. 104–5.

FURTHER READING

Barry, B. (2001). *Culture and Equality*. Polity.

Baumeister (2000). *Liberalism and the Politics of Difference*. Edinburgh University Press.

Kukathas, C. (1992). 'Are There Any Cultural Rights?' *Political Theory*: 20(1) 105–39.

Kymlicka, W. (1995). *Multi-Cultural Citizenship*. OUP.

Kymlicka, W. (2001). *Politics in the Vernacular: Nationalism; Multiculturalism and Citizenship*. OUP.

Kymlicka, W. and S. Ian, ed. (1997). *Ethnicity and Group Rights*. Nomos.

Margalit, A. (1990). 'National Self-determination.' *Journal of Philosophy*: 87(9) 439–61.

Parekh, B. (1997). 'Dilemmas of a Multicultural Theory of Citizenship.' *Constellations*: 4(1) 54–62.

Parekh, B. (1999). 'Political Theory and the Multicultural Society.' *Radical Philosophy*: 95 27–32.

Rawls, J. (1993). *Political Liberalism*. New York, Columbia Univiversity Press.

Rawls, J. (1997). 'The Idea of Public Reason.' *Deliberative Democracy*, Bohman, James ed., Cambridge, MIT Press.

Raz, T. (1998). 'Multiculturalism.' *Ratio Juris*: 11(3).

Young, I.M. (1997). 'Deferring Group Representation.' *Nomos* **XXXIX**: 349–76.

Young, I.M. (1997). 'A Multicultural Continuum:. A Critique of Will Kymlicka's Ethnic-Nation Dichotomy.' *Constellations*: 4(1) 48–53.

Young, I.M. (2002). *Inclusion and Democracy*. OUP.

Part 5
NATIONALISM

Introduction

PRIMA FACIE, THE STRUCTURE of liberal thought suggests that the constituency of the moral should aspire to the universal; that is, all deserve equal consideration. In the first reading of this part, Roger Scruton attempts to undermine this position, by showing it is at best incomplete. What completes it is something that is, in spirit, antithetical to liberalism: namely, nationalism.

Scruton criticises liberalism for answering the question as to the source of unity and the question as to the source of legitimacy in the same terms. In many liberalisms, these are the terms of the social contract. The idea is that 'unconditioned rational choosers' contract together to form an association *and* to obey its rules. Against this Scruton argues that the liberal self is not metaphysically plausible. What is presupposed is a self for whom rational considerations already form a motive for action. A better notion of self would draw on some prior story; specifically, a 'non-political idea of membership'. That is, there is a prior sense of unity that drives individuals towards the social contract. Membership that is not part of the social contract surfaces in the ideas of 'nationalism' and 'race' (the latter Scruton construes as a cultural rather than a biological matter). This is a 'form of union' with those who have come before us and will come after us, and it is a source of obligations. Where Scruton differs from those communitarians who criticise liberalism along similar lines (he mentions, as examples, Sandel, Walzer and Dworkin), is that he regards these obligations as rather stringent. As he puts it, the real price of community is 'sanctity, intolerance, exclusion, and a sense that life's meaning depends upon obedience, and also on vigilance against the enemy'.

In the rest of the paper, Scruton brings his considerable learning to bear on the consequences of this 'non-political unity'. He draws out four of its characteristic features: a shared language, shared associations, shared history and a common culture. He is also explicit about two further ways in which non-political unity can supplement the liberal account. The first is that liberalism cannot solve a problem that goes back at least to Rousseau (Rousseau 1987: ii, vi, vii). In order to sign a contract individuals would have to regard themselves as part of a group, but they are not supposed to regard themselves as part of a group until they have signed the contract. The second, more characteristic of the general communitarian critique, is that liberalism cannot command the kind of loyalty to the state that will inspire people to come to its defence or safeguard its public institutions.

Scruton's challenge is not only to liberals, but also communitarians who seek to challenge liberalism without leaving the political left. If nationalism does imply intolerance, then the position of such communitarians is undermined. In particular, nationalism is incompatible with the tolerant multiculturalism to which modern liberal democracies aspire. Hence, the question for the left to ask is whether a form of nationalism can be found to which people can commit themselves (to solve the problems for liberalism that Scruton and others have identified) which is compatible with tolerance and pluralism.

Alasdair MacIntyre's book, *After Virtue* (MacIntyre 1981), has been one of the most influential in the field of moral philosophy in recent times. In it, MacIntyre argued that modern morality consisted of the remnants of previous moral systems. As these systems did not fit together, and as we no longer have the beliefs necessary to underpin those systems, attempts to stitch them into a defensible system are bound to fail. The alternative, MacIntyre argued, is to return to a form of virtue ethics on the Aristotelian model. Hence, it is characteristic of MacIntyre's approach to focus on particular character traits. Hence, in the essay reprinted here, he considers whether or not the trait of patriotism (viewed with suspicion since the 1960s) is a virtue.

MacIntyre contrasts two views. The moral viewpoint involves impersonal judgement – 'to judge as any rational person would judge, independently of his or her interests, affections and social position'. Patriotism is defined 'in terms of a kind of loyalty to a particular nation which only those possessing that particular nationality can exhibit'. Given this clash, it follows that patriotism is immoral, hence a vice rather than a virtue. However, this 'liberal universalist' morality is not the only option. If morality is, as virtue ethics suggests, intimately tied to the goings-on in particular communities, then a special attachment to such communities 'could not meaningfully be contrasted with or counterposed to what morality required of me'. This position, however, seems to suffer from an inherent conservatism; it seems to exempt 'some fundamental structure of that community's life from criticism'. MacIntyre's reply can be divided in two. The first is to distinguish what is and what is not exempt from criticism by the patriot. Once this is done, it turns out to have enough critical edge – MacIntyre claims – to satisfy the reasonable critic. Second, he turns the tables on the liberal. If liberal morality is to survive, it needs to command people's allegiance. Does it have the resources to provide a ground for such allegiance? If, for example, liberal morality is simply a rational calculation of reciprocity of interest, then it will make sense to default at precisely those times of threat when allegiance is required most.

What we are left with, then, are two views. Either we are liberal universalists, in which case patriotism is a vice but we are in permanent danger of dissolution; or we take the second option, in which case patriotism is a virtue but our public morality is different from that which we think it is. In a final twist, MacIntyre suggests that the survival in 'the large scale modern polity' that is (at least) America requires us to 'live out' the 'conceptual confusion' of these two views.

That our deep moral views are conceptually confused is a hard bullet to bite. It is plausible that a morality founded simply on self-interest will founder when reciprocity breaks down and defaulting becomes rational (although even this has been disputed (Gauthier 1986)). However, is self-interest the only standard of rationality in practical reason to which the liberal can appeal? Could people act on the motive of a commitment to just institutions? (Rawls 1999: section 86.) Or the desire to be, or at least to be seen to be, reasonable? (Scanlon 1982.) Or should, radically, liberal morality eschew particular attachments altogether?

In his contribution, David Miller outlines the position defended at greater length in his subsequent book, *On Nationality* (Miller 1995). Miller defines nationality in terms of three interconnected propositions, involving personal identity, the notion of an ethical community and the notion of a political community. What kind of an identity is a *national* identity? How does it differ from other forms of identity? Miller lists five conditions. The first is that 'national communities are constituted by belief: a nationality exists when its members believe it does'. As this is only one part of the definition, Miller must mean it as necessary and not sufficient. Its importance lies in the fact that it takes the place of other possible candidates: sharing a certain race or language. The second is historical continuity. Here Miller makes a claim, also made by Scruton, that belonging to a nation gives us obligations to the yet to come and the dead. In a sense it is missing the point to ask what it is that grounds this obligation (we have the obligation because we belong to the nation and we belong to the nation because we have this obligation). However, the absence of grounds here leaves the nationalist in a weak position to convince the sceptic. The third is that the identity is active: in particular, nations determine their own politics. The fourth is that nations must be tied to a particular geographical area, and the fifth is that the individuals who comprise a nation must believe themselves to share 'certain traits that mark them off from other peoples'. Even with the proviso that these may be cultural rather than racial, this is likely to worry the liberal as it militates against the current general aspirations to multiculturalism. According to Miller, immigrants must 'take on the essential elements of national character'.

Miller returns to the question of immigration after providing what many in this area see as the strongest argument for nationalism: that it provides the social solidarity that liberal states require to survive, but which liberalism cannot provide. Miller then squarely confronts what he calls 'the liberal objection': that his view is incompatible with the tolerant multiculturalism to which liberal states aspire. Would the liberal be right to assert this incompatibility? Might not, for example, the 'essential elements of national character' be tolerance (or even celebration) of difference? Miller gives a nuanced answer. Although nationalism should aim to be inclusive, and to allow for the flourishing of sub-groups within it, 'one cannot aspire to unlimited tolerance in this area'. However, even here it is unclear how much of a problem this need be for the liberal. With his nod to Mill, it looks as if Miller has in mind only that sub-groups should adopt principles of tolerance and equal respect that are at the heart of liberalism (and incompatible with certain kinds of fundamentalism).

In the remainder of the paper Miller uses the fact that his definition of national identity is partly framed on facts outside of any individual psychology (for example, geographical area and historical continuity) to provide answers to two further problems. First, as to whether the nationalist needs to concede a right to indefinite succession and second, as to whether our nationality depends on our sentiments. In both cases he is able to answer in the negative.

How different, then, is Miller's nationalism from liberalism? It is different chiefly, I think, in that it takes us to have obligations to which we have not consented to individuals who do not stand in reciprocal relations to us (that is, those from different generations). Such obligations fit uneasily into a liberal outlook. A second difference is less clear cut. Miller argues that a national identity can stand above a group identity and be impartial between them. This, as argued above, looks to be standard second-order impartialist liberalism. However, calling it a 'national identity' brings out something that liberals might be loathe to agree to: that it is, itself, a conception of the good and not a wholly neutral position.

REFERENCES

Gauthier, D. (1986). *Morals By Agreement*. Oxford, Clarendon Press.
MacIntyre, A. (1981). *After Virtue*. London, Duckworth.
Miller, D. (1995). *On Nationality*. Oxford, Clarendon Press.
Rawls, J. (1999). *A Theory of Justice*. Oxford, Oxford University Press.
Rousseau, J.J. (1987). *The Social Contract*. Indianapolis, Hackett.
Scanlon, T.M. (1982). 'Contractualism and Utilitarianism.' *Utilitarianism and Beyond*. B. Williams and A. Sen (eds.). Cambridge, Cambridge University Press.

17

IN DEFENCE OF THE NATION

Roger Scruton

[. . .]

I shall consider the unity of the body politic, rather than the legitimacy of the institutions used to govern it. The full liberal theory sees the state itself as the source of that unity, whereas, I shall argue, unity is, in the normal instance, social rather than political and ought also to be national.

The liberal theory has both a descriptive and a prescriptive version. It tells us sometimes that this is how things *are* in the modern world, sometimes that this is how things *ought* to be. As a prescriptive theory it commands widespread acceptance, defended by Spinoza, Locke and Kant, and perhaps even embodied [. . .] in the US Constitution. A version has recently been advanced by John Gray, not in order to attack conservatism, but in order precisely to embody the insights of conservatism in a modified theory of the liberal state.[1] In all cases, however, an understandable concern for liberal ideas of legitimacy, has given rise to a quite untenable theory of political unity – and one which, if upheld as *realpolitik*, would almost certainly lead to the collapse of liberal jurisdiction.

Before considering the liberal theory of unity, however, it is useful to return to the theory of legitimacy from which it derives. The appeal of liberal theories lies in the ease with which they can be given a 'foundational' character, in terms which seem to presuppose no religious or metaphysical commitment on the part of those who subscribe to them. Two ideas have been particularly important in developing the 'deep' theory of the liberal state: the social contract, and the 'unconditioned rational chooser'. Defenders of the social contract argue that all obligation has its foundation in consent, and that we are under a political obligation only to the extent that we are bound by some contractual relation to comply with it. Those who base their liberalism on an idea of pure rational choice argue that a state is legitimate only to the extent that a rational being, consulting the principles of rational choice alone, and without reference to his distinguishing conditions, would choose to live within its jurisdiction. Sometimes the two theories are combined – as in Rawls, for whom, however, the second theory has gradually gained ascendancy. Both theories refuse to acknowledge 'prescriptive right' – that is, obligations which were never 'undertaken'. And both are founded on a conception of the human person that is psychologically, morally, and metaphysically highly questionable.

The objection to the 'liberal individualist' conception of the person has recently surfaced even in the literature of liberalism, usually distorted, as in Walzer, Sandel and Charles Taylor, so as to seem like a further move in a 'leftward' direction.[2] But its original proponent – Hegel [. . .] – was no left-winger. Indeed, in the matter under discussion, he was probably as reactionary as I. In Hegel's view, man owes his identity as a rational chooser to a process of development that implicates him inescapably in obligations which he did not choose. These obligations of piety are both pre-contractual and pre-political. (Hegel assigns them to the 'family', though, as his own argument shows, that is too narrow a designation.) The legitimacy of the state depends in part upon its ability to recuperate and articulate these non-political obligations, which form the original of its own non-contractual order.

The person who, on releasing himself into the freely contracting world of 'civil society', dishonours the pieties that nurtured him is not more, but less rational than the one who respects them. The blithe momentary Benthamite cuts away the ground from the rational choices that he pretends to be making, by depriving himself of every value other than his own pleasure – a commodity whose worth vanishes in the possession of it. He may, once he has risen to full autonomy, possess himself of another source of morality: the universalizing imperative of Kant, which derives its authority from reason alone. But the Kantian imperative sets a limit to goals, and does not provide them. Its capacity to become a *motive*, and so to be incorporated into the agent's acts and projects, depends upon what Hegel called a dialectical relation with those instincts, prejudices and pieties which it serves to qualify. Kant had imagined that reason could be its *own* motive: that the categorical imperative could be freed from all 'empirical determinations', and yet be sovereign. But in this he was wrong, for reasons which subsequent philosophers have made clear. Choice must start somewhere: and even if this starting point is later described, from the point of view of reason, as mere prejudice, this is not to condemn it, but on the contrary, to show the indispensability of prejudice in the make-up of a rational agent.

I mention those arguments only to remind the reader that the questions at issue are, at bottom, metaphysical, and that the assurance of liberals, that they have access to the truth of man's condition, ought to be set against the extreme implausibility of their metaphysical convictions. The same dubious metaphysics which informs the liberal theory of legitimacy motivates the liberal theory of unity. Every political order depends, and ought to depend, upon a non-political idea of membership. And to the extent that it emancipates itself from that idea, I claim, to that extent does it lose its motivating force, just as individuals lose their moral identity and will, to the extent that their prejudices, pieties and moral instincts are cancelled by the abstract imperatives of the 'pure rational chooser'. This is not to say that the full liberal theory of the state does not, in some sense, *describe* the society of the future. It prognosticates the death of political order, by its very ability to evaporate into abstract nothingness the prejudices upon which society depends. The result of this, I believe, will not be the birth of the liberal polity, but its final extinction. For as prejudice dwindles, tolerance is left unguarded by conviction, and falls prey to the ever-vigilant schemes of the fanatic.

MEMBERSHIP

It is often argued that the idea of the nation is a recent invention, coming to the fore either as a reaction to the Enlightenment,[3] or as part of the Enlightenment itself: the necessary replacement for an aristocratic entitlement and a dynastic crown.[4] Certainly there is a *doctrine* – 'nationalism' – which owes its being to the controversies of the late eighteenth century.[5] But an idea is not born with the doctrine that perverts it, nor does the fact wait attendance on our first conceiving it. Nations were realities by the time Shakespeare wrote his histories,[6] and the national idea is already luminous in those histories, even if detached from the bellicose doctrines that have polluted it in recent times. It was to the national idea that Cardinal Richelieu appealed in 1617, when he ruled that, in matters of state, no French Catholic should prefer a Spaniard to a French Protestant.[7] It was a nation, in some sense, which established its empire in South America. And, when the King James Bible has God say to Abraham 'And in thy seed shall all the nations of the earth be blessed' (Genesis 22:18), this is surely not so far from the national idea of recent history.

Nobody who defends the national idea is now likely to explain himself in terms of kinship or race: and not only through fear of the thought-police. The idea that mankind divides into biological 'races' has been put to such absurd use by the Gobinistes and their followers, and entangled itself with so much nonsense and pseudo-science, as to have lost all credibility.[8] Even if there were some element of truth in the theory, it could give no comfort to the nationalist, since races, if they exist, are not confined within national boundaries, and have no characteristic language, culture or history. Indeed biological races are defined without reference to history: there is no other justification for the concept. The idea therefore offers nothing to those searching for a historical identity, upon which to found a state which owes its legitimacy to birthright alone.

Nevertheless, it is difficult to avoid terms like 'race', not least because they accurately reflect *ways of conceiving* social unity. The Jewish self-identification as 'children of Israel' is an important instance. That the Jews form no homogeneous genetic entity is evident. Nevertheless, they identify themselves in terms of a common descent, and this is a feature of their pre-political unity which cannot be discarded without detriment to their cohesion. Our own terms for 'nation' also originate in ideas of common descent: *natio, patria, národ,* etc. German has as its normal term for pre-political unity, *Volk,* a word which is now neutral as to who begat whom, but which originally had connotations of family and tribe. Interesting, too, are the Arabic words for nation. One – *watan* – derives from *watana,* to dwell, and identifies a people purely in terms of its dwelling place. Another, *Umm,* the classical term still used in such phrases as *al-umam al-mutahidah* (The United Nations), derives from the same root as the words for 'source' and 'mother'. Yet another, *qawm* – the more usual term when it comes to questions of nationalism and national identity, and which means, in pre-political parlance, kinsfolk or fellow tribesmen – derives from the root *qāma,* meaning to stand up, to arise, to be proud, to attack, to be. In this root – which occurs in the description of God as *al-qayyum,* the Everlasting one – is condensed a whole philosophy of man's social nature, and one that should be borne in mind by the student of modern 'Arab nationalism'. For a *qawmah* is also an uprising, a 'revolution', and it is through such a 'standing up' against adversaries, the Arab nationalist believes, that a people is born.

In a loose sense, therefore, the term 'race' may still perform a function, even for those who have discarded the eugenic superstitions of the racists. It denotes a continuity across generations, based in kinship and intermarriage, but supported also by a consciousness of common descent. This common descent creates the obligation of inheritance: we must receive from our forefathers what we also pass to our children. Only the idea that the inheritance is entirely *biological,* rather than cultural, renders the concept suspect to those of open mind. The belief in racial inheritance, construed as an endlessly transferable set of benefits and burdens, is universally encountered, and not to be despised merely because it seems to conflict with the liberal conception of politics: the fault may lie, after all, with the liberal conception of politics. It would not be the first time that the conflict between liberalism and human-nature had to be resolved in favour of humanity.

Concepts of race are kind-concepts. As is evident, we are not dealing with a natural kind, nor indeed with any other kind usually studied by contemporary philosophy. A race is an 'intentional' kind – one formed partly in obedience to a conception of itself.[9] And the simplest way to understand it is through the notion of membership, which I touched on above, in considering the relation between aesthetic experience and culture.

The ceremony of membership has an important function, besides that of confirming rights and duties acquired by descent. It can be offered to strangers, and used to incorporate them, as limbs of the collective body, despite their lack of kinship. Of course, this privilege is a rare one, and all tribes are sensible of the dangers which ensue, when membership is offered on easy terms to those who have not proved their capacity for a lifetime's commitment. One way – maybe the principal way – in which membership is understood, is as a form of union with the unborn and the dead. Through membership I see the world as it will be seen by those who are yet to be. Hence I rise to an exalted perspective, a perspective above my own perishable being. Through the ceremonies of membership 'my eyes are opened', and I see the world no longer as an object of my own paltry needs and appetites, but as it really and eternally is (or, to be more philosophical, as it really and eternally seems). Through the ceremony of membership, therefore, the gods enter the world, and make themselves known. Hence 'immersive' membership, of the kind exemplified by the practice of initiation, is closely tied to religion. (Etymologically, a *religio* is a 'binding'.) Communities which experience immersive membership tend to define themselves, like the Jews, in religious terms. But the Jews also display the *revisionary* potential of religion. The gods themselves, once seriously believed in, have a tendency to detach themselves from the localities which gave birth to them, and to exert their sovereignty more extendedly, perhaps over all mankind. Indeed, when a religion is monotheistic, directed towards an all-wise and all-powerful creator, worship must be open to all who have the capacity for obedience. A people can be 'chosen', like the Jews, as the instruments of God's purpose or as a 'race of suppliants', but not as solely entitled to worship him. In such a case, therefore, the experience of membership, and the religious doctrine, have a tendency to separate, and to acquire independent histories.[10] It is one mark of a 'nation', in the modern sense, that this separation has occurred, so that membership can be defined without reference to religious obedience. (Cf. the injunction of Cardinal Richelieu, referred to above.)

At the opposite pole from tribal initiation stands the free contract of partnership, in which individuals meet on terms, and recognize no obligations that are not contained in the contract itself. In such cases association dissolves with the extinction of the mutual purpose. Such relations are only doubtfully described as relations of membership: for their character is entirely summarized by an agreement between individuals, who create no entity beyond themselves.

At the same time, however, there are associations, often verging on the contractual, which introduce new corporate entities and which are rightly understood as forms of membership. Clubs, corporations and trusts are treated by the law in special ways which reflect their corporate nature. Legal personality (which is sometimes accorded and sometimes withheld) is not a convenient fiction, but the transcription of a real and independent moral identity created by the ties of membership. Even when the law recognizes nothing but a contract (as in the 'unincorporated association'), the individuals may experience their relation as a form of corporate personality, with a common will and common goals. Contracts are means; membership is always at least partly an end in itself; and what begins in a contract (joining a club, for example) may outlast the dissolution of the contractual tie.

[. . .]

ALIENATION

For there is no gainsaying that 'modernity' has involved an attempt to revise the experience of membership in a contractual direction. Yet there is no evidence that mankind has become happier (even if it has become more prosperous) as a result. The complaint against 'alienation' may, of course, be so much self-indulgence: after all, it issues from people who are 'not at home in the world'. Nevertheless, we ought for that very reason to take it seriously: when self-indulgence becomes the norm, something is wrong with the society that engenders it.

Two things are usually identified as the root of alienation: capitalism, and scientific thought (including the technology that springs from it). For the liberal there is a certain paradox here. For 'capitalism' is (by and large) a rude name for the sum of market relations – in other words, economic relations established by consent. And science is simply a name for the sum of propositions thought to be true, and believed for no other reason. Science and the market are the two fundamental forms of man's relation to an objective world: the two ways of recognizing the world's objectivity, either as thing (and therefore object of knowledge and use), or as person (and therefore subject of consent). It is perhaps a sign of original sin that these two indispensable links to an objective reality should be experienced as a 'fall' into something 'alien'.

One explanation of this 'fall' is provided by my discussion of membership. The relations established by a market, like those created by science, have a *universal* character. A contract requires no bond, no anterior attachment, between the parties, and its meaning is exhausted by its terms. Moreover, terms are dictated 'impersonally', by the rational self-interest of all who have access to the market. 'All' means everyone; defenders of the market are *ipso facto* defenders of free trade, wishing to multiply the benefits of a free economy through universal access. The alienating quality of the market consists partly in the fact that the 'alien' has utter equality with the friend. No *special* relationship exists to provide the meaning of the transaction, and I throw myself into the system only to set aside the claims of affection in the interests of agreement. There is a loneliness here, born of the very idea that consent is sovereign: the very same loneliness detected by de Tocqueville, at the heart of American democracy.

The desire for some new kind of economic relation is therefore invariably couched in terms of a 'communitarian' ideal – such as 'market socialism' – in which co-operatives, and the relations of trust and loyalty among their members, are proposed as antidote. This involves a move away from contract, towards economic relations which are 'bonded' and circumscribed by duties, in the manner of a feudal tenure. It is also a move in a particularist direction. The market offends by its universality: it pays no attention to people, but only to the abstract person, the 'rational economic man'. The communitarian economy 'restores man to himself' by recognizing his social nature, his *Gattungswesen*, his *membership*.[11]

Similarly with scientific thought. The categories of science arise directly from our rational interest in truth. Science is therefore *common* to all rational beings, and the peculiar possession of none of them. When I engage in scientific enquiry, I free my perception of the world from intentional concepts, and therefore from those categories whose sense derives from a particular community or particular way of life. I no longer see the world under the aspect of 'belonging'. I am not 'at home' in the world of science, for precisely the reason that I am just as much at home there, and just as little, as everyone else.

Two antidotes have been proposed to this condition: the search for a 'subjective' relation to the world (a search which begins in modern times with Kierkegaard, and which leads to Husserl, Heidegger and Patočka); and the search for a 'cultural' mode of knowledge, one that is formed in the image of membership. In the modern world, those two searches tend in a single direction. For the purely individualistic conception of 'subjectivity' again opens the way to solitude and alienation: it stands in need of 'redemption', and redemption either takes a religious form, as in the 'leap of faith' of Kierkegaard, or else involves a *Heimkehr* to the breast of some implied community – some Little Gidding of the imagination – as in the 'culture' of Arnold, Leavis and Eliot. In the opposition between science and culture, therefore, we find precisely the same contrast as that which exists between the free market and the 'moral economy' (to use E.P. Thompson's phrase): the contrast between a universalized relation to the world, and a relation circumscribed by some particular attachment. The same contrast galvanized and tormented the French Revolutionists, who could never decide whether the 'nation' which they had so unwisely deified consists of a contractual partnership of all-comers, or of a 'people', bound by destiny and by the unchosen ties of membership.

The contractual view of society is in one sense supremely rational: it recommends a negotiated solution to every conflict and suggests a path to every goal. Of course, it does nothing to *provide* goals, which must be brought ready-made to the contractual encounter. It is silent about the meaning of life, and has nothing to offer to the lost and the disaffected. That, for the liberal, is its strength. To demand anything else from politics is to demand what cannot be obtained, except at enormous human cost – and perhaps not even then. Political institutions exist in order to mediate and adjudicate, not in order to mobilize and conscript.

Unfortunately, however, the political sphere cannot stand so serenely above the loyalties which feed it. The spirit of contract enters human relations, precisely in order that the liberal state should stand in judgement over them. Those relations are therefore voided of their residue of membership, and become provisional, rescindable, uncertain of themselves, with no authority beyond the transient 'sovereignty' of choice. Such is the celebrated transition from status to contract, described by Sir Henry Maine.[12]

The sanctity of human bonds is, however, inseparable from their reality as *bondage*. Rebuilt in contractual form they become profane, a system of façades, a Disneyland version of what was formerly dignified and monumental. What meaning they have no longer inheres in them as an objective and personal countenance, but merely shines momentarily, as we sweep the light of our desire across their disenchanted surfaces. Nobody, not even the liberal, is happy with this: only the crudest reformer actually *welcomes* what has happened to marriage, for example, in the wake of its desacralization. But the liberal sees no remedy to this misfortune: and for the true liberal there *is* none, besides some new habit of mind which enables us to live with the problem. Of course, there are those – Sandel, Walzer and Dworkin, for example[13] – who propose 'communitarian' ways of thinking, as a further move in the direction which a sophisticated liberalism requires. But none of them is prepared to accept the real price of community: which is sanctity, intolerance, exclusion, and a sense that life's meaning depends upon obedience, and also on vigilance against the enemy. Or at least, in so far as liberals have perceived this, they have deplored it, and tried to attribute these features to some *bad* form of community, in order to save the *good* form which is their heart's desire. If the 'nation' has often been identified as the *bad* form of social membership, this is partly because, in existing circumstances, loyalty to the nation is a real possibility. To fix one's desires on the irrecoverable enables one to persist in the liberal posture, of recommending nothing.

NATIONALISM

The experience of membership is precisely *not* political, but social. It arises, and ought to arise, independently of the state, and it should not be the state's concern either to impose or to forbid any particular form of it, or any particular experience of the sacred and the profane. So says the liberal, and the conservative partly agrees with him. Both are wary of the attempt to *achieve* social unity by political directives, even if they differ as to how it should be *safeguarded*. A core experience of membership, once lost, cannot be recovered by conscription. It is not for the state to manufacture the deeper forms of loyalty, and the attempt to do so is inherently totalitarian. It involves, and has always involved, the replacement of religion by ideology, of civil association by conscription and of law by conspiratorial power. This is so evident to us, in our time, as to go without saying. Nevertheless, the fault, I suggest, lies not in the national idea, but rather in the use that has been made of it. As an *ideology*, force-fed to the multitude, so as to enlist them in a new obedience, nationalism is the enemy of the liberal state. It is also the enemy of nationality, extinguishing, in its furious purposefulness, the purposeless bonding that holds men together in peace.

But the same is true of *every* ideology – including those universalist ideologies which are, in the modern world, set against the 'national idea'. As ideologies and instruments of conscription, 'equality' and 'liberation' have proved to be as much the enemies of freedom as the notion of a 'master race'. Indeed, it is only ignorance that could permit the belief that Soviet communism, founded on universalist principles, has involved less crime, less suffering, less insolence and indignity, than the particularist politics of the Nazis.

At the same time, there is little doubt that the ideology of nationalism has so formed contemporary perception of its leading idea, as to have made it difficult to separate the 'nation' from the tragi-comedy of pre-war Europe and of the present Middle East. Elie Kedourie and Kenneth Minogue have argued vigorously for the view that the ideology comes first, and has therefore given shape to the concept of nationhood. Minogue summarizes what is now a familiar liberal argument in the following words:

> The point we have to emphasize about modern nationalism is that the politics comes first, and the national culture is constructed later. We have found nationalisms without nations, aspirations substituted for reality. Instead of a dog beginning to wag its political tail, we find political tails trying to wag dogs. The Irish government tries to promote an Irish culture, the Nigerian government tries to persuade Ibos, Hausa, Fulanis and Yorubas that they are part of a Nigerian or an African nation . . .
>
> This amounts to saying that the concept of the nation is almost entirely empty of content, until a content is arbitrarily supplied from local circumstances.[14]

As we shall see, Minogue's last claim is untenable. Nevertheless, he is right to suggest that the national idea has been used to *conscript* people to nationhood: to impose a social unity by political means. In this respect, however, the full liberal theory of the state makes a comparable error. It too believes that there is, or ought to be, no source of political unity other than the political process itself: it differs in claiming that unity cannot be imposed, and that, in the right conditions, it emerges from, and expresses, an act of common consent. Until sustained by a national idea, however, the liberal state is, I believe, a solvent of unity and therefore contains the seeds of its own destruction.

WANDERING AND SETTLED PEOPLES

[. . .]

In a recent work Régis Debray has offered a powerful picture of religious doctrine (and its ideological substitutes, such as Marxism) as *formes a priori de la sociabilité (ou de l'existence politique)*.[15] Doctrine, he argues, is both necessary to the formation of a pre-political 'we', and also consequent upon it: *une idéologie est un drapeau, mais on ne se rallie pas à un drapeau au vu de ses couleurs, on adopte le drapeau parce qu'on s'incorpore à la troupe*.[16] As Debray notices, this resuscitation of the Marxian theory of ideology – not so as to criticize ideology, but rather so as to endorse it, in terms similar to those used by Burkean conservatives in defending 'prejudice' – has profoundly anti-liberal implications. If it is true, then what hope do we have of establishing the kind of polity [. . .], in which confession, doctrine and 'conceptions of the good' are all required to vacate their thrones to the sovereign rule of law?

But Debray's thesis is false: not because the foundation of loyalty is, or can be, purely political, as the full liberal theory requires, but because there are other forms of non-political unity than those founded in doctrine. Race is one of them; nationality another. *Pace* Kedourie and Minogue, there is a perfectly coherent idea of membership based in those relations between people which come from *occupying the same place*. People who are not, like the Jews, 'strangers and sojourners' in the land, may have things in common sufficient to constitute them as a 'kind'. The most important of these is territory. People gathered in the same place must accord to each other rights of occupation if they are to live in peace. The network of those rights defines a portion of the earth as 'ours'. Peoples from elsewhere are strangers to our rights, uninterested in preserving them, and liable, in times of war, to cancel them. There arises a common interest in defence, which has territory as its object. Until territory is *ours*, there is no real 'mine' or 'thine'.

If territory is to fall, in this way, under a common but divisible right of ownership, there must be a content to the collective 'we', which settles the terms and the boundaries of membership. Certain factors, naturally associated with joint occupation, contribute to this 'we':[17]

1 Shared language. There is no more dramatic mark of the stranger than his inability to speak my language. My language is not only mine. It is public, and shared, learned from and taught to those who are dearest. My language is always *our* language; the first thing that I inherit from my forefathers and the first that I pass on to my child. Attachment to language is the root of national culture, and, in favourable conditions, may be used to define the boundaries of nationhood. (Cf. the history of Polish, Turkish and especially Arab nationalism in our times.[18])

Language may also be imposed, either to break down loyalties inimical to the political order (Bulgaria, the Soviet Union, the USA until recently), or in order to consolidate a political order that has been newly established (Israel, and also Ireland – in which the attempt met with failure).

2   Shared associations. Settled people have more opportunity for association than those who wander. They can meet not only in family, festival, team and army, but also in places given to membership: churches, clubs, schools, localities of work and leisure. They have an opportunity for institution-building, and for attaching their institutions to the land. Their mutual ties lose the solemn and immersive nature of the ties formed by those who pass each other in the desert. They become looser, freer, and more 'civil', and at the same time fitted for corporate life. Societies differ, of course, as to which associations are permitted, and as to their ability to perpetuate themselves as institutions. The Hegelian idea of civil society is one of maximal association, under a rule of law which permits and encourages the incorporation of all lasting forms of membership. We can see a nation as partly constituted by the long-standing associations which are formed and inherited within it.

3   Shared history. People united by language, association and territory triumph and suffer together. They have common friends and common enemies. A historical *narrative* is manifest in the very associations which serve to combine them, and the memory of it is attached to the landscape, the towns, the institutions and the climate by which they are surrounded.

4   Common culture. There is both the desire and the need to consolidate community in the core experience of membership, as these are safeguarded and enhanced by faith, ritual and worship. For a wandering people this is the root of identity, and the sole durable source of a pre-political 'we'. In certain circumstances, however, membership can develop away from its 'angel infancy' and smile more inclusively, if also more coldly, on the surrounding world. The process – described by Spengler as a transition from 'culture' to 'civilization' – may perhaps foretell (as Spengler thought) the ruin of a people. Nevertheless it is the process that formed the nation states of Europe, and which conditions all that we have or hope for in the modern world. It is precisely this which permits the full loyalty of nationhood, and, with it, the moderating institutions of a liberal state.

A nation, like a race, is a kind formed through a conception of itself. The members of a nation do not merely share those four things (or some significant sub-set of them), but also *concede* them to each other as of right. Membership involves an acquiescence in the claims of others, and a recognition of a shared identity. Others of my nation have a right to the common territory, provided, at least, they are prepared to risk their life in defence of it. This self-consciousness of a nation is part of its moral character.

It endows nations with a life of their own, a destiny, even a personality. People who think of themselves as a collective 'we' understand their successes and failures as 'ours', and apportion collective praise and blame for the common outcome. Hence there arises what Solzhenitsyn has called 'repentance and self-limitation in the life of nations':

> Those who set the highest value on the existence of the nation, who see in it not the ephemeral fruit of social formations but a complex, vivid, unrepeatable organism not invented by man, recognise that nations have a full spiritual life, that they can soar to the heights and plunge to the depths, run the whole gamut from saintliness to utter wickedness (although only individuals ever reach the extremes).[19]

There is something drastic in that utterance, as in the self-castigations which fill the Old Testament, and from which our forefathers acquired the idea of a collective and inherited guilt. But Solzhenitsyn's words correspond to a recurrent thought in the life of nations, one which reveals the force and the depth of every true non-political loyalty. Only when moderated by law, and by conceptions of corporate personality, do sentiments of such intensity become negotiable. And that is why the nation needs law as much as law needs the nation.

[. . .]

LOYALTY AND JURISDICTION

If we consult the standard works of liberal theory, we do not as a rule find any discussion of social membership or social unity. It is assumed that the principles which determine the legitimacy of the ruling institutions will also settle the question as to who is governed by them. Advocates of the social contract, for example, suppose men to be gathered together by the very contract which settles their future obligations. But how were they gathered, and who did the gathering? On what basis are those unborn to be admitted to the contract? How do we distinguish those who are entitled to contract, from those who are 'barging in'? There is no satisfactory position for the contract theorist to take, short of universalism: if the contract is open to anyone, it is open to all. Anything short of world government is therefore tainted with illegitimacy. That is just another way of saying that, until moderated by a non-political loyalty, the contractarian view of the state is without application.

Similarly for democracy. When politicians address the people at an election (when they 'go to the country' as it is said in British parliamentary discourse), they ask a definite question: what do *we* want? The 'we' in question is the class of those entitled to vote. But how they acquired that entitlement, who conferred it and what justifies it, are questions whose answers are inseparable from the history of a nation.

Nor are liberals consistent in their repudiation of the national idea, as is shown by a characteristic liberal attitude to immigration, and to those like myself who wish to prevent or limit it. The argument is advanced that we have no right to close our doors against immigrants from our former colonies, since it was we who exploited them, or who reduced them to the state of economic and cultural dependence which ensures that their best – perhaps their only – prospects are now on British soil. If you examine the use of 'we' in that sentence, you will find a perfect instance of the national idea, as I have described it: the idea of a moral unity between people, based in territory, language, association, history and culture, and so bound up with the self-consciousness of those who are joined by it, as to make subsequent generations answerable for the sins of their forefathers, and entitled to the benefits which their ancestors forewent.

Supposing we accept the need for a non-political loyalty. Why should that loyalty be *national*? The answer is contained in the nature of the modern state. All law requires jurisdiction: that is, a principle for determining who is, and who is not, subject to its edicts. It is a peculiar feature of wandering peoples that they tend to be governed by laws which are co-terminous with their religious confessions, and which derive their authority from the same divine source. When the people are 'strangers and sojourners' this gives rise to an enormous problem of law-enforcement, as instanced by the Jews.

[. . .]

The safety, continuity and stability necessary to a rule of law are unobtainable until territory is secure. And only a territorial idea of jurisdiction will permit the final separation of law from confessional attachment. Territorial jurisdiction exists in two forms: that of empire, and that of the sovereign state. The first is parasitic on the second, since only if there is a 'metropolitan power' can there be an empire. Empires provide the most striking examples that the world has known of trans-national rules of law: the Roman Empire, for example, the Russian Empire during the nineteenth century (especially in Finland and the Baltic states), and the British Empire in India and Africa. Even the Ottoman Empire, despite its disabilities and the imperfection of the *millet* system, made moves towards the rule of law, while the Austro-Hungarian Empire [. . .] is the true paradigm [. . .] of a political unity which casts its mantle over many nations. There are two reasons, however, why liberals should be reluctant to countenance empire as their preferred form of jurisdiction. First, empires have now ceased to be founded on the rule of law: the Soviet Empire, for example, has persisted by *extinguishing* law and adjudication in all the territories which fall beneath its control. (Law is replaced by a Potemkin substitute, from which the sovereign Party is exempt, and to the extent that a rule of law can be reasserted – as in modern Hungary – to that extent is the Empire *threatened*.) Secondly, an empire *imposes* law on its subject peoples. The unity between them is an artificial unity, dependent upon the force exerted by the central power. This force in turn depends upon the cohesion of that power, and its territorial jurisdiction at home. And this depends upon a loyalty adapted to the defence of territory: in other words, on the persistence of something like a national idea. Hence the appeal to empire as the foundation of law may not, in the end, be distinct from the appeal to nationality. The collapse of the Roman Empire was caused precisely by the collapse of Rome, by the loosening of *'asabiyah* in the Empire's heart.

It is at this point, I think, that a liberal ought to bite the bullet, and confess to the advantages of the national idea. It establishes a social loyalty suited to territorial jurisdiction; and without territorial jurisdiction, there is no possibility of a liberal state. It is for this reason that the history of the *Rechtsstaat* and the history of the national idea are inseparable. In trying to understand this fact liberals have sometimes distinguished – as does Lord Acton in a famous essay – between nationality based in race and language, and nationality 'formed by the state', which is 'the only one to which we owe political duties . . . and the only one which has political rights'.[20] It seemed to Acton that the coincidence of national loyalty and legal obligation could be secured only if the nation were in some sense the creature of the law which governs it. (At the same time, he advocated empire, as the best guarantee of the freedom of nationalities, and therefore of the rights of individuals.) But the question is not which comes first – the law or the nation – but rather what determines the unity and durability of each. The national *Rechtsstaat* should be seen in terms of a continuing process of interaction, between a national loyalty and a territorial jurisdiction. The first is social rather than political, just like the loyalty of the Jews. Nationality and jurisdiction interpenetrate, and it is not absurd to envisage their relation in terms of that between body and soul (a special case, for Aristotle, of the relation between matter and form). To notice, as Acton does, their inseparability, is not to deny their distinctness. And to assign the unity of the body politic entirely to its legal part (as the liberal theory does), is as grave an error as to suppose, like Locke, that personal identity has nothing to do with the identity and continuity of the body.

[. . .]

NOTES

1   John Gray, 'The Politics of Culture Diversity,' *The Salisbury Review*, Vol. 6, No. 4, July 1988.

2   Michael Walzer, *Exodus and Revolution*, New York, 1985; Michael Sandel, *Liberalism and the Limits of Justice*, Cambridge, 1982; Charles Taylor, *Philosophy and the Human Sciences*, 2 vols., Cambridge, 1985.

3   So argues, for example, Sir Isaiah Berlin, in 'Nationalism: Past Neglect and Present Power', in *Against the Current*, New York, 1980.

4   Such, perhaps, is the nationalism of Sieyès and the Revolutionists.

5   See Elie Kedourie, *Nationalism*, London, 1960.

6   See R. A. D. Grant, 'Shakespeare as a Conservative Thinker', in R. Scruton, ed., *Conservative Thinkers*, London, 1988.

7   See the commentary by H. T. Buckle, *History of Civilization in England*, third edition, London, Vol. 1, p. 491.

8   See the painstaking demolition by Jacques Barzun, *Race: a study in modern superstition*, London, 1938.

9   On intentional kinds, see my *Sexual Desire*, London, 1986, Chapter 1.

10 The dilemma that this poses for the contemporary Jew is interestingly unfolded in Alan Montefiore, 'The Jewish Religion – Universal Truth and Particular Tradition', *Tel Aviv Review*, Vol. 1, 1988, pp. 166–86.

11 In order to save Feuerbach and Marx from any suspicion of 'race thinking', *Gattungswesen* is normally translated as 'species-being' – which does little justice to the climate of opinion that gave birth to the term.

12 Sir Henry Maine, *Ancient Law*, Cambridge, 1861.

13 See note 2 and also R. Dworkin, *Law's Empire*, London, 1986.

14 Kenneth Minogue, *Nationalism*, New York, 1967, p. 154.

15 Régis Debray, *Critique de la Raison Politique*, Paris, 1981, p. 178.

16 Ibid., p. 208.

17 The canonical Marxist theory of nationality acknowledges the same basic features as I do: 'The nation is a human community, stable and historically constituted, born from a common language, territory, economic life and psychological conditioning, which together are translated into a community of culture' – J. Stalin, *Communism and Russia*, 1913.

18 See especially Albert Hourani, *Arabic Thought in the Liberal Age*, Oxford, 1962, in which the reader can clearly see the way in which liberal conceptions of law, and sovereignty, and national ideas of 'asabiyah, have emerged simultaneously in the modem Arabic world, and stood always in a relation of mutual questioning and dependence.

19 Alexander Solzhenitsyn, 'Repentance and Self-limitation in the Life of Nations', in *From Under the Rubble*, London, 1976.

20 Lord Acton, 'Nationality' in *The History of Freedom and Other Essays*, ed. J. N. Figgis and R. V. Laurence, London, 1907.

18

IS PATRIOTISM A VIRTUE?

Alasdair MacIntyre

I

One of the central tasks of the moral philosopher is to articulate the convictions of the society in which he or she lives so that these convictions may become available for rational scrutiny. This task is all the more urgent when a variety of conflicting and incompatible beliefs are held within one and the same community, either by rival groups who differ on key moral questions or by one and the same set of individuals who find within themselves competing moral allegiances. In either of these types of case the first task of the moral philosopher is to render explicit what is at issue in the various disagreements and it is a task of this kind that I have set myself in this chapter.

For it is quite clear that there are large disagreements about patriotism in our society. And although it would be a mistake to suppose that there are only two clear, simple and mutually opposed sets of beliefs about patriotism, it is at least plausible to suggest that the range of conflicting views can be placed on a spectrum with two poles. At one end is the view, taken for granted by almost everyone in the nineteenth century, a commonplace in the literary culture of the McGuffey readers, that 'patriotism' names a virtue. At the other end is the contrasting view, expressed with sometimes shocking clarity in the nineteen sixties, that 'patriotism' names a vice. It would be misleading for me to suggest that I am going to be able to offer good reasons for taking one of these views rather than the other. What I do hope to achieve is a clarification of the issues that divide them.

A necessary first step in the direction of any such clarification is to distinguish patriotism properly so-called from two other sets of attitudes that are all too easily assimilated to it. The first is that exhibited by those who are protagonists of their own nation's causes because and only because, so they assert, it is their nation which is *the* champion of some great moral ideal. In the Great War of 1914–18 Max Weber claimed that Imperial Germany should be supported because its was the cause of *Kultur*, while Emile Durkheim claimed with equal vehemence that France should be supported because its was the cause of *civilisation*. And here and now there are those American politicians who claim that the United States deserves our allegiance because it champions the goods of freedom against the evils of communism. What distinguishes their attitude from patriotism is twofold: first it is the ideal and not the nation which is the primary object of their regard; and secondly insofar as their regard for the ideal provides good reasons for allegiance to their country, it provides good reasons for anyone at all to uphold their country's cause, irrespective of their nationality or citizenship.

Patriotism by contrast is defined in terms of a kind of loyalty to a particular nation which only those possessing that particular nationality can exhibit. Only Frenchmen can be patriotic about France, while anyone can make the cause of *civilisation* their own. But it would be all too easy in noticing this to fail to make a second equally important distinction. Patriotism is not to be confused with a mindless loyalty to one's own particular nation which has no regard at all for the characteristics of that particular nation. Patriotism does generally and characteristically involve a peculiar regard not just for one's own nation, but for the particular characteristics and merits and achievements of one's own nation. These latter are indeed valued *as* merits and achievements and their character as merits and achievements provides reasons supportive of the patriot's attitudes. But the patriot does not value in the same way precisely similar merits and achievements when they are the merits and achievements of some nation other than his or hers. For he or she – at least in the role of patriot – values them not just as merits and achievements, but as the merits and achievements of this particular nation.

To say this is to draw attention to the fact that patriotism is one of a class of royalty-exhibiting virtues (that is, if it *is* a virtue at all), other members of which are marital fidelity, the love of one's own family and kin, friendship, and loyalty to such institutions as schools and cricket or baseball clubs. All these attitudes exhibit a peculiar action-generating regard for particular persons, institutions or groups, a regard founded upon a particular historical relationship of association between the person exhibiting the regard and the relevant person, institution or group. It is often, although not always, the case that associated with this regard will be a felt gratitude for the benefits which the individual takes him or herself to have received from the person, institution or group. But it would be one more mistake to suppose patriotism or other such attitudes of loyalty to be at their core or primarily responses of gratitude. For there are many persons, institutions and groups to which each of us have good reason to feel grateful without this kind of loyalty being involved. What patriotism and other such attitudes involve is not just gratitude, but a particular kind of gratitude; and what those who treat patriotism and other such loyalties as virtues are committed to believing is not that what they owe their nation or whomever or whatever it is simply a requital for benefits received, based on some relationship of reciprocity of benefits.

So although one may as a patriot love one's country, or as a husband or wife exhibit marital fidelity, and cite as partially supporting reasons one's country's or one's spouse's merits and one's own gratitude to them for benefits received these can be no more than *partially* supporting reasons, just because what is valued is valued precisely as the merits of *my* country or spouse or as the benefits received by *me* from *my* country or spouse. The particularity of the relationship is essential and ineliminable, and in identifying it as such we have already specified one central problem. What *is* the relationship between patriotism as such, the regard for this particular nation, and the regard which the patriot has for the merits and achievements of his or her nation and for the benefits which he or she has received? The answer to this question must be delayed for it will turn out to depend upon the answer to an apparently even more fundamental question, one that can best be framed in terms of the thesis that, if patriotism is understood as I have understood it, then 'patriotism' is not merely not the name of a virtue, but must be the name of a vice, since patriotism thus understood and morality are incompatible.

II

The presupposition of this thesis is an account of morality which has enjoyed high prestige in our culture. According to that account to judge from a moral standpoint is to judge impersonally. It is to judge as any rational person would judge, independently of his or her interests, affections and social position. And to act morally is to act in accordance with such impersonal judgments. Thus to think and to act morally involves the moral agent in abstracting him or herself from all social particularity and partiality. The potential conflict between morality so understood and patriotism is at once clear. For patriotism requires me to exhibit peculiar devotion to my nation and you to yours. It requires me to regard such contingent social facts as where I was born and what government ruled over that place at that time, who my parents were, who my great-great-grandparents were and so on, as deciding for me the question of what virtuous action is – at least insofar as it is the virtue of patriotism which is in question. Hence the moral standpoint and the patriotic standpoint are systematically incompatible.

Yet although this is so, it might be argued that the two standpoints need not be in conflict. For patriotism and all other such particular loyalties can be restricted in their scope so that their exercise is always within the confines imposed by morality. Patriotism need be regarded as nothing more than a perfectly proper devotion to one's own nation which must never be allowed to violate the constraints set by the impersonal moral standpoint. This is indeed the kind of patriotism professed by certain liberal moralists who are often indignant when it is suggested by their critics that they are not patriotic. To those critics however patriotism thus limited in its scope appears to be emasculated, and it does so because in some of the most important situations of actual social life either the patriotic standpoint comes into serious conflict with the standpoint of a genuinely impersonal morality or it amounts to no more than a set of practically empty slogans. What kinds of circumstances are these? They are at least twofold.

The first kind arises from scarcity of essential resources, often historically from the scarcity of land suitable for cultivation and pasture, and perhaps in our own time from that of fossil fuels. What your community requires as the material prerequisites for your survival as a distinctive community and your growth into a distinctive nation may be exclusive use of the same or some of the same natural resources as my community requires for its survival and growth into a distinctive nation. When such a conflict arises, the standpoint of impersonal morality requires an allocation of goods such that each individual person counts for one and no more than one, while the patriotic standpoint requires that I strive to further the interests of my community and you strive to further those of yours, and certainly where the survival of one community is at stake, and sometimes perhaps even when only large interests of one community are at stake, patriotism entails a willingness to go to war on one's community's behalf.

The second type of conflict-engendering circumstance arises from differences between communities about the right way for each to live. Not only competition for scarce natural resources, but incompatibilities arising from such conflict-engendering beliefs may lead to situations in which once again the liberal moral standpoint and the patriotic standpoint are radically at odds.

The administration of the *pax Romana* from time to time required the Roman *imperium* to set its frontiers at the point at which they could be most easily secured, so that the burden of supporting the legions would be reconcilable with the administration of Roman law. And the British empire was no different in its time. But this required infringing upon the territory and the independence of barbarian border peoples. A variety of such peoples – Scottish Gaels, Iroquois Indians, Bedouin – have regarded raiding the territory of their traditional enemies living within the confines of such large empires as an essential constituent of the good life; whereas the settled urban or agricultural communities which provided the target for their depredations have regarded the subjugation of such peoples and their reeducation into peaceful pursuits as one of their central responsibilities. And on such issues once again the impersonal moral standpoint and that of patriotism cannot be reconciled.

For the impersonal moral standpoint, understood as the philosophical protagonists of modern liberalism have understood it, requires neutrality not only between rival and competing interests, but also between rival and competing sets of beliefs about the best way for human beings to live. Each individual is to be left free to pursue in his or her own way that way of life which he or she judges to be best; while morality by contrast consists of rules which, just because they are such that any rational person, independently of his or her interests or point of view on the best way for human beings to live, would assent to them, are equally binding on all persons. Hence in conflicts between nations or other communities over ways of life, the standpoint of morality will once again be that of an impersonal arbiter, adjudicating in ways that give equal weight to each individual person's needs, desires, beliefs about the good and the like, while the patriot is once again required to be partisan.

Notice that in speaking of the standpoint of liberal impersonal morality in the way in which I have done I have been describing a standpoint whose truth is both presupposed by the political actions and utterances of a great many people in our society and explicitly articulated and defended by most modern moral philosophers; and that it has at the level of moral philosophy a number of distinct versions – some with a Kantian flavour, some utilitarian, some contractarian. I do not mean to suggest that the disagreements between these positions are unimportant. Nonetheless the five central positions that I have ascribed to that standpoint appear in all these various philosophical guises: first, that morality is constituted by rules to which any rational person would under certain ideal conditions give assent; secondly, that those rules impose constraints upon and are neutral between rival and competing interests – morality itself is not the expression of any particular interest; thirdly, that those rules are also neutral between rival and competing sets of beliefs about what the best way for human beings to live is; fourthly, that the units which provide the subject-matter of morality as well as its agents are individual human beings and that in moral evaluations each individual is to count for one and nobody for more than one; and fifthly, that the standpoint of the moral agent constituted by allegiance to these rules is one and the same for all moral agents and as such is independent of all social particularity. What morality provides are standards by which all actual social structures may be brought to judgment from a standpoint independent of all of them. It is morality so understood, allegiance to which is not only incompatible with treating patriotism as a virtue, but which requires that patriotism – at least in any substantial version – be treated as a vice.

But is this the only possible way to understand morality? As a matter of history, the answer is clearly 'No'. This understanding of morality invaded post-Renaissance Western culture at a particular point in time as the moral counterpart to political liberalism and social individualism and its polemical stances reflect its history of emergence from the conflicts which those movements engendered and themselves presuppose alternatives against which those polemical stances were and are directed. Let me therefore turn to considering one of those alternative accounts of morality, whose peculiar interest lies in the place that it has to assign to patriotism.

III

According to the liberal account of morality *where* and *from whom* I learn the principles and precepts of morality are and must be irrelevant both to the question of what the content of morality is and to that of the nature of my commitment to it, as irrelevant as *where* and *from whom* I learn the principles and precepts of mathematics are to the content of mathematics and the nature of my commitment to mathematical truths. By contrast on the alternative account of morality which I am going to sketch, the questions of *where* and *from whom* I learn my morality turn out to be crucial for both the content and the nature of moral commitment.

On this view it is an essential characteristic of the morality which each of us acquires that it is learned from, in and through the way of life of some particular community. Of course the moral rules elaborated in one particular historical community will often resemble and sometimes be identical with the rules to which allegiance is given in other particular communities, especially in communities with a shared history or which appeal to the same canonical texts. But there will characteristically be *some* distinctive features of the set of rules considered as a whole, and those distinctive features will often arise from the way in which members of that particular community responded to some earlier situation or series of situations in which particular features of difficult cases led to one or more rules being put in question and reformulated or understood in some new way. Moreover the form of the rules of morality as taught and apprehended will be intimately connected with specific institutional arrangements. The moralities of different societies may agree in having a precept enjoining that a child should honour his or her parents, but what it is so to honour and indeed what a father is and what a mother is will vary greatly between different social orders. So that what I learn as a guide to my actions and as a standard evaluating them is never morality as such, but always the highly specific morality of some highly specific social order.

To this the reply by the protagonists of modern liberal morality might well be: doubtless this is how a comprehension of the rules of morality is first acquired. But what allows such specific rules, framed in terms of particular social institutions, to be accounted moral rules at all is the fact they are nothing other than applications of universal and general moral rules and individuals acquire genuine morality only because and insofar as they progress from particularised socially specific applications of universal and general moral rules to comprehending them as universal and general. To learn to understand oneself as a moral agent just is to learn to free oneself from social particularity and to adopt a standpoint independent of any particular set of social institutions and the fact that everyone or almost everyone has to learn to do this by starting out from a standpoint deeply infected by social particularity and partiality goes no way towards providing an alternative account of morality. But to this reply a threefold rejoinder can be made.

First, it is not just that I first apprehend the rules of morality in some socially specific and particularised form. It is also and correlatively that the goods by reference to which and for the sake of which any set of rules must be justified are also going to be goods that are socially specific and particular. For central to those goods is the enjoyment of one particular kind of social life, lived out through a particular set of social relationships and thus what I enjoy is the good of *this* particular social life inhabited by me and I enjoy *it* as what *it* is. It may well be that it follows that I would enjoy and benefit equally from similar forms of social life in other communities; but this hypothetical truth in no way diminishes the importance of the contention that my goods are as a matter of fact found *here*, among *these* particular people, in *these* particular relationships. Goods are never encountered except as thus particularised. Hence the abstract general claim, that rules of a certain kind are justified by being productive of and constitutive of goods of a certain kind, is true only if these and these and these particular sets of rules incarnated in the practices of these and these and these particular communities are productive of, or constitutive of, these and these and these particular goods enjoyed at certain particular times and places by certain specifiable individuals.

It follows that *I* find *my* justification for allegiance to these rules of morality in *my* particular community; deprived of the life of that community, *I* would have no reason to be moral. But this is not all. To obey the rules of morality is characteristically and generally a hard task for human beings. Indeed were it not so, our need for morality would not be what it is. It is because we are continually liable to be blinded by immediate desire, to be distracted from our responsibilities, to lapse into backsliding and because even the best of us may at times encounter quite unusual temptations that it is important to morality that *I* can only be a moral agent because *we* are moral agents, that I need those around me to reinforce my moral strengths and assist in remedying my moral weaknesses. It is in general only within a community that individuals become capable of morality, are sustained in their morality and are constituted as moral agents by the way in which other people regard them and what is owed to and by them as well as by the way in which they regard themselves. In requiring much from me morally the other members of my community express a kind of respect for me that has nothing to do with expectations of benefit; and those of whom nothing or little is required in respect of morality are treated with a lack of respect which is, if repeated often enough, damaging to the moral capacities of those individuals. Of course, lonely moral heroism is sometimes required and sometimes achieved. But we must not treat this exceptional type of case as though it were typical. And once we recognise that typically moral agency and continuing moral capacity are engendered and sustained in essential ways by particular institutionalised social ties in particular social groups, it will be difficult to counterpose allegiance to a particular society and allegiance to morality in the way in which the protagonists of liberal morality do.

Indeed the case for treating patriotism as a virtue is now clear. *If* first of all it is the case that I can only apprehend the rules of morality in the version in which they are incarnated in some specific community; and *if* secondly it is the case that the justification of morality must be in terms of particular goods enjoyed within the life of particular communities; and *if* thirdly it is the case that I am characteristically brought into being and maintained as a moral agent only through the particular kinds of moral sustenance afforded by my community, *then* it is clear that deprived of this community, I am unlikely to flourish as a moral agent. Hence my allegiance to the community and what it requires of me – even to the point of requiring me to die to sustain its life – could not meaningfully be contrasted with or counterposed to what morality required of me. Detached from my community, I will be apt to lose my hold upon all genuine standards of judgment. Loyalty to that community, to the hierarchy of particular kinship, particular local community and particular natural community, is on this view a prerequisite for morality. So patriotism and those loyalties cognate to it are not just virtues but central virtues. Everything however turns on the truth or falsity of the claims advanced in the three preceding if-clauses. And the argument so far affords us no resources for delivering a verdict upon that truth or falsity. Nonetheless some progress has been achieved, and not only because the terms of the debate have become clearer. For it has also become clear that this dispute is not adequately characterised if it is understood simply as a disagreement between two rival accounts of morality, as if there were some independently identifiable phenomenon situated somehow or other in the social world waiting to be described more or less accurately by the contending parties. What we have here are two rival and incompatible moralities, each of which is viewed from within by its adherents as morality-as-such, each of which makes its exclusive claim to our allegiance. How are we to evaluate such claims?

One way to begin is to be learned from Aristotle. Since we possess no stock of clear and distinct first principles or any other such epistemological resource which would provide us with a neutral and independent standard for judging between them, we shall do well to proceed dialectically. And one useful dialectical strategy is to focus attention on those accusations which the adherents of each bring against the rival position which the adherents of that rival position treat as of central importance to rebut. For this will afford at least one indication of the issues about the importance of which both sides agree and about the chacterisation of which their very recognition of disagreement suggests that there must also be some shared beliefs. In what areas do such issues arise?

IV

One such area is defined by a charge which it seems reasonable at least prima facie for the protagonists of patriotism to bring against morality. The morality for which patriotism is a virtue offers a form of rational justification for moral rules and precepts whose structure is clear and rationally defensible. The rules of morality are justifiable if and only if they are productive of and partially constitutive of a form of shared social life whose goods are directly enjoyed by those inhabiting the particular communities whose social life is of that kind. Hence qua member of this or that particular community I can appreciate the justification for what morality requires of me from within the social roles that I live out in my community. By contrast, it may be argued, liberal morality requires of me to assume an abstract and artificial – perhaps even an impossible – stance, that of a rational being as such, responding to the requirements of morality not qua parent or farmer or quarterback, but qua rational agent who has abstracted him or herself from all social particularity, who has become not merely Adam Smith's impartial spectator, but a correspondingly impartial actor, and one who in his impartiality is doomed to rootlessness, to be a citizen of nowhere. How can I justify to myself performing this act of abstraction and detachment?

The liberal answer is clear: such abstraction and detachment is defensible, because it is a necessary condition of moral freedom, of emancipation from the bondage of the social, political and economic status quo. For unless I can stand back from every and any feature of that status quo, including the roles within it which I myself presently inhabit, I will be unable to view it critically and to decide for myself what stance it is rational and right for me to adopt towards it. This does not preclude that the outcome of such a critical evaluation may not be an endorsement of all or some of the existing social order; but even such an endorsement will only be free and rational if I have made it for myself in this way. (Making just such an endorsement of much of the economic status quo is the distinguishing mark of the contemporary conservative liberal, such as Milton Friedman, who is as much a liberal as the liberal liberal who finds much of the status quo wanting – such as J. K. Galbraith or Edward Kennedy – or the radical liberal.) Thus liberal morality does after all appeal to an overriding good, the good of this particular kind of emancipating freedom. And in the name of this good it is able not only to respond to the question about how the rules of morality are to be justified, but also to frame a plausible and potentially damaging objection to the morality of patriotism.

It is of the essence of the morality of liberalism that no limitations are or can be set upon the criticism of the social status quo. No institution, no practice, no loyalty can be immune from being put in question and perhaps rejected. Conversely the morality of patriotism is one which precisely because it is framed in terms of the membership of some particular social community with some particular social, political and economic structure, must exempt at least some fundamental structures of that community's life from criticism. Because patriotism has to be a loyalty that is in some respects unconditional, so in just those respects rational criticism is ruled out. But if so the adherents of the morality of patriotism have condemned themselves to a fundamentally irrational attitude – since to refuse to examine some of one's fundamental beliefs and attitudes is to insist on accepting them, whether they are rationally justifiable or not, which is irrational – and have imprisoned themselves within that irrationality. What answer can the adherents of the morality of patriotism make to this kind of accusation? The reply must be threefold.

When the liberal moralist claims that the patriot is bound to treat his or her nation's projects and practices in some measure uncritically, the claim is not only that at any one time certain of these projects and practices will be being treated uncritically; it is that some at least must be permanently exempted from criticism. The patriot is in no position to deny this: but what is crucial to the patriot's case is to identify clearly precisely what it is that is thus exempted. And at this point it becomes extremely important that in outlining the case for the morality of patriotism – as indeed in outlining the case for liberal morality – we should not be dealing with strawmen. Liberalism and patriotism are not positions invented by me or by other external commentators: they have their own distinctive spokesmen and their own distinctive voices. And although I hope that it has been clear throughout that I have only been trying to articulate what those voices would say, it is peculiarly important to the case for patriotic morality at this point that its actual historical protagonists be identified. So what I say next is an attempt to identify the common attitudes on this point of Charles Péguy and Charles de Gaulle, of Bismarck and of Adam von Trott. You will notice that in these pairs one member is someone who was at least for a time a member of his nation's political establishment, the other someone who was always in a radical way outside that establishment and hostile to it, but that even those who were for a time identified with the status quo of power, were also at times alienated from it. And this makes it clear that whatever is exempted from patriot's criticism the status quo of power and government and the policies pursued by those exercising power and government never need be so exempted. What then is exempted? The answer is: the nation conceived *as a project*, a project somehow or other brought to birth in the past and carried on so that a morally distinctive community was brought into being which embodied a claim to political autonomy in its various organised and institutionalised expressions. Thus one can be patriotic towards a nation whose political independence is yet to come – as Garibaldi was; or towards a nation which once was and perhaps might be again – like the Polish patriots in the 1860s. What the patriot is committed to is a particular way of linking a past which has conferred a distinctive moral and political identity upon him or her with a future for the project which is his or her nation which it is his or her responsibility to bring into being. Only this allegiance is unconditional and allegiance to particular governments or forms of government or particular leaders will be entirely conditional upon their being devoted to furthering that project rather than frustrating or destroying it. Hence there is nothing inconsistent in a patriot's being deeply opposed to his country's contemporary rulers, as Péguy was, or plotting their overthrow as Adam von Trott did.

Yet although this may go part of the way towards answering the charge of the liberal moralist that the patriot must in certain areas be completely uncritical and therefore irrationalist, it certainly does not go all the way. For everything that I have said on behalf of the morality of patriotism is compatible with it being the case that on occasion patriotism might require me to support and work for the success of some enterprise of my nation as crucial to its overall project, crucial perhaps to its survival, when the success of that enterprise would not be in the best interests of mankind, evaluated from an impartial and impersonal standpoint. The case of Adam von Trott is very much to the point.

Adam von Trott was a German patriot who was executed after the unsuccessful assassination attempt against Hitler's life in 1944. Trott deliberately chose to work inside Germany with the minuscule, but highly placed, conservative opposition to the Nazis with the aim of replacing Hitler from within, rather than to work for an overthrow of Nazi Germany which would result in the destruction of the Germany brought to birth in 1871. But to do this he had to appear to be identified with the cause of Nazi Germany and so strengthened not only his country's cause, as was his intention, but also as an unavoidable consequence the cause of the Nazis. This kind of example is a particularly telling one, because the claim that such and such a course of action 'is to the best interests of mankind' is usually at best disputable, at worst cloudy rhetoric. But there are a very few causes in which so much was at stake – and that this is generally much clearer in retrospect than it was at the time does not alter that fact – that the phrase has clear application: the overthrow of Nazi Germany was one of them.

How ought the patriot then to respond? Perhaps in two ways. The first begins by re-emphasising that from the fact that the particularist morality of the patriot is rooted in a particular community and inextricably bound up with the social life of that community, it does not follow that it cannot provide rational grounds for repudiating many features of that country's present organised social life. The conception of justice engendered by the notion of citizenship within a particular community may provide standards by which particular political institutions are found wanting: when Nazi anti-Semitism encountered the phenomena of German Jewish ex-soldiers who had won the Iron Cross, it had to repudiate German particularist standards of excellence (for the award of the Iron Cross symbolised a recognition of devotion to Germany). Moreover the conception of one's own nation having a special mission does not necessitate that this mission may not involve the extension of a justice originally at home only in the particular institutions of the homeland. And clearly particular governments or agencies of government may defect and may be understood to have defected from this mission so radically that the patriot may find that a point comes when he or she has to choose between the claims of the project which constitutes his or her nation and the claims of the morality that he or she has learnt as a member of the community whose life is informed by that project. Yes, the liberal critic of patriotism will respond, this indeed *may* happen; but it may not and it often will not. Patriotism turns out to be a permanent source of moral danger. And this claim, I take it, cannot in fact be successfully rebutted.

A second possible, but very different type of answer on behalf of the patriot would run as follows. I argued earlier that the kind of regard for one's own country which would be compatible with a liberal morality of impersonality and impartiality would be too insubstantial, would be under too many constraints, to be regarded as a version of patriotism in the traditional sense. But it does not follow that some version of traditional patriotism may not be compatible with some other morality of universal moral law, which sets limits to and provides both sanction for and correction of the particularist morality of the patriot. Whether this is so or not is too large and too distinct a question to pursue in this present paper. But we ought to note that even if it is so – and all those who have been both patriots and Christians *or* patriots and believers in Thomistic natural law *or* patriots and believers in the Rights of Man have been committed to claiming that it is so – this would not diminish in any way the force of the liberal claim that patriotism is a morally dangerous phenomenon.

That the rational protagonist of the morality of patriotism is compelled, if my argument is correct, to concede this does not mean that there is not more to be said in the debate. And what needs to be said is that the liberal morality of impartiality and impersonality turns out also to be a morally dangerous phenomenon in an interestingly corresponding way. For suppose the bonds of patriotism to be dissolved: would liberal morality be able to provide anything adequately substantial in its place? What the morality of patriotism at its best provides is a clear account of and justification for the particular bonds and loyalties which form so much of the substance of the moral life. It does so by underlining the moral importance of the different members of a group acknowledging a shared history. Each one of us to some degree or other understands his or her life as an enacted narrative; and because of our relationships with others we have to understand ourselves as characters in the enacted narratives of other people's lives. Moreover the story of each of our lives is characteristically embedded in the story of one or more larger units. I understand the story of my life in such a way that it is part of the history of my family or of this farm or of this university or of this countryside; and I understand the story of the lives of other individuals around me as embedded in the same larger stories, so that I and they share a common stake in the outcome of that story and in what sort of story it both is and is to be: tragic, heroic, comic.

A central contention of the morality of patriotism is that I will obliterate and lose a central dimension of the moral life if I do not understand the enacted narrative of my own individual life as embedded in the history of my country. For if I do not so understand it I will not understand what I owe to others or what others owe to me, for what crimes of my nation I am bound to make reparation, for what benefits to my nation I am bound to feel gratitude. Understanding what is owed to and by me and understanding the history of the communities of which I am a part is on this view one and the same thing.

It is worth stressing that one consequence of this is that patriotism, in the sense in which I am understanding it in this paper, is only possible to certain types of national community under certain conditions. A national community, for example, which systematically disowned its own true history or substituted a largely fictitious history for it or a national community in which the bonds deriving from history were in no way the real bonds of the community (having been replaced for example by the bonds of reciprocal self-interest) would be one towards which patriotism would be – from any point of view – an irrational attitude. For precisely the same reasons that a family whose members all came to regard membership in that family as governed only by reciprocal self-interest would no longer be a family in the traditional sense, so a nation whose members took up a similar attitude would no longer be a nation and this would provide adequate grounds for holding that the project which constituted that nation had simply collapsed. Since all modern bureaucratic states tend towards reducing national communities to this condition, all such states tend towards a condition in which any genuine morality of patriotism would have no place and what paraded itself as patriotism would be an unjustifiable simulacrum.

Why would this matter? In modern communities in which membership is understood only or primarily in terms of reciprocal self-interest, only two resources are generally available when destructive conflicts of interest threaten such reciprocity. One is the arbitrary imposition of some solution by force; the other is appeal to the neutral, impartial and impersonal standards of liberal morality. The importance of this resource is scarcely to be underrated; but how much of a resource is it? The problem is that some motivation has to be provided for allegiance to the standards of impartiality and impersonality which both has rational justification and can outweigh the considerations provided by interest. Since any large need for such allegiance arises precisely and only when and insofar as the possibility of appeals to reciprocity in interests has broken down, such reciprocity can no longer provide the relevant kind of motivation. And it is difficult to identify anything that can take its place. The appeal to moral agents qua rational beings to place their allegiance to impersonal rationality above that to their interests has, just because it is an appeal to rationality, to furnish an adequate reason for so doing. And this is a point at which liberal accounts of morality are notoriously vulnerable. This vulnerability becomes a manifest practical liability at one key point in the social order.

Every political community except in the most exceptional conditions requires standing armed forces for its minimal security. Of the members of these armed forces it must require both that they be prepared to sacrifice their own lives for the sake of the community's security and that their willingness to do so be not contingent upon their own individual evaluation of the rightness or wrongness of their country's cause on some specific issue, measured by some standard that is neutral and impartial relative to the interests of their own community and the interests of other communities. And, that is to say, good soldiers may not be liberals and must indeed embody in their actions a good deal at least of the morality of patriotism. So the political survival of any polity in which liberal morality had secured large-scale allegiance would depend upon there still being enough young men and women who rejected that liberal morality. And in this sense liberal morality tends towards the dissolution of social bonds.

Hence the charge that the morality of patriotism can successfully bring against liberal morality is the mirror-image of that which liberal morality can successfully urge against the morality of patriotism. For while the liberal moralist was able to conclude that patriotism is a permanent source of moral danger because of the way it places our ties to our nation beyond rational criticism, the moralist who defends patriotism is able to conclude that liberal morality is a permanent source of moral danger because of the way it renders our social and moral ties too open to dissolution by rational criticism. And each party is in fact in the right against the other.

V

The fundamental task which confronts any moral philosopher who finds this conclusion compelling is clear. It is to enquire whether, although the central claims made on behalf of these two rival modern moralities cannot both be true, we ought perhaps not to move towards the conclusion that both sets of claims are in fact false. And this is an enquiry in which substantial progress has already been made. But history in its impatience does not wait for moral philosophers to complete their tasks, let alone to convince their fellow-citizens. The *polis* ceased to be the key institution in Greek politics even while Aristotle was still restating its rationale and any contemporary philosopher who discusses the key conceptions that have informed modern political life since the eighteenth century is in danger of reliving Aristotle's fate, even if in a rather less impressive way. The owl of Minerva really does seem to fly at dusk.

Does this mean that my argument is therefore devoid of any immediate practical significance? That would be true only if the conclusion that a morality of liberal impersonality and a morality of patriotism must be deeply incompatible itself had no practical significance for our understanding of our everyday politics. But perhaps a systematic recognition of this incompatibility will enable us to diagnose one central flaw in the political life characteristic of modern Western states, or at least of all those modern Western states which look back for their legitimation to the American and the

French revolutions. For polities so established have tended to contrast themselves with the older regimes that they displaced by asserting that, while all previous polities had expressed in their lives the partiality and one-sidedness of local customs, institutions and traditions, they have for the first time given expression in their constitutional and institutional forms to the impersonal and impartial rules of morality as such, common to all rational beings. So Robespierre proclaimed that it was an effect of the French Revolution that the cause of France and the cause of the Rights of Man were one and the same cause. And in the nineteenth century the United States produced its own version of this claim, one which at the level of rhetoric provided the content for many Fourth of July orations and at the level of education set the standards for the Americanisation of the late nineteenth-century and early twentieth-century immigrants, especially those from Europe.

Hegel employs a useful distinction which he marks by his use of words *Sittlichkeit* and *Moralität*. *Sittlichkeit* is the customary morality of each particular society, pretending to be no more than this. *Moralität* reigns in the realm of rational universal, impersonal morality, of liberal morality, as I have defined it. What those immigrants were taught in effect was that they had left behind countries and cultures where *Sittlichkeit* and *Moralität* were certainly distinct and often opposed and arrived in a country and a culture whose *Sittlichkeit* just is *Moralität*. And thus for many Americans the cause of America, understood as the object of patriotic regard, and the cause of morality, understood as the liberal moralist understands it, came to be identified. The history of this identification could not be other than a history of confusion and incoherence, if the argument which I have constructed in this lecture is correct. For a morality of particularist ties and solidarities has been conflated with a morality of universal, impersonal and impartial principles in way that can never be carried through without incoherence.

One test therefore of whether the argument that I have constructed has or has not empirical application and practical significance would be to discover whether it is or is not genuinely illuminating to write the political and social history of modern America as in key part the living out of a central conceptual confusion, a confusion perhaps required for the survival of a large-scale modern polity which has to exhibit itself as liberal in many institutional settings, but which also has to be able to engage the patriotic regard of enough of its citizens, if it is to continue functioning effectively. To determine whether that is or is not true would be to risk discovering that we inhabit a kind of polity whose moral order requires systematic incoherence in the form of public allegiance to mutually inconsistent sets of principles. But that is a task which – happily – lies beyond the scope of this chapter.

19

IN DEFENCE OF NATIONALITY

David Miller

My story begins on the river bank of Kenneth Grahame's imagination.

> 'And beyond the Wild Wood again?' [asked the Mole]: 'Where it's all blue and dim, and one sees what may be hills or perhaps they mayn't, and something like the smoke of towns, or is it only cloud drift?'
>
> 'Beyond the Wild Wood comes the Wide World,' [said the Rat]. 'And that's something that doesn't matter, either to you or me. I've never been there, and I'm never going, nor you either, if you've got any sense at all. Don't ever refer to it again, please.'[1]

The Rat, so very sound in his opinions about most things, boats especially, seems in this moment to reveal exactly what so many people find distasteful about national loyalties and identities. He displays no overt hostility to foreign lands and their ways. But the combination of wilful ignorance about places beyond the Wild Wood, and complete indifference to what is going on there, seems particularly provoking. Aggressive nationalism of the 'my country right or wrong' variety is something we might at least argue with. But the narrowing of horizons, the contraction of the universe of experience to the river bank itself, seems to amount to the triumph of sentiment over reasoned argument.

NATIONALITY UNDER ATTACK

Philosophers, especially, will have great difficulty in coming to grips with the kind of national attachments for which I am using the Rat's riverbankism as an emblem. Philosophers are committed to forms of reasoning, to concepts and arguments, that

301

are universal in form. 'What's so special about this river bank?' a philosophical Mole might have asked in reply. 'Why is this river bank a better place than other river banks beyond the Wood?' To which the Rat could only have said, 'This is *my* place; I like it here; I have no need to ask such questions.'

The Rat, clearly, is no philosopher. Yet in contemplating his frame of mind we might be led to recall the words of one who was:

> there are in *England*, in particular, many honest gentlemen, who being always employ'd in their domestic affairs, or amusing themselves in common recreations, have carried their thoughts little beyond those objects, which are every day expos'd to their senses. And indeed, of such as these I pretend not to make philosophers. ... They do well to keep themselves in their present situation; and instead of refining them into philosophers, I wish we cou'd communicate to our founders of systems, a share of this gross earthly mixture, as an ingredient, which they commonly stand much in need of, and which wou'd serve to temper those fiery particles, of which they are composed.[2]

Plainly the Rat is well supplied with gross earthy mixture, literally and metaphorically, and the question is whether any philosophical system can make use of what he has to offer. The sort that can is the Humean sort. By this I mean a philosophy which, rather than dismissing ordinary beliefs and sentiments out of hand unless they can be shown to have a rational foundation, leaves them in place until strong arguments are produced for rejecting them. The Rat's beliefs cannot be deduced from some universally accepted premise; but that is no reason for rejecting them unless the arguments for doing so seem better founded than the beliefs themselves. In moral and political philosophy, in particular, we build upon existing sentiments and judgements, correcting them only when they are inconsistent or plainly flawed in some other way. We don't aspire to some universal and rational foundation such as Kant tried to provide with the categorical imperative.

It is from this sort of stance (which I shall not try to justify) that it makes sense to mount a philosophical defence of nationality. There can be no question of trying to give rationally compelling reasons for people to have national attachments and allegiances. What we can do is to start from the premise that people generally do exhibit such attachments and allegiances, and then try to build a political philosophy which incorporates them. In particular we can do two things: we can examine the critical arguments directed against nationality – arguments trying to undermine the validity of national loyalties – and show that they are flawed; and we call try to assuage the tension between the ethical particularism implied by such commitments and ethical universalism, by showing why it may be advantageous, from a universal point of view, that people have national loyalties.[3]

Philosophers may protest that it is a caricature of their position to suggest that the only reasons for belief or action that they will permit to count are those that derive from an entirely impersonal and universal standpoint. It is common now to distinguish between agent-neutral and agent-relative reasons and to give each some weight in practical reasoning.[4] But what motivates this concession is mainly a concern for individuals' private goals and for their integrity: people must be given the moral space, as it were, to pursue their own projects, to honour their commitments, to live up to their personal ideals. National allegiances, and the obligations that spring from them, are harder to fit into this picture, because they appear to represent, not a different segment of moral life, but a competing way of understanding the concepts and principles that make up the impartial or agent-neutral standpoint (consider, for example, the different conceptions of distributive justice that emerge depending on whether you begin from a national or a universal starting-point). That is why such loyalties appear to pose a head-on challenge to a view of morality that is dominant in our culture, as Alasdair MacIntyre has argued.[5]

It is a curious paradox of our time that while nationalism is politically on the advance, its would-be defenders (in the West at least) find themselves on the defensive. I have just given one reason for this: the view that national allegiances cannot withstand critical scrutiny, so a rational person cannot be a nationalist. There is also a more mundane reason: nationality is widely felt to be a backward-looking, reactionary notion; It is felt to stand in the way of progress. In the European context, for instance, we are invited to look forward to a 'Europe of the regions' in which Catalonia, Brittany, Bavaria, Scotland and the rest co-exist harmoniously under a common administrative umbrella, free from the national rivalries which have plunged us into two world wars. Progress means the overcoming of nationality. In the Oxford branch of the Body Shop (and doubtless in the branches in Paris, Tokyo and elsewhere) you can buy a lapel badge that quotes H.G. Wells: 'Our true nationality is mankind.' H.G. Wells and the Body Shop in tandem epitomize the modern idea of progress, whose disciples were described by George Orwell in such a wonderfully acid way: 'all that dreary tribe of high-minded women and sandal-wearers and bearded fruit-juice drinkers who come flocking towards the smell of "progress" like bluebottles to a dead cat'.[6] If you are one of these bluebottles, and most of us are to some degree, then you will think that ordinary national loyalties amount to reactionary nostalgia and queue up to sport the H.G. Wells slogan.

WHAT IS A NATION?

So the would-be nationalist has two challenges to meet: the philosophical challenge and the progressive challenge. And now it is time to spell out more precisely the notion of nationality that I want to defend.[7] Nationality as I shall understand it comprises three interconnected propositions. The first concerns personal identity, and claims that it may properly be part of someone's identity that they belong to this or that national grouping; in other words that if a person is invited to specify those elements that are essential to his identity, that make him the person that he is, it is in order to refer to nationality. A person who in answer to the question 'Who are you?' says 'I am Swedish' or 'I am Italian' (and doubtless much more besides) is not saying something that is irrelevant or bizarre in the same way as, say, someone who claims without good evidence that he is the illegitimate grandchild of Tsar Nicholas II. Note that the claim is a permissive one: national identity may, but need not, be a constitutive part of personal identity.

The second proposition is ethical, and claims that nations are ethical communities. They are contour lines in the ethical landscape. The duties we owe to our fellow-nationals are different from, and more extensive than, the duties we owe to human beings as such. This is not to say that we owe *no* duties to humans as such; nor is it to deny that there may be other, perhaps smaller and more intense, communities to whose members we owe duties that are more stringent still than those we owe to Britons, Swedes, etc. at large. But it is to claim that a proper account of ethics should give weight to national boundaries, and that in particular there is no objection in principle to institutional schemes that are designed to deliver benefits exclusively to those who fall within the same boundaries as ourselves.

The third proposition is political, and states that people who form a national community in a particular territory have a good claim to political self-determination; there ought to be put in place an institutional structure that enables them to decide collectively matters that concern primarily their own community. Notice that I have phrased this cautiously, and have not asserted that the institution must be that of a sovereign state. Historically the sovereign state has been the main vehicle through which claims to national self-determination have been realized, and this is not just an accident. Nevertheless national self-determination *can* be realized in other ways, and as we shall see there are cases where it must be realized other than through a sovereign state, precisely to meet the equally good claims of other nationalities.

I want to stress that the three propositions I have outlined – about personal identity, about bounded duties and about political self-determination – are linked together in such a way that it is difficult to feel the force of any one of them without acknowledging the others. It is not hard to see how a common identity can support both the idea of the nation as an ethical community and the claim to self-determination, but what is more subtle – and I shall try to bring this out as I go along – is the way in which the political claim can reinforce both the claim about identity and the ethical claim. The fact that the community in question is either actually or potentially self-determining strengthens its claims on us both as a source of identity and as a source of obligation. This interlinking of propositions may at times seem circular; and the fact that the nationalist case cannot be spelt out in neat linear form may confirm philo-sophical suspicions about it. But I believe that if we are to understand the power of nationality as an idea in the modern world – the appeal of national identity to the modern self – we must try to understand its inner logic.

So let me now begin to look more closely at national identities themselves, and in particular ask what differentiates them from other identities – individual or communal – that people may have. What does it mean to think of oneself as belonging to a national community?

The first point to note, and it has been noted by most of those who have thought seriously about the subject, is that national communities are constituted by belief: a nationality exists when its members believe that it does. It is not a question of a group of people sharing some common attribute such as race or language. These features do not of themselves make nations, and only become important insofar as a particular nationality takes as one of its defining features that its members speak French or have black skins. This becomes clear as soon as one looks at the candidates that have been put forward as objective criteria of nationhood, as Ernest Renan did in his famous lecture on the subject:[8] to every criterion that has been proposed there are clear empir-ical counter-examples. The conclusion one quickly reaches is that a nation is in Renan's memorable phrase 'a daily plebiscite'; its existence depends on a shared belief that its members belong together, and a shared wish to continue their life in common. So in asserting a national identity, I assume that my beliefs and commitments are mirrored by those whom I take to share that identity, and of course I might be wrong about this. In itself this does not distinguish nationality from other kinds of human relationship that depend on reciprocal belief.

The second feature of nationality is that it is an identity that embodies historical continuity. Nations stretch backwards into the past, and indeed in most cases their origins are conveniently lost in the mists of time. In the course of this history various significant events have occurred, and we can identify with the actual people who acted at those monuments, reappropriating their deeds as our own. Often these events involve military victories and defeats: we imagine ourselves filling the breach at Harfleur or reading the signal hoisted at Trafalgar. Renan thinks that historical tragedies matter more than historical glories. I am inclined to see in this an under-standable French bias, but the point he connects to it is a good one: 'sorrows have greater value than victories; for they impose duties and demand common effort'.[9] The historic national community is a community of obligation. Because our forebears have toiled and spilt their blood to build and defend the nation, we who are born into it inherit an obligation to continue their work, which we discharge partly towards our contemporaries and partly towards our descendants. The historical community stretches forward into the future too. This then means that when we speak of the nation as an ethical community, we have in mind not merely the kind of community that exists between a group of contemporaries who practise mutual aid among themselves and which would dissolve at the point at which that practice ceased; but a community which, because it stretches back and forward across the generations, is not one that the present generation can renounce. Here we begin to see something of the depth of national communities which may not be shared by other more immediate forms of association.

The third distinguishing aspect of national identity is that it is an active identity. Nations are communities that do things together, take decisions, achieve results and so forth. Of course this cannot be literally so: we rely on proxies who are seen as embodying the national will: statesmen, soldiers, sportsmen, etc. But this means that the link between past and future that I noted a moment ago is not merely a causal link. The nation becomes what it does by the decisions that it takes – some of which we may now regard as thoroughly bad, a cause of national shame. Whether this active identity is a valuable aspect of nationality, or whether as some critics would allege merely a damaging fantasy, it clearly does mark out nations from other kinds of grouping, for instance churches or religious sects whose identity is essentially a passive one in so far as the church is seen as responding to the promptings of God. The group's purpose is not to do or decide things, but to interpret as best it can the messages and commands of an external source.

The fourth aspect of a national identity is that it connects a group of people to a particular geographical place, and here again there is a clear contrast with most other group identities that people affirm, such as ethnic or religious identities. These often have sacred sites or places of origin, but it is not an essential part of having the identity that you should permanently occupy that place. If you are a good Muslim you should make a pilgrimage to Mecca at least once, but you need not set up house there. A nation, in contrast, must have a homeland. This may of course be a source of great difficulties, a point I shall return to when considering objections to the idea of nationality, but it also helps to explain why a national community must be (in aspiration if not yet in fact) a political community. We have seen already that nations are groups that act; we see now that their actions must include that of controlling a chunk of the earth's surface. It is this territorial element that makes nations uniquely suited to serve as the basis of states, since a state by definition must exercise its authority over a geographical area.

Finally it is essential to national identity that the people who compose the nation are believed to share certain traits that mark them off from other peoples. It is incompatible with nationality to think of the members of the nation as people who merely happen to have been thrown together in one place and forced to share a common fate, in the way that the occupants of a lifeboat, say, have been accidentally thrown together. National divisions must be natural ones; they must correspond to real differences between peoples. This need not, fortunately, imply racism or the idea that the group is constituted by biological descent. The common traits can be cultural in character: they can consist in shared values, shared tastes or sensibilities. So immigration need not pose problems, provided only that the immigrants take on the essential elements of national character. Indeed it has proved possible in some instances to regard immigration as itself a formative experience, calling forth qualities of resourcefulness and mutual aid that then define the national character – I am thinking of the settler cultures of the New World such as the American and the Australian. As everyone knows, there is nothing more illustrious for an Australian today than to have an ancestor who was carried over in chains by the First Fleet.

When I say that national differences must be natural ones, I mean that the people who compose a nation must believe that there is something distinctive about themselves that marks them off from other nations, over and above the fact of sharing common institutions. This need not be one specific trait or quality, but can be a range of characteristics which are generally shared by the members of nation A and serve to differentiate them from outsiders. In popular belief these differences may be exaggerated. Hume remarked that the vulgar think that everyone who belongs to a nation displays its distinctive traits, whereas 'men of sense' allow for exceptions; nevertheless aggregate differences undoubtedly exist.[10] This is surely correct. It is also worth noting that people may be hard pressed to say explicitly what the national character of their people consists in, and yet have an intuitive sense when confronted with foreigners of where the differences lie.[11] National identities can remain unarticulated, and yet still exercise a pervasive influence on people's behaviour.

These five elements together – a community constituted by mutual belief, extended in history, active in character, connected to a particular territory, and thought to be marked off from other communities by its members' distinct traits – serve to distinguish nationality from other collective sources of personal identity. I shall come in a moment to some reasons why such identities may be thought to be particularly valuable, worth protecting and fostering, but first I should emphasize what has so far merely been implicit, namely the mythical aspects of national identity. Nations almost unavoidably depend on beliefs about themselves that do not stand up well to impartial scrutiny. Renan once again hit the nail on the head when he said that 'to forget and – I will venture to say – to get one's history wrong, are essential factors in the making of a nation'.[12] One main reason for this is that the contingencies of power politics have always played a large part in the formation of national units. States have been created by force, and, over time, their subject peoples have come to think of themselves as co-nationals. But no one wants to think of himself as roped together to a set of people merely because the territorial ambitions of some dynastic lord in the thirteenth century ran thus far and no further. Nor indeed is this the right way to think about the matter, because the effect of the ruler's conquests may have been, over time, to have produced a people with real cultural unity. But because of the historical dimension of the nation, together with the idea that each nation has its own distinct character, it is uncomfortable to be reminded of the forced nature of one's national genesis. Hence various stories have been concocted about the primeval tribe from which the modern nation sprang. The problem is, of course, particularly acute in the case of states created relatively recently as a result of colonial withdrawal, where it is only too obviously the case that the boundaries that have been drawn reflect the vagaries of imperial competition. It is easy for academic critics to mock the attempts made by the leaders of these states to instil a sense of common nationhood in their people. I myself recall, when teaching in Nigeria in the mid-1970s, reading with some amusement earnest newspaper articles on the question whether the country did or did not need a national ideology – it seeming obvious that a national ideology was not something you could just decide to adopt.

NATIONALITY DEFENDED

The real question, however, is not whether national identities embody elements of myth, but whether they perform such valuable functions that our attitude, as philosophers, should be one of acquiescence if not positive endorsement. And here I want to argue that nationality answers one of the most pressing needs of the modern world, namely how to maintain solidarity among the populations of states that are large and anonymous, such that their citizens cannot possibly enjoy the kind of community that relies on kinship or face-to-face interaction.[13] That we need such solidarity is something that I intend to take for granted here.[14] I assume that in societies in which economic markets play a central role, there is a strong tendency towards social atomization, where each person looks out for the interests of herself and her immediate social network. As a result it is potentially difficult to mobilize people to provide collective goods, it is difficult to get them to agree to practices of redistribution from which they are not likely personally to benefit, and so forth. These problems can be avoided only where there exists large-scale solidarity, such that people feel themselves to be members of an overarching community, and to have social duties to act for the common good of that community, to help out other members when they are in need, etc.

Nationality is de facto the main source of such solidarity. In view of the broadly Humean approach that I am adopting, where our moral and political philosophy bends to accommodate pre-existing sentiments, this in itself would be enough to commend it. But I should like to say something more positive about nationality before coming to the difficulties. It is precisely because of the mythical or imaginary elements in national identity that it can be reshaped to meet new challenges and new needs. We have seen that the story a nation tells itself about its past is a selective one. Depending on the character of contemporary politics, the story may gradually alter, and with it our understanding of the substance of national identity. This need not take the crude form of the rewriting of history as practised in the late Soviet Union and elsewhere (airbrushing pictures of Trotsky out of the Bolshevik central committee and so on). It may instead be a matter of looking at established facts in a new way. Consider, as just one example, the very different interpretation of British imperialism now current to that which prevailed at the time of my father's birth in Edwardian Britain. The tone has changed from one of triumphalism to one of equivocation or even mild apology. And this goes naturally along with a new interpretation of British identity in which it is no longer part of that identity to shoulder the white man's burden and carry enlightenment to the heathen.

From a political standpoint, this imaginary aspect of nationality may be a source of strength. It allows people of different political persuasions to share a political loyalty, defining themselves against a common background whose outlines are not precise, and which therefore lends itself to competing interpretations. It also shows us why nationality is not a conservative idea. A moment's glance at the historical record shows that nationalist ideas have as often been associated with liberal and socialist programmes as with programmes of the right. In their first appearance, they were often associated with liberal demands for representative government put forward in opposition to established ruling elites. Linda Colley's studies of the emergence of British nationalism in the late eighteenth and early nineteenth centuries show that nationalist ideas were developed by middle-class and popular movements seeking to win a place in the public realm, and resisted by the state and the landowning class that supported it.[15] This picture was repeated in its essentials throughout Europe.[16] It is easy to see why a conservative may resist nationalism.[17] Nationality invokes the activist idea of a people collectively determining its own destiny, and this is anathema to the conservative view of politics as a limited activity best left in the hands of an elite who have been educated to rule. Two of the most swingeing of attacks on nationalism have come from acolytes of Michael Oakeshott, Elie Kedourie and Kenneth Minogue.[18] Minogue regards nationalism as essentially a revolutionary theory and 'therefore a direct enemy of conservative politics'. He offers a reductive psychological explanation of its appeal: 'Nationalist theories may thus be understood as distortions of reality which allow men to cope with situations which they might otherwise find unbearable.'[19]

Nationality, then, is associated with no particular social programme: the flexible content of national identity allows parties of different colours to present their programmes as the true continuation of the national tradition and the true reflection of national character.[20] At the same time it binds these parties together and makes space for the idea of loyal opposition, an individual or faction who resist prevailing policy but who can legitimately claim to speak for the same community as the government of the day. But its activist idea of politics as the expression of national will does set it against conservatism of the Oakeshott–Kedourie–Minogue variety.

THE LIBERAL OBJECTION

I have referred to the liberal origins of the idea of nationality, but the first objection that I want to consider amounts essentially to a liberal critique of nationality. This holds that nationality is detrimental to the cultural pluralism that liberals hold dear; it is incompatible with the idea of a society in which different cultural traditions are accorded equal respect, and whose vitality springs from competition and exchange between these traditions. The classic statement of this critique can be found in Lord Acton's essay on 'Nationality' in which he argues in favour of a multinational state in which no one nation holds a dominant place.[21] Such a state, he claims, provides the best guarantee of liberties, 'the fullest security for the preservation of local customs' and the best incentive to intellectual progress.

This argument derives from the assumption that national identities are exclusive in their nature; that where a state embodies a single nationality, the culture that makes up that nationality must drive out everything else. There is no reason to hold this assumption. Nationality is not of its nature an all-embracing identity. It need not extend to all the cultural attributes that a person might display. So one can avow a national identity and also have attachments to several more specific cultural groups: to ethnic groups, religious groups, work-based associations and so forth. A line can be drawn between the beliefs and qualities that make up nationality, and those that fall outside its scope. The place where the line is drawn will be specific to a particular nationality at a particular time, and it will be a subject for debate whether its present position is appropriate or not. For instance one may argue in a liberal direction that a person's religion, say, should be irrelevant to their membership of this nation, or argue in a nationalist direction that language is not irrelevant, that each member should at least be fluent in the national tongue. The Acton argument supposes that no such line can be drawn. It supposes, contrary to all evidence, that one cannot have a pluralist society in which many ethnic, religious etc. groups co-exist but with an over-arching national identity in common.

Indeed one can turn Acton's argument around, as J.S. Mill did by anticipation in his chapter on 'Nationality' in *Representative Government*. Unless the several groups that compose a society have the mutual sympathy and trust that stems from a common nationality, it will be virtually impossible to have free institutions. There will, for instance, be no common interest in stemming the excesses of government, politics becomes a zero-sum game in which each group can hope to gain by the exploitation of the others.

This was Mill's argument, and there is plenty of subsequent evidence to back it up. But I want now to consider a more subtle variation on the theme that nationality and liberalism are at odds. This concedes that national identity and group identity can be kept separate, but points to the fact that national identities are always in practice

biased in favour of the dominant cultural group, the group that historically has dominated the politics of the state. The state may be liberal in the sense that it does not
suppress minority groups, but it does not accord equal respect and equal treatment to
cultural minorities. Practical examples of this would include what is prescribed in the
curricula in state-run schools, the content of what is broadcast through the national
media, and so forth. The national identity includes elements drawn from the dominant
culture, this is reproduced politically through the state, and minority groups are put
at a disadvantage both in various practical respects and in the less tangible sense that
their cultures are devalued by public neglect.

Concrete versions of this critique will be familiar to most readers. I want to reply
to it first by conceding that it is descriptively true in many historical cases – national
identities have very often been formed by taking over elements from the group culture
that happens to be dominant in a particular state – but then adding that it is not integral to national identities that they should be loaded in this way. I have stressed the
malleability of nationality already, and one thing we may be doing in the course of
redefining what it means to be British, French, etc. is to purge these identities of
elements that necessarily entail the exclusion of minority groups. Here there is one
particular aspect of nationality that needs underlining. Although in standard cases a
national identity is something one is born into – and I have argued that this factor of
historical continuity is a source of strength – there is no reason why others should not
acquire it by adoption. In this respect it contrasts with ethnic identities which generally speaking can only be acquired by birth. Although a priori a nation might define
itself tightly by descent, in practice nations extend membership more or less freely to
those who are resident and show willingness to exhibit those traits that make up
national character. So although this does impose certain constraints on them, minority
groups, particularly those migrating to the society in question, have the option of
acquiring a new identity alongside their existing ones. Nationality, precisely because
it aims to be an *inclusive* identity, can incorporate sub-groups in this way without
demanding that they forsake everything they already hold dear.

Indeed one can take this further and say that what best meets the needs of minority
groups is a clear and distinct national identity which stands over and above the specific
cultural traits of all the groups in the society in question. The argument here has been
well put by Tariq Modood, who has particularly in mind the position of Muslims in
British society. He writes:

As a matter of fact the greatest psychological and political need for clarity about
a common framework and national symbols comes from the minorities. For clarity
about what makes us willingly bound into a single country relieves the pressure
on minorities, especially new minorities whose presence within the country is not
fully accepted, to have to conform in all areas of social life, or in arbitrarily chosen

areas, in order to rebut the charge of disloyalty. It is the absence of comprehensively respected national symbols in Britain, comparable to the constitution and the flag in America, that allows politicians unsympathetic to minorities to demand that they demonstrate loyalty by doing x or y or z, like supporting the national cricket team in Norman Tebbit's famous example.[22]

To make my position clear here, I do not suppose that the superimposition of national identity on group identity that I am arguing for can be wholly painless on either side. While national identities are thinned down to make them more acceptable to minority groups, these groups themselves must abandon values and ways of behaving that are in stark conflict with those of the community as a whole. National identity cannot be wholly symbolic; it must embody substantive norms. This will be readily apparent if a formal constitution occupies a central place in such an identity, as I believe it should. Forms of belief and behaviour inconsistent with those laid down in the constitution will be ruled out. So, as I have argued elsewhere,[23] one cannot aspire to unlimited tolerance in this area. But the view I am defending does appear consistent with the kind of politically sensitive liberalism exhibited by J.S. Mill.

THE BALKAN OBJECTION

This, I hope, sufficiently addresses the liberal objection to nationality. Now I want to come to a second objection which might be termed the Balkan objection. This claims that the principle of nationality cannot in practice be realized, but meanwhile the belief that it can leads to endless political instability and bloodshed. This is because would-be nationalities are so entangled with one another that there is no way of drawing state boundaries that can possibly satisfy all claims. Minority group B secedes from state A in search of national self-determination, but this only provokes group C *within* B to attempt secession in its turn and so on *ad infinitum*. I call this the Balkan objection because of a view one frequently hears expressed nowadays that so long as the peoples of that region were governed from afar by the Austro-Hungarian and Turkish empires different ethnic groups lived and worked happily side-by-side, but once those empires were weakened and the idea of national self-determination was let loose, impossible conflicts were generated.[24] Events in Yugoslavia seem to confirm the view, and any day now I expect to hear President Tito's reputation being salvaged on the same terms as that of Emperor Franz Josef.

The principle of nationality as formulated earlier holds that people who form a national community in a particular territory have a good claim to political self-determination. This principle should not be confused with a certain liberal view of the state which makes individual consent a necessary and sufficient condition of a state's authority. If each person must consent to the existence of the state, it follows that the borders of states should be drawn wherever people want them to be drawn. The practical implication is that any sub-community in any state has the right to secede from that state provided that it is in turn willing to allow any sub-sub-community the equivalent right and so on indefinitely.[25] This view confronts the Balkan problem in its most acute form: where populations are intermingled, consistent application of the consent principle points directly towards an anarchic outcome in which no stable frontiers can be established.

The principle of nationality is quite different from this. Central to the idea of nationality is not individual *will*, but individual *identity*, even though some formulations confuse these two – Renan's idea of the nation as 'a daily plebiscite' which I cited earlier is *in this respect* misleading. When we encounter a group or community dissatisfied with current political arrangements the question to ask is not 'Does this group now want to secede from the existing state?' but 'Does the group have a collective identity which is or has become incompatible with the national identity of the majority in the state?' There are broadly three answers that might be given to this question. First, it may turn out that the dissatisfied group is an ethnic group which feels that materially speaking it is not getting a fair deal from the existing set-up and/or that its group identity is not being properly respected in national life. Black Americans would exemplify this: what is needed in such cases is domestic political reform, perhaps of a quite radical and painful kind, not dreams of secession. Second, the group may have a national identity, but one that is not radically incompatible with the identity of the majority community, there being common elements as well as elements of difference. The dissenting group thinks of itself as sharing a common historical identity with the majority, but also as having its own distinct national character which is currently not recognized.[26] This may (I say this with some trepidation) represent the position of the Scots and Welsh in Britain, or the Bretons in France, and the appropriate outcome is again not outright secession (which violates the shared identity) but a constitutional arrangement which gives the sub-community rights of self-determination in those areas of decision which are especially central to its own sense of nationhood.

Finally there are cases where the state as presently constituted contains two or more nations with radically incompatible identities. The reason for this might be that one community takes as constitutive of its identity some feature such as language or race not shared with the others, or that its historical self-understanding includes military conquest of the territory now occupied by the second community, or some other such factor. In these cases there is no realistic possibility of formulating a shared identity, and the minority group has a prima facie case for secession. But to make the case a conclusive one, further conditions must be met.[27] First, there has to be some way of redrawing the borders such that two viable states are created and this in itself may pose insoluble problems. Second, the territory claimed by the seceding community should not contain minorities whose own identity is radically incompatible with the new majority's, so that rather than creating a genuine nation-state, the secession would simply reproduce a multi-national arrangement on a smaller scale. Third, some consideration must be given to small groups who may be left behind in the rump state; it may be that the effect of secession is to destroy a political balance and leave these groups in a very weak position. It is, for instance, a strong argument against the secession of Quebec from the Canadian federation that it would effectively destroy the double-sided identity that Canada has laboured to achieve, and leave French-speaking communities in other provinces isolated and politically helpless.

What I am trying to stress is that the principle of nationality does not generate an unlimited right of secession. What it says is that national self-determination is a good thing, and that states and their constitutions should be arranged so that each nation is as far as possible able to secure its common future. Since homogeneous nation-states are not everywhere feasible, often this will require second-best solutions, where each nationality gets partial self-determination, not full rights of sovereignty. Equally, there may be cases where communities are intertwined in such a way that no form of national self-determination is realistically possible, and the best that can be hoped for is a modus vivendi between the communities, perhaps with a constitutional settlement guaranteed by external powers.

JUSTICE AND SENTIMENT

That, somewhat elliptically, is my answer to the Balkan objection. The final objection I want to consider arises from the second aspect of the idea of nationality, the claim that nations are ethical communities. It runs as follows. You say that nations are ethically significant, that the duties we owe to fellow-members are greater in scope than those we owe to outsiders. Yet you base this on a shared sense of identity which is based not upon concrete practices but upon sentimental ties, on historical understandings which you have conceded to be imaginary in part. But how can duties of justice, especially, depend in this way on our feelings about others? Does this not make justice an entirely subjective idea, and abandon its role as a critical notion which serves to correct both our beliefs and our behaviour?

Observe to begin with that our sense of national identity serves to mark out the universe of persons to whom special duties are owed; it may do this without at the same time determining the content of those duties. In particular my recognition of X as a co-national to whom I have obligations may depend upon a sense of nationality with sentimental content, but it does not follow that my duties to X depend on my feelings about X as a person. An analogy with the family makes this clear. A family does not exist as such unless its members have certain feelings towards one another, yet obligations within the family are not governed by sentiment. I may feel more sympathy for one child than another, yet in allocating the family's resources I ought to consider their needs impartially.

It appears nonetheless that obligations in this account are being derived from the existence of a certain kind of community, while in the national case the community is sentiment-based. It would follow that if nation A embodies a strong sense of fellow-feeling whereas nation B embodies a relatively weak sense, then obligations within A are more extensive than those within B, and this seems paradoxical. What this over-looks, however, is the role played by political culture within national identity. It is not merely that I feel bound to a group of people defined in national terms; I feel bound to them as sharing in a certain way of life, expressed in the public culture. The content of my obligations stems immediately from that culture. Various interpretations of the public culture are possible, but some of these will be closer to getting it right than others, and this also shows to what extent debates about social justice are resolvable. It follows that what social justice consists in will vary from place to place, but not directly in line with sentiments or feelings. A Swede will acknowledge more extensive obligations to provide welfare for fellow-Swedes than an American will for fellow-Americans; but this is because the public culture of Sweden, defining in part what it means to be Swedish, is solidaristic, whereas the public culture of the US is individualistic. It is not part of the story that Swedes must have more sympathetic feelings for other individual Swedes than Americans do for other Americans.

This may still sound an uncomfortably relativistic view to some. What I have argued is that nationalists are not committed to the kind of crude subjectivism which says that your communal obligations are whatever you feel them to be. Membership of a national community involves identifying with a public culture that is external to each of us taken individually; and although we may argue with one another about how the culture should be understood, and what practical obligations stem from it, this is still a question to which better or worse answers can be given.

CONCLUSION

Philosophers may find it restricting that they have to conduct their arguments about justice with reference to national identities at all. My claim is that unless they do they will lose contact entirely with the beliefs of the people they seek to address; they must try to incorporate some of Hume's gross earthy mixture, the unreflective beliefs of everyday life. Nonetheless there is a tension here. We should return to Kenneth Grahame's Rat who on his first appearance seems to stand for unlimited acquiescence in the everyday world of the river bank. As the story draws towards its conclusion, however, a more troubled Rat emerges. Disturbed first by the departure of the swallows to Southern climes, he then encounters a seafaring rat who regales him with tales of the colourful and vibrant world beyond the river bank. The Rat is mesmerized. His eyes, normally 'clear and dark and brown', turn to 'a streaked and shifting grey'. He is about to set out for the South with stick and satchel in hand, and has to be physically restrained by the Mole, who gradually leads his thoughts back to the everyday world, and finally leaves him writing poetry as a kind of sublimation of his wandering instincts.

The Rat's earlier refusal to contemplate the Wide World, it emerges, was a wilful repression of a part of himself that it was dangerous to acknowledge. Something of the same dilemma confronts the philosophical nationalist. He feels the pull of national loyalties, and he senses that without these loyalties we would be cast adrift in a region of great moral uncertainty. Yet he is also alive to the limitations and absurdities of his and other national identities. He recognizes that we owe something to other human beings merely as such, and so he strains towards a more rationally defensible foundation for ethics and politics. There is no solution here but to strive for some kind of equilibrium between the everyday and the philosophical, between common belief and rational belief, between the river hank and the Wide World. But, as the cases both of the Rat and of David Hume in their different ways demonstrate, this is far easier said than done.

NOTES

1 K. Grahame, *The Wind in the Willows* (London, Methuen, 1926), pp. 16–17.
2 D. Hume, *A Treatise of Human Nature*, ed. L.A. Selby-Bigge, 3rd edn revised P.H. Nidditch (Oxford, Clarendon Press, 1978), p. 272.
3 I have attempted the second especially in 'The Ethical Significance of Nationality', *Ethics*, 98 (1987–8), 647–62. I am mainly concerned with the first in the present chapter.
4 See for Instance T. Nagel, *Equality and Partiality* (New York and Oxford, Oxford University Press, 1991) whose organizing idea is the contrast between personal and impersonal ethical standpoints.
5 A. MacIntyre, 'Is Patriotism a Virtue?' (Lawrence, University of Kansas, Department of Philosophy, 1984).
6 G. Orwell, *The Road to Wigan Pier* (Harmondsworth, Penguin, 1962), p. 160.
7 I speak of 'nationality' rather than 'nationalism' because the latter term usually carries with it unwelcome assumptions about what nations are entitled to do to advance their interests; however there is no alternative to 'nationalist' as an adjective. An alternative approach would be to follow Neil MacCormick in distinguishing different conceptions of nationalism; like MacCormick's, the conception I want to defend includes the condition that in supporting my nation's interests, I should respect others' national identities (and the claims that follow from them) as well. See N. MacCormick, 'Nation and Nationalism' in *Legal Right and Social Denmcracy* (Oxford, Clarendon Press, 1982) and N. MacCormick, 'Is Nationalism Philosophically Credible?' in W. Twining (ed.), *Issues of Self-Determination* (Aberdeen, Aberdeen University Press, 1991).
8 E. Renan, 'What is a Nation?' in A. Zimmern (ed.), *Modern Political Doctrines* (London Oxford University Press, 1939).

9 Ibid., p. 203.

10 D. Hume, 'Of National Characters' in *Essays Moral, Political, and Literary*, ed. E. Miller (Indianapolis, Liberty Classics, 1985), pp. 197–8.

11 'It is only when you meet someone of a different culture from yourself that you begin to realize what your own beliefs really are' (Orwell, *Wigan Pier*, p. 145).

12 Renan, 'What is a Nation?', p. 190.

13 I should make it clear that this consideration could not be put forward as a reason for having or adopting a national identity. A national identity depends upon a prereflective sense that one belongs within a certain historic group, and it would be absurd to propose to the subjects of state X that because things would go better for them if they adopted a shared national identity, they should therefore conjure one up. The argument points to benefits that national allegiances bring with them as by-products. Others who have defended nationality in this way include B. Barry. 'Self-Government Revisited' in D. Miller and L. Siedentop (eds), *The Nature of Political Theory* (Oxford, Clarendon Press, 1983), reprinted in B. Barry, *Democracy, Power and Justice* (Oxford, Clarendon Press, 1989); and Nagel, *Equality and Partiality*, ch. 15.

14 I have argued this with specific reference to socialism in 'In What Sense Must Socialism Be Communitarian?', *Social Philosophy and Policy*, 6 (1988–9), 51–73; but I believe the point holds more generally.

15 See especially L. Colley, 'Whose Nation? Class and National Consciousness in Britain 1750–1830', *Past and Present*, 113 (1986), 97–117.

16 See E.J. Hobsbawm, *Nations and Nationalism since 1780* (Cambridge, Cambridge University Press, 1990).

17 It is also true, however, that conservatives of a different persuasion may embrace national identities as a source of social cohesion and authority; see in particular R. Scruton, 'In Defence of the Nation' [Chapter 17 of this volume]. 'Communitarianisms: Left, Right and Centre', in D. Avnon and A. de-Shalit (eds) *Liberalism and its Practice* (London, Rouledge, 1999) looks more closely at what distinguishes this kind of conservative nationalism from other forms of communitarianism.

18 E. Kedourie, *Nationalism* (London, Hutchinson, 1966); K. Minogue, *Nationalism* (London, Batsford, 1967).

19 Minogue, *Nationalism*, p. 148.

20 There is a fine and suitably controversial example of this in Margaret Thatcher's recent attempt to present her political views as the logical outcome of British history and national character.

> I always said and believed that the British character is quite different from the characters of people on the Continent – quite different. There is a great sense of fairness and equity in the British people, a great sense of individuality and initiative. They don't like being pushed around. How else did this really rather small people, from the times of Elizabeth on, go out in the larger world and have such an influence upon it? . . .
>
> I set out to destroy socialism because I felt it was at odds with the character of the people. We were the first country in the world to roll back the frontiers of socialism, then roll forward the frontiers of freedom. We reclaimed our heritage.
>
> (M. Thatcher, 'Don't Undo My Work', *Newsweek*, vol. 119, no. 17, 27 April 1992, p. 14)

21   Lord Acton, 'Nationality' in *The History of Freedom and Other Essays*, ed. J.N. Figgis (London, Macmillan, 1907).

22   T. Modood, 'Establishment, Multiculturalism and British Citizenship', *Political Quarterly*, 65 (1994), 64–5.

23   D. Miller, 'Socialism and Toleration' in S. Mendus (ed.), *Justifying Toleration* (Cambridge, University Press, 1988); *Market, State and Community* (Oxford, Clarendon Press, 1989), ch. 11.

24   One can find it expressed, for example, in Kedourie, *Nationalism*, chs 6–7.

25   See, for instance, H. Beran, 'A Liberal Theory of Secession', *Political Studies*, 32 (1984), 21–31 – though Beran would deny the consequence I wish to infer from this doctrine.

26   If this is allowed, it follows that there can be no simple answer to the question 'How many nations are there in area A?'. Nations are not discrete and easily counted entities like billiard balls. The criteria that I have offered to define them admit of degree, and that is why it is possible to have a smaller nationality nesting within a larger one.

27   The conditions given are intended to be necessary rather than sufficient. I have addressed the issue of justified secession at greater length in 'The Nation-State: A Modest Defence' in C. Brown (ed.), *Political Restructuring in Europe: Ethical Perspectives* (London, Routledge, 1993).

FURTHER READING

Goodin, R.E. (1987–8). 'What is so Special About Our Fellow Countrymen?', *Ethics*, 98: 663–86.

Margalit, A. and Raz, J. (1990). 'National Self Determination'. *Journal of Philosophy* 87: 439–61.

Miller, D. (1995). *On Nationality*. Oxford, Clarendon Press.

Miller, D. (2000). *Citizenship and National Identity*. Cambridge, Polity Press.

Tamir, Y. (1993). *Liberal Nationalism*. Princeton, Princeton University Press.

Part 6
DEMOCRACY

Introduction

DEMOCRACY MEANS 'RULE BY THE PEOPLE'. Recent history tells us that this can be manifested – or at least be thought to be manifested – in many ways. Even if we could agree that liberal democracy most clearly manifests the ideal embodied in the meaning of the word, the system is not as unproblematic as we unreflectively think. There are at least two problems. First, in the absence of unanimity, democracies need a procedure for making decisions as to what policies to pursue. The usual answer to this is some form of majority rule. This, however, condemns significant numbers to being governed by the will of others, rather than by a will they directly endorse. The problem is worst for persistent minorities, that is, those whose representatives have no chance of enacting or even influencing policy. They are, in practice, disenfranchised. Second, democracies count everybody's vote as equal. You can have read all the manifestos, consulted widely as to the effects of proposed policy, and yet your vote will only count as much as that of the person who votes according to whim. Democracy is not a perfect system (even if one might say with Churchill that it is 'the worse form of Government except all those other forms that have been tried from time to time').

Recently, philosophers have been looking at forms of democracy that might lessen the two problems described above. In the first reading of this part, Jon Elster describes and then criticises three views of democratic politics. He presents these, as he says, 'in a somewhat stylized form' in order to focus on what he sees as the key weaknesses in their structure. The first view sees voting as a matter of private choice, the second and third more as a public function.

The first view Elster considers sees voting as a mechanism for aggregating given preferences. This is, I suspect, how most people currently see voting. Citizens have preferences that enable them to rank a range of outcomes. They express these by voting, and an ordering of preferences is discovered for the whole population. Elster has two sets of objections to this. The first is that, for various reasons, 'the preferences people choose to express may not be a good guide to what they really prefer'. That is, there are reasons for thinking that relying on what people say they want will not result in an ordering that reflects what they really want. The second set of objections stems from Elster's view that one of the tasks of politics is to 'create justice'. This can only be done if the preferences expressed pass some measure of acceptability. The fact that they are adaptive or counteradaptive, that they are not formed autonomously or are immoral, all count against acceptability. The aggregation of expressed preferences is not, in Elster's terms, 'appropriate in the forum'.

The second view does not take preferences as given, but as transformed by public discussion. It is argued that the nature of public reasoning and debate means that what will emerge is a set of preferences that are shaped by concern for the common good. Although Elster is sympathetic to this view, he brings six strong objections against it. These are motivated by two underlying worries. The first is the clash between this view and the real constraints of political decision-making. As Elster says, in a non-moral environment (which we can suppose real-world politics is, at least in part) there may be an obligation to deviate from the behaviour this view mandates. Not doing so might result in a situation that was worse overall. The second worry is that efforts to protect the process of rational discussion from undesirable elements such as adaptive preferences, conformity, wishful thinking and the like 'could easily reintroduce an element of domination'.

Finally, Elster considers the view that politics is justified in terms of the beneficial effects it has on the participants. Elster has little difficulty in showing that, given that this justification would have to be transparent to the participants, the view is incoherent. Performing an activity with a certain goal might do us good, but that it would do us good cannot be the goal. The ease by which this is shown might give us pause. Certainly, Elster was explicit that he was considering stylised versions of the views. One element of this is that the views are considered as justifying democracy either instrumentally or in terms of its intrinsic value. Perhaps it can be both or perhaps (even) this distinction should not be rigidly drawn. Some of Elster's closing remarks suggest he might be sympathetic to this.

The paper by Joshua Cohen defends 'deliberative democracy', by which he means 'an association whose affairs are governed by the public deliberation of its members'. Cohen argues for this by drawing on John Rawls' ideal of justice and just institutions. The result is a political ideal defined through three principles: 'When properly conducted, then, democratic politics involves *public deliberation focused on the common good*, requires some form of *manifest equality* among citizens, and *shapes the identity and interests* of citizens in ways that contribute to the formation of a public conception of a common good'. This raises the question of the conditions under which such deliberation should be conducted; what are the conditions (for example) by which we can include reason and exclude coercion? Cohen answers this with an extensive account of 'an *ideal deliberative procedure*'. Important in this is the claim the members of the association are committed to resolve their differences by providing reasons 'they sincerely believe to be persuasive to others'. The effect of this is that, in politics, people are precluded from putting forward positions that favour their self-interest, unless they can find reasons that would appeal to others. The radical nature of Cohen's proposal is further illustrated in his reply to the objection that people's expressed preferences do not match their real preferences, because of the phenomenon of 'adaptive preferences'. It is built into the ideal deliberative procedure, that 'relations of power and subordination are neutralised'.

Cohen defends his conception against criticisms of sectarianism, incoherence, injustice and irrelevance. What emerges is a compelling vision of pubic life that has its roots in Rousseau (Rousseau 1987). There is, as Cohen admits, more that needs to be said in defence of the conception. One might wonder, for example, about the link between public reason and the motivation of participants. Is the desire to be reasonable, and to be seen to be reasonable, sufficient to weigh against naked self-interest? There is also a fundamental worry, that, whether possible or not, an ideal deliberative procedure is not desirable. There are Marxist worries that it has nothing to say about class identities and class interest (Miller 1974). In addition, Iris Marion Young has argued that such universal conceptions discriminate against certain group interests. She puts forward a radical pluralism, which denies the notion of a common ground on which people can work out their disagreements (Young 1989). Obviously, if that is so, then an ideal deliberative procedure could not be defended. However, we might also think that if that is so, then no conception of politics as a forum governed by reason could be defended.

In a provocative essay, Michael Walzer argues that political philosophy (in the guise of the Supreme Court) should exercise restraint in meddling in politics. There has always been a tension between democracy and any view (such as liberalism) that aims to safeguard individual rights. For democracies can (and sometimes do) vote for courses of action that trample on, or put aside, those rights. Democracy is, Walzer argues, a matter of what the people will, not a matter of what is right (as judged by philosophical argument). Of course, some rights need to be enforced, namely, those rights that enable the democratic process to function. But, argues Walzer, 'As soon as the philosophical list of rights extends beyond the twin bans on legal discrimination and political repression, it invites judicial activity that is radically intrusive on what might be called democratic space'. The answer is for judges to operate 'judicial restraint'; to pre-empt or overrule legislative decisions 'only in rare and extreme cases'.

Walzer has certainly raised a question here for those people who are committed liberals and democrats. Democracy is a sphere in which opinions compete with each other, and, in that sphere, philosophical truth has no special place. However, the opposition might not be as stark as he makes out. There are two possibilities that the liberal democrat could explore. First, it might be that the two rights Walzer argues ought to be enforced (that is, the bans on discrimination and repression) are themselves sufficient to justify a great deal of interference by the judiciary in 'democratic space' (Gutmann 1983). Thus, it may be that in making the concession about the enforcement of these rights, Walzer has already deprived himself of the ground on which to argue for restraint. Second, the liberal could argue for building constraints into the democratic procedure such that it is impossible (or at least unlikely) that the outcome of democratic deliberations could be a violation of rights. For example, a democratic procedure could be such that citizens voted not to express their prior preferences, but on what they took to be the most just of a range of alternatives (Waldron 1990). If this were the case then restrictions on the violations of rights would be built into voting itself, and there would be no need for judicial review. This second line of reply would, however, require a huge change in our conception of politics.

REFERENCES

Gutmann, A. (1983). 'How Liberal is Democracy?' *Liberalism Reconsidered*. D. Maclean and C. Mills. Totowa, Rowman and Allanheld: 25–50.

Miller, R. (1974). 'Rawls and Marxism.' *Philosophy and Public Affairs* 3(2): 167–91.

Rousseau, J.J. (1987). *The Social Contract*. Indianapolis, Hackett.

Waldron, J. (1990). 'Rights and Majorities: Rousseau Revisted.' *Nomos* XXXII: 44–75.

Young, I.M. (1989). 'Polity and Group Difference: A Critique of the Ideal of Universal Citizenship.' *Ethics* 99: 250–74 [Chapter 14 of this collection].

20

THE MARKET AND THE FORUM

Three varieties of political theory

Jon Elster

I want to compare three views of politics generally, and of the democratic system more specifically. I shall first look at social choice theory, as an instance of a wider class of theories with certain common features. In particular, they share the conception that the political process is instrumental rather than an end in itself, and the view that the decisive political act is a private rather than a public action, viz. the individual and secret vote. With these usually goes the idea that the goal of politics is the optimal compromise between given, and irreducibly opposed, private interests. The other two views arise when one denies, first, the private character of political behaviour and then, secondly, goes on also to deny the instrumental nature of politics. According to the theory of Jürgen Habermas, the goal of politics should be rational agreement rather than compromise, and the decisive political act is that of engaging in public debate with a view to the emergence of a consensus. According to the theorists of participatory democracy, from John Stuart Mill to Carole Pateman, the goal of politics is the transformation and education of the participants. Politics, on this view, is an end in itself – indeed many have argued that it represents the good life for man. I shall discuss these views in the order indicated. I shall present them in a somewhat stylized form, but my critical comments will not I hope, be directed to strawmen.

I

Politics, it is usually agreed, is concerned with the common good, and notably with the cases in which it cannot be realized as the aggregate outcome of individuals pursuing their private interests. In particular, uncoordinated private choices may lead to outcomes that are worse for all than some other outcome that could have been attained by coordination. Political institutions are set up to remedy such *market failures*, a phrase that can be taken either in the static sense of inability to provide public goods or in the more dynamic sense of a breakdown of the self-regulating properties usually ascribed to the market mechanism.[1] In addition there is the redistributive task of politics – moving along the Pareto–optimal frontier once it has been reached.[2] According to the first view of politics, this task is inherently one of interest struggle and compromise. The obstacle to agreement is not only that most individuals want redistribution to be in their favour, or at least not in their disfavour.[3] More basically consensus is blocked because there is no reason to expect that individuals will converge in their views on what constitutes a just redistribution.

I shall consider social choice theory as representative of the private-instrumental view of politics, because it brings out supremely well the logic as well as the limits of that approach. Other varieties, such as the Schumpeterian or neo-Schumpeterian theories, are closer to the actual political process, but for that reason also less suited to my purpose. For instance, Schumpeter's insistence that voter preferences are shaped and manipulated by politicians[4] tends to blur the distinction, central to my analysis, between politics as the aggregation of given preferences and politics as the transformation of preferences through rational discussion. And although the neo-Schumpeterians are right in emphasizing the role of the political parties in the preference-aggregation process,[5] I am not here concerned with such mediating mechanisms. In any case, political problems also arise within the political parties, and so my discussion may be taken to apply, to such lower-level political processes. In fact, much of what I shall say makes better sense for politics on a rather small scale – within the firm, the organization or the local community – than for nationwide political systems.

In very broad outline, the structure of social choice theory is as follows.[6] (1) We begin with a *given* set of agents, so that the issue of a normative justification of political boundaries does not arise. (2) We assume that the agents confront a *given* set of alternatives, so that for instance the issue of agenda manipulation does not arise. (3) The agents are supposed to be endowed with preferences that are similarly *given* and not subject to change in the course of the political process. They, are, moreover, assumed to be causally independent of the set of alternatives. (4) In the standard version, which is so far the only operational version of the theory, preferences are assumed to be purely ordinal, so that it is not possible for an individual to express the intensity of his preferences, nor for an outside observer to compare preference intensities across individuals. (5) The individual preferences are assumed to be defined over all pairs of individuals, i.e. to be complete, and to have the formal property of transitivity, so that preference for A over B and for B over C implies preference for A over C.

Given this setting, the task of social choice theory is to arrive at a social preference ordering of the alternatives This might appear to require more than is needed: why not define the goal as one of arriving at the choice of one alternative? There is, however, usually some uncertainty as to which alternatives are really feasible, and so it is useful to have an ordering if the top-ranked alternative proves unavailable. The ordering should satisfy the following criteria. (6) Like the individual preferences, it should be complete and transitive. (7) It should be Pareto-optimal, in the sense of never having one option socially preferred to another which is individually preferred by everybody. (8) The social choice between two given options should depend only on how the individuals rank these two options, and thus not be sensitive to changes in their preferences concerning other options. (9) The social preference ordering should respect and reflect individual preferences, over and above the condition of Pareto-optimality. This idea covers a variety of notions, the most important of which are *anonymity* (all individuals should count equally), *non-dictatorship* (*a fortiori* no single individual should dictate the social choice), *liberalism* (all individuals should have some private domain within which their preferences are decisive), and *strategy-proofness* (it should not pay to express false preferences).

The substance of social choice theory is given in a series of impossibility and uniqueness theorems, stating either that a given subset of these conditions is incapable of simultaneous satisfaction or that they uniquely describe a specific method for aggregating preferences. Much attention has been given to the impossibility theorems, yet from the present point of view these are not of decisive importance. They stem largely from the paucity of allowable information about the preferences, i.e. the exclusive focus on ordinal preferences.[7] True, at present we do not quite know how to go beyond ordinality. Log-rolling and vote-trading may capture some of the cardinal aspects of the preferences, but at some cost.[8] Yet even should the conceptual and technical obstacles to intra- and inter-individual comparison of preference intensity be overcome,[9] many objections to the social choice approach would remain. I shall discuss two sets of objections, both related to the assumption of given preferences. I shall argue, first, that the preferences people choose to express may not be a good guide to what they really prefer; and secondly that what they really prefer may in any case be a fragile foundation for social choice.

In actual fact, preferences are never 'given', in the sense of being directly observable. If they are to serve as inputs to the social choice process, they must somehow be *expressed* by the individuals. The expression of preferences is an action, which presumably is guided by these very same preferences.[10] It is then far from obvious that the individually rational action is to express these preferences as they are. Some methods for aggregating preferences are such that it may pay the individual to express false preferences, i.e. the outcome may in some cases be better according to his real preferences if he chooses not to express them truthfully. The condition for strategy-proofness for social choice mechanisms was designed expressly to exclude this possibility. It turns out, however, that the systems in which honesty always pays are rather unattractive in other respects.[11] We then have to face the possibility that even if we require that the social preferences be Pareto-optimal with respect to the expressed preferences, they might not be so with respect to the real ones. Strategy-proofness and collective rationality, therefore, stand and fall together. Since it appears that the first must fall, so must the second. It then becomes very difficult indeed to defend the idea that the outcome of the social choice mechanism represents the common good, since there is a chance that everybody might prefer some other outcome.

[. . .]

A second, perhaps more basic, difficulty is that the real preferences themselves might well depend causally on the feasible set. One instance is graphically provided by the fable of the fox and the sour grapes.[12] For the 'ordinal utilitarian', as Arrow for instance calls himself,[13] there would be no welfare loss if the fox were excluded from consumption of the grapes, since he thought them sour anyway. But of course the cause of his holding them to be sour was his conviction that he would in any case be excluded from consuming them, and then it is difficult to justify the allocation by invoking his preferences. Conversely, the phenomenon of 'counter-adaptive preferences' – the grass is always greener on the other side of the fence, and the forbidden fruit always sweeter – is also baffling for the social choice theorist, since it implies that such preferences, if respected, would not be satisfied – and yet the whole point of respecting them would be to give them a chance of satisfaction.

Adaptive and counter-adaptive preferences are only special cases of a more general class of desires, those which fail to satisfy some substantive criterion for acceptable preferences, as opposed to the purely formal criterion of transitivity. I shall discuss these under two headings: autonomy and morality.

Autonomy characterizes the way in which preferences are shaped rather than their actual content. Unfortunately I find myself unable to give a positive characterization of autonomous preferences, so I shall have to rely on two indirect approaches. First, autonomy is for desires what judgment is for belief. The notion of judgment is also difficult to define formally, but at least we know that there are persons who have this quality to a higher degree than others: people who are able to take account of vast and diffuse evidence that more or less clearly bears on the problem at hand, in such a way that no element is given undue importance. In such people the process of belief formation is not disturbed by defective cognitive processing, nor distorted by wishful thinking and the like. Similarly, autonomous preferences are those that have not been shaped by irrelevant causal processes – a singularly unhelpful explanation. To improve somewhat on it, consider, secondly, a short list of such irrelevant causal processes. They include adaptive and counter-adaptive preferences, conformity and anti-conformity, the obsession with novelty and the equally unreasonable resistance to novelty. In other words, preferences may be shaped by adaptation to what is possible, to what other people do or to what one has been doing in the past – or they may be shaped by the desire to differ as much as possible from these. In all of these cases the source of preference change is not in the person, but outside him – detracting from his autonomy.

Morality, it goes without saying, is if anything even more controversial. (Within the Kantian tradition it would also be questioned whether it can be distinguished at all from autonomy.) Preferences are moral or immoral by virtue of their content, not by virtue of the way in which they have been shaped. Fairly uncontroversial examples of unethical preferences are spiteful and sadistic desires, and arguably also the desire for positional goods, i.e. goods such that it is logically impossible for more than a few to possess them.[14] The desire for an income twice the average can lead to less welfare for everybody, so that such preferences fail to pass the Kantian generalization test.[15] Also they are closely linked to spite, since one way of getting more than others is to take care that they get less – indeed this may often be a more efficient method than trying to excel.[16]

To see how the lack of autonomy may be distinguished from the lack of moral worth, let me use *conformity* as a technical term for a desire caused by a drive to be like other people, and *conformism* for a desire to be like other people, with anti-conformity and and-conformism similarly defined. Conformity implies that other people's desires enter into the causation of my own, conformism that they enter irreducibly into the description of the object of my desires. Conformity may bring about conformism, but it may also lead to anti-conformism, as in Theodore Zeldin's comment that among the French peasantry 'prestige is to a great extent obtained from conformity with traditions, so that the son of a non-conformist might be expected to be one too'.[17] Clearly, conformity may bring about desires that are morally laudable, yet lacking in autonomy. Conversely, I do not see how one could rule out on a priori grounds the possibility of autonomous spite, although I would welcome a proof that autonomy is incompatible not only with anti-conformity, but also with anti-conformism.

We can now state the objection to the political view underlying social choice theory. It is, basically, that it embodies a confusion between the kind of behaviour that is appropriate in the market place and that which is appropriate in the forum. The notion of consumer sovereignty is acceptable because, and to the extent that, the consumer chooses between courses of action that differ only in the way they affect him. In political choice situations, however, the citizen is asked to express his preference over states that also differ in the way in which they affect other people. This means that there is no similar justification for the corresponding notion of the citizen's sovereignty, since other people may legitimately object to social choice governed by preferences that are defective in some of the ways I have mentioned. A social choice mechanism is capable of resolving the market failures that would result from unbridled consumer sovereignty, but as a way of redistributing welfare it is hopelessly inadequate. If people affected each other only by tripping over each other's feet, or by dumping their garbage

329

into one another's backyards, a social choice mechanism might cope. But the task of politics is not only to eliminate inefficiency, but also to create justice – a goal to which the aggregation of pre-political preferences is a quite incongruous means.

This suggests that the principles of the forum must differ from chose of the market. A long-standing tradition from the Greek *polis* onwards suggests that politics must be an open and public activity, as distinct from the isolated and private expression of preferences that occurs in buying and selling. In the following sections I look at two different conceptions of public politics, increasingly removed from the market theory of politics. Before I go on to this, however, I should briefly consider an objection that the social choice theorist might well make to what has just been said. He could argue that the only alternative to the aggregation of given preferences is some kind of censorship or paternalism. He might agree that spiteful and adaptive preferences are undesirable, but he would add that any institutional mechanism for eliminating them would be misused and harnessed to the private purposes of power-seeking individuals. Any remedy, in fact, would be worse than the disease. This objection assumes (i) that the only alternative to aggregation of given preferences is censorship, and (ii) that censorship is always objectionable. Robert Goodin, in his paper 'Laundering preferences', challenges the second assumption, by arguing that laundering or filtering of preferences by self-censorship is an acceptable alternative to aggregation. I shall now discuss a challenge to the first assumption, viz. the idea of a *transformation* of preferences through public and rational discussion.

II

Today this view is especially associated with the writings of Jürgen Habermas on 'the ethic of discourse' and 'the ideal speech situation'. As mentioned above, I shall present a somewhat stylized version of his views, although I hope they bear some resemblance to the original.[18] The core of the theory, then, is that rather than aggregating or filtering preferences, the political system should be set up with a view to changing them by public debate and confrontation. The input to the social choice mechanism would then not be the raw, quite possibly selfish or irrational, preferences that operate in the market, but informed and other-regarding preferences. Or rather, there would not be any need for an aggregating mechanism, since a rational discussion would tend to produce unanimous preferences. When the private and idiosyncratic wants have been shaped and purged in public discussion about the public good, uniquely determined rational desires would emerge. Not optimal compromise, but unanimous agreement is the goal of politics on this view.

There appear to be two main premises underlying this theory. The first is that there are certain arguments that simply cannot be stated publicly. In a political debate it is pragmatically impossible to argue that a given solution should be chosen just because it is good for oneself. By the very act of engaging in a public debate – by arguing rather than bargaining – one has ruled out the possibility of invoking such reasons.[19] To engage in discussion can in fact be seen as one kind of self-censorship, a pre-commitment to the idea of rational decision. Now, it might well be thought that this conclusion is too strong. The first argument only shows that in public debate one has to pay some lip-service to the common good. An additional premise states that over time one will in fact come to be swayed by considerations about the common good. One cannot indefinitely praise the common good 'du bout des lèvres', for – as argued by Pascal in the context of the wager – one will end up having the preferences that initially one was faking.[20] This is a psychological, not a conceptual premise. To explain why going through the motions of rational discussion should tend to bring about the real thing, one might argue that people tend to bring what they mean into line with what they say in order to reduce dissonance, but this is a dangerous argument to employ in the present context. Dissonance reduction does not tend to generate autonomous preferences. Rather one would have to invoke the power of reason to break down prejudice and selfishness. By speaking with the voice of reason, one is also exposing oneself to reason.

To sum up, the conceptual impossibility of expressing selfish arguments in a debate about the public good, and the psychological difficulty of expressing other-regarding preferences without ultimately coming to acquire them, jointly bring it about that public discussion tends to promote the common good. The *volonté générale*, then, will not simply be the Pareto-optimal realization of given (or expressed) preferences,[21] but the outcome of preferences that are themselves shaped by a concern for the common good. For instance, by mere aggregation of given preferences one would be able to take account of some negative externalities, but not of those affecting future genera-tions. A social choice mechanism might prevent persons now living from dumping their garbage into one another's backyards, but not from dumping it in the future. Moreover, considerations of distributive justice within the Pareto constraint would now have a more solid foundation, especially as one would also be able to avoid the problem of strategy-proofness. By one stroke one would achieve more rational pref-erences, as well as the guarantee that they will in fact be expressed.

I now want to set out a series of objections – given altogether – to the view stated above. I should explain that the goal of this criticism is not to demolish the theory, but to locate some points that need to be fortified. I am, in fact, largely in sympathy with the fundamental tenets of the view, yet fear that it might be dismissed as Utopian, both in the sense of ignoring the problem of getting from here to there, and in the sense of neglecting some elementary facts of human psychology.

The *first objection* involves a reconsideration of the issues of paternalism. Would it not, in fact, be unwarranted interference to impose on the citizens the obligation to participate in political discussion? One might answer that there is a link between the right to vote and the obligation to participate in discussion, just as rights and duties are correlative in other cases. To acquire the right to vote, one has to perform certain civic duties that go beyond pushing the voting button on the television set. There would appear to be two different ideas underlying this answer. First, only those should have the right to vote who are sufficiently *concerned* about politics to be willing to devote some of their resources – time in particular – to it. Secondly, one should try to favour *informed* preferences as inputs to the voting process. The first argument favours participation and discussion as a sign of interest, but does not give it an instrumental value in itself. It would do just as well, for the purpose of this argument, to demand that people should pay for the right to vote. The second argument favours discussion as a means to improvement – it will not only select the right people, but actually make them more qualified to participate.

These arguments might have some validity in a near-ideal world, in which the concern for politics was evenly distributed across all relevant dimensions, but in the context of contemporary politics they miss the point. The people who survive a high threshold for participation are disproportionately found in a privileged part of the population. At best this could lead to paternalism, at worst the high ideals of rational discussion could create a self-elected elite whose members spend time on politics because they want power, not out of concern for the issues. As in other cases, to be discussed later, the best can be the enemy of the good. I am not saying that it is impossible to modify the ideal in a way that allows both for rational discussion and for low-profile participation, only that any institutional design must respect the trade-off between the two.

My *second objection* is that even assuming unlimited time for discussion, unanimous and rational agreement might not necessarily ensue. Could there not be legitimate and unresolvable differences of opinions over the nature of the common good? Could there not even be a plurality of ultimate values?

I am not going to discuss this objection, since it is in any case preempted by the *third objection*. Since there are in fact always time constraints on discussions – often the stronger the more important the issues – unanimity will rarely emerge. For any constellation of preferences short of unanimity, however, one would need a social choice mechanism to aggregate them. One can discuss only for so long, and then one has to make a decision, even if strong differences of opinion should remain. This objection, then, goes to show that the transformation of preferences can never do more than supplement the aggregation of preferences, never replace it altogether.

This much would no doubt be granted by most proponents of the theory. True, they would say, even if the ideal speech situation can never be fully realized, it will nevertheless improve the outcome of the political process if one goes some way towards it. The *fourth objection* questions the validity of this reply. In some cases a little discussion can be a dangerous thing, worse in fact than no discussion at all, viz. if it makes some but not all persons align themselves on the common good. [. . .]

A *fifth objection* is to question the implicit assumption that the body politic as a whole is better or wiser than the sum of its parts. Could it not rather be the case that people are made more, not less, selfish and irrational by interacting politically? The cognitive analogy suggests that the rationality of beliefs may be positively as well as negatively affected by interaction. On the one hand there is what Irving Janis has called 'group-think', i.e. mutually reinforcing bias.[22] On the other hand there certainly are many ways in which people can, and do, pool their opinions and supplement each other to arrive at a better estimate.[23] Similarly autonomy and morality could be enhanced as well as undermined by interaction. Against the pessimistic view of Reinhold Niebuhr that individuals in a group show more unrestrained egoism than in their personal relationships,[24] we may set Hannah Arendt's optimistic view:

> American faith was not all based on a semireligious faith in human nature, but on the contrary, on the possibility of checking human nature in its singularity, by virtue of human bonds and mutual promises. The hope for man in his singularity lay in the fact that not man but men inhabit the earth and form a world between them. It is human worldliness that will save men from the pitfalls of human nature.[25]

Niebuhr's argument suggests an aristocratic disdain of the *mass*, which transforms individually decent people – to use a characteristically condescending phrase – into an unthinking horde. While rejecting this as a general view, one should equally avoid the other extreme, suggested by Arendt. Neither the Greek nor the American assemblies were the paradigms of discursive reason that she makes them out to be. The Greeks were well aware that they might be tempted by demagogues, and in fact took extensive precautions against this tendency.[26] The American town surely has not always been the incarnation of collective freedom, since on occasion it could also serve as the springboard for witch hunts. The mere decision to engage in rational discussion does not ensure that the transactions will in fact be conducted rationally, since much depends on the structure and the framework of the proceedings. The random errors of selfish and private preferences may to some extent cancel each other out and thus be less to be feared than the massive and coordinated errors that may arise through group-think. On the other hand, it would be excessively stupid to rely on mutually compensating vices to bring about public benefits as a general rule. I am not arguing against the need for public discussion, only for the need to take the question of institutional and constitutional design very seriously.

A *sixth objection* is that unanimity, were it to be realized, might easily be due to conformity rather than to rational agreement. I would in fact tend to have more confidence in the outcome of a democratic decision if there was a minority that voted against it, than if it was unanimous. I am not here referring to people expressing the majority preferences against their real ones, since I am assuming that something like the secret ballot would prevent this. I have in mind that people may come to change their real preferences, as a result of seeing which way the majority goes. Social psychology has amply shown the strength of this bandwagon effect,[27] which in political theory is also known as the 'chameleon' problem.[28] It will not do to argue that the majority to which the conformist adapts his view is likely to pass the test of rationality even if his adherence to it does not, since the majority could well be made up of conformists each of whom would have broken out had there been a minority he could have espoused.

[. . .]

My *seventh objection* amounts to a denial of the view that the need to couch one's argument in terms of the common good will purge the desires of all selfish arguments. There are in general many ways of realizing the common good, if by that phrase we now only mean some arrangement that is Pareto-superior to uncoordinated individual decisions. Each such arrangement will, in addition to promoting the general interest, bring an extra premium to some specific group, which will then have a strong interest in that particular arrangement.[29] The group may then come to prefer the arrangement because of that premium, although it will argue for it in terms of the common good. Typically the arrangement will be justified by a causal theory – an account, say, of how the economy works – that shows it to be not only *a* way, but the only way of promoting the common good. The economic theories underlying the early Reagan administration provide an example. I am not imputing insincerity to the proponents of these views, but there may well be an element of wishful thinking. Since social scientists disagree so strongly among themselves as to how societies work, what could be more human than to pick on a theory that uniquely justifies the arrangement from which one stands to profit? The opposition between general interest and special interests is too simplistic, since the private benefits may causally determine the way in which one conceives of the common good.

These objections have been concerned to bring out two main ideas. First, one cannot assume that one will in fact approach the good society by acting as if one had already arrived there. The fallacy inherent in this 'approximation assumption'[30] was exposed a long time ago in the economic 'theory of the second best':

> It is *not* true that a situation in which more, but not all, of the optimum conditions are fulfilled is necessarily, or is even likely to be, superior to a situation in which fewer are fulfilled. It follows, therefore, that in a situation in which there exist many constraints which prevent the fulfilment of the Paretian optimum

conditions, the removal of any one constraint may affect welfare or efficiency either by raising it, by lowering it or by leaving it unchanged.[31]

The ethical analogue is not the familiar idea that some moral obligations may be suspended when other people act non-morally.[32] Rather it is that the nature of the moral obligation is changed in a non-moral environment. When others act non-morally, there may be an obligation to deviate not only from what they do, but also from the behaviour that would have been optimal if adopted by everybody.[33] In particular, a little discussion, like a little rationality or a little socialism, may be a dangerous thing.[34] If, as suggested by Habermas, free and rational discussion will only be possible in a society that has abolished political and economic domination, it is by no means obvious that abolition can be brought about by rational argumentation. I do not want to suggest that it could occur by force – since the use of force to end the use of force is open to obvious objections. Yet something like irony, eloquence or propaganda might be needed, involving less respect for the interlocutor than what would prevail in the ideal speech situation.

As will be clear from these remarks, there is a strong tension between two ways of looking at the relation between political ends and means. On the one hand, the means should partake of the nature of the ends, since otherwise the use of unsuitable means might tend to corrupt the end. On the other hand, there are dangers involved in choosing means immediately derived from the goal to be realized, since in a non-ideal situation these might take us away from the end rather than towards it. A delicate balance will have to be struck between these two, opposing considerations. It is in fact an open question whether there exists a ridge along which we can move to the good society, and if so whether it is like a knife-edge or more like a plateau.

The second general idea that emerges from the discussion is that even in the good society, should we hit upon it, the process of rational discussion could be fragile, and vulnerable to adaptive preferences, conformity, wishful thinking and the like. To ensure stability and robustness there is a need for structures – political institutions or constitutions – that could easily reintroduce an element of domination. We would in fact be confronted, at the political level, with a perennial dilemma of individual behaviour. How is it possible to ensure at the same time that one is bound by rules that protect one from irrational or unethical behaviour – and that these rules do not turn into prisons from which it is not possible to break out even when it would be rational to do so?[35]

III

It is clear from Habermas's theory, I believe, that rational political discussion has an *object* in terms of which it makes sense.[36] Politics is concerned with substantive decision-making, and is to that extent instrumental. True, the idea of instrumental politics

335

might also be taken in a more narrow sense, as implying that the political process is one in which individuals pursue their selfish interests, but more broadly understood it implies only that political action is primarily a means to a non-political end, only secondarily, if at all, an end in itself. In this section I shall consider theories that suggest a reversal of this priority, and that find the main point of politics in the educative or otherwise beneficial effects on the participants. And I shall try to show that this view tends to be internally incoherent, or self-defeating. The benefits of participation are by-products of political activity. Moreover, they are *essentially* by-products, in the sense that any attempt to turn them into the main purpose of such activity would make them evaporate.[37] It can indeed be highly satisfactory to engage in political work, but only on the condition that the work is defined by a serious purpose which goes beyond that of achieving this satisfaction. If that condition is not fulfilled, we get a narcissistic view of politics – corresponding to various consciousness-raising activities familiar from the last decade or so.

My concern, however, is with political theory rather than with political activism. I shall argue that certain types of arguments for political institutions and constitutions are self-defeating, since they justify the arrangement in question by effects that are essentially by-products. Here an initial and important distinction must be drawn between the task of justifying a constitution *ex ante* and that of evaluating it *ex post* and at a distance. I argue below that Tocqueville, when assessing the American democracy, praised it for consequences that are indeed by-products. In his case, this made perfectly good sense as an analytical attitude adopted after the fact and at some distance from the system he was examining. The incoherence arises when one invokes the same arguments before the fact, in public discussion. Although the constitution-makers may secretly have such side effects in mind, they cannot coherently invoke them in public.

[. . .]

Politics in this respect is on a par with other activities such as art, science, athletics or chess. To engage in them may be deeply satisfactory, if you have an independently defined goal such as 'getting it right' or 'beating the opposition'. A chess player who asserted that he played not to win but for the sheer elegance of the game, would be in narcissistic bad faith – since there is no such thing as an elegant way of losing, only elegant and inelegant ways of winning. When the artist comes to believe that the process and not the end result is his real purpose, and that defects and irregularities are valuable as reminders of the struggle of creation, he similarly forfeits any claim to our interest. The same holds for E. P. Thompson, who, when asked whether he really believed that a certain rally in Trafalgar Square would have any impact at all, answered: 'That's not really the point, is it? The point is, it shows that democracy's alive ... A rally like that gives us self-respect. Chartism was terribly good for the Chartists, although they never got the Charter.'[38] Surely, the Chartists, if asked whether they thought they would ever get the Charter, would not have answered: 'That's not really the point, is it?' It was because they believed they might get the Charter that they engaged in the struggle for it with the seriousness of purpose that also brought them self-respect as a side effect.[39]

IV

I have been discussing three views concerning the relation between economics and politics, between the market and the forum. One extreme is 'the economic theory of democracy', most outrageously stated by Schumpeter, but in essence also underlying social choice theory. It is a market theory of politics, in the sense that the act of voting is a private act similar to that of buying and selling. I cannot accept, therefore, Alan Ryan's argument that 'On any possible view of the distinction between private and public life, voting is an element in one's public life.'[40] The very distinction between the secret and the open ballot shows that there is room for a private–public distinction within politics. The economic theory of democracy, therefore, rests on the idea that the forum should be like the market, in its purpose as well as in its mode of functioning. The purpose is defined in economic terms, and the mode of functioning is that of aggregating individual decisions.

At the other extreme there is the view that the forum should be completely divorced from the market, in purpose as well as in institutional arrangement. The forum should be more than the distributive totality of individuals queuing up for the election booth. Citizenship is a quality that can only be realized in public, i.e. in a collective joined for a common purpose. This purpose, moreover, is not to facilitate life in the material sense. The political process is an end in itself, a good or even the supreme good for those who participate in it. It may be applauded because of the educative effects on the participants, but the benefits do not cease once the education has been completed. On the contrary, the education of the citizen leads to a preference for public life as an end in itself. Politics on this view is not *about* anything. It is the agonistic display of excellence,[41] or the collective display of solidarity, divorced from decision-making and the exercise of influence on events.

In between these extremes is the view I find most attractive. One can argue that the forum should differ from the market in its mode of functioning, yet be concerned with decisions that ultimately deal with economic matters. Even higher-order political decisions concern lower-level rules that are directly related to economic matters. Hence constitutional arguments about how laws can be made and changed, constantly invoke the impact of legal stability and change on economic affairs. It is the concern with substantive decisions that lends the urgency to political debates. The ever-present constraint of *time* creates a need for focus and concentration that cannot be assimilated to the leisurely style of philosophical argument in which it may be better to travel hopefully than to arrive. Yet within these constraints arguments form the core of the political process. If thus defined as public in nature, and instrumental in purpose, politics assumes what I believe to be its proper place in society.

NOTES

1 Elster (1978, Ch. 5) refers to these two varieties of market failure as *suboptimality* and *counterfinality* respectively, linking them both to collective action.
2 This is a simplification. First, as argued in Samuelson (1950), there may be political constraints that prevent one from attaining the Pareto-efficient frontier. Secondly, the very existence of several points that are Pareto-superior to the *status quo*, yet involve differential benefits to the participants, may block the realization of any of them.
3 Hammond (1976) offers a useful analysis of the consequences of selfish preferences over income distributions, showing that 'without interpersonal comparisons of some kind, any social preference ordering over the space of possible income distributions must be dictatorial'.
4 Schumpeter (1961, p. 263): 'the will of the people is the product and not the motive power of the political process'. One should not, however, conclude (as does Lively 1975, p. 38) that Schumpeter thereby abandons the market analogy, since on his view (Schumpeter 1939, p. 73) consumer preferences are no less manipulable (with some qualifications stated in Elster 1983a, Ch. 5).
5 See in particular Downs (1957).
6 For fuller statements, see Arrow (1963), Sen (1970), and Kelly (1978), as well as the contribution of Aanund Hylland to Elster and Hylland (1986).
7 Cf. d'Aspremont and Gevers (1977).
8 Riker and Ordeshook (1973, pp. 112–13).
9 Cf. the contributions of Donald Davidson and Allan Gibbard to Elster and Hylland (1986).
10 Presumably, but not obviously, since the agent might have several preference orderings and rely on higher-order preferences to determine which of the first-order preferences to express, as suggested for instance by Sen (1976).
11 Pattanaik (1978) offers a survey of the known results. The only strategy-proof mechanisms for social choice turn out to be the dictatorial one (the dictator has no incentive to misrepresent his preferences) and the randomizing one of getting the probability that a given option will be chosen equal to the proportion of voters that have it as their first choice.
12 Cf. Elster (1983b, Ch. III) for a discussion of this notion.
13 Arrow (1973).
14 Hirsch (1976).
15 Haavelmo (1970) offers a model in which everybody may suffer a loss of welfare by trying to keep up with the neighbours.
16 One may take the achievements of others as a parameter and one's own as the control variable, or conversely try to manipulate the achievements of others so that they fall short of one's own. The first of these ways of realizing positional goods is clearly less objectionable

than the second, but still less pure than the non-comparative desire for a certain standard of excellence.

17 Zeldin (1973, p. 134).
18 I rely mainly on Habermas (1982). I also thank Helge Høibraaten, Rune Slagstad, and Gunnar Skirbekk for having patiently explained to me various aspects of Habermas's work.
19 Midgaard (1980).
20 For Pascal's argument, cf. Elster (1979, Ch. II.3).
21 As suggested by Runciman and Sen (1965).
22 Janis (1972).
23 Cf. Hogarth (1977) and Lehrer (1978).
24 Niebuhr (1932, p. 11).
25 Arendt (1973, p. 174).
26 Finley (1973); see also Elster (1979, Ch. II.8).
27 Asch (1956) is a classic study.
28 See Goldman (1972) for discussion and further references.
29 Schotter (1981, pp. 26 ff., pp. 43 ff.) has a good discussion of this predicament.
30 Margalit (1983).
31 Lipsey and Lancaster (1956–7, p. 12).
32 This is the point emphasized in Lyons (1965).
33 Cf. Hansson (1970) as well as Føllesdal and Hilpinen (1971) for discussions of 'conditional obligations' within the framework of deontic logic. It does not appear, however, that the framework can easily accommodate the kind of dilemma I am concerned with here.
34 Cf. for instance Kolm (1977) concerning the dangers of a piecemeal introduction of socialism – also mentioned by Margalit (1983) as an objection to Popper's strategy for piecemeal social engineering.
35 Cf. Ainslie (1982) and Elster (1979, Ch. II.9).
36 Indeed, Habermas (1982) is largely concerned with maxims for *action*, not with the evaluation of states of affairs.
37 Cf. Elster (1983b, Ch. III) for a discussion of the notion that some psychological or social states are essentially by-products of actions undertaken for some other purpose.
38 *Sunday Times*, 2 November 1980.
39 Cf. also Barry (1978), p. 47).
40 Ryan (1972, p. 105).
41 Veyne (1976) makes a brilliant statement of this non-instrumental attitude among the elite of the Ancient World.

REFERENCES

Ainslie, G. (1982) 'A behavioral economic approach to the defense mechanisms', *Social Science Information* 21, 735–80.
Arendt, H. (1973) *On Revolution*, Harmondsworth: Pelican Books.
Arrow, K. (1963) *Social Choice and Individual Values*, New York: Wiley.
—— (1973) 'Some ordinal-utilitarian notes on Rawls's theory of justice', *Journal of Philosophy* 70, 245–63.
Asch, S. (1956) 'Studies of independence and conformity: I. A minority of one against a unanimous majority', *Psychology Monographs* 70.

Barry, B. (1978) 'Comment', in S. Benn *et al.* (eds.), *Political Participation*, Canberra: Australian National University Press, pp. 37–48.

d'Aspremont, C. and Gevers, L. (1977) 'Equity and the informational basis of collective choice', *Review of Economic Studies* 44, 199–210.

Downs, A. (1957) *An Economic Theory of Democracy*, New York: Harper.

Elster, J. (1978) *Logic and Society*, Chichester: Wiley.

—— (1979) *Ulysses and the Sirens*, Cambridge: Cambridge University Press.

—— (1983a) *Explaining Technical Change*, Cambridge: Cambridge University Press; Oslo: Universitetsforlaget.

—— (1983b) *Sour Grapes*, Cambridge: Cambridge University Press.

Elster, J. and Hylland, A. (eds.) (1986) *Foundations of Social Choice Theory*, Cambridge: Cambridge University Press.

Finley, M.I. (1973) *Democracy: Ancient and Modern*, London: Chatto and Windus.

Føllesdal, D. and Hilpinen, R. (1971) 'Deontic logic: an introduction', in R. Hilpinen (ed.), *Deontic Logic: Introductory and Systematic Readings*, Dordrecht: Reidel, pp. 1–35.

Goldman, A. (1972) 'Toward a theory of social power', *Philosophical Studies* 23, 221–68.

Goodin, R.E. (1986) 'Laundering preferences', in Elsrer and Hylland (eds, 1986), pp. 75–101.

Haavelmo, T. (1970) 'Some observations on welfare and economic growth', in W.A. Eltis, M. Scott and N. Wolfe (eds.), *Induction, Growth and Trade: Essays in Honour of Sir Roy Harrod*, Oxford: Oxford University Press, pp. 65–75.

Habermas, J. (1982) Diskursethik – notizen zu einem Begründingsprogram. Mimeographed.

Hammond, P. (1976) 'Why ethical measures need interpersonal comparisons', *Theory and Decision* 7, 263–74.

Hansson, B. (1970) 'An analysis of some deontic logics', *Nous* 3, 373–98.

Hirsch, F. (1976) *Social Limits to Growth*, Cambridge, Mass.: Harvard University Press.

Hogarth, R.M. (1977) 'Methods for aggregating opinions', in H. Jungermann and G. de Zeeuw (eds.), *Decision Making and Change in Human Affairs*, Dordrecht: Reidel, pp. 231–56.

Janis, I. (1972) *Victims of Group-Think*, Boston: Houghton Mifflin.

Kelly, J. (1978) *Arrow Impossibility Theorems*, New York: Academic Press.

Kolm, S.-C. (1977) *La transition socialiste*, Paris: Editions du Cerf.

Lehrer, K. (1978) 'Consensus and comparison. A theory of social rationality', in C.A. Hooker, J.J. Leach and E.F. McClennen (eds.), *Foundations and Applications of Decision Theory*. Vol. 1: *Theoretical Foundations*, Dordrecht: Reidel, pp. 283–310.

Lipsey, R.G. and Lancaster, K. (1956–7) 'The general theory of the second-best', *Review of Economic Studies* 24, 11–32.

Lively, J. (1975) *Democracy*. Oxford: Blackwell.

Lyons, D. (1965) *Forms and Limits of Utilitarianism*, Oxford: Oxford University Press.

Margalit, A. (1983) 'Ideals and second bests', in S. Fox (ed.), *Philosophy for Education*, Jerusalem: Van Leer Foundation, pp. 77–90.

Midgaard, K. (1980) 'On the significance of language and a richer concept of rationality', in L. Lewin and E. Vedung (eds.), *Politics as Rational Action*, Dordrecht: Reidel, pp. 83–97.

Niebuhr, R. (1932) *Moral Man and Immoral Society*, New York: Scribner's.

Pattanaik, P. (1978) *Strategy and Group Choice*, Amsterdam: North-Holland.

Riker, W. and Ordeshook, P.C. (1973) *An Introduction to Positive Political Theory*, Englewood Cliffs, N.J.: Prentice Hall.

Runciman, W.G. and Sen, A. (1965) 'Games, justice and the general will', *Mind* 74, 554–62.

Ryan, A. (1972) 'Two concepts of politics and democracy: James and John Stuart Mill', in M. Fleisher (ed.), *Machiavelli and the Nature of Political Thought*, London: Croom Helm, pp. 76–113.

Samuelson, P. (1950) 'The evaluation of real national income', *Oxford Economic Papers* 2, 1–29.

Schotter, A. (1981) *The Economic Theory of Social Institutions*, Cambridge: Cambridge University Press.

Schumpeter, J. (1939) *Business Cycles*, New York: McGraw-Hill.

—— (1961) *Capitalism, Socialism and Democracy*, London: Allen and Unwin.

Sen, A.K. (1970) *Collective Choice and Social Welfare*, San Francisco: Holden-Day.

—— (1976) 'Liberty, unanimity and rights', *Economica* 43, 217–45.

Veyne, P. (1976) *Le pain et le cirque*, Paris: Seuil.

Zeldin, T. (1973) *France 1848–1945*, Vol. 1. Oxford: Oxford University Press.

21

DELIBERATION AND DEMOCRATIC LEGITIMACY

Joshua Cohen

In this essay I explore the ideal of a 'deliberative democracy'.[1] By a deliberative democracy I shall mean, roughly, an association whose affairs are governed by the public deliberation of its members. I propose an account of the value of such an association that treats democracy itself as a fundamental political ideal and not simply as a derivative ideal that can be explained in terms of the values of fairness or equality of respect.

The essay is in three sections. In section I, I focus on Rawls's discussion of democracy and use that discussion both to introduce certain features of the deliberative democracy, and to raise some doubts about whether their importance is naturally explained in terms of the notion of a fair system of social cooperation. In section II, I develop an account of deliberative democracy in terms of the notion of an *ideal deliberative procedure*. The characterization of that procedure provides an abstract model of deliberation which links the intuitive ideal of democratic association to a more substantive view of deliberative democracy. Three features of the ideal deliberative procedure figure prominently in the essay. First, it helps to account for some familiar judgements about collective decision-making, in particular about the ways that collective decision-making ought to be different from bargaining, contracting and other market-type interactions, both in its explicit attention to considerations of the common advantage and in the ways that that attention helps to form the aims of the participants. Second, it accounts for the common view that the notion of democratic association is tied to notions of autonomy and the common good. Third, the ideal deliberative procedure provides a distinctive structure for addressing institutional questions. And in section III of the paper I rely on that distinctive structure in responding to four objections to the account of deliberative democracy.

I

The ideal of deliberative democracy is a familiar ideal. Aspects of it have been high-lighted in recent discussion of the role of republican conceptions of self-government in shaping the American constitutional tradition and contemporary public law.[2] It is represented as well in radical democratic and socialist criticisms of the politics of advanced industrial societies.[3] And some of its central features are highlighted in Rawls's account of democratic politics in a just society, particularly in those parts of his account that seek to incorporate the 'liberty of the ancients' and to respond to radical democrats and socialists who argue that 'the basic liberties may prove to be merely formal'. In the discussion that follows I shall first say something about Rawls's remarks on three such features, and then consider his explanation of them.[4]

First, in a well-ordered democracy, political debate is organized around alternative conceptions of the public good. So an ideal pluralist scheme, in which democratic politics consists of fair bargaining among groups each of which pursues its particular or sectional interest, is unsuited to a just society (Rawls 1971, pp. 360–1).[5] Citizens and parties operating in the political arena ought not to 'take a narrow or group-interested standpoint' (p. 360). And parties should only be responsive to demands that are 'argued for openly by reference to a conception of the public good' (pp. 226, 472). Public explanations and justifications of laws and policies are to be cast in terms of conceptions of the common good (conceptions that, on Rawls's view, must be consistent with the two principles of justice), and public deliberation should aim to work out the details of such conceptions and to apply them to particular issues of public policy (p. 362).

Second, the ideal of democratic order has egalitarian implications that must be satis-fied in ways that are manifest to citizens. The reason is that in a just society political opportunities and powers must be independent of economic or social position – the political liberties must have a fair value[6] – and the fact that they are independent must be more or less evident to citizens. Ensuring this manifestly fair value might, for example, require public funding of political parties and restrictions on private polit-ical spending, as well as progressive tax measures that serve to limit inequalities of wealth and to ensure that the political agenda is not controlled by the interests of economically and socially dominant groups (Rawls 1971, pp. 225–6, 277–8; 1982, pp. 42–3). In principle, these distributional requirements might be more stringently egali-tarian than those fixed by the difference principle (1982, p. 43).[7] This is so in part because the main point of these measures is not simply to ensure that democratic poli-tics proceeds under fair conditions, nor only to encourage just legislation, but also to ensure that the equality of citizens is manifest and to declare a commitment to that equality 'as the public intention' (1971, p. 233).

Third, democratic politics should be ordered in ways that provide a basis for self-respect, that encourage the development of a sense of political competence, and that contribute to the formation of a sense of justice;[8] it should fix 'the foundations for civic friendship and [shape] the ethos of political culture' (Rawls 1971, p. 234). Thus the importance of democratic order is not confined to its role in obstructing the class legislation that can be expected from systems in which groups are effectively excluded from the channels of political representation and bargaining. In addition, democratic politics should also shape the ways which the members of the society understand themselves and their own legitimate interests.

When properly conducted, then, democratic politics involves *public deliberation focused on the common good*, requires some form of *manifest equality* among citizens, and *shapes the identity and interests* of citizens in ways that contribute to the formation of a public conception of common good. How does the ideal of a fair system of social co-operation provide a way to account for the attractiveness and importance of these three features of the deliberative democratic ideal? Rawls suggests a formal and an informal line of argument. The formal argument is that parties in the original position would choose the principle of participation[9] with the proviso that the political liberties have their fair value. The three conditions are important because they must be satisfied if constitutional arrangements are to ensure participation rights, guarantee a fair value to those rights, and plausibly produce legislation that encourages a fair distribution according to the difference principle.

Rawls also suggests an informal argument for the ordering of political institutions, and I shall focus on this informal argument here:

> Justice as fairness begins with the idea that where common principles are necessary and to everyone's advantage, they are to be worked out from the viewpoint of a suitably defined initial situation of equality in which each person is fairly represented. The principle of participation transfers this notion from the original position to the constitution . . . [thus] preserv[ing] the equal representation of the original position to the degree that this is feasible.
>
> (Rawls 1971, pp. 221–2)[10]

Or, as he puts it elsewhere: 'The idea [of the fair value of political liberty] is to incorporate into the basic structure of society an effective political procedure which *mirrors* in that structure the fair representation of persons achieved by the original position' (1982, p. 45; emphasis added). The suggestion is that, since we accept the intuitive ideal of a fair system of co-operation, we should want our political institutions themselves to conform, in so far as it is feasible, to the requirement that terms of association be worked out under fair conditions. And so we arrive directly at the requirement of equal liberties with fair value, rather than arriving at it indirectly, through a hypothetical choice of that requirement under fair conditions. In this informal argument, the original position serves as an *abstract model* of what fair conditions are, and of what we should strive to mirror in our political institutions, rather than as an initial-choice situation in which regulative principles for those institutions are selected.

I think that Rawls is right in wanting to accommodate the three conditions. What I find less plausible is that the three conditions are natural sequences of the ideal of fairness. Taking the notion of fairness as fundamental, and aiming (as in the informal argument) to model political arrangements on the original position, it is not clear why, for example, political debate ought to be focused on the common good, or why the manifest equality of citizens is an important feature of a democratic association. The pluralist conception of democratic politics as a system of bargaining with fair representation for all groups seems an equally good mirror of the ideal of fairness.

The response to this objection is clear enough: the connection between the ideal of fairness and the three features of democratic politics depends on psychological and sociological assumptions. Those features do not follow directly from the ideal of a fair system of co-operation, or from that ideal as it is modelled in the original position. Rather, we arrive at them when we consider what is required to preserve fair arrangements and to achieve fair outcomes. For example, public political debate should be conducted in terms of considerations of the common good because we cannot expect outcomes that advance the common good unless people are looking for them. Even an ideal pluralist scheme, with equal bargaining power and no barriers to entry, cannot reasonably be expected to advance the common good as defined by the difference principle (1971, p. 360).

But this is, I think, too indirect and instrumental an argument for the three conditions. Like utilitarian defences of liberty, it rests on a series of highly speculative sociological and psychological judgements. I want to suggest that the reason why the three are attractive is not that an order with, for example, no explicit deliberation about the common good and no manifest equality would be unfair (though of course it might be). Instead it is that they comprise elements of an independent and expressly political ideal that is focused in the first instance[11] on the appropriate conduct of public affairs – on, that is, the appropriate ways of arriving at collective decisions. And to understand that ideal we ought not to proceed by seeking to 'mirror' ideal fairness in the fairness of political arrangements, but instead to proceed by seeking to mirror a system of ideal deliberation in social and political institutions. I want now to turn to this alternative.

II[12]

The notion of a deliberative democracy is rooted in the intuitive ideal of a democratic association in which the justification of the terms and conditions of association proceeds through public argument and reasoning among equal citizens. Citizens in such an order share a commitment to the resolution of problems of collective choice through public reasoning, and regard their basic institutions as legitimate in so far as they establish the framework for free public deliberation. To elaborate this ideal, I begin with a more explicit account of the ideal itself, presenting what I shall call the 'formal conception' of deliberative democracy. Proceeding from this formal conception, I pursue a more substantive account of deliberative democracy by presenting an account of an *ideal deliberative procedure* that captures the notion of justification through public argument and reasoning among equal citizens, and serves in turn as a model for deliberative institutions.

The formal conception of a deliberative democracy has five main features:

D1 A deliberative democracy is an ongoing and independent association, whose members expect it to continue into the indefinite future.

D2 The members of the association share (and it is common knowledge that they share) the view that the appropriate terms of association provide a framework for or are the results of their deliberation. They share, that is, a commitment to coordinating their activities within institutions that make deliberation possible and according to norms that they arrive at through their deliberation. For them, free deliberation among equals is the basis of legitimacy.

D3 A deliberative democracy is a pluralistic association. The members have diverse preferences, convictions and ideals concerning the conduct of their own lives. While sharing a commitment to the deliberative resolution of problems of collective choice (D2), they also have divergent aims, and do not think that some particular set of preferences, convictions or ideals is mandatory.

D4 Because the members of a democratic association regard deliberative procedures as the source of *legitimacy*, it is important to them that the terms of their association not merely be the results of their deliberation, but also be *manifest* to them as such.[13] They prefer institutions in which the connections between deliberation and outcomes are evident to ones in which the connections are less clear.

D5 The members recognize one another as having deliberative capacities, i.e. the capacities required for entering into a public exchange of reasons and for acting on the result of such public reasoning.

A theory of deliberative democracy aims to give substance to this formal ideal by characterizing the conditions that should obtain if the social order is to be manifestly regulated by deliberative forms of collective choice. I propose to sketch a view of this sort by considering an ideal scheme of deliberation, which I shall call the 'ideal deliberative procedure'. The aim in sketching this procedure is to give an explicit statement of the conditions for deliberative decision-making that are suited to the formal conception, and thereby to highlight the properties that democratic institutions should embody, so far as possible. I should emphasize that the ideal deliberative procedure is meant to provide a model for institutions to mirror – in the first instance for the institutions in which collective choices are made and social outcomes publicly justified – and not to characterize an initial situation in which the terms of association themselves are chosen.[14]

Turning them to the ideal procedure, there are three general aspects of deliberation. There is a need to decide on an agenda, to propose alternative solutions to the problems on the agenda, supporting those solutions with reasons, and to conclude by settling on an alternative. A democratic conception can be represented in terms of the requirements that it sets on such a procedure. In particular, outcomes are democratically legitimate if and only if they could be the object of a free and reasoned agreement among equals. The ideal deliberative procedure is a procedure that captures this principle.[15]

I1 Ideal deliberation is *free* in that it satisfies two conditions. First, the participants regard themselves as bound only by results of their deliberation and by the preconditions for that deliberation. Their consideration of proposals is not constrained by the authority of prior norms or requirements. Second, the participants suppose that they can act from the results, taking the fact that a certain decision is arrived at through their deliberation as a sufficient reason for complying with it.

I2 Deliberation is *reasoned* in that the parties to it are required to state their reasons for advancing proposals, supporting them or criticizing them. They give reasons with the expectation that those reasons (and not, for example, their power) will settle the fate of their proposal. In ideal deliberation, as Habermas puts it, 'no force except that of the better argument is exercised' (1975, p. 108). Reasons are offered with the aim of bringing others to accept the proposal, given their disparate ends (D3) and their commitment (D2) to settling the conditions of their association through free deliberation among equals. Proposals may be rejected because they are not defended with acceptable, reasons, even they could be so defended. The deliberative conception emphasizes that collective choices should be *made in a deliberative way*, and not only that those choices should have a desirable fit with the preferences of citizens.

I3 In ideal deliberation parties are both formally and substantively *equal*. They are formally equal in that the rules regulating the procedure do not single out individuals. Everyone with the deliberative capacities has equal standing at each stage of the deliberative process. Each can put issues on the agenda, propose solutions, and offer reasons in support of or in criticism of proposals. And each has an equal voice to the decision. The participants are substantively equal in that the existing distribution of power and resources does not shape their chances to contribute to deliberation, nor does that distribution play an authoritative role in their deliberation. The participants in the deliberative procedure do not regard themselves as

347

bound by the existing system of rights, except in so far as that system establishes the framework of free deliberation among equals. Instead they regard that system as a potential object of their deliberative judgement.

I4 Finally, ideal deliberation aims to arrive at a rationally motivated *consensus* – to find reasons that are persuasive to all who are committed to acting on the results of a free and reasoned assessment of alternatives by equals. Even under ideal conditions there is no promise that consensual reasons will be forthcoming. If they are not, then deliberation concludes with voting, subject to some form of majority rule.[16] The fact that it may so conclude does not, however, eliminate the distinction between deliberative forms of collective choice and forms that aggregate non-deliberative preferences. The institutional consequences are likely to be different in the two cases, and the results of voting among those who are committed to finding reasons that are persuasive to all are like to differ from the results of an aggregation that proceeds in the absence of this commitment.

Drawing on this characterization of ideal deliberation, can we say anything more substantive about a deliberative democracy? What are the implications of a commitment to deliberative decisions for the terms of social association? In the remarks that follow I shall indicate the ways that this commitment carries with it a commitment to advance the common good and to respect individual autonomy.

Common good and autonomy

Consider first the notion of the common good. Since the aim of ideal deliberation is to secure agreement among all who are committed to free deliberation among equals, and the condition of pluralism obtains (D3), the focus of deliberation is on ways of advancing the aims of each party to it. While no one is indifferent to his/her own good, everyone also seeks to arrive at decisions that are acceptable to all who share the commitment to deliberation (D2). (As we shall see just below, taking that commitment seriously is likely to require a willingness to revise one's understanding of one's own preferences and convictions.) Thus the characterization of an ideal deliberative procedure links the formal notion of deliberative democracy with the more substantive ideal of a democratic association in which public debate is focused on the common good of the members.

Of course, talk about the common good is one thing: sincere efforts to advance it are another. While public deliberation may be organized around appeals to the common good, is there any reason to think that even ideal deliberation would not consist in efforts to disguise personal or class advantage as the common advantage? There are two responses to this question. The first is that in my account of the formal idea of a deliberative democracy, I stipulated (D2) that the members of the association are committed to resolving their differences through deliberation, and thus to providing reasons that they sincerely expect to be persuasive to others who share that commitment. In short, this stipulation rules out the problem. Presumably, however, the objection is best understood as directed against the plausibility of realizing a deliberative procedure that conforms to the ideal, and thus is not answerable through stipulation.

The second response, then, rests on a claim about the effects of deliberation on the motivations of deliberators.[17] A consequence of the reasonableness of the deliberative procedure (I2) together with the condition of pluralism (D3) is that the mere fact of having a preference, conviction or ideal does not by itself provide a reason in support of a proposal. While I may take my preferences as a sufficient reason for advancing a proposal, deliberation under conditions of pluralism requires that I find reasons that make the proposal acceptable to others who cannot be expected to regard my preferences as sufficient reasons for agreeing. The motivational thesis is that the need to advance reasons that persuade others will help to shape the motivations that people bring to the deliberative procedure in two ways. First, the practice of presenting reasons will contribute to the formation of a commitment to the deliberative resolution of political questions (D2). Given that commitment, the likelihood of a sincere representation of preferences and convictions should increase, while the likelihood of their strategic misrepresentation declines. Second, it will shape the content of preferences and convictions as well. Assuming a commitment to deliberative justification, the discovery that I can offer no persuasive reasons on behalf of a proposal of mine may transform the preferences that motivate the proposal. Aims that I recognize to be inconsistent with the requirements of deliberative agreement may tend to lose their force, at least when I expect others to be proceeding in reasonable ways and expect the outcome of deliberation to regulate subsequent action.

Consider, for example, the desire to be wealthier come what may. I cannot appeal to this desire itself in defending policies. The motivational claim is the need to find an independent justification that does not appeal to this desire and will tend to shape it into, for example, a desire to have a level of wealth that is consistent with a level that others (i.e. equal citizens) find acceptable. I am of course assuming that the deliberation is known to be regulative, and that the wealth cannot be protected through wholly non-deliberative means.

Deliberation, then, focuses debate on the common good. And the relevant conceptions of the common good are not comprised simply of interests and preferences that are antecedent to deliberation. Instead, the interests, aims and ideals that comprise the common good are those that survive deliberation, interests that, on public reflection, we think it legitimate to appeal to in making claims on social resources. Thus the first and third of the features of deliberative democracy that I mentioned in the discussion of Rawls [. . .] comprise central elements in the deliberative conception.

The ideal deliberative scheme also indicates the importance of autonomy in a deliberative democracy. In particular, it is responsive to two main threats to autonomy. As a general matter, actions fail to be autonomous if the preferences on which an agent acts are, roughly, given by the circumstances, and not determined by the agent. There are two paradigm cases of 'external' determination. The first is what Elster (1982) has called 'adaptive preferences'.[18] These are preferences that shift with changes in the circumstances of the agent without any deliberate contribution by the agent to that shift. This is true, for example, of the political preferences of instinctive centrists who move to the median position in the political distribution, wherever it happens to be. The second I shall call 'accommodationist preferences'. While they are deliberately formed, accommodationist preferences represent psychological adjustments to conditions of subordination in which individuals are not recognized as having the capacity for self-government. Consider Stoic slaves, who deliberately shape their desires to match their powers, with a view to minimizing frustration. Since the existing relations of power make slavery the only possibility, they cultivate desires to be slaves, and then act on those desires. While their motives are deliberately formed, and they act on their desires, the Stoic slaves do not act autonomously when they seek to be good slaves. The absence of alternatives and consequent denial of scope for the deliberative capacities that defines the condition of slaves supports the conclusion that their desires result from their circumstances, even though those circumstances shape the desires of the Stoic slaves through their deliberation.

There are then at least two dimensions of autonomy. The phenomenon of adaptive preferences underlines the importance of conditions that permit and encourage the deliberative formation of preferences: the phenomenon of accommodationist preferences indicates the need for favourable conditions for the exercise of the deliberative capacities. Both concerns are met when institutions for collective decision-making are modelled on the ideal deliberative procedure. Relations of power and subordination are neutralized (I1, I3, I4), and each is recognized as having the deliberative capacities (D5), thus addressing the problem of accommodationist preferences. Further, the requirement of reasonableness discourages adaptive preferences (I2). While preferences are 'formed' by the deliberative procedure, this type of preference formation is consistent with autonomy, since preferences that are shaped by public deliberation are not simply given by external circumstances. Instead they are the result of 'the power of reason as applied through public discussion'.[19]

Beginning, then, from the formal ideal of a deliberative democracy, we arrive at the more substantive ideal of an association that is regulated by deliberation aimed at the common good and that respects the autonomy of the members. And seeking to embody the ideal deliberative procedure in institutions, we seek *inter alia*, to design institutions that focus political debate on the common good, that shape the identity and interests of citizens in ways that contribute to an attachment to the common good, and that provide favourable conditions for the exercise of deliberative powers that are required for autonomy.

III

I want now to shift the focus. While I shall continue to pursue the relationship between the ideal deliberative procedure and more substantive issues about deliberative democratic association, I want to do so by considering four natural objections to the conception I have been discussing, objections to that conception for being sectarian, incoherent, unjust and irrelevant. My aim is not to provide a detailed response to the objections, but to clarify the conception of deliberative democracy by sketching the lines alone which a response should proceed. Before turning to the objections, I enter two remarks about what follows.

First, as I indicated earlier, a central aim in the deliberative conception is to specify the institutional preconditions for deliberative decision-making. The role of the ideal deliberative procedure is to provide an abstract characterization of the important properties of deliberative institutions. The role of the ideal deliberative procedure is thus different from the role of an ideal social contract. The ideal deliberative procedure provides a model for institutions, a model that they should mirror, so far as possible. It is not a choice situation in which institutional principles are selected. The key point about the institutional reflection is that it should *make deliberation possible*. Institutions in a deliberative democracy do not serve simply to implement the results of deliberation, as though free deliberation could proceed in the absence of appropriate institutions. Neither the commitment to nor the capacity for arriving at deliberative decisions is something that we can simply assume to obtain independent from the proper ordering of institutions. The institutions themselves must provide the framework for the formation of the will; they determine whether there is equality, whether deliberation is free and reasoned, whether there is autonomy, and so on.

Second, I shall be focusing here on some requirements on 'public' institutions that reflect the ideal of deliberative resolution. But there is of course no reason to expect as a general matter that the preconditions for deliberation will respect familiar institutional boundaries between 'private' and 'public' and will all pertain to the public arena. For example, inequalities of wealth, or the absence of institutional measures designed to redress the consequences of those inequalities, can serve to undermine the equality required in deliberative arenas themselves. And so a more complete treatment would need to address a wider range of institutional issues (see Cohen and Rogers 1983, chs 3, 6; Cohen 1988).

Sectarianism

The first objection is that the ideal of deliberative democracy is objectionably sectarian because it depends on a particular view of the good life – an ideal of active citizenship. What makes it sectarian is not the specific ideal on which it depends, but the (alleged) fact that it depends on some specific conception at all. I do not think that the conception of deliberative democracy suffers from the alleged difficulty. In explaining why not, I shall put to the side current controversy about the thesis that sectarianism is avoidable and objectionable, and assume that it is both.[20]

Views of the good figure in political conceptions in at least two ways. First, the *justification* of some conceptions appeals to a notion of the human good. Aristotelian views, for example, endorse the claim that the exercise of the deliberative capacities is a fundamental component of a good human life, and conclude that a political association ought to be organized to encourage the realization of those capacities by its members. A second way in which conceptions of the good enter is that the *stability* of a society may require widespread allegiance to a specific conception of the good, even though its institutions can be justified without appeal to that conception. For example, a social order that can be justified without reference to ideals of national allegiance may none the less require widespread endorsement of the ideal of patriotic devotion for its stability.

A political conception is objectionably sectarian only if its *justification* depends on a particular view of the human good, and not simply because its stability is contingent on widespread agreement on the value of certain activities and aspirations. For this reason the democratic conception is not sectarian. It is organized around a view of political justification – that justification proceeds through free deliberation among equal citizens – and not a conception of the proper conduct of life. So, while it is plausible that the stability of a deliberative democracy depends on encouraging the ideal of active citizenship, this dependence does not suffice to show that it is objectionably sectarian.

Incoherence

Consider next the putative incoherence of the ideal. We find this charge in an important tradition of argument, including Schumpeter's *Capitalism, Socialism, and Democracy* and, more recently, William Riker's work on social choice and democracy. I want here to say a word about the latter, focusing on just one reason that Riker gives for thinking that the ideal of popular self-government is incoherent.[21]

Institutionalizing a deliberative procedure requires a decision rule short of consensus – for example, majority rule. But majority rule is globally unstable: as a general matter, there exists a majority-rule path leading from any element in the set of alternatives to any other element in the set. The majority, standing in for the people, wills everything and therefore wills nothing. Of course, while anything can be the result of majority decision, it is not true that everything will be the result. But, because majority rule is so unstable, the actual decision of the majority will not be determined by preferences themselves, since they do not constrain the outcome. Instead decisions will reflect the particular institutional constraints under which they are made. But these constraints are 'exogenous to the world of tastes and values' (Riker 1982, p. 190). So the ideal of popular self-government is incoherent because we are, so to speak, governed by the institutions, and not by ourselves.

I want to suggest one difficulty with this argument that highlights the structure of the deliberative conception. According to the argument I just sketched, outcomes in majority-rule institutions reflect 'exogenous' institutional constraints, and not underlying preferences. This suggests that we can identify the preferences and convictions that are relevant to collective choices apart from the institutions through which they are formed and expressed. But that is just what the deliberative conception denies. On this conception, the relevant preferences and convictions are those that could be expressed in free deliberation, and not those that are prior to it. For this reason, popular self-government *premises* the existence of institutions that provide a framework for deliberation; these arrangements are not 'exogenous constraints' on the aggregation of preferences, but instead help to shape their content and the way that citizens choose to advance them. And, once the deliberative institutions are in place, and preferences, convictions and political actions are shaped by them, it is not clear that instability problems remain so severe as to support the conclusion that self-government is and empty an incoherent ideal.

Injustice

The third problem concerns injustice. I have been treating the ideal of democracy as the basic ideal for a political conception. But it might be argued that the ideal of democracy is not suited to the role of fundamental political ideal because its treatment of basic liberties is manifestly unacceptable. It makes those liberties dependent on judgements of majorities and thus endorses the democratic legitimacy of decisions that restrict the basic liberties of individuals. In responding to this objection I shall focus on the liberty of expression,[22] and shall begin by filling out a version of the objection which I put in the words of an imagined critic.[23]

'You embrace the ideal of a democratic order. The aim of a democratic order is to maximize the *power of the people* to secure its wants. To defend the liberty of expression you will argue that that power is diminished if the people lack the information required for exercising their will. Since expression provides information, you will conclude that abridgements of expression to be barred. The problem with your argument is that preventing restrictions on expression also restricts the power of the people, since the citizens may collectively prefer such restrictions. And so it is not at all clear as a general matter that the protection of expression will maximize popular power. So while you will, of course, not want to prevent everyone from speaking all the time, you cannot defend the claim that there is even a presumption in favour of the protection of expression. And this disregard for fundamental as is unacceptable.'

This objection has force against some conceptions on which democracy is a fundamental ideal, particularly those in which the value of expression turns exclusively on its role as a source of information about how best to advance popular ends. But it does not have any force against the deliberative conception, since the latter does not make the case for expression turn on its role in maximizing the power of the people to secure its wants. That case rests instead on a conception of collective choice, in particular on a view about how the 'wants' that are relevant to collective choice are formed and defined in the first place. The relevant preferences and convictions are those that arise from or are confirmed through deliberation. And a framework of free expression is required for the reasoned consideration of alternatives that comprises deliberation. The deliberative conception holds that free expression is required for *determining* what advances the common good, because what is good is fixed by public deliberation, and not prior to it. It is fixed by informed and autonomous judgements, involving the exercise of the deliberative capacities. So the ideal of deliberative democracy is not hostile to free expression; it rather presupposes such freedom.

But what about expression with no direct bearing on issues of public policy? Is the conception of deliberative democracy committed to treating all 'non-political expression' as second-class, and as meriting lesser protection? I do not think so. The deliberative conception construes politics as aiming in part at the formation of preferences and convictions, not just at their articulation and aggregation. Because of this emphasis on reasoning about preferences and convictions, and the bearing of expression with no political focus on such reasoning, the deliberative view draws no bright line between political speech and other sorts of expression. Forms of expression that do not address issues of policy may well bear on the formation of the interests, aims, and ideals that citizens bring to public deliberation. For this reason the deliberative conception supports protection for the full range of expression, regardless of the content of that expression.[24] It would violate the core of the ideal of free deliberation among equals to fix preferences and convictions in advance by restricting the content of expression, or by barring access to expression, or by preventing the expression that is essential to having convictions at all. Thus the injustice objection fails because the liberties are not simply among the topics for deliberation; they help to comprise the framework that makes it possible.[25]

Irrelevance

The irrelevance objection is that the notion of public deliberation is irrelevant to modern political conditions.[26] This is the most important objection, but also the one about which it is hardest to say anything at the level of generality required by the present context. Here again I shall confine myself to one version of the objection, though one that I take to be representative.

The version that I want to consider starts from the assumption that a direct democracy with citizens gathering in legislative assemblies is the only way to institutionalize a deliberative procedure. Premising that, and recognizing that direct democracy is impossible under modern conditions, the objection concludes that we ought to be led to reject the ideal because it is not relevant to our circumstances.

The claim about the impossibility of direct democracy is plainly correct. But I see no merit in the claim that direct democracy is the uniquely suitable way to institutionalize the ideal procedure.[27] In fact, in the absence of a theory about the operations of democratic assemblies – a theory which cannot simply stipulate that ideal conditions obtain – there is no reason to be confident that a direct democracy would subject political questions to deliberative resolution, even if a direct democracy were a genuine institutional possibility.[28] In the absence of a realistic account of the functioning of citizen assemblies, we cannot simply assume that large gatherings with open-ended agendas will yield any deliberation at all, or that they will encourage participants to regard one another as equals in a free deliberative procedure. The appropriate ordering of deliberative institutions depends on issues of political psychology and political behaviour; it is not an immediate consequence of the deliberative ideal. So, far from being the only deliberative scheme, direct democracy may not even be a particularly good arrangement for deliberation. But, once we reject the idea that a direct democracy is the natural or necessary form of expression of the deliberative ideal, the straightforward argument for irrelevance no longer works. In saying how the ideal might be relevant, however, we come up against the problem I mentioned earlier. Lacking a good understanding of the workings of institutions, we are inevitably thrown back on more or less speculative judgements. What follows is some sketchy remarks on one issue that should be taken in this spirit.

At the heart of the institutionalization of the deliberative procedure is the existence of arenas in which citizens can propose issues for the political agenda and participate in debate about those issues. The existence of such arenas is a public good, and ought to be supported with public money. This is not because public support is the only way, or even the most efficient way, of ensuring the provision of such arenas. Instead, public provision expresses the basic commitment of a democratic order to the resolution of political questions through free deliberation among equals. The problem is to figure out how arenas might be organized to encourage such deliberation.

In considering that organization, there are two key points that I want to underscore. The first is that material inequalities are an important source of political inequalities. The second point – which is more speculative – is that deliberative arenas which are organized exclusively on local, sectional or issue-specific lines are unlikely to produce the open-ended deliberation required to institutionalize a deliberative procedure. Since these arenas bring together only a narrow range of interests, deliberation in them can be expected at best to produce coherent sectional interests, but no more comprehensive conception of the common good.

These two considerations together provide support for the view that political parties supported by public funds play an important role in making a deliberative democracy possible.[29] There are two reasons for this, corresponding to the two considerations I have just mentioned. In the first place, an important feature of organizations generally, and parties in particular, is that they provide a means through which individuals and groups who lack the 'natural' advantage of wealth can overcome the political disadvantages that follow on that lack. Thus they can help to overcome the inequalities in deliberative arenas that result from material inequality. Of course, to play this role, political organizations must themselves be freed from the dominance of private resources, and that independence must be manifest. Thus the need for public funding. Here we arrive back at the second point that I mentioned in the discussion of Rawls's view – that measures are needed to ensure manifest equality – though now as a way of displaying a shared commitment to deliberative decisions, and not simply as an expression of the commitment to fairness. Second, because parties are required to address a comprehensive range of political issues, they provide arenas in which debate is not restricted in the ways that it is in local, sectional or issue-specific organizations. They can provide the more open-ended arenas needed to form and articulate the conceptions of the common good that provide the focus of political debate in a deliberative democracy.

There is certainly no guarantee that parties will operate as I have just described. But this is not especially troubling, since there are no guarantees of anything in politics. The question is how we can best approximate the deliberative conception. And it is difficult to see how that is possible in the absence of strong parties, supported with public resources (though, of course, a wide range of other conditions are required as well).

IV

I have suggested that we take the notion of democratic association as a fundamental political ideal, and have elaborated that ideal by reference to an ideal deliberative procedure and the requirements for institutionalizing such a procedure. I have sketched a few of those requirements here. To show that the democratic ideal can play the role of fundamental organizing ideal, I should need to pursue the account of fundamental liberties and political organization in much greater detail and to address a wide range of other issues as well. Of course, the richer the requirements are for institutionalizing free public deliberation, the larger the range of issues that may need to be removed from the political agenda; that is, the larger the range of issues that form the background framework of public deliberation rather than its subject matter. And, the larger that range, the less there is to deliberate about. Whether that is good news or bad news, it is in any case a suitable place to conclude.

NOTES

I have had countless discussions of the subject matter of this paper with Joel Rogers, and wish to thank him for his unfailingly sound and generous advice. For our joint treatment of the issues that I discuss here, see Cohen and Rogers (1983), ch. 6. The main differences between the treatment of issues here and the treatment in the book lies in the explicit account of the ideal deliberative procedure, the fuller treatment of the notions of autonomy and the common good, and the account of the connection of those notions with the ideal procedure. An earlier draft of this paper was presented to the Pacific Division Meetings of the American Philosophical Association. I would like to thank Loren Lomasky, Alan Hamlin and Philip Pettit for helpful comments on that draft.

1 I originally came across the term 'deliberative democracy' in Sunstein (1985). He cites (n. 26) an article by Bessette, which I have not consulted.

2 For some representative examples, see Sunstein (1984, 1985, 1986), Michelman (1986). Ackerman (1984, 1986).

3 I have in mind, in particular, criticisms which focus on the ways in which material inequalities and weak political parties restrict democracy by constraining public political debate or undermining the equality of the participants in that debate. For discussion of these criticisms, and of their connections with the ideal of democratic order, see Cohen and Rogers (1983), chs 3, 6; Unger (1987), ch. 5.

4 In the discussion that follows, I draw on Rawls (1971, esp. sections 36, 37, 43, 54; 1982).

5 This rejection is not particularly idiosyncratic. Sunstein, for example, argues (1984, 1985) that ideal pluralism has never been embraced as a political ideal in American public law.

6 Officially, the requirement of fair value is that 'everyone has a fair opportunity to hold public office and to influence the outcome of political decisions' (Rawls 1982, p. 42).

7 Whatever their stringency, these distributional requirements take priority over the difference principle, since the requirement of fair value is part of the principle of liberty; that is, the first principle of justice (Rawls 1982, pp. 41–2).

8 The importance of democratic politics in the account of the acquisition of the sense of justice is underscored in Rawls (1971), pp. 473–4.

9 The principle of participation states that 'all citizens are to have an equal right to take part in, and to determine the outcome of, the constitutional process that establishes the laws with which they are to comply' (Rawls 1971, p. 221).

10 I assume that the principle of participation should be understood here to include the requirement of the fair value of political liberty.

11 The reasons for the phrase 'in the first instance' are clarified below.

12 Since writing the first draft of this section of the paper, I have read Elster (1986) and Mania (1987), which both present parallel conceptions. This is especially so with Elster's treatment of the psychology of public deliberation (pp. 112–13). I am indebted to Alan Hamlin for bringing the Elster article to my attention. The overlap is explained by the fact that Elster, Manin and I all draw on Habermas. See Habermas (1975, 1979, 1984). I have also found the discussion of the contractualist account of motivation in Scanlon (1982) very helpful.

13 For philosophical discussions of the importance of manifestness or publicity, see Kant (1983), pp. 135–9; Rawls (1971), p. 133 and section 29; Williams (1985), pp. 101–2, 200.

14 The distinction between the ideal procedure and an initial-choice situation will be important in the later discussion of motivation formation and institutions.

15 There are of course norms and requirements on individuals that do not have deliberative justification. The conception of deliberative democracy is, in Rawls's term, a 'political conception', and not a comprehensive moral theory. On the distinction between political and comprehensive theories, see Rawls (1987), pp. 1–25.

16 For criticism of the reliance on an assumption of unanimity in deliberative views, see Maxim (1987), pp. 359–61.

17 Note the parallel with Elster (1986) indicated in note 12. See also the discussion in Habermas (1975), p. 108, about 'needs that can be communicatively shared', and Habermas (1979), ch. 2.

18 For an interesting discussion of autonomous preferences and political processes, see Sunstein (1986, pp. 1145–58; 1984, pp. 1699–1700).

19 Whitney vs. California, 274 US 357 (1927).

20 For contrasting views on sectarianism, see Rawls (1987); Dworkin (1985), pt 3; MacIntyre (1981); Sandel (1982).

21 See Riker (1982); for discussion of Riker's view see Coleman and Ferejohn (1986); Cohen (1986b).

22 For discussion of the connection between ideals of democracy and freedom of expression, see Meiklejohn (1948), Tribe (1978; 1985, ch. 2) and Ely (1980, pp. 93–4, 105–16). Freedom of expression is a special case that can perhaps be more straightforwardly accommodated by the democratic conception than liberties of conscience, or the liberties associated with privacy and personhood. I do think, however, that these other liberties can be given satisfactory treatment by the democratic conception, and would reject it if I did not think so. The general idea would be to argue that other fundamental liberties must be protected if citizens are to be able to engage in and have equal standing in political deliberation without fear that such engagement puts them at risk for their convictions or personal choices. Whether this line of argument will work out on the details is a matter for treatment elsewhere.

23 This objection is suggested in Dworkin (1985), pp. 61–3. He cites the following passage from a letter of Madison's: 'And a people who mean to be their own Governors, must arm themselves with *the power which knowledge gives*' (emphasis added).

24 On the distinction between content-based and content-neutral abridgements, the complexities of drawing the distinction in particular cases, and the special reasons for hostility to content-based abridgements, see Tribe (1978), pp. 584–682; Stone (1987), pp. 46–118.

25 I am not suggesting that the deliberative view provides the only sound justification for the liberty of expression. My concern here is rather to show that the deliberative view is capable of accommodating it.

26 For an especially sharp statement of the irrelevance objection, see Schmitt (1985).

27 This view is sometimes associated with Rousseau, who is said to have conflated the notion of democratic legitimacy with the institutional expression of that ideal in a direct democracy. For criticism of this interpretation, see Cohen (1986a).

28 Madison urges this point in the *Federalist Papers*. Objecting to a proposal advanced by Jefferson which would have regularly referred constitutional questions 'to the decision of the whole of society', Madison argues that this would increase the danger of disturbing the public tranquillity by interesting too strongly the public passions'. And 'it is the reason, alone, of the public that ought to control and regulate the government ... [while] the passions ought to be controlled and regulated by the government'. I endorse the form of the objection, not its content. (Federalist Papers 1961, pp. 315–17.)

29 Here I draw on Cohen and Rogers (1983), pp. 154–7. The idea that parties are required to organize political choice and to provide a focus for public deliberation is one strand of arguments about 'responsible parties' in American political-science literature. My understanding of this view has been greatly aided by Perlman (1987), and, more generally, by the work of my colleague Walter Dean Burnham on the implications of party decline for democratic politics. See, for example, Burnham (1982).

REFERENCES

Ackerman, B.A. 1984: The Storrs Lectures: Discover the constitution. *Yale Law Journal*, 93: 1013–72.

—— 1986: Discovering the constitution. Unpublished manuscript.

Burnham, W.D. 1982: *The Current Crisis in American Politics*. Oxford: Oxford University Press.

Cohen, J. 1986a: Autonomy and democracy: reflections on Rousseau. *Philosophy and Public Affairs*, 15: 275–97.

—— 1986b: An epistemic conception of democracy. *Ethics*, 97: 26–38.

—— 1988: The material basis of deliberative democracy. *Social Philosophy and Policy*, 6(2): 25–50.

Cohen, J. and Rogers, J. 1983: *On Democracy*. Harmondsworth: Penguin.

Coleman, J. and Ferejohn, J. 1986: Democracy and social choice. *Ethics*, 97 (October): 6–25.

Dworkin, R. 1985: *A Matter of Principle*. Cambridge, Mass.: Harvard University Press.

Elster, J. 1982: Sour grapes. In A. Sen and B. Williams (eds), *Utilitarianism and Beyond*. Cambridge: Cambridge University Press, 219–38.

—— 1986: The market and the forum: three varieties of political theory. In J. Elster and A. Hylland (eds), *The Foundations of Social Choice Theory*. Cambridge: Cambridge University Press, 103–32. [Reprinted as Chapter 20 of this volume].

Ely, J.H. 1980: *Democracy and Distrust: A Theory of Judicial Review*. Cambridge, Mass.: Harvard University Press.

Federalist Papers 1961: ed. C. Rossiter. New York: American Library.

Habermas, J. 1975: *The Legitimation Crisis of Late Capitalism*, tr. T. McCarthy. Boston, Mass.: Beacon Press; London: Heinemann.

—— 1979: *Communication and the Evolution of Society*, tr. T. McCarthy. Boston, Mass.: Beacon Press.

—— 1984: *The Theory of Communicative Action*, vol. 1, tr. T. McCarthy. Boston, Mass.: Beacon Press.

Kant, I., tr. T. Humphrey 1983: To perpetual peace: a philosophical sketch. In *Perpetual Peace and other Essays*. Indianapolis: Hackett.

MacIntyre, A. 1981: *After Virtue*. Notre Dame, Ind.: University of Notre Dame Press.

Manin, B. 1987: On legitimacy and political deliberation. *Political Theory*, 15: 338–68.

Meiklejohn, A. 1948: *Free Speech and its Relation of Self-Government*. New York: Harper and Row.

Michelman, F.I. 1986: The Supreme Court, 1985 Term – Foreword: Traces of Self-Government. *Harvard Law Review*, 100: 4–77.

Perlman, L. 1987: Parties, democracy and consent. Unpublished.

Rawls, J. 1971: *A Theory of Justice*. Cambridge, Mass.: Harvard University Press; also Oxford, Clarendon Press (1972).

—— 1982: The basic liberties and their priority. *Tanner Lectures on Human Values*, Salt Lake City: University of Utah Press, vol. III.

—— 1987: The idea of an overlapping consensus. *Oxford Journal of Legal Studies*, 7: 1–25.

Riker, W. 1982: *Liberalism Against Populism: A Confrontation Between the Theory of Democracy and the Theory of Social Choice*. San Francisco: W.H. Freeman.

Sandel, M. 1982: *Liberalism and the Limits of Justice*. Cambridge: Cambridge University Press.

Scanlon, T.M. 1982: Contractualism and utilitarianism. In A.K. Sen and B. Williams (eds), *Utilitarianism and Beyond*. Cambridge: Cambridge University Press, 103–28.

Schmitt, C. 1985: *The Crisis of Parliamentary Democracy*, tr. E. Kennedy. Cambridge, Mass.: MIT Press.

Schumpeter, J.A. 1954: *Capitalism, Socialism and Democracy*. London: Unwin.

Stone, G. 1987: Content-neutral restrictions. *University of Chicago Law Review*, 54: 46–118.

Sunstein, C. 1984: Naked preferences and the constitution. *Columbia Law Review*, 84: 1689–1732.

—— 1985: Interest groups in American public law. *Stanford Law Review*, 38: 29–87.

—— 1986: Legal interference with private preferences. *University of Chicago Law Review*, 53: 1129–84.

Tribe, L. 1978: *American Constitutional Law*. Mineola NY: Foundation Press.

—— 1985: *Constitutional Choices*. Cambridge, Mass.: Harvard University Press.

Unger, R. 1987: *False Necessity*. Cambridge: Cambridge University Press.

Williams, B. 1985: *Ethics and the Limits of Philosophy*. London: Fontana, Collins; Cambridge, Mass.: Harvard University Press.

22

PHILOSOPHY AND DEMOCRACY

Michael Walzer

The prestige of political philosophy is very high these days. It commands the attention of economists and lawyers, the two groups of academics most closely connected to the shaping of public policy, as it has not done in a long time. And it claims the attention of political leaders, bureaucrats, and judges, most especially judges, with a new and radical forcefulness. The command and the claim follow not so much from the fact that philosophers are doing creative work, but from the fact that they are doing creative work of a special sort – which raises again, after a long hiatus, the possibility of finding objective truths "true meaning," "right answers," "the philosopher's stone," and so on. I want to accept this possibility (without saying very much about it) and then ask what it means for democratic politics. What is the standing of the philosopher in a democratic society? This is an old question; there are old tensions at work here: between truth and opinion, reason and will, value and preference, the one and the many. These antipodal pairs differ from one another, and none of them quite matches the pair "philosophy and democracy." But they do hang together; they point to a central problem. Philosophers claim a certain sort of authority for their conclusions; the people claim a different sort of authority for their decisions. What is the relation between the two?

I shall begin with a quotation from Wittgenstein that might seem to resolve the problem immediately. "The philosopher," Wittgenstein wrote, "is not a citizen of any community of ideas. That is what makes him into a philosopher."[1] This is more than an assertion of detachment in its usual sense, for citizens are surely capable, sometimes, of detached judgments even of their own ideologies, practices, and institutions. Wittgenstein is asserting a more radical detachment. The philosopher is and must be an outsider standing apart, not occasionally (in judgment) but systematically (in thought). I do not know whether the philosopher has to be a political outsider. Wittgenstein does say *any* community, and the state (polis, republic, commonwealth, kingdom, or whatever) is certainly a community of ideas. The communities of which the philosopher is most importantly not a citizen may, of course, be larger or smaller than the state. That will depend on what he philosophizes about. But if he is a political philosopher – not what Wittgenstein had in mind – then the state is the most likely community from which he will have to detach himself, not physically, but intellectually and, on a certain view on morality, morally too.

This radical detachment has two forms, and I shall be concerned with only one of them. The first form is contemplative and analytic; those, who participate in it take no interest in changing the community whose ideas they study. "Philosophy leaves everything as it is."[2] The second form is heroic. I do not want to deny the heroic possibilities of contemplation and analysis. One can always take pride in wrenching oneself loose from the bonds of community; it is not easy to do, and many important philosophical achievements (and all the varieties of philosophical arrogance) have their origins in detachment. But I want to focus on a certain tradition of heroic action, alive, it seems, in our own time, where the philosopher detaches himself from the community of ideas in order to found it again – intellectually and then materially too. For ideas have consequences, and every community of ideas is also a concrete community. He withdraws and returns. He is like the legislators of ancient legend, whose work precludes ordinary citizenship.[3]

In the long history of political thought, there is an alternative to the detachment of philosophers, and that is the engagement of sophists, critics, publicists, and intellectuals. To be sure, the sophists whom Plato attacks were citiless men, itinerant teachers, but they were by no means strangers in the Greek community of ideas. Their teaching drew upon, was radically dependent upon, the resources of a common membership. In this sense, Socrates was a sophist, though it was probably crucial to his own understanding of his mission, as critic and gadfly, that he also be a citizen: the Athenians would have found him less irritating had he not been one of their fellows. But then the citizens killed Socrates, thus demonstrating, it is sometimes said, that engagement and fellowship are not possible for anyone committed to the search for truth. Philosophers cannot he sophists. For practical as well as intellectual reasons, the distance that they put between themselves and their fellow citizens must be widened into a breach of fellowship. And then, for practical reasons only, it must be narrowed again by deception and secrecy. So that the philosopher emerges, like Descartes in his *Discourse*, as a separatist in thought, a conformist in practice.

He is a conformist, at least, until he finds himself in a position to transform practice into some nearer approximation to the truths of his thought. He cannot be a participant in the rough and tumble politics of the city, but he can be a founder or a legislator, a king, a nocturnal councillor, or a judge – or, more realistically, he can be an advisor to such figures, whispering in the ear of power. Shaped by the very nature of the philosophical project, he has little taste for bargaining and mutual accommodation. Because the truth he knows or claims to know is singular in character, he is likely to think that politics must be the same: a coherent conception, an uncompromising execution. In philosophy as in architecture, and so in politics, wrote Descartes: What has been put together bit by bit, by different masters, is less perfect than the work of a single hand. Thus, "those old places which, beginning as villages, have developed in the course of time into great towns, are generally . . . ill-proportioned in comparison with those an engineer can design at will in an orderly fashion."[4] Descartes himself disclaims any interest in the political version of such a project – perhaps because he believes that the only place where he is likely to reign supreme is his own mind. But there is always the possibility of a partnership between philosophical authority and political power. Reflecting on that possibility, the philosopher may, like Thomas Hobbes, "recover some hope that one time or other, this writing of mine may fall into the hands of a sovereign, who will . . . by the exercise of entire sovereignty . . . convert this truth of speculation into the utility of practice."[5] The crucial words in these quotations from Descartes and Hobbes are "design at will" and "entire sovereignty." Philosophical founding is an authoritarian business.

II

A quick comparison may be helpful here. Poets have their own tradition or withdrawal and engagement, but radical withdrawal is not common among them. One might plausibly set alongside Wittgenstein's sentences the following lines of C. P. Cavafy, written to comfort a young poet who has managed after great effort to finish only one poem. That, Cavafy says, is a first step, and no small accomplishment:

> To set your foot upon this step
> you must rightfully be a citizen
> of the city of ideas.[6]

Wittgenstein writes as if there were (as there are) many communities, while Cavafy seems to suggest that poets inhabit a single, universal city. But I suspect that the Greek poet means in fact to describe a more particular place: the city of Hellenic culture. The poet must prove himself a citizen there; the philosopher must prove that he is not a citizen anywhere. The poet needs fellow citizens, other poets and readers of poetry, who share with him a background of history and sentiment, who will not demand that everything he writes be explained. Without people like that, his allusions will be lost and his images will echo only in his own mind. But the philosopher fears fellowship, for the ties of history and sentiment corrupt his thinking. He needs to look at the world from a distance, freshly, like a total stranger. His detachment is speculative, willful, always incomplete. I do not doubt that a clever sociologist or historian will detect in his work, as readily as in any poem, the signs of its time and place. Still, the philosopher's ambition (in the tradition that I am describing) is extreme. The poet, by contrast, is more modest – as Auden has written:

> A poet's hope:
> to be like some valley cheese
> local, but prized elsewhere.[7]

The poet may be a visionary or a seer: he may seek out exile and trouble; but he cannot, short of madness, cut himself off from the community of ideas. And perhaps for that reason, he also cannot aspire to anything quite like sovereignty over the community. If he hopes to become a "legislator for mankind," it is rather by moving his fellow citizens than by governing them. And even the moving is indirect. "Poetry makes nothing happen."[8] But that is not quite the same thing as saying that it leaves everything as it is. Poetry leaves in the minds of its readers some intimation of the poet's truth. Nothing so coherent as a philosophical statement, nothing so explicit as a legal injunction; a poem is never more than a partial and unsystematic truth, surprising us by its excess, teasing us by its ellipsis, never arguing a case. "I have never yet been able to perceive," wrote Keats, "how anything can be known for truth by consecutive reasoning."[9] The knowledge of the poet is of a different sort, and it leads to truths that can, perhaps, be communicated but never directly implemented.

III

But the truths discovered or worked out by political philosophers can be implemented. They lend themselves readily to legal embodiment. Are these the laws of nature? Enact them. Is this a just scheme of distribution? Establish it. Is this a basic human right? Enforce it. Why else would one want to know about such things? An ideal city is, I suppose, an entirely proper object of contemplation, and it may be the case that "whether it exists anywhere or ever will exist is no matter" – that is, does not affect the truth of the vision. But surely it would be better if the vision were realized. Plato's claim that the ideal city is "the only commonwealth in whose politics [the philosopher] can ever take part" is belied by his own attempt to intervene in the politics of Syracuse when an opportunity arose, or so he thought, for philosophical reformation.[10] Plato never intended, of course, to become a citizen of the city he hoped to reform.

The claim of the philosopher in such a case is that he knows "the pattern set up in the heavens." He knows what ought to be done. He cannot just do it himself, however, and so he must look for a political instrument. A pliable prince is, for obvious practical reasons, the best possible instrument. But in principle any instrument will do – an aristocracy, a vanguard, a civil service, even the people will do, so long as its members are committed to philosophical truth and possessed of sovereign power. But clearly, the people raise the greatest difficulties. If they are not a many-headed monster, they are at least many-headed, difficult to educate and likely to disagree among themselves. Nor can the philosophical instrument be a majority among the people, for majorities in any genuine democracy are temporary, shifting, unstable. Truth is one, but the people have many opinions; truth is eternal, but the people continually change their minds. Here in its simplest form is the tension between philosophy and democracy.

The people's claim to rule does not rest upon their knowledge of truth (though it may, as in utilitarian thought, rest upon their knowledge of many smaller truths: the account that only they can give of their own pains and pleasures). The claim is most persuasively put, it seems to me, not in terms of what the people know but in terms of who they are. They are the subjects of the law, and if the law is to bind them as free men and women, they must also be its makers. This is Rousseau's argument. I do not propose to defend it here but only to consider some of its consequences. The argument has the effect of making law a function of popular will and not of reason as it had hitherto been understood, the reason of wise men, sages, and judges. The people are the successors of gods and absolutist kings, but not of philosophers. They may not know the right thing to do, but they claim a right to do what they think is right (literally, what pleases them).[11]

Rousseau himself pulled back from this claim, and most contemporary democrats would want to do so too. I can imagine three ways of pulling back and constraining democratic decisions, which I will outline briefly, drawing on Rousseau, but without attempting any explicit analysis of his arguments. First, one might impose a formal constraint on popular willing: the people must will generally.[12] They cannot single out (except in elections for public office) a particular individual or set of individuals from among themselves for special treatment. This is no bar to public assistance programs designed, say, for the sick or the old, for we can all get sick and we all hope to grow old. Its purpose is to rule out discrimination against individuals and groups who have, so to speak, proper names. Second, one might insist on the inalienability of the popular will and then on the indestructibility of those institutions and practices that guarantee the democratic character of the popular will: assembly, debate, elections, and so on. The people cannot renounce now their future right to will (or, no such renunciation can ever be legitimate or morally effective).[13] Nor can they deny to some group among themselves, with or without a proper name, the right to participate in future willing.

Clearly, these first two constraints open the way for some kind of review of popular decision-making, some kind of enforcement, against the people if necessary, of nondiscrimination and democratic rights. Whoever undertakes this review and enforcement will have to make judgments about the discriminatory character of particular pieces of legislation and about the meaning for democratic politics of particular restrictions on free speech, assembly, and so on. But these judgments. though I do not want to underestimate either their importance or their difficulty, will be relatively limited in their effects compared to the sort of thing required by the third constraint. And it is on the third constraint that I want to focus, for I do not believe that philosophers in the heroic tradition can possibly be satisfied with the first two. Third, then, the people must will what is right. Rousseau says, must will the common good, and goes on to argue that the people will will the common good if they are a true people, a community, and not a mere collection of egoistic individuals and corporate groups.[14] Here the idea seems to be that there exists a single set – though not necessarily an exhaustive set – of correct or just laws that the assembled people, the voters or their representatives, may not get right. Often enough, they get it wrong, and then they require the guidance of a legislator or the restraint of a judge. Rousseau's legislator is simply the philosopher in heroic dress, and though Rousseau denies him the right to coerce the people, he insists on his right to deceive the people. The legislator speaks in the name of God, not of philosophy.[15] One might look for a parallel deception among contemporary judges. In any case, this third constraint surely raises the most serious questions about Rousseau's fundamental argument, that political legitimacy rests on will (consent) and not on reason (rightness).

IV

The fundamental argument can be put in an appropriately paradoxical form: it is a feature of democratic government that the people have a right to act wrongly – in much the same way that they have a right to act stupidly. I should say, they have a right to act wrongly within some area (and only, following the first two constraints, if the action is general over the area and does not preclude future democratic action within the area). Sovereignty is always sovereignty somewhere and with regard to some things, not everywhere and with regard to everything. The people can rightfully, let us say, enact a redistributive income tax, but they can only redistribute their own income, not those of some neighboring nation. What is crucial, however, is that the redistributive pattern they choose is not subject to authoritative correction in accordance with philosophical standards. It is subject to criticism, of course, but insofar as the critic is a democrat he will have to agree that, pending the conversion of the people to his position, the pattern they have chosen ought to be implemented.

Richard Wollheim has argued in a well-known article that democratic theory conceived in this way is not merely paradoxical in some loose sense; it is a strict paradox.[16] He constructs the paradox in three steps.

(1) As a citizen of a democratic community, I review the choices available to the community and conclude that A is the policy that ought to be implemented.

(2) The people, in their wisdom or their willfulness, choose policy B, the very opposite of A.

(3) I still think that policy A ought to be implemented, but now, as a committed democrat, I also think that policy B ought to be implemented. Hence, I think that both policies ought to be implemented. But this is incoherent.

The paradox probably depends too much upon its verbal form. We might imagine a more modest first person – so that the first step would go like this:

(1) I conclude that A is the policy that the people ought to choose for implementation.

Then there would be nothing incoherent about saying:

(3) Since the people didn't choose A, but chose B instead, I now conclude that B ought to be implemented.

This is not very interesting, but it is consistent, and I think it makes sense of the democratic position. What underlies Wollheim's version of the first step is a philosophical, and probably an antidemocratic, argument that has this form:

(1) I conclude that A is the right policy, and that it ought to be implemented *because it is right.*

But it is not at all obvious that a policy's rightness is the right reason for implementing it. It may only be the right reason for hoping that it will be implemented and so for defending it in the assembly. Suppose that there existed a push-button implementation system, and that the two buttons, marked A and B, were on my desk. Which one should I push, and for what reasons? Surely I cannot push A simply because I have decided that A is right. Who am I? As a citizen of a democratic community, I must wait for the people's decision, who have a right to decide. And then, if the people choose B, it is not the case that I face an existential choice, where my philosophical arguments point toward A and my democratic commitments point toward B, and there is no way to decide between them. There is a way to decide.

The distinction that I am trying to draw here, between having a right to decide and knowing the right decision, might be described in terms of procedural and substantive justice. Democrats, it might be said, are committed to procedural justice, and can only hope that the outcomes of just procedures will also be substantively just. But I am reluctant to accept that formulation because the line between procedure and substance seems to me less clear than it suggests. What is at stake in discussions about procedural justice is the distribution of power, and that is surely a substantive matter. No procedural arrangement can be defended except by some substantive argument, and every substantive argument (in political philosophy) issues also in some procedural arrangement. Democracy rests, as I have already suggested, on an argument about freedom and political obligation. Hence it is not only the case that the people have a procedural right to make the laws. On the democratic view, it is right that they make the laws – even if they make them wrongly.

Against this view, the heroic philosopher might argue that it can never be right to do wrong (not, at least, once we know or can know what is right). This is also, at least incipiently, an argument about the distribution of political power, and it has two implications. First, that the power of the people ought to be limited by the rightness of what they do; and second, that someone else ought to be empowered to review what the people do and step in when they move beyond those limits. Who else? In principle, I suppose, anyone who knows the truth about rightness. But in practice, in any ongoing political order, some group of people will have to be found who can be presumed to know the truth better or more consistently than the people as a whole do. This group will then be awarded a procedural right to intervene, grounded on a substantive argument about knowledge and moral truth.

Popular legislation might be reviewed democratically: in ancient Athens, for example, citizens concerned about the legitimacy of a particular decision of the assembly could appeal from the assembly as a whole to a smaller group of citizens, selected by lot and empanelled as a jury. The jury literally put the law on trial, with individual citizens acting as prosecutors and defense attorneys, and its verdict took precedence over the legislative act itself.[17] In this case, obviously, no special wisdom was claimed; the same argument or the same sort of argument would justify both the act and the verdict. More often, however, groups of this sort are constituted on aristocratic rather than democratic grounds. The appeal is from popular consciousness, particular interests, selfish or shortsighted policies to the superior understanding of the few: Hegel's corps of civil servants, Lenin's vanguard party, and so on. Ideally, the group to which the appeal is made must be involved in the community of ideas, oriented to action within it, but attuned at the same time to philosophers outside. In but not wholly in, so as to provide a match for the philosopher's withdrawal and return.

V

In the United States today, it is apparent that the nine judges of the Supreme Court have been assigned something like this role. The assignment is most clearly argued in the work of a group of contemporary law professors, all of whom are philosophers

too or, at least, much influenced by political philosophy.[18] Indeed, the revival of political philosophy has had its most dramatic impact in schools of law – and for a reason
that is not difficult to make out. In a settled democracy, with no revolution in prospect,
judges are the most likely instruments of philosophical reformation. Of course, the
conventional role of Supreme Court judges extends no further than the enforcement
of a written constitution that itself rests on democratic consent and is subject to democratic amendment. And even when the judges act in ways that go beyond upholding
the textual integrity of the constitution, they generally claim no special understanding
of truth and rightness but refer themselves instead to historical precedents, long-established legal principles, or common values. Nevertheless, the place they hold and the
power they wield make it possible for them to impose philosophical constraints on
democratic choice. And they are readily available (as the people are not) for philosophical instruction as to the nature of those constraints. I am concerned here with
judges only insofar as they are in fact instructed – and with philosophers before judges
because a number of philosophers seem so ready to provide the instruction. The
tension between judicial review and democracy directly parallels the tension between
philosophy and democracy. But the second is the deeper tension, for judges are likely
to expand upon their constitutional rights or to sustain a program of expansion only
when they are in the grip of a philosophical doctrine.

Now, judges and philosophers are (mostly) different sorts of people. One can
imagine a philosopher-judge, but the union is uncommon. Judges are in an important
sense members of the political community. Most of them have had careers as office-
holders, or as political activists, or as advocates of this or that public policy. They have
worked in the arena; they have participated in debates. When they are questioned at
their confirmation hearings, they are presumed to have opinions of roughly the same
sort as their questioners – commonplace opinions, much of the time, else they would
never have been nominated. Once confirmed, to be sure, they set themselves at some
distance from everyday politics; their special standing in a democracy requires a certain
detachment and thoughtfulness. They don the robes of wisdom, and those robes
constitute what might be called a philosophical temptation: to love wisdom better than
the law. But judges are supposed to be wise in the ways of a particular legal tradition,
which they share with their old professional and political associates.

The stance of the philosopher is very different. The truths he commonly seeks are
universal and eternal, and it is unlikely that they can be found from the inside of any
real and historic community. Hence the philosopher's withdrawal: he must deny himself the assurances of the commonplace. (He does not have to be confirmed.) To what
sort of a place, then, does he withdraw? Most often today, he constructs for himself
(since he cannot, like Plato, discover for himself) an ideal commonwealth, inhabited by
beings who have none of the particular characteristics and none of the opinions or commitments of his former fellow-citizens. He imagines a perfect meeting in an "original

position" or "ideal speech situation" where the men and women in attendance are liberated from their own ideologies or subjected to universalizing rules of discourse. And then, he asks what principles, rules, constitutional arrangements these people would choose if they set out to create an actual political order.[19] They are, as it were, the philosophical representatives of the rest of us, and they legislate on our behalf. The philosopher himself, however, is the only actual inhabitant of the ideal commonwealth, the only actual participant in the perfect meeting. So the principles, rules, constitutions, with which he emerges are in fact the products of his own thinking, "designed at will in an orderly fashion," subject only to whatever constraints he imposes upon himself. Nor are any other participants required, even when the decision procedure of the ideal commonwealth is conceived in terms of consensus or unanimity. For if there were another person present, he would either be identical to the philosopher, subject to the same constraints and so led to say the same things and move toward the same conclusions, or he would be a particular person with historically derived characteristics and opinions and then his presence would undermine the universality of the argument.

The philosopher returns from his retreat with conclusions that are different from the conclusions of any actual democratic debate. At least, they have, or he claims for them, a different status. They embody what is right, which is to say for our present purposes, they have been agreed upon by a set of ideal representatives, whereas the conclusions reached through democratic debate are merely agreed upon by the people or by their actual representatives. The people or their representatives might then be invited to revise their own conclusions in the light of the philosopher's work. I suppose that this is an invitation implicitly extended every time a philosopher publishes a book. At the moment of publication, at least, he is a proper democrat: his book is a gift to the people. But the gift is rarely appreciated. In the political arena, the philosopher's truths are likely to be turned into one more set of opinions, tried out, argued about, adopted in part, repudiated in part, or ignored. Judges, on the other hand, may well be persuaded to give the philosopher a different sort of hearing. Their special role in the democratic community is connected, as I have already said, to their thoughtfulness, and thoughtfulness is a philosophical posture: judicial status can only be chanced by a little real philosophy. Moreover, judges are admirably placed to mediate between the opinions (temporarily) established in the democratic arena and the truths worked out in the ideal commonwealth. Through the art of interpretation, they can do what Rousseau's legislator does through the art of divination.[20]

VI

Consider the case of "rights." Our ideal representatives in philosophical seclusion come up with a list of rights that attach to each individual human being. Let us assume that the list is, as it commonly is among contemporary philosophers, deeply meditated and serious. The enumerated rights form a coherent whole, suggesting what it might mean to recognize in another man or woman the special qualities of moral agency and personality. The philosophical list differs from the list currently established in the law, but it also overlaps with the law and with what we can think of as the suburbs of the law, the cluster of opinions, values, and traditions to which we escape, if we can, whenever we find the inner city of the law constraining. Now the philosopher – I mean still the heroic philosopher, the philosopher as founder – invites the judges to attempt a more organized escape, from the law, through the suburbs, to the ideal common-wealth beyond. The invitation is all the more urgent in that rights are at stake. For rights have this special characteristic: their violation requires immediate relief or reparation. And judges are not merely the available, they are also the appropriate instruments of relief and reparation.[21]

In effect, the philosopher proposes a decision procedure for judges modeled on that of the ideal commonwealth. This is in part flattery, but it also has a factual rationale. For the discussions of judges among themselves really do resemble the arguments that go on in the ideal commonwealth (in the mind of the philosopher) much more closely than democratic debate can ever do. And it seems plausible to say that rights are more likely to be defined correctly by the reflection of the few than by the votes of the many.[22] So the philosopher asks the judges to recapitulate in their chambers the argu-ment he has already worked out in solitary retreat, and then to give that argument "the utility of practice" first by locating it in the law or in the traditions and values that surround the law and then by deciding cases in its terms. When necessary, the judges must preempt or overrule legislative decisions. This is the crucial point, for it is here that the tension between philosophy and democracy takes on material form.

The legislature is, if not the reality, then at least the effective representation of the people assembled to rule themselves. Its members have a right to act within an area. Judicially enforced rights can be understood in two different but complementary ways with regard to this area. First, they are boundaries circumscribing it. From this view, a simple equation follows: the more extensive the list of rights, the wider the range of judicial enforcement, the less room there is for legislative choice. The more rights the judges award to the people as individuals, the less free the people are as a decision-making body. Or, second, rights are principles that structure activities within the area, shaping policies and institutions. Then judges do not merely operate at the boundaries, however wide or narrow the boundaries are. Their judgments represent deep penetra-tion raids into the area of legislative decision.[23] Now, all three of the constraints on popular willing that I described earlier can be conceived in either of these ways, as defense or as penetration. But it is clear, I think, that the third constraint simultane-ously narrows the boundaries and permits deeper raids. As soon as the philosophical list of rights extends beyond the twin bans on legal discrimination and political repression, it invites judicial activity that is radically intrusive on what might be called democratic space.

But this, it can be objected, is to consider rights only in the formal sense, ignoring their content. And their content may well enhance rather than circumscribe popular choice. Imagine, for example, a philosophically and then judicially recognized right to welfare.[24] The purpose of such a right is plain enough. It would guarantee to each citizen the opportunity to exercise his citizenship, and that is an opportunity he could hardly be said to have, or to have in any meaningful fashion, if he were starving to death or desperately seeking shelter for himself and his family. A defensible right, surely, and yet the argument I have just sketched still holds. For the judicial enforcement of welfare rights would radically reduce the reach of democratic decision. Henceforth, the judges would decide, and as cases accumulated, they would decide in increasing detail, what the scope and character of the welfare system should be and what sorts of redistribution it required. Such decisions would clearly involve significant judicial control of the state budget and, indirectly at least, of the level of taxation – the very issues over which the democratic revolution was originally fought.

This sort of thing would be easier for committed democrats if the expanded list of rights were incorporated into the constitution through a popularly controlled amending process. Then there would exist some democratic basis for the new (undemocratic) power of philosophers and judges. The people would, I think, be ill-advised to agree to such an incorporation and to surrender so large a part of their day-to-day authority. In the modern state, however, that authority is exercised so indirectly – it is so far, in fact, from being day-to-day authority – that they might feel the surrender to be a minor matter. The rights they gain as individuals (in this case, to welfare services from a benevolent bureaucracy) might in their view far outweigh the rights they lose as members. And so it is not implausible to imagine the constitutional establishment of something like, say, Rawls's two principles of justice.[25] Then the entire area of distributive justice would effectively be handed over to the courts. What a range of decisions they would have to make! Imagine a class action suit testing the meaning of the difference principle. The judges would have to decide whether the class represented in the suit was really the most disadvantaged class in the society (or whether all or enough of its members fell within that class). And if it was (or if they did), the judges would then have to decide what rights followed from the difference principle under the material conditions currently prevailing. No doubt, they would be driven to consult experts and officials in making these decisions. It would make little sense for them to consult the legislature, however, for to these questions, if rights are really at issue, there must be a right answer – and this answer is more likely to be known by philosophers, judges, experts, and officials than by ordinary citizens or their political representatives.[26]

Still, if the people came to feel oppressed by the new authorities that they had established, they could always disestablish them. The amending process would still be available, though it might be the case that the gradual erosion of legislative energy would make it less available in practice than it was in principle.[27] Partly for this reason, and partly for reasons to which I will now turn, I want to argue that philosophers should not be too quick to seek out the judicial (or any other) instrument, and that judges, though they must to some extent be philosophers of the law, should not be too quick to turn themselves into political philosophers. It is a mistake to attempt any extensive incorporation of philosophical principles into the law either by interpretation or amendment. For that is, in either case, to take them out of the political arena where they properly belong. The interventions of philosophers should be limited to the gifts they bring. Else they are like Greeks bringing gifts, of whom the people should beware, for what they have in mind is the capture of the city.

VII

"The philosopher is not a citizen of any community of ideas. That is what makes him into a philosopher." I have taken these sentences to mean that the political philosopher must separate himself from the political community, cut himself loose from affective ties and conventional ideas. Only then can he ask and struggle to answer the deepest questions about the meaning and purpose of political association and the appropriate structure of the community (of every community) and its government. This kind of knowledge one can have only from the outside. Inside, another kind of knowledge is available, more limited, more particular in character. I shall call it political rather than philosophical knowledge. It answers the questions: What is the meaning and purpose of *this* association? What is the appropriate structure of *our* community and government? Even if we assume that there are right answers to these last questions (and it is doubtful that the particular questions have right answers even if the general questions do), it is nevertheless the case that there will be as many right answers as there are communities. Outside the communities, however, there is only one right answer. As there are many caves but only one sun, so political knowing is particular and pluralist in character, while philosophical knowing is universalist and singular. The political success of philosophers, then, would have the effect of enforcing a singular over a pluralist truth, that is, of reiterating the structure of the ideal commonwealth in every previously particularist community. Imagine not one but a dozen philosopher kings: their realms would be identically fashioned and identically governed, except for those adjustments required by an ineradicably particularist geography. (If God were a philosopher king, He would have allocated to each community an identical or equivalent set of geographic conditions.) The case would be the same with a dozen communities founded in the original position: there is only one original position. And it would be the same again with a dozen communities shaped by undistorted communication among an idealized set of members: for it is a feature of undistorted communication, as distinct from ordinary talk, that only a very few things can be said.[28]

Now, we may or may not be ready to assign value to particularism and pluralism. It is not easy to know how to decide. For pluralism implies a range of instances – a range of opinions, structures, regimes, policies – with regard to each of which we are likely to feel differently. We might value the range or the idea of a range and yet be appalled by a large number of the instances, and then search for some principle of exclusion. Most pluralists are in fact constrained pluralists, and the constraints they defend derive from universal principles. Can it still be said that they value pluralism? They merely like variety, perhaps, or they are not ready yet to make up their minds about every case, or they are tolerant, or indifferent. Or they have an instrumentalist view: many social experiments will lead one day (but that day is far off) to a single truth. All these are philosophical perspectives in the sense that they require a standpoint outside the range. And from that standpoint, I suspect, pluralism will always be an uncertain value at best. But most people stand differently. They are inside their own communities, and they value their own opinions and conventions. They come to pluralism only through an act of empathy and identification, recognizing that other people have feelings like their own. Similarly, the philosopher might come to pluralism by imagining himself a citizen of every community rather than of none. But then he might lose that firm sense of himself and his solitude that makes him a philosopher, and the gifts he brings might be of less value than they are.

I do not mean to underestimate those gifts. But it is important now to suggest that the value of universal truth is as uncertain when seen from inside a particular community as is the value of pluralism when seen from outside every particular community. Uncertain, I mean to say, not unreal or negligible: for I do not doubt that particular communities improve themselves by aspiring to realize universal truths and by incorporating (particular) features of philosophical doctrine into their own ways of life. And this the citizens also understand. But from their standpoint, it will not always be obvious that the rights, say, of abstract men and women, the inhabitants of some ideal commonwealth, ought to be enforced here and now. They are likely to have two worries about any such enforcement. First of all, it will involve overriding their own traditions, conventions, and expectations. These are, of course, readily accessible to philosophical criticism; they were not "designed at will in an orderly fashion" by a founder or a sage; they are the result of historical negotiation, intrigue, and struggle. But that is just the point. The products of a shared experience, they are valued by the people over the philosopher's gifts because they belong to the people and the gifts do not – much as I might value some familiar and much-used possession and feel uneasy with a new, more perfect model.

The second worry is more closely connected to democratic principle. It is not only the familiar products of their experience that the people value, but the experience itself, the process through which the products were produced. And they will have some difficulty understanding why the hypothetical experience of abstract men and women should take precedence over their own history. Indeed, the claim of the heroic philosopher must be that the first sort of experience not only takes precedence over but effectively replaces the second. Wherever universal truth has been established, there is no room for negotiation, intrigue, and struggle. Hence, it looks as if the political life of the community is to be permanently interrupted. Within some significant part of the area over which citizens had once moved freely, they are no longer to move at all. Why should they accept that? They might well choose politics over truth, and that choice, if they make it, will make in turn for pluralism. Any historical community whose members shape their own institutions and laws will necessarily produce a particular and not a universal way of life. That particularity can be overcome only from the outside and only by repressing internal political processes.

But this second worry, which is the more important of the two, is probably exaggerated. For philosophical doctrine, like the law itself, requires interpretation before it can be enforced. Interpretations must be particular in character, and they invite real and not merely hypothetical argument. Unless the philosopher wins "entire sovereignty" for himself, then, his victory will not in fact interrupt or cut off political activity. If his victory were to take the form that I have been imagining, it would merely shift the focus of political activity from legislatures to courts, from law-making to litigation. On the other hand, insofar as it is a victory at all, it has to have some universalizing tendencies: at least, it has to impose some constraints on the pluralizing tendencies of a free-wheeling politics. The more the judges are "strict constructionists" of philosophical doctrine, the more the different communities they rule will look alike and the more the collective choices of the citizens will be confined. So the exaggeration makes a point: the citizens have, to whatever degree, lost control over their own lives. And then they have no reason, no democratic reason, for obeying the decrees of the judges.

VIII

All this might be avoided, of course, if the judges adopted a policy of "judicial restraint," preempting or overruling legislative decisions only in rare and extreme cases. But I would suggest that judicial restraint, like judicial intervention, draws its force from some deeper philosophical view. Historically, restraint has been connected with skepticism or relativism.[29] It is of course true that philosophical views change, and judges must be leery of falling in with some passing fashion. But I am inclined to think that judicial restraint is consistent with the strongest claims that philosophers make for the truths they discover or construct. For there is a certain attitude that properly accompanies such claims, and has its origin in the ideal commonwealth or the perfect meeting from which the claims derive. This attitude is philosophical restraint, and it is simply the respect that outsiders owe to the decisions that citizens make among themselves and for themselves. The philosopher has withdrawn from the community. It is precisely because the knowledge he seeks can only be found outside this particular place that it yields no rights inside.

At the same time, it has to be said that since the philosopher's withdrawal is speculative only, he loses none of the rights he has as an ordinary citizen. His opinions are worth as much as any other citizen's; he is entitled like anyone else to work for their implementation, to argue, intrigue, struggle, and so on. But when he acts in these ways, he is an engaged philosopher, that is, a sophist, critic, publicist, or intellectual, and he must accept the risks of those social roles. I do not mean that he must accept the risk of death; that will depend upon the conditions of engagement in his community, and philosophers, like other citizens, will hope for something better than civil war and political persecution. I have in mind two different sorts of risks. The first is the risk of defeat, for though the engaged philosopher can still claim to be right, he cannot claim any of the privileges or rightness. He must live with the ordinary odds of democratic politics. The second is the risk of particularism, which is, perhaps, another kind of defeat for philosophy. Engagement always involves a loss – not total but serious enough – of distance, critical perspective, objectivity, and so on. The sophist, critic, publicist, or intellectual must address the concerns of his fellow citizens, try to answer their questions, weave his arguments into the fabric of their history. He must, indeed, make himself a *fellow* citizen in the community of ideas, and then he will be unable to avoid entirely the moral and even the emotional entanglements of citizenship. He may hold fast to the philosophical truths of natural law, distributive justice, or human rights, but his political arguments are most likely to look like some makeshift version of those truths, adapted to the needs of a particular people: from the standpoint of the original position, provincial; from the standpoint of the ideal speech situation, ideological.

Perhaps we should say that, once engaged, naturalized again into the community of ideas, the philosopher is like a political poet, Shelley's legislator, not Rousseau's. Though he still hopes that his arguments reach beyond his own community, he is first of all "local." And so he must be ready to forsake the prerogatives of distance, coherent design, and entire sovereignty, and seek instead with "thoughts that breathe and words that burn," to reach and move his own people. And he must give up any more direct means to establish the ideal commonwealth. That surrender is philosophical restraint.

Judicial restraint follows (and so does vanguard restraint and bureaucratic restraint). The judges must hold themselves as closely as they can to the decisions of the democratic assembly, enforcing first of all the basic political rights that serve to sustain the character of that assembly and protecting its members from discriminatory legislation. They are not to enforce rights beyond these, unless they are authorized to do so by a democratic decision. And it does not matter to the judges as judges that a more extensive list of rights can be, or that it has been, validated elsewhere. Elsewhere does not count.

Once again, I do not want to deny that rights can be validated elsewhere. Indeed, the most general truths of politics and morality can only be validated in the philosophical realm, and that realm has its place outside, beyond, separate from every particular community. But philosophical validation and political authorization are two entirely different things. They belong to two entirely distinct spheres of human activity. Authorization is the work of citizens governing themselves among themselves. Validation is the work of the philosopher reasoning alone in a world he inhabits alone or fills with the products of his own speculations. Democracy has no claims in the philosophical realm, and philosophers have no special rights in the political community. In the world of opinion, truth is indeed another opinion, and the philosopher is only another opinion-maker.

NOTES

1. *Zettel*, ed. G. E. M. Anscombe and G. H. von Wright (Berkeley: University of California Press, 1970), no. 455.
2. L. Wittgenstein (trans. G. E. M. Anscombe), *Philosophical Investigations* (New York: Macmillan, 1958), para. 124.
3. For an account of this special form of philosophical heroism, see Sheldon S. Wolin, *Hobbes and the Epic Tradition of Political Theory* (Los Angeles: Univ. of California Press, 1970).
4. René Descartes, *Discourse on Method*, trans. Arthur Wollaston (Harmondsworth: Penguin, 1960), pp. 44–45.
5. Thomas Hobbes, *Leviathan*, Part II, ch. 31 (end).
6. C. P. Cavafy, "The First Step," in *The Complete Poems of Cavafy*, trans. Rae Dalven (New York: Harcourt Brace Jovanovich, 1976), p. 6.
7. W. H. Auden, "Shorts II," *Collected Poems*, ed. Edward Mendelsohn (New York: Random House, 1976).
8. "In Memory of W. B. Yeats," in *The English Auden: Poems, Essays and Dramatic Writings*, 1927–1939, ed. Edward Mendelsohn (New York: Random House, 1977).
9. *The Letters of John Keats*, ed. M. B. Forman (London: Oxford Univ. Press, 1952), p. 67.
10. *The Republic of Plato*, trans. F. M. Cornford (New York: Oxford Univ. Press, 1945), 591A–592B.
11. Thus an Athenian orator to the assembly: "It is in your power, rightly, to dispose of what belongs to you – well, or, if you wish, ill." Quoted in K. J. Dover, *Greek Popular Morality in the Time of Plato and Aristotle* (Berkeley: Univ. of California Press, 1974), pp. 290–291.
12. *The Social Contract*, book II, chs. iv and vi.
13. This follows, I think, from the argument that the general will is inalienable, though Rousseau wants to make even more of inalienability than this – as in his attack on representation, book III, ch. xv.

14 *Social Contract*, book II, ch. iii and *passim*.

15 *Social Contract*, book II, ch. vii.

16 Richard Wollheim, "A Paradox in the Theory of Democracy," in *Philosophy, Politics and Society* (Second Series), ed. Peter Laslett and W. G. Runciman (Oxford: Basil Blackwell, 1962), pp. 71–87. I should stress that the argument here is about implementation, not obedience. What is at issue is how or for what reasons policies should be chosen for the community as a whole. Whether individual citizens should uphold this or that policy once it has been chosen, or assist in carrying it out, is another question.

17 A. H. M. Jones, *Athenian Democracy* (Oxford: Basil Blackwell, 1960), pp. 122–123.

18 See, for example, Ronald Dworkin, *Taking Rights Seriously* (Cambridge, MA: Harvard Univ. Press, 1977); Frank Michelman, "In Pursuit of Constitutional Welfare Rights," *University of Pennsylvania Law Review* (1973) 121: 962–1019; Owen Fiss, "The Forms of Justice," *Harvard Law Review* (1979) 93: 1–58; Bruce Ackerman. *Social Justice in the Liberal State* (New Haven: Yale Univ. Press, 1980).

19 In this mode of argument, John Rawls is obvious the great pioneer. But the specific use of the new philosophy with which I am concerned is not advocated by him in *A Theory of Justice* or in any subsequent articles.

20 Like Rousseau's legislator again, the judges have no direct coercive power of their own: in some ultimate sense, they must always look for support among the people or among alternative political elites. Hence the phrase "judicial tyranny," applied to the enforcement of some philosophically but not democratically validated position, is always a piece of hyperbole. On the other hand, there are forms of authority, short of tyranny, that raise problems for democratic government.

21 The special invitation and the sense of urgency are most clear in Dworkin, *Taking Rights Seriously*. But Dworkin seems to believe that the ideal commonwealth actually exists, so to speak, in the suburbs. The set of philosophically validated rights can also be validated, he argues, in terms of the constitutional history and the standing legal principles of the United States, and when judges enforce these rights they are doing what they ought to be doing, given the sort of government we have. For a different reading of our constitutional history, see Richard Ely, *Democracy and Distrust* (Cambridge, MA: Harvard Univ. Press, 1980). Ely argues for something very much like the two constraints that I have defended. For him, too, the ideal commonwealth lies somewhere beyond the U.S. Constitution. It is the proper goal of parties and movements, not of courts.

22 For a careful and rather tentative argument to this effect, see T. M. Scanlon, "Due Process" in *Nomos* XXII, ed. R. Pennock and J. Chapman (New York: New York Univ. Press, 1977), pp. 120–121.

23 Fiss provides some clear examples in "Forms of Justice."

24 Cf. Michelman "Welfare Rights," and also "On Protecting the Poor Through the Fourteenth Amendment," *Harvard Law Review* (1969) 83.

25 For a proposal to this effect, see Amy Gutmann, *Liberal Equality* (Cambridge, England: Cambridge Univ. Press, 1980), p. 199.

26 Dworkin, *Taking Rights Seriously*, especially Chapters 4 and 13.

27 Judicial interventions on behalf of individual rights broadly understood may also lead to an erosion of popular energies – at least on the left. For a brief argument to this effect, see my article "The Left and the Courts," *Dissent* (Spring, 1981).

28 Even if we were to connect philosophical conclusions to some set of historical circumstances, as Habermas does when he imagines "discursive will-formation" occurring "at a given stage in the development of productive forces," or as Rawls does when he suggests

that the principles worked out in the original position apply only to "democratic societies under modern conditions," it remains true that the conclusions are objectively true or right for a range of particular communities, without regard to the actual politics of those communities. See Habermas, *Legitimation Crisis* (Boston: Beacon, 1975), p. 113: Rawls, "Kantian Constructivism in Moral Theory," *The Journal of Philosophy*, 77 (September, 1980), p. 518.

29 See, for example, Ely, *Democracy and Distrust*, pp. 57–59.

FURTHER READING

Gutmann, A. (1983). "How Liberal is Democracy?" *Liberalism Reconsidered*. D. Maclean and C. Mills. Totowa, Rowman and Allanheld: 25–50.

Harrison, R. (1993). *Democracy*. Routledge.

Miller, R. (1974). "Rawls and Marxism." *Philosophy and Public Affairs* 3(2): 167–91.

Waldron, J. (1990). "Rights and Majorities: Rousseau Revisited." *Nomos* XXXII: 44–75.

Young, I. M. (1989). "Polity and Group Difference: A Critique of the Ideal of Universal Citizenship." *Ethics* 99: 250–74 [Reprinted as Chapter 14 of this volume].

Part 7
PUNISHMENT

Introduction

RECENT YEARS HAVE SEEN a rise in public awareness of the problems surrounding the criminal justice system. There have been debates on many aspects of the system such as sentencing policy, the release of individuals deemed to be dangerous, the efficacy of custodial sentences, alternatives to custody and the role of the police. Not entirely coincidentally, there has also been an active philosophical debate which has attempted to find, in H.L.A. Hart's terms, a 'general justifying aim' of judicial punishment (Hart 1959). A few philosophers have concluded that there is no such justification and that state punishment is unjust and should be abolished (Bianchi 1986). Fewer still, however, claim that state punishment is justified in its current form. This is a philosophical debate with urgent practical consequences, and there are few areas in which philosophy has such a direct effect on public policy.

There are broadly three places in which a justification for punishment has been sought. The first – deterrence theory – is grounded in the consequentialist thought that state punishment is justified to the extent that it reduces the level of crime. The second finds the justification in the reform and rehabilitation of the offender. The third, retributivism, claims punishment is justified on the grounds that offenders are getting what they deserve. One question that has been dominant in much of the recent literature is the extent to which these theories respect the person of the offender. That is, it is thought that systems of punishment must obey the Kantian injunction to treat the offender as an end, and not solely as a means. Deterrence theory is found wanting as punishment is inflicted on the offender as a means of reducing the level of crime. The objection can be dramatised by showing that deterrence theory would justify the punishment of the innocent (in cases in which this is the most efficient way of reducing the level of crime), however the objection applies equally to punishment of the guilty. Even in this case, the humanity of the offender is not being addressed and the punishment is simply a means to a logically independent end.

Of the reform and rehabilitation theories, the objection applies most directly to those that put no constraints on how reform is effected. Techniques that bypass the offender's rational agency (mandatory drug treatments, for example) fall to the Kantian objection. Techniques that do address the offender's rational agency face other objections. If punishment is a function of reform, the length of sentences should vary with the reform of the offender rather than the seriousness of the crime, which offends our conception of justice.

Retributive theories seem best placed to deal with the Kantian objection as they directly address the offender's agency. However, the concept on which retributivism places a great deal of weight (desert) may not be able to provide the independent justification the theory requires. If 'the offender deserves to be punished' is no more or less than 'the offender ought to be punished', then we have an intuition with no independent reason to support it. Recently, a number of theorists have attempted to find an independent account of desert in the idea of punishment as communication.

The communication theory, of which Antony Duff is the foremost advocate, justifies punishment as the expression of censure of an offender's behaviour. The basic thought behind the theory is that it is part of taking moral matters seriously that we are committed to censuring those who flout its rules. Institutional punishment is the form this takes when (as is appropriate) the state takes on that role. In 'Punishment, Communication and Community' Duff outlines his theory (which he has defended in more detail elsewhere (Duff 1986)) and considers two significant issues that arise from it. The first of these is the role of 'hard treatment'. State punishment treats offenders in ways such that, were private individuals to do the same, it would count as a significant wrong. Most obviously, the state deprives offenders of their freedom, sometimes for considerable periods of time. Why should the communication of censure take this form? Duff considers two sorts of response: those that take hard treatment to be internal to the communication of censure and those that take it to be a supplement to the censure. His own view is a version of the former; for Duff, hard treatment is to be construed as a form of secular penance. In a similar way to that in which the abbot of a monastery can ask an erring monk to perform certain tasks as a penance, so does the state ask the same of offenders. Is, however, a monastery an appropriate guide to the actions of a modern, secular state? Duff's view is, as he admits, 'fundamentally inconsistent with some of the more strenuous and metaphysical versions of liberal individualism'. The question, explored here and in the next reading, is the extent to which the view is compatible with any reasonably robust liberalism.

The second significant issue that concerns Duff is the conditions that need to be in place for the theory to work. Censure is only appropriate if the state stands in the right sort of moral relation to the offender. If offenders rightly take themselves to be in an equal, or even higher, moral position to the state then censuring is not appropriate. Furthermore, although the censure might be sincerely meant as admonition, it might be heard as 'the expression of patronising pity'. These are real problems, as offenders tend to be those for whom society has provided least opportunity for a successful life (Carlen 1989). Even if it would be naive to assume that a background could be found in the real world against which this ideal theory would work, Duff points out that the theory can at least provide us with a critical tool for assessing current imperfections.

Andrew von Hirsch is also a communication theorist. Like Duff, he needs to face the question of why this communication has the form it does: namely, hard treatment. Von Hirsch is more overtly liberal than Duff, and thus is keener to draw limits to the state's control over the individual. Duff's talk of penance, according to von Hirsch, 'ascribes to the state a role beyond its proper standing . . . given its functions and its relationship to citizens'. Rather, von Hirsch thinks we should recognise our own fallibility when it comes to staying within the law and see hard treatment as a 'prudential supplement' to censure: as an additional factor in our calculations as to whether or not to offend. This solution, although consonant with liberalism, would appear to face a fatal dilemma. Either the prudential supplement is a real disincentive or it is not. If it is, then the 'moral voice' is drowned out and we are left with what is basically a deterrence theory. If it is not a disincentive, then it is not clear what the function of hard treatment is. Von Hirsch grasps the first horn of the dilemma, using it as an argument for greatly reducing sentencing levels. This is only touched on in this reading, although von Hirsch has argued for this elsewhere (von Hirsch 1993).

In the final section of this reading, von Hirsch looks at the problem of the moral standing of the state with respect to offenders. The problem here is that social deprivation is a factor in drawing many offenders into crime. If we concede that being born into a socially deprived milieu that is difficult to escape is not the offender's fault, it becomes difficult to see that the state has good grounds for censure. Von Hirsch contrasts his view (that one could ascribe a reduced culpability to the offender) with a view he ascribes to Duff (that the state might have no moral grounds for censure). Here and elsewhere, von Hirsch's work is informed by the actual practices of state punishment. It is certainly less ambitious than Duff's view, and, to that extent, more suited to this non-ideal world. Nonetheless, one might wonder, in both cases, whether social conditions are such (or ever could be such) that the communication of censure would be recognised as such by offenders. Furthermore, one might wonder whether focusing on the individual offender (while justified in terms of treating the offender as a person) is the right way to justify an institution that has such an important structural function in the running of the state.

There are circumstances in which we are within our rights to inflict coercion, even violence, on another: namely, in direct self-defence. Hence, if punishment could be shown to be grounded in self-defence, with the offender as attacker, the infliction of punishment would be within our rights. Daniel Farrell provides a careful argument along these lines. He draws two distinctions. The first is between 'special deterrence' (punishment directed at a particular offender for a particular crime) and 'general deterrence' (punishment directed at types of people for crimes in general). The second is between 'the less radical approach' (which is grounded in an intuitively acceptable principle of distributive justice) and the 'more radical approach' (which goes beyond this principle). The desirable position for Farrell (which is where his argument takes him) is to justify general deterrence through the less radical approach. The disagreement between the communication theorists and Farrell is fundamental. Farrell builds his case on the fact that, in a Lockean state of nature, we have a right to threaten those who we believe are going to attack us. Communication theorists would argue that this gets us off on the wrong foot. In a community, threat would be inappropriate; instead, we ought to address our attacker's reason (Duff 1996: 15–17). It is interesting to reflect on which of these two sources of justification we prefer, and why.

REFERENCES

Bianchi, H. (1986). 'Abolition: Assensus and Sanctuary.' *A Reader on Punishment*. R.A. Duff and D. Garland, eds. Oxford, Oxford University Press (1994): 336–51.

Carlen, P. (1989). 'Crime, Inequality and Sentencing.' *A Reader on Punishment*. R.A. Duff and D. Garland, eds. Oxford, Oxford University Press (1994): 306–32.

Duff, R.A. (1986). *Trials and Punishments*. Cambridge, Cambridge University Press.

Duff, R.A. (1996). 'Penal Communications: Recent Work in the Philosophy of Punishment.' *Crime and Justice: A Review of Research* 20: 1–97.

Hart, H.L.A. (1959). 'Prolegomenon to the Principles of Punishment.' *Punishment and Responsibility*. Oxford, Oxford University Press: 1–27.

von Hirsch, A. (1993). *Censure and Sanctions*. Oxford, Clarendon Press.

23

PUNISHMENT, COMMUNICATION AND COMMUNITY

Antony Duff

One theme in the "retributivist revival" of the last two decades has been that of punishment as a communicative practice. The central retributivist slogan is that punishment is justified as being *deserved* for the crime which is punished: the concept of desert is supposed to indicate the justificatory relationship between past crime and present punishment in virtue of which punishment is an intrinsically appropriate response to crime. For "negative" retributivists, who argue only that punishment must not be *un*-deserved, criminal desert is supposed to provide a necessary, but not a sufficient, condition for punishment; for "positive" retributivists, who argue that punishment is justified just insofar as it is deserved, criminal desert is supposed to provide a sufficient condition for punishment.[1] For either kind of retributivist, however, the central task is to explain this idea of desert – this supposed justificatory relationship between past crime and present punishment: what does it mean to say that crime deserves punishment, or that the guilty deserve to suffer punishment: how does crime call for punishment, or make punishment appropriate?[2] One kind of answer to such questions has portrayed punishment as a communicative process: what crime deserves or makes appropriate is a response which punishment communicates to the criminal.

I want to explore two aspects of such a communicative conception of punishment: but I must first explain in a little more detail what it amounts to. This task will occupy section 1 of this chapter. Section 2 will discuss the role of penal "hard treatment" within a communicative conception of punishment: I will contrast two accounts of that role (von Hirsch's and mine), which appeal respectively to a liberal and to a communication view of the proper nature and function of the state. Finally, section 3 will raise (but will not try to answer) some questions about the moral and political conditions which must be satisfied if criminal punishment is in practice to be justified in the way that, on a communicative conception, it should ideally be justified.

1 PUNISHMENT AS COMMUNICATION

The thought that punishment serves or should serve a communicative purpose is neither new, nor necessarily retributivist.

It is at least a close relative of the familiar thought that punishment serves an expressive function.[3] However, I think it matters that we should talk of "communication", rather than of "expression": for the idea of communication involves, as that of expression need not, the idea of a *reciprocal* and *rational* activity. Expression requires only one who expresses; if there is someone at whom it is directed, that person need figure only as its passive recipient; and if it aims (as it need not) to bring about any effect on its recipient, that intended effect could be entirely non-rational – it need not be mediated by the recipient's reason or understanding. By contrast, communication requires someone to, or with, whom we try to communicate; that person must (if the communication is to be successful) be an active participant in the process, who receives and responds to the communication; and that reception and response must (are intended to) be rational, in that communication appeals to the other's rational understanding, and seeks a response mediated by that understanding. That punishment should be a mode of rational communication (primarily with the offender) is, I believe, an implication of a more general conception of law, and of how a state should treat its citizens – of the view that it should treat and address its citizens as rational, responsible agents.[4]

Now non-retributive theories can, of course, talk of communication. Most obviously, a deterrent theory can portray punishment as a mode of rational communication, which offers potential criminals prudential reason to obey the law: what the punishment of actual offenders communicates – to others, but also to those offenders – is that the threat of punishment is to be taken seriously.[5] What is distinctive about a retributivist version of communication?

Two features distinguish it. First, whereas for a consequentialist (a deterrence theorist for instance) punishment may communicate with anyone who might be usefully affected by the communication, and in particular with the public at large or with those members of it who are tempted by crime, for retributivists the communication must be focused primarily (though not exclusively) on the offender who is being punished: if we are to avoid (as retributivists are keen to avoid) the Kantian accusation of using the offender "merely as a means", we must focus punishment on him, as response to him which is justified by his past offence. Secondly, for a consequentialist *what* is communicated by punishment may be any message which can be expected to assist the further aims that punishment should serve – for instance the message that crime is likely to be followed by sanctions which provides prudential reasons for obeying the law. For a retributivist, by contrast, the message which is communicated by punishment must be a message focused on, and justified by, the offender's past offence: it must be a message appropriate to that past offence.

What kind of message could that be? One obvious answer, on which I will focus here, is that what is communicated should be the censure or condemnation which the crime deserves. Whatever puzzles there might be about the general idea that crimes "deserve" punishment, puzzles of which some anti-retributivists make quite a meal,[6] there is surely nothing puzzling about the idea that wrongdoing deserves censure. An honest response to another's culpable wrongdoing – a response that respects and treats her as a responsible moral agent – is to criticise or censure that conduct; and if we think we have the moral standing to pass moral comment on her conduct (a matter to be discussed in section 3 below), we may indeed sometimes think that we *ought* to censure her – that we owe it to those she wronged, to the values she flouted, and also to her, to censure her. So too, a society which declares certain kinds of conduct to be wrong, as criminal, can and should then censure those who nonetheless engage in such conduct (subject to the qualification about moral standing). Censure addresses the wrongdoers as a responsible citizen; it is owed to him, as an honest response to his crime; to his victims (if there are any), as expressive of a concern for their wronged status; and to the whole society, whose values the law claims to embody.

Now censure can be communicated in various ways. In particular, in the context of the criminal law, it can be communicated by the formal conviction which follows proof of guilt in a criminal trial; or it could be communicated by a system of purely symbolic punishments – punishments which are burdensome or unwelcome *solely* in virtue the censure which they communicate. It *can* also be communicated by the kind of "hard treatment" punishments that characterise our existing penal systems:[7] punishments – for example, imprisonment, fines, compulsory community service – which are (at least typically) burdensome or unwelcome independently of their condemnatory meaning. For given the appropriate kind of conventions, an appropriate institutional setting, all appropriate shared understanding between those who are punished and those who punish (or in whose name punishment is imposed), hard treatment punishments can carry this kind of meaning (but I will have more to say later about the conditions under which they can be expected to be understood in this way).

However, to say that hard treatment punishment *can* carry such a meaning, that censure *can* be communicated in this way, is clearly a long way from saying that this is how censure *should* be formally communicated to those who break the law; or that a society or a state has the right to use this method of communicating censure. Thus the familiar task for those who offer any kind of communicative (or for that matter expressive) account of punishment is to explain and justify the role of hard treatment.

This leads me into the first of my two main topics. Various accounts could be offered of the proper role of hard treatment punishments within a roughly communicative, and roughly retributivist, account of punishment.[8] They differ primarily in whether they try to justify hard treatment in terms of the communicative purpose of punishment itself; or accept that it requires some other, separate kind of justification.

For present purposes, I will focus on the contrast between the account I have argued for, which is of the first kind, and that which von Hirsch offers, which is of the second kind: this contrast will also lead its into aspects of the tension between communitarian, and liberal political theories.

2 PENAL HARD TREATMENT: PENANCE OR PRUDENTIAL SUPPLEMENT?

On the account I have developed and defended elsewhere, the communicative purpose of criminal punishment runs all the way down, even to the justification (at, I should emphasise, the level of ideal theory) of particular kinds of hard treatment punishment. The aim of penal hard treatment should ideally be to bring the criminal to understand, and to repent, the wrong he has done: it tries to direct (to force) his attention onto his crime, aiming thereby to bring him to understand that crime's character and implications as a wrong, and to persuade him to accept as deserved the censure which punishment communicates – an acceptance which must involve repentance. Punishment also provides a vehicle through which he can strengthen or deepen that repentant understanding of his wrongdoing, and express it to others: a vehicle, that is, both for the attempt at self-correction and self-reform that sincere repentance involves, and for the communication to others (to those he has wronged, to his fellow citizens) of that sincere repentance. Finally, by undergoing such penitential punishment the wrongdoer can reconcile himself with his fellow citizens, and restore himself to full membership of the community from which his wrongdoing threatened to exclude him. Punishment is, in other words, a secular penance; and the particular modes of punishment should be suitable to such an enterprise of penitential communication.[9]

I should emphasise four initial points about this account. First, it is retributivist in that it justifies punishment as an intrinsically appropriate response to a past crime – a response that seeks to communicate to the offender, and to persuade her to understand and accept, the fact, nature, and implications of the wrong she has done. Unlike many more traditional retributivist accounts, it also looks to the future: punishment aims to induce a process of repentance, self-reform, and reconciliation. However, this is not to say that it seeks to combine retributivist and consequentialist elements in a "mixed" penal theory. Whereas on a consequentialist account the relationship between punishment and the ends which justify it is purely *contingent* (punishment is justified if it is a contingently efficient means of securing some independently identifiable end), on my account that relationship is *internal*: for the end to be achieved (the offender's repentant understanding of her crime) is such that punishment (the attempt to induce such an understanding by the communication of censure) is an intrinsically appropriate way to achieve it.

Secondly, this account is intended to provide, not a justification of punishment as it actually operates in our existing penal systems (which cannot in general be seen as administering such communicative, penitential punishments), but an account of what punishment should *ideally* be: an account against which we can measure, and no doubt find seriously wanting, our existing penal practices. I take this to be a general feature of normative theories of punishment: that they should aim to provide, not a comforting justification of the penal status quo, but a critical, ideal standard against which our penal actualities should be judged.[10]

Thirdly, this account does not warrant grossly oppressive kinds of punishment which seek to break or grind the offender down until he repents: for his punishment must, if it is to communicate the kind and degree of censure he deserves, be proportionate to his offence; and it must address and appeal to him as a rational moral agent, whose moral understanding it seeks to arouse but should not seek to coerce. This implies (as is anyway obvious enough) that punishment is necessarily fallible: it aims or aspires to induce repentance and self-reform but, like any attempt at moral persuasion, leaves the offender free to remain unpersuaded *and* unrepentant. Punishments which fail to persuade the offender are in one sense unsuccessful: but they can still be justified as attempts (even as attempts which we might reasonably believe are doomed to fail) to communicate with and to persuade a moral agent who is within the realm of our shared moral discourse; and they can succeed in communicating even if they fail to persuade.

Fourthly, such communicative punishment is best exemplified, not by the kinds of long prison sentence which loom so large in penal discussion; nor by the fines which, though the penalty of choice for very many offenders, are usually ill-suited to this communicative purpose: but by such "punishments in the community" as community service orders and probation (as well as by "mediation" schemes whose aim is to bring the offender to recognise the nature and implications of what she has done, and thus to make material or symbolic reparation for it).

Now I think that punishments *can*, even in our own radically imperfect penal systems, serve such a communicative and penitential purpose.[11] Such an account nonetheless seems to many to be quite implausible as an account even of the ideal aims of a system of state punishment. I want to focus here on some of von Hirsch's objections, concerning the proper aims and purposes of the state – since these lead us into the issues in political theory that I want to discuss.[12]

Von Hirsch allows that in certain particular contexts punishment could have the kind of communicative and penitential character that I ascribe to criminal punishment: for instance, in the context of a monastic order. Three features of such a context might seem crucial. First, it involves a community membership of which is typically optional (or should be optional, if we are not to have serious doubts about its legitimacy): members are free to leave; and alternative modes of life are available which do not make such stringent or intrusive moral demands. Secondly, the community is structured and united by a rich set of shared spiritual values: to belong to the community is to be committed not just to behaving towards one's fellows in appropriate ways, but to orienting one's soul towards the proper values. Thirdly, it can then be plausible that breaches of the community's norms do threaten to separate the offender not just from others within the community, but from his own good – which, as he himself sees it (else he would not want to remain a member) consists in full membership of the community; and that penance imposed on him by the community or its proper authority can serve to bring him to a proper repentance (partly because they appeal to what he already believes and accepts), restoring him to full membership of the community – and thus to his own good. Monasteries do, by their very nature, have a proper interest in the spiritual condition and well-being of their members – an interest which those members accept in virtue of their membership; and that interest can properly be exercised in, *inter alia*, the application of penitential punishments.

However, matters are quite different in all three respects when we turn to the context of a modern state. First, membership of the state, and consequent subjection to its laws, are not optional: we are born into a state; and if we have any alternative at all, it is emigration to another state. Secondly, even if we can identify any shared values which help to structure the political community whose law it is (and there is certainly more scope here than there is in the case of a monastery for the identity and character of the "community" to be determined by institutional structures and power relationships, rather than by genuinely shared values), they are (and should be) far more modest and limited in their scope than are those which structure a monastic community: in particular, they do not and should not, as values of a political society, include spiritual values to do with the conditions of its members' souls. Thirdly, we therefore cannot see breaches of the law as separating the offender from her own good (we must recognise, if we also disapprove of, the fact that for many individuals and subgroups their good as they intelligibly understand it is not bound up with the values defined and protected by the law); nor can we see punishments imposed by the state as restoring the offender to membership of a community in which she herself finds her own good.

This kind of objection clearly appeals both to some obvious facts about modern political society, and to certain familiar, roughly liberal, values. Modern Western states of the kinds in which we live (excluding officially theocratic states) do not constitute the sorts of intimate spiritual community in which penance finds its natural home: nor *should* they do so, since that would be profoundly at odds with the liberal values of respect for individual freedom and autonomy, of pluralism and of privacy, and profoundly dangerous to individual good.

By contrast, my account might seem to embody a (to liberal ears) disturbingly intrusive and oppressive form of communitarianism. It locates the individual's identity and her good in her membership, not just of *some* community, but of the larger political community under whose laws she must live – in her relationship to the shared values by which that community is supposedly structured, and which its laws supposedly embody. It gives the state, as the institutional embodiment or structure of that political community, a proper interest not just in her (external) conduct towards her fellow citizens, but in her (internal) moral condition – an interest strong and extensive enough to justify it in trying to improve her moral condition by punitive coercion.

What then can a liberal critic like von Hirsch say about penal hard treatment – if he is still to justify it (as he wants to); if he is to preserve (as he wants to) the thought that punishment should serve primarily as a mode of moral communication which seeks to communicate to the offender the censure which his wrongdoing deserves; and if he is to avoid (as he wants to) the Hegelian objection that to use penal hard treatment *purely* as a mode of prudential deterrence is to treat the citizen (any potential criminal) "like a dog instead of with the Freedom and respect due to him as a man"?[13] Von Hirsch's answer is that penal hard treatment should serve as a prudential *supplement* to the law's normative voice. It serves as a deterrent, in that it aims to reduce crime by creating a prudential disincentive that might dissuade from crime at least some of those who are insufficiently motivated by the law's moral appeal. However, it should not replace or drown (as a system of purely deterrent hard treatment punishments replaces or drowns) the moral tones of censure: it offers an *additional*, prudential reason for obedience, as being suitable to moral agents like ourselves who are susceptible to moral censure but also susceptible to temptation – a reason which is not (or should not be) intended to be persuasive by itself (as the reasons offered by purely deterrent punishments are intended to be), but which can add additional persuasive force to the law's primarily moral appeal. It follows from this, of course, that hard treatment punishments must be strictly limited in their severity, if they are not to drown the law's moral voice: von Hirsch suggests that current levels of penal severity should be reduced towards a system that would allow no prison term of more than three years (or five years for homicide).[14]

One significant merit of such an account is that it portrays punishment as something we could plausibly impose on, and threaten against, *ourselves*. Purely deterrent justifications of punishment are liable to portray it as something that "we", the law-abiding and moral, must threaten against "them", the dangerously immoral or amoral, in order to coerce them into obeying "our" laws – laws for which they otherwise have no respect.[15] Von Hirsch's account, by contrast, aims to portray punishment as a system of prudentially supplemented censure that we could, as moral agents who recognise our own imperfections and inadequacies, plausibly impose on ourselves to help us to act as we know we ought to act (but fear we will not always act without such prudential incentives).

However, one objection to this solution to the problem of justifying penal hard treatment is that it is liable to be undermined by the tension between preserving the communication of censure to moral agents as the primary purpose of punishment, and using hard treatment as a prudential supplement, which will have some additional crime-preventive efficacy. On the one hand, whilst the threat of a three-year prison term is certainly dramatically less coercive than are the maximum sentences currently provided (even in relatively liberal penal systems) for offences other than homicide, it still seems rather too severe to serve as a mere prudential supplement – as merely "an aid to carrying out what [the agent] himself recognizes as the proper course of conduct":[16] it seems more apt to replace, than to supplement, the moral voice of the law. On the other hand, if we seriously tried to reduce the severity of hard treatment punishments to a level at which they would provide no more than a subordinate prudential supplement to the law's moral voices, it is not at all clear that such punishments would have a preventive efficacy significantly greater than would flow from a system of purely symbolic punishments – an efficacy great enough to justify the creation and maintenance of the whole apparatus of penal hard treatment.

This account is perhaps most plausible in relation to relatively minor crimes, and the relatively light punishments they would attract. The fine I would receive for speeding or for dangerous driving might well not by itself, as a purely prudential disincentive (independently of its character as a punishment), suffice to dissuade me: but the prospect of it could provide a useful, modest supplement to the moral appeal of the law – an appeal to which I know I am sometimes liable to be insufficiently attentive. This is not too far removed from the kind of private punishment that someone might threaten against herself to encourage herself to do what she knows she ought to do. However, matters seem very different when we turn to much more serious kinds of crime. The prospect of three years' imprisonment might dissuade some potential murderers or rapists from committing such crimes: but if we ask how that prospect could figure in their deliberations or motivations, the only plausible answer is surely that it would replace, rather than supplement, the law's moral appeal to the wrongfulness of such conduct.

The problem about penal hard treatment, for communicative theorists, is that the obvious rationale to offer for communicating censure by hard treatment rather than by purely symbolic punishments is deterrence – recognising that too many potential criminals will be unmoved or insufficiently moved by the prospect of symbolically communicated censure, we create for them a prudentially persuasive reason to obey the law: but such a rationale is unacceptable to those who take seriously the Hegelian (and Kantian) objection that to secure obedience to the law by the threat of deterrent sanctions is to fail to respect the moral agency of those whom we threaten. Von Hirsch seeks to resolve this problem by transforming deterrence into a subordinate prudential supplement, of a kind that we might impose on ourselves: but I think his resolution fails.

Can my attempt to resolve this problem, by incorporating hard treatment *within* the aim of moral communication, fare any better? In particular, can it meet the liberal charge that it is inconsistent with the liberal values of respect for individual autonomy and privacy, and with a liberal conception of the proper role of the state – and of the limits that should be set on its exercise of its coercive punitive power?

My account is certainly and fundamentally inconsistent with some of the more strenuous and metaphysical versions of liberal individualism, which take their stand on the separate and distinct identity of each individual, allocating to the individual an extensive private sphere which includes her moral beliefs and attitudes; and which found political relationships and institutions on the model of a social contract. Social contracts are made between strangers, who wish to regulate their external dealings with each other; and whilst they may include clauses which require not just certain kinds of mutual non-interference, but also certain kinds of positive mutual assistance, they presuppose separateness and distance between the parties. They are of course likely to include penalty clauses, attaching agreed sanctions to breaches of the contract: but those provisions, when they do not aim to remedy the harm done by the breach,[17] can be most plausibly understood in deterrent terms – they provide prudential disincentives to breaches of the contract, and thus make the contract itself (and the parties' confidence in it) more secure.

The idea of punishment as secular penance would obviously be entirely alien to such an understanding of society and the state. So too, however, would be the idea of punishment as a mode of moral communication, for two reasons.

First, such moral communication – even if it aims only to communicate censure – must presuppose richer and closer relationships between the people concerned than this austere contractualist model provides. It presupposes a shared language of values (which itself requires some genuinely shared values) in which the communication can take place. It also presupposes that those involved have a proper interest in the moral character of each others' conduct, *and* a relationship with each other which gives them the moral standing to comment thus forcibly on that conduct. It presupposes, that is, a moral community, whose members see themselves as bound (or can at least intelligibly claim of each other that they *should* see themselves as bound) by certain shared values which inform their common life; a community whose members also have, in virtue of that common life, the standing to criticise each others' conduct in the light of those values.

Secondly, the purpose internal to censure as a communicative act is not just that the other should hear what is said, nor just that she should understand it, but that she should *accept* it: that she should come to see, if she does not already see, the censure as a justified response to the wrong she has done.[18] But to accept censure as justified is to recognise that I have done wrong; to recognise that I have done wrong should (if that recognition is sincere and whole-hearted) be to repent that wrong; and to repent my past conduct commits me to an attempt to reform my future conduct. The purpose internal to a practice of censure is thus not merely to transmit a message; nor merely to modify the external conduct of those who are censured: but to induce an appropriate moral change in their attitudes and dispositions – a purpose that can find no place within the austere contractualist model sketched above.

A conception of punishment as communicative is thus (in one of the many variegated senses of the term) "communitarian": it appeals to a linguistic and moral community whose members, in virtue of their shared language, values and form of life, can claim and have the moral standing to criticise each others' conduct. It is important to notice, however, that such a community can be a *liberal* community, in that it can recognise as being of foundational importance some of the central values to which liberal theorists typically appeal. In particular, it can recognise individual autonomy (autonomy understood, of course, as autonomy *within* a shared form of life, which alone can give the notion any substantive sense) as a fundamental value – as something to be both promoted and respected; it can likewise recognise individual freedom and privacy – the preservation for each citizen of an extensive sphere within which they are free from coercion or intrusion by others and by the state – as essential values.

This kind of communitarianism thus rejects that metaphysical conception of the person, as an individual who can be identified (and treated as the basis of value) independently of their social context, which some forms of liberalism have taken to be foundational. To reject such a *metaphysical* conception, however, is not necessarily to reject the *normative* claims of liberalism, which can (suitably reinterpreted in line with a communitarian metaphysics) be detached from such dubious metaphysical foundations.

This account also rejects, or at least seeks to limit, some of the more extreme claims of normative liberalism. It insists that the community (and the state that should give institutional form to the central values and aims of the community) must respect the autonomy of its members or citizens: thus in the context of criminal law and punishment, the citizens must be addressed as moral agents whose obedience and allegiance are to be sought by modes of rational moral persuasion, but must not be coerced or manipulated. But it also allows the state to use the coercive apparatus of criminal punishment not just to provide prudential incentives for obedience, but to try to reach the offender's moral conscience and understanding – which many liberals would count as a dangerously intrusive, and potentially oppressive, use of the coercive power of the state. However, three points about this conception of punishment, about the nature of criminal law and of (communicative) punishment in a community which takes autonomy seriously, should do something to allay such concerns. None are inconsistent with the idea that hard treatment punishments can and should serve the aims of penitential communication: rather, they will help to structure a more precise articulation of that idea, which will show it to be fully consistent (at the level, I emphasise again, of ideal theory) with a proper regard for individual autonomy, freedom, and privacy.

First, a community which takes autonomy seriously (and the related values of individual freedom and privacy, and of a plurality of conceptions of the good life) will set strict limits on the scope of the criminal law: given the law's peremptory nature, and its demand that the individual citizen subject their own judgement to its authority, it should be used to prohibit only kinds of conduct which seriously treated interests or values which are of central importance to the community and its members.[19] This is one difference between the criminal law (as on this view it should be) and the laws of a monastic order: that the laws of a monastic order will be far more extensive (and far more intrusive) in scope than those of a liberal community.

Secondly, the criminal law, and the criminal justice system, do have a proper interest in the moral character (the moral attitudes and values) of the citizens: the law condemns, and seeks to persuade to self-reform, those whose criminal conduct manifests a serious disrespect for the legally protected rights and interests of others, and for the values which the law protects. But that interest is strictly limited to those aspects of the citizen's moral character which are fully displayed in (indeed constituted by) criminal conduct: it is only the offender's actualised criminal dispositions that properly concern the criminal law.[20] This is then another difference between the criminal law (as it should be) and the laws of a monastic order: a monastic order has a proper interest in every aspect of its members' spiritual and moral condition, whereas the criminal law has a very much more restricted proper interest in the moral condition of its citizens.

Thirdly, a respect for autonomy will preclude any attempt to *force* a citizen to change her moral attitudes, or to bring about such a change by any means other than those of rational moral persuasion – it precludes both the coercion and the manipulation of attitudes or beliefs. Thus although the aim of communicative punishment is to induce an appropriate change in the offender's attitudes and dispositions, that change must in the end be one that he himself brings about, because he sees it to be necessary (the aim, we could say, is not merely "reform" but *self*-reform); and although punishment is, obviously, coercive, what it should aim to force on the offender is not the desirable change in his attitudes, dispositions and future conduct, but the awareness that his community thinks such a change necessary. He is forced to hear the punitive message: but it must be up to him whether or not he accepts that message, and the opportunity for repentance and reconciliation which his punishment provides. (A further, and related, constraint is that an offender's punishment should not be continued until he (appears to) repent: partly because that would clearly constitute an attempt at coercive change; partly because if his punishment is to communicate an appropriate censure of his crime, it must be roughly proportionate to the seriousness of that crime.)

A penal system structured by such (liberal-communitarian) values and constraints could, in principle, use hard treatment punishments to serve the communicative and penitential aims which (on my account) punishment should serve – and to serve those aims in a way which respects the autonomy, the moral standing and the privacy of conscience of those who are punished (as of all citizens). It would differ quite significantly from our own penal system in its use of penal hard treatment: it would make much less use of imprisonment (which, as communicating the message that exclusion from the community is the only appropriate moral response to the offender's crime, must be reserved for the most serious community-destroying crimes); it would make less use of fines (which lack an appropriately meaningful relationship to many of the offences for which they are currently imposed); it would make far more use of a wide range of non-custodial punishments – including but not limited to community service orders and probation (which are better suited to the task of bringing offenders to understand the nature and implications of their crimes, and of constituting appropriate penalties for those crimes). But its punishments would still involve penal hard treatment, in that they would be at least typically burdensome or unwelcome independently of their condemnatory meaning.

I have argued so far that a fully communicative account of punishment, which portrays penal hard treatment as an integral part of the communicative penal process, can be defended against von Hirsch's liberal criticisms: it is not fundamentally inconsistent with the values (or with a communitarian version of the values) of autonomy, freedom, and privacy on which his criticisms rest. However, such liberal worries have more, although now non-foundational,[21] force when we turn from the level of ideal theory at which I have so far been arguing, to that of practical actuality. Are we really to urge those who administer our penal system to see themselves as properly engaged in an enterprise of moral persuasion and reform: to allow and urge judges to find new and creative kinds of punishment which will be communicatively appropriate to the individual offender; to urge prison officers to seek to persuade their charges of the need for repentance and moral reform; to urge those who administer non-custodial punishments to see their task as that of administering secular penances? The dangers of any such programme (of distortion, of oppression, of manipulation) are all too obvious – though again this is more true if we look at our prisons, and less true if we look at the ways in which some programmes of non-custodial punishment are administered; and those dangers might throw a more attractive light on a less ambitious communicative account like von Hirsch's.

I will not, however, pursue this question here. It concerns the practical possibility (and the moral dangers) of seeking to actualise an ambitiously communicative conception of punishment in an existing penal system like our own, and focuses on the internal workings of that system: how far could we realistically expect, given the nature and structure of that system, that punishments would actually be administered or received in the way, in the spirit, with the restraint and respect, which this conception of punishment requires? But there are deeper worries than this about the applicability of this (or, I would argue, of any plausible) justifying account of punishment to our actual world; and it is to these that I now turn.

3 COMMUNICATION AND MORAL STANDING

The question raised (but left unanswered) at the end of the previous section concerned the internal operations of a would-be communicative practice of punishment: how far could we realistically expect that the actual administrations of punishment would satisfy the conditions for just and justified punishment specified by a communicative theory? The deeper worries to which I referred concern the conditions which must be satisfied if any such practice is to be legitimate, whatever its internal operations: conditions whose existence must be presupposed by any such practice, but whose existence is also, in our present situation, doubtful.[22] I think that worries of this kind should undermine our confidence in the applicability of any plausible justifying theory of criminal punishment which takes the demands of justice seriously:[23] but a communicative theory raises them in a particular, and perhaps illuminating, form.

I want to note two such conditions here: one concerns "moral standing"; the other what we might call the accent of penal communication – the voice in which it is administered and can be received. Both conditions reflect the fact that the possibility, and the legitimacy, of a communicative process depend on there existing an appropriate relationship between the parties concerned. They also remind us that the question of the justification of punishment is not just the question of whether, from some abstract point of view, criminals deserve to be punished, or of whether their punishment would achieve some good, but also and crucially the question of whether some particular person or body can justly and justifiably punish them.

If, as an individual, I criticise another's conduct on moral grounds, the justifiability of my action depends on two kinds of condition. First, did she actually (and culpably) commit the wrong for which I criticise and condemn her (a question which of course involves a host of subordinate questions about the facts, the proper interpretation, and the moral character of her conduct)? Secondly, and even if she did do such a culpable wrong, do I have the moral standing to criticise or condemn her for it? This second question is clearly crucial, but also (at least to a significant degree) independent of the first: the person I criticise could reject my criticism, not on the grounds that she did not do the wrong I accuse her of doing (she might admit that), but on the grounds that it is not for *me* to judge or to criticise her.

We can note two such grounds. She might argue, on the one hand, that I lack the appropriate relationship to her, or to the action in question, for that action to be any of my business: she is not answerable to me, though she may be answerable to others, for what she has done; my criticism is not a piece of justified moral comment, but an unwarranted interference (just what kind of relationship is required for moral criticism to be legitimate depends crucially, of course, on the nature of the wrong I accuse her of doing). Or, alternatively, she might argue that though her conduct is indeed my business (for instance because it directly affected me), my previous dealings with her deprive me of the moral standing to criticise her: if I have unrepentantly betrayed her, or wrongfully deceived her, I am not now well placed to criticise her for betraying or deceiving me in a similar way. (Notice again that this is not to claim that my past conduct to her *justifies* or *excuses* her present conduct to me, rendering it non-culpable: it is to claim that I lack the moral standing to criticise her.)

Communicative punishments censure or criticise the conduct of those who are punished. They are formally imposed by the courts, and administered by officials of the penal system: but they are supposedly imposed and administered on behalf of, in the name of, the political community whose laws the offender has breached; the content of the communication is not "*I* (the judge, the prison officer, the probation officer) censure your conduct", but "*We* (the whole community, to which you belong, and by whose laws you are bound) censure your conduct". We therefore need to ask what is required to constitute an appropriate "we"; and whether "we" have the moral standing to criticise and censure this person's conduct.

The first of these questions concerns some of the conditions required for the existence of a political community – as a linguistic community which shares a normative language, and so also a set of substantive values,[24] rich enough to render mutually intelligible the normative demands that the law makes on all citizens, and the normative judgments it makes on their conduct. If the law is to be *their* law, as citizens of the political community (rather than being an alien imposition on them), it must express values that are widely shared; and those values, and the language in which they are expressed, must be at least accessible to all the citizens, as values which they *could* share – and which others can properly claim that they *should* share.

This requirement might not be *enormously* demanding, if the law is as modest in scope as I suggested it should be on a liberal-communitarian view. It is certainly consistent, on such a view, with wide differences in forms of life, in normative concepts, in values, within the same political community: perhaps what it requires is something more like a Rawlsian overlapping consensus than a Habermassian ideal speech community. But it is nonetheless a substantive requirement, as reflecting an important precondition of legal obligation (for I can be obligated only by laws that reflect values which are accessible to me, and which I could reasonably be expected to accept);[25] and we need to ask how far it is satisfied by any actual legal system – including our own. Answers to this question are likely to be complicated and messy, rather than simple and straightforward: we might expect to find that some aspects of the law satisfy this requirement, whilst others do not, at least in relation to some groups. But insofar as this requirement is not fully satisfied, the law's claim to obligate all citizens (and thus to condemn and punish them legitimately for breaches of its demands) is weakened or undermined.

However, even if a satisfactory answer can be provided to the first question (about the existence of a linguistic and political community which constitutes an appropriate "we"), there remains the second question – about whether "we" also have the moral standing to condemn, through the courts, the conduct of this defendant. For just as my own previous and unrepented conduct towards the person I would now criticise can disqualify me from having the standing to criticise her, so can the (collective and institutional, rather than personal and informal) behaviour of a political community towards some of its members deprive it of the standing to condemn at least some of their conduct through the law. Someone who has been not merely unfortunately disadvantaged, but unjustly excluded from many of those opportunities and benefits that others enjoy, seeks by criminal means some modest improvement in her unjustly disadvantaged lot – for instance by committing a social security fraud: I think there is then a real question about whether "we" – the comfortably included – have the standing to condemn her, insofar as we either benefit from those political and economic structures which treat her thus unjustly, or are passively complicit in those injustices; in which case there is also a real question about whether the courts have the moral standing to condemn and punish her.

I should emphasise that to raise this question is not to suggest that the courts might lack moral standing to condemn *any* crime that such a person might commit: just as my previous deception of another person, whilst it might disqualify me from condemning her deception of me, need not disqualify me from condemning other kinds of wrong that she commits (an act of gratuitous cruelty, perhaps), so the courts could be morally disqualified from condemning some, but not all, kinds of crime committed by one who has been unjustly disadvantaged. Nor is it to suggest that her crime (her social security fraud) is either justified or excusable: it is rather to raise the issue of who has the standing to judge it at all. Nor, finally, is it to suggest that *no one* has the standing to judge, or indeed to condemn, her conduct: for instance, those whose situation is similar to hers might have that standing; and might indeed justly condemn her, on the grounds that hers is not an appropriate response to the injustices which she, and they, admittedly suffer.

We should also note, however, that the two questions I have so far raised in this section (about the existence of an appropriate political community, and about its moral standing to judge a defendant's conduct) are closely connected in at least the following way: that a radical enough failure to satisfy the conditions of moral standing (to have behaved towards this person in a way that entitles "us" to judge her) also undermines the conditions of community between her and "us" – between her and those for whom and in whose voice the law speaks. We can reasonably expect, if we are not overcome by a radical MacIntyrean scepticism about the contemporary existence or possibility of moral community,[26] to find that *some* political community of the appropriate sort exists, whose law the actual law can plausibly claim to be: a community whose members do indeed share the values which the law embodies. But this is not yet to say that that community includes as full members *all* those whom the law claims to bind and to have the standing to judge and punish – that every defendant who appears before the courts will be a member of the "we" in whose name he is judged; and those who suffer persistent, systematic, and serious injustice under an existing set of political, economic, and legal structures may indeed be excluded from that "we". In one sense they are members of the political community: since they live within it, they have a legitimate claim to be treated as full members of it, and suffer injustice in so far as they are not thus treated. In another sense, however, they may be excluded (or may reasonably exclude themselves) from the community: they are not accorded the respect, the concern, which is due to fellow citizens; in response to which they may no longer see themselves as bound by the laws or demands of a community which thus excludes them.

These points about the moral standing to punish can, I think, help us to understand the problem of "doing justice in an unjust society".[27] Sometimes the issue here is taken to be that of whether the law should recognise some special defence of acute (unjust) social disadvantage[28] which implies that the unjustly disadvantaged defendant is indeed answerable before the law for her conduct, but should perhaps be able to plead some special justification or excuse. We must also ask, however (which is the force of the questions I have raised here) whether such a defendant *is* answerable before the courts for this conduct. This is to ask, in part, whether she was genuinely obligated to obey the law which she allegedly broke:[29] but it is also and relatedly to ask in part about the existence of all appropriate political community to which she belongs and whose law this is; and to ask whether the courts have the moral standing to judge her.

The questions I have raised so far in this section concern the moral standing of those who would punish offenders, or on whose behalf and in whose name offenders are to be punished. They are thus independent of, and prior to, the question of whether the *content* of the penal communication is, from some abstract point of view, justified or appropriate – the question of whether this person did culpably commit the criminal wrong for which his punishment would censure him: they concern, as I have emphasised, not the issue of whether this person acted rightly or wrongly, justifiably or unjustifiably, excusably or inexcusably (from either a legal or a moral point of view), but the question of who has the appropriate standing to judge that issue. I want now, finally, to raise a further and related question, concerning not so much the moral standing of those who punish, but the accent or tones in which they speak the language of punishment, and in which they can be heard to speak by those who are punished.

There is a multitude of ways in which communications can be misunderstood; and whilst some misunderstandings reflect some fault or failing on the part of the listener, many others are, from her point of view, quite reasonable. Some such reasonable misunderstandings have to do with the content of the communication: the language, the concepts, the structures of thought, might be obscure, equivocal, or simply unfamiliar to the listener. Others, however, have rather to do with the accent or voice in which the speaker speaks – or is heard to speak. What is sincerely intended as an expression of sympathetic fellow feeling might be heard as an expression of patronising pity; what is intended as a polite and tentative request might be heard instead as a peremptory order; what a teacher intends to be a constructive but tentative suggestion in discussion with a student might be heard instead as a dogmatic instruction that that is what the student must write in her essay or her exam if she wants a good mark. Such misunderstandings depend, of course, on a variety of factors: on the expectations which the hearer brings to the particular situation; on the personal, social, or institutional contract within which the interchange is set; on the speaker's (whether actual, or as perceived by the listener) position and attitudes in relation to the listener; on the past dealings between the speaker (or the institutional structures from within which she speaks) and the listener; and so on. All of these contextual factors help to determine just what it is that the listener hears.[30]

A sensitive speaker will of course be alert to the possibility of such misunderstandings, and might sometimes rightly feel that she should refrain from speaking at all: not because the content of what she said would (as she intends it) be wrong or inappropriate; nor because she lacks the standing to say it, but because he realises that it is likely to be misunderstood – that she is likely to be heard to speak in the (inappropriate) accent of condescending pity rather than in the (appropriate) accent of fellow feeling, or in the accent of peremptory instruction rather than in that of polite request. The prospective misunderstanding might not be one for which she (or the hearer) could be criticised, or one that she could avoid: this is particularly likely to be true in institutional contexts, when what the listener hears will be conditioned in crucial part by his perception of, and past dealings with, the institution from within which and with whose institutional voice she must speak. But if such misunderstanding is likely enough, and would be damaging enough to the aims of her communicative enterprise, it might be that she should not speak.

What has this to do with criminal punishment? Nothing, if we do not see punishment as a communicative enterprise: but a lot, if we do see it as communicative. For we must then ask, not just whether the content of the penal communication (either in the abstract, or as intended by those who punish) is appropriate to the wrongful conduct of the person to be punished; nor just whether those who would judge and punish him (or in whose name he is to be judged and punished) have the moral standing to do so: but also whether he can be reasonably expected to receive and to interpret the penal message with the meaning, in the accents, that it should have and is intended to have. The mere fact that an offender will, predictably, misinterpret his punishment does not of course render its imposition unjustified. We, or the court, might be confident that a career robber will interpret his latest conviction and prison sentence not as an expression of the condemnation which (in the eyes of the law and the community) his conduct deserves (for he has no interest in such moralising), but simply as one of the hazards of his chosen profession: but so long as we can properly attribute that interpretation to his wilful refusal to face up to the wrongful character of his conduct (a refusal which his punishment is intended, albeit perhaps with little hope of success, to persuade him to rethink), we can still hold that he is justly punished. Not all such predictable misunderstandings can, however, be thus blamed on the offender.

A penal practitioner (a probation officer, for instance, or a prison governor) might see her proper task as being to engage in the kind of communicative enterprise that I have sketched. But she might also recognise that, in a particular case or perhaps even in general, that task is not one that she can now perform: that in the context in which she must try to perform it (a context structured by the whole institutional apparatus of the criminal justice system, and by the offenders' histories of past dealings with various parts of that system), her communicative endeavours are almost bound to be misinterpreted by those towards whom they are directed; they will be interpreted (and, given those past histories, not unreasonably so) not as attempts at moral communication, but as the coercive – perhaps also hypocritical – impositions of an alien or oppressive institutional structure.

If this would happen only in a (relatively) few particular cases, it would create a problem within the penal system for the practitioners who must deal with those cases, but it would not threaten the legitimacy of the system as a whole. If, however, something like this would be a predictable general result of an attempt to transform our existing penal practices into the kind of communicative enterprise that I have suggested punishment ought (in ideal theory) to be; if what were intended to be (and would be justified only as being) the accents of moral communication would predictably and not unreasonably be heard in other quite inappropriate tones: then the problem – at least for an ambitiously communicative theory of punishment – is much more serious. We would have to conclude that such a conception of punishment cannot – at least at present – be actualised as the conception which structures our penal practices.

In this section, I have suggested various conditions which would need to be satisfied for punishment to serve, as I believe it should ideally serve, as a mode of moral communication that aims to induce repentance and self-reform in the offender: conditions which have to do, not so much with the internal workings of a penal system, but with the social and political context on which such a system depends. I have not tried to answer the question of whether or how far those conditions are satisfied in a society such as our own; nor am I at all sure what the answer (or rather, the answers, since we cannot suppose that any one unitary answer will be available) should be. It will not, we can be sure, be a very reassuring answer: but I find that I veer back and forth between, on the one hand, a wholly pessimistic view that under present – and foreseeable – conditions criminal punishment simply cannot be or become such a mode of moral communication; and the slightly more optimistic view that, once we grasp the fact that "the criminal justice system" is less a monolithic and unitary institution than a set of diverse and partly autonomous sub-systems and practices, we will also see that there may be room, in some contexts, for at least modest efforts at a communicative penalty.

Some will no doubt think that an ideal account of punishment which raises such complex questions about its own practicability, which is as far removed from penal actuality as I admit that mine is, and which sets such demanding preconditions for the legitimacy of punishment, should simply be rejected as a philosopher's dream: a dream that might be interesting to those who enjoy the intellectual game of imagining ideal communities, but that has nothing to say to those who want to engage with the real world of crime and punishment. If we want to see punishment as a morally communicative process at all, we should abandon such ambitious communicative aims in favour of a more modest model like von Hirsch's, which does not aim to use penal hard treatment itself as part of the communicative process. Or, alternatively, we should abandon the idea of moral communication in the penal sphere altogether, in favour of some other justifying theory (some other version of retributivism; a suitably side-constrained deterrent theory; an account of punishment as "social defence"?) which has more chance of being practically realisable.

However (and unsurprisingly), that does not seem to me to be the right way forward, for two reasons. First, *if* such an ambitious communicative theory is plausible, as part of an ideal account of how a state should deal with its citizens and how they should deal with each other, then the impracticability of that ideal does not render it irrelevant to practice: it should, at the very least, serve as a standard against which the radical imperfections of penal actuality can be assessed and highlighted. Secondly, I think that *any* justifying account of punishment (or any account which is to have any moral credibility) must face versions of the questions which I have posed for a communicative theory. Any such account faces a version of the question of moral standing – the question of who has the right or the standing to judge and to punish those who break the law. Furthermore, I take it to be a basic principle (a principle independent of any particular theory of punishment) for a state which is to treat its citizens as rational and autonomous agents that punishment, like any other application of the state's coercive power, must not only be justified, but must be justified *to* those on whom it is imposed. But if that is so, then a communicative endeavour (the justification of the punishment) must be involved in any infliction of punishment, under any acceptable theory of punishment; and if that is so, any acceptable theory of punishment must face some version of the questions I have raised about the preconditions of legitimate and effective communication.

NOTES

1   On "negative" and "positive" retributivisms, see D. Dolinko, "Some Thoughts about Retributivism", (1991) 101 *Ethics* 537–59.

2   See P. Ardal, "Does Anyone Ever Deserve to Suffer?", (1984) 91–92 *Queens Quarterly* 241–57; D. Husak, "Why Punish the Deserving?", (1991) 26 *Nous* 447–64; T. Honderich, *Punishment: The Supposed Justifications* (Cambridge, Polity, revd. edn. 1989), ch. 2 Honderich, "Culpability and Mystery", in R. A. Duff and N. E. Simmonds (eds.), *Philosophy and the Criminal Law* (Franz Steiner, 1984), pp. 71–7.

3   See, famously, J. Feinberg, "The Expressive Function of Punishment" (1965) 49 *The Monist* 397–408; also I. Primoratz, "Punishment as Language", (1989) 64 *Philosophy* 187–205. For critical discussion, see A. J. Skillen, "How to Say Things with Walls, (1980) 55 *Philosophy* 509–23; M. Davis, "Punishment as a Language: Misleading Analogy for Desert Theorists", (1991) 10 *Law and Philosophy* 310–22.

4   See my *Trials and Punishments* (Cambridge, Cambridge University Press, 1986), especially chs. 3, 4, 9, 10.

5   For other, more sophisticated, consequentialist accounts of punishment which give communication an important role, see N. Lacey, *State Punishment* (London, Routledge, 1988); J Braithwaite and P. Pettit, *Not Just Deserts* (Oxford: Oxford University Press, 1990).

6   See e.g. Honderich, 'Culpability and Mystery", n. 2 above.

7   On "hard treatment", see Feinberg, n. 3 above.

8   See, for instance, J. R. Lucas, *On Justice* (Oxford, Oxford University Press, 1980), pp. 132–6; M. M. Faalls, "Retribution, Reciprocity and Respect for Persons", (1987) 6 *Law and Philosophy* 25–51; I. Primoratz, n. 3 above. J. Kleinig, "Punishment and Moral Seriousness", (1991) 25 *Israel Law Review* 401–21; J. Hampton, "Correcting Harms versus Righting Wrongs: The Goal of Retribution", (1992) 39 *UCLA Law Review* 201–44.

9   See my *Trials and Punishments*, n. 4 above; and "Penal Communications", (1996) 20 *Crime and Justice* 1–97.

10 See J. G. Murphy, "Marxism and Retribution", (1973) 2 *Punishment and Public Affairs* 217–43.

11 For examples of such punishment, see my "Penal Communications", n. 9 above, at 52–3, 63–4; and my "Alternatives to Punishment – or Alternative Punishments?", in W. Cragg (ed.) *Retributivism and it Critics* (Franz Steiner, 1992) 43–68.

12 See his *Censure and Sanctions* (Oxford, Oxford University Press, 1993), especially chs. 2, 8; see also U. Narayan, "Appropriate Responses and Preventive Benefits: Justifying Censure and Hard Treatment in Legal Punishment" (1993) 13 *Oxford Journal of Legal Studies* 166–82.

13 Hegel, *The Philosophy of Right*, trans. T. Knox (Oxford, Oxford University Press, 1942), at p. 246; see von Hirsch, n. 12 above, at pp. 12–14, and my *Trials and Punishments*, n. 4 above, at pp. 178–86.

14 See *Censure and Sanctions*, n. 12 above, ch. 5; for more detailed criticism of his account, see my "Penal Communications", n. 9 above, at 41–5.

15 See further my "Inclusion and Exclusion: Citizens, Subjects and Outlaws" (1998) 51 *Current Legal Problems*.

16 Von Hirsch, n. 12 above, at p. 13.

17 An idea which underpins one recent version of retributivism, according to which punishment serves to restore that fair balance of benefits and burdens which crime disturbs: see Murphy, n. 10 above.

18 This is not to say that we can never properly criticise or censure someone who will, we are sure, remain unmoved and unpersuaded: of course we can, and we might think it important to do so. But our censure still has the character of an attempt (an attempt that we think is doomed to fail) to persuade him to recognise the wrong he has done.

19 See, e.g., Lacey, n. 5 above, ch. 5.

20 Thus I am not grounding criminal liability in "character" *rather than* in action or "choice" (which could open the way to extensive and intrusive inquiries into every aspect of offenders' characters): liability should rather be grounded in "character" (moral attitudes and dispositions) *as displayed in action*; see my "Choice, Character and Criminal Liability" (1993) 12 *Law and Philosophy* 345–83.

21 By which I mean that they concern, not the basic principles and conceptions on which this communicative theory rests, but the dangers involved in trying to apply it in our actual world.

22 The worries thus concern, we can say, the preconditions rather than the conditions of justified punishment: see my "Law, Language and Community: Some Preconditions of Criminal Liability" (1998) 18 *Oxford Journal of Legal Studies* 189–206.

23 See, e.g., Murphy, n. 10 above; also A. W. Norrie, *Law, Ideology and Punishment* (Dordrecht, Kluwer, 1991).

24 See L. Wittgenstein, *Philosophical Investigations*, trans. G. E. M. Anscombe (Oxford, Blackwell, 1963) para. 242: "If language is to be a means of communication, there must be agreement not only in definitions but also (queer as this may sound) in judgements".

25 I realise that to talk of what a person "could reasonable be expected to accept" conceals a multitude of questions about what can make such (normative) expectations reasonable or unreasonable: but I cannot pursue those questions here.

26 See A. MacIntyre, *After Virtue*, 2nd edn. (London, Duckworth. 1985).

27 See, e.g., B. Hudson, *Penal Policy and Social Justice* (London, Macmillan, 1993), and von Hirsch, n. 12 above, at pp. 97–9, pp. 106–8; this is also a theme which underpins much of Alan Norrie's work – see *Crime, Reason and History* (Wiedenfeld and Nicolson, 1993). For more detailed discussion of some of the issues I raise here, see my "Principle and Contradiction in the Criminal Law", in Duff (ed.) *Philosophy and Criminal Law: Principle and Critique* (Cambridge, Cambridge University Press, 1998), pp. 156–204.

28 See, e.g., B. Hudson, "Beyond Proportionate Punishment: Difficult Cases and the 1991 Criminal Justice Act", (1995) 22 *Crime, Law and Social Change* 59–78.

29 See my "Principle and Contradiction in the Criminal Law", n. 27 above, at pp. 187–9.

30 Though for convenience I have spoken in this paragraph of "content" and "context" as if they were two quite separate elements in a communicative exercise, a more thorough (and Wittgensteinian) account would start to break down the distinction between "content" and "context": the content, the sense, of what is said cannot be divorced from the context in which it is said. See C. Travis, *The Uses of Sense* (Oxford, Oxford University Press. 1989).

24

PUNISHMENT, PENANCE AND THE STATE

A reply to Duff

Andrew von Hirsch

1 INTRODUCTION: DUFF'S AND MY VIEWS CONTRASTED

Antony Duff and I share, as he points out in his chapter, a *communicative* perspective on the criminal sanction's general justification:[1] punishment, we both believe, should be conceptualised as a form of censure. Penal censure has important moral functions that are not reducible to crime prevention. A response to criminal wrongdoing that conveys blame gives the individual the opportunity to respond in ways that are typically those of an agent capable of moral deliberation: to recognise the wrongfulness of the action; feel remorse; make efforts to desist in future – or else, to try to give reasons why the conduct was not actually wrong. What a purely "neutral" sanction not embodying blame would deny, even if no less effective in preventing crime, is precisely this recognition of the person's status as a moral agent. A neutral sanction would treat offenders and potential offenders much as beasts in a circus, as creatures which must merely be conditioned, intimidated, or restrained.

Can the institution of punishment, however, be explained *purely* in terms of censure? Punishment conveys blame, but does so in a special way – through visitation of deprivation ("hard treatment") on the offender. That deprivation is the vehicle through which the blame is expressed. But why use *this* vehicle, rather than simply expressing blame in symbolic fashion? It is on this latter issue that Duff and I part company. Duff maintains that the hard treatment component of the penal sanction can itself be explained in reprobative terms; he treats the deprivations involved in punishment as providing a kind of secular penance – for reasons he explains in his chapter and in earlier writings.[2]

I take a different view: that the reason for having the hard treatment element in punishment has to do with helping to keep predatory behaviour within tolerable limits.

Had the criminal sanction no usefulness in preventing crime, there should be no need to visit material deprivations on those who offend. True, one might still wish to devise another way of issuing authoritative judgements of blame, for such predatory behaviour as occurs. But those judgements, in the interest of keeping state-inflicted suffering to a minimum, would no longer be linked to purposive infliction of suffering.

If the institution of legal punishment thus serves to prevent crime as well as to censure, how is this consistent with treating offenders and potential offenders as moral agents? The hard treatment in punishment, I have argued, serves as a prudential reason for obedience to those insufficiently motivated by the penal censure's moral appeal. But this should *supplement* rather than replace the normative reasons for desisting from crime conveyed by penal censure – that is, provide an *additional* reason for compliance to those who are capable of recognising the law's moral demands, but who are also tempted to flout them.[3] The law thus addresses ourselves, not a distinct "criminal" class of those considered incapable of grasping moral appeals. And it addresses us neither as perfectly moral agents (we are not like angels), nor as beasts which only can be coerced through threats; but rather, as moral but fallible agents who need some prudential supplement to help us resist criminal temptation. However, this account calls for moderation in the overall severity in punishment levels. The harsher the penalty system is, the less plausible it becomes to see it as including a moral appeal rather than constituting a system of bare threats.[4]

Behind this disagreement about hard treatment lies different views of the function of the *state* in the area of criminal justice. In a previous discussion,[5] I have questioned whether administering penances is a proper role for a liberal state. Duff gives his response in the present volume, and sketches further some of his ideas concerning the state's role in punishment. My aim here is to comment on some of his arguments, and spell out my own views on punishment and the state.

2 SOME POINTS OF CLARIFICATION

Before proceeding, two points of clarification are in order. One concerns the role of crime-prevention under my view; the other, the function of penances under Duff's.

The question of sufficient deterrence

Duff suggests that my "prudential supplement" model may provide insufficient deterrence for a penal system [see Chapter 23, pp. 393–4]. But I do not claim that a penal system based on my theory would necessarily deliver as much crime prevention as, say, the tougher penal policies generally prevailing today (although that is difficult to judge, given the limited state of present knowledge concerning marginal deterrent effects).[6] I merely assert that my model would be capable to a degree of preventing crime, while nevertheless treating offenders as moral agents. If severer overall penalty levels are thought necessary to prevent crime more effectively, adopting those higher penalty levels would simply constitute a deviation from my model – and thus not fully justifiable in its terms. How problematic this would be would depend on how much more severe those overall penalty levels were. The theory nevertheless would remain useful as a heuristic model: to point toward a reduction of overall sentence levels, to the extent practicable.[7]

Duff's objection would be a disturbing one only if my theory were to fail to support any substantial sanctions at all. But it is not clear why that should be true. I have argued that if the penalty scale is inflated sufficiently, the resulting sanctions may become almost wholly coercive, and render largely meaningless the communicative content of the sanction.[8] This, however, would not seem to rule out moderate but still significant penalties. Inflating the penalty scale sufficiently could also undermine the penitential functions of which Duff speaks, for comparable reasons. But this, again, would not necessitate insubstantial criminal penalties.

Functions of penance

Duff claims that, on his penance perspective, punishment can be accounted for wholly in communicative terms. But what communicative functions are involved in the hard treatment aspects of punishment?

One function, of which Duff speaks, is that of *forcing the offender's attention*: the unpleasantness of the sanction may compel the actor to attend to the disapproval visited through the sanction [Chapter 23, p. 390]. The moral logic of this function needs explanation, however. Ordinarily, when A censures B for some misdeed failing, it is up to B to decide whether or not to pay attention; A is not entitled to use force to get B to attend properly. Coercive attention-getting is warranted only when A holds a special position of moral authority over B. Perhaps, an abbot has such authority over the members of his monastery, in view of his special role as spiritual mentor, and in view of the fact that his charges have submitted themselves to his authority. Whether the *state* has that authority, however, is precisely the issue in dispute between Duff and myself. But at least, attention-getting *is* a communicative role, and thus can be part of a communicative theory of state punishment (provided that the state can be shown to have the requisite authority).

A second function for a penance may be that of *providing an appropriate psychological setting for feelings of shame and regret*. The material discomforts of the penance might be seen as a way of evoking the moral discomfort that the penitent offender should feel. This too, gives hard treatment a communicative character – of doing something to try to persuade the offender to think and feel in a certain way.

A third possible function of penances is that of *expiation*, but that is different. Expiation involves more that creating the right psychological setting; it involves the idea that undergoing certain discomforts is the *appropriate* manner through which repentance ought to be achieved. The deprivations of the punishment are not just ways of evoking regret for the deed; but are seen as required (that is, *morally* required) for the purging of guilt. This function does make the link to hard treatment necessary rather than contingent: even the already-penitent offender needs to undergo some painful experience to "work through" his penance. The difficulty however, is that it is not clear why this is a communicative function. Moral communication involves conveying a normative judgement to someone; perhaps, trying to persuade him of the correctness of that judgement; and perhaps also, trying to get him to feel certain emotions that comport with that judgement. But if all of that could occur without invocation of hard treatment, it is far from clear what further *communicative* role necessitates offenders' actually having to undergo the pains of expiation.

Duff's explanation of expiation and its function do not illuminate. He asserts that the pains of punishment can "reconcile [the offender] with his fellow citizens, and restore himself to full membership in the community from which his wrongdoing threatened to exclude him" [Chapter 23, p. 390]. I find this puzzling for several reasons. First, Duff is relying here on a broad notion of community which refers to a group's having a shared set of behavioral norms; it is these shared norms that give members, and the institutions acting in their behalf, the basis for criticising the conduct of those who flout them. The state thus can act on behalf of a "community" of citizens in this sense, just as a university disciplinary committee can act on behalf of the university's community of scholars in taking action against a colleague who has committed a serious academic infraction. But what justifies an abbot in imposing expiatory penances is not merely that the monastery represents a community of shared values, but that it is one of a special kind, having very specific (and ambitious) moral purposes. Secondly, the connection between community and exclusion is unclear. If expiation is needed to restore the offender to "full membership", then the offender's wrongdoing must have removed him *pro tanto* from membership. But why should offending result in communal exclusion? The family, for example, represents a small community of a kind. Yet many parents feel strongly that misconduct by their children, while warranting criticism or even punishment, should *not* be grounds for actual or emotional loss of membership, even for brief periods; it is only the frigid parent that refuses to speak to his errant child. Thirdly, even if wrongdoing and separation from the community are linked, it is far from clear why *expiatory* penances are needed to restore the person's membership. If the offender comes to recognise and repent of his wrongdoing, for example, why should that not be enough to make him morally "one of us" again? Why is it also necessary for the penitent wrongdoer to undergo something nasty?

It is my suspicion that the expiatory function is not a communicative function at all. It seems, rather, to reflect the traditional retributive sense that suffering is needed to "wipe clean" the moral blemish of wrongdoing. Perhaps, I am mistaken; but if so, Duff needs to explain more clearly whether expiation is an essential element in his conception of penance; and if it is, how it might satisfactorily be explained in purely communicative terms.[9]

3 STANDING TO IMPOSE PENANCES AND THE STATE ROLE

Duff [Chapter 23, p. 392] mentions two dimensions of "moral standing", namely, (a) that the censurer has the requisite relationship to the actor to make the wrongfulness of the latter's conduct his proper business; and (b) "clean hands" – that the censurer is not disqualified through his own misconduct from standing in judgement on the actor. There is, however, a third dimension of standing that Duff does not address and that is crucial for present purposes: namely, that of how deeply the censurer may properly involve himself in seeking to bring about the morally appropriate response from the wrongdoer he censures. That may depend on his relationship to the wrongdoer.

Consider simple acts of censure: someone has acted inconsiderately toward me, and I respond in reprobative manner. How far I may properly go in trying to elicit the morally appropriate response from him may depend on the character of our relationship. If a stranger negligently steps on my foot, I may give a simple blaming response (say, tell him he ought to be more careful), but it would be inappropriate of me to ask him why he acted in this inconsiderate manner, whether he feels regret, and so forth. A close friend, however, may have standing to make such further inquiries.

This dimension of standing also affects the appropriateness of imposing penances. There is no doubt the head of a monastic community has standing to visit a penance upon an erring monk. For a university disciplinary committee to undertake this role, however, would be more questionable. Yes, the committee is entitled to censure the faculty member, after the proper procedures have been undergone; and in appropriate cases that censure may properly embody some form of deprivation – say, a period of suspension. It might also be hoped that the penalty elicits sentiments of regret, etc. But if the committee characterises the sanction as a penance whose discomforts provide the vehicle for achieving a penitent understanding, one might well think they had overstepped their proper role.[10]

Duff concedes [Chapter 23, pp. 399–405] that the state operates differently from a monastic institution, in that membership is not optional; that the shared values underlying the criminal law are conduct-related and more restricted in scope, and that the state is not properly concerned with the person's own spiritual good *per se*. Notwithstanding these differences, however, he still wants to give the state the abbot-like function of imposing penances. My essential objection remains that (for reasons to be outlined below) this ascribes to the state a role behind its proper standing (in the sense of that term just suggested), given its functions and its relationship to citizens.

Duff does attempt [Chapter 23, pp. 390–1] to make his position more consistent with liberalism by imposing two kinds of side-constraints on penances: (a) a limitation of scope: penances may only be imposed for conduct threatening certain basic values of peaceable social coexistence, and (b) penances may not involve bringing about penitent attitudes through coercion. The second limitation is implict anyway in any proper notion of a penance: the abbot wants to bring forth the person's *own* penitent attitudes, not brainwash the person. The first limitation also seems insufficient, as it does not address the standing issue spoken of here: that even with respect to harmful conduct, the functions of which Duff speaks might go behind the state's proper remit. I would scarcely be reassured if a university disciplinary committee sought to impose penances, but only for specified kinds of unprofessional conduct.

4 PENANCE AND THE STATE'S ROLE: SOME HYPOTHETICALS

What more can be said on this issue of the state's penal role? Two hypotheticals might help to bring the differences between penances and state-administered punishments into sharper relief.

1. Suppose a penalty system, with quite moderate sanction levels, were instituted in State X; and that (given the relatively peaceable nature of the populace) it sufficed to help maintain low rates of offending. Suppose, however, that an in-depth survey of convicted offenders were to disclose that the sanctions had very little success in eliciting from them sentiments of shame, repentance, and the like; to the extent that such persons desisted from re-offending, that was mainly due to growing older, or to motives of wishing to avoid the unpleasantness or the stigma of further punishment. From my perspective, this scenario would represent a modest success. The sanctions do reflect and give public expression to a moral valuation of the conduct. Offenders are being treated as moral agents, by being given the *opportunity* of responding as such agents should. And the prudential disincentive embodied in the hard treatment has some apparent effect and yet is not so severe as to "drown out" the censuring message. While one might regret that actual offenders are so seldom penitent, this would not suffice to warrant a judgement of failure.

On Duff's view, however, this outcome of this scenario would seem to represent a failure – because the penalties, intended as penances, so seldom elicit the desired penitential response.[11] Now, if a comparable scenario occurred in a monastery, the abbot would quite rightly be concerned that he was failing: because his central concern is with the moral attitudes of his charges. But it would seem strange to carry over such a judgement to a liberal state, whose central mission seems so much less concerned with attitude than with conduct.

2. Consider a yet more peaceable society, in which punishment scarcely seems needed to prevent crime at all. Offending is relatively rare, being kept in check by people's moral inhibitions, plus fear of the social stigma associated with having been found to have offended. Not much difference in criminality could then be expected between instituting a system of state punishments and relying instead only on formal symbolic censure plus informal social controls. Suppose, however, that there was occasional offending in this society, and that something more than symbolic censure – some measure of hard treatment – was needed to help the few actual offenders achieve a penitent understanding of their misdeeds. Should one, than, insist on punishment with its attendant deprivations?

On my view, the answer would emphatically be no. The justification for the hard treatment would fall away, since it would not ordinarily be needed to help people overcome the temptations of offending.[12] On Duff's view, however, a system of punishments would seem to be called for – simply to provide penances for those few persons who do offend.

In the context of the monastic institution, this latter conclusion would make sense. Even if transgressions were rare in the institution, that would not suffice; if there are any infractions of monastic discipline, it would be the abbot's duty to attend to the consciences of those involved, and institute the purifying process of penance to help them achieve repentance. But for a liberal state, this would seem a strange conclusion. Duff does assert, as noted earlier, that the state should not be concerned with conscience or moral attitudes *per se*, but only with these as expressed through harmful conduct. But the present hypothetical should bring into relief why this concession is not enough. We *are* speaking of harmful conduct here, but the question remains what aspects of the conduct should be the state's main concern. In a situation where harm prevention is no longer significantly at issue, I cannot see why it is the business of the state to establish so coercive and burdensome an institution as punishment, merely to assist the consciences of some offenders.

5 REHABILITATION AND PENANCE

Offender rehabilitation in the 1960s to 1980s tended to steer clear of attempts to moralise. The offender would be enlisted in a programme designed to improve his skills or resolve his psychological difficulties. The offence itself was seldom discussed. This reticence is now being questioned. Changing the offender's behaviour, current thinking about rehabilitation (or some of it) holds, requires one to talk to the offender about what he did, discuss the reasons why he did it, encourage the offender to consider other persons' interests, and try to get him to understand why his behaviour failed to do so.[13] Confronting the offender with his behaviour is again coming to be seen as a legitimate part of rehabilitation.

In cruder versions, such strategies have been conceived in purely utilitarian terms: how much the offender is to be "shamed" would depend purely on what will work to prevent reoffending.[14] However, other penologists[15] see these strategies as constrained by strong proportionality limits: the duration and intensity of the sanction (including its treatment elements) should depend on the gravity of the offence. Thus restricted, these newer rehabilitation methods can be made consistent with a proportionality-oriented sentencing theory.[16]

But why is confronting the offender morally the legitimate business of the state? The seeming answer would be that this helps induce offenders to refrain from reoffending. It is thus a crime-prevention aim, and crime prevention (at least on my model) is a legitimate state function within appropriate desert limits. And while researchers are now less optimistic than they once were about the effectiveness of rehabilitative programmes, there seems to be reason to believe that certain programmes, carefully targeted to amenable offenders, might work to a modest extent to reduce recidivism.[17]

However, matters are not quite so simple, as becomes apparent when we consider recent research on another crime-prevention aim, incapacitation. That research has suggested that – even if imprisonment does "work" in the sense of preventing the imprisoned offender from reoffending while confined – it still may not succeed in reducing the public's net exposure to crime. Locking up the potential recidivist will not necessarily put others less at risk, if (for example) there are large numbers of other potential offenders not currently in prison or being sentenced who can replace his criminal activities. Incapacitation research is thus focusing increasingly on the issue of *net* effects on crime.[18] Where this question of net preventative impact asked of rehabilitation, the implications could be disturbing. If treatment works only for certain selected types of offenders carefully screened for amenability,[19] then the numbers of persons thus "reformed" might simply be too small to have a substantial impact on the incidence of crime. In that case, rehabilitation ceases to "work" as a conventional crime-prevention strategy, notwithstanding successes with particular individuals.

Perhaps, however, rehabilitation might have a somewhat different role, closer to the old notion of "reforming" offenders. The aim would not so much be to reduce overall rates of crime, as to induce some persons to live different lives. On this perspective, a predatory lifestyle is a bad way of living – bad not only in its destructive effects on victims, but in the values that it embodies. Inducing offenders to give up this kind of life and to treat others more decently might arguably (albeit controversially)[20] be seen as worthwhile, even if no net preventative impact ensues.

Were we to go this far, would we have embraced Duff's position? We would be utilising a means of which he speaks: namely, using the vehicle of hard treatment to confront the offender, and bring about a recognition of wrongdoing and efforts to change. And the end seems close to his: namely, moral reform of the offender.

Nevertheless, we would still actually be a long way from Duff. Reform of the offender, in the scenario just mentioned, is not being offered as the basis of the whole penal system, but merely as an incidence of a penal system which principally may derive its support from other grounds. The main reasons offered for punishment could still be those of my suggested kind – that the system conveys censure and provides a significant disincentive against criminal behaviour. The constraints applicable to punishments, namely, those of proportionality, derive from those aims.[21] If punishment fails or is not needed to promote these basic aims, then (as the hypotheticals in section 4 have indicated) it should not be retained, not even to "reform" some offenders. Offender reform, in the sense just described, is thus merely an additional permissible activity.[22]

6 THE CONSTITUTIVE GROUNDS FOR STAFF PUNISHMENT

What view of the state is implicit in the arguments I have sketched in this paper? It is one that is far from the restricted contractualist liberalism to which Duff refers [Chapter 23, pp. 392–3]. It admits that sentences may – so long as they observe proportionality constraints – seek a variety of objectives, including that of trying to induce an offender to desist from crime by fashioning a sanction designed to help him to recognise the wrongfulness of his conduct. But functions such as these presuppose the legitimacy of the criminal sanction, and that legitimacy should rest on more restricted claims.

The justification for the criminal sanction concerns its *constitutive* grounds: the reasons why such an institution should exist at all. What the foregoing illustrations (see section 4) are meant to suggest, is that those constitutive grounds should concern certain *public* functions: of expressing a valuation of certain kinds of (harmful) conduct[23] and of providing a (modest) disincentive against it.

These basic expressive and preventative functions are matters which concern the character of the minimum norms for peaceable co-existence,[24] and their enforcement. If the institution of the criminal sanction is incapable of carrying out these public functions (or if those functions can be performed without having to resort to the coercive and unpleasant features of punishment) then that institution would lose its *raison d'être*. In that event, the pains of punishment cannot be sustained solely on the grounds that its pains help it function as a penance for certain wrongdoers.

My just-stated argument about constitutive grounds is designed to address only certain coercive state institutions. The assumption is that, in a free society, such institutions should exist only where necessary for certain fairly narrowly defined purposes, including those of the kind just described. Where sustainable on those grounds, these coercive institutions might also be given certain *supplemental* functions, perhaps concerned with the offender's moral well-being (see section 5). But the latter functions cannot alone support the existence of the criminal sanction. This perspective also should not restrict the availability of a plethora of state and communal institutions aimed at providing resources to citizens and encouraging co-operation among citizens. It is not the idea of a minimal state on which my arguments rest, but a certain minimalism concerning state *coercion*. My ultimate difficulty with Duff's view is that I do not grasp the conception of the state, and of "community" on which it rests.

7 WHAT DIFFERENCE DOES IT MAKE? CRITERIA FOR PROPORTIONALITY OF SENTENCE

It is common ground between Duff and myself that the principle of proportionality of sentence is of central importance: punishments should be proportionate in their severity to the seriousness of the crime. On both our views, the principle derives from the censuring features of punishment: if punishment conveys blame, then the quantum of punishment should depend on the degree of blameworthiness (i.e. seriousness) of the offender's criminal conduct.

However, the criteria for proportionality appear to operate differently according to the two perspectives. My position calls for a rather demanding standard of proportionality: conduct of equal reprehensibleness should be punished with comparable severity, and penalties should also be ranked according to crime seriousness. With criminal prohibitions seen as public admonitions, and sanctions as public acts of censure, what counts is the degree of blameworthiness of the offence, and the degree of disapproval conveyed through the severity of the sanction.[25] This conception, as mentioned in section 5, can still allow rehabilitative efforts that are designed to confront the offender personally, and to try to induce some awareness of wrongdoing in him. But given the preeminently public nature of the sanction, and the public character of its constitutive grounds (see section 6), the degree of seriousness of the offence should act as a strong constraint on how much the offender may be punished to achieve such reformative effects. The offender may not, for example, be held in a given penal regime for longer than someone having committed a similarly blameworthy offence, even were the extra time helpful in inducing "reform" on his part.

Duff also calls for proportionality in punishment, and thus opposes any tactic of confining the offender indefinitely until he repents [Chapter 23, p. 391]. But his penance rationale does seem to dilute proportionality requirements. Suppose Offender A has a thicker skin than Offender B, and would require a tougher penance to help him achieve the desired penitential response. Since under Duff's view the imposition of penance is the *constitutive* aim of the criminal sanction, and not merely a permissible collateral aim of an institution resting on other constitutive grounds, it would seem difficult to resist punishing A more than B. This would not be seen as a limited (but possibly, permissible[26]) departure from proportionality requirements. Instead, imposing differential amounts of punishment on the two offenders – at least, when the differences are not great – would be seen as involving no moral cost at all.

In the context of a monastery, this latter conclusion could be acceptable. Suppose Brother A and Brother B commit sins of comparable gravity, and the abbot (in view of their differences in character and sensitivity) gives A a more onerous penance. Were A to have the temerity to complain that he has been unfairly treated, the abbot might rightly respond that penances are concerned with helping to promote a penitent response, and that the differences were designed to help bring such a response about. This type of argument seems misplaced, however, in the context of state-imposed punishment.

8 PUNISHMENT AND SOCIAL DEPRIVATION

Both Duff and I discuss the problem of social deprivation and punishment. I have suggested that social deprivation might possibly be a basis for ascribing reduced culpability to the offender, on grounds that such deprivation (if sufficiently serious) makes compliance with the law so much more difficult.[27] Duff, however, argues that social deprivation might undermine the state's moral authority to punish. The two claims are not necessarily exclusive; it might be possible to view social deprivation as a mitigating factor that reduces the offender's culpability; but also, in extreme cases, deny the state the standing to punish at all. Let me just make some brief comments on these differing perspectives and their implications.

1 On a culpability-reduction view, deprived offenders' claim to mitigation would depend on the extent of the social deprivation that exists: for it is that which (arguably) affects the offender's degree of blameworthiness. On Duff's moral standing view, however, the issue shifts to *how much at fault* the state or its more prosperous citizens are for the existence of such deprivation – indeed, Duff [Chapter 23, p. 401] speaks of complicity in social injustice. This means there is no direct link between social deprivation and exculpation; all would depend on the intermediate step of identifying governmental or class villainy or neglect. It will be far from easy to develop workable doctrines that enable one to judge when this kind of fault is present.[28] It also will mean that absent such fault, the state's standing to punish could not be called into question. Consider, for example, a country which is very poor but which nevertheless has a decent government making gallant efforts to alleviate poverty, efforts which,

alas, are largely unavailing because of the country's limited economic resources. Since this government would have "clean hands", it would have standing to punish even the most deprived offenders.

2 On a culpability-reduction view, how much mitigation is granted would be a matter of degree, depending on the extent of the social deprivation involved and how it bears specifically on culpability. Only the most extreme conditions – for example, stealing to avoid starvation – would support complete exculpation.[29] On Duff's moral-standing perspective, however, the punishability of deprived persons would be an all-or-nothing matter: either the state is or it is not sufficiently at fault to lose standing to punish deprived offenders or certain classes of them.

3 At the end of his chapter, Duff raises the question of what should happen if it is concluded that the state lacks the standing to have a penance-based system of punishment. First, he suggests that a fallback position might be one such as mine, where state punishments are conceived of as conveying blame and providing some kind of disincentive. Then, however, he takes this concession back, on the grounds that such a fallback position would raise the same basic issue of the state's having insufficiently "clean hands" to censure deprived violators. But this may not be correct, for the criteria for "clean hands" standing may vary with how ambitious a communicative role is at issue. We rightly expect the head of a religious institution to lead an exemplary existence because his involvement in the moral lives of his charges is so deep. The less morally ambitious role presupposed by a penal theory such as mine could arguably permit less stringent "clean hands" requirements of moral standing.[30]

If matters are bad enough, of course, then the state may lose moral standing even to play the more modest role which my position would ascribe to it. In that event, however, there would appear to be no morally acceptable alternative basis for criminal sanctions. If an unjust state lacks the moral standing to censure lawbreakers, then it cannot avoid injustice merely by resorting to purely deterrent or incapacitative sanctions – for these are plainly objectionable on grounds of not treating offenders as moral agents at all. If the state is all that rotten, the appropriate response is revolution (or emigration, for those who can), and not finding alternate grounds for giving moral support to state sanctions.

NOTES

1 "General justification" addresses the question "why punish at all?"; it concerns, that is, the reasons justifying the existence of the institution of legal punishment; see H. L. A. Hart, *Punishment and Responsibility* (Oxford, Oxford University Press, 1986), ch. 1. For the criteria for allocating quanta of punishment, see section 7 below.

2 R. A. Duff, *Trials and Punishments* (Cambridge, Cambridge University Press, 1986), ch. 9; R. A. Duff, "Penal Communications", (1996) 20 *Crime and Justice: A Review of Research* 1–97.

3   A. von Hirsch, *Censure and Sanctions* (Oxford, Oxford University Press, 1993), ch. 2; see also U. Narayan, "Adequate Responses and Preventive Benefits: Justifying Censure and Hard Treatment in Legal Punishment", (1993) 13 *Oxford Journal of Legal Studies* 166–82.

4   Von Hirsch, n. 3 above.

5   Ibid., at pp. 72–7.

6   For a survey of recent deterrence research, see A. von Hirsch, A. E. Bottoms *et al.*, *Criminal Deterrence and Sentence Severity* (Oxford and Portland, Oregon Hart Publishing, 1999). This survey concludes that while there is a modicum of evidence pointing to possible deterrent effects of varying the *certainty* of punishment (e.g., the likelihood of an offender's being apprehended and convicted), there is still little firm evidence concerning the marginal deterrent effects of altering *severity* levels.

7   Duff's penance view actually would need to address this same issue of "sufficient" deterrence, even though his account does not explicitly invoke crime-preventative aims – for the sanction levels that would serve as penances might also be substantially lower than existing penalty levels. So to the extent Duff wishes to use his view as a support for a state punishment system, the same question arises: does it justify a practicably adequate level of sanctions? His answer, presumably, would be the same as mine: that it may or may not do so; and to the extent it does not, then practically "needed" sanction levels could not wholly be justified on his terms.

8   Von Hirsch, n. 3 above.

9   A possible account might be that the expiatory pains offer the offender the opportunity to communicate *back* his penitent understanding of the wrong. Indeed, Duff suggests this view in his Response (see below). If there is to be any communication back, however, it cannot be compulsory to have any meaning; and I am unconvinced how this communication can be located in the attitude of the offender to an imposed hard treatment. Treating the expiatory pains of punishment as a kind of enforced apology also raises the problem of compulsory attitudinising, which I have suggested may be a form of demeaning treatment; see von Hirsch, n. 3 above pp. 83–4.

What this leaves unexplained, moreover, is why expiatory hard treatment is *necessary* for communicating-back regret. Possibly, it might be a way of signalling such sentiments. But there are other ways: for example, the offender's simply expressing regret in a sincere fashion, or else, subjecting himself to deprivations voluntarily (e.g. deciding himself to put on the sackcloth and ash). Why then, should the offender be *made* to undergo the penalty for this purpose – especially when his acquiescence is needed anyway in order to convey true penitence?

10 In his Response (see below), Duff suggests departmental colleagues might seek to elicit penitential attitudes from an erring member. Perhaps, this might be appropriate for a small tightly-knit department – precisely in virtue of its character as such. But in larger institutional contexts (for example, that of a disciplinary committee acting on behalf of a large university) this seems a strange role.

11 True, Duff points out that penances need not *always* indeed in eliciting penitence from the wrongdoers on whom they are imposed. But if the institutions of state-imposed penance almost *never* induced the desired response from offenders, one would have to query whether it was performing what he consider to be its desired function.

12 See more fully von Hirsch, n. 3 above p. 14.

13 S. Rex, "A New Form of Rehabilitationalism?", in A. von Hirsch and A. Ashworth (eds.), *Principled Sentencing*, 2nd edn. (Oxford, Hart Publishing, 1998) pp. 34–41.

14 See J. Braithwaite's view of "reintegrative shaming" in his *Crime, Shame and Reintegration* (Cambridge, Cambridge University Press, 1989); for a critique of Braithwaite, see A. von Hirsch and A. Ashworth, "Not Just Deserts: A Response to Braithwaite and Pettit" (1992) 13 *Oxford Journal of Legal Studies* 83, 96, and also von Hirsch, n. 3 above, ch. 3.

15 See Rex, n. 13 above, pp. 38–39.

16 For how treatment efforts can be made consistent with a model through observance of proportionality constraints, see also von Hirsch, n. 3 above. Certain limits on the modalities of treatment are also called for, designed to assure that they are not intrusive or demeaning – for example, a bar against forcing the offender to express attitudes or views to which he does not subscribe; see ibid. at ch. 9.

17 Rex, n. 13 above pp. 35–8.

18 See von Hirsch and Ashworth (eds.), n. 13 above pp. 13–27.

19 Recent research indicates that successes tend to occur *selectively*, for treatment modalities targeted to particular sub-groups, selected for amenability, ibid. at pp. 26–41.

20 One might possibly argue that this is a species of moralistic paternalism, since the aim is in part to promote the moral well-being of the offender himself. However, the conduct with which the rehabilitative intervention is concerned is of the kind that is injurious to others.

21 Von Hirsch, n. 3 above, ch. 2; von Hirsch and Ashworth, n. 18 above, at pp. 168–79.

22 That is also why one would be entitled to retain the penal system even if few offenders could successfully be reformed; why one can legitimately take the risk of failure of treatment. With Duff's rationale, by contrast, systematic failure of offender-reform efforts would put the legitimacy of the whole system into question (see my first hypothetical in section 4 above).

23 Holding that expressing a public valuation is a central role of punishment does not require one to accept German theorists' notion of "positive general prevention". According to that theory, the public message embodied in punishment, and its supposed resulting effect of reinforcing citizens' moral inhibitions, constitutes the chief justification of the criminal sanction. This theory cannot be correct, because it would be morally impermissible to censure or punish A *merely* to provide a moral message to B, C, and D. Essential to the case for penal censure, under both Duff's theory and my own, is that the actor has engaged in an act of wrongdoing, and the censure is the kind of response that treats the actor as a moral agent, by giving him the opportunity to respond in characteristically moral ways. For fuller discussion, see T. Hoernle and A. von Hirsch, "Positive Generalpraevention und Tadel" (1995) 142 *Goldtdammer's Archiv fuer Strafrecht* at 261–82.

24 I am assuming, here, a theory of criminalisation which restricts the scope of criminal sanction primarily to conduct which does or risks immediate injury to others; see, e.g. N. Jareborg, "What Kind of Criminal Law Do We Want? in A. Snare (ed.), *Beware of Punishment* (Oslo, Pax Forlag, 1995), at pp. 17–36.

25 See von Hirsch, n. 3, above, at pp. 15–17. For the reasons why these proportionality requirements hold, even on a general justification for punishment (such as mine) that relies on crime prevention as well as censure, see ibid., at pp. 16–17.

26 I have suggested elsewhere that it might be possible to see proportionality (in my strong sense) is a requirement of fairness, and yet permit *limited* departures from it, on grounds that these would involve no great degree of injustice (albeit concededly some) and permit pursuit of other aims seen as especially urgent. See my discussion of "hybrid models" in ibid., at pp. 54–6.

27 See *ibid.* pp. 106–28.

28 In speaking of fault here, Duff seems to treat the state as something akin to a person, rather than a complex set of institutions, many with diverse and even conflicting policies.

29 See von Hirsch, n. 3 above, at p. 108n.

30 In that event, one might conclude that punishment remains justifiable on my censure-plus-disincentive rationale, but that rehabilitative interventions of the kind discussed in section 5 are no longer acceptable. While retaining the minimal moral standing needed to condemn the harmful conduct typical of law violations, the system may lack the standing to confront offenders personally with their wrongdoing. Indeed, some radical criminologists of the 1960s and 1970s objected to such efforts of "offender reform", precisely on such grounds.

APPENDIX

RESPONSE TO VON HIRSCH

Antony Duff

I'm grateful for the chance to respond briefly to some of the points that Andrew von Hirsch has raised. I must admit at once that much was left under-explained in my chapter (and will still be left under-explained here), in particular about the kind of communitarianism to which I appeal, and about the implications of the non-satisfaction of the preconditions of justified punishment which I discuss in section 3 of my chapter. However, whilst it is clear that the disagreement between von Hirsch and me depends in part on our different ideal conceptions of the state and of political community, I can indicate how I would hope to meet a few of his main criticisms and questions.

1 THE COMMUNICATIVE FUNCTIONS OF PUNISHMENT

Von Hirsch rightly suggests [Chapter 24, pp. 410–12] that expiation is an important dimension of hard treatment punishments, and that its communicative significance lies, on my account, in what it enables the offender to communicate to others: a punishment which is (or becomes) *voluntarily* accepted and undergone communicates to the offender's fellow citizens his own repentant recognition of the wrong he has done. In this respect punishment is a kind of enforced apology. Like other modes of apology, whether informal or formal, it has two aspects: its public form, which conventionally bears a certain meaning (for instance, the words spoken in a formal apology); and its individual character and meaning as something undertaken or undergone by this particular wrongdoer (the terms in which *he* understands and undergoes it).

Now communicative punishment essentially involves the former aspect, and *aspires* to take on the latter aspect: the offender is required or forced to undergo the punishment, with its public meaning; and the hope is that he will come to accept it as an appropriate way to strengthen and to express his repentance. That acceptance, how-ever, which would turn his punishment into a genuine expiation, cannot be coerced or compelled: by which I mean that whatever is coerced or compelled cannot count as genuine expiation, since it would not express the offender's own authentic under-standing and repentance of his wrong, and that it would be wrong to try to coerce it, since that would be incompatible with a proper respect for the offender as a moral agent.

If the offender remains unrepentant, his punishment has thus failed in one of its aims: but it can still succeed as a communication with him. Furthermore, I think we owe it to the offender to treat him *as if* his punishment constituted a genuine expiation, just as we owe it to those non-intimate fellow citizens who may informally apologise to us to treat their apologies as (if they were) sincere: that is the proper meaning of the idea that the offender who has been punished has "paid his debt"; and it guards against the danger that offenders will effectively be coerced into inauthentic expressions of remorse by the prospect of some remission of punishment if they are seen to repent.

However, even if I can claim that punishment as (in part) expiation need not involve – at the level of ideal theory – an improper attempt to coerce or manipulate the offender's understanding and attitudes, this will no doubt do nothing to assuage von Hirsch's worries about the role that my account allows to the state.

2 STATES, MONASTERIES, AND DEPARTMENTS

The monastic example of penitential punishment is both useful and dangerous for my account. It is useful because this is a context in which punishment can clearly be seen to have the ambitiously communicative character of a penance; and I want to argue that criminal punishment should ideally share – to a *limited* extent – this character. But it is also dangerous, because it can be taken to imply that the criminal justice system and its penal officials should take the kind of intrusive and all-encompassing interest in the moral condition of the citizens that a monastery and its abbot properly take in the spiritual condition of its inhabitants. I tried in my chapter to indicate some of the stringent limits which should constrain a (liberal-communitarian) system of criminal law and punishment, and thus distinguish it from a monastery's rules and penances: limits both on the scope of the criminal law, and on the extent to which punishment should seek to address or impinge on the offender's moral character. Von Hirsch regards these limits as insufficient, even in the context of an ideal theory of punishment: whilst I cannot hope to persuade either him or a sceptical reader here, I can perhaps explain my account a little further by commenting on the case of punish-ment within an academic institution, and on the two hypothetical cases with which von Hirsch challenges me.

Von Hirsch would not want his "departmental chair . . . to impose penances", even if these were "only for specified kinds of unprofessional conduct" [Chapter 24, p. 413] and I agree that to talk in this context of "penance" is likely, given the religious connotations of the term, to grate on our ears. However, I think that a decent academic department, one whose members share a commitment both to the academic values which structure their activity and to each other as colleagues, would have a place for a secular, academic version of penance.

Note first that the department will have a proper interest only in strictly limited aspects of its members' conduct and attitudes, those which bear directly on their performance of their academic job. If I am doing my job badly, my colleagues (or the departmental chair acting in their name) have the standing to intervene – to comment, to criticise, to demand; but if I am misbehaving in my non-academic life, they have no such standing to intervene (this is not to say that some of them could not have such standing as my friends; but they do not have it as my colleagues). Furthermore, a liberal-minded department will tolerate, indeed encourage, a fair degree of diversity of professional attitudes and conduct, different approaches to teaching and to research, different ways of living and working as an academic. Nor will it seek, as a department, to delve into its members' deeper motivations or attitudes: its concern will be limited to their professional conduct and their attitudes directly manifested in that conduct.

Suppose then that a member of the department commits some serious academic wrong in her dealings with her colleagues or her students. Her colleagues will rightly criticise her (for it is their business; they have the standing to do so); they might *demand* that she listen to their criticism, explain herself to them, and apologise for what she has done; they might impose some appropriate academic sanction on her. The point of this whole process is not just (as von Hirsch would agree) to communicate to her the censure her wrongdoing deserves; nor such communication plus (as von Hirsch might add) the provision of a supplementary prudential disincentive against a repetition of the wrongdoing. It is rather, I suggest, to remind or persuade her of the nature and seriousness of that wrongdoing, and of the need to re-establish her standing within the department by assuring her colleagues and students that she is sorry for what she has done. Her colleagues' response is to her as someone who is, and who must remain (unless the wrong is so serious that expulsion is the only proper response), a colleague – someone whose relationship with the department and with the values which structure its academic life needs to be reinforced or re-established after the wrong she has done; and this is properly achieved by this process of criticism and punishment.

I am not suggesting that either an academic department or a monastery is an ideal model of society. What I do suggest is that, while a department should take a far less all-embracing, far less intrusive interest in its members' moral condition than a monastery takes in the spiritual condition of its members, we can see a proper place

425

within it for a secular version of penance; and that this can help us to see the role that penitential punishment could play in other contexts, including that of the criminal law.

3 VON HIRSCH'S HYPOTHETICALS

What then of the two hypotheticals with which von Hirsch challenges me [Chapter 24, pp. 413–14]? One offers us a society in which hard treatment punishments (of only modest severity) serve as effective prudential supplements, but (almost) never secure the penitential response that should on my account be their aim; the other a society in which only very few offenders would need hard treatment punishment to elicit such a penitential response.

My initial (and I hope not merely evasive) response is that before we can discuss the role that punishment has or could have in such societies, we need to know a lot more about them – about the kinds of people who make them up, about the character of their social and moral relationships. For any normative account of punishment depends on a view not just of "human nature", but of human nature in some concrete social, context; it must locate punishment within the political, social and moral relationships and institutions which structure that context. The social context of von Hirsch's hypotheticals, however, is radically under-specified.

Thus in the first hypothetical, we are to imagine people who are in general susceptible to moral persuasion and censure, at least outside the context of the criminal justice system; and who are in principle open to moral persuasion through the kinds of punishment they suffer (else their punishments could not communicate censure to them, and give them "the *opportunity* of responding as [moral] agents should" [Chapter 24, p. 413]); but who are in fact (almost) never thus persuaded. But why is this? Is it because of the kinds of punishment which are imposed, or the manner and spirit in which they are imposed – in which case I need suggest only that their penal system needs reforming? Or is it because of some odd feature of their moral psychology – in which case we need to know more about that feature?

In the second hypothetical, we are to imagine people who for the most part do not need the apparatus of penitential hard treatment punishments, but a few of whom would occasionally need it, to "achieve a penitent understanding of their misdeeds" [Chapter 24, p. 414]. But why is this? Does this have to do with the seriousness of those misdeeds, or with the nature of their relationships to their fellow citizens, or with some particular feature of their moral psychology? Again, we need a fuller account of the moral psychology of the offenders, and of their moral lives and relationships outside the context of punishment.

Depending on what that account turned out to be, I might suggest that in the first case there would indeed be no adequate justification for a system of hard treatment punishment; or that the character, manner, and institutional context of punishment should be reformed so that it might achieve its proper penitential aims. In the second, I might suggest that there would again, though on different grounds, be no adequate justification for a system of hard treatment punishments (because we should not create a large, complex, and dangerous penal institution for the sake of a few unusual offenders); or that it could still be justified, as still serving – for all offenders – the penitential ends that punishment should serve.

The point to emphasise here, however, is that any plausible justifying account of punishment will portray it as being necessary and justified, not a priori for any and every kind of (rational, human?) being, but for particular kinds of being (human beings like ourselves in relevant respects). If such an account is to be challenged, on the grounds that it has counter-intuitive or disturbing implications when applied to imagined beings radically different from ourselves, we need first to be clear whether and how it would apply to such beings – and we cannot guarantee in advance that it should so apply.

25

THE JUSTIFICATION OF GENERAL DETERRENCE

Daniel Farrell

Aside from any "backward-looking" or retributivistic aims we may happen to have, there are at least two things we are typically trying to do when we punish someone for disobeying the law: we are trying to keep *them* from disobeying the law again, and we are trying to keep others from following their example. In many cases, we may have reason to believe that both of these aims will be served quite effectively by one and the same penalty: the "two-to-five" that we give the mugger for his first offence may arguably be likely both to deter him and to serve as an effective warning to others not to do likewise. In other cases, though, what we think is necessary for effectively deterring potential wrongdoers may be considerably more than what we think is necessary in order to keep the wrongdoer we are punishing from doing wrong again. The most dramatic example of this latter sort of case, of course, is capital punishment. For holding aside complications that are irrelevant to the present point, it seems that the most we would ever have to do to keep a convicted murderer from murdering again would be to imprison him for life. If, however, we had reason to believe that certain potential murderers could be deterred from murdering if we executed those convicted of the relevant sorts of murderers, we might be tempted to resort to execution despite the fact that we are willing to concede that this is not necessary in order to keep the person executed from murdering again.

It is sometimes said that in treating convicted capital criminals in this way we would be wronging them, since we would be "using" them as a means to our own social ends. We may believe, of course, on retributive grounds, that capital criminals *deserve* to die, so that might be our reason for executing them. The effect our action has on potential murderers would then be just a happy side-effect. If, however, we do not accept this retributive rationale, and yet do believe that capital punishment, is both necessary and morally justifiable as a way of reducing capital crime, we will face the challenge that is implicit in our remarks above: that of explaining by what right we use convicted capital criminals in order to deter potential capital criminals.

In what follows I want to suggest what I think is a novel way of meeting this challenge. I shall begin by showing why so-called "special" or "individual" deterrence is immune to doubts of the sort just imagined for the justification of general deterrence. I shall then show why the sorts of considerations that justify special deterrence are apparently unable to provide us with a justification of general deterrence. Finally, I shall show how it is that general deterrence may nonetheless be upheld. In doing all this, I shall take the liberty of extending ordinary usage, at least to a degree. I shall call the view that wrongdoers may be punished beyond what is necessary to keep them from doing wrong again – *if* so punishing them can plausibly be said to be likely to deter others from doing wrong themselves – a form of "weak retributivism." Obviously, weak retributivism, thus conceived, is nothing like the retributivism of the "classical" or "fierce" retributivist, who holds that the guilty may be punished simply because of what they have done. Still, inasmuch as it suggests that, in and of itself, wrongdoing makes a crucial moral difference with respect to how one may justifiably be treated – makes one, that is to say, a suitable object of social use – the view implicit in our ordinary thinking about the justification of general deterrence does appear to have at least something in common with certain forms of the retributive view. For it suggests that one's wrongful choices make one liable, morally, to treatment to which one would ordinary not be liable. And this, as I explain below, might plausibly be thought of as introducing a kind of weak or watered-down retributivism into what is otherwise a clearly non-retributive approach to punishment.

I

Suppose we ignore for a moment the problem of justifying the institution of punishment and reflect, instead, on the problem of articulating the rights and wrongs of various defensive actions in something like a Lockean state of nature. One right most of us would claim in such a situation is the right to resist, directly, others' attempts to violate our rights. If, for example, in a situation of the sort we have in mind, we imagine someone coming at me with a meat-cleaver, with the express intention of killing me so as to make it easier to rob me, most of us would say I have the right to resist him, even, if necessary, with deadly force. I shall call this presumed right my right to *direct self-defense*.

More problematic, I think, but equally widely accepted, is what I shall call the right to *indirect* self-defense. Suppose the offender described above has come at me with the aforementioned meat-cleaver on a good number of occasions in the past, and it has become clear to me that he is going to continue these attacks. And suppose, as well, I have discovered that this particular individual has an intense aversion to physical pain. In particular, suppose I have learned that if I can make him believe that I will subject him to a certain amount of pain if he continues his attacks, he will discontinue them.

In these circumstances, it seems to me, I have a right to threaten the offender with the infliction of serious physical suffering if he continues his attacks. What's more, if it transpires that I cannot convince him that I am in earnest without actually inflicting such suffering, subsequent to one of his attacks, I have, I believe, a right to inflict it. After all, we are supposing that short of killing him, this is the only way of keeping him from continuing to try to kill me. And why should I have to run the risk of thus being killed, unjustifiably, if I can obviate that risk by subjecting him to a certain amount of physical pain?

Someone might deny that I have the right in question, his argument being that I have no right to harm an attacker in the required way given that by hypothesis doing so is not necessary for preventing the current attack (we are supposing I have already prevented it). Let him consider, then, the following sort of case. Suppose the circumstances are exactly as above, except that at the time of the most recent (unsuccessful) attack, I know exactly when the next attack will be and also that, when it occurs, I will be incapacitated by some recurrent illness. All I have time to do, let us suppose, as I resist the current attack, is either rebuff the attacker as I usually do or rebuff him and subject him to some intense physical pain. I know, let us suppose, that if subjected to the additional physical pain, he will not attack again, but that if not subjected to this pain, he will attack again, at a time when I will be sick with fever and unable to resist. If I am justified in resisting him during any given attack – with death, if necessary – how can it be that I may not do what I have to do to prevent his next attack, given that I know I will be unable to defend myself when he launches that attack?

Suppose it is granted that under the appropriate circumstances one has the right to both "direct" and "indirect" self-defense. What are the implications for the theory of punishment? Obviously, it might be thought that if the claims above are right, they can be applied more or less straightforwardly to that side of the institution of punishment that concerns itself with what is usually called "special" or "individual" deterrence: with the enterprise, that is, of trying to prevent convicted criminals from repeating their crimes. For if, in a Lockean state of nature, I would have the right to what we have called indirect self-defense, surely society, acting as my agent, can exercise that right on my behalf.

I think the analogy suggested here is sound: attempts at special deterrence are indeed instances of what I have called indirect self-defense. What is problematic is the question of whether the intuitions suggested above are themselves sound – that is, whether so-called "indirect self-defense" really is justifiable – and also the question of whether the defense of punishment along these lines really is free of any "backward-looking" or weakly retributivistic elements. That it might seem to be free of such elements, of course, is due to the fact that we have justified it, if we have, strictly on grounds of self-defense. And it is not clear, offhand, that there is anything "backward-looking," or even weakly "retributivistic," about acting in self-defense.

Upon reflection, however, it should be clear that the proposed principles of self-defense are certainly "backward-looking" in at least this sense: we would not ordinarily say that one is justified in doing just anything – to anyone – in defense of her life or liberty; we would say that one is justified in resisting *an unjust aggressor*, in certain ways, in defense of her life or liberty. Thus, to take just one example, it is not at all clear that we would feel justified in killing an aggressor's children, even if that were the only way of keeping her from killing us. And we would certainly say that we are much more clearly justified in killing the murderous aggressor, in order to protect ourselves from her, than in killing her children, even if the latter would do the job just as well as the former.

What this suggests, of course, is that we intuitively believe that self-defense, like punishment, must be "aggressor-oriented." We believe, that is to say, for reasons to be discussed below, that in unjustly aggressing against us, an aggressor loses her right not to be treated in certain ways. We do not believe, however, that *anyone else* loses those rights – the aggressor's children, for example – even if we also believe that by treating them in the relevant ways we can save ourselves from that aggressor.

All of this is connected, I think, in a fairly straightforward way, with the question of whether the principles of self-defense – and, thereby, the principles for justifiable special deterrence – are in some sense "retributivistic." For just as the pursuit of general deterrence seems to require the assumption that wrongdoers are morally liable for "social use" – in ways in which those who have not done wrong are not held to be liable – so too, we might say, special deterrence seems to require a somewhat similar assumption. For as we have seen, even in cases of self-defense, and hence in cases of special deterrence, we think of unjust aggressors as more appropriately treated in certain ways than nonaggressors, even when we believe that treating the nonaggressors in those ways will serve exactly the same purposes as treating, the aggressors in those ways. Of course, we would not say that we are "using" aggressors when we treat them as we do, for purposes of indirect self-defense, and this is due to a significant difference between special and general deterrence. It is the case, however, as we have just seen, that the initiation of unjust aggression makes a person liable to certain sorts of treatment: treatment to which other, nonaggressing individuals are not ordinarily thought to be liable.

But now why should we suppose that our intuitions about justifiable self-defense are anything more than that – intuitions – and why, in particular, should we suppose that they are deserving of anything more than anthropological interest? The most insightful answer to this question, it seems to me, is that in the sorts of situations we have been imagining, self-defense is a matter of distributive justice.[2] To see this, notice that in cases of the relevant sort, the victim is faced with a choice of two ways of distributing certain harms: she call refrain from resisting can the aggressor, thereby sparing the aggressor harm while suffering harm herself, or she can resist, thereby saving herself from harm (at least if her resistance is successful) by subjecting the aggressor to harm. Now if one is inclined to think, as I believe most of us are, that in a situation of this sort the victim is entitled to take the latter tack, one must say, at least roughly, why one believes that this is so. And one not implausible way of doing this, I think, is to argue as follows: inasmuch as it is the aggressor who has (knowingly and willingly) brought it about that the victim must make the relevant choice, justice entitles the victim to choose that the aggressor, rather than the victim, will suffer the harm that, by hypothesis, one or the other of them must suffer.

The principle that is implicit here is by no means uncontroversial.[3] Notice, though, that it has at least this much to be said for it: it explains our intuitions about ordinary cases of self-defense, and it explains as well our intuitions about defense of the innocent against unjust aggression. The first of these points will be clear from our remarks above. To appreciate the second point, we simply need to imagine a case where, as bystanders, we are in a position of either intervening on behalf of a potential victim of aggression or standing by and letting the victim be wronged. I think most of us would say that in such a case one has a right to intervene. We would call this, of course, not "self-defense" but "defense of the innocent against unjust aggression." We do believe that it is justifiable, however, and it is not implausible to suppose that we believe this for precisely the reasons the account above suggests.

Suppose one agrees that this appeal to the notion of distributive justice provides a plausible basis for the intuitions that underlie our thinking about the justifiability of actions taken in self-defense and also about the justifiability of actions taken in defense of others. It should be clear that far from removing the suspicion that there is something weakly retributivistic in our thinking about these matters, this account actually reinforces those suspicions and to some extent explains them. For what this account tells us is that a person's (informed) choices make her liable to suffering certain harms if, in light of those choices, it is inevitable that someone be harmed and she is one of the individuals who can be harmed in order that someone else be saved. And this, I shall say, is one version of the thesis of "weak retributivism": one must suffer, once one has done wrong, not (simply) because of one's decision to do wrong, as in classical or "fierce" retributivism: rather, one must suffer if one's decision to do wrong makes it necessary that someone must suffer and that sufferer must either be the wrongdoer or some innocent victim.

II

Thus far I have argued that special deterrence can plausibly be thought of as a form of self-defense, and I have argued as well that even if this is so, punishment with this end has an interestingly retributivistic aspect. I now want to consider punishment in the interests of general deterrence – capital punishment, for example, where what we hope to achieve is not merely prevention of a like offense by the offender in question but prevention of such offenses by other, like-minded individuals as well. Offhand, it seems clear that if general deterrence is morally permissible, this is not because it is permissible on grounds of distributive justice exactly like those suggested above. After all, our argument above was that we are justified in special deterrence because the aggressor is the one responsible for our having to choose between her suffering or our suffering and because in cases like this justice entitles us to choose that she suffer rather than that we suffer. In the case of general deterrence, by contrast, it would seem to be just false to suppose that any given offender can plausibly be said to be responsible for the choice we have to make. We do indeed have to decide, if the assumptions behind the pursuit of general deterrence are sound, between harming convicted criminals or letting innocent victims be harmed. However, we cannot say, straightforwardly, that this choice was forced on us by any particular criminal. It is, to be sure, a choice we face because of the existence of people *like* her – that is, because of the existence of her and of like-minded individuals. But to say this is quite different from saying that it is a choice we face because of an unjustifiable choice that she made and as a result of which we have apprehended her.[4]

There are, of course, a number of other tacks that we might take in attempting to justify the pursuit of our general-deterrence aims. One approach would be to modify the principle of distributive justice mentioned above, so that it extends to cases like those that now interest us: to allege, for example, that we may justifiably act to harm not just those who have faced us with the choice of harms but those, also, who have done the *sort* of thing that requires us to concern ourselves with this distribution-problem in the first place. Thus, we would allege, on this account, that justice allows us to "use" those who have perpetrated certain harms and that it allows us to do this simply because they have perpetrated those harms. There is no attempt to explain this claim, or otherwise defend it, on this approach; it is simply taken to be obvious that this is something that justice allows.

I shall call this view *undefended extensive weak-retributivism*. I introduce it here not because, at present, I propose to defend or to attack it, but because it provides us with a convenient point of reference for the evaluation of certain other views. The point is that if this is as much as we can say about the justification of general-deterrence penalties, there really is something deeply – though still "weakly" – retributivistic about this side of our institution of punishment. For what this view is saying

433

is that, in the nature of things, it is simply *more appropriate* that those who have perpetrated certain wrongs should suffer than that those who would otherwise be the victims
of similar wrongs should suffer, and that it is more appropriate simply because the
members of the one group have done that kind of thing while the members of the other
group have not.[5]

[. . .]

III

Let us begin by calling to mind a fact about the institution of punishment that we have
so far ignored: in the institution of punishment as we know it, people who are "used"
for the purpose of general deterrence are not people who just happen to have done
things such that, once they have been done, the rest of us see that by punishing the
doers of these deeds we can prevent other people from doing similar sorts of things in
future. Rather, in the institution of punishment as we know it, potential criminals are
warned, in advance of their crimes, that if they perpetrate those crimes, we will hold
them liable for "use" in the appropriate ways. And this, I think most us would say, is
crucial to that institution. It might indeed be wrong to use a person as general deterrence requires its to use him, if we have not in fact warned him that we will thus use
him if he does wrong to us. If he *has* been warned, however, he can hardly object to
our carrying out our threats when he ignores them – or so it might be said – especially
if we have good reason to believe that thus warning and punishing people will serve
the ends we intuitively believe that this will serve.

Holding aside for a moment any merits it may have, the view suggested here is
clearly problematical in at least one rather obvious way: in suggesting that the crucial
element in the justification of general deterrence is the fact that the relevant criminals
have been forewarned in the relevant ways, it at least appears to beg exactly the
question that interests us. We do not ordinarily think that telling someone we will
do X if they do Y justifies us in actually *doing* X if they do Y, unless we believe that
we have a right to do X, if they do Y, in the first place. That is to say, if we have
reason to believe that we are not justified in doing X to someone, should they do Y,
then it is not at all clear that we are justified in doing X to them, if they do Y, simply
because we have told them, in advance of their doing Y, that we would do X if they
did Y. To suppose otherwise, it would seem, would be to suppose that we can justify
what we otherwise would have no right to do simply by telling the relevant parties
that we intend to do it.[6]

Of course, it seems relevant, intuitively, that the persons in question have no right
to do things like Y in the first place. And we shall have more to say about the relevance

of this fact below. Notice, though, that it is not at all clear, offhand, exactly how this is relevant. We are supposing that despite the fact that a murderer had no right to murder, it is problematic as to whether or not we have a right to kill him in order to prevent other potential murderers from murdering. And if all we can say, by way of showing that we have this right, is that we have told him we would kill him if he killed, it seems we have not said nearly enough. For our question is exactly what makes us think we have a right to tell him this, meaning to do what we say we will do if *he* does what we have warned him not to do.

Now notice, by way of attempting an answer to this question, that our aim in making the relevant threats is not what one very simple-minded view would suggest: in making such threats, we are not *simply* trying to put ourselves into a position of being able to rationalize the application of the threatened penalties if and when our threats are ignored. No doubt, if and when we have to keep our threats, we will feel that our having threatened the relevant penalties is one thing that justifies us in applying them. Nonetheless, to think that our aim in making the threats is simply to justify thus carrying them out would be to overlook the fact that our real aim in making them could conceivably be achieved even if our threats were never ignored and hence never had to he carried out. For our real aim is to convince potential wrong-doers that their prospective wrongdoing would be a bad bargain. And this, of course, could conceivably be achieved, and with complete success, even if no one ever ignored our threats and hence even if no one ever had to be punished.

Suppose we gloss this way of thinking about the point of our general-deterrence threats as follows: suppose we say that in making the relevant threats we are attempting to restrain certain sorts of conduct by *putting a price* on actions of the relevant sorts. It will be clear from what we have already said that there are at least two very different moral problems that might be said to be associated with the use of such a "pricing system" in the control of people's conduct: the problem of saying what it is that justifies us in *making* the relevant threats – or setting the relevant prices – in the first place, thereby effectively limiting the freedom of choice of the persons threatened; and the problem of saying what it is that justifies us in actually carrying out these threats in cases where they are ignored. It would be a mistake, of course, to suppose that these are entirely independent problems. For now, however, it will be useful to think of them as if they were: to think of the relevant threats, that is, as comprised of things that we *say* we will do rather than as things that we necessarily intend to do, and to think of the carrying out of those threats as something that is itself not necessarily justified just because the threats were justified when we made them.

It might appear that the first of these problems is fairly easy to meet. No doubt, threats do need to be justified, even when, for all the person threatened knows, they are bluffs. For threats, if they are believed, are a way of limiting a person's freedom of action, and this, we generally suppose, is something which is *prima facie* wrong. In cases of the sort that interest us, however, coercive control of some sort is itself at least *prima facie* warranted, since in such cases we are dealing with potential violations of innocent persons' rights. If we suppose, therefore, as we are doing, that threats of harm are likely to reduce such violations and, moreover, are necessary if we are to reduce them to a tolerable level, it would seem that such threats are perfectly justifiable. After all, our threats are directed only to potential wrongdoers – that is, they are threats to do harm only to those who wrong us in certain ways – and, for all we have so far, they are not threats that will necessarily be carried out.

The problem with this, of course, is that it overlooks the fact that the threats we will be making will be "uniform" or "generic" threats rather than what we might call "individualized" threats: we will be threatening everyone with the same penalty (or spectrum of possible penalties) for each kind of crime, that is to say, basing our threats on considerations discussed below, rather than threatening specific persons with specific penalties, these latter being based on estimates of what seems necessary to deter each particular person from wronging us in some particular way. And this might be said to be objectionable, even by those who accept the basic thrust of the argument above, since we might be said to have no right even to so much as *threaten* a person with anything more than is arguably necessary to deter *him* or *her* from wronging us.

Now let us suppose that in a very simple social setting, we might very well be obligated to individualize our threats in the way this objection requires. It certainly does not follow that in a society like our own, the justification of generic threats is impossible, with the result that our argument for general deterrence cannot even get off the ground. For in a society as complex as our own, it would be virtually impossible, consistent with ever doing anything else, to individualize our threats in the way the objection above requires. If we simplify things for a moment, therefore, and suppose that, realistically, we must either issue uniform threats or else construct, at incalculable expense, an unimaginable bureaucracy that does nothing but issue particular threats to particular people, it seems reasonable to suppose that we are, after all, justified in issuing uniform threats.[7]

But now what about the justifiability of carrying out our threats, supposing they have been justifiably made? Obviously, our threats will sometimes be ignored. And given that all the argument above purports to show is that we are justified in *saying* we will do thus and such to those who wrong us, we now need an argument for the justifiability of actually doing it once our threats have been ignored.

Superficially, of course, the case for the justifiability of keeping threats which we have justifiably made seems clear enough. For if we suppose that in cases of the sort that interest us we have to carry out our threats, when they are ignored, in order for them to be effective in other cases, it would seem that we have a right to carry them out in order to keep them credible. For if they are not credible, we are not defended. And we have supposed that we have a right to be defended.

This argument obviously won't do, however, at least as it stands. For our critic could rightly contend that we have got things backwards here. If, as he contends, there are independent grounds for believing that there are certain things we have no right to do, we cannot justify the doing of them simply by showing we had a right to *say* we would do them – at least if what this latter right comes down to is just a right literally to say something, with no implication at all, for all we have said so far, about whether we would be justified in saying it *meaning to do it.*[8]

Now our critic's objection presumably rests on the fact that, using generic threats, we will, in some cases at least, have threatened to do more than we will actually have to do, to any particular wrongdoer once she has been apprehended, in order to keep that particular wrongdoer from wronging us again. It is not entirely clear, however, when one reflects on the matter, why this is supposed to make it wrong for us to carry out our threats. On one way of understanding it, of course, the objection might be put as follows: in doing more to any given wrongdoer than special deterrence requires, we are invariably wronging that wrongdoer, because we are thereby "using" her for our own ends. This formulation of the critic's point is not very compelling, however, at least as it stands. No doubt, there is a straightforward sense in which, on the pricing-system model, we are indeed "using" convicted criminals when we carry out our threats: we are, having announced that we would do so, using the fact of their conviction as an occasion for making an example of them, with the hope, thereby, of deterring similar wrongdoing on the part of others. Whether or not in doing this are thereby *wronging* convicted criminals, however, and in that sense "using" them, is precisely what is at issue here. Thus, while the point about how we are "using" people when we resort to our pricing system is sound, it is not a point that can be turned against that system until it is shown that to use people in this way is wrong.

Our critic could, of course, take a slightly different tack here and just *assert* – what is no doubt at the back of his mind in all this – that we simply have *no right* to do more, in any given case, than is necessary to deter the offender in question from acting similarly again and, moreover, that we have no right to do more even when we have warned him that we would do more if he acted against us. Unfortunately, in the absence of any argument, this claim simply begs the question that interests us, which is precisely the question of whether we ever *do* have a right to do more, in any given case, than is necessary to prevent the wrongdoer in question from wronging us again.

If this were all that could be said about the matter, of course, we would simply have reached a standoff, with our critic alleging that we do not have a right to use people in the relevant ways, even if we have warned them that they will be so used while we allege that, sometimes at any rate, we do. There is, however, something more that we can say. Imagine that you are attacked by someone, unjustifiably, in a Lockean state of nature, and suppose that as a result of her attack you are in a condition which will not only make you unable to resist *her* subsequent attacks but which will also make you unable to resist the attacks of other (potential) attackers as well. We have already seen that if our principle of distributive justice is sound, you are justified in such a case in harming the original attacker in order to prevent her from initiating another attack. If this is so, however, why are you not also justified in harming her in order to prevent *others* from doing what they would not have been able – or inclined – to do except for the damage that she has inflicted on you? If, that is to say, you are more vulnerable – *to attacks from others* – because of her attack, and if you can counter just this degree of added vulnerability by harming her now that she has harmed you, then, by the principle of distributive justice introduced above, it seems you would, at least within certain limits, be justified in harming her in order to prevent harms that she has brought it about that you will suffer if you do *not* harm her.[9]

It might be objected to this, of course, that it is unreasonable – and not at all consonant with our earlier principle – to hold an attacker liable for harms she had no way of knowing she would instigate by her wrongful conduct. At best, it might be said, we can justly penalize such a person – in the way general deterrence requires – only if we can convincingly expand our earlier principle to include both harms that are created knowingly and those that are not. And this, of course, would be a radical extension of that principle and one that is not at all as intuitively plausible as our earlier principle appeared to be.

We can avoid this objection, however, if we can put ourselves into the position of being able to say, to any given wrongdoer, that she did indeed have plenty of reason to believe that, by wronging us, she was increasing our vulnerability to harm from others. And this we can do by calculating, in advance of any actual wrongdoing, the approximate degree of harm to which we will have been made vulnerable by any given attack, and then publicly announcing the results of our calculations. To be sure, these calculations will be rough ones, and, moreover, any given wrongdoer may be able to say that she was unaware of the fact that by acting against us she would be putting us in a position of the relevant sort. Still, if we can possibly say that the attacker *ought* to have known what we know – if we can say, for example, that there was plenty of available evidence and that any reasonable person would have known what we know – then, it seems to me, we will justly hold her liable despite her claims of ignorance.

So the critic of general-deterrence penalties is wrong to say that we may never do, to any given offender, more than we have to do in order to keep that offender from wronging us again: if, by not penalizing an offender to some degree beyond what special deterrence would warrant, we will be vulnerable to wrongdoing, from others, which we would not have faced in the absence of this particular wrongdoer's attack, and if we can plausibly say that the wrongdoer in question either knew or ought to have known that this would be so, we may, within certain as yet unexplored limits, justifiably harm that wrongdoer beyond what is necessary to keep him or her from wronging us again. And this, of course, if it is right, not only suggests that the critic of general-deterrence penalties is wrong in this particular respect; it also suggests a general conception of what we are doing in announcing and applying general-deterrence penalties and why we are justified in doing it. For if our argument is right, we are, contrary to our tentative conclusion in Section II above, justified in imposing at least *some* penalties, over and above what special deterrence warrants, *by virtue of the same principle that justifies our special-deterrence efforts themselves*: namely, the principle of distributive justice introduced above, which tells us that when someone wrongfully (and wittingly) puts us in the position of having to decide whether they shall suffer or some innocent party shall suffer, we are entitled to choose that they should bear the suffering.

Have we shown, then, that the pursuit of general deterrence can be vindicated by the principle of distributive justice introduced above? Unfortunately, we have not. For, clearly, our argument thus far presupposes that the wrongdoer in question is both causally and morally responsible for our increased vulnerability to others' wrongdoing. Suppose that in a certain set of circumstances this is not the case. Suppose, for example, that while my vulnerability will not be heightened as a result of a given wrongdoer's attack – if, that is, I do not retaliate against her – I have good reason to believe that if I do retaliate, I will increase my overall security. Or suppose that while my vulnerability *has* been heightened by her attack, I realize that I can enhance my previous level of security, vis-à-vis others, by doing even more to her than I need to do to bring myself back to where I was, "security-wise," prior to her attack. It will be tempting, of course, to retaliate, in the first sort of case, and, in the second, to do more than I have to do in order to get back to where I was. If I do retaliate, however, in the one case, or do in fact do more, in the other, than our principle of distributive justice allows, and if I wish to say that I am justified in doing so, this can only be, for all we have said so far, because I am implicitly relying on the view that we earlier called "undefended extensive weak-retributivism." For by hypothesis the wrongdoer in question is not responsible for my being in a position where I have to decide either to harm her (at least to the degree to which I am tempted to harm her) or let myself be harmed by others. If we assume, therefore, that I may justifiably harm her as a means of reducing the probability that I will be harmed by others, it must be, for all we have said so far, simply because she is a wrongdoer the harming of whom will do me some good. And this, of course, is simply undefended extensive weak-redistributivism. This doctrine may be sound, and it may not be in need of further defense. Our hope, however, was to provide some further defense, showing, thereby, either that general deterrence is not as retributivistic as it seems or, at any rate, that, if it is, it is justifiable nonetheless. And this is something we have thus far not been able to do.

IV

Let us call the approach to the justification of general deterrence that rests upon our special principle of distributive justice "the less radical approach," and let us call the approach that would allow us to set and enforce deterrent penalties beyond what this less radical approach allows "the more radical approach." Although I shall not be able to show it here, I think it can be shown that the latter approach really does require us to embrace a form of "extensive" weak-retributivism which cannot itself be grounded on any deeper or more general moral basis – a basis like that provided by our special principle of distributive justice, for example, which underlies the less radical of our strategies, which has intuitive appeal in its own right, and which is capable of accounting for all sorts of cases in addition to the sorts of cases that interest us here. Our thought, of course, was that this approach might be shown to be justifiable by virtue of the fact that its implementation is preceded by threats or "warnings," these latter having been issued on the assumption that issuing and enforcing them would significantly reduce the number of wrongful attacks to which we would be subjected. As we have seen, however, in the absence of an account of why it is that what may not be done *without* threats may sometimes be done once threats have been made, it is not at all clear how our having threatened a penalty justifies us in imposing it if and when it is ignored. An account of the relevant sort may be forthcoming, of course, but, unfortunately, nothing that we have been able to say here suggests how such an account would go. Rather, what we have seen here is that those penalties that may be threatened, and then imposed, are precisely those that, in theory at least, might have been imposed even in the absence of the relevant threats.[10]

There is, of course, still before us, the very important problem of attempting to say something about the limits that must be observed, on either of these approaches, in the pursuit of our general-deterrence aims. And in a moment I shall go on to discuss this question in connection with what I am calling the less radical approach to the justification of general deterrence. Notice here, though, that as far as the more radical approach is concerned, it would seem that in the absence of a general moral principle grounding this approach, it will be rather difficult to say anything convincing about the limits within which we must stay when pursuing general deterrence on the grounds that this approach suggests. The most that one could hope to do here, it seems to me, would be to produce more or less plausible intuitions about what those limits are. And, obviously, the problem with thus resting one's claims on intuition is that someone else could just as well summon up opposing intuitions in defense of an opposing view.

In connection with what I am calling the "less radical" approach, by contrast, I think we can say something rather more compelling about the limits to which we may justifiably go in pursuit of our general-deterrence aims. For, of course, on this approach we *do* have a general moral principle to guide us in what we say: the principle of distributive justice introduced above, according to which we have a right to protect ourselves – and other innocents – against harms that some wrongdoer's actions have made it necessary that either the wrongdoer himself must suffer or that some innocent party must suffer instead. Our question here is simply what limits this principle entails for the sorts of cases that interest us.

Now in attempting to answer this question, it will be useful to begin by calling to mind a fact that we have thus far ignored: the harms that the less radical approach to general deterrence allows us to impose do not *have* to have been threatened, or otherwise announced in advance, in order to be justifiably imposed. This, of course, is because that approach, being based on our special principle of distributive justice, allows us to impose suffering on someone who has wrongfully (and wittingly) confronted us with a certain choice – namely, to hurt them or to run the risk of being hurt ourselves – even if we have not previously told them that we would choose their suffering, rather than our suffering, if it came down to this. Of course, it may be that we are obligated to warn people that we plan to act on this principle if there is time to want them and if thus warning them will not entail any avoidable disadvantages to ourselves. And, in any case, it will certainly make sense to warn them that we plan to act on this principle, since, just warning them of this may be enough to dissuade some of them from wronging us. Still, it is important to note that, in principle, we are free to act against wrongdoers in the rather extensive ways our special principle of distributive justice allows, even if we have not warned them that we would do so.[11]

But, now, suppose we ask what our situation would be like if we did not say, in advance of any wrongdoing against us, that we plan to act against wrongdoers in the relevant ways *and* if we did not say, in advance, roughly what we thought this would involve. We will be wronged at some point, we may suppose, and hence will have to decide what steps to take once we have been wronged. Presumably, one limit on what we may do in a situation like this will be set by the fact that, ordinarily, at any rate, we think of ourselves as being entitled to do no more, when we are acting to prevent avoidable harms on the basis of our special principle of distributive justice, than we *have* to do in order to protect ourselves against the harms made likely by any given wrongdoer's attack. How, then, will we calculate what we thus have to do in order to protect ourselves against these harms? Obviously, this is an empirical matter: we need to ask what harms we will face, if we do not react to a given degree, that we would not have faced if we had never been attacked in the first place. Notice, though, that in any given case this is likely to be an empirical question that it will be very hard to answer. Indeed, it seems fair to say that in many cases it will be impossible to answer. Of course, it is reasonable to assume, in light of this, that we are entitled, in such cases, to *estimate* what is required for protecting ourselves against the relevant sorts of harms. Notice, though, that our estimates, given that we have made no threats, must be estimates based on the details of each particular case. And these, while in principle quite possible, will themselves be extremely difficult to make.

Now suppose we were to try to get around these difficulties in an obvious way: by announcing, in advance of any actual wrongdoing against us, exactly what we intend to do in response to acts of wrongdoing – where acts are classified into categories in some appropriate way – in order to ensure that we are none the worse off by virtue of these acts having occurred. There will certainly be limits on what we may thereby announce (and enforce) as penalties – limits, it seems to me, which will be set by two different sorts of considerations. On the one hand, it is clear that since we are basing our right to retaliate on the principle of distributive justice suggested above, there will be certain "absolute" or "a priori" limits, which will be set by the fact that we do not have a right to do just *anything*, no matter how severe, to avoid an evil that someone else has made it necessary for us to avoid, but, rather, that we have a right to do *certain* things to avoid evils that others have set for us but not to do other things. An example will make this clear. If we suppose that someone, by his wrongful action, has made it inevitable that either I (an innocent person) must die or that he must die, our principle tells us that I may choose that he die rather than I. If, by contrast, he has made it inevitable that either I suffer a mild inconvenience or he dies, most of us would say that I would be wrong to cause his death just so that I may be spared the mild inconvenience.

The question, of course, is exactly what I may and may not do in thus defending myself (and other innocents) against the likely consequences of others' wrongdoing. Unfortunately, this is a question to which I have, at present, no useful answer. Different people will no doubt have radically different intuitions about what is and is not appropriately done – in defense of oneself (and others) against various degrees of wrongdoing – and I am currently not in possession of a general account that would enable us to sort through these intuitions in order to create a cohesive whole. Notice, though, that the problem of resolving these difficulties is not *simply* a problem for the defender of general deterrence, as we are conceiving the latter here. Rather, it is a problem that is endemic to the general theory of self-defense and, even more generally, to that part of the theory of distributive justice that deals with the distribution of harms made inevitable by someone's wrongful conduct. Thus, while there are indeed large and very pressing problems here, they are not problems that are created by the approach to general deterrence that we are exploring here.

There are other considerations, though, which are relevant to what we may justifiably threaten when we make the threats that I am supposing the less radical approach to the justification of general deterrence allows, and these are considerations which might be thought to raise difficulties that are peculiar to the approach to general deterrence that we are following here. These latter considerations have to do with the fact, to which we have alluded above, that in defending ourselves against the harmful consequences of others' wrongful actions, we are entitled, or so we ordinarily suppose, to do only as much as we have to do, in any given case, in order to prevent those consequences. In cases of the sort that interest us, of course, the relevant consequences include the likely acts of those who might be affected by what we do or do not do in light of the current attack. Hence, in such cases a great deal more will be justified, at least in principle, than the ordinary picture of justifiable self-defense intuitively suggests. Still, there are definite limits here which are quite distinct, in theory at least, from the absolute or a priori, limits discussed above. We might call these second sorts of limits "case-relative" or "a posteriori" limits, inasmuch as they seem to be set by the exigencies of each particular case.[12]

Now if we were supposing that, on the less radical approach that currently interests us, the pursuit of general deterrence would be effected on a case-by-case basis – with estimates of what's necessary for "self-defense" being made successful to any given attack and being tailored to the ascertainable facts of the particular case at hand – the existence of limits of this second or a posteriori kind would pose no special theoretical problems. We are supposing, of course, that it will generally be impossible to say, in any given case, exactly what we have to do in order to keep ourselves from suffering increased vulnerabilities as a result of the wrongdoer's attack in that particular case. But this difficulty can be handled, I think, without compromising the principles on which our current approach is grounded, by supposing, as we did above, that our right to defend ourselves in such situations allows us to estimate the penalties that are required, at least when it is impossible to determine them exactly. This is no different, it seems to me, than saying that in cases of direct self-defense we are entitled to estimate what we have to do to stop an immediate attack if, under the circumstances, it is impossible to determine *exactly* what we have to do to stop it.

The real problem that is raised by limits of this second (a posteriori) sort is a rather different one. To see this, we need to notice that, proceeding as we are supposing we will proceed, it will sometimes happen that what we have *threatened* to do, vis-à-vis a given type of crime, will be more than we in fact *need* to do in order to protect ourselves against avoidable vulnerabilities created by the person who has wronged us in the case at hand. If, in such cases, we apply the penalty that was threatened, rather than limiting ourselves to what is in fact required for "self-defense," it would seem that we will be violating the principle with which our current reflections began: the principle that tells us that in defending ourselves against the harmful consequences of others' wrongful actions, we are justified in doing, within the a priori limits discussed above, only as much as we need to do in order to protect ourselves against vulnerabilities created by any given wrongdoer's wrongdoing in any given case.

It may well be that this line of argument is essentially correct: ideally, we ought not to do, in any given case, anything more than we need to do in order to block avoidable vulnerabilities that have been created by that particular case. Suppose it could be shown, though, that, *as a matter of fact*, we are actually likelier to prevent the relevant sorts of vulnerabilities, even as they arise in any given case, if we react to wrongful aggression not on a case-by-case basis but on the basis of a pre-announced schedule of penalties which has itself been established on the basis of an honest empirical estimate of what we must do to contain the likely effects of such aggression. This is a big assumption, of course, and an entirely empirical one. However, if we suppose that it is sound, we may ask whether we are not, in light of it, entitled to resort to the sort of strategy we have been favoring, despite the fact that such a strategy will inevitably require us to do more, in certain cases, than we need to do in order to protect ourselves from vulnerabilities that we face because of the particular case at hand. And the answer, it seems to me, is that we *are* entitled, on these assumptions, to choose the one strategy over the other and that we are so entitled not (simply) on utilitarian grounds but (also) on grounds provided by the principle of distributive justice that has guided our reflections in everything we have said above. For at the heart of that principle is the idea that in cases of the sort that interest us, we have a right to protect ourselves, and other innocents, against the harmful consequences of others' wrongful acts. And how could this right, properly interpreted, not include a right to announce and enforce fixed penalties of the sort we are supposing might be necessary if we (and other innocents) are to be protected against the relevant sorts of harms?

Suppose these last assertions are accepted as sound. I do not think that in accepting them we undermine the distinction between the so-called "less radical" and "more radical" approaches to the justification of general deterrence. For that distinction has to do with whether we are aiming, in our general-deterrence efforts, at preventing harmful consequences of particular wrongful acts, or at preventing wrongful acts as such, independently of their connection with any other wrongful act. And this distinction remains, it seems to me, despite our concession that, even on the former approach, we will occasionally be inflicting penalties, in any given case, that are somewhat more severe than those we actually need to inflict in order to prevent the harmful consequences that would otherwise be caused by the agent's actions in that particular case. No doubt, if, on the former approach, our threatened penalties generally tend to be considerably beyond what is actually required, in any given case, for the purpose of "self-defense," we would not be justified in continuing to impose them. If, however, our penalties are *not* typically beyond the relevant limits, and if, moreover, when they are over those limits, they are not egregiously so, it seems to me there is no objection to them, on grounds of moral principle, and that in holding them unobjectionable we have not deprived ourselves of being able to distinguish the less radical approach to general deterrence from the more radical approach described above.

V

I have suggested, in the previous section, that there are two different sorts of limits that our general-deterrence penalties must honor, at least if we follow the less radical approach to the justification of general deterrence suggested above, and I have tried to show, as well, how, consistent with the recognition of these limits, we could justifiably announce the relevant penalties in advance and then impose them, after the fact, once they are ignored. It is perhaps worth emphasizing, in concluding, that penalties that honor the spirit of our principle of distributive justice, and that consequently are aimed at making up only for whatever added vulnerability we would face in the absence of such penalties, might themselves be considerably less rigorous than those penalties that would be necessary to protect us from attacks that the given wrongdoer is not responsible for but that we *could* prevent if we were willing to do enough to him and to people like him. Thus, it could be, as a matter of empirical fact, that capital punishment is never necessary for controlling vulnerabilities that are created by any particular capital criminal but that capital punishment *is* necessary if we are to prevent certain capital crimes. In that case, we would have a very dramatic illustration of the difference between what can be justified on our less radical approach to the justification of general deterrence and what can be justified on the more radical approach.

It will perhaps be obvious, then, that a theory of general deterrence that is based on our principle of distributive justice will be less "retributivistic" than one that is not and that allows itself to go beyond what that principle allows, at least in this sense: on the latter, but not on the former, people may be "used" not just to prevent vulnerabilities that *they themselves* have created but also to prevent vulnerabilities that exist independently of their actions. If general deterrence is objectionable, therefore, on the grounds that it requires us to wrongfully harm some people – namely, convicted criminals – as a way of helping others, perhaps it will be precisely when we thus resort to harming some in order to help others without the excuse of doing so because of the fact that the former have made it necessary for us to harm them or to see innocent people be harmed. Whether or not general deterrence *is* objectionable when thus pursued, and is objectionable on the grounds suggested here, is, unfortunately, a question that must be left for another time.

NOTES

1   Note that what makes the pursuit of general deterrence "weakly retributivistic," at least on the view suggested here, is not the fact that the advocate of general-deterrence penalties makes legal guilt a necessary condition of the imposition of such penalties but, rather, that the advocate of such penalties makes legal guilt a sufficient condition for "using" people in ways in which we would not use *innocent* people even if we believed that so using them

would have results that would be just as beneficial, socially, as the results of similarly using convicted criminals. As I understand his argument in "Prolegomenon to the Principles of Punishment" (*Punishment and Responsibility* [New York: Oxford University Press, 1968], pp. 1–27), H. L. A. Hart makes much of the *necessity* of (legal) culpability for just punishment but nothing at all of the fact, explored here, that in the pursuit of general deterrence we are inclined to think of culpability as also sufficient, for given certain empirical facts, for the justification of using the culpable individual for the advancement of our social ends.

2 Here I follow Philip Montague in "Punishment and Societal Self-Defense," in *Criminal Justice Ethics*, Vol. 2. No. 1 (Winter/Spring, 1983).

3 For some tentative and admittedly inconclusive reflections on the bases of this principle, see Judith Jarvis Thomson, "Remarks on Causation and Liability," *Philosophy and Public Affairs*, 13 (1984), pp. 101–133, which came to my attention only after the present paper was substantially completed.

4 I am simplifying here in ways that are explained below. It might in fact happen that a given offender *is* responsible for my being vulnerable to attacks from others – or, at any rate, for my being more vulnerable than I would otherwise have been – in which case the principle to which we have appealed above would be relevant. Our interest at the moment, however, is not in cases such as these but in cases where no one attacker is responsible for the other (potential) attacks with which I am faced but where I can diminish the likelihood of these other attacks occurring by doing more harm to any given attacker than is required for defending myself – directly or indirectly – *from her*. This, as we shall see, is the sort of case that presents the most difficult challenge for the defender of general deterrence as a form of social control.

5 This is not, of course, an uncommon view, nor is it, intuitively, an implausible one. For an oblique but rather compelling statement of it, see Steven Goldberg, "Does Capital Punishment Deter?" in Richard A. Wasserstrom (ed.), *Today's Moral Problems*, second edition (New York: Macmillan Publishing Co., 1979), pp. 547–548.

6 See Alan Goldman, "The Paradox of Punishment," *Philosophy and Public Affairs*, 9 (1979), pp. 54–56, and also Richard W. Burgh, "Do the Guilty Deserve Punishment?" *The Journal of Philosophy*, 79 (1982), pp. 198 ff.

7 I return to this question below and remove the simplifying assumption. Notice here, though, that the present argument is merely intended to be an in-principle argument for the permissibility of uniform threats. It leaves open the question, considered immediately below, of whether we are justified in *carrying out* such threats, once they are ignored, and also the question, considered at length in Section IV, of whether these threats may be as harsh as maximally effective general deterrence requires. The point is simply that in our special sense of "threat", generic threats seem to be justifiable, and they seem to be justifiable, given certain empirical assumptions, on grounds of self-defense.

8 Things are actually somewhat more complicated than I am allowing here, since someone might argue that we are sometimes entitled not only to *say* we will do what (we know) we may not do but also to say we will do it *meaning to do it* (i.e., fully intending to do it). I argue against this view in "Strategic Planning and Moral Norms: The Case of Deterrent Nuclear Threats" (unpublished ms.).

9 Notice that this reasoning can actually take us much further than is indicated in the text. For suppose the wrongdoer in question makes you more vulnerable not by incapacitating you but by making it the case that others are likelier to attack you if you do not harm her beyond what is necessary to deter *her* from subsequent attacks. If the wrongdoer is both causally and morally responsible for the situation in which you are thus placed – and, of

course, in certain situations she will be and in others she will not – it would seem that our principle of distributive justice would justify your harming her beyond what is necessary for preventing her from harming you again.

Notice, too, that I am speaking of your saving *yourself* here, rather than some other innocent party, only for the sake of simplicity. Exactly the same points as were made in Section I above also apply here: our principle is one that justifies us in saving innocents from harms that wrongdoers have brought it about that either the innocents must suffer or that the wrongdoers must suffer. It is, that is to say, a principle governing the defense of the innocent against unjust aggression and not simply a principle of self-defense.

10 We did say, of course, that under certain circumstances we might have to have made certain information available to potential wrongdoers if we were going to be clearly justified in harming them – for purposes of general deterrence – on the basis of our special principle of distributive justice. (See above, p. 438.) Our point, however, was not that we needed to have announced the relevant penalties in advance in order to be justified in imposing them but, rather, that we might need to have done certain other things, in advance, in order to ensure that wrongdoers could rightly be said to have known, when they acted, that they were endangering us in so acting. See below for further reflections that are relevant here.

11 See above, however, note 10, for an important *caveat*.

12 We might think of limits of the first sort as setting an a priori "upper bound" on what we may do, in any given case, in pursuit of the relevant general-deterrent aims and of limits of the second sort as varying, within the limits set by the first, depending on what is *in fact* required, in any given case, to keep us from being made more vulnerable than we would have been if we had never been wrongfully attacked in the first place.

FURTHER READING

Duff, R.A. (1986). *Trials and Punishments*. Cambridge, Cambridge University Press.

Duff, R.A. and Garland, D. (1994). *A Reader on Punishment*. Oxford, Oxford University Press.

Duff, R.A. (1996). "Penal Communications: Recent Work in the Philosophy of Punishment." *Crime and Justice A Review of Research* 20: 1–97.

Hart, H.L.A. (1959). "Prolegomenon to the Principles of Punishment." *Punishment and Responsibility*. Oxford, Oxford University Press: 1–27.

von Hirsch, A. (1993). *Censure and Sanctions* Oxford, Clarendon Press.

von Hirsch, A. and Ashworth, A. (1998). *Principled Sentencing: Readings on Theory and Policy* (2nd edn). Oxford: Hart Publishing.

Walker, N. (1991). *Why Punish?* Oxford, Oxford University Press.

INDEX

Note: figures and tables are indicated by *italicized* page numbers.

Acton, Lord 284, 310
advocacy issues 138, 195
After Virtue (MacIntyre) 268
agents 303, 326; moral 292–3, 294, 396, 408, 409, 410
Ake, Christopher 126–7
Althusser, Louis Pierre 23, 60
America/Americans 299–300, 313, 315, 336; *see also* United States
Anarchy State and Utopia (Nozick) 69, 70
anti-reductionism 11, 56, 57, 59, 61–4
Arendt, Hannah 207, 333
Aristotle 144, 182, 188, 201, 284, 292, 299, 352
Arrow, K. 328
associations 225, 267, 275–6, 281, 356–7
atomism 56–8, *57*, 138, 139, 195, 196, 199, 201, 203–4
Auden, W.H. 364
Augsburg, Peace of (1530) 257
Australia 246
Austrian school 13
autonomy 239–40, 392, 396–7; and democracy 342, 348–51; and liberalism 257, 260, 272; and preferences 328–9, 331, 333

Barry, Brian 216–18
behavior 17, 29, 103, 107
beliefs 217, 248–55, 269, 290
Bell, D.D. 150–1
Bellah, Robert 207
Bentham, Jeremy 199, 239, 272
Bismark, Otto, Fürst von 295
Blum, Walter 86
Bourdieu, Pierre 24–5
Britain 249–50, 309; empire 283, 289

Canada 246, 314
capitalism 27–8, 50, 51, 59, 62, 276; and societies 26–7, 64, 221

Capitalism, Socialism, and Democracy (Schumpeter) 352
Catholicism 27, 161
causation 30, 41, 121
Cavafy, C.P. 363
censure in communicative punishment 384–5, 389, 390, 393, 394, 395, 400, 403–4, 408, 412
chartism 337
children, protection of 256–7, 261
choice(s) 31, 101, 103, 107, 251, 271, 272, 329–30, 354, 369; and preferences 248, 252, 326–7; private 325–6; *see also* rational choice theory; social choice theory
Churchill, Winston S. 321
citizens/citizenship 139, 201–2, 329, 337, 396; conceptions of 215–16, *216*, 223, 224–31, 296; and democracy 223, 321–3, 345–6; differentiated 215, 220, 224–31; and dignity 198, 208, 209; and equality 219–20, 222, 232, 343; as generality 221–4, 228; rights and liberties 166, 175, 176, 201, 372; universality of 215, 219–36
civil society 281
class issues 33, 59, 323
coalitions 229–30
coercion 198, 322, 393
coercive structure 103–4, 105, 107, 109–10
Cohen, G.A. 54, 70–1, 126
Cohen, Joshua 322–3
collectivity 8, 59, 60, 138, 195–6; decision-making 221, 342
Colley, Linda 309
common good 139, 186, 189, 191, 199, 201, 203, 206, 331; in democracies 321, 322, 325, 342, 343, 344, 348, 366; and social choice mechanism 328, 331, 332–3, 334

communicative ethics concept 228
communicative punishment 387, 391, 394, 396,
   399, 403–4, 405; aims/functions 397, 423–4;
   and language issues 395, 400–1, 402–3;
   monastic/academic examples 391–2, 397,
   412–13, 414, 418, 424–6; and moral standing
   399–405, 412; theory 384, 385, 388–90, 399;
   see also censure
communism and free market 138
communitarian–liberal debate 135–9, 182–91, 267;
   cross-purposes 195–210
communitarianism 137, 182–91, 196, 276–7, 278,
   392, 423; and metaphysics 188–9, 396
community/communities 195, 198, 199, 278, 298;
   and criminal justice 392, 396, 401, 411, 423;
   and morality 289, 291, 292–3, 402; and nations
   304–6; political 401, 402, 423; *see also*
   society/societies
comprehensive doctrines 136, 161, 162, 164, 171,
   175; definition 165–6
Comte, Auguste 13
conflict 289, 290, 298
conformity/conformism 329
consequentialism 41, 383, 388; laws 9, 44, 50
conservatism 268, 271, 280, 309
constitutional issues 137, 138, 155–6
contract(s) 277; bonds/bondage 278, 297; social
   271, 276, 282, 395
conversation 200
Cooley, Charles Horton 13
Coser, Lewis 24
crime 385, 390; causes/theories 29, 385, 402;
   homicide 428, 435; prevention 408–10, 415,
   416, 428; *see also* communicative punishment;
   deterrence; offenders; punishment
Criminal Justice Act (1988) 253–4
criminal justice system 383, 384, 385, 404, 405,
   426
criminal law 146–7, 148, 250, 253, 396–7, 426
Critique of the Gotha Programme (Marx) 34
Critique of Political Economy, A (Marx),
   "Preface" 41–2, 47
cultural diversity 216, 239–42; and equality 242–7;
   and rights issues 235, 244–5, 248–61
cultural relativism 258
culture 273, 277, 315; and autonomy 239–40; and
   unity 267, 281

Darwin, Charles 45, 48, 49
de Gaulle, Charles 295
Debray, Régis 280
decision-making 221, 224, 342; deliberative 350,
   351; and groups 228–31, 248; political 322,
   337, 365–6
deliberative democracy 322–3, 342–57; common
   good and autonomy 348–51; objections to
   352–6; procedures 322–3, 342, 346, 347–8,
   350, 351; theory of 346–7

democracy(ies) 190, 223, 230, 282–3, 322–3,
   325; constitutional 137, 138; definition/theories
   227, 321, 337, 366–7; ideal of 343–4; political
   constraints 323, 365–7, 369, 371, 375–7;
   see also deliberative democracy
democratic politics 343–5, 361–77; constitutions
   336, 337, 372; and decision-making 366–8; and
   fairness 344–5; and justice 368–70; and rights
   370–3
democratic societies 161, 174, 176, 204–5; and
   groups 224–31; and public discussion 164, 221,
   321–2
democratic space 323, 372
deontology: egalitarian 70, 119, 120, 121, 122,
   129; liberal 135, 136, 152–4, 184, 240
Descartes, René 362–3
desert(s) 135–6, 140, 145, 148, 182, 383–4, 387;
   see also retributivists/retributivism
despotism 201–2, 203
deterrence 147, 393, 409–10, 428, 433;
   forewarning/threats 434–7; justification of
   428–45; special/general 385, 429, 431, 433,
   434, 438–9, 444, 445; theory 383, 384, 385,
   388, 405; *see also* punishment
Diderot, Denis 12
difference principle 91–3, 100–1, 148, 149, 372;
   in Germany and US 108–9; and incentives
   argument 105–6
disabled, rights of 216, 234, 252
Discourse (Descartes) 362–3
discrimination 29, 234, 323
discussion 330, 331, 332–4, 335; time constraints
   issue 332–3, 338; *see also* public debate
distribution 116, 120, 121, 125–6, 251; levelling
   down 70, 124–5
distributive justice 69, 73–9, 217–18, 331, 372;
   and morality 116, 148; principles of 75, 126,
   385; and retributive justice 144, 145–9, 445;
   and self-defense 431–2, 433, 438–9, 441–4;
   theories 145–9
diversity: cultural 216, 239; of doctrines 161; and
   liberalism 218, 239–47, 255–61
doctrines 161, 168, 170; religious 280; of
   sufficiency 82–97; *see also* comprehensive
   doctrines
"Domain of the Political and Overlapping
   Consensus, The" (Rawls) 136
drugs 255, 383
dualism 187–8, 190
Duff, Anthony 384
Durkheim, Émile 13, 17, 287
duties 304, 314
Dworkin, Ronald 195, 196, 267, 278

economies/economics 27, 45, 168, 195, 276;
   consumers/consumption 86–7, 329–30;
   equality/inequality 82, 83, 89–90, 108;
   growth/structure 11, 42, 43, 45; market 104,

108; power and production 42, 43, 44, 277; theories 13, 334, 337

egalitarians/egalitarianism 69–70, 83, 87–9, 90; Divided World scenario 118–19, 122, 129; and equality/priority issue 91–2, 123–5, 129; and Levelling Down Objection 122, 124–9; Telic/Deontic 70, 117–22, 124, 127, 129

Eighteenth Brumaire of Louis Bonaparte (Marx) 29

empires 283–4, 289

Enlightenment 12, 273

entitlement(s) 140; theories 78–9, 144

entrepreneurs 74–5, 77

equality 69, 70, 119; cultural 217, 242–5; levelling down 70, 122, 124–5, 126, 127–9; and liberalism 140, 168, 256; and morality 82–97, 119; political 224; and priority 115–29; Rawls's family scenario 92–3, 115–16; theory/principle 117, 140–1, 243

Espinas 13

Ethics 2

ethics 137, 138, 268, 304, 335

explanation: functional 9, 10; typology 56–61

exploitation and subordination 51

Eysenck, H.J. 17

fairness 150, 174, 251, 344–5; and justice 140, 144, 160, 161, 166, 167, 169, 170, 171, 184, 344

family 199, 298, 314–15; as model of community 182, 411–12; structure 103, 104

Farrell, Daniel 385

Feinberg, Joel 140–1, 145

feminists/feminism 222, 233–4, 235, 260–1

Ferraro, Geraldine 187

Field, Alexander J. 24

"Forces and Relations of Productions" (Elster) 47–8

forum–market distinctions in politics 325–7

Foster, John 28

Foucault, Michel 24

France 287, 300

freedom 174, 279, 284, 290; cultural 201–7, 258; individual 195, 201, 392; moral 294; political 202, 217; religious 249; of speech 257, 366

French revolution 277, 300

French Structuralism 30

Friedman, Milton 196, 294

friendship 154–8, 199, 201

functionalism 23–30, 46; analysis 23, 24, 30; explanation 8, 9, 10, 41, 43–4, 46, 48, 49, 51

Galbraith, J.K. 294

game theory 8, 22, 30–6, 47, 52; assurance games 9, 34, 35; and Marxism 34, 46, 51; strategies 32–4

Garibaldi, Giuseppi 295

Germany 287, 296; philosophy 13, 27, 108–9

Gifford lectures (1996) 70

Ginsberg, Morris 13

Gobinistes 273

Goethe, Johann Wolfgang von 26

Goodin, Robert 330

good(s) 135, 136, 137, 150, 392

Grahame, Kenneth 301, 315

gratitude and loyalty 287–8

Gray, John 271

Great War (1914–18) 286–7

group(s) 36, 344; concept of 224–6; cultural 244–5, 245–7, 313; differentiation 215–16, 219–36; equality/inequalities 219, 232–6, 244–55; oppression/segregation 224, 226–8, 232, 235–6; representation 224–31; theories of rights 248–61

Gurvitch, Georges 13

Gutmann, Amy 137–8, 224

Habermas, Jürgen 228, 325, 330, 335, 347

Hart, H.L.A. 383

Hayek, F.A. 13, 15, 16, 19, 55, 79

Hegel, Georg Wilhelm Friedrich 23, 60, 182, 272, 300, 368

Heidegger, Martin 225, 277

historical continuity 269, 305

historical materialism 41, 45–6, 46–7, 49, 51, 52

history 41, 169, 273, 283; and non-political unity 267, 281; rewriting of 309; theory of 59

Hobbes, Thomas 12, 17, 152, 199, 221, 239, 363

Hodja, Enver 196

holism 8, 14, 19, 138, 139, 195, 210; radical 56, 57, 59–61

Homans, George 13, 17

House of Mirth, The (Wharton) 253

Humboldt, Wilhelm von 196

Hume, David 307, 315, 316

Husserl, Edmund 277

identity 198–9, 241, 275–6, 323; collective/group 310–12, 313; defining 225–6; I/we 201, 280, 281–2, 283; individual/personal 155, 244, 269, 274, 284, 313, 392; national 269, 270, 273, 304, 305–8, 310–12, 313, 314, 316

ideologies 279, 280, 308

incoherence 352–3, 367

India 246

individualism 12, 15, 138, 183, 195–6, 290; liberal 135, 221, 255, 272, 384, 395; *see also* methodological individualism

Individualism (Lukes) 7

individualist–collectivist question 196

individuals 242–3, 244; interaction 56–7, 58; and justice 76–7; responsibility 150–1; rights/freedom 69, 195

inequality(ies) 3, 69, 71, 121, 127; and democracy 351, 356; and egalitarianism 120–3; gender 105,

233–6; and justice 71–2, 74, 84–5, 105, 121, 343; and poverty 90–1; social 219–20, 229, 232–6, 246

injustice 216, 322

Inquiry 49

institutions 241, 256, 304; democratic 173, 230, 351, 355–6; free 161, 164, 310; political 166, 241, 277, 335, 344, 345, 352–3

intentionality 8, 30

interaction 56–7, 58

intolerance 189, 267

Janis, Irving 333

Jews 280, 283, 284; anti-Semitism 296; rights and laws 249, 251, 258–9; self-identity 274, 275

Jones, Peter 249

judges 373, 375–7; roles in democratic politics 368–77

jurisdiction 282–4

justice 119–20, 126, 140–1, 151–2, 160, 215, 314–15, 368; conceptions/theory of 136–7, 161, 165, 169–71, 195; as fairness 140, 144, 160, 161, 166, 167, 169, 170, 171, 184, 344; liberal 138, 185, 191; and overlapping consensus 160–76; political conception of 160–76; and possession 140, 141, 142, 152; principles of 71, 72, 100, 103, 137, 145, 152–3, 160; Rawls's theory 120, 143–4, 149; *see also* distributive justice

Justice and the Politics of Difference (Young) 215

Kalven, Harry 86

Kant, Immanuel 35, 152, 161, 271, 272, 302

Kantian constructivism 152, 184

Kantian tradition 329

Karl Marx's Theory of History (Cohen) 41, 42, 44, 50

Keats, John 364

Kedourie, Elie 279, 280, 309

Kennedy, Edward 294

Kierkegaard, Søren 277

knowledge, theory of 19

Kymlicka, Will 216, 239, 260

Lamarck, Jean Baptiste 45, 48

language 246, 267; and nationalism 269, 273, 280–1, 284; and punishment 395, 400–1, 402–3

law(s) and legislature 45, 86, 198, 217, 283; and constitution 337, 372; constraints/restraints 369, 371, 375–7; in democratic politics 365, 371–3; and group differences 232, 248–61; and justice 368–70, 409; moral 152–3, 297; in multicultures 244–5, 248–9, 254–5

law(s) and legislature moral 152–3, 297

Leibniz, Gottfried Wilhelm 23

Lévi-Strauss, Claude 19

L'Homme machine (La Mettrie) 17

liberal democrats 323

liberalism 137–8, 158, 161, 196, 384, 396; and citizenship 215–16, *216*, 246–7; and communitarianism 135–9, 182–91, 195–210, 400; deontological 135, 151, 240; and diversity 218, 255–61; and nationalism 267–70; and nonliberalism 240–1; and patriotism 289–90, 294–6; political 166, 167–8, 169, 172–3; procedural 197–8, 202–10; and rights 231, 258; and the state 271–2, 279–80; theories 183, 197, 271, 272–3, 282

Liberalism and the Limits of Justice (Sandel) 135, 140–58

libertarians 196

liberty 104, 175, 201, 353–4; and equality 83, 140, 344; principles 140–1; and rights 166, 172–3, 174, 175, 176

Linger, Roberto 188

Locke, John 18, 69, 199, 221, 239, 271, 284

Lockean state of nature 385, 429, 430, 437

loyalty 282–4, 287–8, 293, 294–7, 316

McGuffey Readers 286

Machiavelli, Niccolò 198, 221

MacIntyre, Alasdair 138, 182–91, 195, 268, 303

Main Functional Paradigm 23, 24

Maine, Sir Henry 278

Making Sense of Marx (Elster) 55, 58

Malinowski, B. 13

Mandeville, Bernard 23

Mansbridge, Jane 224

marginal utility 85–6, 94–7

market socialism 276–7

market–forum differences 325–8

markets: failures 326, 329; free 138, 276

Marx, Karl 25–7, 42, 54, 60, 182, 196

Marxism 1–2, 23–30, 49, 54, 217, 220; and game theory 30–6, 41, 46, 47, 50, 51; and justice 70, 323; and social theories 23, 41, 279, 280

Menger, Carl 13

Merton, Robert K. 23, 24

metaphysical conceptions 185, 188–9, 272–3, 396

methodological collectivism 60

methodological individualism 7–8, 10, 11, 12–19, 54–64, 57, 195; definition of 22–3; and game theory 32–3; vs anti-reductionism 61–4

migration 79, 269, 307, 311–12

Mill, John Stuart 13, 104, 161, 239, 261, 310, 325; doctrine of liberty 196, 260

Miller, David 269–70

Minogue, Kenneth 279, 280, 309

minorities 189, 321; and identity 280–2, 311–12, 314; rights 231–6, 245–7, 249

Modood, Tariq 311–12

monism 242–3

Montesquieu, Charles Louis, Baron de 12, 198

morality 128, 189, 268, 272; and equality 82–97, 92–3, 116, 119; liberal 268, 290, 294, 295, 298, 299; and patriotism 286–300, 303; and preferences 329, 333; rules/standards 290, 291, 292, 294
multiculturalism: and equality 242–61; and nationalism 267–8, 269
Muslims 249, 251, 311–12

Nagel, Thomas 91–3, 195; and equality 92–3, 115–16, 123, 125
nationalism 267–70, 273, 278–9
'Nationality' (Acton) 310
nationhood/nationality 269, 273–6, 278, 280, 284; alienation 276–8; concepts/etymologies 274, 275, 279, 303–8; criticism/defence of 298–9, 301–3, 308–9; definition/principles/propositions 269, 304–8, 312–14; and justice 282–4, 314–15; and liberalism 310–12; membership 273–6, 278–9, 280; and nomadic/settled peoples 280–2; and patriotism 295, 298; territorial issues 306–7
natural history 48, 49
natural liberty principle 140–1, 149–51
Nazi Germany 296
need(s) 84, 125–6; and priority/urgency 92–3, 123; sufficiency 84, 91–2
Nicaragua 230
Niebuhr, Reinhold 333
nondespotism 201–2, 203
Norman, Richard 126
Nozick, Robert 70, 72, 116, 182, 196
Nozick–Rawls argument on desert issue 140–51

Oakeshott, Michael 309
obligation(s) 267, 269, 270, 271–2, 275; moral 335; and nationality 303, 305, 315; and rights 332
offenders 383, 388; and censure 384, 385, 391, 400, 403–4; as moral/rational agents 383, 408, 409, 410, 413, 424, 426; reform/rehabilitation 383, 391, 404, 414–16; repentance/expiation 404, 411–12, 423–4; and social deprivation 385, 402, 418–19
Olson, Mancur 33
"On the Jewish Question" (Marx) 100
On Liberty (Mill) 260
On Nationality (Miller) 269
ontology 15, 138, 195, 198, 199, 206, 210
opportunity 168, 217, 248, 253
oppressed/oppression 220, 224, 227–8; concept 226–7; and inequality 230–1, 232
Orwell, George 303

Parekh, Bhikhu 252, 257, 259, 260
parenthood 256–7, 261
Pareto, V. 13, 17; principle 326, 327, 328, 331, 334

Parfit, Harry 70
participation, principle of 344
particularism 373–4
Pascal, Blaise 331
Pateman, Carole 325
Patočka, Jan 277
patriotism 139, 182, 198–9, 201, 297; allegiances 295, 298, 303; definition 268, 286–7; and freedom 202–7; and loyalty 288–9, 294–5; and morality 293–9; as vice/virtue debate 286–300
Péguy, Charles 295
penal systems/policies 4, 389, 390, 398, 404, 409, 413
penance(s) 384, 390–9, 408, 409, 410–16
philosophy 188, 301–2; moral 268, 286, 299; see also political philosophy
Philosophy and Public Affairs 2
Plato 362, 364, 369
pluralism 137, 144, 164, 172–3, 218, 392; cultural 240, 310; and democracy 161, 164, 323, 349, 374–5
Pluralist Egalitarians 117–18, 121
poets and detachment 363–4
Political Liberalism 136, 137
political philosophy 160, 250, 302, 308, 323; and democracy 361–77; and justice 160–76, 369–77
Political Studies 49
political theory 219, 325–38, 336; see also social choice theory
politics 3, 158, 167, 231, 337; coalitions 33, 229–30; forum–market distinctions 325–38; instrumental 335–6; party funding issue 343, 356; and restraint 323, 369, 371, 375–7; theories of 330, 337
polity(ies) 219–36, 299, 300
Popper, Karl 13–14, 15, 19, 55, 195
Posner, Richard 24
post-Cartesianism 199
preferences 326–7, 328–31, 333; adaptive/counter-adaptive 322, 328, 330, 350; and choices 248, 252; in democratic politics 321, 350, 354
Prioritarians 123–4
priority and equality 92–3, 115–29
Priority View 123–4, 125
Prisoners' Dilemma 34, 35
productivity 42–3, 44, 45; strike actions 8–9; see also economies/economics
property 59, 77–8, 146–7
Przeworski, Adam 54
Psychology of Politics, The (Eysenck) 17
public debate 321, 325, 330, 331, 332
punishment 147–8, 383, 393, 394, 411; hard-treatment 384, 389, 390–9, 405, 408–9, 414, 416, 426–7; institutional 384, 398, 415; justifications of 136, 383, 389, 391, 393, 399, 405, 414, 416, 423, 427, 429;

penalties/sentences 383, 393–4, 398, 410, 413, 416, 417–18; penitential 404, 411–12, 423–4, 424–6; prudential supplements 384–5, 393–4, 409; theories of 148, 384, 385, 388–90, 399, 430; *see also* censure; communicative punishment; offenders; penance(s)
Pure Egalitarians 117–18

Race Relations Acts 250
race(s) 29, 267, 273, 274, 280; concepts of 274, 281; and nationalism 269, 284
Raphael, D.D. 125–6
Rastafarians 255
rational choice theory 22, 30–1, 271–2
Rawls, John 1, 2, 3, 69, 70–1, 72, 116, 126, 216; and arbitrariness 140, 142, 149–51; basic-structure objection 100–10; and democratic politics 342, 343, 349; desert issue 140–51; Difference Principle 91–3; and justice 120, 137, 143–4, 184, 195, 322, 344–5, 372; liberalism 182, 188, 190, 191, 239; and theories 136, 142–3, 144, 145–9, 272
Raz, Jo 216, 239, 240
reason 36, 162–4, 174, 322
reciprocity 120, 168, 288
redistribution 69, 71, 75–6, 326, 366
reductionism 10–11, 61; type- 10, 62, 63, 64
relationships 287, 288
religion(s) 23, 189, 258–9, 273, 275, 280; and customs debate 249–50
Renan, Ernest 305, 307, 313
Representative Government (Mill) 310
repression 189, 323
republicanism 139, 189, 202–10, 221, 223
resources 69, 88–9, 117, 126, 216–18
respect 243–4, 269
Rethinking Multiculturalism (Parekh) 216–17
retributivists/retributivism 126, 145–9, 383, 387, 390, 428–32, 433, 440
revolutions 299–300; and game theory 28–9, 47
Richelieu, Cardinal 273, 275
rights 69, 77, 203, 244, 272, 280, 377; in democratic politics 332, 344, 370–3; of disabled 216, 234, 252; and equality 121; human 186, 376; individual 69, 75–7, 195, 284; liberal 186–7, 189; and liberties 17, 166, 172–3, 174, 175, 176; and multiculturalism 244–5, 248–61; tolerance 255–61; universal 231–6; violation of 78–9, 323; of women 215, 233–6
Riker, William 352
Robespierre, Maximilien de 300
Roemer, John 54
Roman Empire 283, 284, 289
Rousseau, Jean-Jacques 221, 267, 365, 366, 370, 376
rule of/by law 175–6, 205, 280, 283–4
Russell, Bertrand 18
Ryan, Alan 337

Saint-Simon, Comte de 12–13
Sandel, Michael 135–6, 137–8, 182, 251, 267, 272; and communitarian–liberalism debate 182–91, 195, 197, 278
Sartre, Jean-Paul 25, 36, 188
Scanlon, T.M. 195
Schumpeter, Joseph Alois 326, 337
science(s) 24, 30, 276–7; social theory 41, 195, 197
Scruton, Roger 267–8
sectarianism 322, 352
segregation and exclusion 224, 235
self: conception of 135–6, 151, 153–4, 183, 267; deontological 156–8; and Rawls's theory of the person 142–3, 147, 150
self-censorship 330, 331
self-defense 429–32, 438–9
self-determination 304, 312–14
self-government 343, 352
self-interest 139, 229, 268, 298, 323
self-knowledge 154–8
self-ownership 69, 70, 78
self-respect 244
self-rule 207–10
Sen, Amartya 34, 195, 199
Shelley, Percy Bysshe 376
Sikhs 249, 253–4
Simmel, Georg 13
Singer, Peter 251
Skinner, B.F. 196
Smith, Adam 294
social choice theory 325, 326–30; objections 329, 331–5
social mobility 26–7, 29
social movements 229, 232, 235–6
social phenomena 12, 15, 58, 60; typology of explanation 56–7, 56
society/societies 232, 277, 286, 334, 335, 352, 392; democratic 74–5, 161, 171–2, 174, 198, 241–2; free 198, 201–2, 203, 208, 416–17; liberal 241–2, 257; multicultural issues 242–5, 246, 311–12; structure 100–10, 169
Socrates 362
solidarity 33–5, 308, 337
Solzhenitsyn, Alexander 282
sophists 362
South America 273
Spinoza, Benedict de 271
state(s) 27–8, 59, 161, 164; and justice system 409, 412–14, 415, 416, 419, 423, 424–6; and liberalism 271–2, 279–80; and nationality 312–13; penal systems 383, 384, 385, 392; and religion 175; and secession 313–14; sovereign 283, 304, 314, 366
Strong Functional Paradigm 23, 24
structuralism 8, 30, 59
Subjection of Women, The (Mill) 261
subjectivity 277, 315

sufficiency, doctrine of 82–97
Sweden 315

Tamir, Yael 251, 259
Tarde, Gabriel 13, 17
taxation 69, 71, 76–7, 78, 101, 343
Taylor, Charles 35–6, 257, 260, 272
teleology 8, 9, 24, 28, 59–60, 117, 240; objections to telic view 121–3; *see also* egalitarians/egalitarianism
Temkin, Larry 127
territory 280, 283, 284
Theories of Surplus-Value (Marx) 25, 26
Theory of History (Marx) 41
Theory of Justice, A (Rawls) 1, 2, 70, 72, 101, 135, 136, 160, 171–2, 215
Thompson, E.P. 28, 277, 336
Tocqueville, Alexis de 198, 276, 336
token-reductionism 10, 62, 64
truth(s) 277, 369–70, 373–5, 377

Unger, Roberto 182
uniformity 242–3
United States 108, 249, 287, 300, 333, 334; constitution 223, 271, 343; and group/cultural rights 230–1, 244, 246, 255; republican thesis 204–6, 209; Supreme Court 368–9
unity 267, 271, 280, 283, 284; social 278, 282; theory of 272–3
universalists/universalism 4, 215, 220, 235–6, 268, 282, 302

utilitarians/utilitarianism 13, 123, 161, 171, 328; and equality 115–16, 117–18
utility(ies) 87–9, 117–18; law of diminishing 86–7; marginal 85–6

values 117–18, 163, 168–9, 190–1
Vanity Fair (Thackeray) 253
Vico, Giambattista 12
von Hirsch, Andrew 384, 387, 390, 391, 393, 394, 398
von Trott, Adam 295, 296
voting processes 321, 325, 326–30, 332, 334, 337

Walzer, M. 195, 267, 272, 278, 323
Watkins, J.W.N. 13, 14
Weber, Max 13, 19, 286–7
welfare, social 79, 92–3, 115–16, 117–18, 195
Wells, H.G. 303
Wind in the Willows, The (Grahame) 301, 302, 315–16
Wittgenstein, Ludwig 361–2, 363
Wollheim, Richard 366–7
women: rights 215, 233–6, 250; roles 182, 222–3; subjection 260–1
workers/workplace 33, 43, 226, 233–6
worth, concept of 145, 146, 147

Young, Iris Marion 215–16, 323
Yugoslavia 312

Zeldin, Theodore 329